UNITED STATES ARMY IN WORLD WAR II

The War in the Pacific

LEYTE: THE RETURN TO THE PHILIPPINES

by

M. Hamlin Cannon

MILITARY INSTRVCTION

CENTER OF MILITARY HISTORY

UNITED STATES ARMY

WASHINGTON, D.C., 1996

Library of Congress Catalog Card Number: 53-61979

First Printed 1954—CMH Pub 5-9

For sale by the Superintendent of Documents, U.S. Government Printing Office
Washington, D.C. 20402

UNITED STATES ARMY IN WORLD WAR II
Kent Roberts Greenfield, General Editor

Advisory Committee
(As of 1 May 1953)

James P. Baxter
President, Williams College

John D. Hicks
University of California

William T. Hutchinson
University of Chicago

S. L. A. Marshall
Detroit News

Charles S. Sydnor
Duke University

Brig. Gen. Verdi B. Barnes
Army War College

Brig. Gen. Leonard J. Greeley
Industrial College of the Armed Forces

Brig. Gen. Elwyn D. Post
Army Field Forces

Col. Thomas D. Stamps
United States Military Academy

Col. C. E. Beauchamp
Command and General Staff College

Charles H. Taylor
Harvard University

Office of the Chief of Military History
Maj. Gen. Albert C. Smith, Chief*

Chief Historian	Kent Roberts Greenfield
Chief, War Histories Division	Col. G. G. O'Connor
Chief, Editorial and Publication Division	Col. B. A. Day
Chief, Editorial Branch	Joseph R. Friedman
Chief, Cartographic Branch	Wsevolod Aglaimoff
Chief, Photographic Branch	Maj. Arthur T. Lawry

*Maj. Gen. Orlando Ward was succeeded by General Smith on 1 February 1953.

. . . to Those Who Served

Foreword

With the Leyte Campaign the War in the Pacific entered a decisive stage. The period of limited offensives, bypassing, and island hopping was virtually over. American troops in greater numbers than ever before assembled in the Pacific Theater, supported by naval and air forces of corresponding size, fought and overcame Japanese forces of greater magnitude than any previously met.

Though the spotlight is on the front-line fighting, the reader will find in this volume a faithful description of all arms and services performing their missions. The account is not exclusively an infantry story. It covers as well the support of ground fighting on Leyte by large-scale naval operations and by land-based air power under the most adverse conditions. In addition, careful attention to logistical matters, such as the movement of supplies and the evacuation of the wounded, gives the reader a picture of the less spectacular activities of an army in battle.

ORLANDO WARD
Maj. Gen., U. S. A.
Chief of Military History

Washington, D. C.
30 January 1953

The Author

M. Hamlin Cannon received the degree of Doctor of Philosophy in History from the American University of Washington, D. C. He is already known to American historians for his writings on Mormon and Civil War history which have appeared in historical journals. During World War II he served with the Navy in Australia and New Guinea.

Preface

The landing of the American forces on Leyte on 20 October 1944 brought to fruition the long-cherished desire of General Douglas MacArthur to return to the Philippine Islands and avenge the humiliating reverses suffered in the early days of World War II. The successful conclusion of the campaign separated the Japanese-held Philippine Archipelago into two parts, with a strong American force between them. More important, it completed the severance of the Japanese mainland from the stolen southern empire in the Netherlands Indies from which oil, the lifeblood of modern warfare, had come.

The Leyte Campaign, like other campaigns in the Pacific, was waged on the land, in the air, and on and under the sea. In this operation all branches of the American armed forces played significant roles. Therefore, although the emphasis in this volume is placed upon the deeds of the United States Army ground soldier, the endeavors of the aviator, the sailor, the marine and the Filipino guerrilla have been integrated as far as possible into the story in order to make the campaign understandable in its entirety. At the same time, every effort has been made to give the Japanese side of the story.

Obviously, to include every exploit of every branch of the armed forces, of the Filipinos, and of the Japanese would be far beyond the compass of a single volume. A careful selectivity was necessary throughout in order to avoid the Scylla of omission while skirting the Charybdis of oversimplification. Despite these precautions, because of the nature of the available documentary evidence, I may have unwittingly fallen into some of the very pitfalls that I tried to avoid.

I wish to express my sincere gratitude and thanks to the many people who have given fully of their time and talents in the preparation of this volume.

Especial thanks are due to Dr. John Miller, jr., who, during his tenure as Chief of the Pacific Section, Office of the Chief of Military History, carefully reviewed the final draft of the manuscript. His sound advice and constructive criticism eliminated many a roadblock. I wish, also, to thank Dr. Louis Morton, Chief of the Pacific Section, under whose direction this volume was started; he made constructive criticism of several of the chapters. Dr. Kent Roberts Greenfield, Chief Historian, Department of the Army, devoted much time and effort to reviewing the manuscript and his many penetrating comments on the various chapters were invaluable.

Appreciation is due to the people of the Historical Records Section, Departmental Records Branch, Office of the Adjutant General, who helped to locate source material and furnished working space for me and the records. To Mrs. Lois Aldridge, Mrs. Frances Bowen, Mrs. Clyde Christian, Miss Margaret Emerson, Mrs. Ellen Garrison, Mr. Robert Greathouse, Miss Matilda Huber, Mrs. Margarite Kerstetter, Mr. Wilbur Nigh, Miss Sue D. Wallace, and Miss Thelma K. Yarborough—thanks.

I wish also to thank the members of the U. S. Air Force Historical Division, Air University, and the Naval History Branch, Naval Records and History Division, Office of the Chief of Naval Operations, for placing at my disposal the pertinent air and naval records.

Thanks are also due to the members of the historical sections of the U. S. Navy and the U. S. Air Force and to the many participating commanders of various branches of the U. S. armed forces who read all or parts of the manuscript.

The late W. Brooks Phillips started the editing of the manuscript. He was succeeded by Col. B. A. Day, Chief of the Editorial and Publication Division, and Mrs. Loretto Stevens. Mrs. Stevens also prepared the final copy for the printer. Miss Mary Ann Bacon prepared the index.

Mrs. Martha Willoughby, in addition to accomplishing the arduous task of interpreting my handwriting, typed many of the drafts of the manuscript and saw that the subject and predicate agreed. Mrs. Wynona Hayden, Mrs. Stella Hess, and Mrs. Michael Miller also typed parts of the manuscript. Miss Elizabeth Armstrong painstakingly typed the final copy.

Mr. Wsevelod Aglaimoff and Lt. Col. Robert F. O'Donnell, as well as other members of the Cartographic Branch, spent many months in research for and preparation of the maps. At the time this volume was being prepared for publication, no reliable maps of Leyte were available. The maps for this volume are based on the highly inaccurate maps used by the troops during the operation. The relief in particular, as shown on these maps, has little in common with the terrain configuration which confronted the troops. Thus, both military and geographical information as given on the maps in the volume should be regarded only as an approximation of the actual situation at the time of the battle.

Major Arthur T. Lawry selected and edited the photographs used in this volume. Lt. Roger Pineau (USNR) furnished me the photograph of General Suzuki. Mr. Israel Wice and his capable assistants in the General Reference Branch were helpful at crucial stages of the manuscript.

My sincere appreciation and thanks go to Maj. Gen. Harry A. Maloney, Chief of Military History, and to his successors, Maj. Gen. Orlando Ward and Maj. Gen. Albert C. Smith, as well as to members of their staffs, for their understanding and co-operation.

Washington, D. C.   M. HAMLIN CANNON
15 June 1953

Contents

Tables

Charts

Maps

Illustrations

All illustrations but one are from Department of Defense files. The photograph of Lt. Gen. Sosaku Suzuki on page 51 was contributed by Lt. Roger Pineau (USNR).

LEYTE: THE RETURN TO THE PHILIPPINES

CHAPTER I

The Strategic Plan

"It is with the deepest regret that I must inform you that conditions over which I have no control have necessitated the surrender of troops under my command." [1] With this message of 20 May 1942, from Lt. Col. Theodore M. Cornell, U.S. Army, to Bernardo Torres, Governor of Leyte, the control which the United States had held over the island since 1898 came to an end. Nearly two and a half years were to elapse before the sound of naval guns in Leyte Gulf would announce to the world the opening of the Leyte Campaign, the first phase of the re-entry of American forces into the Philippine Archipelago.

The primary purpose of the Leyte Campaign was to establish an air and logistical base in the Leyte area in order to support operations in the Luzon–Formosa–China coast area and particularly to nullify Japanese strength in Luzon. Leyte is one of the Visayan Islands, which constitute the geographical heart of the Philippines. It was hoped that the fertile Leyte Valley, broad and flat, could be utilized for major airfields and base sites from which large-scale operations could be launched against the rest of the Philippines.

Preliminary Discussion

Behind the decision to go into Leyte lay a series of strategically significant victories, which had followed a staggering initial reverse. American prewar plans for the Pacific had originally been based on the assumption that only the United States and Japan would be at war and that the U.S. Pacific Fleet would be in existence.[2] But the destruction of the fleet at Pearl Harbor and the entrance of Germany and Italy into the war nullified these plans. The strategy of the Joint Chiefs of Staff [3] in early 1942, therefore, was concerned chiefly with trying to limit the rapid advance of the Japanese and with keeping the line of communications to Australia open. The Pacific Theater was divided into command areas—the Southwest Pacific Area, with General Douglas MacArthur as

---

[1] Philippine Municipal Government Reports, Folder 2, App. DD, Guerrilla File 6910.23 (B), Military Intelligence (MI) Library.

[2] Louis Morton, "American and Allied Strategy in the Far East," *Military Review*, XXIX (December, 1949), 38.

[3] The Joint Chiefs of Staff were General George C. Marshall, Chief of Staff, United States Army; Admiral Ernest J. King, Commander in Chief, U.S. Fleet, and Chief of Naval Operations; General Henry H. Arnold, Commanding General, Army Air Forces; and Admiral William D. Leahy, Chief of Staff to the Commander in Chief—the President of the United States. The Joint Chiefs were responsible for the conduct of the war in the Pacific, subject to the decisions of the Combined Chiefs of Staff. The latter were representatives of the United States and the United Kingdom. The Joint Chiefs represented the United States.

Supreme Commander (he referred to himself, however, as Commander in Chief), and the Pacific Ocean Area (which included the Central Pacific), with Admiral Chester W. Nimitz as Commander in Chief.[4]

In 1942 and 1943 the Allied forces had halted the Japanese at Papua and Guadalcanal and started to push them back. On 8 May 1943 the Joint Chiefs approved a "Strategic Plan for the Defeat of Japan," which was endorsed by the Combined Chiefs in December. The objective of the plan was to secure the unconditional surrender of Japan, an objective that might necessitate an invasion of the Japanese home islands. As such an invasion promised to be a "vast undertaking," it would be necessary to secure a large supply base from which a great aerial offensive could be mounted against Japan. According to the original plan this base was to be located in China, but the Mariana Islands were afterward substituted for China. The plan called for the acquisition of successive island bases which could be used as "steppingstones," preferably those which would shorten the sea route, provide for its security, and at the same time deny to the Japanese bases from which they might interfere with the Allied line of communications. The main effort was to be through the waters of the Pacific Ocean. Nimitz' operations were to be conducted west through the Japanese mandated islands while MacArthur's proceeded northwest along the New Guinea coast. The two series of operations were to be mutually supporting.[5]

Although no specific islands were named in the Strategic Plan, the Philippine Archipelago, because of its strategic position and long possession by the United States, naturally loomed large in the planning. The Philippines lie athwart all sea routes south from Japan to the economically important Netherlands Indies—rich in rubber, tin, oil, and rice. The capture of the Philippines would help to sever this line of communications and would furnish an excellent staging area for attacks against China, Formosa, or Japan. Aside from strategic considerations, the liberation of the Islands was important for reasons of Far Eastern politics and prestige.[6] The obligation of the United States to the subjugated Filipino people could not be lightly ignored. Furthermore, General MacArthur was imbued with a burning determination to return to the Philippine Islands and avenge the humiliating defeats suffered by the American forces in 1941 and 1942.

By the spring of 1944 the operations in the Pacific were going so well that the successes had exceeded even the most optimistic hopes of any of the planning officers. On 12 March the Joint Chiefs ordered General MacArthur to prepare plans for a return to Mindanao, southernmost island of the Philippines, with a target date of 15 November 1944.[7] General MacArthur on 15 June issued a plan for his future operations. The entrance into the Philippines was to be accomplished in two phases. The first would be a preliminary operation on 25

---

[4] Memo, Gen Marshall and Admiral King for President, 30 Mar 42, no sub, and two incls, "Directive to the Commander in Chief of the Pacific Ocean Area" and "Directive to Supreme Commander in the Southwest Pacific," OPD ABC 323.31 POA (1–29–42), 1–B.

[5] JCS 287/1, Strategic Plan for the Defeat of Japan, 8 May 43; CCS 417, Over-all Plan for the Defeat of Japan, 2 Dec 43.

[6] United States Strategic Bombing Survey [USSBS], Military Analysis Division, *Employment of Forces Under the Southwest Pacific Command* (Washington, 1947), p. 32.

[7] JCS to CINCSWPA, CM-IN 5137, 12 Mar 44. CM-IN and CM-OUT numbers used in the footnotes of this volume refer to numbers on copies of those messages in General Marshall's Message Log, on file in the Staff Communications Office, Office of the Chief of Staff, U.S. Army.

October into the Sarangani Bay area in southern Mindanao in order to establish land-based air forces to augment the carrier-based air support for the principal effort. The major effort was to be an amphibious landing operation with forces mounted from New Guinea for the seizure on 15 November of airfields and bases on Leyte.[8] The latter was to follow quickly on the heels of the first operation in order to take full advantage of the surprise tactics.

Leyte occupies a commanding position in the Philippine Islands. Because of its central location, its repossession by the United States would not only divide the Japanese forces in the Philippines but would also provide an excellent anchorage in Leyte Gulf, together with sites for bases and airfields from which land-based aircraft could bomb all parts of the Philippines, the coast of China, and Formosa. To an even greater extent than Mindanao, Leyte could be made into an excellent springboard from which to launch subsequent operations against the Japanese in Formosa or in the rest of the Philippines.

In his planning, General MacArthur recognized that the Leyte operation, his most ambitious to date, would require "massed carrier-based air support" and all of the "combined amphibious and naval forces available at the time."[9]

By June 1944 General MacArthur's forces had pushed up the New Guinea coast to the island of Biak, about nine hundred nautical miles southeast of Davao, Mindanao, while those of Admiral Nimitz were poised to strike at Saipan some twelve hundred miles northeast of Davao. In most of their previous campaigns the Americans had struck with overwhelming force at weakly held Japanese garrisons. Since the tide of war was now so favorable to the Allied cause, the Joint Chiefs thought that the Pacific timetable of pending operations might be accelerated. On 13 June they had therefore asked MacArthur and Nimitz their opinions with regard to three ways proposed for speeding up operations: "(a) By advancing target dates of operations now scheduled through operations against Formosa; (b) By by-passing presently selected objectives prior to operations against Formosa; and (c) By by-passing presently selected objectives and choosing new ones including the home islands." Although the Philippine Islands were not explicitly named as targets that might be bypassed, they were certainly included by implication.[10]

On 18 June General MacArthur replied to the query of the Joint Chiefs,[11] and on 4 July Admiral Nimitz made known his opinions.[12] On the advancement of the target dates, both commanders were in complete agreement—it was impossible unless certain conditions could be changed. The logistic resources in the Southwest Pacific were being strained to the limit to meet the fixed target dates, while the strengthening of Japanese garrisons made it unlikely that the Central Pacific could make its present scheduled dates.

With respect to bypassing objectives prior to the seizure of Formosa, MacArthur thought it would be "unsound" to bypass the Philippines and launch an attack across the Pacific directly against Formosa—an attack which would have the benefit of no appreciable land-based air support and

[8] GHQ SWPA, RENO V, 15 Jun 44.
[9] Ibid.

[10] Rad, JCS to CINCSWPA and CINCPOA, CM-OUT 50007, 13 Jun 44.
[11] Rad, CINCSWPA to CofS, CM-IN 15058, 18 Jun 44.
[12] Rad, CINCPOA to COMINCH, CM-IN 2926, 4 Jul 44.

which would be based upon the Hawaiian Islands, 5,100 miles away. In his opinion it was essential to occupy Luzon and establish land-based aircraft thereon before making any move against Formosa.[13] Nimitz stated that in a series of informal discussions between his and MacArthur's planning officers, the latter anticipated the seizure in early September of Morotai Island, 300 statute miles southeast of Mindanao. This was to be followed in late October by a limited occupation of the Sarangani Bay area on Mindanao, which was to be used primarily as a base for short-range aircraft. The major operation was to be the occupation of Leyte about 15 November. Nimitz thought that this timing was "optimistic." He felt that the critical and decisive nature of the Leyte operation required "practically all available covering and striking forces, fire support forces, and all available assault shipping." If successful, however, the Americans would achieve air supremacy over the Philippines. Therefore, since the inclusion of the Leyte operation with that of Mindanao would expedite subsequent operations, Nimitz considered it "advisable."[14]

As to the feasibility of bypassing present objectives and choosing new ones, including the Japanese home islands, the two commanders were not in complete agreement. MacArthur pronounced the concept "utterly unsound," since the available shipping was limited to a seven-division lift and there was insufficient air support. Nimitz thought that no decision should be made until after further developments.

The proposals disturbed General MacArthur, who concluded his message to the Joint Chiefs with the following peroration:

It is my opinion that purely military considerations demand the reoccupation of the Philippines in order to cut the enemy's communications to the south and to secure a base for our further advance. Even if this were not the case and unless military factors demanded another line of action it would in my opinion be necessary to reoccupy the Philippines.

The Philippines is American Territory where our unsupported forces were destroyed by the enemy. Practically all of the 17,000,000 Filipinos remain loyal to the United States and are undergoing the greatest privation and suffering because we have not been able to support or succor them. We have a great national obligation to discharge.

Moreover, if the United States should deliberately bypass the Philippines, leaving our prisoners, nationals, and loyal Filipinos in enemy hands without an effort to retrieve them at earliest moment, we would incur the gravest psychological reaction. We would admit the truth of Japanese propaganda to the effect that we had abandoned the Filipinos and would not shed American blood to redeem them; we would undoubtedly incur the open hostility of that people; we would probably suffer such loss of prestige among all the peoples of the Far East that it would adversely affect the United States for many years. . . .[15]

In reply, General George C. Marshall, Chief of Staff, cautioned MacArthur to "be careful not to let personal feelings and Philippine politics" override the great objective, which was to end the war. He also pointed out that "bypassing" was not "synonymous with abandonment."[16]

Admiral William F. Halsey, the commander of the Third Fleet, and his staff, when they heard of the proposal, were enthusiastic about the possibility of bypassing the more immediate objectives. But in contrast to Admiral Ernest J. King, Chief of Naval Operations, who wished to move di-

[13] Rad cited n. 11.
[14] Rad cited n. 12.

[15] Rad cited n. 11.
[16] Rad, CofS to CINCSWPA, CM-OUT 55718, 24 Jun 44.

CONFERENCE AT PEARL HARBOR *brings together (left to right) General Douglas MacArthur, President Franklin D. Roosevelt, Admiral William D. Leahy and Admiral Chester W. Nimitz.*

rectly to Formosa, bypassing the Philippines, Halsey felt it necessary and profitable to go into the Philippine Archipelago, which he considered to be "the vulnerable belly of the Imperial dragon." [17] Halsey stated that when Rear Adm. Robert B. Carney, his chief of staff, was asked by King, "Do you want to make a London out of Manila?" Carney replied, "No, sir. I want to make an England out of Luzon." [18]

The Joint Chiefs of Staff concluded that none of the currently selected objectives could be bypassed. They continued, however, to search for means by which the tempo of the war in the Pacific might be accelerated.

In the latter days of July, General Marshall invited General MacArthur to visit Pearl Harbor in order to confer with Admiral Nimitz on future plans for the war in the Pacific. MacArthur arrived on 26 July. To his surprise, the President of the United States was present. President Roosevelt invited him and Admirals Halsey and Nimitz to dinner. After dinner the President drew out a map and, pointing to Leyte, is reported to have said, "Well, Douglas, where do we go from here?" [19]

[17] William F. Halsey, *Admiral Halsey's Story* (New York, 1947), pp. 194–99.

[18] *Ibid.,* p. 195.

[19] Information was furnished by Capt. Samuel Eliot Morison, USNR, 22 January 1951, who stated that Roosevelt had related the incident to him. Lt. Gen. Robert C. Richardson, who was not present, states that MacArthur told him that the President pointed to Mindanao when he made his remark. Ltr, Gen Richardson to Gen Marshall, 1 Aug 44, Book 21, OPD Exec 9.

Although MacArthur had been given no intimation that strategy was going to be discussed, he launched into a long talk on the necessity of taking Luzon before moving against Formosa. Nimitz did not enter into the conversation. The following morning the discussions were continued. Admiral William D. Leahy, who was present, later declared: "Both General MacArthur and Admiral Nimitz felt that they did not require any additional reinforcements or assistance" for the scheduled operations.[20] This Admiral Leahy considered most unusual.

Admiral Nimitz reported to Admiral King that the conferences "were quite satisfactory. The general trend of the discussion . . . was along the line of seeing MacArthur into the Central Philippines. . . ."[21]

There was no strong disagreement between General MacArthur and Admiral Nimitz. Admiral Leahy said, "I personally was convinced that they together were the best qualified officers in our service for this tremendous task, and that they could work together in full agreement toward the common end of defeating Japan."[22]

Strong efforts were already under way to accelerate operations in the Pacific. A shortage of shipping appeared to be the bottleneck which halted all attempts to speed up the operational target dates. General MacArthur at Brisbane had been directing the

whole of his planning toward the reoccupation of the Philippine Islands, and on 10 July had issued a plan for all operations into the archipelago. According to this plan the conquest of the Islands was to be accomplished in four major phases.

The initial phase envisaged footholds in the southern and central Philippines for the establishment of bases and airfields from which subsequent operations could be supported. The first operation, planned for 1 November 1944, was to be the seizure of the Sarangani Bay area in southern Mindanao for the purpose of establishing land-based air forces to augment the carrier-based air support for the advance into Leyte. The Leyte operation, the main effort of this series, was to come on 22 November. Major air, naval, and logistic bases were to be constructed on the shores of Leyte Gulf for the control of Leyte, Samar, and Surigao Strait, and for the neutralization of the Japanese aerial strength on Luzon.[23] The other phases covered the occupation of Luzon and the consolidation of the Philippines.

On 26 July the Joint Chiefs agreed that the primary purpose of the occupation of the Leyte–Mindanao area was to establish air forces there in order to reduce the enemy air strength on Luzon. Some of Admiral Nimitz' assault craft which were suitable for shore-to-shore operations were to be transferred to General MacArthur. The Joint Chiefs, therefore, asked their planners to submit their views on the possibility of advancing the target date for Leyte to 15 November by compressing the intervals between contemplated operations or by the elimination of certain scheduled operations.[24]

---

[20] Interv with Admiral Leahy, 5 Oct 50, OCMH.
[21] Memo, COMINCH for CofS, 9 Aug 44, OPD ABC 384 Pacific (1–17–43).
[22] Interv with Admiral Leahy, 5 Oct 50, OCMH. See also, Fleet Admiral William D. Leahy, *I Was There* (New York, 1950), pp. 247–52. In answer to an inquiry about the conference made to the director of the Franklin D. Roosevelt Library, the author was informed that "a careful search of the papers of Franklin D. Roosevelt in this Library has not revealed any materials that would be pertinent to the subject. . . ." Ltr, Herman Kahn to author, 20 Oct 50, OCMH.

[23] GHQ SWPA, MUSKETEER Plan, 10 Jul 44.
[24] Rad, JPS to Staff Planners of CINCPOA and CINCSWPA, CM-OUT 71483, 27 Jul 44.

In furtherance of this directive, planning officers from Washington met with General MacArthur and his staff in Brisbane in the early part of August and discussed means of accelerating the target date for Leyte. General MacArthur told them that a substantial interval between the operations at Sarangani Bay and Leyte was necessary. His reasons were as follows: (1) the assault shipping that was used for the Sarangani Bay operation would have time to turn around, reload, and then be used for the Leyte operation; (2) in the interval six combat air groups could be installed in the Sarangani Bay area to support the Leyte operation; and (3) the carriers would have sufficient time to execute two strikes before the Leyte operation.[25]

The planners from Washington, however, felt that there was sufficient assault shipping in the Pacific without using the same craft for both the Sarangani Bay and the Leyte operations. An enumeration of the vessels assigned to the Southwest Pacific and the Central Pacific gave the areas more than a six-division lift. As Brig. Gen. Frank N. Roberts, chief of the Strategy and Policy Group, Operations Division, War Department General Staff, in Washington, told Col. William L. Ritchie, his deputy, who was in Brisbane, "If you sit down and look at those figures a bit you will see that there should be sufficient assault lift for Leyte just on playing the numbers racket, without touching the shipping on Sarangani." [26]

Both Washington and Brisbane recognized that the operations in the Leyte–Surigao area were necessary in order to provide air bases, depot areas, and a fleet anchorage for any future advance whether in the Philippines, against Formosa, or by a direct route into the Japanese homeland. Consequently, the planners never seriously entertained any idea of bypassing this area, although they continued to probe for means which would accelerate the target date.

The determination of the target date was dependent upon the availability of assault shipping and the desire of General MacArthur to have each successive advance supported by land-based aircraft. The existing shipping was needed for operations already scheduled. The planners concluded that additional shipping could be made available if certain phases of the campaigns of Central Pacific forces into the Palaus, scheduled to start on 15 September, were canceled or set ahead of schedule. The alternatives were to modify the concept of providing land-based air support for subsequent operations or to execute the Sarangani Bay and Leyte operations simultaneously.[27] There the matter rested. Apparently the Joint Chiefs had decided that the time was not opportune for an acceleration of the target dates.

On 27 August General MacArthur furnished General Marshall a timetable for future operations by his forces. On 15 September a division and a reinforced regiment were to seize Morotai in order "to protect the western flank" and to provide land-based aircraft for advances northward. On 15 October a division less one regimental combat team was to land in the Talaud Islands northwest of Morotai in order "to neutralize the [Japanese] western flank," to establish air bases from which the neutralization of Mindanao and the western Visayan Islands could be accomplished, and to set up a base for airborne troops. On 15 November two divisions were to land in the

---

[25] Tel conf, Washington and Brisbane, 7 Aug 44, WD–TC 797.
[26] Tel conf, Washington and Brisbane, 10 Aug 44, WD–TC 809.

[27] *Ibid.*

Sarangani Bay area in order to construct bases for land-based aircraft that were to support the Leyte operation. On 7 December a regimental combat team and a parachute battalion were to drop on Mindanao and establish an airfield for fighter cover for the aerial neutralization of the western Visayan Islands and southern Luzon. On 20 December five divisions were to land on Leyte for the purpose of providing "major air and logistic bases for operations to the northward." The plan was predicated on the assumption that there would be available in the Pacific sufficient amphibious lift and fleet support.[28]

Plans Agreed Upon

On 1 September 1944 the Joint Chiefs of Staff in their 171st meeting reviewed the situation in the Pacific. The time had come when it was necessary to issue a directive for future operations in that area. After much discussion, the Joint Chiefs left in abeyance the question of what operation should follow Leyte but "directed the Joint Staff Planners to prepare, as a matter of urgency, a directive to the Commander in Chief, Southwest Pacific Area, and the Commander in Chief, Pacific Ocean Areas, to carry out the Leyte operation." [29]

Accordingly, on 8 September, the two commanders were given the following missions: General MacArthur, after conducting the necessary preliminary operations, was to take the Leyte–Surigao area on 20 December, with Admiral Nimitz furnishing fleet support and additional assault ship-

ping. Both commanders were to arrange for co-ordination of plans and mutual support of operations; to co-ordinate plans with General Joseph W. Stilwell, Commanding General, United States Army forces, China, Burma and India, in order to get maximum support from that theater; and to arrange with General Henry H. Arnold, Commanding General, Twentieth Air Force, for supporting operations.[30]

Concurrently with the issuance of this directive, momentous events were taking place in the Pacific. Admiral Halsey was in command of scheduled operations against the Palau Islands. On 7 and 8 September aircraft from his carriers struck at Yap and the Palau Islands, against which Admiral Nimitz had scheduled operations, and for the next two days bombed Mindanao. On the 12th and 14th the bombers hit the central Philippines in support of the operations against the Palau Islands and Morotai.

Admiral Halsey advised Admiral Nimitz that, as a result of the strikes, few serviceable planes in the Philippines were left to the Japanese, the bulk of the enemy's oil supplies was destroyed, there was "no shipping left to sink," the "enemy's non-aggressive attitude [was] unbelievable and fantastic," and "the area is wide open." [31] Halsey also told Nimitz that one of his downed carrier pilots had been told by his Filipino rescuers that there were no Japanese on Leyte.[32] He therefore felt that it was time to accelerate the operations in the Pacific, and he strongly recommended that the intermediate opera-

---

[28] Rad, CINCSWPA to CofS, CM-IN 24770, 27 Aug 44.

[29] Min, JCS 171st Mtg, 1 Sep 44.

[30] Rad, JCS to CINCSWPA and CINCPOA, CM-OUT 27648, 8 Sep 44.

[31] Rad, Com3dFlt to CINCPOA, CM-IN 13120, 14 Sep 44.

[32] Rad, Com3dFlt to CINCPOA, CINCSWPA, and COMINCH, CM-IN 12893, 13 Sep 44.

tions—Yap, Talaud, and the Sarangani Bay area on Mindanao—be canceled. Leyte could be seized immediately and cheaply without any intermediate operations. Halsey's fleet could cover the initial landing until land-based aircraft could be established. The force intended for the occupation of Yap could be made available to General MacArthur.[33]

When this message was received, the Combined Chiefs of Staff were attending a conference in Quebec. The recommendations were transmitted to Quebec by Admiral Nimitz, who offered to place at MacArthur's disposal the III Amphibious Force, including the XXIV Corps, which was loading at Pearl Harbor for Yap. General Marshall so informed General MacArthur and asked his opinion on the proposed change of target date.[34]

The message reached MacArthur's headquarters at Hollandia, on New Guinea, while MacArthur was en route to Morotai and observing radio silence. His chief of staff advised General Marshall that although the information from the rescued pilot that there were no Japanese on Leyte was incorrect, the intermediate operations could be eliminated. The 1st Cavalry Division and the 24th Infantry Division with sufficient service troops were available for the Leyte operation; adequate air strength could be pro-

vided; the logistic support was practicable; and the XXIV Corps could be used.[35]

General Marshall received this answer at Quebec on 15 September while he, Admiral Leahy, Admiral King, and General Arnold were at a formal dinner given by Canadian officers. The Americans withdrew from the table for a conference. Within an hour and a half after the message arrived, the Joint Chiefs ordered MacArthur and Nimitz to cancel the three intermediate operations of Yap, Talaud, and Sarangani, co-ordinate their plans, and invade Leyte on 20 October.[36]

Later that evening, as he was on his way to his quarters after the dinner, General Marshall received this message: "Subject to completion of arrangements with Nimitz, we shall execute Leyte operation on 20 October. . . . MacArthur." [37]

On 3 October the Joint Chiefs of Staff directed General MacArthur to occupy Luzon on 20 December 1944, the date originally set for the entrance into Leyte.[38] The decision had been made. General MacArthur was to return to the Philippine Islands in force.

---

[33] Rad, Com3dFlt to CINCPOA, CM-IN 12893, 14 Sep 44.
[34] *Biennial Report of the Chief of Staff of the United States Army, July 1, 1943, to June 30, 1945, to the Secretary of War* (Washington, 1945), p. 71.

[35] Rad, CINCSWPA to JCS, CINCPOA, and Com3dFlt, CM-IN 12636, 14 Sep 44.
[36] Rad, JCS to CINCSWPA, CINCPOA, and Com3dFlt, 15 Sep 44, OCTAGON 31–A, CofS CM-OUT Log, 15 Sep 44; *Biennial Report,* p. 71, cited n. 34; General of the Air Force Henry H. Arnold, *Global Mission* (New York, 1949), pp. 529–30.
[37] Rad, CINCSWPA to JCS, CM-IN 17744, 15 Sep 44.
[38] Rad, JCS to CINCSWPA *et al.,* CM-OUT 40792, 3 Oct 44.

CHAPTER II

The Nature of the Target

The Philippine Islands, the largest island group in the Malay Archipelago, were discovered by Ferdinand Magellan in 1521. They became a Spanish possession in 1565 and remained so until 10 December 1898 when they were ceded to the United States by the Treaty of Paris as a result of the Spanish-American war. In the spring of 1942 Japan secured military domination over the Islands.

The Philippine Archipelago lay in the geographical heart of the Far Eastern theater of war. As a pivotal point of control the Islands were centrally placed in relation to Japan, China, Burma, French Indochina, Thailand, British Malaya, and the Netherlands Indies. Being the most northerly part of the Malay Archipelago, the Philippines were also close to the vital areas of Japan and the Chinese-held areas of the Asiatic mainland. Located southeast of the continent, they occupy much the same position with respect to the mainland of Asia that the West Indies do with respect to North America.

The Islands are among the remnants of a great continent that once extended over the space now occupied by the entire East Indies. There are some 7,100 islands and islets in the Philippine Archipelago, which has a land area of 114,830 square miles. Of these, about 460 have an area of one square mile or more and 2,773 are named. The Philippine Islands are divided into three main groups—Luzon and adjacent islands in the northern sector; the Visayan Islands in the central portion, comprising Samar, Leyte, and numerous others; and finally, in the southern part, Mindanao and the Sulu Archipelago. The Philippines had a prewar population of about 16,000,000, of whom 14,550,000 were Christians, 678,000 were Mohammedans, 626,000 were pagans, and about 64,000 were Buddhists and Shintoists.[1]

Geography of Leyte

The northeastern Visayan group, which consists mainly of Leyte and Samar, was selected as the point of entrance into the Philippines. Leyte had the higher potential military value. The air distance from the capital city of Tacloban to Manila is 295 miles. Leyte is a natural gateway to the rest of the Philippines, and its possession would greatly facilitate and support further operations to the north as well as expedite control over the remaining islands in the Visayan group.[2]

---

[1] MI Sec, WDGS, Survey of the Philippines, 3 vols., 15 Feb 43; Div of Naval Intel, Office, Chief of Naval Opns, ONI 93, Field Monograph of the Philippines, Jan 44; Allied Geographical Sec, GHQ SWPA, Terrain Study 84, Leyte Province, 17 Aug 44; ASF Manual M365–1, Civil Affairs Handbook, Philippine Islands, 25 Apr 44.

[2] Sixth Army Opns Rpt Leyte, p. 5. Unless otherwise stated the material on terrain is based upon this report, pages 5–7.

Leyte roughly resembles a molar tooth with its crown toward Samar and its roots pointing to Mindanao. The eighth largest island in the Philippines, with an area of 2,785 square miles, it runs generally from north to south, with an approximate length of 115 miles and a width of 15 to 45 miles. It is situated on one of the principal submerged shelves of the Philippine Archipelago, and the waters over the shelf have an average depth of 22 fathoms.

The Terrain

The island is mainly volcanic in origin. A range of mountains, the topographical backbone of the island, extends southeast from Biliran Strait in the north to Cabalian Bay in the south and separates the Leyte and Ormoc Valleys. All of southern Leyte is mountainous and, militarily speaking, of little importance. The northwest coast is also rugged, and except for the port of Palompon has little tactical significance. The heavily forested central mountain range is composed of numerous knifelike ridges and spurs and deep ravines and serves as an effective natural barrier between the island's eastern and western coastal areas. It is a major obstacle to the rapid movement of troops and can be utilized very effectively in defending the island.

Leyte Valley, a broad and fertile plain, stretches across the northeastern part of the island from Leyte Gulf to Carigara Bay. More than twenty-five miles wide along the shore of the gulf, it is gradually narrowed by the mountain ranges to the north and south to less than ten miles as it reaches Carigara Bay. Most of the island's population live in this valley, and here too are most of the principal cities and airfields.

The main road net of the island runs through Leyte Valley, a great number of streams interlacing it. The numerous rice paddies, centuries old, disrupt the natural drainage of the valley. Rarely is the water level more than a few inches below the surface. Even in the drier months, vehicular movement is limited to the existing roads. In 1944 these were poor, inadequate, and ill suited for heavy military traffic. The best of them had only a light bituminous surface and were neither wide enough nor strong enough for two-way military traffic.[3] It was hoped that Leyte Valley could be developed into a large air and logistical base to support further operations, but it was not well suited for this purpose.

The shore line of Leyte Valley along Leyte Gulf and San Pedro Bay affords the best landing beaches on the island. This coast is dangerous for beach landings during northeast monsoon periods, when heavy surf, high winds, and torrential rains imperil men, equipment, and shipping. July, August, and September are the best months for landing. In general there are good firm sand beaches, onto which landing craft can go directly. A road parallels the shore line, but there are few exit roads from the beach to this road and beyond. In many places close to the shore there are swamps and rice paddies which prevent rapid egress from the beach. There are other good landing beaches on the east coast of Ormoc Bay, but they are crossed by innumerable creeks and streams.

Leyte Gulf is large and open, offering an excellent anchorage for a considerable number of vessels, including those of largest size. Carigara Bay, to the north of the island, is

---

[3] S. D. Sturgis, Jr., Brigadier General, U.S. Army Air Engineer, USAF, *Engineer Operations in the Leyte Campaign,* reprinted from *The Military Engineer,* November and December, 1947, and January, 1948, p. 4.

twenty miles wide, but shallow waters, swamps, and the hilly terrain of its eastern and western sides restrict its value for military operations. A narrow neck of the central mountain range separates the bay from the northern end of Ormoc Valley. San Juanico Strait, which separates Leyte from Samar in the north, connects Carigara Bay and San Pedro Bay, the latter being a northern extension of Leyte Gulf. The strait is thirteen and a half miles long with an average width of a quarter to a half mile. Small landing craft can navigate the channel, but there are strong tidal currents which cause violent rips and swirls at many points.

Wedged in between the central mountain range and the hill mass of the northwest coast of Leyte, the Ormoc Valley, about five miles wide in its largest part, extends from Ormoc Bay to the north for fifteen miles where a narrow neck of the central ridge separates it from Carigara Bay. Through the valley runs a narrow road, its northern portion marked by steep grades and sharp curves. Halfway along, a branch road zigzags its course to Port Palompon on the west coast. Although most of the southern part of the valley is under cultivation, there are large patches of forest, scrub growth, and cogon grass in the north.[4]

The largest city on the island, the provincial capital, is Tacloban, which lies at the head of San Pedro Bay. As the only sizable port in the area, it handles most of the outbound shipping, mainly from Leyte and Samar. Its prewar population was about 31,000. Other important towns are Carigara and Barugo on the north coast; Baybay and Ormoc, the leading ports on the west coast; and Palo, Tanauan, and Abuyog along the east coast. All the more significant

towns are situated on the main road system of the island, and the larger coastal barrios (villages) have roads of a sort.

The road system is divided into a northern and a southern coastal road net. The former, which is the better, was designed for the transportation of agricultural produce from the northern interior areas to Tacloban. The latter is composed of narrow, roundabout roads that are constantly in need of repair. The two systems are joined by a road, scarcely better than a trail, which runs west of Abuyog and corkscrews its way through heavily forested mountains to Baybay. Another road, long, narrow, and broken in parts, goes north from Baybay to Ormoc and thence through the Ormoc Valley to Carigara.

The Tacloban airstrip, the principal airfield on the island, was located on the Cataisan Peninsula, which lies just southeast of Tacloban. The Japanese had constructed another airfield, known as the Dulag airstrip, two miles west of Dulag; three others—the Buri, Bayug, and San Pablo airstrips— near Burauen, five miles west of Dulag; and still another at Valencia in the Ormoc Valley, eight miles north of Ormoc.

Control of the island of Leyte is dependent upon control of the Leyte and Ormoc Valleys and their adjacent hills and mountains. Thus, before a successful movement into Leyte Valley could be assured, control of the high ground in the vicinity of Palo would be essential. Continued dominance over the valley is dependent upon control of the high ground at its northwestern end in the vicinity of Pinamopoan on Carigara Bay, possession of which would preclude infiltration from Ormoc Valley. The control of Ormoc Valley and use of the excellent anchorage and harbor facilities of Ormoc Bay is dependent upon control of the low-

---

[4] Allied Geographical Sec, GHQ SWPA, Terrain Study 84, Leyte Province, 17 Aug 44, p. 43.

land in the vicinity of Ormoc city and the commanding hills to the east.

The People

In 1939 the total population of Leyte was 915,853, of whom more than 912,000 were native Visayans of Malaysian stock. The largest other group consisted of 3,076 Chinese, half of whom were engaged in retail trade. There was a sprinkling of other national groups—40 Spaniards, 20 Germans, 81 from other European countries, 56 Americans, and 73 Japanese.

Because of their insular position and somewhat primitive culture, the inhabitants are primarily an agricultural and fishing people. The principal crops are rice, sugar cane, corn, and copra. Judged by Occidental standards, the mode of farming is backward and shows little tendency to progress. The Filipinos who have been exposed to industrial life, however, have been able to adapt themselves to employment in the limited trade crafts and manufacturing on the island.

According to his own standards, the Filipino lives well enough. His chief foods are rice or corn, fish, camotes (sweet potatoes), and occasionally chicken or other meat. The men's clothing is simple; the average man has several changes of cheap cotton shirts and pants made of imported cotton cloth or, in the more remote districts, from homespun material.

Most of the dwelling houses are made of bamboo and sheathed with palm leaves on roof and sides. The material is gathered locally and tied with rattan. The houses rarely consist of more than two rooms, and many are raised on piling, with space for the family pig and chickens underneath. In one of the rooms, or outdoors, is an open fireplace with a mud and stone hearth for cooking. There is little furniture, and in three out of four families the personal possessions would not be worth more than ten dollars.

Less than 5 percent of the people have a rising standard of living. This higher standard is exemplified by a better type of habitation, which ranges from a three-room house to a dwelling similar to that of the American middle class. The diet of more prosperous Filipinos is basically the same as that of the poorer class, but it offers a greater variety. Clothing follows the Occidental fashion. The wealthiest people and those with foreign education or contacts, who make up less than 1 percent of the population, dress and live in the same manner as Occidentals.

The Japanese, during their occupation, governed through the old administrative organization of the province. They and their puppet officials also set up larger governing bodies that exercised superior jurisdiction. On 6 February 1944 the puppet president of the Philippine Republic, José Laurel, appointed a commissioner who held supervisory power over the local governments in the Visayan Provinces.

The governor of the province of Leyte, who previously had been an elected official, was appointed by the president. He was the chief operative and administrative head of the province and on all provincial administrative matters his decision was final. The treasurer of the province, who reported directly to the governor, was its chief financial officer and tax assessor. He collected all taxes and license fees, national and local, and prepared financial statements for the governor but he had no say in administrative matters. The law officer of the province was legal adviser to the governor and to the municipal authorities. He could advise only on administrative matters.

The Japanese Military Administration maintained liaison between the Japanese Army and the civil government. The military police collected military intelligence and information and disseminated propaganda. The Japanese allowed only one political party on the Islands—the *Kalibapi*—to which all government officials were required to belong. This party was one of the principal propaganda agencies, being the prime mover of the pacification programs in the province, and exercised general supervision over the local neighborhood associations. The latter helped in maintaining law and order, assisted the constabulary, and aided in the distribution of scarce commodities.

It should be emphasized that during most of the occupation there were few Japanese on Leyte. Southern Leyte in general maintained the same Filipino institutions and officials as in the prewar years. The heel of the Japanese conqueror pressed but lightly on most of the people of Leyte. Beginning in early 1944, however, the Japanese Army forces on the island were reinforced. From that time forward the Filipinos had their crops appropriated and in other ways were subjected to the will of the Japanese. Misery, hunger, and poverty became commonplace and a resistance movement grew.

The Resistance Movement on Leyte

The Organizing of Guerrilla Bands

A period of uncertainty and confusion followed the surrender of the American and Filipino forces in the Philippines in the spring of 1942. Civilians and members of the armed forces who did not surrender to the Japanese Army fled into the hills. Some went because they wanted to continue the fight, others because they felt that the chaotic conditions on the Islands would afford unequaled opportunities for looting and pillaging.

Once in the hills, the men formed themselves into guerrilla bands.[5] At first all of the bands, because of their lack of money and supplies, freely raided farms and storehouses for food and equipment whenever they had the opportunity. Moreover, there were real bandit groups who frequently and wantonly raped the countryside. For a time all of the groups were discredited by the people. Gradually, however, strong men emerged who formed the guerrilla bands into semimilitary organizations. The leader of each band, who was generally an ex-member of the armed forces, gave himself a "bamboo commission," usually considerably higher than the one he had hitherto possessed.

The following oath of allegiance taken by the members of one of the bands is probably typical:

I do solemnly swear that I shall obey orders from my superior officer; that I shall fight the enemy of the Government of the Commonwealth of the Philippines and the United States of America whosoever and wherever he maybe [sic] in the territory of the Philippines; that I shall never allow myself nor any arm or ammunition to be caught by the

---

[5] Unless otherwise stated, material on the guerrillas is based upon the Guerrilla Papers, a collection of disorganized, miscellaneous records by and about the guerrillas in the Philippine Islands. It is located in the Documents Files Section, G–2, Department of the Army.

The records of the Leyte guerrillas are incomplete, inadequate, and controversial. Some of the guerrilla bands had no records, and all that is known of others is from violently prejudiced sources. Consequently, the full story of the guerrillas can probably never be told.

GUERRILLAS PREPARE FOR INSPECTION AT CONSUEGRA

enemy; that I shall never turn traitor to my country nor the United States of America; and muchless [sic] reveal to the enemy any secret of the Army to which I honorably belong; that I shall never abandon a wounded brother in arms; that I join the United Forces in the Philippines without personal or party interest, but with the determination to sacrifice myself and all that is mine for FREEDOM and DEMOCRACY; that I shall protect the lives and property of all loyal Filipinos everywhere.

I make this LOYALTY OATH without mental reservation or purpose of evasion.

SO HELP ME GOD.[6]

For some time the various guerrilla bands on Leyte operated separately, and there was little or no co-operation between them. They were united, however, in their hatred of the Japanese. Jealousy and strife between groups were rampant, but circumstances

gradually compelled the smaller bands to submit to absorption, either by force or persuasion, into the larger and more powerful groups. The fact that there were few Japanese on the island enabled the guerrillas and loyal provincial officials to organize the governments of most of the barrios.

All of the guerrillas declared that their primary purpose was to aid the civilians, maintain peace and order, and keep the Japanese from abusing the people. They also assumed control over various phases of public activities—the allotment of food supplies, the issue of emergency currency, and the punishment of criminals. The guerrillas in northern Leyte depended upon voluntary contributions to support them, while those in southern Leyte levied a loyalty tax. Hard money having been driven out of circulation, the guerrilla units tried to issue paper, which was acceptable only in those regions where

---

[6] 24th Div G–2 Jnl, 22 Oct 44.

the particular unit was active. There was no widespread circulation or acceptance of any of the guerrilla money.

The most important of the guerrilla leaders on Leyte were Lt. Col. Ruperto K. Kangleon and Brig. Gen. Blas E. Miranda. Colonel Kangleon had served for twenty-seven years in the Philippine Army and was a graduate of the Philippine Academy and General Service School. General Miranda,[7] a former member of the Philippine Constabulary, was very hostile to the Japanese and to anyone who surrendered to them. He killed many former prisoners, whom the Japanese had released, on the pretext that they were enemy spies. Miranda was especially bitter toward Kangleon, a former prisoner of the enemy.

Official recognition from General MacArthur's headquarters was slow in reaching the guerrillas on Leyte, a fact that brought about misunderstandings. General MacArthur had early established contact with Col. Macario Peralta on Panay and Col. Wendell Fertig on Mindanao. In the middle of February 1943 MacArthur sent Lt. Comdr. Charles Parsons, USNR, to the Islands by submarine. Before his departure, General Headquarters had established the policies to be followed. The prewar military districts, as of December 1940, were to be revived.[8] Since General MacArthur had received information that Colonel Fertig had successfully created an effective guerrilla organization on Mindanao and Colonel Peralta one on Panay, he recognized them

as commanders of the 10th and 6th Military Districts, respectively. Radio communication from MacArthur's headquarters informed Peralta and Fertig of the appointments on 21 February 1943. Commander Parsons also carried formal letters, dated 13 February 1943, making these appointments.

Parsons safely reached the Philippines in early March and established friendly relations with Colonel Fertig. While on Mindanao he made several local trips, one to southern Leyte where he heard of Colonel Kangleon who had escaped from the Butuan prison camp and returned to his home. Parsons visited Kangleon with the promise that he would be made commander of the 9th Military District (Leyte and Samar), and succeeded in persuading him to join the guerrilla movement on Leyte.[9]

Until area commanders could be selected for the 7th, 8th, and 9th (Leyte) Districts, Peralta and Fertig had been authorized by MacArthur's headquarters, through Parsons, to organize the guerrillas on neighboring islands, as well as on their own. Each thought he was to organize the guerrillas on Leyte. Peralta made contact with General Miranda on northwestern Leyte; Fertig got in touch with Colonel Kangleon. Both Peralta and Fertig told their contacts to organize Leyte with the official sanction of General MacArthur's headquarters. Consequently, Kangleon and Miranda each thought the other to be a usurper.[10]

Miranda was adamant in his refusal to treat with Kangleon. Colonel Kangleon thought that Miranda should be ordered to "forget his established kingdom," but if this failed, he declared, the 92d Division,

---

[7] Miranda's rank is obscure. At various times he is referred to as lieutenant, major, colonel, and brigadier general.

[8] MI Sec, GHQ AFPAC, Intelligence Series, Vol. II, Intelligence Activities in the Philippines During the Japanese Occupation (hereafter cited as Intelligence Activities in the Philippines), App. 7.

[9] Intelligence Activities in the Philippines, p. 56.

[10] Ibid., pp. 16–18.

commanded by himself, would "force . . . Miranda to join us." [11]

The situation became extremely tense, since both Kangleon and Miranda felt much bitterness. In August 1943 Kangleon sent a force against Miranda and during a clash between the two parties some of the men were killed. Miranda was routed and many of his followers joined Kangleon.[12] The power of Miranda was broken. Kangleon incorporated the other guerrillas on the island into the 92d Division, and Leyte was then unified under his command.

On 21 October 1943 General MacArthur recognized Colonel Kangleon as the Leyte Area Commander, and in a letter accompanying the appointment he told Kangleon what he expected of him. "I desire that you establish and maintain direct communication with this headquarters at your earliest opportunity and thereafter you keep me informed of major developments involving enemy movement, dispositions and other activity within your area and observation." [13]

Japanese Punitive Expeditions

In the latter part of 1943 the Japanese military authorities tried to conciliate the guerrillas, offering, in return for their surrender, not only freedom from punishment but also jobs and the opportunity to resume their normal family life. A great many guerrillas took advantage of this offer of amnesty and surrendered.[14] Among the guerrilla units that surrendered to the Japanese were those of Maj. Marcos G. Soliman and other subordinates of General Miranda's command.[15] They gave themselves up in January 1944, but General Miranda himself refused to surrender and left for either Cebu or Bohol.

After their attempts at pacification, the Japanese launched more frequent and intensive patrols against the guerrillas. The garrison troops that had been stationed on Leyte were reinforced. Southern Leyte, which had known few Japanese, was "reinvolved" on 8 December 1943. The guerrillas withdrew and hid in the interior. It was thought that after a month the troops would leave and be replaced by constabulary officers. But after two weeks the Japanese turned their attention to the civilians. Some they arrested and imprisoned for days without food and water, others they tortured and executed. Houses were broken into, property was looted, and food was stolen. Spies were brought in from neighboring islands to locate the guerrilla hideouts.

Since the people begged for action, Colonel Kangleon held a meeting of his unit commanders on 24 January 1944. With his officers in unanimous accord, he issued an order to fight, commencing on 1 February 1944. All officers and enlisted men of his command signed a loyalty oath that they

[11] Memo, Col Kangleon for K–50–OCTOPUS (probably for MacArthur), 23 May 43, Guerrilla Papers.

[12] The estimates on the number of deaths vary considerably. In a letter to President Manuel Quezon by Senator Carlos Garcia, dated 16 October 1943, the deaths are mentioned as "several"; a manuscript by Mrs. Charlotte Martin, who was on Leyte, says "many lives were lost"; and 1st Lt. Jack Hawkins, USMC, a guerrilla, stated in December 1943 that "over three hundred casualties were suffered by the contesting sides." Guerrilla Papers.

[13] GHQ FEC, MI Sec, GS, Messages in the Guerrilla Resistance Movement in the Philippines, Kangleon 201 File, DRB AGO.

[14] Office of Strategic Services, Research and Analysis Br, Rpt, Guerrilla Resistance in the Philippines, 21 Jul 44, Guerrilla Papers.

[15] ATIS, GHQ SWPA, Current Translations, 148, 6 Feb 45.

would not allow either themselves or their weapons to be captured.

From 1 February until 12 June, according to Colonel Kangleon, the guerrillas in southern Leyte had only 10 casualties. In a report dated 18 May 1944, the Japanese casualties were listed as 434 killed, of whom 4 were officers, and 205 wounded.

The Japanese commander in Leyte made quite a different report. He stated that from 1 January to 31 August his forces had taken part in 561 engagements with the guerrillas. They had seized 7 vehicles; 7 generators; 37 radios and other items of wireless equipment; 1,556 weapons, including rifles, bayonets, and homemade shotguns; and 55,348 rounds of ammunition, as well as sticks of dynamite. The Japanese declared that they had taken 2,300 prisoners of war, including 3 Americans; that 6 Americans and 23,077 Filipinos had surrendered; 1,984 guerrillas had been killed; and that the Japanese casualties amounted to 7 officers and 208 enlisted men killed, and 11 officers and 147 men wounded.[16]

In the month of October 1944 General MacArthur's Military Intelligence Section estimated that the strength of the guerrilla 92d Division was as follows: Headquarters, Leyte Area Command, 23 officers and 107 enlisted men; 94th Regiment, 71 officers and 1,210 enlisted men; 95th Regiment, 78 officers and 954 enlisted men; 96th Regiment, 37 officers and 710 enlisted men; total strength, 209 officers and 2,981 enlisted men.[17]

Colonel Kangleon stated that as a result of guerrilla activities the Japanese sent out fewer patrols, staying mainly in the towns. The civilians, he claimed, were therefore able to plant and harvest their crops. Despite these brave words the guerrillas were definitely on the defensive, since Japanese intelligence had accurate information on their movements and strength. Nevertheless, the Japanese also knew that the guerrillas had established communication with General MacArthur in Australia and that they were sending important information to General Headquarters. This service the Japanese were unable to cut off.

Liaison Between Leyte and Australia

After his arrival in Australia in March 1942, General MacArthur had maintained radio contact with Corregidor until 6 May, but because of conditions in the Philippines radio communication with other parts of the Islands was all but impossible.[18] Before its fall, Corregidor maintained radio contact with military commanders on the other islands. Afterward, a few men escaped and made their way to Australia. The sum of information they brought was not large, but it included the welcome news that guerrilla units were in existence all over the Islands. In the summer of 1942 General Headquarters began to receive messages from the guerrillas in the Philippines, though at first General MacArthur was not sure that the messages actually came from the guerrillas.

In August 1942 MacArthur decided to get in touch with the members of the resistance movement in the Philippines, and for this purpose he enlisted the services of Maj.

[16] ATIS, SWPA, Enemy Publications 359, Guerrilla Activities in the Philippines, 2 parts, 28 Apr 45, *passim,* DRB AGO. Any resemblance between the Japanese figures and those in Kangleon's reports is purely coincidental.

[17] MI Sec, GHQ SWPA, G–2 Info Bull, The Resistance Movement on Leyte Island, 7 Oct 44, Doc Files Sec, G–2, Dept of Army.

[18] Intelligence Activities in the Philippines, p. 5.

Jesus Antonio Villamor, who had escaped from the Islands and who volunteered to return.[19] From August to December methods were devised and plans were made for sending an intelligence party to the Philippines.[20] On 27 December 1942 Major Villamor received orders to return secretly to the Islands by submarine with three other Filipino officers and two enlisted men.[21] They were instructed to establish an intelligence and secret service network throughout the Philippines; develop a chain of communications within the Philippines and to Australia, together with an escape route from the Islands for the evacuation of important personages; build up an organization for subversive activities, propaganda, limited resistance, and sabotage; and make an intelligence survey to obtain information on Japanese political, military, and civil intentions as well as the strength and disposition of Japanese military, naval, and air forces.[22]

Armed with these instructions, Major Villamor returned to the Philippine Islands. Slowly but carefully, from December 1942 to November 1943, he established an intelligence network that covered Luzon and the Visayan Islands. His story is told in part as follows:

I established this network principally with the idea that this net would be entirely independent of all intelligence nets previously established by the guerrillas, believing that in all probability you [General MacArthur] could rely more on guerrilla intelligence activities

for the present. I wanted to establish something that would really be underground and as secret as possible. For that reason, I took my time about it. I took as much as two months to train each individual man. I tried to impress on each man that after he left my place, he would be on his own and that no matter what happened to me or to the rest of the net, he would carry on. I assured him that both GHQ and I would have faith in him.[23]

Kangleon was largely responsible for the Leyte radio network. This intelligence network did not cover the entire island but only those positions over which he had control. General MacArthur did not furnish any considerable supplies for this net until shortly before his return in October 1944.[24] On 3 July 1944 Kangleon received seventy tons of supplies; an additional shipment of supplies and men followed on 20 July.[25] This allotment was in addition to money sent him. The funds available to Kangleon consisted of $50,000 in prewar currency ("only a few hundred" of which were spent by him), $225,000 in "bogus Japanese" currency, and $479,198 in emergency currency printed in the Islands and used for "army" purposes.[26]

Several clandestine radio stations were in operation on or near Leyte in June 1944. These were primarily contact stations established originally to integrate more closely the activities of the various guerrilla units with the directives of Colonel Kangleon's headquarters, which was in touch with General Headquarters. After the Leyte Area Command was recognized by General MacArthur, the first radio was sent to Leyte, but the Japanese captured it early in 1944 before

[19] Lt. Gen. Lewis H. Brereton considered Villamor "the most daring of the Filipino pilots." Lewis H. Brereton, *The Brereton Diaries* (New York, 1946), p. 58.

[20] Interv with Maj Villamor, 12 Oct 50.

[21] The party consisted of Major Villamor, 1st Lt. R. C. Ignacio, 2d Lt. D. C. Yuhico, 2d Lt. E. F. Quinto, Sgt. P. Jorge, and Sgt. D. Malie.

[22] AIB, GHQ SWPA, Instructions to Maj Villamor, 27 Dec 42, Guerrilla Papers.

[23] Villamor Rpt on Intel Net in Philippines, Guerrilla Papers.

[24] Intelligence Activities in the Philippines, p. 77.

[25] *Ibid.*, App. 2. The number of men and the amount and kinds of supplies are not given.

[26] *Ibid.*, App. 1.

it could be put to use. Kangleon received a new set from Mindanao. There were two coastwatcher stations in operation—one in southern Leyte and the other on Dinagat Island. These furnished MacArthur information on the activities of the Japanese in the area. Colonel Kangleon also used the radio set in southern Leyte to maintain contact with Colonel Fertig on Mindanao.[27]

As a result of information received from the intelligence network, on Leyte and in other areas, together with information from other sources, General MacArthur's intelligence officers were able to piece together a reasonably accurate picture of the Japanese units on Leyte, their strength, dispositions, and fortifications.

Kangleon's network, however, was not as active as most of the others in the Philippines that were operated by coastwatchers and guerrillas. From March 1944, when Kangleon's network was established, to Oc-

tober 1944, when the American forces returned, the monthly totals of messages received by General Headquarters from Leyte were as follows: March, 6; April, 7; May, 7; June, 12; July, 13; August, 13; September, 17; and October, 26.[28]

The guerrillas of the Philippine Islands made far-reaching contributions to the war effort. They were an extremely valuable source of intelligence; their activities forced the Japanese to retain in the Philippines comparatively large forces which would otherwise have been sent south; it is estimated that they killed from eight thousand to ten thousand Japanese troops; and, finally, they bolstered the morale, spirit, and loyalty of the Filipino people.[29] They kept alive the hope and belief that the forces of the United States would return and redeem the Islands.

---

[27] *Ibid., passim.*

[28] GHQ FEC, MI Sec, GS, A Brief History of the G–2 Section, GHQ SWPA, and Affiliated Units, Plate 10, facing p. 32, copy in OCMH.

[29] Office, Chief of Naval Opns, Guerrilla Activities in the Philippines, 14 Sep 44, file OP–16 FE.

CHAPTER III

Plans Are Made and Forces Are Readied

Estimate of the Enemy Situation

American knowledge of the Japanese forces on Leyte was derived from many sources.[1] The guerrillas on Leyte and other islands in the archipelago sent information to Australia on the movements, dispositions, fortifications, and defenses of the Japanese. Commander Parsons, on his submarine trips to the Islands, brought back with him important intelligence. Just before the invasion an intelligence officer from Sixth Army and one from the Seventh Fleet secretly went ashore from a submarine and gathered material on Japanese coastal fortifications and defenses in the beach area.

Much effort was expended before the invasion in mapping the island, but this work was based on prewar maps and the results were very inaccurate. Since much of the island was under heavy fog for long periods, the photomaps that were produced had little value. They missed many important terrain features and misplaced others by thousands of yards. In general, however, the maps of the beachhead areas were accurate.

In the spring of 1944 General MacArthur's headquarters received information that the Japanese were starting to reinforce their Philippine garrisons. An early estimate, made in June, put the number of enemy troops on the island at 20,000, a sharp increase over the 5,900 of the previous month. The increase resulted from the movement to Leyte from Samar of the veteran *16th Division*, which had fought at Bataan, and the arrival of 4,000 naval troops from the Palau Islands.[2] For the next month reports flowed in to General Headquarters that the *16th Division* was building coastal defenses and air-raid shelters, and improving the airfields and garrison defenses of the island.[3]

In July 1944 the Americans received information that all was not going well in the Japanese homeland. From a radio interception they learned that Premier Hideki Tojo and his entire cabinet had resigned on 18 July. The Japanese message stated: "The situation is the result of the period of

---

[1] Unless otherwise stated this section is based upon a report by Col H. V. White, G–2 Sixth Army, sub: G–2 Est of Enemy Sit, 20 Sep 44, Sixth Army Opns Rpt Leyte, pp. 167–70.

[2] GHQ SWPA Philippine Monthly Combined Sitrep, 15 Jun 44, GHQ G–3 Jnl, 15 Jun 44.

[3] GHQ SWPA Philippine Islands, G–2 Est of Enemy Sit 4, 11–17 Jun 44, GHQ G–3 Jnl, 17 Jun 44; GHQ SWPA Philippine Islands, G–2 Est of Enemy Sit 5, 18–24 Jun 44, GHQ G–3 Jnl, 24 Jun 44; AAF SWPA Intel Sum, Ser 216, GHQ G–3 Jnl, 13 Jun 44; GHQ SWPA Philippine Islands, G–2 Est of Enemy Sit 6, 25 Jun–1 Jul 44, GHQ G–3 Jnl, 1 Jul 44; GHQ SWPA Philippine Islands, G–2 Est of Enemy Sit 7, 2–8 Jul 44, GHQ G–3 Jnl, 8 Jul 44; AAF SWPA Intel Sum, Ser 225, GHQ G–3 Jnl, 14 Jul 44.

'sweating blood' and we sincerely regret causing anxiety to the Emperor. We thank the people at home and at the front for co-operating with the government. . . ." [4] The tenor of the announcement and of sub-sequent statements made it abundantly clear, however, that the Japanese were de-termined to do their utmost toward prose-cuting the war to a successful conclusion.

Meanwhile, all the Japanese garrisons in the Philippines were reinforced. The senior headquarters in the western Pacific was transferred from Singapore to Manila, and the brigades in the Islands were being de-veloped to divisional strength. Of the esti-mated 180,000 troops, 80,000 were believed to be on Luzon, 50,000 in the Visayan Is-lands, and 50,000 on Mindanao. It was also believed that the enemy air strength on the Islands was being greatly increased. There were 100 to 120 airfields in operation and between 700 and 1,500 aircraft, of which half were combat planes and the others training aircraft.[5]

In September 1944 Sixth Army G–2 estimated that the Japanese forces on Leyte consisted mainly of *16th Division* units and service troops—a total of 21,700 troops. The *35th Army* had just been activated on Cebu and was to be charged with the de-fense of all the Visayan Islands. It was esti-mated that the Leyte garrison consisted of the following combat troops: *20th Infantry Regiment*, 3,000; *33d Infantry Regiment*, 3,000; *16th Division Reconnaissance Regi-ment*, 1,000; elements of *102d Division*, 1,700; *7th Independent Tank Company*, 125; and *16th Division Headquarters* troops, 1,800. The total amounted to 10,625

men. In addition there were 1,000 base-defense troops and 10,075 service troops.

It was believed that the Japanese would commit one division on the day of the land-ing and the equivalent of another division, assembled from the tactical reserves on the island, not later than three days after the landing. For the next ten days, five to eight regiments might be sent in from neighboring islands. These would constitute the "maxi-mum numbers of reinforcements predicated upon the existence of conditions most favor-able to the enemy." [6] The enemy had an undetermined number of tanks and armored cars. The only artillery known to be avail-able were some coastal defense guns em-placed along the east coast and some artillery pieces on the hills overlooking Tacloban.

Sixth Army believed that on Leyte there were five operational airfields; three prob-ably operational or under construction; seven nonoperational; and one seaplane base. The two most important operational airstrips were the one at Tacloban with forty-five hardstandings and the one at Dulag with twenty hardstandings. The Tac-loban airstrip could accommodate both bombers and fighters. At the time of the in-vasion, it was estimated that the Japanese could oppose the amphibious movement and the landing with 442 fighters and 337 bombers from airfields scattered throughout the Philippines.

Although the possibility existed that the Japanese Fleet, which was based in waters near the home islands, might move to the Philippines, such a move was considered doubtful. It was believed that the principal and immediate threats consisted of a strong cruiser-destroyer task force; submarines; and motor torpedo boats and similar craft.

---

[4] AAF SWPA Intel Sum, Ser 228, GHQ G–3 Jnl, 25 Jul 44.

[5] Notes, WIDEAWAKE Conference, 20 Jul 44, GHQ G–3 Jnl, 24 Jul 44.

[6] Sixth Army G–2 Est of Enemy Sit, 20 Sep 44, Sixth Army Opns Rpt Leyte, p. 170.

Sixth Army concluded that the town of Tacloban, with its important port and airfield, was the key to the Japanese defense of the island. Consequently, a strong perimeter defense of the town and the surrounding area was expected. Since it was impossible for the Japanese, with a limited number of their troops on the island, to defend all of the east coast, strong forces and emplaced defensive positions were likely to be concentrated at road junctions and at the operational airfields. Mobile reserves would almost certainly be held in readiness at key points in Leyte Valley, ready to be rushed to the east coast areas under attack. It was assumed that strong defenses were already established in the Ormoc area and along the northeast coast of Ormoc Bay, since the port of Ormoc could be used to bring in reserves from the other islands in the archipelago. A strong garrison was expected at Carigara to protect the northern approaches to Leyte Valley and to repel any amphibious landing through Carigara Bay.

The plan for the liberation of Leyte called for more men, guns, ships, and aircraft than had been required for any previous operation in the Pacific. For the first time ground troops from the Central Pacific and Southwest Pacific were to join and fight the foe under a common commander. General MacArthur, who had left Luzon in a motor torpedo boat, was to return to the Philippines with a vast armada—the greatest seen in the Pacific up to that time.

The Tactical Plan

The Southwest Pacific Area was the command responsibility of General MacArthur. He had under his command Allied Air Forces, Lt. Gen. George C. Kenney commanding; Allied Naval Forces, Vice Adm.

Thomas C. Kinkaid commanding; Allied Land Forces, Gen. Sir Thomas Blamey commanding; United States Army Services of Supply (SWPA), Maj. Gen. James L. Frink commanding; and ALAMO Force, which was virtually Sixth Army, Lt. Gen. Walter Krueger commanding.

On 31 August 1944 General MacArthur issued his first formal directive covering projected operations in the Philippines. The Leyte operation was known as KING II. The Southwest Pacific forces were to "seize objectives in the Mindanao, Leyte and Samar areas in order to establish air, naval and logistic bases to cover subsequent operations to complete the reoccupation of the Philippines." The assigned target dates were as follows: southern Mindanao, 15 November 1944; northwestern Mindanao, 7 December; and Leyte Gulf-Surigao Strait area, 20 December. The Sixth Army, covered by Admiral Halsey's Third Fleet and supported by the Allied Air and Naval Forces, was directed to carry out the three operations.[7] On 15 September General Krueger received word that the Talaud and Mindanao operations had been canceled and that the target date—designated as "A Day"—for the Leyte operation had been advanced to 20 October.[8]

The American Forces

The immediate task assigned the forces of the Southwest Pacific, supported by the Third Fleet, was the seizure and control of the Leyte Gulf–Surigao Strait area in order to establish air, naval, and logistic bases to support further operations into the Philippines. Before the invasion, air and naval operations were to be conducted so as to dis-

[7] GHQ SWPA Warning Instns 5, 31 Aug 44.
[8] GHQ SWPA Warning Instns 5/1, 15 Sep 44.

organize Japanese ground and air defenses. The ground operation was divided into three phases. In the first phase overwater movement and minor amphibious operations to secure entrance into Leyte Gulf were to take place. The main effort, which constituted the second phase, was to involve a major assault to caputre the airfields and base sites in Leyte Valley and to open up San Juanico and Panaon Straits. In the final phase, the remaining portions of the island in Japanese hands and the western part of southern Samar were to be secured, and Surigao Strait was to be opened.[9] The target date had been set for 20 October 1944.

General plans for the operation had long since been worked out, but not until 20 September did General MacArthur issue his final plan for the occupation of Leyte. It was based upon the assumption that American forces were or would be established along the Marianas–Ulithi–Palaus–Morotai line and that the Japanese land and air forces in the Philippines and Formosa would have been "seriously crippled and that the Japanese Fleet would elect to remain in Empire waters" with only "light forces remaining in the vicinity of the Philippines." The Japanese were expected to have one well-supplied division in the area with only limited ability to reinforce it from others of the Visayan Islands and with all subsequent supply deliveries cut off. It was assumed that Japanese defenses would be concentrated in the vicinity of the airfields in the Leyte Valley and at Tacloban.

The command organization was as follows: General MacArthur was Supreme Commander, but during the amphibious movement and landing Admiral Kinkaid,

as commander of the Naval Attack Force, was to be in command of all amphibious operations. *(Chart 1)* Army officers, who took control of their forces ashore, were to continue under the Commander, Naval Attack Force, until the next senior Army commander assumed control. Upon his arrival ashore and after notification to Admiral Kinkaid, General Krueger was to take control of the ground troops. General Kenney, as commander of the Allied Air Forces, would report directly to General MacArthur.

Admiral Halsey, as commander of the Third Fleet, was to co-ordinate his operations with those of General MacArthur but he was responsible to Admiral Nimitz, Commander in Chief, Pacific Ocean Area. The Third Fleet was composed of Vice Adm. Marc Mitscher's Fast Carrier Task Force, together with miscellaneous elements. Mitscher's force was divided into four carrier groups.[10]

The Allied Naval Forces, which consisted principally of the U. S. Seventh Fleet under Admiral Kinkaid, was to transport and establish ashore the ground assault force. The Central Philippine Attack Force consisted of three task forces. Task Force 77, commanded by Admiral Kinkaid, was to furnish direct air and naval support and was composed of battleships, light and heavy cruisers, destroyers, destroyer escorts, carriers, escort carriers, gunboat and mortar flotillas, mine sweepers, auxiliary vessels, and underwater demolition teams. The transports and cargo ships of the Northern Attack Force, Task Force 78, under Rear Adm. Daniel E. Barbey, and the Southern

---

[9] GHQ SWPA Stf Study, KING II, 4th ed., 20 Sep 44. This study was not a directive but a basis for planning the operation.

[10] CINCPAC–CINCPOA Opn Plan 8-44, quoted in Annex A, CINCPAC–CINCPOA Opns in POA, Oct 44, pp. 56–57, A–16–3/FF12, Ser 00397, 31 May 45.

CHART 1—OPERATIONAL ORGANIZATION FOR THE LEYTE CAMPAIGN

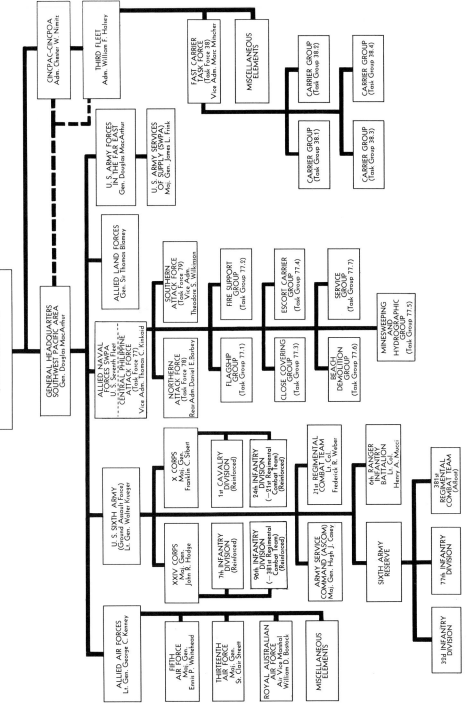

Attack Force, Task Force 79, under Vice Adm. Theodore S. Wilkinson, were to transport and set ashore the ground troops. Task Force 79 had been lent to General MacArthur by Admiral Nimitz for the operation.

The Allied Air Forces, principally the Far East Air Forces under General Kenney, was to neutralize hostile air and naval forces within range of the Philippines. The Allied Air Forces consisted of the Fifth Air Force, commanded by Maj. Gen. Ennis P. Whitehead; the Thirteenth Air Force, commanded by Maj. Gen. St. Clair Streett; the Royal Australian Air Force Command under Air Vice Marshal William D. Bostock; and miscellaneous elements. On order, the Fifth Air Force was to be prepared to take over the mission of furnishing direct air support to the ground troops.

The United States Army Services of Supply, Southwest Pacific Area, commanded by General Frink, was to furnish logistic support for the operation. The Eighth U.S. Army, commanded by Lt. Gen. Robert L. Eichelberger, and the Allied Land Forces, commanded by General Blamey, were to take over missions previously assigned the Sixth Army and to assist the latter in training, staging, and mounting the troops for the Leyte operation.

The ground troops who were to attack Leyte constituted a field army—the Sixth Army, which had fought its way up the New Guinea coast since April 1943 as ALAMO Force. On 25 September 1944 ALAMO Force was dissolved and Sixth Army assumed its tactical missions. General Krueger was commanding general for all these campaigns. The principal component parts of Sixth Army were X and XXIV Corps. The former consisted of the 1st Cav-

alry and 24th Infantry Divisions, under Lt. Gen. Franklin C. Sibert, a seasoned commander who had successfully fought the Japanese on New Guinea at Wakde–Sarmi. The XXIV Corps, under Maj. Gen. John R. Hodge, who had defeated the Japanese on Guadalcanal, New Georgia, and Bougainville, was composed of the 7th and 96th Infantry Divisions. In reserve were the 32d and 77th Infantry Divisions. The Sixth Army Service Command was to perform engineer functions on the island and give general logistic support.

Approximately 174,000 troops were made available for the initial assault phase of the operation. About 51,500 of these made up the XXIV Corps and 53,000 the X Corps. In addition to these troops, the reserve 32d and 77th Divisions had a strength of about 14,500 and 14,000 troops, respectively. All of the assault divisions were reinforced with tank battalions, amphibian truck and tractor battalions, joint assault signal companies, and many attached service units. A total of about 202,500 ground troops was committed to the Leyte operation.[11]

Headquarters, Sixth Army, had never participated as such in any campaign, but as Headquarters, ALAMO Force, it had directed the operations up the New Guinea coast. Both the X and XXIV Corps were yet to be battle tested, though all their divisions with one exception had participated in previous campaigns against the Japanese. The 1st Cavalry Division had taken part in the Admiralty Islands campaign; the 7th Division had defeated the Japanese at Attu and Kwajalein; the 24th Division had fought in the Hollandia campaign; the 32d Division had won the Papua Campaign and

---

[11] Sixth Army FO 25, 23 Sep 44, Annexes 6a–6f.

been victorious at Aitape on New Guinea; and the 77th Division had shared in the victory at Guam. Only the 96th Division was yet to be combat tested.[12]

General MacArthur's Warning Instructions 5 and Operations Instructions 70 were used by each of the major commanders as a basis for his own operations orders. Although each order was derived from the one next above it, all were planned concurrently. There was need for constant intertheater, interservice, and intraservice conferences and discussions on all phases of the plans as they evolved. Frequently the planning was made easier by using the work done on plans for other operations. For example, the logistical plan for the canceled Yap operation was adapted with very little change to the Leyte operation. The general schemes of maneuver and the employment of support forces which had been found valuable in previous operations were also adapted with minor variations to the plans for Leyte.

Air Support

The Navy was to bear the brunt of furnishing air support in the early stages of the campaign. By arrangement with Admiral Nimitz, the Carrier Task Force from Admiral Halsey's Third Fleet was to strike northern Luzon and Okinawa or Formosa, or both, from A Day minus 10 to A minus 7. From A minus 4 through A Day, strikes were to be made on Luzon, the Cebu–Negros area, and the Leyte area in support of the landings. As soon as the Palau air base facilities would permit, shore-based air

forces from the Central Pacific were to operate in the Bicol area.[13]

The Allied Naval Forces was to furnish carrier aircraft as protection for convoys and naval task forces and, supplemented by aircraft of the Third Fleet and the Allied Air Forces, to provide direct air support for the landings. In addition, it was to furnish protective air support and cover by carrier aircraft prior to A Day for the preliminary landings in Leyte Gulf and for the mine sweeping.[14]

General MacArthur assigned air support missions to the Allied Air Forces. General Kenney's airmen were (1) to make aerial reconnaissance; (2) in co-ordination with Third Fleet carrier-based aircraft, to neutralize hostile naval and air forces within range of the Philippines from A minus 9 in order to cover the movement of naval forces, the landing, and subsequent operations; (3) within capabilities and when requested by Admiral Kinkaid, to protect convoys and naval forces and provide direct support of the landings and subsequent operations; and (4) to destroy Japanese shipping and installations in the Sulu and Arafura Seas and the East Indies.[15]

On 24 September General Kenney issued his order for the Leyte operation and assigned missions to the Allied Air Forces. He designated General Whitehead's Fifth Air Force as the Air Assault Force. It was to support the operation by intensified air activities against enemy installations, destroy hostile air and surface forces in the Celebes Sea and assigned areas in the Philippine Archipelago, and provide air defense for

---

[12] Hist Div, Dept of the Army, Combat Chronicle, An Outline History of U.S. Army Divisions, *passim*, OCMH.

[13] CTF 77 Opns Plan, Ser 00022A, 26 Sep 44, GHQ G–3 Jnl, 6 Oct 44; CINCPAC-CINCPOA Opn Plan 8–44, cited n. 10, above.

[14] GHQ SWPA Opns Instns 70, 21 Sep 44.

[15] *Ibid.*

existing bases and forces in transit to Leyte within range of its capabilities. It was also to be prepared to establish, on order, land-based air forces on Leyte. The Thirteenth Air Force was to support the missions of the Fifth Air Force, while the Royal Australian Air Force Command was to destroy Japanese installations and sources of raw materials in the Netherlands Indies.[16]

Aircraft from other theaters agreed to aid in the operation. The Fourteenth Air Force from the China–Burma–India Theater and the Twentieth Air Force from the Central Pacific were to conduct strikes against Formosa. The Southeast Asia Command was asked to schedule air offensives against Burma and Malaya just prior to A Day.[17]

Naval Support

The Seventh Fleet under Admiral Kinkaid was assigned the following mission: "by a ship to shore amphibious operation, [to] transport, protect, land and support elements of the 6th Army in order to assist in the seizure, occupation and development of the Leyte area of the Southern Philippines." [18] *(Chart 2)*

The Seventh Fleet was designated the Naval Attack Force. For the operation Admiral Kinkaid organized two attack forces: the Northern Attack Force (VII Amphibious Force), under Admiral Barbey, and the Southern Attack Force (III Amphibious Force), under Admiral Wilkinson. In addition, several subordinate units were created: a bombardment and fire support group under Rear Adm. Jesse B. Oldendorf; and a close covering group, an escort carrier

group, a mine-sweeping group, and twelve underwater demolition teams. The Northern Attack Force was to transport and land the X Corps, while the Southern Attack Force was to do the same for the XXIV Corps.

The task groups of the two attack forces were to sortie from the mounting areas at Manus in the Admiralties and Hollandia in Netherlands New Guinea and rendezvous en route to the objective area. Both were "to land main elements as nearly simultaneously as practicable at H Hour on 20 October." Meanwhile, an advance group on 17 October was to land the 6th Ranger Infantry Battalion on the islands guarding the approaches to Leyte Gulf. The task groups were to regulate their speed of advance so that they would arrive at the entrance of the approach channel to Leyte Gulf at specified times. The mine-sweeping group and certain units of the bombardment and fire support group which were to render fire support for initial mine-sweeping operations were to arrive at 0600 on 17 October. They were to be followed fifteen minutes later by the attack group assigned to the island approaches. At 1000 on the same day the rest of the bombardment and fire support group were to arrive. Beginning at 2300 on 19 October the transports and LST's of the two attack forces were scheduled to arrive in successive groups. Their time of arrival was also set so that each group would reach its transport area in sufficient time to dispatch the assault waves to the beach at the designated hour.[19]

On arrival in the objective area, the bombardment and fire support group was to divide into northern and southern fire support units, which were then to move to their respective target areas. The northern fire

---

[16] AAF SWPA Opns Instns 71, 24 Sep 44.
[17] FEAF, History of Far East Air Forces, I, 117, AAF Hist Archives.
[18] CANF SWPA Opns Plan 13-44, 26 Sep 44.

[19] *Ibid.,* Apps. 1 and 2 to Annex C.

CHART 2—ORGANIZATION OF THE CENTRAL PHILIPPINE ATTACK FORCE

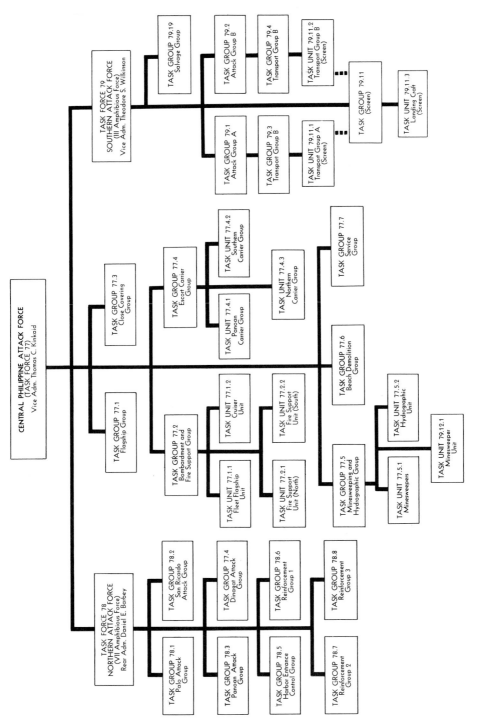

support unit consisted of 3 old battleships—the *Mississippi, Maryland,* and *West Virginia*—and 3 destroyers. The southern fire support unit was composed of 3 battleships—the *Tennessee, California,* and *Pennsylvania*—13 destroyers, 3 light cruisers, 3 heavy cruisers, and 1 small seaplane tender.

The destroyers in the two target areas were to furnish protection to the mine sweepers and the underwater demolition teams. The latter were to cover the northern and southern beaches before A Day and search out and destroy any obstacles, either Japanese-made or natural, in the waters surrounding the landing beach areas. The mine sweepers were to start clearing Leyte Gulf of fixed or floating mines on 17 October, three days before the main assault. On the following days, including 20 October, they were to make more intensive sweeps of the channels and landing beach areas, with the vessels going as close to shore as possible without endangering gear.[20]

Admiral Oldendorf was to direct the bombardment and fire support. The bombardment was to start on 17 October in preparation for the landings on the island approaches. The gunfire before 20 October was for the purpose of rendering unserviceable both airfields and Japanese aircraft on the ground, in addition to destroying guns and emplacements, fuel storage and ammunition dumps, naval forces and shipping, beach defenses and strong points, troops, torpedo launching ramps, and torpedo barges. Close fire support was to be given to the underwater demolition teams and destructive fire was to be delivered against enemy forces attempting overwater movements. Finally, night harassing fire was

scheduled to prevent any night attempts of the Japanese to reconstruct the fortifications and airfields.

On 20 October the naval gunfire support units were to cover the approach of the transports to the unloading areas and to furnish necessary counterbattery fire; thoroughly cover the landing beach areas from the low-water line to approximately 400 yards inland; and closely support the landings with rockets, 4.2-inch mortars, and gunfire of all caliber from the ships. After the landings, the naval gunfire units were to deliver fire on call and prevent the Japanese from either reinforcing or evacuating the island.[21]

The Joint Chiefs of Staff had directed Admiral Nimitz to support General MacArthur's operation against Leyte. Admiral Nimitz ordered Admiral Halsey's Third Fleet to "destroy enemy naval and air forces in or threatening the Philippine Area." The Third Fleet was also to protect the air and sea communications along the Central Philippines axis. If an opportunity to destroy major portions of the Japanese Fleet should arise or could be created, such destruction was to be the primary task of all naval forces from the Central Pacific. Admiral Halsey and General MacArthur were to arrange the necessary measures for the co-ordination of their operations.[22]

In support of the Leyte operation the Third Fleet was to contain or destroy the Japanese Fleet and to destroy enemy aircraft and shipping in the Formosa, Luzon, Visayan, and Mindanao areas from 9 October through 17 October, and from A Day for as long as necessary during the next thirty

---

[20] *Ibid.,* App. 3 to Annex E.

[21] *Ibid.,* App. 1 to Annex E.
[22] CINCPAC–CINCPOA Opn Plan 8-44, cited n. 10, above.

days, in order to "maintain their continued neutralization." From 18 October until such time as the escort carriers could assume direct support, the Third Fleet was to destroy enemy ground defenses and installations in Leyte and adjacent areas. Finally, the Third Fleet was to provide direct support by fast carrier aircraft for the landing and subsequent operations.[23]

Submarines from both the Southwest Pacific and Central Pacific were to support the operations by maintaining an offensive reconnaissance over the most probable Japanese route of advance, maintaining observation and lifeguard services and furnishing weather reports and strategic patrols. Submarines from the Central Pacific were to patrol in the Formosa, Luzon, Tokyo Bay, and Sasebo areas, while those from the Seventh Fleet patrolled in the area of Makassar Strait, the Celebes Sea, and the Sulu Sea. Submarines from both areas were to maintain a strong patrol in the Hainan–northern Luzon areas.[24]

The naval gunfire, the air support, and the artillery fire were to be carefully co-ordinated. At every level from battalion to army representatives from each support arm were to co-ordinate the use of their support arms against targets in their respective zones of action. Requests for support were to be screened as they passed through the various echelons for approval. Commanders in the field felt that the passage of requests through many channels was time consuming and consequently sometimes nullified what might have been an immediate advantage. However, requests for support were usually acted upon within an hour.

---

[23] GHQ SWPA Opns Instns 70, 21 Sep 44.
[24] CANF SWPA Opns Plan 13-44, 26 Sep 44.

The Ground Forces

The ground forces designated for the Leyte operation came from two different theaters—the X Corps from the Southwest Pacific and the XXIV Corps from the Central Pacific. The XXIV Corps, originally intended for the Yap operation, had been substituted for the XIV Corps, originally intended for Leyte. As the new assignment of the XXIV Corps placed it under the operational control of General MacArthur, it was necessary that agreements on the co-ordination of operations be reached by the commanders in chief of the two areas. The XXIV Corps, with its original shipping, had been turned over to General MacArthur. During the combat phase at Leyte, General MacArthur was to furnish the replacements required by the XXIV Corps, but subsequent replacements were to be supplied by Admiral Nimitz.[25]

The initial assault for the island of Leyte was to begin in the dim half dawn of 17 October, when elements of the 6th Ranger Infantry Battalion were to land under the protection of naval gunfire and seize the small islands that guarded the entrance to Leyte Gulf. (*Map 1*) Harbor lights were to be placed on Homonhon Island and the northern tip of Dinagat Island in order to guide the passage of the convoy into the gulf. Since it was believed that there were valuable mine charts on Suluan, that island was added to the objectives of the 6th Rangers.

General Krueger had wanted to use either the reinforced 158th Infantry Regiment or

---

[25] Memo, Rear Adm Forrest P. Sherman, Plans Off POA, and Maj Gen Stephen J. Chamberlin, ACofS G–3 SWPA, for CINCSWPA and CINC-POA, 21 Sep 44, Sixth Army G–3 Jnl, 21 Sep 44.

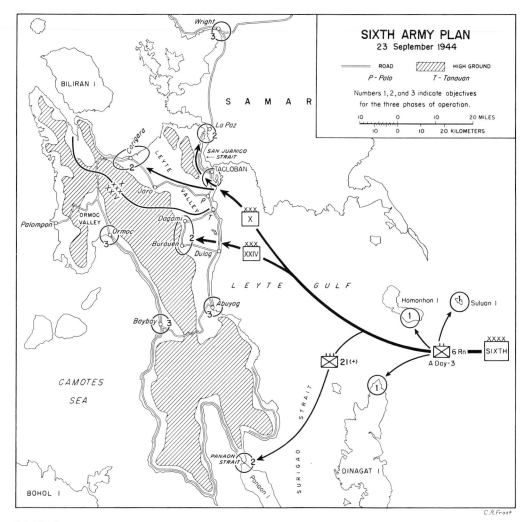

MAP 1

the reinforced 112th Cavalry Regimental Combat Team to secure the island approaches to Leyte Gulf and the Panaon Strait area. The 21st Infantry, which was assigned the mission of securing the Panaon Strait area, then could have remained with the 24th Division, its parent unit, and the 6th Ranger Battalion could have been used wherever and whenever needed. In addition, these missions would have been put in

the hands of a general officer who had an experienced staff to assist him. Neither of the desired regiments, however, could be made available for the Leyte operation because of shortage of troops and previous commitments.[26]

While the Rangers were seizing the small islands, the mine sweepers and underwater

---

[26] *Ibid.*

demolition teams were to start clearing the gulf of natural and man-made obstacles. The fire support units were to move in and start softening up the beaches. The completion of these missions would conclude the first phase of the operation.

The second phase comprised "a major amphibious assault to attack and destroy hostile forces in the coastal strip Tacloban–Dulag inclusive, and to seize airdromes and base sites therein; a rapid advance through Leyte Valley to seize and occupy the Capoocan–Carigara–Barugo area; [and finally] open San Juanico and Panaon Straits...." [27]

In the very early hours of 20 October the Northern and Southern Attack Forces were to move to their appointed beach areas and be prepared to disembark their assault troops. The reinforced 21st Infantry Regiment was to go ashore at 0930 in the vicinity of Panaon Strait at the extreme southeast tip of Leyte and secure control of that entrance to Sogod Bay. To the north at 1000, the X Corps was to land with two divisions abreast in the Marasbaras and Palo areas. About fifteen miles farther south, in the Dulag area, the XXIV Corps was to go ashore simultaneously with two divisions abreast. The two corps would be so widely separated and their objectives so divergent that initially they could not be mutually supporting. Even within the zones of action of the two corps, the missions assigned the divisions would limit the ability of the divisions to support each other. [28]

As General Krueger felt that the Japanese would offer the greatest resistance in the north, the initial objectives of the X Corps were limited to the seizure of Palo and the capture of Tacloban and its airfield. The northernmost unit, the 1st Cavalry Division, actually an infantry square division, was to land with brigades abreast in the Marasbaras area, advance to the north, and seize Tacloban and its airstrip, the most important objective for A Day. Thereafter, the division was to secure control over San Juanico Strait. To the left of the 1st Cavalry Division, the 24th Division was to go ashore with regiments abreast in the Palo area, seize Palo, and then advance northwest through the Leyte Valley. The two divisions were to converge on Carigara, at the northern end of Leyte Valley on Carigara Bay. [29]

In the XXIV Corps zone, the 96th Division with regiments abreast was to land in the area between Dulag and San Roque, and to secure that portion of Highway 1 in its zone, Catmon Hill, and, finally, the Dagami–Tanauan area. On its left the 7th Division with regiments abreast was to go ashore in the Dulag area. One element was to go south and seize the Highway 1 bridge and crossings of the Daguitan (Marabang) River at Dao while the main force of the division was to advance along the axis of the Dulag–Burauen road and capture Burauen. The 7th Division would then be in a position to move north toward Dagami. All hostile airfields in its zone of action were to be seized and occupied. The division was to be prepared, on corps order, to seize Abuyog, to the south, and Baybay, on the west coast, destroying enemy forces on the west coast and in the southern portion of Leyte. [30]

Completion of these missions of the X and XXIV Corps would bring to an end the second phase of the Leyte operation. By this time, General Krueger hoped, the back of the Japanese resistance would be broken.

---

[27] Sixth Army FO 25, 23 Sep 44.

[28] *Ibid.;* Sixth Army Opns Rpt Leyte, p. 23.

[29] X Corps FO 1, 30 Sep 44; 1st Cav Div FO 1, 2 Oct 44; 24th Inf Div FO 1, 1 Oct 44.

[30] XXIV Corps FO 3, 28 Sep 44; 96th Div FO 2, 10 Oct 44; 7th Div FO 9, 1 Oct 44.

With Leyte Valley and its airfields and base sites firmly in the hands of the Sixth Army, General Krueger's forces would be in a position to apply firmly the pincers on the remaining Japanese on the island. The X Corps was to drive south down the Ormoc Valley to Ormoc while the XXIV Corps was to move north from Baybay along the shores of Ormoc Bay and make juncture with the X Corps. The remnants of the Japanese forces, driven into the mountains of western Leyte, would be unable to continue an organized resistance.[31]

The eastern shores of Leyte were chosen for the initial landing, since the beaches on this side were the best on the island, and were the logical entrance to the important airfields, base sites, and roads in Leyte Valley.

Since the large number of naval vessels required considerable room for landing the assault troops and for maneuvering, the landing beach areas of the two corps were widely separated. In addition, the value of the road net which connected Dulag with the Burauen airfields formed an important consideration in the determination of the landing beach sites of the XXIV Corps. "This latter factor—which took precedence over the potentiality of strong enemy resistance from Catmon Hill—had determined the selection of beaches in the Dulag area."[32]

Although it was recognized as necessary for elements of the XXIV Corps to advance south to Abuyog and then overland to Baybay in order to destroy the enemy forces on the west coast, these maneuvers would leave great gaps in the battle line if only four divisions were at first employed. General Krueger therefore asked General Headquarters

of the Southwest Pacific for additional combat troops, and during the progress of the campaign General MacArthur made them available.[33]

The Sixth Army was also troubled about its reserve force. Although the 32d Division at Morotai and Hollandia and the 77th Division at Guam had been designated as Sixth Army Reserve, it would be impossible for these units to arrive at Leyte before the middle of November. The shortage of amphibious shipping made it necessary to mount these divisions on the turnaround of assault shipping. Since the floating reserve would have to come from one of the assault divisions, it was difficult to determine from which division to take it. It was decided that the 96th Division, considering its mission, could best spare such a unit, and the 381st Infantry of that division was therefore selected.[34]

To summarize the mission of the Sixth Army: on 17 October, the 6th Ranger Infantry Battalion would seize Suluan, Dinagat, and Homonhon Islands, in the entrance to Leyte Bay. At 0930 on 20 October, the 21st Infantry Regiment was to land in the vicinity of Panaon Strait and secure control of that entrance to Sogod Bay. At 1000 on the same day the Sixth Army with the X and XXIV Corps abreast would make a major amphibious landing on Leyte. In the north the X Corps, with the 1st Cavalry Division and the 24th Infantry Division abreast, after moving ashore in the Marasbaras and the Palo areas, would capture Tacloban, its airfield, and Palo. In the south the XXIV Corps with the 96th and 7th Infantry Divisions abreast would go ashore to secure control in the Dulag area.[35]

---

[31] Sixth Army FO 25, 23 Sep 44.
[32] Sixth Army Opns Rpt Leyte, p. 23.

[33] *Ibid.*
[34] *Ibid.*
[35] *Ibid.,* p. 20.

The Logistical Plan

Construction

The decision to land on Leyte at the beginning of the rainy season and to construct a major supply and air base thereon presented a serious problem to the engineers. The poor soil, inadequate roads, and heavy rains were obstacles that had to be met and in some way overcome if the operation was to be a logistical success. General MacArthur recognized the need for making use of Leyte as a logistical base by creating for the first time in the Southwest Pacific an army service command and by detailing his chief engineer, Maj. Gen. Hugh J. Casey, to be its commander. ASCOM, as it was called, was to provide the logistical services required for the operation and to build and operate the Army base facilities until the United States Army Services of Supply (SWPA) could take over. This transfer was expected to take place about thirty days after the assault troops first landed on the shores of Leyte.[36]

General MacArthur directed the Sixth Army to establish the following air facilities in the Leyte area: by A plus 5, facilities for two fighter groups, one night fighter squadron, one photo squadron, one medium bomber group plus one squadron, three patrol bomber squadrons, and one Marine reconnaissance squadron; by A plus 30, additional facilities for two light bomber groups, one air-sea rescue squadron, one tactical reconnaissance squadron, and one fighter squadron; additional facilities by A plus 45 for one fighter group, one patrol bomber squadron, two heavy bomber groups, and one laboratory squadron; and by A plus 60, further facilities for one photo

squadron, one patrol bomber squadron, two troop carrier groups, and one combat mapping squadron.[37]

The final Sixth Army plan for the Leyte operation directed ASCOM to establish naval facilities in the Leyte area as well as the aforementioned air facilities; to make topographic and hydrographic surveys, followed by suitable changes in the plans for the construction of bases, docks, roads, and airdromes; to unload all units, supplies, and matériel arriving in the area and to store and issue supplies to ground and air units; and, in co-operation with the Philippine Civil Affairs Units, recruit and direct native labor.[38]

The construction program as planned for Leyte brought strong remonstrances from the Sixth Army engineers. On 10 August Col. William J. Ely, the executive officer, protested against the employment of Leyte as a major supply and air force base. The reasons for his objections were prophetic. The operation was to be launched during the season of heavy rains in an area where high winds and typhoons occurred. The harbor was so shallow and so obstructed by patches of coral that the approaches would have to be as much as 800 feet long. The fact that the flat Leyte Valley was interlaced by many streams and flooded with rice paddies indicated that the soil was "most unstable." The condition of the soil and drainage would require the hauling, frequently for long distances, of considerable quantities of rock for the construction of roads. The existing roads and bridges, in most places so narrow as to permit only one-way traffic, would soon disintegrate under the constant heavy rains and the pounding of military vehicles. Colonel Ely forecast

---

[36] *Ibid.*, p. 24.

[37] *Ibid.*, p. 19.
[38] Sixth Army FO 25, 23 Sep 44.

that, in the light of past experience with poor conditions of soil and drainage, the construction and enlargement of the airstrips would be difficult. The shortage of engineer troops decreased the possibility of providing major air and supply bases in sufficient time to properly support further operations. He concluded that "the construction mission cannot be satisfactorily accomplished with the engineer troops available, particularly during the first 90 days." Colonel Ely gloomily summarized, "Perhaps we can mud and muddle through again on a shoestring but the shoestring must be frayed by this time and if it broke we may lose our shirt as well as our shoe."

If the strategic plan were fixed, he recommended that one or more of the following measures be adopted: (1) increase the number of engineer construction troops; (2) shift the operation to an area where major air and supply bases could be constructed without encountering the adverse weather and port conditions existing on Leyte; (3) "decrease the tempo of the strategic plan"; and finally (4) decrease the scope of the air and supply requirements. Nothing was to be gained "by undertaking an overambitious program from the beginning that cannot be completed on a time schedule that will assure early and adequate support to future operations." [39]

Col. Samuel D. Sturgis, Jr., Sixth Army Engineer, forwarded Colonel Ely's report with a strong concurrence to General Mac-Arthur's engineer, but General Headquarters decided to proceed with the original logistical plans for the operation. [40]

Supplies

The supplies required for the operation involved staggering quantities. For an invasion force of 150,000 men, the War Department figures showed that, for the landing period alone, 1,500,000 tons of general equipment, 235,000 tons of combat vehicles, 200,000 tons of ammunition, and 200,000 tons of medical supplies were required. Thereafter, 332,000 tons of equipment would be required every thirty days. [41] According to the final plan, issued by General Krueger on 30 September 1944, [42] the units of the Sixth Army, X Corps, and Sixth Army Service Command, under General Casey, which were to arrive at Leyte between 20 and 30 October were to take ashore a minimum of ten days' supply of all classes (except engineer supplies, which were to be for at least thirty days), and two units of fire. [43] In this way the strain on ASCOM supply units would be lessened, and ASCOM, it was hoped, would have time to establish dumps and make the necessary supply installations. In addition to supplies accompanying the assault troops, sufficient quantities were to be brought into Leyte by 30 October to bring the total supplies for the troops to the following figures, expressed in days: thirty days of food, clothing, and equipment; fifteen days of motor transport fuel and distillate; and thirty days of other petroleum products. There were also to be five units of fire for combat troops and three for service troops. The original plan had called for a thirty-day supply of all petroleum products to be brought in by A plus 10,

---

[39] Memo, Col Ely, Exec Off, Sixth Army Engineer, for Col Samuel D. Sturgis, Jr., Sixth Army Engineer; Air Evaluation Board SWPA, The Leyte Campaign, pp. 400–403.

[40] Interv with Maj Gen George H. Decker, formerly CofS Sixth Army, 7 Sep 51.

[41] MI, GS, GHQ FEC, History of the United States Army Forces in the Far East 1943–1945, p. 69.

[42] Sixth Army Admin O 14, 30 Sep 44.

[43] Sixth Army Admin O 14, Annex 4, 30 Sep 44.

but this quantity was reduced when General Krueger adopted a plan for the installation by A plus 7 of bulk fuel storage. The XXIV Corps supply levels were to remain the same as those planned for the now-canceled Yap operation, since the corps was already loaded with supplies which were considered adequate for the Leyte invasion.[44]

There were certain differences in the loads carried by the X and the XXIV Corps. The XXIV Corps embarked with a thirty-day supply of rations and medical supplies, twenty days of clothing, weapons, vehicles, fuels, lubricants, construction matériel, and seven units of fire for all artillery and five units for other types of weapons. Since the type of equipment loaded had been selected for the Yap operation, amphibian vehicles were favored over wheeled vehicles. Less than 50 percent of the Table of Equipment allowance of general purpose vehicles and dump trucks accompanied the units. Furthermore, many badly needed items of organizational equipment were carried by the rear echelons, which did not arrive until January 1945, after Leyte had been secured.[45]

The supplies which were to accompany the troops during the initial phases of the Leyte operation were to come from bases in New Guinea and the Central Pacific. Resupply shipping—to be called for as needed—was to be loaded at bases in the United States, Australia, and, if necessary, New Guinea.[46] In addition, ten loaded liberty ships were to be held in floating reserve, eight at Hollandia and two in the Palaus. Two of these were loaded with aviation gasoline, two with fuel oil and lubricants,

two with ammunition for the air forces and four with ammunition for the ground forces. Admiral Nimitz was to furnish two of the four last mentioned. Except for the LST's transporting the XXIV Corps, each LST arriving on 20 October was to carry thirty tons of technical supplies for the air forces. All LST's arriving from A plus 1 through A plus 4 were to carry forty tons of similar supplies.[47] General MacArthur charged the Commanding General, United States Army Services of Supply (SWPA), with providing the Sixth Army with all supplies, except air force technical supplies, that would be needed for the operation.[48]

An Army garrison force for Yap under Maj. Gen. Roscoe B. Woodruff had been scheduled to go with the XXIV Corps, and at Admiral Nimitz' suggestion this force was designated to accompany the corps to the new target, Leyte, though the Southwest Pacific Area had never used an organization of this type.[49] It was hoped that the force might be useful in taking over "housekeeping" duties and the development of rear areas, thus relieving the assault commander of those responsibilities. Incidentally, General Krueger made little use of the garrison force. Units which furnished logistic support for carrier operations were also included and were to be assigned to the Seventh Fleet. Admiral Nimitz was to continue furnishing logistic support to the XXIV Corps until relieved by General MacArthur.[50]

---

[44] Sixth Army Opns Rpt Leyte, p. 24.
[45] XXIV Corps Opns Rpt Leyte, p. 35.
[46] Ibid.

[47] Sixth Army Admin O 14, 30 Sep 44.
[48] GHQ SWPA Opns Instns 70, Annex 4, 21 Sep 44, Sixth Army G-3 Jnl, 21 Sep 44.
[49] Ibid., p. 18.
[50] Rad, CINCPOA to CINCSWPA, 16119, 19 Sep 44, Sixth Army G-3 Jnl, 19 Sep 44; Info Rad, CINCSWPA to CINCPOA, CX 18072, 20 Sep 44, Sixth Army G-3 Jnl, 21 Sep 44.

Shipping

On 21 September, Pacific Ocean Areas and Southwest Pacific Area reached an agreement on resupply of ammunition for the XXIV Corps. Arrangements were made for loaded ships from San Francisco to be sent to the Leyte area periodically to alleviate the shipping shortage.[51] It was expected that at least twenty-two cargo ships would so arrive from San Francisco during the operation.

The change in target dates and the substitution of the XXIV Corps for the XIV Corps reduced the amount of amphibious shipping available for the Leyte operation. Consequently representatives of the Sixth Army, the VII Amphibious Force, and the Fifth Air Force met at General Krueger's headquarters to work out the details for a new shipping schedule. They made minor changes in the dates for the movement of convoys, and rearranged echelons, eliminating one.[52] The shipping for the XXIV Corps and the ten resupply ships were to remain the same as planned for Yap.[53]

The amphibious shipping allocated to MacArthur was to be made available for such turnaround shipping as would be required. The date of release of the amphibious vessels in order to mount subsequent operations would be announced later, but none were to be released for return to Nimitz' control without permission from MacArthur. An additional division lift, which was not included, was to return the 77th Division from Guam to Guadalcanal or to a location indicated by Admiral Nimitz.[54]

On 25 September Sixth Army submitted to General Headquarters a schedule of cargo loadings of heavy shipping for the Leyte operation and made suggestions as to heavy shipping for direct movement of troops. All troops and supply ships with the assault convoy which were to depart from Hollandia must arrive in that area not later than A minus 9.[55]

The shipping instructions specified that the ships were to be loaded for selective discharge; all resupply ships transporting rations, clothing, vehicles, weapons, and ammunition would be duplicate loaded; loaded floating reserve ships would be provided; medical supplies would be top loaded to avoid breakage and damage; and sufficient stevedore gear would be placed aboard each ship to handle its cargo. On 25 and 26 September General Krueger's transportation officer submitted to General Headquarters the heavy shipping requirements for the overwater movement of cargo and troops, respectively. It was considered necessary to utilize "all types of shipping from Navy LSM's, LST's, and assault transports to army controlled merchant ships and troop carriers." [56] Additional shipping was obtained by making use of that which had carried the 1st Marine Division and the 81st Division to Peleliu and Angaur in the Palau Islands.[57] The shipping specified above was assembled at Manus and Hol-

---

[51] Memo, Adm Sherman, Plans Off POA, and Gen Chamberlin, ACofS G–3 SWPA, for CINCSWPA and CINCPOA, 21 Sep 44, Sixth Army G–3 Jnl, 22 Sep 44.

[52] Sixth Army Opns Rpt Leyte, p. 19.

[53] GHQ SWPA Opns Instns 70, Annex 4, 21 Sep 44, Sixth Army G–3 Jnl, 21 Sep 44.

[54] Ltr, GHQ SWPA to Comdr Allied Naval Forces, 23 Sep 44, Sixth Army G–3 Jnl, 26 Sep 44.

[55] Ltr, Lt Col James W. Hill, Asst AG Sixth Army to CINCSWPA and CG USASOS, 25 Sep 44, sub: Heavy Shipping Requirements for King II Operation, Sixth Army G–3 Jnl, 25 Sep 44.

[56] Sixth Army Opns Rpt Leyte, Rpt of Transportation Off, p. 270.

[57] CTF 77 Attack Plan A304–44, 2 Oct 44.

landia and was assigned to the 1st Cavalry Division and the 24th Division, which were embarking, respectively, at those two ports. The XXIV Corps, after leaving the Hawaiian Islands, was brought to Manus where it remained in its original shipping.

On 8 October General Krueger asked the commanding generals of X Corps, XXIV Corps, and ASCOM, together with the commanding officers of the 6th Ranger Infantry Battalion and the 21st Infantry Regiment, whether they would be able to meet the target date for Leyte.[58] Upon receiving affirmative replies, he laconically informed General Headquarters: "Sixth Army Forces designated for KING TWO Operations are ready to meet KING TWO Target Date." [59]

---

[58] Rads, CG Sixth Army to CG X Corps, CG XXIV Corps, CG ASCOM, CO 21st Inf Regt, and CO 6th Ranger Inf Bn, Sixth Army G–3 Jnl, 8 Oct 44.

[59] Rad, CG Sixth Army to GHQ SWPA, Sixth Army G–3 Jnl, 10 Oct 44.

CHAPTER IV

The Return

For more than two years the high command of the Southwest Pacific had anticipated the promised return to the Philippines. That objective had governed nearly all of the planning and most of the earlier invasions. Now the day had arrived. Plans had been made and troops and cargo were aboard ships. The fleets of the Pacific Ocean Areas and the Southwest Pacific Area were about to join forces in a mighty assault against the Philippines.

The Convoy Forms

That part of the VII Amphibious Force which carried the 24th Infantry Division and the Sixth Army Service Command assembled at the harbor of Hollandia, Netherlands New Guinea. In this force were over 470 ships, ranging in size from small rocket-launching craft to 5,000-man troopships, loaded and now waiting for the message to weigh anchor and head for the Far Shore, as Leyte was designated. They were scheduled to pick up that part of the force which was carrying the 1st Cavalry Division from Manus Island and then rendezvous with the III Amphibious Force.

At 1600 on Friday, the thirteenth of October, the word was given and the great fleet at Hollandia got under way for the target—Leyte—1,300 miles distant.[1] Mine-sweeping task groups had preceded it on 11 and 12 October.[2] By sundown the convoy was formed and the ships were darkened. On 14 October the ships of the convoy crossed the equator without ceremony. General quarters (battle drill) and abandon ship drills were held. The part of the force carrying the 1st Cavalry Division was sighted during the day. On the following day the two units joined and the convoy proceeded. On 17 October the convoy made visual contact with the tractor groups of the III Amphibious Force. This force had come from Hawaii with the XXIV Corps to help in the liberation of Leyte.[3]

XXIV Corps Afloat

In the early morning hours of 13 September the headquarters of XXIV Corps at Schofield Barracks, Oahu, Hawaii, was awake and active. Breakfast was served at 0330, and all men who had been informed the day before that they were to embark for an unknown shore shouldered their barracks bags and carried them to waiting trucks. By 0700 the men had been loaded on the trucks, which took them to the narrow-gauge Oahu railroad. In flat cars they traveled some twenty miles to Honolulu Harbor. The

[1] Opns Rpt CTF 78 to COMINCH, Ser 00911, 10 Nov 44.

[2] Rpt, Capt Ray Tarbuck, USN, 3 Nov 44, GHQ SWPA G–3 Jnl, 30 Oct 44. (Hereafter cited as Tarbuck Rpt.)

[3] Opns Rpt CTF 78 to COMINCH, Ser 00911, 10 Nov 44.

usual seeming delays followed, but eventually the hot, tired, and perspiring headquarters men boarded the *George F. Clymer* and were assigned bunks. The *Clymer* was but one unit of a large convoy that stretched toward the horizon in every direction. At 1115 on 15 September the convoy got under way for a destination believed to be Yap. As the ships departed, word was received that the Yap operation had been canceled and that Leyte was to be their destination. For the men on board, life fell into the monotonous routine common to all transports. Reading, card and dice games, eating, sleeping, and interminable "bull sessions" helped to pass the time.

On the 25th of the month the *Clymer* anchored at Eniwetok Island, an anchorage already crowded with hundreds of transports, warships, and cargo vessels. The men were allowed to go ashore, where they were given beer and other refreshments. The XXIV Corps was notified that it would leave for Manus, in the Admiralty Islands, where further orders would be received and the staging completed. The LST flotilla left on 26 September and two days later the transports followed. Maps, terrain studies, and aerial photographs were distributed and studied en route.[4] At the same time the XXIV Corps issued a tentative field order which was distributed to lower unit commanders, who then held conferences and issued tentative verbal field orders.[5]

Early in October the convoy crossed the equator. On many of the ships ceremonies were held transforming pollywogs into shellbacks, with the result that some of the men preferred standing to sitting for a few days. On 3 October the convoy arrived at Manus.[6] The assault troops of the XXIV Corps were transferred from AKA's to LST's. The 96th Division on 9 October issued a final field order for the Leyte operation. This order allowed the regimental headquarters less than forty-eight hours to complete final orders, plans, and maps, and distribute them to the headquarters of the assault battalions.[7]

On 11 October the LST transports carrying the assault battalions filed out of the Manus anchorage, and on 14 October the rest of the convoy again formed and started on the last stretch of the journey.[8] Its progress was satisfactory, and on 15 October the President of the United States sent his best wishes for the success of the operation to President Sergio Osmeña of the Philippine Commonwealth, who was at sea with the expedition.[9] When the III Amphibious Force rendezvoused with the Seventh Fleet, the largest convoy ever seen in the Pacific up to that time was formed.[10]

Composition of the Convoy

Thirty-four months had been spent in building and preparing these combatant and amphibious vessels. Practically none of them were in existence at the time Corregidor was besieged. Most of the 183 vessels of Task Force 77 were warships, while Task Forces 78 and 79, the amphibious forces, consisted mainly of transports, cargo ships, and a wide variety of landing ships and craft. Fully 518 ocean-going vessels were included in Task Forces 78 and 79.[11]

Of the vessels assigned to participate in the operation, 157 were combatant ships: 6 old battleships, 5 heavy cruisers, 6 light

---

[4] 96th Inf Div Opns Rpt Leyte, p. 20.
[5] 7th Inf Div Opns Rpt Leyte, p. 2.
[6] XXIV Corps Opns Rpt Leyte, p. 4.

[7] 96th Div Opns Rpt Leyte, p. 25.
[8] XXIV Corps Hist Rpt for 1944, Sec Histories, History of the Adjutant Generals Section from 8 April to 31 December 1944, pp. 10–11.
[9] Tarbuck Rpt.
[10] *Ibid.*
[11] CTF 77 Opns Rpt, Ser 00302–C, 31 Jan 45.

cruisers, 18 escort carriers, 86 destroyers, 25 destroyer escorts, and 11 frigates. There were 420 transport vessels, including 5 command ships, 40 attack transports, 10 LSD's, 151 LST's, 79 LCI's, 21 LCT's, and 18 high-speed transports. The remainder included patrol, mine-sweeping, hydrographic, and service ships.[12]

The convoy did not include the combatant ships of Admiral Halsey's Third Fleet. The main striking force of the Third Fleet was Task Force 38, composed of four powerful carrier task groups, under Admiral Mitscher. Each group contained fast carriers, cruisers, destroyers, and the newest American battleships.[13]

After forming, the convoy proceeded toward the target. At this time a disquieting report was received from the meteorologists on board the ships: a typhoon was headed toward the Leyte Gulf area. Such a disturbance could be fatal to the expedition. A severe storm did in fact lash the gulf area from 14 through 17 October, but it gradually abated and the morning of A Day, 20 October, was clear. This favorable weather augured well for a successful landing.

Softening the Target

Early Strikes

Allied aircraft had already visited the Philippine Archipelago. The first aerial strikes since 1942 were made in the early fall of 1944. On 1 September B–24's from New Guinea bases initiated their first large-scale air attack against airdromes in the Davao area, though bad weather prevented the protective fighter escort from attacking the target. The airborne defense encountered was surprisingly light—only three intercepting fighters opposed the strike. The bombers dropped 100 tons of bombs, destroying 34 planes on the ground and killing about 100 men.[14] Two American bombers were shot down and six received minor damages.[15] General MacArthur believed that the Japanese were conserving their air strength in order to concentrate it against anticipated Allied landings.[16]

On 4 September the first aerial reconnaissance flights were made over Leyte. During the period 9–14 September, Admiral Mitscher launched a large-scale, carrier-based air assault against the Japanese air defenses in the Philippine Islands in order to protect the Palau and Morotai landings. On 9 September aircraft from the carriers attacked airdromes and installations in the Mindanao area, destroying 60 aircraft on the ground and 8 in the air. On 12 September the attack was directed against the Visayan Islands. Of an estimated air strength of 225 aircraft in the sector, 125 were destroyed on the ground and 75 in the air. During the night of 12 September the Japanese flew in reinforcements from Luzon. A Third Fleet strike on 13 September against the reinforced air strength destroyed an estimated 135 aircraft on the ground and 81 in the air. On the 14th, the Third Fleet planes encountered no enemy air opposition but destroyed from 10 to 15 aircraft on the ground. The air strength which the enemy had conserved for an

---

[12] CINCPAC and CINCPOA Rpt Opns in POA in Oct 44, Ser 002397, 31 May 45.

[13] USSBS, *Employment of Forces Under the Southwest Pacific Command*, p. 40.

[14] Japanese Studies in World War II, 14, Naval Air Operations in the Philippine Area, 1942–45, p. 18. (Monograph numbers cited in this volume are file designations used by OCMH.)

[15] GHQ SWPA Sum of Enemy Sit 894, GHQ G–3 Jnl, 2 Sep 44.

[16] *Ibid.*

anticipated American invasion was thus decimated. About 500, or approximately 57 percent of the 884 aircraft believed to be in the Philippines, were rendered nonoperational or destroyed. This successful knocking out of the Japanese air strength in the Philippine Islands was an important factor in the decision to speed up the landing at Leyte by two months.

On 21 September Central Pacific carrier-based aircraft directed their attention to the Luzon area. In spite of their vigorous defense of the Luzon airfields, the Japanese lost an estimated 110 aircraft in the air and 95 on the ground. These included not only combat aircraft but also reconnaissance, transport, and training planes. The remaining air strength in the area was estimated to be 350 aircraft, of which 10 percent were in Mindanao, 20 percent in the Visayan Islands, and 70 percent in Luzon.

At the same time, the carrier-based aircraft made strong strikes against enemy shipping in the central and southern Philippines. It was estimated that from 1 September to 15 September 105 merchant vessels were sunk in those waters by carrier planes, destroyers, cruisers, and submarines. Although exact information was lacking on the number of enemy vessels present in the Visayan and Mindanao areas, it was thought that 50 percent of the Japanese merchant marine in those areas was eliminated. A successful attrition of the Japanese air and naval strength in the Philippines had been accomplished.[17]

The Third Fleet's carriers then started to neutralize the approaches to the Philippine Islands. The carrier-based aircraft launched strikes against enemy aircraft staging areas in the Ryukyus, of which Okinawa is the largest and most important. As a result of attacks on 10 October, they destroyed an estimated 23 enemy planes in the air and 88 on the ground or in the water. Admiral Halsey reported that his flyers sank 1 subtender, 1 mine sweeper, 1 destroyer escort, 2 minecraft, 4 midget submarines, 20 cargo ships, and 45 other craft. In addition, nearly as many ships, mostly of small size, were damaged.[18] On 11 October the flyers struck at Luzon.

Air and Naval Action
in the Formosa Area

The plans of the Third Fleet called for strong carrier-based strikes against Formosa on 12 and 13 October. The four task groups of Task Force 38 were assigned targets in the southern Formosa, northern Formosa, central Formosa, and the Takao areas, respectively. (Takao is a port city on the southwest coast of Formosa.) After a fast run on the night of 11–12 October the carriers of Task Force 38 arrived in position off Formosa in the early morning. Although the Japanese were aware of the approach of the task force, they made no attacks against it before dawn. As the first fighters started sweeps over their respective areas, heavy opposition developed, but it dropped markedly during the day. From 12 to 14 October the Japanese lost some 280 aircraft,[19] while the Americans lost 76. As a result of the operation, the Japanese lost half of their naval air strength. This loss gave assurance that

---

[17] GHQ SWPA, Philippine Islands, G–2 Est of Enemy Sit 16, 3–9 Sep 44; 905, 13–14 Sep 44; 914, 22–23 Sep 44; 916, 24–25 Sep 44; and 907, 15–16 Sep 44; GHQ G–3 Jnl, 9–25 Sep 44.

[18] CINCPAC and CINCPOA Rpt on Opns in POA in Oct 44, Ser 002397, 31 May 45.
[19] Japanese Studies in WW II, 102, Philippine Area Naval Operations, Oct–Dec 44, Part II, The Battle of Leyte Gulf, pp. 4–11. (Hereafter cited as Philippine Naval Opns.)

the U. S. forces would have air superiority over the Leyte area on A Day.[20]

On the evening of 13 October the American heavy cruiser *Canberra* was torpedoed eighty-five miles off Formosa. Admiral Halsey kept his forces in the area another day in order to afford protection to the *Canberra*. Attacks, therefore, continued against enemy aircraft, airfields, and installations. By this time, Japanese reinforcements had arrived. On the evening of 14 October an aerial torpedo hit the heavy cruiser *Houston*.

Admiral Halsey decided to capitalize on the damage inflicted on the two cruisers. He ordered two task groups, which included the battleships, to retire eastward out of sight; he sent another of the task groups to conduct intermittent air raids against northern Luzon; and he assigned the remaining task group to protect the crippled *Canberra* and *Houston*. Halsey instructed this last task group to send out messages in the clear begging piteously for assistance. He hoped that by this ruse, which he called the "Lure of the Streamlined Bait," the Japanese fleet would be led to believe that this task group was all that remained of the task force and would therefore sweep down for the kill. The two task groups which had retired eastward would then appear and engage the enemy. The Japanese swallowed the bait and dispatched destroyers and cruisers toward the "crippled" American force. Unfortunately, their search planes uncovered the two task forces off Formosa, and the Japanese surface ships hastily withdrew.

The enemy pilots made such greatly exaggerated claims of success that *Imperial General Headquarters* decided to order out the *2d Diversion Attack Force* against the

Americans. The flying units of *Carrier Divisions 3* and *4* were transferred to the *2d Air Fleet*. These air units proceeded to Formosa on the 12th of October. *Carrier Divisions 3* and *4*, however, remained in the Inland Sea until they sortied forth for the Battle of Leyte Gulf.[21] The exaggerated claims of the Japanese air force were accepted jubilantly on the home islands. The people felt that the American Navy had indeed been given a death blow, and the Finance Ministry distributed "celebration sake" to all households in the country to commemorate the event. The Tokyo radio made the unfounded claim that "a total of 57 enemy warships including 19 aircraft carriers and four battleships were sunk or heavily damaged by the Japanese forces . . . the enemy task forces lost the majority of their strength and were put to rout. . . ."[22] It also predicted that the Allied losses would delay the invasion of the Philippine Islands by two months.[23]

Admiral Halsey's reaction was to report that "all 3d Fleet Ships reported by radio Tokyo as sunk have now been salvaged and are retiring towards the enemy."[24]

The convoy, as it steamed toward Leyte, received the news of the United States success with considerable satisfaction. At this time, however, Admiral Halsey announced that the Third Fleet was being deployed for action, since he was expecting the Japanese to rise to his bait. Consequently the Third Fleet, except for the current strike at Luzon, could not furnish any more carrier support for the operation.[25] The Third Fleet task

---

[20] USSBS, Naval Analysis Div, *The Campaigns of the Pacific War* (Washington, 1946), p. 283.

[21] Philippine Naval Opns, pp. 5, 85–86.

[22] AAF SWPA Intel Sum, Ser 247, GHQ G–3 Jnl, 29 Oct 44.

[23] AAF SWPA Intel Sum, Ser 246, GHQ G–3 Jnl, 22 Oct 44.

[24] Rad, Com3rdFlt to CINCPAC–CINCSWPA, 170352 Oct 44, GHQ G–3 Jnl, 17 Oct 44.

[25] Rad, Com3rdFlt to CINCPAC and var., H 2692, 0321, 15 Oct 44, AAF Hist Archives.

group which went to the Luzon area successfully struck at enemy airfields and shipping. From 17 to 19 October it destroyed an estimated ninety-nine enemy aircraft on the ground and ninety-five in the air.[26]

Realignment of Air Support

On the heels of Admiral Halsey's announcement that no assistance in connection with the Leyte landings could be expected from the Third Fleet, Far East Air Forces stated that the Fifth Air Force would support the Leyte operation as a "priority mission." [27] At the same time the Seventh Fleet requested intensive reconnaissance of San Bernardino and Surigao Straits in the Leyte area. This mission was assigned to the Fifth Air Force, which was also charged with neutralizing the Visayan airfields. The Thirteenth Air Force was to expedite the basing on Morotai of heavy bombers which could be called forward in support when requested by the Fifth Air Force. From 18 to 19 October the carrier aircraft of the Seventh Fleet protected the convoy and struck at small vessels and airfields in northern Mindanao as well as defense and communications installations and airfields on Leyte.[28]

Although the missions Admiral Halsey had assigned his carriers apparently prevented any aircraft of the Third Fleet from participating in direct support of the landings, Halsey nevertheless ordered one of the task groups to strike at the Leyte, Samar, Cebu, and Negros areas on 18–19 October and to provide direct air support for the

Leyte operation on 20 October.[29] Moreover, by 18 October news was received that the Japanese had discovered the ruse and withdrawn their warships from the Formosa area, thus leaving Admiral Halsey's forces free to protect the operation by covering San Bernardino and Surigao Straits.[30]

The carrier force of the Seventh Fleet was to bear the brunt of the tactical air support. By the afternoon and night of 17 October the weather had cleared, and flying conditions were perfect as the carriers moved into their operation areas the following morning. The force was divided into three units: one unit operated in the southern part of Leyte Gulf to protect the landings at Panaon Strait; another operated near the entrance to the gulf in order to support the landings of the Southern Attack Force at Dulag; and the last operated southeast of Samar Island to support the landings of the Northern Attack Force at Tacloban.

During 18 and 19 October, aircraft from the carriers struck at enemy airfields on Cebu, Negros, and Panay Islands. There was very little enemy activity from the Japanese airfields in the Leyte area, since they were still sodden from the recent storms. In the two days' strikes, the Seventh Fleet aircraft destroyed an estimated thirty-six enemy planes and damaged twenty-eight more.[31]

Japanese Plan of Defense

The air blows on the Philippines served as a warning that the Americans were ready to return to the Islands—an event long ex-

---

[26] Air Evaluation Bd SWPA Rpt, Leyte Campaign—Philippines, 1944, p. 16.

[27] Hist of FEAF, pp. 261–63, AAF Hist Archives.

[28] Air Evaluation Bd SWPA Rpt, p. 16.

[29] Rad, Com3rd Flt to CTG 38.1, 160216, 16 Oct 44, GHQ G–3 Jnl, 17 Oct 44.

[30] Tarbuck Rpt.

[31] CTG 77.4 Opns Rpt, Ser 00120, 15 Nov 44.

pected by the Japanese. By the end of June 1944, the Japanese military situation had considerably worsened. The outer circle of Japan's perimeter had been pierced and the impetus of the American drive showed no signs of slackening. (*Map 2*)

The Allied nations had hit the Japanese from east and west and seriously interfered with their seaborne commerce. Japan was in grave danger of being separated from her stolen southern area—the source of her raw materials. Units within this area were also being forcibly isolated from each other. The fall of Saipan had brought about a "most serious crisis." Premier Tojo was removed and Kuniaki Koiso formed a new cabinet.[32]

In the summer of 1944 *Imperial General Headquarters* had started to strengthen the Philippines, the Ryukyus, the Kurile Islands, and Japan itself—the "first line of sea defense." If the Allies landed forces in any of these areas, the Japanese would concentrate their land, air, and sea forces and attempt to repel the landing force. These operations were known as the *SHO* (Victory) *Operations*. Defense of the Philippines was *SHO* I.[33]

The Japanese strategy was simple. Japan wished to remain in the war, and to do so she must at all costs keep open the lines of communication to the sources of her raw materials in the Netherlands Indies.

In the first part of August 1944, the headquarters of the *14th Area Army*, which was to be charged with the defense of the Philippine Archipelago, was organized under the command of the *Southern Army*, while the *35th Army*, which was to defend the Visayan Islands, was established under the command of the *14th Area Army*.[34]

The Philippine Islands were under the jurisdiction of the *Southern Army*, whose command organization was extremely complex. (*Chart 3*) The supreme commander was Field Marshal Count Hisaichi Terauchi. There were four area armies in the *Southern Army*: the *2d Area Army* occupied Netherlands New Guinea, thence west to Timor; the *7th Area Army* was at Singapore; the *Burma Area Army* was at Rangoon; and the *14th Area Army*, commanded by Lt. Gen. Shigenori Kuroda, was in the Philippines with its headquarters at Manila. The *Southern Army* also had two air armies and three garrison armies: the *3d Air Army* in Singapore; the *4th Air Army*, consisting of two air divisions in the Philippines and one air division in western New Guinea; and a garrison army stationed in Thailand, another in French Indochina, and a third in Borneo. The commander of the *14th Area Army* maintained a staff liaison with the *4th Air Army* but otherwise had no control over it.

The *1st Air Fleet*, under the command of the *Southwest Area Fleet*, was stationed in the Philippines, with headquarters at Manila. Admiral Soemu Toyoda, commander in chief of the *Combined Fleet* with headquarters at Tokyo, controlled the entire naval forces, including the *Southwest Area Fleet*.[35]

---

[32] Japanese Studies in WW II, 72, Hist of *Army Section, Imperial General Headquarters,* 1941–45, p. 131. (Hereafter cited as Hist of *Army Sec, Imperial GHQ.*)

[33] *Ibid.,* pp. 131–32.

[34] Japanese Studies in WW II, 6, *14th Area Army* Plans, 1944. (Hereafter cited as *14th Area Army* Plans.)

[35] The organization of Japanese forces is discussed in detail in Hist of *Army Sec, Imperial GHQ.*

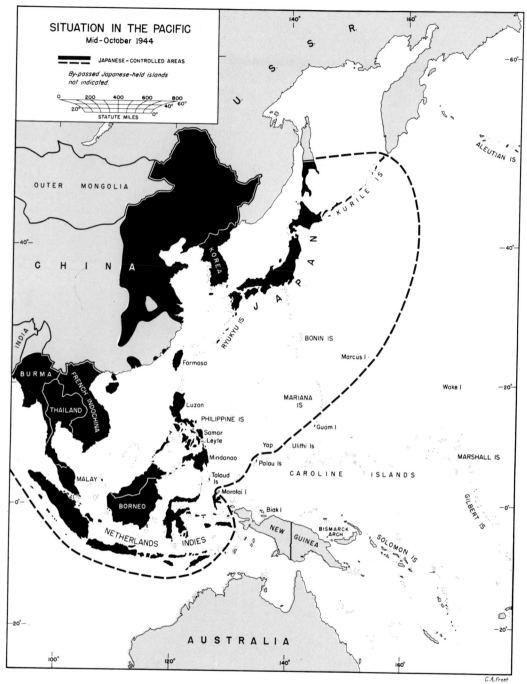

SITUATION IN THE PACIFIC
Mid-October 1944

JAPANESE-CONTROLLED AREAS

By-passed Japanese-held islands
not indicated.

STATUTE MILES

MAP 2

CHART 3—JAPANESE ARMY ORGANIZATION OF MAJOR UNITS FOR THE LEYTE OPERATION

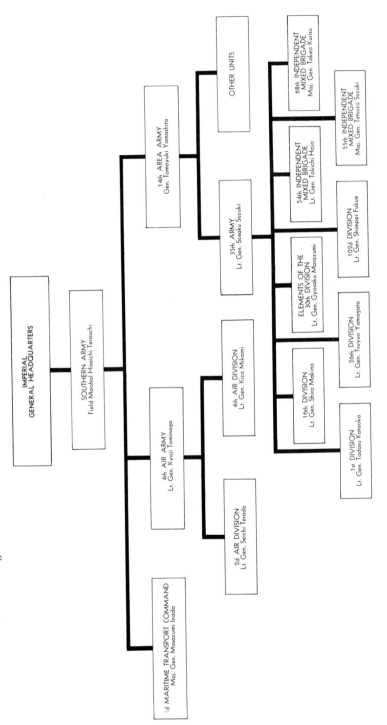

Plans for the 14th Area Army

The Japanese during the summer of 1944 anticipated that the United States forces would return to the Philippine Islands, but when and where were two questions for which not even Tokyo Rose, the Japanese radio propagandist, had the answers. Consequently, the Japanese wished to keep their troops sufficiently mobile that reinforcements might be rushed to the point of contact. The original plan called for the main defensive effort of the ground forces to be made on Luzon, since there were too few Japanese troops in the archipelago to defend all of the Philippines. The Japanese Navy and Air Forces, however, were to carry out "decisive" actions in the central and southern Philippines.[36]

To General Kuroda fell the task of making and executing plans for the defense of the Philippines by the *14th Area Army*. General Kuroda was essentially a realist. He stated in June 1947 that in October 1944 he had told Maj. Gen. Seizo Arisue, Chief of Army Intelligence, *Imperial General Headquarters*, that "it would be best for Japan to negotiate an immediate peace before the Americans could destroy our nation by air power."[37] Kuroda thought that all available land forces should be concentrated in the Luzon area in order to counterattack any American landing within the Luzon perimeter. However, because of their predominant aerial strength, the Americans in their next attempt could unless they made "some terrible mistake . . . land in force and once ashore, could take the Philip-pines."[38] General Kuroda's plan was never considered. *Imperial General Headquarters'* plan for the defense of the Philippines called for the employment of ten divisions and five brigades: five divisions and two brigades in Luzon, four divisions and two brigades in the southern Philippines, and one division and one brigade in China and Formosa. The two units last mentioned would be rushed to the Philippines as soon as the American landing became imminent.[39] When the Americans landed, all of these units, acting in concert, were to participate in fighting a decisive battle against the American troops. This plan was never carried out in its entirety.

The Japanese occupation troops of the Philippine Islands had grown soft and had "no particular will to fight." In the spring of 1944, there were only minor units available to set up an organized defense.

Imperial General Headquarters and the *Southern Army* thought that because of the many islands in the archipelago emphasis should be placed on air power. Air attacks could destroy the American forces before they arrived at the landing areas or at least before they could make appreciable gains. The way could then be opened to turn a defense into an offensive.[40] General Kuroda threw cold water on this plan by bluntly stating:

That concept is good, but you cannot fight with concept alone. Words alone will not sink American ships and that becomes clear when you compare our airplanes with theirs. That is why the major battles have been occurring on land. We can say that the power of our air force is negligible at this time. No matter

[36] Hist of *Army Sec, Imperial GHQ,* pp. 140–41.
[37] Interv, 2d Lt Stanley L. Falk with General Kuroda, at Sugamo Prison, Tokyo, 13 Jun 47, copy in OCMH.

[38] *Ibid.*
[39] Hist of *Army Sec, Imperial GHQ,* pp. 132–33, 135, 140, and errata sheet to above.
[40] Maj Gen Yoshiharu Tomochika, The True

how much the *Fourteenth Army* devotes their efforts toward air power, in actuality, should there be a decisive fight, they must fight on land. The preparation and conduct of an operation, and the responsibilities thereof cannot be conducted by airplanes and air units. The land army should initiate its own preparations. For example, for what purpose were the group of air bases constructed at Davao and Tacloban? Even though they are built, they aren't used. It amounts to construction for the use of the enemy.[41]

During the month of August, the Japanese devoted their main efforts toward strengthening the air force. After the first of September more emphasis was placed on building up the ground troops while the air preparations continued to some extent. The *Southern Army* in late August ordered about one half of a division to Sarangani and one division to Davao against the wishes of the *14th Area Army*. This meant a reshuffling of the troops that had been moving and repairing defenses since the first part of August. "The order was carried out begrudgingly." [42]

Lt. Gen. Sosaku Suzuki, the commander of the *35th Army*, thinking that the American Army would land on 1 October, said: "Contrary to what has been announced by *General Headquarters* our air force cannot be prepared and equipped in time, nor can the *Combined Fleet* be depended upon. The situation grows worse and for this reason the land force preparations must be hastened. Yet, in spite of that, we must not discourage the air forces and should do as much as possible to prepare aggressive aerial opposition." [43]

In the middle of September, *Imperial General Headquarters* decided to replace General Kuroda with General Tomoyuki Yamashita. Not only did General Kuroda have a concept of the Philippine operations that differed from that of his superiors, but he was charged with neglecting his duty as field army commander.[44] Lt. Col. Seiichi Yoshie of the Personnel Bureau of the War Ministry, who had been sent to the Philippines to investigate personnel matters in the *Southern Army,* said of the incident:

Stories reached the War Ministry that Lt. Gen. Kuroda was devoting more time to his golf, reading and personal matters than to the execution of his official duties. It appeared that his control over staff officers and troops was not sufficiently strong and that there was a good deal of unfavorable criticism of his conduct among the troops. There were also indications that discipline was becoming very lax.

On 4 September 1944, I left Tokyo under orders . . . to investigate. As a result I obtained many statements substantiating the unfavorable stories in regard to Lt. Gen. Kuroda. The recommendations of all the staff was that Lt. Gen. Kuroda be relieved as soon as possible, and be replaced by Gen. Yamashita . . . who was a superb tactician and excellent leader.[45]

General Yamashita, who was in Manchuria, received notification of his appointment on 23 September, and on the 9th of October he assumed command of the *14th Area Army.*[46] On his arrival in the Philippines, he found conditions were "unsatisfactory." Of the eleven members of the old staff only five were left and the new staff

---

Facts of the Leyte Operation, p. 8, typescript of translation in OCMH.
[41] *Ibid.*
[42] *Ibid.,* p. 9.
[43] *Ibid.,* p. 8.

[44] *Ibid.*
[45] Statement of Lt Col Seiichi Yoshie, Circumstances Leading to the Relief of General Kuroda, 1 Oct 51, copy in OCMH.
[46] *United States* vs *Tomoyuki Yamashita,* Testimony of Yamashita, XXVIII, 3518–19, DRB AGO.

GEN. TOMOYUKI YAMASHITA

LT. GEN. SOSAKU SUZUKI

officers were unfamiliar with conditions in the Philippine Islands.[47] The state of affairs was well exemplified by a remark of his new chief of staff, Lt. Gen. Akira Muto, who arrived in the Philippines on 20 October from Sumatra, where he had been in command of the *2d Imperial Guards Division*.[48] Upon being told that the Americans had landed on Leyte, Muto is said to have replied, "Very interesting, but where is Leyte?"[49]

Maj. Gen. Toshio Nishimura, one of three assistants to Yamashita, states that the planning for the Leyte campaign was "very bad." The supply situation, however, was favorable. Since Manila was the main depot not only for the Philippines but also for other places in the south such as Borneo and Singapore, a sufficient amount of everything needed was at hand.[50]

There were two tactical concepts of defense of the islands in July and August 1944. One was termed the policy of "annihilation at the beachhead" and the other the policy of "resistance in depth." The respective merits of the two concepts were bitterly debated by their partisans. The proponents of resistance in depth thought that the beach defenses, which had been constructed with a great deal of labor, were useless, since it was believed they could not withstand naval bombardment. On the other hand, the friends of annihilation at the beachhead felt that semipermanent beach fortifications could withstand bombardment. *Imperial*

[47] *Ibid.,* XXVIII, 3519–20.

[48] *Ibid.,* Testimony of Muto, XXII, 2998.

[49] A. Frank Reel, *The Case of General Yamashita* (Chicago, 1949), pp. 18–19.

[50] USSBS Interrog 418, Interrog of Maj Gen Toshio Nishimura, 19–22 Nov 45, MS, OCMH.

General Headquarters, after studying the battle lessons of the Pacific Campaign and the actual effect of naval bombardment, decided to adopt the resistance in depth tactics and instructed the entire army forces to comply. Consequently, the various group commanders abandoned their beach defenses with regret and began to build strong fortifications in selected areas of the interior.[51]

The control of the Visayan Islands and Mindanao was vested in the *35th Army,* which was the equivalent of an American army corps. General Suzuki, its commander, compromised between the two concepts of defense. At a meeting of the *35th Army* unit commanders in the middle of August 1944, he stated that although the main battle was to be fought away from the beaches some troops should remain to resist the American landings and "therefore part of the troops must suffer premature losses." [52]

The *16th, 102d, 30th,* and the *100th Divisions,* which were in Leyte, Panay, and Mindanao, were placed under the *35th Army,* whose headquarters was at Cebu.[53]

The Suzu Plan

On 17 August General Suzuki issued the Suzu orders for the defense of the Visayan Islands and Mindanao by the *35th Army.* The *100th Division* was to protect the Davao area on Mindanao while the *16th Division* would defend Leyte. Most of the *30th Division* and two infantry battalions were made mobile units which could be rushed to annihilate the American force wherever it landed. However, if the Americans landed simultaneously on Davao and Leyte, the main force of the *30th Division* was to be sent to Davao and the other mobile units would go to Leyte.

In late August, Suzuki received orders to dispose his troops as follows: a reinforced division in the Davao area, three battalions in the Sarangani Bay area, three battalions in the vicinity of Zamboanga, two battalions in the Jolo Islands, a "strong unit" in the vicinity of Surigao, and one division in the Leyte Gulf area. The *55th Independent Mixed Brigade* was to be assigned to the *35th Army.* Units of the *16th Division* which were in Luzon were sent to the *16th Division* on Leyte. These elements, which consisted of one engineer company, an independent transportation unit, and a medical unit, were placed under the commander of the *33d Infantry Regiment.*[54]

Lt. Gen. Shiro Makino, commanding the *16th Division,* which was the major force on Leyte, had directed his efforts since April 1944 toward the construction of defensive positions on the island. The first line of defense, which was on the east coast in the Dulag area, was practically completed by the middle of October. The third defensive line was in the middle of Leyte Valley in the vicinity of Dagami. The second line of defense was between the two others, while the bulk of supplies was assembled in the central mountain range at Jaro.

The distribution of the other troops at the time of the American landings was as follows: one battalion of the *9th Infantry Regiment* in the Catmon Hill and Tanauan district, and the main strength of the *33d Infantry Regiment* in the Palo and Tacloban area. The larger part of the *33d Infantry Regiment,* which was less adequately trained

---

[51] Tomochika, True Facts of Leyte Opn, p. 6.
[52] *Ibid.*
[53] *Ibid.*

[54] Japanese Studies in WW II, 11, *35th Army* Operations 1944–45, pp. 14–20. (Hereafter cited as *35th Army* Opns.)

than the other regiments, had arrived on Leyte in mid-September from Luzon. Its officers were unfamiliar with the terrain and did not fortify their positions.[55]

On 17 October General Makino, having heard that American warships had approached Leyte Gulf, alerted the *16th Division* for the impending battle and ordered all units to "shatter the enemy landing attempts." [56] On 18 October the *14th Area Army* received a report from the *16th Division* which indicated that the latter was not certain the vessels sighted off Leyte were an enemy attacking force. They might be ships seeking safety from the storms, or vessels damaged in the naval battle off Formosa. Consequently, *14th Area Army* was not sure that an attack was imminent at Leyte.[57]

Plans for the 4th Air Army

The principal assignment of the *4th Air Army* was to attack American transports and interdict American shipping and, if given the opportunity, to attack the American combatant vessels. The *4th Air Army* was also to give aerial support to the movement of reinforcements.[58]

In October the *4th Air Army* issued a plan for anticipated operations. In co-operation with the Army and the Navy, the *4th Air Army* would attempt to destroy the American forces when they struck the Philippines. The Army air force in concert with the naval air units would try to destroy

carrier-based planes and air bases. In operations against the American fleet, the Army and Navy air units were to have "a unified and tactful commitment." If the naval air units could not co-operate the Army air force was to venture a surprise attack with a few planes. Dusk, night, and dawn attacks were to be made against Allied air bases and all means exerted to foil Allied attempts to establish advance bases in the Philippines. The main strength of the fighter units was to move into the central and southern Philippines in order to destroy the principal American landing force. The mission of the Japanese *4th Air Army,* operating from Mindanao, Celebes, and northern Borneo, would be restricted to checking the current attempts on the part of the Americans to establish bases on Halmahera and western New Guinea and the destruction of the planes there. For this purpose the Japanese air force would use bases in the southern Philippines.

When the American convoy was sighted moving toward the Philippines, the heavy bombers were to deploy to the central and southern Philippines and make preparations for an immediate attack on the convoy after it had arrived in the harbor. The fighter units were to attack Allied aircraft and, if the circumstances were propitious, were also to attack the convoy. If the Americans should attempt simultaneous landings at various points, the Japanese Army air forces would "try to annihilate the landing parties one by one," [59] acting in concert with the Japanese Navy.

Capt. Toshikazu Ohmae, the chief of staff to the commander in chief of the Japanese *Third Fleet,* was highly critical of the liaison

---

[55] Tomochika, True Facts of Leyte Opn, p. 6.

[56] *16th Division* Order 821, Tacloban, 17 October 1944, translation in App. C to Annex Y, 7th Div Opns Rpt Leyte, DRB AGO.

[57] Japanese Studies in WW II, 7, *14th Area Army Operations on Leyte,* p. 4 (Hereafter cited as *14th Area Army* Opns Leyte.)

[58] USSBS Interrog 506, Interrog of Maj. Gen. Yoshiharu Tomochika, Oct–Dec 44, p. 2, typescript copy in OCMH.

[59] Japanese Studies in WW II, 5, *4th Air Army Operations,* 1944–45, pp. 1–50. (Hereafter cited as *4th Air Army* Opns.)

between the Army and Navy air forces. "The Army and Navy always quarreled with each other. In theory they were supposed to cooperate and on the higher levels it would work, but personalities were the trouble." [60]

Japanese Navy Plans

On 21 July 1944 Admiral Toyoda received a directive which laid down the basic policies for subsequent "urgent operations." A great deal of the contracting empire was abandoned. The Southwest Area, which embraced the region from Manila to Singapore, was ordered to "maintain security of resources areas, hold vital sectors for their defense, and place emphasis on protection for fleet anchorages." Thus the Japanese planned to restrict battle "to the homeland and to the island chain which protected the last links" of the empire with the south. The forces in the Japanese home islands, the Ryukyu chain, Formosa, and the Philippine Islands were told to take "all measures to expedite the establishment of conditions to cope with decisive battle. In event of enemy attack, summon all strength which can be concentrated and hold vital sectors, in general intercepting and destroying the enemy within the operational sphere of planes of our base air force." [61]

The success of Admiral Halsey's carrier strikes against Formosa had considerably weakened the strength of Japanese carrier-based planes, and less than one half of the Army planes remained. The necessity of sending reinforcements to Formosa also weakened considerably the Japanese aerial defense of the Philippines. The enemy became almost completely dependent upon the remaining land-based planes. [62] Within their capabilities the Japanese had made their plans and readied their forces, as the American convoy steamed towards Leyte to do battle.

Securing the Channel Approaches

Landings of the 6th Ranger Infantry Battalion

The forward part of the convoy, which was carrying the 6th Ranger Infantry Battalion, commanded by Lt. Col. Henry A. Mucci, had experienced stormy weather since leaving Hollandia, but by dawn of the 17th the storm had slackened, though the ocean was still choppy. The transports carrying the reinforced 6th Ranger Battalion, preceded by three mine sweepers, entered Leyte Gulf. [63]

The USS Crosby, carrying Company D, arrived on schedule off Suluan Island, the outermost of the islands guarding Leyte Gulf. For twenty minutes the cruiser Denver shelled the island. Under lowering skies and in a driving rain which rendered impossible the anticipated air support, [64] Company D, under 1st Lt. Leslie M. Gray, disembarked from the transport and headed for the island in landing craft. The mission of the unit was to secure mine charts which were believed to be located in a lighthouse

---

[60] USSBS, *Interrogations,* I, 160.

[61] James A. Field, Jr., *The Japanese at Leyte Gulf: The SHO Operation* (Princeton, N. J., 1947), p. 8.

[62] USSBS, *Interrogations,* I, 219; II, 500–504.

[63] Unless otherwise noted the account of the activities of the 6th Ranger Infantry Battalion is taken from the 6th Ranger Infantry Battalion Operations Report Leyte.

[64] Rad, CTG 77.2 to CTF 78, 17 Oct 44, GHQ G–3 Jnl, 17 Oct 44.

on the island. At 0805 the boats touched shore.

The landing was unopposed. The men immediately filed south 500 yards on a trail along the coast and then headed east toward the lighthouse. On the way, four buildings, one of which contained a Japanese radio, were found and set ablaze. The company then continued along the trail. Suddenly the enemy fired from a concealed position, killing one man and wounding another. When Company D went into attack formation, the enemy force disappeared into the heavy jungle bordering the trail. The march was resumed and the company reached its objective without further incident. The lighthouse, which had been damaged by naval bombardment, and adjoining buildings were deserted.[65]

In searching the documents found in the lighthouse, the company failed to turn up the hoped-for enemy mine charts.[66] It returned to the beachhead area and, finding that the landing boats had been hopelessly battered and broken up by the surf, formed a perimeter for the night.

As Company D was moving along the coast of Suluan Island, naval fire blasted away at the extreme northwest coast of Dinagat Island. At 0900 the first assault waves of the 6th Rangers, minus Companies D and B, started for the beach. Although coral reefs approximately one hundred yards offshore grounded the boats so that the men had to wade the remainder of the distance, the companies were all ashore by 1230. No Japanese were on the island and the troops accomplished their mission, the erection of a navigation light at Desolation Point to guide the movement of the main portion of the convoy.

Company B of the 6th Rangers was to have landed on Homonhon Island at the same time landings were made on Suluan and Dinagat. Its mission, too, was the emplacement of a navigation light, but bad weather and choppy seas kept the troops confined to the ship throughout the 17th.[67] On the morning of the 18th, the ship's address system clanged out general quarters. The men went below, put on their gear, and checked their weapons. At 0900 the troops were told to prepare to disembark. They bolted up the ladders and spilled out over the deck to the davits.[68] The boats were lowered and the first wave started for the beach. At the same time the guns from the destroyer and frigate which had escorted the transport concentrated fire against the shore line for twelve minutes. Three minutes later, the boats grounded on a coral reef forty yards from the beach, and the men waded the remaining distance to shore. They encountered no resistance and at 1038 the company commander, Capt. Arthur D. Simons, notified the battalion commander, "Beachhead secured, supplies ashore. No resistance. No casualties."[69] The company set up a channel light.

By 18 October, steady white lights were beaming from Dinagat and Homonhon Islands to guide the convoy in to Leyte Island. The one on Dinagat had a visibility of twelve miles and that on Homonhon a visibility of ten.[70]

[65] Co D, 6th Ranger Inf Bn, Opns Rpt Leyte.

[66] Msg, CTG 78.4 to *Tancier,* 18 Oct 44, Sixth Army G–3 *Wasatch* Jnl, 18 Oct 44.

[67] Rad, GHQ to CofS, 17 Oct 44, GHQ G–3 Jnl, 18 Oct 44.

[68] Co B, 6th Ranger Inf Bn, Opns Rpt Leyte, p. 1.

[69] *Ibid.*

[70] Rad, CTG 78.5 to CTF 77, 19 Oct 44, Sixth Army G–3 *Wasatch* Jnl, 19 Oct 44.

PATROL OF COMPANY F, 6TH RANGERS, *at Desolation Point (above), and investigating a native village on Dinagat Island (below).*

Mine Sweeping

The mine-sweeping plans contemplated that the mine-sweeping group would arrive on 17 October simultaneously with the troops that were to storm Suluan, Dinagat, and Homonhon Islands. On 11 October the slow-moving mine sweepers lifted anchor at Manus and departed for the objective area. They rendezvoused near the Palaus with the Dinagat force, which had left Hollandia on 12 October. On 15 October they were joined by the carriers and the beach demolition and bombardment and fire support groups which had sortied from Manus on 12 October. On 14 October information was received from guerrilla sources that there were no underwater obstacles off the beaches between Abuyog and Tacloban. Although the northern Surigao Strait was mined, it was considered doubtful whether the same condition existed at the southern entrances of Leyte Gulf.[71] The mine-sweeping groups that had left Hollandia on 11 October arrived in Leyte Gulf during the storm of the evening of 16 October. Some of the mine sweepers had been delayed by the storm but were able to arrive in time to begin sweeping the channels.[72]

In the early dawn of 17 October the mine sweepers began their work on the channel approaches to Suluan Island.[73] By 0630 they had accomplished their task and then began to sweep the waters of the landing areas in Leyte Gulf until the storm forced them to suspend operations. At 1259 they resumed sweeping with great difficulty. Until A Day, intensive area and tactical mine sweeping continued. The sweepers started at dawn each day and worked continuously until nightfall. By 19 October it was known that the Japanese had heavily mined the approaches to Leyte Gulf but that there were no mines within the gulf itself. The northern part of the main channel into the gulf, however, was not considered safe.[74] By the same date sweeping had been completed in the southern half, 186 mines having been destroyed. At about 0135 on 19 October, the destroyer supporting the mine-sweeping units which were in the gulf struck a floating mine and while maneuvering away from the area struck another. The ship was disabled and retired from action. By A Day, a total of 227 mines had been destroyed and a passage approximately six miles wide had been cleared just north of Dinagat Island. All ships were therefore directed to enter Leyte Gulf through that portion of the strait.[75]

As the mine sweepers came close to the land, boats containing Filipinos moved out to welcome the advance party of liberators. The reception they met was not enthusiastic. Admiral Oldendorf, the commanding officer of the bombardment and fire support group, "suspected that some might have come seeking information so detained them aboard their respective ships. . . . Directed no further patriots be taken aboard ship." [76]

Underwater Demolition Teams

The naval plans for the amphibious phase of the operation contemplated the use of seven underwater demolition teams—three to cover the northern coast beaches and

---

[71] Rad, Parsons to CTF 77, 78, and 79, 14 Oct 44, Sixth Army G–3 *Wasatch* Jnl, 14 Oct 44.

[72] CTF 77 to COMINCH, Opns Rpt Leyte, Ser 00302–C, 31 Jan 45, p. 8.

[73] Sixth Army Opns Rpt Leyte, p. 31.

[74] Rad, CTG 77.5 to CTF 77, 19 Oct 44, Sixth Army G–3 *Wasatch* Jnl, 19 Oct 44.

[75] Rpt, COMINCH, Amph Opns—Invasion of the Philippines, COMINCH P–008, pp. 1–3.

[76] CTG 77.2 to CTF 77, Sixth Army G–3 *Wasatch* Jnl, 19 Oct 44.

four to cover the southern beaches. The teams, starting A minus 2 (18 October), were to locate underwater obstructions and detonate mines. On 18 and 19 October the underwater demolition teams made a reconnaissance of the landing areas, accompanied by destroyers which bombarded the shores. The two days' reconnaissance disclosed no underwater obstacles or mines in the vicinity of the proposed landing beaches.

The Convoy Enters Leyte Gulf

By the evening of 19 October the preliminary operations were almost completed. The beaches had been surveyed and found suitable for landing; mines had been cleared from most of the main approach channel; and the entrances to Leyte Gulf had been secured.[77]

All ships were to be prepared to attach paravanes (mine-cable cutting devices) on signal at any time after noon on 19 October.[78] Since the mine sweepers had not sufficiently cleared the gulf, paravanes were attached preparatory to entering it. The mine sweepers were to have escorted the convoy into the area, but since they would not be ready for about two hours, the entry was ordered to be made without them. The convoy hugged the Dinagat shore line so closely that the distance from the center of the formation to the shore was only 3,800 yards.[79] Some of the ships did not see the signal light which had been placed on Dinagat Island by the 6th Rangers and were delayed on that account.

The convoy advanced without incident toward the target area. On the 18th Admiral Kinkaid radioed General MacArthur that the operations were going well, though the storm had somewhat delayed matters, and the General was made "welcome to our city."[80] MacArthur in reply said that he was "glad indeed to be in your domicile and under your flag. It gives me not only confidence but a sense of inspiration," and, probably thinking of the many arduous months of planning and amphibious operations, he added, "As Ripley says believe it or not we are almost there."[81]

As the convoy came ever closer to the target, the atmosphere aboard the vessels became more and more tense. By 1800 on 19 October most of the vessels had arrived outside the gulf. The Far Shore was now near and could be seen vaguely in the distance. On board one of the vessels Protestant and Catholic evening prayers were broadcast over the address system. Some of the men felt that it gave them a lift, but many felt that they were being administered the last rites of their church.[82]

All vessels arrived on schedule. Because the mine barrier in the entrance had not been completely cleared, the ships entered the gulf somewhat to the south of the center of the entrance, avoiding the main channel and keeping close to the northern point of Dinagat Island. Fears that strong ebb tides might impede progress of the slower vessels through the entrance proved groundless. Paravanes were retained until arrival in the transport areas, but no mines were encountered.[83]

---

[77] Rpt, CTF 77 to COMINCH, Amph Opn P–008, pp. 1–3.

[78] CTG 79.1 Movement Order, A173–44, 9 Oct 44, GHQ G–3 Jnl, 16 Oct 44.

[79] Opns Rpt CTG 79.1 to CTF 79, Ser 00454, 26 Oct 44, GHQ G–3 Jnl, 15 Nov 44.

[80] Msg, CTF 77 to CINCSWPA, Sixth Army G–3 Wasatch Jnl, 18 Oct 44.

[81] Msg, CINCSWPA to CTF 77, Sixth Army G–3 Wasatch Jnl, 18 Oct 44.

[82] Tarbuck Rpt.

[83] Opns Rpt CTF 79 to Com7thFlt, Ser 00323, 13 Nov 44, p. 71.

Naval plans called for bombardment of the enemy-held shores on A minus 2 (18 October), but because the water areas had not been completely swept for mines by that time, ships could not reach the bombardment area. On A minus 1, bombardment was chiefly for the purpose of providing effective support and coverage for the underwater demolition teams. However, many of the defenses and installations of the enemy on or near the landing beaches, including buildings and supply dumps, were neutralized or destroyed.

By the afternoon of 19 October, when it had become apparent to the Japanese that the Americans had returned to the Philippine Islands, General Suzuki put his defense plan into effect. He ordered the *16th Division* to annihilate the American force, and, failing that, to interfere as much as possible with the use of Leyte airfields by the American Army. The mobile units, including two battalions from the *30th Division,* were to speed to Leyte as fast as possible. Finally, the headquarters of the *35th Army* was to move to Ormoc on the west coast of Leyte on the 23d or 24th of October.[84]

Through the night of 19–20 October, destroyers near the shore continued to shell the Japanese forces on land. The American forces were safely within Leyte Gulf—A Day had arrived.

---

[84] Japanese Studies 11, *35th Army* Opns, p. 24.

CHAPTER V

A Day: 20 October 1944

Bombardment of the Shores of Leyte

The waters of Leyte Gulf were glassy calm as the convoys bearing the assault forces steamed into their appointed positions off the shores of Leyte in the very early morning hours of 20 October 1944.

There were three stages of the naval gunfire support: the pre-A-Day bombardment, A-Day bombardment, and close supporting missions to be delivered after H Hour and to continue until 24 October. A portion of the fire support group in support of the underwater demolition teams had bombarded the southern landing beaches and the town of Dulag on 18 October, a process which was repeated on the following day in support of the underwater demolition teams on the northern landing beaches.[1]

At 0600 on A Day, 20 October, the battleships assigned to the Southern Attack Force opened fire on the beaches. A lone Japanese plane appeared at 0612 over the northern beaches, circled the convoy, and despite gunfire from the *Maryland* and *West Virginia* disappeared unscathed.[2] At 0700 the battleships of the Northern Attack Force commenced firing. For two hours the six battleships, three to each attack force, fired on the beaches. Since no specific targets

could be discerned or determined, the gunfire was directed at areas. Many enemy supply dumps and minor military installations were destroyed. An observer reported:

Gray smoke plumes are rising from the shores. Battleship *Mississippi* is now working on the northern beaches. She is joined by the *Maryland* whose fire has apparently caused a large shore explosion. Jap ack-ack is fired at spotting planes but the performance is weak.

Battleships move inshore and renew their constant thunder. Helldivers and Avengers from our CVE's are heading toward the shore. . . .[3]

At 0900 the battleships ceased their fire and the cruisers and destroyers moved in closer to the shore to deliver their scheduled bombardment.[4]

At 0850 gunfire was suspended in the vicinity of Catmon Hill, the most prominent coastal terrain feature near Dulag, in order to allow an air strike against installations in the interior by the planes from the CVE's of the amphibious force. During the day a total of 500 sorties by more than 140 planes were flown in direct support. Twelve direct support missions were carried out, nine against selected targets requested by ground troops and three against targets of opportunity. Dawn and dusk fighter sweeps were made against airfields.[5] The aircraft from

---

[1] CTF 79 Opns Rpt, Ser 00323, 13 Nov 44. (All naval records cited are in the Office of Naval Records and Library.)

[2] COMBATDIV4 Opns Rpt, Ser 0322, 28 Dec 44.

[3] Tarbuck Rpt.

[4] COMBATDIV 4 Opns Rpt, Ser 0322, 28 Dec 44.

[5] COMINCH P–008, pp. 2–8.

CONVOY OFF LEYTE *at dawn on A Day.*

the carriers, which were beyond the range of the guns of enemy coastal defenses, did not attempt secondary missions upon the completion of a mission in the target area.[6]

The principal bombing and strafing targets were revetments, dispersal areas, supply dumps, and bivouac areas, together with aircraft on islands near Leyte. Grounded planes were strafed and destroyed. The commander of the escort carriers made the surprising estimate that aircraft from his carriers had destroyed 125 planes on the ground and damaged an additional 90 more in the first three days of this "close support at a distance."[7] Aircraft did not

bomb the shore line, since gunfire from the vessels within the gulf was considered more effective.

At 0900 the cruisers commenced bombarding the beaches. They were joined at 0930 by the destroyers. At 0945 the cruisers and destroyers lifted their fire and directed it at the inland areas, at the flanks of the landing beaches, and at important roads and towns.[8]

At 0800 the first anchor chains of the vessels had rattled out; LCVP's were quickly swung over the sides; boats circled mother ships and moved to their rendezvous areas.[9] The LCI mortar and LCI rocket ships took their places at the head of the

[6] Com3dAmph Force Opns Rpt, Ser 00317, 11 Nov 44.

[7] CTG 77.4 (Com Escort Carrier Group), Opns Rpt, COMINCH P–008, 30 Apr 45, Part 2, pp. 9, 10.

[8] CTF 78 Opns Rpt, Ser 00911, 10 Nov 44.

[9] 24th Div Opns Rpt Leyte, p. 4. Unless otherwise stated all records of tactical units are in DRB AGO.

assault waves. It was now 0945, fifteen minutes before H Hour. The LCI's raced simultaneously to the shores of Leyte, raking the landing beaches with rocket and mortar fire. The bombardment grew heavier and more monotonous. Hundreds of small boats, flanked by rocket ships and destroyers, headed toward the beaches; thousands of rockets hit the beaches with the rumble of an earthquake. It was impossible to distinguish one explosion from another in the unbroken roar.[10] Over a smooth sea a hot, brilliant, tropical sun beat down. The American forces were ready to land.

X Corps Goes Ashore

Hours earlier reveille had sounded on board the transports and the troops had dressed by the red lights in the holds where they were quartered. There was very little talking. Many of the men sat on their bunks giving their weapons a final check. Others lay back and smoked in silence. A few sought the chaplains.[11]

Missions of Sixth Army Summarized

The Sixth Army had been ordered to seize and establish beachheads in the Dulag and Tacloban areas and to secure the airfields in order to provide naval and air bases; and to seize such objectives in the Panaon Strait area as would permit safe passage of naval forces through the strait to the Camotes Sea.[12] To carry out the operation General Krueger had assigned the 21st Infantry Regiment, 24th Infantry Division, to gain control of Panaon Strait; the XXIV Corps was to secure the Dulag area and its airstrip;

and the 1st Cavalry Division of X Corps was to land in the Marasbaras area and, by advancing north, capture the Tacloban airdrome, the most important A-Day objective for the Sixth Army. At the same time, the 24th Division, less the 21st Infantry, of the X Corps was to seize Palo and advance rapidly to the northwest.[13] The seizure of these areas would secure the important coastal airstrips for future air operations, cut off any Japanese attempts at reinforcement from the southern Philippines through the Mindanao Sea and Sogod Bay, secure the important eastern entrances into the interior, and enable the American forces to control San Pedro Bay and San Juanico Strait.

The northernmost unit of X Corps, the 1st Cavalry Division, was to land in the vicinity of San Jose (also called San Ricardo and San Jose Ricardo) about three miles north of Palo, on White Beach. White Beach extended southward 2,000 yards from the Cataisan Peninsula. There was an interval of 1,500 yards between this beach and the northern limit of Red Beach, which was also 2,000 yards long.[14] The 24th Division, less the 21st Infantry, was to land in the vicinity of the town of Palo, on Red Beach. (*Map 3*)

1st Cavalry Division

White Beach had a fairly good landing surface of white coral sand, but even at high tide it was suitable only for shallow-draft landing craft. Its average width was fifteen yards at low tide, at which time a small irregular bank two to three feet high appeared at the water's edge. The underwater gradient was shallow, extending out half a mile in places. An irregular fringe of coconut trees ran the length of the beach. In the

---

[10] Tarbuck Rpt.
[11] 24th Div Opns Rpt Leyte, p. 4.
[12] GHQ SWPA Opns Instns 70, 21 Sep 44.

[13] Sixth Army FO 25, 23 Sep 44.
[14] CTF 77 Opns Rpt, Ser 00911, 10 Nov 44.

LANDING BEACHES. *White Beach is in the foreground, with Red Beach, bounded by the Palo River, beyond.*

southern section this fringe was narrow, with very wet and swampy cleared land behind it. Highway 1 roughly paralleled the beach about a mile inland.[15]

The roar of many guns could be heard as the 1st Cavalry Division prepared to disembark into landing boats, which were to rendezvous at the line of departure 5,000 yards from shore. A pall of lazily billowing yellow smoke obscured the shores of Leyte.[16]

The 1st Cavalry Division, commanded by Maj. Gen. Verne D. Mudge, was to land on White Beach with brigades abreast—the 1st Brigade on the left (south) and the 2d Brigade on the right (north)—and advance inland. The 1st Brigade, under Brig. Gen. William C. Chase, was to reconnoiter the

hills on the west side of Tacloban Valley and establish observation posts which would command the entrances to the valley. The 2d Brigade, under Brig. Gen. Hugh F. Hoffman, had the most important mission of the day. It was to advance northwest, capture the Tacloban airdrome and seize the Cataisan Peninsula, reaching Cataisan Point, the northern extremity of the peninsula, by 1400. Col. William J. Bradley's 8th Cavalry Regiment of the 2d Brigade was held afloat in division reserve and was to be prepared to reinforce either the 1st or 2d Brigade.[17]

Flanked by rocket and gunboat LCI's, and preceded by amphibian tanks, the 5th and 12th Cavalry Regiments, which formed the 1st Brigade, and the 7th Cavalry, which with the 8th Cavalry (in reserve) composed

---

[15] CTF 78 Opns Plan 101–44, 3 Oct 44.
[16] 1st Cav Div Opns Rpt Leyte, p. 17.

[17] 1st Cav Div FO 1, 2 Oct 44.

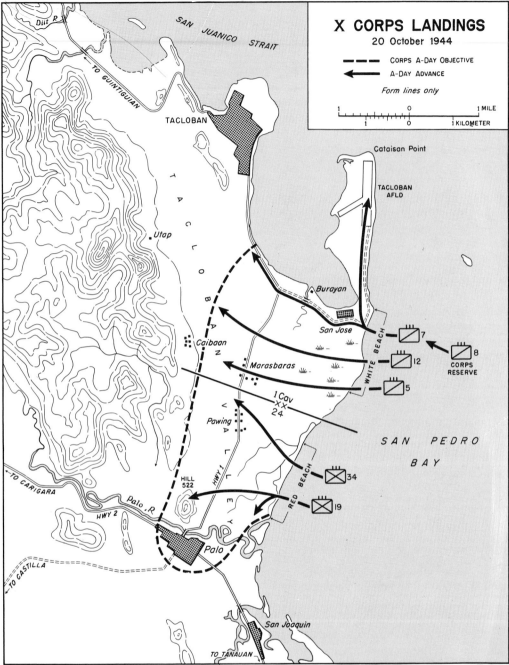

MAP 3

the 2d Brigade, raced for the shores of Leyte. The escorting rocket ships laid down a heavy barrage which covered the beach defenses to a depth of 1,800 yards inland and left the enemy incapable of organized resistance. As the boats neared shore, only small arms and machine gun fire opposed the landing.[18] As planned, the regiments landed abreast, the 7th Cavalry Regiment on the right (north), the 12th Cavalry Regiment in the center, and the 5th Cavalry on the left (south).

The 1st Squadron of the 7th Cavalry was to land north of the 2d Squadron on the northern end of White Beach, which at this point coincided with the narrow neck of land connecting the Cataisan Peninsula to the rest of the island, and then go directly north to secure the entire peninsula and the airstrip. On its left the 2d Squadron, 7th Cavalry, was to land on the right flank of White Beach, push inland, capture San Jose and a bridge across the Burayan River northwest of the town, and seize a beachhead line a thousand yards west of Highway 1 and three thousand yards from White Beach. The Cataisan Peninsula would then be sealed off.

Both squadrons landed on schedule, with only slight opposition, and immediately began to execute their assignments. The 2d Squadron, within fifteen minutes after landing, knocked out two pillboxes on the beach, killing eight Japanese in one and five in the other. It then organized rapidly and pushed on to secure its first objective, the town of San Jose. In the town the squadron engaged in a house-to-house search but found few Japanese. By 1230 twenty-four Japanese had been killed, San Jose was in

American hands, and the Cataisan Peninsula was sealed off. The 7th Cavalry Regiment established its command post on the west side of the town at 1245. The troops of the 2d Squadron then set out in a northwesterly direction astride the hard-surfaced, narrow San Jose–Tacloban road, but they were slowed down by swamps and flooded rice paddies on either side.[19] At 1400 they crossed the Burayan River on a bridge which the *33d Infantry Regiment* had attempted to destroy but had only damaged. The engineers strengthened the bridge so that the medium tanks could cross, and at 1420 the forward movement continued. By 1630 the squadron had reached its objective—a point 3,000 yards from White Beach—and immediately set up its night perimeter.

The 1st Squadron, 7th Cavalry, landed in amphibian tractors on the north end of White Beach a few minutes after initial assault waves of the 2d Squadron, 7th Cavalry, had cleared the beach. It moved west off the beach 100 yards, pivoted to the right, and began to move up the Cataisan Peninsula. The squadron was expected to secure the peninsula and the airstrip with great speed. Engineer units had landed just behind it and were waiting to start work on the airstrip as soon as it was seized. The 1st Squadron met with only light enemy opposition, the chief obstacles being the swamps, unoccupied pillboxes—each of which had to be checked—and the numerous Filipino shacks that afforded possible protection to the enemy. By 1600 the squadron had secured the airstrip and the Cataisan Peninsula.[20] Later in the afternoon the squadron, less Troop A, was withdrawn from the peninsula.

---

[18] Unless otherwise stated the material on the 1st Cavalry Division is taken from 1st Cav Div G–3 Jnl, 20 Oct 44, and 1st Cav Div Opns Rpt Leyte, pp. 2–4.

[19] 7th Cav Regt Opns Rpt Leyte, pp. 2–4.
[20] *Ibid.*

TROOPS OF THE 1ST CAVALRY DIVISION *wade through a swamp to their A-Day objective.*

The 5th and 12th Cavalry Regiments landed on White Beach without incident at exactly 1000. Immediately beyond the narrow landing beach was a deep swamp through which the regiments must move to reach Highway 1. The morass was often waist deep, in places even up to the armpits, and men of the advancing line of troops cursed heartily as they floundered toward the highway.[21] Under such circumstances it was impossible for the men to carry all of their personal equipment, and they had to make three trips in order to complete the crossing of certain areas. At 1100 a reconnaissance platoon of the 5th Cavalry Regiment made physical contact with elements of the 34th Infantry, 24th Division, on its left. By 1500 both cavalry regiments were

on Highway 1. They pushed westward immediately toward the next objective—the foothills west of the highway.[22] Col. Royce E. Drake, the commanding officer of the 5th Cavalry Regiment, went forward with a patrol from F Troop. At 1900, about three quarters of a mile south of Caibaan, the patrol made contact with the enemy. In the ensuing fight ten Japanese and one American were killed and two Americans wounded. At 1915 the 12th Cavalry Regiment closed in on its A–Day objective and formed its night perimeter.[23] The 5th Cavalry Regiment formed its night perimeter at 2135, a few hundred yards short of the objective.[24]

[21] 1st Cav Div Opns Rpt Leyte, p. 17.

[22] 1st Cav Brig Opns Rpt Leyte, p. 2.
[23] 12th Cav Regt Opns Rpt Leyte, pp. 1–2.
[24] 5th Cav S–3 Periodic Rpt 1, 20 Oct 44.

The first elements of the 8th Cavalry Regiment, 2d Cavalry Brigade, the corps reserve, moved to White Beach at 1040, and by 1130 the entire reserve regiment was ashore. The regiment continued in corps reserve throughout the day and spent its first night in the Philippines on the western edge of San Jose.[25]

At 1400 General Mudge assumed command ashore of the 1st Cavalry Division and by 1630 had established the divisional command post at San Jose.[26] Preceded by a ground reconnaissance of the unit commanders, all of the 1st Cavalry Division artillery landed on White Beach at 1330 and immediately established a position in the vicinity of San Jose. Before nightfall all battalions had registered and were prepared to fire, and beginning at 2115 the 61st Field Artillery Battalion throughout the night delivered harassing fire on the hills south of Tacloban.[27] By the end of the day the division had secured the Cataisan Peninsula and the Tacloban airstrip and, after crossing Highway 1, had made physical contact with the right flank of the 24th Infantry Division.[28]

24th Infantry Division [29]

In the southern part of the X Corps zone, to the left of the 1st Cavalry Division, the 24th Infantry Division (less the 21st Infantry), under Maj. Gen. Frederick A. Irving, was to land on Red Beach on the morning of A Day.[30] Although there were no underwater obstacles, mines, or barbed wire along Red Beach, the water was too shallow to permit vessels the size of LST's to come in and make a dry landing. Red Beach was narrow but consisted of firm sand. Back of it was flat, marshy ground covered with palm trees and jungle growth, extending inland in a southwesterly direction from the northern end of the beach. General Makino had converted a small stream bed in this area into a wide and deep tank trap which paralleled the beach for 1,500 yards. Several large, well-camouflaged pillboxes, connected by tunnels and constructed of palm logs and earth, were scattered throughout the area. Between the swamp and a low range of hills one and a quarter miles inland were open fields and rice paddies. The most prominent terrain feature was Hill 522 just north of Palo. This hill commanded the beach area, the town of Palo, and Highway 2, leading into the interior. It was partly wooded, and the *33d Infantry Regiment* had interlaced it with tunnels, trenches, and pillboxes.

From the beach a single deeply rutted and muddy exit road ran south to the Palo River, where it turned westward to Highway 1. The river was just north of the town of Palo and roughly paralleled Highway 2, which ran in a northwesterly direction from Palo into the interior, between the hills dominating this entrance to Leyte Valley.

The 24th Division was to occupy Palo, advance with regiments abreast into the interior in a northwesterly direction,[31] occupy the Capoocan–Carigara–Barugo area, and secure Highway 1 between Palo and Tanauan. The 19th Infantry on the left (south) was to establish an initial beachhead, advance to the west and south, seize Hill 522, and move on and capture Palo. The 34th Infantry on the right (north) was

---

[25] 8th Cav Regt Opns Rpt Leyte, p. 5.
[26] 1st Cav Div Opns Rpt Leyte, p. 19.
[27] 1st Cav Div Arty Opns Rpt Leyte, p. 3, 1st Cav Div Arty Unit Jnl, 20 Oct 44.
[28] 1st Cav Div Msgs to X Corps, 20 Oct 44.
[29] Unless otherwise stated information in this subsection is taken from 24th Div Opns Rpt Leyte, pp. 2–10, and 24th Div G–3 Jnl, 20 Oct 44.
[30] X Corps FO 1, 30 Sep 44.

[31] *Ibid.*

to establish an initial beachhead, then move westward into the interior and be prepared to assist the 19th Infantry in the capture of Hill 522.[32]

The assaulting forces, having been transferred to landing craft, met at the line of departure 5,000 yards from shore. After grouping, they dashed for the landing beaches, each regiment in column of battalions. The division landed at 1000 with regiments abreast according to plan. The Japanese allowed the first five waves to land, but when the other waves were 3,000 to 2,000 yards offshore, they opened strong artillery and mortar fire against them.[33] A number of the landing craft carrying the 1st Battalion, 19th Infantry, were hit and four of them sunk. There were numerous casualties: the commanding officer of Company C was killed; a squad of the Ammunition and Pioneer Platoon was almost wiped out; and the Cannon Company suffered the loss of two section leaders, a platoon leader, and part of its headquarters personnel.

Among the vessels hit by Japanese artillery were four LST's, one of which was set on fire. Of the five remaining, two were driven away and three did not get in until much later. The enemy fired upon the retiring LST's, which carried with them the artillery and most of the tanks. The commanding officer of Headquarters Company and the division quartermaster, together with the latter's executive officer, were wounded. Many of the division headquarters personnel were killed or wounded.

The first elements of the 3d Battalion, 34th Infantry, inadvertently landed 300 yards north of the assigned area and were immediately pinned down by heavy machine gun and rifle fire. The commanding officer of the regiment, Col. Aubrey S. Newman, arrived on the beach and, noting the situation, shouted to his men, "Get the hell off the beach. Get up and get moving. Follow me." [34] Thus urgently prompted, the men followed him into the wooded area.

Company I was able to advance, but Company K ran into a defensive position of five pillboxes along a stream about seventy-five yards from the beach. It successfully stormed these pillboxes with rifles, BAR's, and hand grenades. The 3d Battalion then halted for reorganization. Company L, the reserve company, moved into the line south of Company K to close the gap between the 19th and 34th Infantry Regiments, a gap created when part of the 34th landed too far north.

By 1215 the 34th Infantry had cleared the beach area of the enemy, and the 3d Battalion was ready to advance across an open swamp to a line of trees 150 yards away. A preparatory concentration by 81-mm. mortars, tanks, and heavy machine guns was first laid down. At 1230 the 3d Battalion moved in. Although the going was rough and the mud waist deep, the troops reached the trees at 1300 and waited for the mortars and machine guns to arrive. The 3d Battalion then pushed on an additional 250 yards.

The 2d Battalion, 34th Infantry, passed through the 3d Battalion, crossed Highway 1 at 1550, and dug in for the night 100 yards west of the highway.[35]

The 34th Infantry established contact with the 1st Cavalry Division on the right and the 19th Infantry on the left. The 1st Battalion, 34th Infantry, remained in the beachhead area.

---

[32] *Ibid.*
[33] 19th Inf Regt Opns Rpt Leyte, p. 1.

[34] 24th Div Opns Rpt Leyte, p. 7.
[35] 34th Inf Unit Rpt 1, 20 Oct 44.

To the south the 19th Infantry, with the 3d Battalion in the lead, had also struck heavy opposition on its sector of the beach. Through error the first waves of the regiment landed almost directly behind the 34th Infantry and 800 yards north of the proposed landing point. The later waves landed at the planned spot.

Company K did not land on schedule, because its command boat broke down. Going in under heavy fire, the company had all its officers except one killed or wounded. One of its platoons was unable to make contact with the rest of the company until the following day.

Company L, on the right, met little opposition on landing, established contact with the 34th Infantry, and reached the initial phase line 500 yards in from the beach. Company I, on the left, encountered stiff resistance fifty yards off the beach. The defenses of the *33d Infantry Regiment* in this sector consisted of a tank ditch and light automatic weapons, mortars, 75-mm. guns, and light and heavy machine guns in prepared positions. Company I hit a group of pillboxes and knocked out several of them as well as a 75-mm. gun. In this action Pfc. Frank B. Robinson played a spectacular role. Crawling behind a pillbox, he dropped three grenades into it and then reached down and pulled the machine gun barrel out of line. After a further advance of 200 yards, when a flame thrower aimed at a pillbox failed to ignite, he threw a bundle of lighted papers in front of the pillbox. The operator of the flame thrower then fired through the blaze and the charge was ignited. By openly exposing himself to fire from a third pillbox, Robinson enabled tanks to locate its position.[36]

During the next few hours platoons and squads fought independently. The 3d Battalion, 19th Infantry, drove into the interior about 500 yards, where it reorganized, made contact with adjacent units, and then established its perimeter on Highway 1.[37]

The 1st Battalion, 19th Infantry, had come in under intense fire in which several boats were hit, and numerous casualties occurred. The battalion landed 300 yards north of its selected area, moved in 200 yards, and then made a left, oblique turn in order to reach its predetermined assembly area. Company B suffered several casualties when it ran into strong rifle and pillbox fire, which pinned it down. The company was ordered to break off fighting and move to the northern edge of the Japanese positions. Lt. Col. Frederick R. Zierath, the commanding officer of the battalion, ordered the self-propelled guns to be brought up. They successfully neutralized the pillbox and a supporting position behind it. Company C, landing on the left flank of the battalion, was immediately pinned down by hostile fire. Zierath ordered it to disengage and proceed to the designated assembly area. Company A, which was split by enemy fire, regrouped inland and reached the assembly area just ahead of Company C.

The 2d Battalion, 19th Infantry, arrived at the beach just as the 1st Battalion was bypassing the initial resistance. By noon its first defense was formed around the beachhead. At 1245 Company E, with a rocket launcher, silenced a 75-mm. gun which had been firing on the LST's. In its advance the company located two more 75-mm. guns which had been abandoned. Company G relieved Company E and prepared to move along the beach road southwest toward Palo. As the point started to move out at 1300 it

---

[36] Private Robinson was awarded the Distinguished Service Cross.

[37] 19th Inf Unit Rpt 1, 20 Oct 44.

75-MM. M8 SELF-PROPELLED HOWITZERS *move in to support the infantrymen in their advance from the beach.*

was attacked by approximately a platoon from the *33d Infantry Regiment* which attempted to retake the gun positions. The Japanese were repulsed by rifle fire, leaving eleven dead.

At 1430 Company G, in resuming its advance, ran at once into a series of mutually supporting pillboxes about 500 yards inland, where the beach road turns to meet Highway 1. A stiff rifle fire fight followed, in which the Americans suffered fifteen casualties. Since darkness was approaching, the battalion broke off the action and dug in along the road for the night.

While the 2d Battalion, 19th Infantry, was proceeding cautiously forward the 1st Battalion was working toward Hill 522. This hill, which rose directly from the river's edge north of Palo, overlooked the landing beaches and its upward trails were steep and winding. Hill 522 presented the most significant terrain feature which would have to be overcome before the American forces could push into the interior from Palo and it constituted one of the chief objectives for A Day. Three months earlier General Makino had started to fortify it, impressing nearly all of the male population of Palo for the work. By A Day they had constructed five well-camouflaged pillboxes of rocks, planking, and logs, covered with earth. Numerous tunnels honeycombed the hill; the communications trenches were seven feet deep.

During the preliminary bombardments the Navy had delivered some of its heaviest blows on the hill, and the bombardment was continued by Battery B of the 13th Field

MAJ. GEN. FRANKLIN C. SIBERT *(left)*, *X Corps commander, confers with Maj. Gen. Frederick A. Irving, commander of the 24th Division, at a forward command post.*

Artillery Battalion and Battery A of the 63d Field Artillery Battalion. The 1st Battalion of the 19th Infantry sent reconnaissance parties to locate a northern route to the hill. The plan had been to move inland from the extreme south of the beachhead, but that area was still in Japanese hands. At 1430, when scouts reported finding a covered route on the northern side of the hill, the 1st Battalion immediately moved out in a column of companies. The column had barely started when Company A, in the lead, was held up by enemy fire from the five pillboxes. The remainder of the battalion moved north around Company A, and, skirting the woods, attacked Hill 522 from the northeast, with Company C on the right and Company B on the left.

The men, although tired from the day's activity and strain, made steady progress up the slope. As the troops moved upward, American mortars started to shell the crest of the hill. It was thought that this was artillery fire and a request was made that it be lifted. It came, however, from chemical mortars. After a short delay the firing ceased. At dusk Company B reached the first crest of the hill and was halted by fire from two enemy bunkers. The company thereupon dug in.

At the same time scouts from Company C reached the central and highest crest of the hill and espied about two platoons of Japanese coming up the other side. They shouted for the remainder of the company to hurry. Company C got to the top of the hill barely ahead of the Japanese, and a sharp engagement took place in which about fifty Japanese were killed. Company C held the highest crest of the hill. During this attack,

1st Lt. Dallas Dick was struck in the leg and his carbine was shot from his hands, but he continued to command his unit until his evacuation forty-eight hours later.

During the night the Japanese made frequent but unsuccessful attempts to infiltrate the company area and in the darkness they carried away their dead and wounded. During the action to secure Hill 522, fourteen men of the 1st Battalion were killed and ninety-five wounded; thirty of the latter eventually rejoined their units. General Irving, who had assumed command of the 24th Division ashore at 1420, later said that if Hill 522 had not been secured when it was, the Americans might have suffered a thousand casualties in the assault.

By the end of A Day, the division had crossed Highway 1 and established physical contact with the 1st Cavalry Division on its right flank. In spite of strong opposition on its left flank, the 24th Division had secured Hill 522, which dominated the route into the interior and overlooked the town of Palo, the entrance point into Leyte Valley. Furthermore, the X Corps had now secured a firm beachhead area averaging a mile in depth and extending over five miles from the tip of the Cataisan Peninsula to the vicinity of Palo, and had captured the important Tacloban airstrip on the Cataisan Peninsula.

XXIV Corps Goes Ashore

While the X Corps was engaged in seizing a beachhead and capturing the Tacloban airfield, the XXIV Corps was carrying out its mission more than fourteen miles to the south. (*Map 4*) It was to land in the Dulag–San Jose area and establish a beachhead between Dulag and Tanauan. The Dulag airstrip was the primary objective. The 7th and

96th Divisions—the 7th on the left (south) and the 96th on the right (north)—made the landings. The most prominent terrain feature near the shore line is a short, finger-like hill range between the mouth of the Labiranan River and the village of Pikas. Ranging from 400 feet at its southern extremity, known as Labiranan Head, to 1400 feet at Catmon Hill, southeast of Pikas, this hill mass dominates the surrounding plain for miles around. (The entire hill mass will hereafter be referred to as Catmon Hill.)

The *9th Infantry Regiment*, less one battalion, was guarding the Catmon Hill area while the *20th Infantry Regiment*, less one battalion, was defending the Dulag area.[38]

Immediately northwest of Dulag and just off the beach was a swamp,[39] and along the coast were coconut groves interspersed with rice fields. Many streams and rivers cut across the coastal plain.[40] Between Dulag and Labiranan Head was a good section of firm sand beach, backed by a broad alluvial plain extending ten miles inland.

96th Infantry Division

In the early morning hours of 20 October the Southern Attack Force moved to a location off the shores of Leyte near the town of Dulag. The 96th Division was to land with regiments abreast in the area between the Calbasag River and the town of San Jose—the 382d Infantry on the left (south) and the 383d Infantry on the right (north). The southern half of the division's beachhead area was designated Blue Beaches 1 and 2, and the northern half was known as Orange Beaches 1 and 2. The beaches had

---

[38] *35th Army* Opns, p. 27.

[39] CTF 79 Opns Rpt, Ser 00323, Encl A, 13 Nov 44.

[40] 383d Inf Regt FO 6A, App. A, 30 Sep 44.

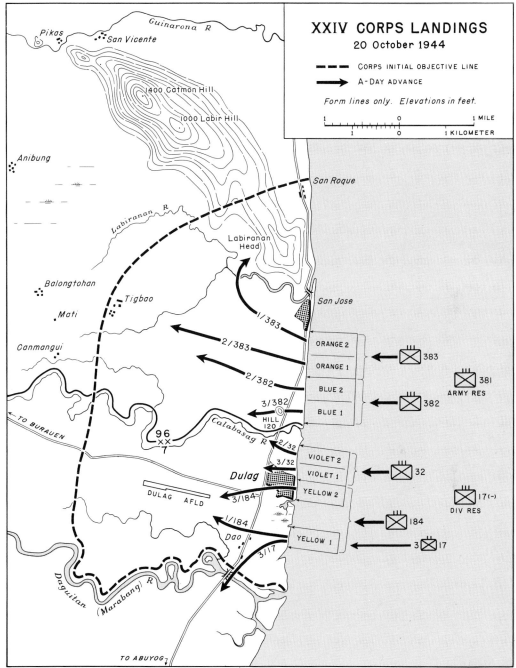

MAP 4

an average length of about 525 yards. The northern extremity of Orange Beach was about ten miles from the southernmost beach of the 24th Division in the X Corps sector.

The order to "land the landing force" of the 96th Division came at 0845, and LVT's immediately began to spill out of the LST's and head for the line of departure. By 0930 the assault waves, preceded by the amphibian tank wave, had arrived at their appointed position 4,500 yards offshore.[41] At the head of the column were LCI gunboats which were to give fire support and act as guides for succeeding waves. The assault waves then headed for Blue and Orange Beaches.

When the landing craft were within 100 yards of the shore, the LCI's fired into the interior and to each side of the landing beaches. Thereupon the amphibian tanks began to fire directly beyond the beaches, in front of the advancing assault forces. The 382d Infantry under Col. Macey L. Dill landed at 0950 on Blue Beach, and the 383d Infantry under Col. Edwin T. May landed ten minutes later on Orange Beach.

The 383d Infantry landed with two battalions abreast—the 2d Battalion on the left and the 1st Battalion on the right. By 1045 both battalions had landed all of their assault troops and had advanced 1,200 yards inland, encountering no resistance except intermittent mortar fire from the *9th Infantry Regiment* in the vicinity of Catmon Hill.[42] Immediately beyond the highway the two battalions reached an unsuspected swamp. The amphibian tanks bogged down at 1045 and were unable to catch up with the assault troops during the rest of the day. Intermittent Japanese fire continued to fall on the beach area. The 2d Battalion crossed

the swamp without encountering the enemy and established its night perimeter 2,600 yards inland from the landing beaches.

The 1st Battalion, 383d Infantry, pushed northwest through the barrio of San Jose, which was on the beach, and along the marshy ground and swamps on the south bank of the Labiranan River for 2,200 yards. It crossed the river at 1610. Company C placed a roadblock at the point where Highway 1 crossed the Labiranan River. After advancing 400 yards farther northwest the battalion ran into fire from elements of the *9th Infantry Regiment*. At 1900 the battalion, still under enemy fire, dug in for the night. At the close of the day's action it was at the base of Labiranan Head in a position which would permit an attack to be launched on that terrain feature from the west.

The 3d Battalion, which had been held afloat in regimental reserve, came ashore at 1045. It mopped up in the rear of the 1st and 2d Battalions and established its night perimeter 800 yards away from the 1st Battalion on the south bank of the Labiranan River. During the day the 383d Infantry Regiment, slowed by the terrain, had advanced 2,600 yards inland.[43]

As heavy enemy artillery and mortar fire fell on the beach, the 382d Infantry also landed with two battalions abreast—the 2d Battalion to the right (north) at Blue Beach 2 and the 3d Battalion to the left (south) at Blue Beach 1. The 2d Battalion, though momentarily stopped by debris on the shore, was able to advance quickly and by 1025 had penetrated 300 yards inland. This gain was increased to 700 yards by 1115. The battalion crossed Highway 1 before it encountered the first defensive positions of the *9th Infantry Regiment,* a series of zigzag

---

[41] CTG 79.2 Opns Rpt, Ser 0032, 4 Nov 44.
[42] 383d Inf Opns Rpt Leyte, p. 1.

[43] *Ibid.*

BEACH AREA *as seen from Hill 120.*

deserted trenches roughly paralleling the beach. Although the 2d Battalion met no enemy opposition, the intense heat and the swampy ground made progress slow. At 1630, when the battalion formed a perimeter for the night, it had pushed inland approximately 2,500 yards.

The amphibian tractors carrying the 3d Battalion, 382d Infantry, were held up by the tank barriers of coconut logs and debris on the beach, and the troops were forced to debark at the water's edge. Several hundred yards off the beach this battalion began to receive heavy fire from Hill 120, which was about 600 yards from the beach. The hill dominated the regimental beach area [44] and was the A-Day objective for the battalion. The fire pinned down the battalion,

which thereupon called for mortar support and naval gunfire. The resulting barrage forced the Japanese out of their positions, and at 1040 the battalion advanced and captured Hill 120.

The 1st Battalion, 382d Infantry, which had been in floating reserve, landed on Blue Beach 1 and moved to the foot of Hill 120 to support the 3d Battalion. Immediately beyond the hill there was a small meadow rimmed by a deep swamp. The enemy fired upon the hill throughout the day but could not dislodge the 3d Battalion. This steady fire and the presence of the swamp limited the A-Day advance of the 3d Battalion to 1,300 yards inland from the landing beach.

At the end of the day, despite the swampy terrain and the harassing fire of the Japanese, the 382d Infantry had advanced approximately 2,500 yards on the northern

---

[44] 382d Inf Unit Jnl, 20 Oct 44.

flank and 1,300 yards on the southern flank. Contact had been established at 1600 with the 32d Infantry, 7th Division, on the left flank, and the 383d Infantry, 96th Division, on the right flank.[45]

At 1630 the assault forces of the 96th Division consolidated their positions and set up defense perimeters for the night. During the day the division had captured the barrio of San Jose, established control over both sides of the Labiranan River, captured Hill 120 overlooking the beach area, and progressed well inland. Although all units of the division fell considerably short of the objective for A Day, this delay was due fully as much to the swampy and difficult terrain as it was to enemy resistance. The 381st Infantry Regiment remained in Sixth Army floating reserve throughout the day.[46]

Maj. Gen. James L. Bradley arrived ashore at 1750, and at 1800 he assumed command of the 96th Infantry Division. The three light artillery battalions of the division had landed and were in position by 1800.

7th Infantry Division

Concurrently with the landings of the 96th Division, the 7th Division, on the left, was establishing a beachhead in its zone of action just south of the 96th Division. At 0800 the assault troops of the 7th Division began to clamber down the nets of their transports into landing boats which were to carry them in the dash for the shore.[47] By

0815 they were boated and at the line of departure.

The 7th Division was to land on Violet and Yellow Beaches. Violet Beach extended 785 yards north from the northern edge of Dulag. The northern half of Yellow Beach, called Yellow Beach 2, which was south of Violet Beach and contiguous to it, was 400 yards long. Between the northern and southern halves of Yellow Beach was a swamp. The southern half of Yellow Beach, Yellow Beach 1, was approximately 425 yards in length and was located south of Dulag and north of the Daguitan River mouth.

The 7th Division was to go ashore between the Calbasag and Daguitan Rivers with regiments abreast—the 32d Infantry on the right (north) and the 184th Infantry on the left (south); the 17th Infantry, less its 3d Battalion, was in reserve. The principal A-Day objectives were the barrio of Dulag and its airstrip. The 3d Battalion, 17th Infantry, was to swing south and secure the bridge and the crossing of the Daguitan River at Dao and the crossing of the Talisay River.

The 32d Infantry, under Col. Marc J. Logie, was to land on the northern and southern portions of Violet Beach, drive into the interior, and protect the right flank of the division. The 184th Infantry, commanded by Col. Curtis D. O'Sullivan, was to land on Yellow Beach 1 and Yellow Beach 2 and then drive inland, directing its main effort toward an early seizure of the airfield west of Dulag. It was also to seize and secure the crossings of the Daguitan River.

After the landing waves had formed at the line of departure, the landing craft started for the beaches, preceded by the

---

[45] 382d Inf Opns Rpt Leyte, p. 2.

[46] 96th Div Opns Rpt Leyte, pp. 33–37.

[47] Unless otherwise stated, the part of this subsection dealing with the 7th Infantry Division is taken from the following: 7th Inf Div Opns Rpt Leyte, pp. 3–5; 7th Inf Div G–3 Jnl, 20 Oct 44; and 7th Inf Div FO 9, 1 Oct 44.

776th Amphibian Tank Battalion. As it got ashore, the tank battalion received hostile mortar and small arms fire that came from a tank barrier of coconut palm logs near the water's edge. The battalion overcame this opposition fifteen minutes after landing and advanced a distance of 200 yards inland to positions from which it could support the infantry.[48] According to plan, the 32d and 184th Infantry Regiments followed abreast. The 32d Infantry landed with two battalions abreast—the 2d on the right and the 3d on the left. The regiment encountered minor resistance at the beach, consisting of light rifle fire and sporadic artillery and mortar fire. By 1023 the 3d Battalion had landed all its assault troops and by 1030 seven assault waves of the 2d Battalion had reached the shore. As the two battalions proceeded inland, they met opposition from the enemy.

The 2d Battalion landed on the edge of a cemetery in which were small groups of the enemy very much alive. By 1100 these were subdued by rifle fire and the battalion was able to advance without difficulty into the interior. At about 1300 the 2d Platoon of Company F, after advancing some 600 yards, ran into fire from three pillboxes concealed in the tall cogon grass on the right flank. Tanks were brought up to knock out the enemy pillboxes. The advance then continued. By 1315 the 2d Battalion made physical contact with elements of the 96th Division on the right. Shortly after 1400 the 2d and 3d Battalions of the 32d Infantry made contact and reached Highway 1.[49]

Companies L and K of the 3d Battalion, 32d Infantry, landed abreast. Company L, on the left, ran into heavy fire from Japanese machine gunners who had waited until the leading elements of the company exposed themselves. The Japanese were entrenched in bunkers emplaced in hedgerows and banana groves. The pillboxes, which were mutually supporting, were located at the ends of the hedgerows and occasionally in the middle of an open field. Each pillbox had machine guns and antitank guns. Company L suffered a number of casualties and was pinned down. The enemy gunners then turned to Company K and stopped its forward movement. In the space of fifteen minutes two officers and six men of the 3d Battalion were killed, and one officer and eighteen men wounded. Of the medium tanks that had come ashore at 1030, three were sent to support Company L and two to support Company K. The latter two were knocked out before they could adjust their fire on the pillboxes. The leading tank sent in support of Company L was knocked out by a direct hit from an antitank gun. With two tanks remaining, it was decided to hit the flanks of the entrenched pillboxes at 1345. A platoon of Company K went to the right and another platoon from the company to the left. Simultaneously the remaining elements of the two companies, coordinating with the tanks, assaulted the pillboxes. The heavy volume of fire kept the enemy guns quiet until they could be finished off with grenades. The pillboxes were knocked out without further casualties.

Paralleling the route of advance of Company L were several hedge fences, behind which were enemy machine guns and mortars. Although under heavy fire, the company was able to break through the first barriers with the aid of the tanks. At 1630, since the enemy fire continued in volume, the 32d Infantry withdrew and established a defensive position for the night. During the day the 32d Infantry had reached a

---

[48] 776th Amph Tank Bn Opns Rpt Leyte, p. 4.
[49] 32d Inf Unit Jnl, 20 Oct 44.

general line along Highway 1. The 2d Battalion had advanced 400 yards beyond the highway and the 3d Battalion 100 yards.[50]

The 184th Infantry landed at 1000, two battalions abreast—the 1st on the southern half of Yellow Beach and the 3d on the northern half. They encountered surprisingly little resistance on either beach and were able to push inland at a much greater speed than had been anticipated. The 3d Battalion drove through the town of Dulag, which lay directly in its path, to the Dulag–Burauen Highway. The 1st Battalion pushed inland and reached the highway at 1210, just fifteen minutes after the 3d Battalion. At 1530 the two battalions established physical contact and maintained it throughout the day as they continued their advance along the highway. At 1255 the 2d Battalion, 184th Infantry, landed on Yellow Beach and went into regimental reserve on the regiment's southern flank. As the advance of the 32d Infantry on the right slowed up, Company G, 184th Infantry, was committed to fill the gap which had developed between the two regiments. At 1835 the 184th Infantry, although it had failed to secure the Dulag airstrip, formed its night perimeter along the edge of the strip.[51] At the end of the day the regiment had no battle casualties, but three men had been overcome by the heat. Eleven Japanese had been killed in the regiment's zone.[52]

The 17th Infantry, less its 3d Battalion, was kept in 7th Division reserve. The 3d Battalion of the 17th had come ashore at 1500 on the southern end of Yellow Beach. The battalion pushed west and south through light opposition, seizing the bridge

over the Daguitan River at Dao, and by 2100 had established a bridgehead south of the river and made contact with the 184th Infantry on the right. At the end of the first day's fighting the 7th Division had gained possession of the Leyte shore in its zone and penetrated inland 600 yards on the right and nearly 2,300 yards on the left. It had also reached the edge of the Dulag airstrip. By nightfall the XXIV Corps had established a firm beachhead line extending along the coast from San Jose on the north to just below Dao on the south.

Seventy miles to the south the 21st Infantry Regiment of the 24th Division, which was detailed to land in the vicinity of Panaon Strait on 20 October at 0930, half an hour before the launching of the great offensive, and to secure control of that entrance to Sogod Bay, successfully accomplished its mission. It encountered no Japanese.

Thus at the end of A Day the Sixth Army had succeeded in landing assault forces all along the eastern coast of Leyte and was in control of Panaon Strait. Its casualties amounted to 49 men killed, 192 wounded, and 6 missing in action. There remained a gap of nearly ten miles between the X and XXIV Corps. The Tacloban airstrip on the Cataisan Peninsula had been secured and the American forces were on the edge of the airstrip at Dulag. Nearly as important as the capture of the airstrip was the seizure of Hill 522, which commanded the entrance to the broad Leyte Valley at Palo. The advance echelon of General Headquarters had opened on Leyte Island at 1200.[53] On the following day, when adequate communication facilities had been established, Generals

[50] 32d Inf Opns Rpt Leyte, p. 4.
[51] 184th Inf Opns Rpt Leyte, p. 2.
[52] 184th Inf Jnl, 20 Oct 44.

[53] Rad, GHQ SWPA to CG Sixth Army, Sixth Army G–3 Rear Jnl, 21 Oct 44.

LT. GEN. WALTER KRUEGER AND COL. RUPERTO K. KANGLEON
of the guerrilla forces head for the beach (above). Krueger talks with men of the 7th Division on the beach near Dulag (below).

Krueger, Sibert, and Hodge assumed command ashore of the Sixth Army, X Corps, and XXIV Corps, respectively.

Most of the *16th Division* had withdrawn during the naval and air bombardment which took place just prior to the landing. The immediate invasion of the troops after this pounding enabled the Americans to secure most of the coastal defenses before the enemy could regroup and return. As a consequence, the only Japanese forces encountered were those left behind to fight a delaying action. The meeting with the enemy in force was yet to come.

Bringing in Supplies

While the assault forces were securing the beaches of Leyte, supplies were being poured in to support the operation. Within an hour after the first assault wave hit the hostile shores, rations, equipment, and other supplies were being rushed to the beaches. Each man going ashore carried a change of clothing in his pack, two days' supply of emergency rations, one day's supply of D rations, and two filled canteens, in addition to his gas mask, weapons, and ammunition.

The Navy was responsible for transporting the troops and supplies to the target area. Ships' companies unloaded the cargo from the cargo vessels and transported it in small craft to the beaches. Many of the ships had been improperly loaded for the journey to Leyte. The cargo should have been so loaded that articles first needed would be the last put on board; instead it had been stowed haphazardly, with little attention given to the problem of unloading.

As a result of the faulty stowage of supplies on the ships, many badly needed items were at the bottoms of the holds, and articles that would not be needed until later in the operation were piled on top of them. The supplies were set ashore in random fashion and then were carelessly thrown on trucks and other vehicles. This sort of handling resulted in a loss of carrying capacity, in slow removal of the loads, and in a consequent delay in the return of vehicles to the landing beaches.

The LSM's were used to very good advantage in the unloading of the APA's and AKA's. Vehicles and supplies could be loaded on them without difficulty, and in addition, two hatches on the LSM's could be worked at the same time. On each of the APA's, AKA's, and LST's which carried troops, a labor crew was detailed to remain on board to assist in the unloading.[54]

At the beach, the Army took over the cargo and moved the supplies to prearranged dumps. On the northern beaches in the X Corps sector, the Army shore party was composed of the 532d and 592d Engineer Boat and Shore Regiments of the 2d Engineer Special Brigade. After landing, these units facilitated the movement of troops, vehicles, and supplies across the beaches and controlled all unloading operations.[55] The 1122d and 1140th Engineer Combat Groups supervised the unloading in the XXIV Corps sector. They were assisted by naval beach parties from the VII Amphibious Force, which brought the cargo ashore.

The beachhead areas at which the supplies were unloaded varied in quality and depth. Most of the beaches on which the 7th and 96th Divisions landed were very good,[56]

---

[54] Extracted Report of Landing on Leyte in the Philippine Islands by an Australian Officer Attached to the Northern Assault Force Landing at Red Beach. Copy in OCMH.

[55] 2d ESB Opns Rpt Leyte, p. 1.

[56] Sixth Army Opns Rpt Leyte, Engr Rpt, p. 232.

UNLOADING SUPPLIES AT DULAG *on A Day (above), and (below) general view of the beach area on 22 October 1944.*

as contrasted with those in the X Corps area where the 24th Infantry Division and 1st Cavalry Division came ashore. The greatest difficulty was encountered along Red Beach, where the 24th Division landed. This stretch of coast line was ill adapted to the unloading of supplies, having poor exits and offering few dispersal areas ashore.[57]

LST's approaching Red Beach were under intense enemy fire. Four of them received direct hits.[58] Nearly all of the LST's were grounded 100 to 200 yards from the beach. Only one of them was able to come within forty to fifty yards of the beach, and it succeeded in unloading its cargo of heavy equipment only with considerable difficulty.[59] Another put off a bulldozer, which disappeared in seven feet of water. With difficulty the other LST's withdrew and returned to the transport area.[60]

The shore parties on both Red and White Beaches (X Corps sector) did not land early enough to effect a proper organization before the cargo began to come in. Although the parties worked hard, they were undermanned, and it was necessary to augment them by "volunteers" in order to unload the large volume of cargo.[61] It had been planned to establish temporary beach dumps at the point of unloading of each LST, but since at Red Beach the LST's could not get ashore, the plans had to be changed. These craft were diverted to the 1st Cavalry Division's White Beach 2,000 yards north. The LSM's and LCM's were able to discharge their vehicles in three or four feet of water. Many of these, being poorly water-proofed, stalled and had to be pulled ashore. Once there, the heavily loaded vehicles churned up the sand, and many of them sank so deeply that they had to be pulled out.[62]

The strong resistance of the Japanese and the difficult terrain limited the depth of the 24th Division's beachhead and prevented the establishment of division dumps beyond the beachhead areas. As a result, most of the supplies and nearly all supporting and service troops had to be concentrated on the first three or four hundred yards of the beachhead. Fortunately there was no bombing or strafing of the area, and although the development of exit roads was slow, the congestion on the beach was cleared before trouble developed.[63]

The diversion of the 24th Division's LST's to the beaches of the 1st Cavalry Division naturally strained the facilities of the beach and shore parties on White Beach. The southern end of White Beach also proved unsuitable for landing LST's, which consequently were shifted to the northern end.[64] However, the Army shore parties organized White Beach immediately upon landing. A two-way road was cleared along the beach with military police directing traffic. Dump areas were marked off by white ribbons, and sign posts were erected. The supplies were unloaded from the landing craft by roller conveyors and "fire brigade methods" directly onto the waiting trucks and trailers.[65] After the ships had been un-

---

[57] Sixth Army Opns Rpt Leyte, G–4 Rpt, p. 218.

[58] Ltr, CG 2d ESB to CG Sixth Army, 22 Oct 44, 2d ESB Jnl and Jnl File.

[59] CTU 78.1.7 Opns Rpt, COMINCH P–008, Part 5, p. 2.

[60] Ltr, CG 2d ESB to CG Sixth Army, 22 Oct 44, 2d ESB Jnl and Jnl File.

[61] CTU 78.2.1 and 78.2.3 Opns Rpt, COMINCH P–008, Part 5, p. 3.

[62] Lts, CG 2d ESB to CG Sixth Army, 22 Oct 44, 2d ESB Jnl and Jnl File.

[63] Maj F. W. Doyle to Brig Gen L. J. Whitlock, Rpt of Observations, KING II Opn, 4 Nov 44, GHQ G–4 Jnl, AGO KCRC.

[64] 2d ESB Opns Rpt Leyte, p. 6.

[65] Maj Doyle to Gen Whitlock, Rpt of Observations, KING II Opn, 4 Nov 44, GHQ G–4 Jnl.

loaded the shore parties consolidated all of the supplies into dumps as rapidly as possible. The rations and ammunition, which were loaded on fifteen LVT's, were kept mobile to the rear of the troops.[66]

When Leyte was substituted for Yap as the target, it had been decided that the 96th Division should unload troops and supplies at Leyte as rapidly as possible. Consequently, supplies were unloaded with little regard for the order in which items would be needed ashore.[67]

There was no general unloading on the beach in the XXIV Corps area until the late afternoon of A Day, when water, rations, and ammunition were sent ashore. For about an hour the unloading proceeded satisfactorily, but the beach soon became congested. The beach parties brought in the supplies faster than they could be handled by the shore parties.[68] At one time more than eighty loaded boats waited over five hours before they could be unloaded. The slowness of the shore parties in unloading the boats was not entirely their fault. Many of the boats were improperly loaded with mixed cargo, a situation which caused the boats to ship water. They were forced to come in to the beach or sink. The shore parties were also handicapped by a lack of workers. A shore party of 250 men included headquarters personnel, military police, and communications men, leaving only fifty or sixty workers. The unloading was further retarded by lack of sufficient mechanical equipment and

failure to make full use of available transportation.[69]

Loose cargo piled up on the beaches faster than it could be taken to the dump sites.[70] A deep swamp, 250 yards inland and parallel to Blue Beach, also limited the extension of dumps in that area. The congestion was relieved the next day, when the supplies were taken to selected dump sites nearly as fast as they could be removed from the boats.

In the Dulag area, the organization of the shore party and its operations were well co-ordinated.[71] In the initial phase the 7th Division employed the "drugstore system" whereby DUKW's carried the supplies directly to the front-line consumers of the division from specially loaded LST's which had been anchored off the landing beaches.[72] By using this method the division was able to deliver critical supplies to the combat troops within an hour after the request was received. At the same time, other supplies and equipment could be put ashore without interruption.

In the wake of the initial assault waves, the engineer troops landed and began at once to clear the beaches, prepare dump sites, and build access roads. The men worked around the clock in six-hour shifts.[73]

Within four hours the 7th Division's shore party was prepared to start full-scale operations, and two hours later began to issue supplies to the assault forces. Since the cargo came ashore in nets, it was possible to use cranes and bulldozers to good advantage. The cargo was initially moved over the

[66] 7th Cav Opns Rpt Leyte, Supplementary Annex, p. 3.

[67] 96th Inf Div Opns Rpt Leyte, p. 73.

[68] Rpt of Sup Off to CO *Funston,* 23 Oct 44, in CO USS *Frederick Funston* Opns Rpt, Ser 0101, 31 Oct 44. The boat crews and beach parties had been fortified with a lunch consisting of turkey salad, ham and cheese, hot steak sandwiches, ice cream, and cold fruit juices. The Army assault troops carried K rations.

[69] Com3dAmph Force Opns Rpt, Ser 00317, 11 Nov 44.

[70] 96th Inf Div Opns Rpt Leyte, pp. 73–75.

[71] CTG 79.1 Opns Rpt, COMINCH P–008, Part 5, p. 15.

[72] 7th Inf Div Opns Rpt Leyte, G–4 Rpt.

[73] CTG 71.1 Opns Rpt, COMINCH P–008, Part 5, p. 15.

landing beaches to regimental beach dumps 500 yards inland, and as vehicles landed they were driven to temporary assembly areas or directly to their organizations.[74] Six hours after the first assault wave hit the beaches the 7th Division abandoned the floating drugstore system, since by that time sufficient supplies had been brought ashore to fill requisitions directly from the dumps.[75]

During the day a total of 107,450 tons of supplies and equipment were discharged over the beaches of the Sixth Army. Although the beaches in some instances were extremely congested, steps had been initiated to relieve the situation.

News of the success of the American forces in establishing a beachhead on Leyte—the first foothold in the Philippine Islands—was joyfully received by the American nation. The President radioed congratulations to General MacArthur and added, "You have the nation's gratitude and the nation's prayers for success as you and your men fight your way back. . . ." [76]

---

[74] 7th Inf Div Opns Rpt Leyte, G–4 Rpt.

[75] 1140th Engr Const Gp Shore Party Opns Rpt Leyte.

[76] The *New York Times,* October 20, 1944.

CHAPTER VI

The Japanese Reaction

The Japanese undertook the defense of Leyte with serene assurance. Their pilots had erroneously reported the naval battle off Formosa as a great victory and declared that only remnants of the once strong American Navy remained. The defeatist attitude of the summer of 1944 vanished.

During the summer there had been disagreement among the Japanese military leaders. *Imperial General Headquarters* felt that the decisive battle should be fought on Luzon and only delaying actions taken in other areas. To this the *14th Area Army* agreed. The *Southern Army,* on the other hand, believed that it would be impossible to wage a successful battle on Luzon if other areas, especially the Visayan Islands, were allowed to fall into American hands. Since these islands, if captured, could be used as Allied air bases, the decisive battle should be fought whenever and wherever the Americans attacked.[1]

Confident that the U. S. fleet had suffered grievously in the battle off Formosa, the Japanese closed ranks and all the commands agreed that the time was most opportune to deliver the *coup de grâce.* The foolhardy Americans would take a severe drubbing, and Japan, after a long series of humiliating and costly defeats, would regain the initiative. It was therefore a jubilant *Imperial General Headquarters* that ordered its

armed forces to do battle with the Americans.

The essence of the *Imperial General Headquarters* plan was simple. The American convoys and carriers were to be given complete freedom in their journey to the Philippine Islands. When they were sufficiently close to make retreat difficult, the main strength of the Japanese Army, Navy, and Air Forces would descend upon them and deliver a knockout blow. If the operation were launched too early, the Americans could annihilate the inferior Japanese air strength before the battle could be fought; if too late, the Americans could escape and the objective would be lost. *Imperial General Headquarters,* therefore, was "patiently waiting" for the opportune moment.[2]

The Air Forces

On the evening of 17 October the *4th Air Army,* upon receiving word that the U. S. forces were in the vicinity of Suluan Island, ordered the entire *2d Air Division* to attack the Americans. The main strength of the fighter units was to be concentrated in the central and southern Philippines areas. Although bad weather prevented a reconnaissance, the increase in American air raids on the central and southern Philippines made it imperative for the Japanese to

---

[1] Japanese Studies in WW II, 21, Hist of *Southern Army,* 1941–45, OCMH.

[2] Hist of *Army Sec, Imperial GHQ,* p. 139.

attack with their main air force. The *2d Air Division* was ordered to move from Clark Field on Luzon to Bacolod on Negros Island. It was unable to do this because of the bad weather, and it was therefore unable to forestall the American landings. The commander of the *4th Air Army* decided on 21 October, as a result of the American landings, to use the entire air force under his command, employing the *7th Air Division* and the *30th Fighter Group,* in addition to the *2d Air Division.* The *12th Air Brigade* of the *30th Fighter Group* had just arrived in the Philippines from Japan, via Shanghai, and it was necessary to employ this brigade immediately because of the impending battle in Leyte Gulf.

All the various units were to launch an attack against the American land forces and shipping by the evening of 23 October. On 24 October there was to be a series of aerial attacks, the first early in the morning with the entire force; the second consisting of two waves; the third by the entire force in the evening; and during the night by waves of heavy and light bombers and assault planes.[3]

The Americans anticipated increased aerial activity over Leyte, and therefore the number of fighters was increased on 24 October to 36, on call from 0545 till dark, with an additional 16 fighters ready for immediate action upon request. Twenty-eight of the 36 were assigned to the attack force commanders and 8, retained by General Krueger, patrolled the beachhead area and provided additional fighters when and where they were needed.

The Leyte area was subjected to a heavy air assault on the same day, 24 October, when an estimated 150 to 200 enemy planes (mostly twin-engined bombers) approached

northern Leyte. Sixty-six were definitely shot down and eighteen others were probably shot down.[4] On the American side, forty combat air patrol and ten direct supporting planes participated in this engagement. Three American aircraft crashlanded—two on the Tacloban airstrip and one in the water.[5] Only a small percentage of the American air activity was directed toward the neutralization of the enemy air force, as most of the available aircraft were attacking the Japanese fleet. The Japanese were determined to "make Leyte the decisive air battlefield as well as the decisive ground and naval battlefield of the Philippines."[6] For the first time since the Allied counteroffensive in the Pacific had started rolling, the Japanese, for an extended period, risked aircraft in great numbers in daylight raids as well as at night. The shipping off Tacloban and Dulag and the Tacloban airfield were the principal targets, though other air installations on the island were hit. An example of the enemy's dogged determination occurred during the evening and night of 27 October. At twilight, twelve enemy fighters and dive bombers dropped 100-pound bombs in the vicinity of Tacloban and tried repeatedly but unsuccessfully to strafe the Tacloban airstrip. After a lull, the Japanese aircraft renewed the aerial assault just before midnight and continued almost uninterruptedly until dawn. Between 2332 and 0125, there were nine raids of two to four planes each; between 0340 and 0450, three raids of two to four planes each; and between 0454 and 0555 five additional planes made an attack on the area.[7] The

---

[3] *4th Air Army* Opns, pp. 38–43.

[4] Sixth Army G–3 Jnl, 24 Oct 44.
[5] Sixth Army G–2 Jnl, 24 Oct 44.
[6] Hist of V Bomber Command, Ch. 4, Jul–Dec 44, p. 73, AAF Hist Archives.
[7] *Ibid.,* pp. 73–75.

JAPANESE AIR ATTACKS *on shipping (above) and supply dumps (below) were a constant threat during the early days of the invasion.*

Tacloban airstrip frequently was "well illu-minated" by burning aircraft.[8]

The *2d Air Division* assaulted American shipping from 24 through 28 October, but because of the increasing necessity for giving air cover to the convoys the main strength of fighters of the *4th Air Army* was used to protect the transportation of reinforcements of the *14th Area Army* of Leyte. From 25 October on, the Bacolod airfield and the air forces protecting the Japanese convoys going to Leyte were attacked by American bombers and suffered serious losses. Since it had to participate in every phase of the action, the losses of the *4th Air Army* were heavy.[9]

After 1 November the Japanese increas-ingly felt the American air power through attacks upon their air bases and shipping. Their fighter units, which had suffered con-siderable losses in protecting the convoys, were ordered to counterattack. They were not successful. At the same time the *4th Air Army* received orders to protect the reinforcement convoys in the Manila area. By this time the Japanese air forces' wings had been clipped and "what had once been a formidable weapon was transformed into a sacrificial army of guided missiles." [10] The suicidal kamikaze pilot became the sole hope of the Japanese air forces.

The Battle of Leyte Gulf

Japanese Naval Plans

On 21 July the chief of the naval general staff, *Imperial General Headquarters,* issued a directive for subsequent "urgent opera-

tions." [11] The operational policy to be fol-lowed by the *Combined Fleet* was as fol-lows:

1. Make utmost effort to maintain and make advantageous use of the strategic *status quo;* plan to smash the enemy's strength; take the initiative in creating favorable tactical opportunities, or seize the opportunity as it presents itself to crush the enemy fleet and attacking forces.

2. Co-operate in close conjunction with the Army, maintain the security of sectors vital to national defense, and prepare for future eventualities.

3. Co-operate closely with related forces to maintain security of surface routes between Japan and vital southern sources of mate-rials.[12]

On 26 July the chief of the naval general staff informed Admiral Toyoda, Com-mander in Chief, *Combined Fleet,* that the future "urgent operations" were to be known as the *SHŌ* (Victory) *Operations.* There would be four *SHŌ Operations.* The first was to cover the defense of the Philippine Archipelago.[13] It was essentially the last chance for Japan to remain in the war. Said Admiral Toyoda of the situation at the time of the battle of Leyte Gulf:

Since without the participation of our Combined Fleet there was no possibility of the land-based forces in the Philippines hav-ing any chance against your forces at all, it was decided to send the whole fleet, taking the gamble. If things went well, we might obtain unexpectedly good results; but if the worst should happen, there was a chance that we would lose the entire fleet. But I felt that that chance had to be taken. . . . Should we lose in the Philippines operations, even though the fleet should be left, the ship-ping lane to the south would be completely cut off, so that the fleet, if it should come back to Japanese waters, could not obtain its fuel

---

[8] Hist of 7th Fighter Sq, 49th Fighter Gp, 86th Fighter Wing, V Fighter Comd, Fifth Air Force, Nov 44, p. 1, AAF Hist Archives.

[9] USBSS, *Campaigns of the Pacific War,* p. 285.

[10] *Ibid.*

---

[11] *Ibid.*

[12] *Ibid.,* App. 87, p. 292.

[13] *Ibid.,* App. 88, p. 294.

supply. If it should remain in southern waters, it could not receive supplies of ammunition and arms. There would be no sense in saving the fleet at the expense of the Philippines.[14]

Since their carrier force was weak, the Japanese had developed a plan based upon the main gunnery strength of the fleet and upon the land-based air forces. Battleships and cruisers from a southern base were to approach Leyte from the south, fight their way to the landing beaches, and destroy Allied assault shipping. A decoy force was to attempt to lure the U.S. carrier task force away from the main action. Shore-based air forces were to inflict maximum damage on the American carrier forces whenever and wherever possible, but once the invasion came they were to conserve their strength until the day of the landings, when all the Allied assault shipping would be concentrated off the beaches and when their attacks on the U.S. carriers would assist the advancing Japanese fleet. The plan was designed to get the Japanese naval gunnery force into a position where it could do the greatest damage. Little attention was paid to getting it out. "The war had reached a point where the Japanese fleet, hopelessly outnumbered and, as imminent events would prove, even more hopelessly outclassed, could not risk the fleet action it had previously desired but was forced to expend itself in suicidal attack upon the United States transports."[15]

Upon receiving information on 17 October that American vessels were off the shores of Suluan Island, Admiral Toyoda immediately alerted his forces. On 18 October Toyoda, after intercepting American messages dealing with the landings on the island approaches to Leyte Gulf, activated

his plan for the defense of the Philippine Islands. The target date (X Day) for the fleet engagement was set for 22 October but logistical difficulties caused a series of delays and on 21 October Admiral Toyoda changed X Day to 25 October. "From the far corners of the shrinking Empire the whole combatant strength of the Japanese Navy converged on Leyte Gulf."[16]

The Naval Battle [17]

The strongest Japanese naval force—the *1st Diversion Attack Force*—moved from the south, reached Brunei Bay in northwest Borneo on 20 October, and after refueling split into two parts and proceeded on its way two days later. The main strength of the *1st Diversion Attack Force,* under Admiral Kurita, sailed northeast up the west coast of Palawan (one of the Visayan Islands), and then turned eastward through the waters of the central Philippines to San Bernardino Strait, while the smaller unit commanded by Vice Adm. Shoji Nishimura moved eastward through the Sulu Sea in order to force an entrance at Surigao Strait. The *2d Diversion Attack Force,* commanded by Vice Adm. Kiyohide Shima, after leaving the Pescadores on 21 October,

---

[14] USSBS, *Interrogations,* II, 317.
[15] USBSS, *Campaigns of the Pacific War,* p. 281.

[16] *Ibid.,* p. 284.
[17] It is not within the scope of this history to deal with the ensuing battle between the Japanese and American Navies. A full discussion of the "greatest naval battle of the Second World War and the largest engagement ever fought on the high seas" would require a volume. Such a study is being prepared by Samuel Eliot Morison in his series of studies on the U.S. Navy's part in the war. Two excellent accounts—James Field's *The Japanese at Leyte Gulf,* and C. Vann Woodward's *The Battle for Leyte Gulf* (New York, 1947)—have already appeared. The present volume attempts to present only those facts needed to understand the effect of the battle on land operations. (Quotation is from Woodward, *Battle for Leyte Gulf,* p. 1.)

sailed south, past western Luzon, and after refueling in the Calamian Islands, just south of Mindoro, proceeded to follow and support the southern part of the *1st Diversion Attack Force* in forcing Surigao Strait.

The *Main Body,* consisting chiefly of partially empty carriers with a destroyer escort, departed on the 20th, and on the evening of the 22d turned southwest toward Luzon. It was commanded by Vice Adm. Jisabuto Ozawa. The *Main Body* was to act as a decoy to draw off the main American strength. The Japanese submarines off Formosa were ordered south toward the eastern approaches to the Philippine Archipelago and the *2d Air Fleet,* shortly before 23 October, began to arrive on Luzon.[18]

There were two American fleets in Philippine waters—the Seventh Fleet under Admiral Kinkaid, whose superior was General MacArthur, and the Third Fleet under Admiral Halsey, whose superior was Admiral Nimitz. The Seventh Fleet, which consisted of 6 old battleships, 16 escort carriers, 4 heavy cruisers, 4 light cruisers, 30 destroyers, and 10 destroyer escorts, had escorted the convoy to Leyte and now stood by to protect it as it unloaded. The Third Fleet was composed of Task Force 38 under Admiral Mitscher. It consisted of four task groups which averaged 23 ships each, divided about as follows: 2 large carriers, 2 light carriers, 2 new battleships, 3 cruisers, and 14 destroyers. The task force was to secure air supremacy over the Philippines, protect the landings, and apply unremitting pressure on Japan. If the opportunity to destroy the major portion of the Japanese fleet should arise or could be created, that destruction was to be its primary task.

The Japanese had 4 carriers, 7 battle-ships, 19 cruisers, 33 destroyers, and 2 battleship-carriers which carried no aircraft; there were 108 planes on the carriers and about 335 shore-based planes in the Luzon area.[19]

On 23 October two American submarines, the *Dace* and the *Darter,* encountered the *1st Diversion Attack Force* and sank two heavy cruisers, the *Atago* and *Maya,* off the western coast of Palawan. The former was Kurita's flagship; its sinking forced the Japanese admiral to transfer hurriedly to another vessel. The submarines also seriously damaged another heavy cruiser.

Upon receiving information that the *Combined Fleet* was steaming toward the Philippines, Admiral Oldendorf's fire support group of the Seventh Fleet moved to the southern end of Leyte Gulf and formed a battle line across the mouth of Surigao Strait while motor torpedo boats patrolled within the strait and about its southern entrance. Halsey's Third Fleet moved toward San Bernardino Strait. The escort carriers from Kinkaid's Seventh Fleet cruised off Leyte Gulf.[20]

On the 24th, after receiving a report from the submarine, the carriers of the Third Fleet sent aircraft to search to the west and southwest. These aircraft sighted the main part of the *1st Diversion Attack Force* south of Mindoro, and sighted and attacked the smaller force under Admiral Nishimura off Negros, slightly damaging a battleship and a destroyer. The aircraft of the carriers from their position off San Bernardino Strait struck repeatedly at Kurita's force while the smaller Nishimura force was left to the battleships in the gulf. One Japanese battle-

---

[18] USSBS, *Campaigns of the Pacific War,* p. 284.

[19] Admiral Frederick C. Sherman, *Combat Command: The American Aircraft Carriers in the Pacific War* (New York, 1950), p. 286.

[20] Field, *Japanese at Leyte Gulf,* pp. 81–82.

ship of the *1st Diversion Attack Force* was sunk, one heavy cruiser rendered impotent, and minor damage was inflicted on other battleships. The Japanese were forced temporarily "to reverse course to westward." [21]

The aircraft from the Japanese *2d Air Fleet* attempted to aid the naval forces which were moving eastward through the Philippines. In co-operation with some aircraft from the *Main Body,* which was now about 100 miles east of Luzon, they attacked the northernmost unit of the American carriers. Halsey's airmen sighted and reported the sacrificial Japanese *Main Body* in the afternoon. Not knowing that this force consisted mainly of empty carriers and believing that the *1st Diversion Attack Force* had been severely damaged, Admiral Halsey withdrew the battleships and carriers of his Third Fleet and steamed north to meet the new threat, leaving San Bernardino Strait wide open. At midnight Kurita's *1st Diversion Attack Force* moved unmolested through San Bernardino Strait and turned south toward Leyte Gulf. The Japanese strategy had worked.

In the early morning hours, Admiral Oldendorf's warships destroyed the Nishimura force as it sailed into Surigao Strait. Of two battleships, one heavy cruiser, and four destroyers, only the cruiser and one destroyer escaped from the strait, and the cruiser, which had been damaged, was sunk by aircraft from the U. S. carriers the next morning.[22] Admiral Shima's *2d Diversion Attack Force,* entering the same strait thirty minutes after Nishimura's force, suffered damage to a light cruiser that was hit by American torpedo boats. Shima's force then made an abortive attack, during which its

flagship was damaged by collision, and withdrew without having engaged. The Third Fleet far to the north fell upon the decoy forces, sank all four carriers of the *Main Body,* and thus "wrote an end to the Japanese carrier air force." [23]

Admiral Kurita's *1st Diversion Attack Force* "for which so much had been sacrificed" [24] encountered Kinkaid's carriers and destroyers off the coast of Samar. Admiral Kinkaid was ill prepared to meet the main thrust of the Japanese Navy, since his carriers were protected only by destroyers and destroyer escorts. His "handling of the exceedingly difficult situation" was "superb." [25] The aircraft from his carriers under Rear Adm. Clifton A. F. Sprague rose to the occasion and gave a "magnificent performance," [26] continually attacking the much stronger *1st Diversion Attack Force.* Kurita's forces sank one carrier, two destroyers, and one destroyer escort but lost three heavy cruisers and had one crippled. The American fighting strength was greatly diminished at the very time it was needed to protect the amphibious shipping that had carried the Sixth Army, and which still lay near the shores of Leyte Gulf. Just as it appeared inevitable that Kurita would move in and deliver the *coup de grâce,* he suddenly broke off the engagement and retired toward San Bernardino Strait. After the war he stated in justification of this strange move: "The conclusion from our [the Japanese] gunfire and anti-aircraft fire during the day had led me to believe in my uselessness, my ineffectual position, if I proceeded into Leyte Gulf where I would come under

---

[21] USBSS, *Campaigns of the Pacific War,* p. 285.
[22] *Ibid.*

[23] *Ibid.*
[24] *Ibid.*
[25] Ltr, Gen Krueger to Maj Gen Orlando Ward, 12 Sep 51, OCMH.
[26] *Ibid.*

even heavier aircraft attack. I therefore concluded to go north and join Admiral Ozawa for coordinated action against your northern Task Forces." [27]

Said Admiral Sprague: "The failure of the enemy main body and encircling light forces to completely wipe out all vessels of this Task Unit can be attributed to our successful smoke screen, our torpedo counterattack, continuous harassment of enemy by bomb, torpedo, and strafing air attacks, timely maneuvers, and the definite partiality of Almighty God." [28]

The battle for Leyte Gulf was over. It had ended in a resounding victory for the Americans, whose losses of 1 light carrier, 2 escort carriers, 2 destroyers, and 1 destroyer escort were small in comparison with the Japanese losses of 3 battleships, 1 large carrier, 3 light carriers, 6 heavy cruisers, 4 light cruisers, and 9 destroyers.[29]

As the Japanese retreated throughout the 25th and 26th of October, carrier- and land-based aircraft struck at the enemy vessels and inflicted fresh injuries upon them.

The Sixth Army summarized its view of the probable consequences if the battle had gone against the U. S. Navy as follows:

Had the [Japanese] plan succeeded the effect on the Allied troops on Leyte in all likelihood would have been calamitous, for these troops would have been isolated and their situation would have been precarious indeed. If it had been victorious in the naval battle, the Japanese fleet could have leisurely and effectively carried out the destruction of shipping, aircraft, and supplies that were so vital to Allied operations on Leyte. An enemy naval victory would have had an adverse effect of incalculable proportions not only upon the Leyte Operation, but upon the overall plan for the liberation of the Philippines as well.[30]

The Sixth Army, however, was depicting the worst of all possible contingencies. Admiral Halsey's conclusion is quite different:

That Kurita's force could have leisurely and effectively carried out the destruction of shipping, aircraft, and supplies in Leyte Gulf was not in the realm of possibilities. . . . Kurita would have been limited to a hit-and-run attack in the restricted waters of Leyte Gulf. He would further have been subjected to the attack of the cruisers present in Leyte Gulf. He would have been limited to minor damage. . . . The statement that an enemy naval victory would have had an effect of incalculable proportions not only on the Leyte operation, but upon the overall plan for the liberation of the Philippines as well, can only be premised on the thought that our naval forces would be almost totally destroyed. The prognostication of such a condition could be reasoned on none of the facts existing during this three days' engagement.[31]

The Japanese Reinforce the Leyte Garrison

The Japanese felt that the honors of the battle were evenly divided and consequently continued with their program of making Leyte the decisive battle of the Philippines. Although the American fleet had soundly whipped the Japanese Navy, the Japanese were still able to send reinforcements in great numbers to their Leyte garrison. Because of the lack of sufficient aerial strength, the Americans were unable to check the steady flow of troops into the port of Ormoc.

---

[27] USBSS, *Interrogations*, I, 44.

[28] CTU 77.4.3 Opns Rpt, Ser 00100, 29 Oct 44, Incl B, p. 2.

[29] Woodward, *Battle for Leyte Gulf*, p. 229.

[30] Sixth Army Opns Rpt Leyte, p. 43.

[31] Ltr, Adm Halsey to Gen Ward, 6 Jul 51, OCMH.

American Aerial Retaliation

The carrier strikes of the Seventh and Third Fleets up to and through A Day had been most successful in forestalling any concentrated effort on the part of the Japanese against the American shipping in Leyte Gulf and the troops on the coastal strand. Thereafter, the Japanese unleashed a furious air assault on the American forces and shipping.[32]

At the same time, American aircraft from the carriers struck at the Japanese troops and their installations in close support of the ground troops. The first called-for air strike was at 0834 on 21 October against bridges over streams that were not fordable along the road leading from Ormoc to Carigara, in order to prevent enemy movement along this road.[33] A total of 121 missions were flown in support of ground units during the first four days, of which only 33 had been requested by the air liaison parties. The targets for these missions included artillery and mortar positions, fuel and supply dumps, bridges, pillboxes, and other installations, together with trucks, armored vehicles, and tanks.[34]

During the initial stages of the campaign, Navy flyers gave efficient close support to the ground forces.[35] The average time required to carry out each of these support missions was approximately one hour, though the usual difficulties of locating friendly troops and pinpointing the target were present. Enthusiastic reports on the effectiveness of this co-operation from naval air were made by the 7th Division. Members of this division, which formerly had been supported by Army and Navy air forces, found Navy air support in the first days on Leyte far more satisfactory than that which the Army Air Forces had been able to provide in the past. They believed that this superiority was due to the system that the Navy had worked out for directing strikes at close-in targets without endangering friendly ground forces, and to the Navy's use of rehearsals with ground units to establish mutual understanding and confidence.[36]

The Battle of Leyte Gulf interfered greatly with the close support rendered by the Navy, since the carrier-based planes had to be withdrawn. The combat air patrol assignments were also disrupted because of surface engagements and the repairing of the CVE's.[37]

At this time the Japanese had about 432,000 men in the Philippines, including air force and construction units. Most of them believed that they were well prepared to meet the Americans. In fact a staff officer of the *14th Area Army,* upon hearing that the Americans had landed on Leyte, is reported to have jumped up and exclaimed: "Good, they have picked the place where our finest troops are located." [38] It was also thought that the American troops on Leyte were "having a difficult time." [39] Nevertheless, General Yamashita, who had succeeded

---

[32] Hist of V Fighter Comd, Ch. 4, Jul–Dec 44, p. 73, AAF Hist Archives.

[33] Sixth Army G–3 *Wasatch* Jnl, 21 Oct 44.

[34] Opns Rpt, CSA Seventh Flt to Comdr Seventh Flt, no ser, 2 Nov 44.

[35] AAF Evaluation Bd POA Rpt 3, The Occupation of Leyte, Philippine Islands, pp. 27 and 15. This report was prepared by Brig. Gen. Martin F. Scanlon, who accompanied the XXIV Corps to Leyte as an air observer for the Army Air Forces in the Central Pacific. By close support is meant operating to the immediate front of the first-line troops.

[36] AAF Bd POA Rpt 3, p. 15.

[37] Opns Rpt, CSA Seventh Flt to Comdr Seventh Flt, no serial, 2 Nov 44.

[38] USSBS Interrog 418, Interrog of Maj Gen Toshio Nishimura, 19–22 Nov 45, p. 6, OCMH.

[39] *14th Area Army* Opns Leyte, pp. 2–3.

Kuroda as the commanding general of the *14th Area Army*, sent the *1st Division* and other units to Leyte. The Japanese felt that "if the decisive battle in Leyte results in failure, it will upset the entire operation in the Philippines and the decisive battle in Luzon will be lost." [40]

By the 25th of October a battalion of the *55th Independent Mixed Brigade* and one of the *57th Independent Mixed Brigade* from Cebu, together with two battalions of the *30th Division*, had arrived on Leyte to reinforce the *16th Division*. Shortly after the Sixth Army landed, the *35th Army* commander, General Suzuki, received orders from General Yamashita to undertake an all-out offensive against the Americans. All Japanese air, naval, and land forces were to participate. [41]

On 22 October the *14th Area Army* asked the *35th Army* how the *26th Division* and *68th Independent Mixed Brigade* were to be utilized if the Japanese decisively won the pending naval battle. The *35th Army* stated that if the Japanese Navy were victorious, the units were to prevent the landing of more Americans at Leyte Gulf, but if it were unsuccessful the troops were to be landed at Carigara Bay. The optimism of the Japanese was high. Said Maj. Gen. Yoshiharu Tomochika, Chief of Staff, *35th Army:* "We were determined to take offensive after offensive and clean up American forces on Leyte Island. . . . We seriously discussed demanding the surrender of the entire American Army after seizing General MacArthur." [42] Then came the Battle of Leyte Gulf.

Despite the setbacks caused by this disastrous sea battle, the Japanese continued to send troops to Leyte through Ormoc. The reinforcement of Leyte consisted of moving five major units, in nine echelons: the *35th Army* moved as many of its units as possible from Mindanao, Cebu, and Panay; the *1st Division* was sent down from Luzon on 1 November; then the *26th Division,* the *68th Independent Mixed Brigade,* and one third of the *8th Division* were sent from Luzon in the order given. [43]

On 27 October the Fifth Air Force took over the mission of supporting the Sixth Army. As the airstrips were not in serviceable condition, only a small detachment— the 308th Bombardment Wing—could be sent in. Aircraft from the carriers continued to give support. The Fifth Air Force felt that it could best check the Japanese reinforcement program, and at the same time give more lasting support to the ground troops, by attacking the Japanese convoys before they arrived in Leyte. The Fifth Air Force intended also to attack large movements of land troops, concentrations, and supply areas. Army Air Forces doctrine assigned close support as the third priority mission of tactical air forces. [44] Since there were always insufficient aircraft for the missions assigned to the air forces, close support of ground troops suffered.

The Allied Air Forces, which had been given the mission of supporting the Leyte operation, directed its main efforts against airfields in bypassed areas. Two fighter groups were on Morotai, one heavy bomber group was on Noemfoor, off the north coast of New Guinea, and two heavy bomber

---

[40] *Ibid.,* p. 6.

[41] 10th I&HS, Eighth Army, Stf Study of the Japanese *35th Army* on Leyte, Part I, pp. 3–4, copy in OCMH.

[42] Tomochika, True Facts of Leyte Opn, p. 13.

[43] *14th Area Army* Opns Leyte, pp. 17–18, 37, 52, 59, 93, 94, and 99.

[44] FM 100–20, 21 Jul 43, Command and Employment of Air Power, p. 16.

AIR STRIKES AGAINST JAPANESE INSTALLATIONS *included attacks on Baco-lod Airfield, Negros Island (above), and on shipping in Zamboanga harbor, Mindanao (below).*

groups were on Biak; they completed 175 sorties in strikes against airfields on Mindanao and the Visayan area. The main targets of attack were on Mindanao and Cebu and in the Negros area.[45] The XIII Bomber Command, which carried the burden of this assault, was to neutralize targets previously hit and protect the southwestern flank of the American forces in the Philippines. The 42d Bombardment Group (medium bombers) in October flew the greatest number of sorties in the history of the group up to that time.[46]

The heavy bombers (B–24's) of the 868th Bombardment Squadron, operating from Noemfoor, had as their main target enemy shipping in the Makassar Strait. At the same time, the B–24's that were within range of the Sulu Sea struck at the Japanese *Southern Fleet* as it retreated after its engagement with the Seventh Fleet. The fighters and medium bombers, which had been used to strike at targets on Mindanao, were alerted to strike any enemy naval vessels that came within range.[47]

While protecting the southwestern flank of the American forces in the Philippines, the XIII Bomber Command was extraordinarily busy on 26 October. Part of the Japanese naval task force, consisting of three battleships, five cruisers, and four destroyers, had withdrawn from the Leyte area and was in the Sulu Sea when sighted by the 307th Bombardment Group. Twenty-eight B–24's of the bombardment group made their principal targets two of the battleships—one of the *Kongo* class and the other of the *Yamato*

class. Three of the planes were shot down as the Japanese skillfully and evasively maneuvered their vessels so that none was sunk. At the same time B–24's from the 5th Bombardment Squadron sighted and sank an enemy light cruiser at a different location in the Sulu Sea.[48]

General MacArthur had originally allocated the attack of all land targets in the Philippines to the Allied Air Forces,[49] and although subsequent events occasioned a modification of this order the Fifth Air Force officially established its advance units on Leyte at 1600 on 27 October and assumed operational control of land-based aircraft.[50] The 308th Bombardment Wing, the advance echelon of the Fifth Air Force, had two major duties included in its mission. It was to obtain air superiority over the Philippines and to isolate the Japanese forces on the battlefield of Leyte. In addition to these two principal tasks it was to render maximum close support to the ground forces, establish night fighter patrols and a system of courier aircraft, and provide maximum protection to Allied naval vessels.[51] Among the Army flyers of the 49th Fighter Group, an advance party of the Fifth Air Force that arrived on 27 October, was Maj. Richard I. Bong, of the 9th Fighter Squadron, the leading ace of the Army Air Forces. He celebrated his arrival by shooting down an enemy plane.[52]

---

[45] AAF Evaluation Bd, SWPA Rpt, Leyte Campaign, p. 32, AAF Hist Archives.

[46] Hist of XIII Bomber Comd, Oct 44, p. 5, AAF Hist Archives.

[47] *Ibid.*

[48] *Jane's Fighting Ships, 1947–48* (New York), pp. 473–78; Hist of XIII Bomber Comd, Oct 44, p. 4, AAF Hist Archives.

[49] Rad, GHQ to CG Sixth Army *et al.,* Sixth Army G–3 Rear Jnl, 28 Oct 44.

[50] Rad, CG Allied Air Forces to CG Fifth Air Force, 27 Oct 44, Sixth Army G–3 Jnl, 1 Nov 44.

[51] Hist of 308th Bombardment Wing, Ch. 3, p. 4, AAF Hist Archives.

[52] Hist of 9th Fighter Sq, Oct 44, AAF Hist Archives.

ANTIAIRCRAFT GUN *in action at Tacloban airstrip, 27 October 1944.*

On 28 October the Army flyers of the 7th Fighter Squadron got their first enemy airplane on Leyte. Since there were "only" three enemy air raids during the night, the men were able to get some much needed sleep.[53]

The 29th of October, however, was a day of heavy action for the Army flyers, as described in a report of the 7th Fighter Squadron:

The 29th was a day that will be long remembered. . . . Two more Nips were added to the unit's score; . . . the 49th Group's 500th victory. But more important at that time was the fact . . . [that] the . . . road between the strip and the camp collapsed under army traffic. . . . The already long hours were lengthened still more as pilots and men were forced to arise between three and four o'clock in the morning, make their way to the barge at Tacloban, cross to the strip by water and then sweat out the pre-dawn raids. At night, the planes landing at dusk had hardly hit the runway before . . . BOFORS [40-mm. antiaircraft guns] went off and the lights went out. Then down to the end of the strip near the gas dumps, and another session of sweating beneath A/A [antiaircraft] awaiting the barge for the trip back to Tacloban and then to camp. Supper was served as late as 10 o'clock . . . a few brave individuals tried an alternate road to the south, swinging out east to White Beach above Dulag and then north along the beach to Tacloban Strip. Japanese snipers soon put a stop to this travel during the hours of darkness.

To add to the "big day"—29 October—the weather observers reported a 50 knot gale on the way. Working after dark, pilots and linemen minus the regular tie downs and using tent ropes and anything available secured the airplanes to jeeps, trucks, trailers and tractors. At night, in camp, the small

[53] Hist of 7th Fighter Sq, Oct 44, pp. 5–6, AAF Hist Archives.

LOCKHEED P–38 *after Japanese raid on Tacloban airstrip.*

typhoon hit and with it went three or four tents, occupants of which awoke to find themselves thoroughly drenched and at odds with the world, Leyte in particular.[54]

Although 29 October was the most difficult day on Leyte for the men of the 7th Fighter Squadron, they were again disheartened the following day, when one of the squadron's pilots was shot down by friendly antiaircraft.[55]

During the first week of November, offensive operations by the Fifth Air Force were primarily against targets in Ormoc Valley and enemy shipping in Ormoc Bay. The barrios of Ormoc, Valencia, and Palompon were the first land targets. Most of the strikes, however, were against Japanese ship-

ping in Ormoc Bay and in the vicinity of the Camotes Islands.[56]

By 4 November a number of P–38's had been destroyed by bombs and strafing, some of which were completely burned up. To cut down the aircraft losses, it was decided to have planes of some of the squadrons use the Bayug airstrip in the Dulag area. But since this was a poor airfield which soon became overcrowded and subject to Japanese air attacks, it was finally abandoned.[57]

On 3 November fifteen P–38's of the 49th Bomber Group struck "one of the most lucrative strafing targets of their history." [58]

---

[54] *Ibid.*, pp. 6–7.
[55] *Ibid.*, p. 7.

[56] Hist of Fifth Air Force, Ch. V, pp. 42–43, AAF Hist Archives; Rad, Sixth Army to GHQ, 3 Nov 44, Sixth Army G–3 Jnl, 3 Nov 44.
[57] *Ibid.*
[58] Hist of V Fighter Comd, Jul–Dec 44, Ch. 4, p. 64, AAF Hist Archives.

In an early morning search for enemy shipping in Ormoc Bay the bombers found nothing, but on their return they sighted a ten-mile-long convoy of trucks, artillery, and tanks extending from Ormoc to Valencia. The convoy was strafed and dispersed, leaving twenty to thirty-five trucks destroyed and many other vehicles, including two tanks, in flames.[59] However, two American planes were shot down by enemy antiaircraft fire, four came in on single engines, and all showed many bullet holes. The bombers made no further strikes against the convoy, "as all aircraft received extremely heavy and accurate ground fire."[60]

The airmen of the Fifth Air Force continued to hit shipping in Ormoc Bay and in the Camotes Islands, and they also achieved success against bridges, airfields, troops, camp areas, and transportation.[61] Although the number of Japanese air raids had diminished by 6 November, the Americans could not yet feel that they were "out of the rough."[62] There was insufficient direct air support for the ground troops throughout the operation and the Japanese continued to send troops into Ormoc. The constant stream of Japanese reinforcements coming into Leyte augured ill for the success of the operation.

The TA Operation

The TA Operation, by which name the Japanese program for the reinforcement of Leyte was known, continued from 23 October through 11 December. The numerical

weakness of the U. S. land-based aircraft enabled the Japanese to land many thousands of troops and tons of supplies on Leyte. Nine convoys in all were sent to the port of Ormoc, on the west coast.[63] As a whole, however, the operation was "literally gruesome" to the Japanese, since their transports and escort vessels were struck again and again by American aircraft.

The first Japanese convoy had three echelons. The first consisted of a landing barge and an auxiliary sailing vessel carrying about 300 troops of the 102d Division. The second echelon, whose composition was identical with the first, carried about 150 troops of the same division. Both safely discharged their troops on 23 and 25 October, respectively. The third echelon was made up of 2 destroyers, together with 4 transports carrying about 2,000 men of the 30th Division. The transports safely unloaded their passengers on 26 October, but American airmen later sank the destroyers and all but one of the transports. The remaining vessel was damaged.

The second convoy consisted of three echelons, composed of 3, 1, and 4 transports respectively. The escorting vessels of the third echelon, the only one that had an escort, consisted of 6 destroyers and 4 coast defense vessels. The escort vessels carried the troops of the 1st Division: the first wave about 1,000 men, the second about 100 headquarters men, and the third approximately 10,000 troops and about 9,000 ship tons of provisions and ammunition. All vessels safely debarked their troops on 1 and 2 November.

The 5 transports of the third convoy carried about 2,000 troops of the 26th Division and approximately 6,600 tons of supplies.

[59] Rad, COMAF5 to Sixth Army, 4 Nov 44, Sixth Army G–3 Jnl, 5 Nov 44.

[60] Msg, 308th Bomb Wing to G–2 Sixth Army, 3 Nov 44, Sixth Army G–3 Jnl, 3 Nov 44.

[61] Hist of Fifth Air Force, Ch. 5, pp. 42–45, AAF Hist Archives.

[62] OPD 319.1, Sec VII, Case 248, DRB AGO.

[63] Activities of the Japanese Navy During the Leyte Operation, p. 94, A715 SWPA, Doc 2543.

JAPANESE CONVOY UNDER ATTACK *in Ormoc Bay. A destroyer escort is blown apart by a direct hit (above), and a large transport is straddled by bomb bursts (below).*

The convoy sailed from Manila on 9 November and was escorted by 1 submarine chaser, 1 torpedo boat squadron, and 4 destroyers. On 10 November, when the convoy reached the mouth of Ormoc Bay, American airmen destroyed all of the escort vessels and transports before they could unload their troops and cargo.

Each of the two echelons of the fourth convoy had 3 transports, but only the first one had an escort—6 destroyers and 4 coast defense vessels. The first echelon carried approximately 10,000 troops of the *26th Division* and about 3,500 tons of supplies, including provisions, ammunition, and four long-range guns. The second echelon carried about 1,000 men of the *1st Division*. Both discharged their troops safely on 9 November, a day earlier than the anticipated arrival of the third convoy, but because of American air action, they were able to get only a limited part of the supplies ashore.

The fifth convoy was organized on the same pattern as its predecessor, but the first wave had a submarine chaser as an escort while the second had a destroyer. This convoy, which left Manila between 11 and 25 November with an unknown number of troops and quantity of supplies, was completely destroyed en route to Leyte.

The sixth convoy, composed of 2 transports, 2 submarine chasers, and 1 patrol boat, carried approximately 2,500 tons of provisions and ammunition. It entered Ormoc harbor on 28 November and had completed most of its unloading when the vessels were either sunk or set afire by U.S. aircraft and motor torpedo boats.

There were four echelons in the seventh convoy. The composition of the first two is unknown, but it is known that the first echelon completed unloading at Ipil just south of Ormoc on 30 November. The third and

fourth echelons, consisting altogether of 3 transports and 2 destroyers, also carried an unknown number of troops and quantity of supplies. As they were unloading at Ormoc on 2 December, the vessels were attacked by American airmen who sank one of the destroyers and damaged the other. The transports and the damaged destroyer returned to Manila.

The 4 transports of the eighth convoy, escorted by 3 destroyers and 2 submarine chasers, carried about 4,000 troops—the main body of the *68th Independent Brigade*—and an unknown quantity of provisions and ammunition. It unloaded some of its troops and a part of the cargo at San Isidro on the west coast of Leyte on 7 December; but immediately thereafter, American aircraft sank the transports and heavily damaged the destroyers.

There were two echelons in the ninth convoy. The first echelon, which consisted of 5 transports, 3 destroyers, and 2 submarine chasers, carried approximately 3,000 troops of the *5th Infantry Regiment, 8th Division,* and about 900 tons of provisions and ammunition. In unloading at Ormoc on 11 December, 1 destroyer was sunk and 1 destroyer and 1 transport were damaged. The remaining vessels then moved to Port Palompon on the west coast of Leyte and completed unloading. The second echelon consisted of only one transport and carried an unknown number of troops and quantity of supplies. It was able on 11 December to elude the American airmen and complete its unloading.[64]

After the war, General Nishimura, who had been on the staff of the *14th Area Army,* made the amazing statement that nearly 80 percent of the vessels sent to Ormoc were

---

[64] Trans of Data on Reinforcement and Support of the Leyte Island Campaign, ATIS Doc 16946.

sunk en route. Although most of the vessels went down close enough to the Leyte shore for the troops to swim ashore, the equipment lost could not be replaced.[65] It is estimated that the Japanese landed more than 45,000 troops and something over 10,000 tons of matériel.[66]

Even though the Japanese had not succeeded completely in their reinforcement program, General Krueger was faced with a far stronger foe than had been anticipated. The Leyte Campaign was to be long and costly and was to upset the timetable for the impending Luzon operation. At the end of A Day the American assault forces had firmly established themselves on the shores of Leyte, but the battle for the island was yet to come.

---

[65] USSBS Interrog 506, Interrog of Maj. Gen. Yoshiharu Tomochica *et al.,* MS, OCMH.

[66] *14th Area Army* Opns Leyte, Appended Table 1.

CHAPTER VII

Southern Leyte Valley: Part One

The SHŌ Operations

In their preliminary planning, the Japanese considered that the defense of Leyte would be only a delaying action. The defenders were to inflict as many casualties as possible upon the invaders and also to prevent them from using the Leyte airfields, but the decisive battle for the Philippines would be fought on Luzon. As late as 10 October the chief of staff of the *35th Army* received the following order from Manila: "Depending on conditions the *35th Army* will prepare to dispatch as large a force to LUZON ISLAND as possible." [1]

On 21 October, after receiving news of the American landings, General Yamashita activated *SHŌ ICHI GO* (Victory Operation Number One). He made it clear that the Japanese Army, in co-operation with "the total force of the Air Force and Navy," was to make a major effort on Leyte and destroy the American forces on the island. The *35th Army* was to concentrate its forces there. The *1st* and *26th Divisions,* the *68th Brigade,* and an artillery unit from the *14th Area Army* would be sent to augment the *35th Army* troops. At the same time General Suzuki received information that the Japanese Air Force and Navy would engage in

"decisive" battles in support. "The morale of the *35th Army* rose as a result."

The Japanese thought that only two American divisions had landed on Leyte, and that if the *1st, 16th, 30th,* and *102d Divisions* engaged the Americans, a decisive victory would be theirs. General Suzuki decided to send forward the following reinforcements to Leyte: the main force of the *30th Division,* only three battalions of which would remain in Mindanao; three infantry battalions of the *102d Division;* and one independent infantry battalion each from the *55th* and *57th Independent Mixed Brigades.* These forces were in addition to the two battalions previously sent on 23 October.

General Suzuki believed that the Americans would attempt to join and strengthen their beachheads in the vicinity of Tacloban and Dulag before they tried to penetrate inland. At the same time, since Catmon Hill and the high ground west of Tacloban Valley were in Japanese hands, the *16th Division* should be able to contain the Americans until reinforcements arrived.

He therefore issued orders based upon these assumptions and also upon the assumption that the Japanese air and naval forces would be victorious. The *35th Army* was to concentrate its reinforcements in the Carigara area. The principal elements of the *16th Division* were to occupy Burauen and Dagami, and the rest of the division would

---

[1] *35th Army* Opns, p. 30. Unless otherwise indicated, the following is based upon this study, pp. 30–34.

occupy Catmon Hill and the western plateau of Tacloban. The *16th Division* was to protect the concentration of the main force of the *35th Army*. The *102d Division* was to occupy the Jaro area and give direct protection to the *1st* and *26th Divisions* and the *68th Brigade*. The *30th Division* was to land at Ormoc Bay in the Albuera area and then advance to the Burauen area in coordination with the *16th Division* and assist the main force of the *35th Army*. The *1st Division* was to land at Ormoc, the *26th Division* and *68th Brigade* were to land at Carigara. If the situation were favorable, however, the *68th Brigade* was to land in the vicinity of Catmon Hill. After the main elements of the *35th Army* had assembled at Carigara and the area southeast of it, they were to move down Leyte Valley and annihilate the American forces in the Tacloban area. All the important airfields, bases, and roads were also in the valley.

The part of Leyte Valley where the Americans hoped air and supply bases could be developed is a broad and level plain inside a quadrangle formed by the main roads linking Tanauan, Dulag, Burauen and Dagami. (*Map 5*) The region extending ten miles westward from the stretch of coast between Dulag and Tanauan to the foothills of the central range is an alluvial plain, interlaced by many streams, in which swamps and rice paddies predominate. Catmon Hill, about half way between Tanauan and Dulag, was the most prominent terrain feature near the shore line.

Catmon Hill is actually a series of hills with many spurs. This hill mass starts at the mouth of the Labiranan River above San Jose where Labiranan Head meets Highway 1, the coastal road, and extends in a general northwest direction to the vicinity of San Vicente and Pikas where it drops abruptly

into the coastal plain. It is covered with cogon grass about six feet high, in the midst of which are found a few trees. The beach areas between the Calbasag River on the south and Tolosa on the north, together with much of southern Leyte Valley, are dominated by this hill mass.[2]

The *16th Division* made use of the caves on Catmon Hill for shelters, artillery positions, and supply dumps, and established well-concealed coconut log pillboxes and observation posts at numerous vantage points on the hills. Some of these pillboxes, with good fields of fire and spider holes, were emplaced in positions to cover the roads.[3] A spider hole was dug about five feet deep, sometimes camouflaged with a removable cover, and was large enough to contain a man and his weapon.

The American prelanding naval bombardment destroyed a number of field pieces of the *22d Field Artillery Regiment,* which was deployed in position along the first line of defense. The gunfire also disrupted the regiment's radio service, and direct communication with the *35th Army* and the *14th Area Army* headquarters was temporarily broken.[4]

After the heavy naval bombardment on A Day and the subsequent landings by American forces in the Dulag area, General Makino moved the command post of the *16th Division* to Dagami, a step which made communications very difficult and inadequate. The troops of the division were then disposed as follows: the *20th Infantry Regiment,* though considerably diminished in number, was holding Julita, and one of its

---

[2] Allied Geographical Sec, GHQ SWPA Terrain Handbook 34, Tacloban, 25 Sep 44, p. 10.

[3] 96th Div Opns Rpt Leyte, p. 88.

[4] 10th I&HS Eighth Army, Stf Study of Opns of Japanese *35th Army* on Leyte, pp. 2–3.

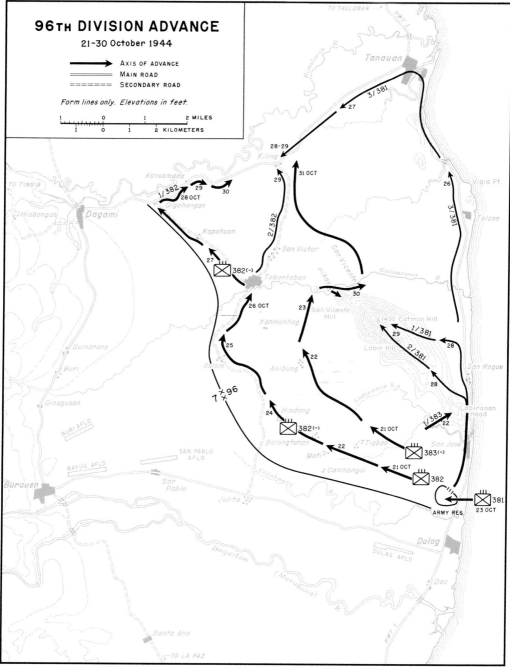

96TH DIVISION ADVANCE

21–30 October 1944

→ AXIS OF ADVANCE
━━━ MAIN ROAD
======= SECONDARY ROAD

Form lines only. Elevations in feet.

MAP 5

LANDING AREAS AND LEYTE VALLEY *as seen from a captured Japanese observation post on Catmon Hill.*

platoons patrolled the Daguitan River banks; the main part of the *9th Infantry Regiment* was at Catmon Hill, while one of its battalions occupied Tabontabon.[5]

At the end of 20 October the Sixth Army was established on the shores of Leyte Gulf. The X Corps was in the north near Palo and Tacloban, and the XXIV Corps was in the vicinity of Dulag, poised for a drive into southern Leyte Valley. General Krueger planned to push rapidly through Leyte Valley and secure its important roads, airfields, and base sites before General Makino could regroup the *16th Division* and offer a firm line of resistance.

Enlarging the 96th Division Beachhead

General Krueger had assigned the mission of seizing southern Leyte Valley to the XXIV Corps. The 96th Division was to seize Catmon Hill and its surrounding area, together with the Dagami–Tanauan road. The 7th Division was to proceed along the Dulag–Burauen road, seize the airfields in that area, and then proceed north to Dagami.

General Bradley's scheme of maneuver for the 96th Division specified a movement into the interior from the beachhead area in a northwesterly direction with regiments abreast—the 383d Infantry on the right (north) and the 382d Infantry on the left (south). The 1st Battalion, 383d Infantry, was to capture Labiranan Head and secure Highway 1 as far north as San Roque. The rest of the regiment was to proceed inland, bypass Catmon Hill at first, and then, after artillery, naval bombardment, and air strikes had neutralized it, to capture Catmon Hill and the adjacent high ground.

The 382d Infantry was to proceed inland in a northwesterly direction and seize Anibung, which was erroneously believed to have an airfield. The regiment was then to be ready to advance either to the north or to the west.[6]

At the end of A Day the assault troops of the 383d Infantry, commanded by Colonel May, were approximately 2,500 yards inland. The forward positions of the 1st Battalion were 400 yards up the sides of the ridge running north from where the troops had crossed the Labiranan River. The 3d Platoon of Company C had established a roadblock at the highway crossing; the 2d Battalion, protecting the regimental southern boundary, had advanced 2,600 yards inland from Orange Beach 1; and the 3d Battalion had established a night perimeter 800 yards southwest of the 1st Battalion on the southern bank of the Labiranan River.[7]

The 382d Infantry, under Colonel Dill, had made a successful landing on A Day. The 2d Battalion, on the right, had pushed inland 2,700 yards, while the 3d Battalion, on the left, had gained 1,300 yards; the 1st Battalion was in reserve. Contact had been established with the 32d Infantry, 7th Division, on the 382d Infantry's left, and with the 383d Infantry on its right.[8]

Labiranan Head

During the night of 20–21 October the 361st Field Artillery Battalion fired upon Labiranan Head in support of the 1st Battalion, 383d Infantry.[9] In addition naval guns, supporting the 96th Division, fired harassing and interdicting missions against

---

[5] *35th Army* Opns, pp. 22–23.

[6] 96th Div FO 2, 10 Oct 44.
[7] 383d Inf Opns Rpt Leyte, p. 3.
[8] 382d Inf Unit Rpt 1, 20 Oct 44.
[9] 361st FA Bn Opns Rpt Leyte.

possible enemy positions and lines of communication.[10] At 0810 on 21 October an air strike was registered on Labiranan Head, followed by a three-hour naval and artillery barrage.

The 382d Infantry was to move inland, maintain contact with the 7th Division, and forestall any Japanese attempt to reach the beaches. Concurrently, the 1st Battalion, 383d Infantry, would advance on Catmon Hill from Labiranan Head while the 2d and 3d Battalions of the regiment would swing around the northwest end of Catmon Hill and squeeze the Japanese in a pincers.

At 1130 an assault force commanded by Capt. Hugh D. Young of the 1st Battalion, 383d Infantry, attacked the Japanese position on Labiranan Head. This assault force, a composite company, consisted of a platoon each from A, B, and C Companies, together with the weapons platoon from C Company. The troops moved up the ridge and within ten minutes after starting destroyed one machine gun and drove off the crew of another. Under cover of mortar fire, the Japanese retired to the next ridge.

In co-operation with the advance of Captain Young's force, the 3d Platoon of Company C, which had established the roadblock at the Highway 1 crossing of Labiranan River on A Day, moved out just below Labiranan Head and hit the Japanese flank. The platoon met a strongly entrenched enemy position which consisted of seven pillboxes guarding ten 75-mm. guns. There were also six coastal guns but only two of these had been even partially assembled. When the men of the platoon got within twenty feet of the enemy position, they received fire from the two flanks and the front. After knocking out a machine gun nest the platoon withdrew.

Lt. Col. Edwin O. List, the commanding officer of the 1st Battalion, then ordered Captain Young to advance northward up a covered draw and secure a small hill in the rear of the enemy force. As the troops advanced up the hill, they observed smoke coming from Labiranan Head. Company D thereupon placed mortar fire on the position which contained the ten 75-mm. guns. At 1430 Captain Young requested that the fire be lifted; this was done, and the advance continued.[11]

At 1600 Captain Young reported that his troops had secured Labiranan Head. At the same time, friendly naval gunfire shelled Young's troops.[12] This gunfire was not stopped, since there were known Japanese positions in the vicinity and it was believed to be of more lasting importance to knock them out than to hold this one position. Captain Young evacuated Labiranan Head and withdrew his troops, who swam across the Labiranan River and formed a night perimeter on the south bank. At the end of the day the front lines of the rest of the 1st Battalion, 383d Infantry, were along the northern banks of the Labiranan River and on the high ground 800 yards west of Labiranan Head.[13]

During the night the 361st, 363d, and 921st Field Artillery Battalions delivered harassing fires on the positions of the *9th Infantry Regiment* on Labiranan Head.[14] The following morning, Captain Young's force rejoined the 1st Battalion, 383d Infantry. The 921st Field Artillery Battalion continued to pound the enemy emplacements until 1200 and then supported the attack as the 1st Battalion, 383d Infantry,

---

[10] 96th Div Arty Opns Rpt Leyte, p. 5.

[11] 382d Inf Unit Jnl, 21 Oct 44.
[12] 96th Div G–3 Jnl, 21 Oct 44.
[13] 383d Inf Opns Rpt Leyte, p. 9.
[14] 921st FA Bn Opns Rpt Leyte, p. 6.

CREW OF A LIGHT ARMORED CAR M8 *prepares to fire on enemy positions in the Labiranan Head sector.*

with Companies A and C as lead companies, moved up the slopes of Labiranan Head. The antitank platoon of the 1st Battalion set up its 37-mm. guns in a position from which it could rake the south side of Labiranan Head from the river and support the advance of Company C on the left. The platoon knocked out four pillboxes and two machine guns and then directed fire on the enemy 75-mm. guns. Companies A and C pushed aside the Japanese and at 1630 reached the crest of the hill, their objective. They immediately dug in, consolidated the position, and then formed a night perimeter from which the entire beach area from San Roque to Dulag could be observed.[15]

At 1930 the Japanese centered a counterattack on Company A on the right flank of the 1st Battalion, 383d Infantry. A combined concentration from the 921st, 361st, and 363d Field Artillery Battalions repelled this assault.[16] While Labiranan Hill was being secured, a force consisting of the 3d Platoon, Company C, the 1st Platoon, Company D, 763d Tank Battalion, the 1st Platoon, Cannon Company, and the battalion Antitank Platoon pushed along Highway 1, secured San Roque, and set up a roadblock.[17] From the 23d to the 26th of October the 1st Battalion, 383d Infantry, patrolled the Labiranan Hill–San Roque area and protected the right flank of the 96th Division as the rest of the division slogged through swamps and rice paddies to the south.

---

[15] 383d Inf Unit Jnl, 22 Oct 44.

[16] 921st FA Bn Opns Rpt Leyte, p. 3.
[17] 383d Inf Opns Rpt Leyte, p. 10.

Battling the Swamps

At 0840 on 21 October the 2d and 3d Battalions, 383d Infantry, which were to go in a northwesterly direction around Catmon Hill and isolate the Japanese force on the hill, moved out westward. They advanced through swamps and rice paddies but met no Japanese during the day. At 1640, when they established a night perimeter, the 2d Battalion was 300 yards north of Tigbao and the 3d Battalion with the regimental command group was 1,100 yards northeast of the barrio and south of Catmon Hill.[18]

The 382d Infantry, while protecting the left flank of the 96th Division, was to advance rapidly into the interior and seize Tigbao.[19] During the night of 20–21 October artillery fire from an unknown source fell in the sector of the 2d Battalion, killing three men and wounding eight others. At 0800, on 21 October, the 2d Battalion, 382d Infantry, moved out, followed at 0812 by the 3d Battalion. These troops, like the 2d and 3d Battalions of the 383d Infantry, were confronted with waist-deep swamps which made the going slow and arduous. The 3d Battalion, 382d Infantry, immediately after moving out, ran into enemy pillboxes constructed of coconut logs and defended by machine guns and riflemen. At first the troops bypassed the pillboxes but at 1030 Company K went back and wiped them out. In addition to the morass through which the troops were moving, numerous empty pillboxes slowed up the advance, since each of them had to be checked.[20] At 1430, because there was a gap between the 2d and 3d Battalions, Colonel Dill committed the 1st Battalion to close the line. The battalions then advanced abreast and kept lateral contact with the 2d and 3d Battalions of the 383d Infantry on their right. At 1630, when the battalions established their night perimeters, they were far short of their objective.[21]

At 1745 Colonel Dill directed all of the battalions of the 382d Infantry to move out at 0800 on 22 October—the 1st Battalion was to capture Tigbao and Bolongtohan and then push on to Hindang; the 2d Battalion was to proceed toward Anibung; and the 3d Battalion, on the right of the 1st Battalion, was to proceed to the northwestern edge of Bolongtohan.[22]

Since it was known that the Japanese were strongly entrenched on Catmon Hill, General Bradley had decided to bypass the hill temporarily. His plan called for the 2d and 3d Battalions of the 383d Infantry to envelop Catmon Hill from the south and then move north to make contact with the 24th Division at Tanauan.[23] On the morning of 22 October, Colonel May of the 383d Infantry asked General Bradley for permission to attack Catmon Hill from the south with his 2d and 3d Battalions. General Bradley refused the request and ordered Colonel May to continue the enveloping movement he had started on 21 October.[24] Later on that morning, therefore, the 2d and 3d Battalions, 383d Infantry, moved out north-northwest. Encountering a deep swamp at 1130, the troops turned northwest. This move did not materially help the situation, since they found that they had exchanged the swamp for rice paddies. The advance units reached Anibung at 1630

---

[18] *Ibid.*, p. 9.
[19] 382d Inf FO 2, 21 Oct 44.
[20] 382d Inf Unit Jnl, 21 Oct 44.

[21] 382d Inf Unit Rpt 2, 21 Oct 44.
[22] 382d Inf Unit Jnl, 21 Oct 44.
[23] 96th Div Opns Rpt Leyte, p. 38.
[24] 96th Div G–3 Jnl, 22 Oct 44.

without encountering any Japanese. By 1800 all units had closed in on the vicinity of Anibung and set up a night perimeter 400 yards north of the barrio.

Few supplies had been brought forward because the vehicles of the battalions had advanced only 200 yards when they bogged down. The troops hand-carried their weapons and communications equipment, while civilians with about eight carabaos [25] helped carry the supplies. In the transportation of supplies forward, ammunition was given priority over rations and water, even though the supply of the latter items, which had been issued to the troops before landing, was nearly exhausted. The men made free use of coconuts for food and drink.[26]

At 0800 on 22 October the three battalions of the 382d Infantry moved out. By 0900 the 1st and 2d Battalions had pushed through Tigbao, whereupon the regimental commander changed the orders for the day. He ordered the 2d Battalion to take Bolongtohan, the 1st Battalion to seize Canmangui, and the 3d Battalion to go into reserve.[27]

The 1st and 3d Battalions of the 382d Infantry made contact with each other at 1152. When patrols from the 1st Battalion did not find any Japanese at Canmangui, the battalion proceeded toward Bolongtohan. Upon nearing Mati, the 1st Battalion encountered an entrenched position of the enemy and by outflanking the position was able to knock it out. The Japanese fought a delaying action and withdrew during the afternoon. At 2000 the battalion formed its night perimeter at Mati. The other battalions of the regiment encountered no Jap-

anese during the day's progress inland, and formed their night perimeters at 1800—the 2d Battalion 800 yards east of Bolongtohan and the 3d Battalion 500 yards southeast of Tigbao. During the day the 382d Infantry had pushed forward approximately 2,000 yards.[28]

At 2300 on 22 October General Makino issued an order for the defense of the island by the Japanese *16th Division*. He organized his troops into the *Northern* and *Southern Leyte Defense Forces*. The *Southern Defense Force* was to protect the Dulag–Burauen road and the airfields in the vicinity of Burauen. It was in the zone of action of the 7th Division. The *Northern Leyte Defense Force* [29] was to remain on Catmon Hill, the high ground south of Tanauan, and the high ground south of Palo. Elements were to be in the vicinity of Tabontabon and Kansamada, and a unit was to protect the artillery positions north of Catmon Hill. The *16th Engineer Regiment* (less three platoons) was to be prepared to demolish the roads connecting Dagami and Burauen and those connecting Dagami and Tanauan, in order to check the advance of American tanks. Simultaneously, the main force of the unit was to secure the road running northwest from Dagami to Tingib. The division reserve and command post were to be in the vicinity of Dagami.[30]

At 0900 on 23 October the 2d Battalion, 383d Infantry, sent a patrol to investigate the enemy situation west of Pikas and near the Guinarona River. At 1130 the patrol reported that there were a few Japanese on a

---

[25] A carabao is a domesticated native water buffalo that is used extensively in the Philippines as a beast of burden.

[26] 383d Inf Opns Rpt Leyte, p. 4.

[27] 382d Inf Unit Jnl, 22 Oct 44.

[28] 382d Inf Unit Rpt 3, 22 Oct 44.

[29] This unit consisted of the *9th Infantry Regiment* (less the *2d Battalion*) and two batteries of the *22d Field Artillery Regiment*.

[30] 96th Inf Div Opns Rpt Leyte, Annex C, Part III, Trans, *KAKI* Operational Order A-387, 22 Oct 44.

hill near Pikas. The 2d and 3d Battalions, 383d Infantry, moved out at 1200 with the 2d Battalion in the lead. At 1430 Company G, the leading company, surprised some Japanese who were swimming in the Guinarona River. They were "literally caught with their pants down." [31] The leading companies were able to rout the enemy and continue the advance despite small forays which were broken up; about fifty of the enemy were killed. At 1810 the 2d Battalion, 383d Infantry, reached the high ground on the north bank of the Guinarona River, 600 yards west of Pikas. A force of approximately 100 Japanese attacked the battalion as it was establishing a night perimeter. Fortunately the Americans, just fifteen minutes before, had put their machine guns and mortars in position and were thus able to fire their weapons immediately and repulse the attack. The 3d Battalion, 383d Infantry, closed in on the area at 1900 and each battalion set up a perimeter for the night. [32]

During the day the regiment received a small quantity of supplies by Filipino and carabao trains and by airdrop from Navy planes. The amount of food came to about one-half ration for each man. On the following day Colonel May ordered the 1st Battalion, 383d Infantry, to remain in position until a supply route could be established. [33]

Early on 24 October General Bradley told Colonel May to hold his present positions and sent out patrols to find roads, trails, and solid ground that could be used as or converted into supply routes to the rear. [34]

The communications between the regiment and the 96th Division were very hard to maintain, since the only radios the troops could move inland were hand-carried sets of short range.

In the early morning hours of 25 October a division reconnaissance patrol, with light tanks and a motorized engineer platoon, went along Highway 1 with the mission of reconnoitering the highway as far north as the Binahaan River and making contact with the X Corps. By 1300 the patrol reached the river near Tanauan and found a damaged bridge. By 1600 the bridge had been repaired and the patrol pushed through Tanauan and made contact with Company K of the 19th Infantry, 24th Division, the first between the X and XXIV Corps since the landing.

The 382d Infantry spent 23 October patrolling. Contact was established and maintained between all of the battalions of the regiment during the day. Although the forward movement was slowed to allow much-needed supplies to come up, an advance of 600 yards was made. As the regiment advanced farther inland it became apparent that the entire area was composed of swamps and rice paddies. The roads were only muddy trails and were impassable for wheeled vehicles. The M29 cargo carriers and LVT's were pressed into service to carry supplies, but the numerous streams and waist-deep swamps soon halted all vehicular traffic. The task of supply and of evacuation of wounded soon assumed staggering proportions. For days the troops had had little food since priority had been given to the indispensable ammunition. Filipino and soldier carrying details were the only means by which the front lines could be supplied. [35]

[31] Orlando R. Davidson, J. Carl Willems, and Joseph A. Kahl, *The Deadeyes, The Story of the 96th Infantry Division* (Washington, 1947), p. 23.

[32] 383d Inf Unit Rpt 4, 23 Oct 44.

[33] 96th Div G–3 Periodic Rpt 3, 24 Oct 44.

[34] 96th Div Opns Rpt Leyte, p. 41.

[35] 382d Inf Opns Rpt Leyte, p. 2.

FILIPINO CIVILIAN GUIDES U.S. TANK *to Japanese positions in Julita.*

On the morning of 24 October General Bradley ordered the 382d Infantry to have its 2d Battalion close in on Anibung. The 3d Battalion was to occupy Hindang and the 1st Battalion was to proceed through Hindang to a position about 500 yards farther north.[36]

At 0830 the 1st and 3d Battalions, 382d Infantry, moved astride the narrow trail that led to Tabontabon, with the 3d Battalion echeloned to the right rear. The 1st Battalion passed through Bolongtohan at 0930 and moved on in a northwesterly direction toward Hindang. At 1105, as the 1st Battalion was pushing through Hindang, it came under enemy rifle fire. The Japanese had dug spider holes under the huts, and a trench extended along the western end of the barrio. The 1st Battalion, assisted by

troops from Company B, 763d Tank Battalion, moved through the town, leaving the 3d Battalion the job of mopping up. The 3d Battalion reached Hindang at 1530 and immediately attacked the enemy force there. The Japanese offered only slight resistance and then fled, abandoning thirty-six well-constructed defensive positions. At 1610 the barrio was secured.

Meanwhile, the 1st Battalion, after driving through Hindang with Companies A and C abreast, came upon a strong enemy position some 200 yards beyond the town on the left flank of Company A. A platoon of the Cannon Company and some light tanks had managed to get forward. The tanks and flame throwers flushed the Japanese into the open where they were met by the fire of American riflemen who were waiting for them. By 1600 the enemy strong

---

[36] 96th Div G–3 Jnl, 24 Oct 44.

point was secured and the battalion moved northwest and formed a night perimeter at 1700.

The 2d Battalion reached Anibung without incident. The airfield believed to be in the vicinity of the barrio proved nonexistent. At the end of the day the regiment had advanced approximately 2,200 yards. The 2d Battalion was at Anibung, the 3d Battalion was just beyond Hindang, and the 1st Battalion was in a position to move northwest against Aslom.[37]

On the morning of 25 October the 1st and 3d Battalions, 382d Infantry, moved out in a northwesterly direction toward Aslom, with the 3d Battalion on the right, while the 2d Battalion moved out in a northwesterly direction toward Kanmonhag. The Japanese had withdrawn during the night, leaving only scattered riflemen to oppose the advance.

In their advance, the battalions were supported by elements of the 763d Tank Battalion. At Aslom the two battalions encountered a strongly fortified position of five gun emplacements and four pillboxes, which the tanks were able to knock out.[38] The 1st Battalion formed its night perimeter near Aslom while the 3d Battalion pushed north 1,500 yards and formed its perimeter.

The 2d Battalion encountered only abandoned pillboxes on its front and left flank during its advance. At 1200 a patrol which reconnoitered Kanmonhag found no resistance, and the battalion pushed on to form its night perimeter on line with the 3d Battalion.[39]

During the first six days of the operation, the casualties of the 96th Division amount-

ed to 5 officers and 89 enlisted men killed, 17 officers and 416 enlisted men wounded, and 13 enlisted men missing in action.[40] In the same period the division had killed an estimated 531 Japanese and had taken one prisoner.[41]

Catmon Hill Area

By the end of 25 October the 1st Battalion of the 383d Infantry was in position to attack Labir Hill, while the 2d and 3d Battalions, remaining in position near Pikas, had sent vigorous patrols into Tabontabon, San Victor, and San Vicente. The 2d and 3d Battalions of the 382d Infantry were beyond Aslom while the 1st Battalion was still at that point. By this time the supply line had been opened up and the main swamps had been traversed. The 96th Division was deep in southern Leyte Valley and had isolated a strong enemy force on Catmon Hill. The way was now open for the division to launch an attack against Tabontabon, bypass the positions of the *9th Infantry Regiment* on Catmon Hill, and secure the remainder of its beachhead area.

Taking Tabontabon

By 23 October the 383d Infantry, less the 1st Battalion, had crossed the Guinarona River and established a position west of Pikas. Having been ordered by General Bradley to hold this position, the regiment limited its activities to patrolling. While awaiting orders to advance, Colonel May decided to give battle training to

---

[37] 382d Inf Unit Rpt 5, 24 Oct 44.
[38] 763d Tank Bn Unit Rpt 1, 25 Oct 44.
[39] 382d Inf Unit Rpt 6, 25 Oct 44.

[40] 96th Div G–1 Daily Strength Rpts, 20–25 Oct 44.
[41] 96th Div G–2 Periodic Rpt 5, 25 Oct 44.

various units by sending them out on patrolling missions to observe the enemy.[42] Tabontabon and San Victor were assigned to the 3d Battalion commander as a training mission for one of his companies, while San Vicente Hill was assigned to the 2d Battalion commander for the same purpose. Tabontabon was a key point, since it was one of the main *16th Division* supply centers.

Company K, which had been selected by the 3d Battalion commander for the first mission, sent patrols into the Tabontabon–San Victor area on the afternoon of 24 October. The patrol sent to Tabontabon found that the *9th Infantry Regiment* had extensively fortified the barrio. There were deep foxholes and machine gun emplacements dug in under the houses. None of the positions appeared to be occupied, but at the end of the town the patrol saw approximately twenty-five Japanese preparing their evening meal. Tabontabon was a fairly large barrio on the Guinarona River, with several blocks of shops and houses, including a church and several two-story buildings, the axis of the town running east and west.

On the basis of information brought by the patrol, it was decided to have Company K move out the following morning to seize Tabontabon. At 0645 on 25 October Company K, reinforced, advanced and at 0730 took covered positions 200 yards east of the barrio. Under the plan for attack the 1st Platoon was to approach the northeastern edge of the village by a covered route, and await the completion of an artillery concentration scheduled for 0800. After the

artillery preparation a squad from the platoon was to enter and reconnoiter for possible enemy positions. At the same time, the 2d Platoon, with a similar mission, was to enter Tabontabon from the southeast side. The 3d Platoon was to be prepared to support the action of either the 1st or the 2d. Machine guns and mortars were placed in such a way as to give direct support to both platoons.

Because of unexplained communication difficulties, the artillery did not deliver its scheduled fire at 0800. Each platoon, however, sent a squad into Tabontabon. As soon as advance elements of both platoons entered the town they came under intense rifle and mortar fire from enemy positions under the houses. It was obvious that the Japanese had heavily reinforced the barrio during the night. The reinforcements consisted of a battalion from the *9th Infantry Regiment*.[43]

The rest of the 1st and 2d Platoons came up and a fire fight ensued. The 3d Platoon was sent in at 1000 to support the 1st Platoon, and in response to a request for reinforcements, a rifle platoon from Company I was brought up at 1040. The commanding officer of Company K advised the 3d Battalion by radio that he could take Tabontabon with an additional rifle company but could not do so with his present force without suffering heavy casualties. The battalion commander ordered him to withdraw. The withdrawal, under supporting fire from the 3d Platoon, Company K, the platoon from Company I, and mortar and machine gun fire from the weapons company, was successfully accomplished at 1155. At 1240 Company K rejoined the battalion.

---

[42] Unless otherwise stated the account of the patrol to Tabontabon is taken from 383d Inf Opns Rpt Leyte, Patrol to Tabontabon, 25 Oct 44, Incl 1.

[43] *35th Army* Opns, p. 28.

General Bradley ordered the 383d Infantry to direct the patrols of the 3d Battalion elsewhere, since the 382d Infantry had been assigned the mission of securing Tabontabon. During the forthcoming attack the 383d Infantry was to protect the flank of the 382d, whose 2d and 3d Battalions were to launch a co-ordinated attack on the town. On 26 October the 2d Battalion of the 382d Infantry moved west and established contact with the 3d at 1200. After an artillery concentration had been placed on the town the two battalions moved out.

By 1600 they had forded the shoulder-deep Guinarona River under heavy enemy fire and had reached the edge of Tabontabon. As the battalions slowly pushed their way to the outskirts of the barrio, they came under heavy fire. Elements of the *9th Infantry Regiment* had dug in under the houses, and connecting trenches honeycombed the streets from one strong point to another. At twilight, after heavy artillery fire, the enemy launched a strong counterattack which forced the battalions to withdraw to the river bank, where they established perimeters for the night.[44] Until midnight, mortar fire from the *9th Infantry Regiment* fell in the 2d and 3d Battalion areas.

At 2100 the 96th Division artillery commenced firing on the town and continued to fire throughout the night. The 1st Battalion, less Company B which had been left at Aslom to guard supplies, had by now joined the rest of the regiment. At 1000 on 27 October the 382d Infantry launched a co-ordinated attack against Tabontabon with the 2d and 3d Battalions. As Companies I and K of the 3d Battalion started to wade the Guinarona River, Colonel Dill,

the regimental commander, called to the men to follow him and then dashed across the bridge, which was swept by enemy rifle fire. The 3d Battalion followed him over the bridge and to the southeast corner of the barrio.[45] The troops met considerable opposition from elements of the *9th Infantry Regiment* who were hidden in the tall cogon grass. After a short fire fight the two battalions worked their way slowly through the western portion of the town and then advanced northwest. Although they met fire from several pillboxes, there was no organized resistance. Night perimeters were set up about a mile northwest of Tabontabon with the 3d Battalion on the left side of the road and the 1st Battalion on the right.[46]

The 2d Battalion, which had hit the center of the town, encountered stiff and determined opposition. Company F proceeded cautiously down one street as Company G went through the middle of the second block on its right. The Japanese had riflemen and machine guns under the houses and on the second floors of the large buildings. By noon the two companies had worked their way through to the northern edge of the town, where they encountered the enemy entrenched in force.

The Japanese had placed machine guns to cover the exits from the barrio. The guns were aimed down each street and so placed that each gun was protected by another. Since in Company G men were dropping from heat exhaustion, Company E was sent in to relieve Company G. At the same time, the 2d Platoon of the Cannon Company moved forward, but its howitzers were unable to direct their fire effectively. Late in the afternoon, since it had become apparent

---

[44] 382d Inf Unit Rpt 7, 26 Oct 44.

[45] Davidson *et al., The Deadeyes*, p. 37.
[46] 382d Inf Unit Rpt 8, 27 Oct 44.

that the 2d Battalion would not be able to secure the town before nightfall, the troops were called back to the center of the town, where the 2d Battalion set up its night perimeter.[47]

During the night the Japanese counterattacked, but American artillery and mortar fire broke up the assault.[48] At 0800 on 28 October the 2d Battalion continued the attack and succeeded in knocking out the enemy resistance northeast of the town, an action which enabled the battalion to move out north of Tabontabon at 1200. Leaving Company G to clear the area immediately outside the town, the 2d Battalion proceeded along the road toward the road junction at Kiling.[49] In spite of determined opposition, the Japanese supply center of Tabontabon had at last been taken and approximately 350 Japanese killed in the area. During the three days of fighting, the 2d Battalion had thirty-four men killed and eighty wounded.

Capture of Catmon Hill

The capture of Catmon Hill falls into two separate and distinct actions—the operations of the 383d Infantry in the San Vicente sector and the assault of the 381st Infantry against Catmon Hill.

On 24 October a Japanese prisoner stated that the fortifications on San Vicente Hill, the northern tip of Catmon Hill, were guarded by elements of the *9th Infantry* and *20th Infantry Regiments* of the Japanese *16th Division*.[50] On the morning of 26 October the regimental commander ordered Company E, 383d Infantry, under Capt.

Jesse R. Thomas, to make a reconnaissance in force of San Vicente Hill.[51] Upon receiving his orders, Captain Thomas made his plans. The 1st Platoon was to move forward and take the left nose of the hill, operating on the right of the 2d Platoon. The 3d Platoon was to move into an assembly area fifty yards behind the line of departure.

On the morning of 26 October the 155-mm. howitzers of the 363d Field Artillery Battalion laid a ten-minute concentration on the crest of the hill. This fire was ineffective, since it was too far ahead of the troops. At 1000 the platoons of Company E moved through the tall cogon grass to the edge of an open field approximately 200 yards from the base of the hill. The men were under orders not to fire until fired upon. As the leading elements of the two platoons entered the field, the *9th Infantry Regiment* opened fire with rifles and mortars. The 3d Platoon then moved up into position along the line of departure, prepared to support the attack. Since the 2d Platoon was not under heavy fire, it was ordered to move to the foot of the hill and take a position from which it could support by fire the advance of the 1st Platoon. Enemy mortars were dropping shells around the center of the area, but American mortars silenced them.

The 2d Platoon reported that it was 100 yards from the base of the hill. The 2d Battalion commander, Lt. Col. James O. McCray, moved into the company command post, about seventy-five yards behind the attacking platoons at the edge of the open field. This sector began to receive

---

[47] Davidson *et al., The Deadeyes,* p. 38.
[48] 382d Inf Unit Rpt 9, 28 Oct. 44.
[49] *Ibid.*
[50] 383d Inf Opns Rpt, p. 5.

[51] The operations report of the 383d Infantry for the Leyte Campaign has an "Account of Eyewitnesses Made Immediately Following the Action," which is Inclosure 2 to the report. Unless otherwise stated these statements are the basis for this account of the action on San Vicente Hill.

SAN VICENTE HILL

heavy fire from the right side of the hill and several men on the edge of the field were hit. Colonel McCray crawled up and started to help drag the wounded men to cover. At the same time he ordered the battalion to open fire against the hill with all weapons except artillery, but an undetermined number of enemy riflemen in the rear of the command post and on the left flank of the company started firing into the command post.

Colonel McCray continued to bring back wounded men. At this time Captain Thomas was overcome by the heat, and the executive officer of Company E, 2d Lt. Owen R. O'Neill, took over. He ordered the withdrawal of the force. It was now 1335 and the company, under continuous fire since 1000, had been unable to advance. Captain Thomas revived and again assumed command, directing the withdrawal and the bringing back of the wounded. The body of Colonel McCray, who had sacrificed his life while dragging the wounded from the hill, was found about twenty yards from the command post. The withdrawal was completed.

From 27 to 29 October, the actions of the 2d and 3d Battalions, 383d Infantry, were limited to reconnaissance patrols in the vicinity of the town of San Vicente and San Vicente Hill in attempts to find the strong positions of the enemy on the hill. At 0930 on 30 October Colonel May ordered the battalions to renew the attack from positions near the Guinarona River. The two units jumped off at 1300. The 3d Battalion advanced along the north bank of the Guinarona River, one company going through Pikas and the rest of the battalion making a wide swing through a coconut palm grove and open fields. The 2d Battalion moved along the south bank of the Guinarona River, one company following a trail from Pikas to San Vicente and the rest of the battalion going directly to San Vicente Hill, which was taken without opposition since the enemy force had withdrawn. The 3d Battalion went through the barrio of San Vicente without difficulty but encountered some small arms fire along the river 300 yards north of the village. Both battalions formed their night perimeters near the river.

At the same time, the eastern slopes of Catmon Hill were being assaulted by elements of the 381st Infantry, which had been in Sixth Army reserve through 26 October. On 27 October Sixth Army had released the 381st Infantry to XXIV Corps control. At 1330 on the same day General Bradley ordered the regiment to relieve on the following day the 1st Battalion, 383d Infantry, which had been on Labiranan Head since 22 October. It was then to attack and capture Catmon Hill.

Catmon Hill had been under steady naval and artillery fire since A Day—20 October. The 96th Division artillery had constantly fired on targets of opportunity by day and harassed enemy positions in the area during the night. Starting at 2100 on 27 October, the 105-mm. howitzers of the 361st Field Artillery Battalion, the 155-mm. howitzers of the 198th Field Artillery Battalion, a battery of 155-mm. howitzers from the 363d Field Artillery Battalion, and the 75-mm. howitzers from the 780th Amphibian Tank Battalion were to deliver harassing fires on the hill until 1030 the following day. At that time all of the artillery units were to commence firing successive concen-

trations beginning at the bottom of the hill and working to the top in fifty-yard bounds. After the 381st Infantry, less the 3d Battalion, attacked at 1200 on 28 October, the artillery was to fire concentrations in front of the troops as they advanced.[52]

In making his plans for the capture of Catmon Hill, Col. Michael E. Halloran, commander of the 381st Infantry, decided to have the 1st Battalion make an enveloping movement from the northeast while the 2d Battalion pushed west along the main ridge. The 1st Battalion, 383d Infantry, from its position on Labiranan Head, would support the attack by fire. On the morning of 28 October the 381st Infantry, less the 3d Battalion, moved into position for the attack. After a thirty-minute preparation by the artillery, the 381st Infantry jumped off to the attack at 1200.

The 1st Battalion, 381st Infantry, moved to the foot of the hill, where it received "a bloody nose" from fire coming out of well-entrenched positions. It withdrew under cover of smoke and established a night perimeter in the vicinity of its line of departure. The 2d Battalion, however, met no enemy resistance and advanced rapidly. At the close of the day the battalion was just short of Labir Hill.[53] During the night the Americans expended 3,000 rounds of artillery ammunition on Catmon Hill, chiefly in front of the 2d Battalion sector. The plans for 29 October called for a morning attack by the 2d Battalion, supported by fire from the 1st Battalion, 383d Infantry, which had not yet been relieved; the 1st Battalion,

---

[52] 96th Div Opns Rpt Leyte, p. 45. Unless otherwise stated the section dealing with the capture of Catmon Hill is based on 381st Inf Opns Rpt Leyte, pp. 3–3c.

[53] 381st Inf Unit Rpt 4, 28 Oct 44; 381st Inf Unit Jnl, 29 Oct 44.

105-MM. SELF-PROPELLED HOWITZER M7 FIRING *on Japanese positions on Catmon Hill.*

381st Infantry, was to seek a new lane of approach and attack at noon.

After a thirty-minute artillery preparation, the 2d Battalion, 381st Infantry, moved out at 0830. With the support of a platoon of light tanks, the battalion easily secured both Labir and Catmon Hills. By 1300 the position had been consolidated. The 1st Battalion, 381st Infantry, supported by the massed fire of forty-five tanks and the Regimental Cannon Company, jumped off at 1200. The troops moved through a heavily fortified area, and at 1600 they established physical contact with the regiment's 2d Battalion.

During the heavy pounding of Catmon Hill, the main body of Japanese troops, the *9th Infantry Regiment,* had withdrawn

from the hill on 26 October, unknown to the Americans, and rejoined the main force of the *16th Division* in the Dagami area.[54]

At last Catmon Hill had been secured. The 1st Battalion, 383d Infantry, was relieved and passed to the Sixth Army reserve. The 381st Infantry's command post was moved north of San Roque, and at 1800 its 3d Battalion rejoined the regiment south of this position. During 30 and 31 October the entire Catmon Hill area was mopped up— fifty-three pillboxes, seventeen caves, and numerous smaller emplaced positions were destroyed by demolition charges. The last enemy stronghold threatening the landing beaches had been removed.

---

[54] *35th Army* Opns, p. 34.

Convergence on Kiling

Since the main force of the 96th Division was centered in the vicinity of Catmon Hill, General Bradley had decided to secure the northern limits of the corps beachhead line—the road running from Tanauan to Dagami—concurrently with the assault on Catmon Hill. On 25 October Colonel Halloran had ordered the 3d Battalion of the 381st Infantry to move north along Highway 1 to Tanauan and thence southwestward along the Tanauan–Dagami road to Dagami. At the same time the 17th Infantry, 7th Division, was advancing north toward Dagami on the Burauen–Dagami road. At 0830 on 26 October the reinforced 3d Battalion of the 381st Infantry moved out.[55] The forward movement was halted by a bridge that had been mined and partially blown out. The battalion forded the river and the advance continued without tanks or vehicles, while engineers from the 321st Engineer Battalion deactivated the mines and repaired the bridge. The tanks and vehicles then rejoined the battalion. Two platoons supported by tanks were sent forward to guard the two bridges south and east of Tanauan. En route, the platoons received some machine gun and rifle fire from a hill between Vigia Point and Tanauan. During the night the enemy made his presence known by three rounds of mortar fire and by sporadic rifle fire on the bridge guards.

At 0800 on 27 October the march was renewed. The troops again came under fire from the hill between Vigia Point and Tanauan. After a delay of two hours, in

which artillery fire was placed on the hill, the advance continued and the entrance into Tanauan at 1145 was unopposed. The battalion then turned southwestward along the Tanauan–Dagami road toward Kiling, which is about midway between Tanauan and Dagami. The 3d Battalion had gone about two miles along the road when it came under fire from 75-mm. guns, mortars, and machine guns. Two hours were required for Company A, 763d Tank Battalion, and two flame-thrower tanks to reduce this resistance.[56] Seven pillboxes and three 75-mm. guns were destroyed and a command post was captured. A night perimeter was established on the road, at 1700, and only sporadic rifle fire occurred during the night.

At 0800 the following day the 3d Battalion, 381st Infantry, moved out and about 1500 the advance element entered Kiling. An attack supported by Battery C, 361st Field Artillery Battalion, was launched against the enemy about 1630. The Japanese countered with heavy machine gun, mortar, and rifle fire. The attack continued without success until 1800, when the 3d Battalion withdrew under a smoke screen and established a night perimeter about 1,000 yards east of Kiling. Battery C, 361st Field Artillery, fired intermittently during the night to prevent any Japanese attack against the perimeter.[57]

At 0800 the following morning—29 October—the 3d Battalion, supported by tanks and artillery, moved out against Kiling. On the outskirts of the barrio the battalion met stubborn and determined resistance where the Japanese, with machine guns, mortars, and rifles, fought "to the last man." The resistance was overcome, and by 1500 the Americans occupied the town,

---

[55] The reinforcements consisted of a platoon from the Cannon Company, 381st Infantry; one platoon from Company A, 321st Engineers; Company A, 763d Tank Battalion; one platoon from Company A, 321st Medical Battalion; and Battery C, 361st Field Artillery Battalion.

[56] 763d Tank Bn S–3 Periodic Rpt 3, 27 Oct 44.
[57] 381st Inf Opns Rpt Leyte, pp. 3–3a.

which was honeycombed with emplacements and entrenchments. At 1600 the 3d Battalion, 381st Infantry, was relieved by the 2d Battalion, 382d Infantry, which had come up from Tabontabon by truck. At 1800 the 3d Battalion, 381st Infantry, returned by truck to the area north of San Roque.[58]

From Tabontabon two important roads lead to the Tanauan–Dagami road. One of these runs in a northeasterly direction and meets the Tanauan–Dagami road at Kiling; the other goes in a northwesterly direction and meets the road at Digahongan about one and a half miles east of Dagami. Colonel Dill ordered the 1st and 3d Battalions, 382d Infantry, to pass through Tabontabon on 27 October and then to proceed northwest along the latter road to Digahongan. They were then to go northeastward along the Tanauan–Dagami road and at Kiling join the 2d Battalion, which was to proceed northeast along the road from Tabontabon to Kiling.

The 1st and 3d Battalions, with the 3d Battalion in the lead, moved out of Tabontabon and advanced about three quarters of a mile to Kapahuan where they established night perimeters. During the night the Japanese charged the perimeter of the 1st Battalion. The attack was repulsed with only three casualties to the battalion, while about one hundred of the enemy were killed.

At 0830 on the 28th the 1st and 3d Battalions jumped off abreast along both sides of the narrow road for Digahongan—the 1st Battalion on the right and the 3d Battalion on the left. At 1200, when the battalions were about two miles northwest of Tabontabon, they encountered a strongly fortified position. The *16th Division* had

built coconut pillboxes and many spider holes, which were supported by two 70-mm. howitzers and a number of 50-mm. mortars. Flame throwers and demolition teams, supported by the artillery, knocked out this fortified area. Taking their dead and wounded, the enemy withdrew. The American troops then advanced under protection of artillery fire toward the road junction at Digahongan, which they reached at 1500. During the day the battalions had been harassed by numerous hidden riflemen, mines, and booby traps.

The 1st Battalion was to move east toward Kiling. The 3d received orders to stay and guard the road junction at Digahongan, nicknamed Foxhole Corners, where it went into night perimeter. At 1600 the battalion successfully repulsed a counterattack by about 200 Japanese. In the meantime the 1st Battalion moved as far east on the Digahongan–Kiling road as Kansamada, where it established a night perimeter. During the night several small enemy groups of six to eight men each tried to enter the battalion lines but were driven off.[59]

The 3d Battalion spent 29 October in patrolling the area around Digahongan and guarding the road junction. It broke up one enemy attack by about thirty men. At 0800 the 1st Battalion moved out from Kansamada toward Kiling against scattered enemy fire but at 1130 the troops were stopped by heavy automatic fire which came from pillboxes astride the road. Shortly afterward the enemy artillery opened up and the 1st Battalion was forced to withdraw about a thousand yards to a point where it established a perimeter.[60] During the fight Lt. Col. Jesse W. Mecham, the commanding

---

[58] *Ibid.*

[59] 382d Inf Unit Rpt 9, 28 Oct 44.
[60] 382d Inf Unit Rpt 10, 29 Oct 44.

officer of the battalion, was mortally wounded. His last order to the battalion was that the troops should not risk their lives to get his body out.[61] That night, however, Maj. Joseph R. Lewis, who had assumed command of the battalion, led a small party forward and recovered the body of Colonel Mecham.

During the night the *9th Infantry Regiment* withdrew. On 30 October the 1st Battalion, 382d Infantry, found no opposition during its advance forward to Kiling and at 1030 established contact with the 2d Battalion, 382d Infantry. The 2d Battalion, less Company G, had moved out of Tabontabon on the northeast road to Kiling on 28 October, spending the night on the outskirts of the town.

The units of the 96th Division spent the next three days in patrolling and mopping up. The division had secured the beachhead area of the XXIV Corps in its zone of action. Its units had seized the Catmon Hill mass, which dominated the landing beaches, had traversed and cleaned out the inland swamps, and had secured the important communications center and supply dump of Tabontabon and the main portion of the significant Tanauan–Dagami road. Since landing they had killed an estimated 2,769 Japanese and taken 6 prisoners in their zone of action.[62] The cost had not been light. Casualties of the 96th Division since 25 October had been 13 officers and 132 enlisted men killed, 30 officers and 534 enlisted men wounded, and 2 officers and 88 enlisted men missing in action.[63]

---

[61] Davidson *et al., The Deadeyes*, p. 41.

[62] 96th Div G–2 Periodic Rpt 13, 2 Nov 44.

[63] Compiled from 96th Div G–1 Daily Strength Rpts, 26 Oct–2 Nov 44.

CHAPTER VIII

Southern Leyte Valley: Part Two

Before the invasion, the Japanese had reached the conclusion that if and when the Americans landed on Leyte it would be in the Dulag area, and their greatest efforts had therefore been directed toward making that area impregnable. General Makino, commanding general of the *16th Division,* had stationed the following units in the Dulag sector: the *20th Infantry Regiment,* commanded by Col. Keijiro Hokoda; elements of the *22d Field Artillery Regiment;* the *54th Air Field Company,* commanded by Comdr. Kazumasa Kumazawa; and the *7th Independent Tank Company.*[1] At 0300 on 21 October, General Makino withdrew from the Dulag area to Dagami and established his command post in that sector.[2] The effective fire of the preliminary naval bombardment had driven the Japanese from the landing beaches.

The Dulag–Burauen Road

The beachhead quadrangle of the XXIV Corps was bounded, generally, by the Dulag–Burauen–Dagami–Tanauan road. The sections of the road bordering the northern edge of the quadrangle (Dagami to Tanauan) and the eastern edge (Tanauan to Dulag) were, in general, in the 96th Division zone of action. The southern and western sides of the quadrangle were assigned to the 7th Division. The road that ran along the coast between Dulag and Tanauan was a one-way thoroughfare which soon disintegrated under the heavy rainfall and military traffic. (*Map 6*)

Besides the Dulag airstrip, which was approximately one mile west of the town, there were three other airfields in the zone of action of the 7th Infantry Division. The San Pablo airstrip was approximately five miles west of Dulag and two miles east of Burauen. Its runway extended generally east to west with a width of 164 feet and a length of 4,920 feet. The field was overgrown with weeds and had not been occupied by the Japanese. The Bayug airstrip was just north of the highway and a half mile east of Burauen. It had a runway approximately 5,000 feet long. The Buri airstrip, the most important one in the 7th Division zone, was about one mile northeast of Burauen, ran in a general east-west direction, and was also 5,000 feet long.[3]

Halfway to Burauen

General Hodge ordered the 7th Division to capture the Dulag airfield and then drive west along the Dulag–Burauen road to seize Burauen and its airfields. After this was

---

[1] 7th Inf Div G–2 Periodic Rpt 2, 21 Oct 44, and Rpt 4, 23 Oct 44.
[2] *35th Army Opns,* p. 27.

[3] Fifth Air Force Opns Instns 6, Engr Annex, 28 Sep 44, Sixth Army G–3 Jnl, 30 Sep 44.

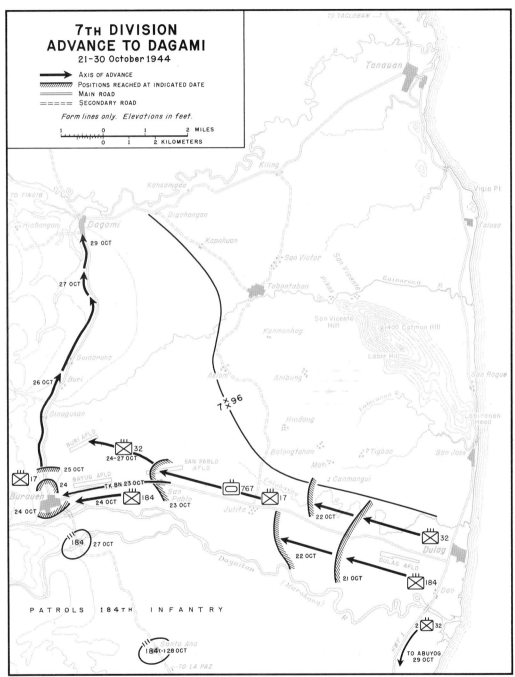

7TH DIVISION
ADVANCE TO DAGAMI
21–30 October 1944

➤	AXIS OF ADVANCE
⊞⊞⊞	POSITIONS REACHED AT INDICATED DATE
▬▬	MAIN ROAD
=====	SECONDARY ROAD

Form lines only. Elevations in feet.

TO TACLOBAN

Tanauan

TO TINGIB

Hinabang

Kiling

Kansamada

Digahongan

Dagami

29 OCT

Kapahuan

Hiabangan

San Victor

27 OCT

Vigia Pt.

Tolosa

San Vicente

Tabontaban

Pikas

Guinarona

26 OCT

Guinarona

Buri

Kanmonhog

San Vicente Hill

1400 Catmon Hill

Labir Hill

San Roque

Ginagusan

Aslom

Anibung

7 X 96

Hindang

Labiranan R.

Labiranan Head

BURI AFLD

24–27 OCT

32

SAN PABLO AFLD

25 OCT

17

24

BAYUG AFLD

TK BN 23 OCT

Burauen

24 OCT

184

24 OCT

San Pablo

23 OCT

767

23 OCT

17

Bolangtohan

Mati

Canmangui

Tigbao

San Jose

Julita

22 OCT

184

27 OCT

Duguiton

22 OCT

Catahaxiy

21 OCT

DULAG AFLD

Dulag

32

184

Dao

PATROLS   184TH   INFANTRY

(Marabang) R.

Santa Ana

184(-) 28 OCT

TO LA PAZ

HWY. 1

2   32

TO ABUYOG

29 OCT

R. Johnstone

MAP 6

DULAG AND BAYUG AIRSTRIPS *as they appeared in 1946. Dulag is above.*

MAJ. GEN. JOHN R. HODGE, *XXIV Corps commander, outlines plans to his staff at corps headquarters in Dulag.*

done, the division was to turn north along the Burauen–Dagami road and capture Dagami.[4] The 32d Infantry was to protect the division's right (north), maintain contact with the 96th Division, and, if necessary, help the 184th Infantry on its left to secure the Dulag airstrip west of the town of Dulag. Securing the airstrip was to be the main effort of the 184th Infantry.[5]

At the end of A Day (20 October), all the assault battalions of the 32d and 184th Infantry Regiments of the 7th Division were ashore. The 32d Infantry was on the right (north) flank and the 184th Infantry on the left (south) flank. The 32d Infantry had advanced just beyond Highway 1 in

the area northwest of Dulag.[6] The 3d Battalion, 184th Infantry, was on the southern edge of the Dulag airstrip, while the 1st Battalion of the regiment was directly left of the 3d, and the 2d Battalion was in reserve.[7] The 3d Battalion, 17th Infantry, protecting the left flank of the XXIV Corps, was across the Daguitan River at Dao;[8] the 1st and 2d Battalions of the same regiment were to remain in division reserve.

The 7th Division had scarcely established itself for the night of 20 October when the Japanese launched two small-scale tank attacks against the perimeter of the division. Since a gap existed between the 184th and

_____

[4] XXIV Corps Opns Rpt Leyte, p. 6.
[5] 7th Inf Div FO 9, 1 Oct 44.

_____

[6] 32d Inf Regt Jnl, 20 Oct 44.
[7] 184th Inf S–3 Periodic Rpt 1, 20 Oct 44.
[8] 17th Inf Unit Jnl, 20 Oct 44.

32d Infantry Regiments, Company G of the 184th was committed to fill the space. As the men of the company were digging in for the night, three tanks from the *7th Independent Tank Company* came down the road and sprayed the area with machine gun fire, but the fire was high and there were no casualties. Though the company fired rifles, bazookas, and mortars against them, the tanks escaped without injury. An hour later, when one of the tanks returned, it was knocked out and its crew were killed by a rifle grenade. An enemy scout car then dashed down the road, and its occupants killed two men and wounded three others.

The 3d Battalion, 184th Infantry, had established its night perimeter on the edge of the Dulag airfield, with its right flank on the Dulag–Burauen road. At 0130 three Japanese medium tanks moved along this road. Pfc. George W. Tilk of Company M stopped one of these, as it came into range, with one shot from his bazooka. The other two tanks continued down the road but on their return trip they were destroyed—one by the battalion supply detail and the other by Pfc. Johnnie Johnson with his bazooka.[9]

The uneasy repose of the 7th Division was again broken at 0400 on 21 October when six enemy tanks attacked the sector of the 3d Battalion, 184th Infantry. Within thirty minutes the battalion knocked out two of the tanks and forced the others to retreat.[10] The next disturbance was at 0530 when about fifty Japanese launched a limited counterattack against the night perimeter of

Company K, 3d Battalion, 32d Infantry, with light machine gun and rifle fire. The Americans broke up the attack with machine guns, mortars, and artillery.[11] Daylight revealed thirty-five enemy dead in front of the company perimeter, and there was evidence that others had been dragged away.

Maj. Gen. Archibald V. Arnold, commander, ordered the 184th and 32d Infantry Regiments of the 7th Division to move west toward the Burauen airstrips abreast. Since a gap of several hundred yards existed between the two regiments, the battalions of the 184th Infantry were ordered to veer to the right. At 0800 the 7th Division attacked, the 184th Infantry on the left and the 32d Infantry on the right. There were four battalions in the assault, from left to right: 1st Battalion, 184th Infantry; 3d Battalion, 184th Infantry; 3d Battalion, 32d Infantry; and 2d Battalion, 32d Infantry.[12]

As the 2d Battalion, 32d Infantry, moved forward, it encountered Japanese entrenched in positions along the hedgerows. Knocking out these positions from hedgerow to hedgerow greatly retarded the advance. The 3d Battalion on the left faced an impassable swamp. In order to establish contact with the 184th Infantry and cover the area, Company I moved around the left side of the swamp, and Company L went around the right; Company K was to cover the gap between the 2d and 3d Battalions until the 2d Battalion could close it.

There was an enemy strong point between the 2d and 3d Battalions of the 32d Infantry, but since Colonel Logie was anxious to

---

[9] Lt Russell A. Gugeler, Battle for Dagami, pp. 10–11, MS in OCMH. The author, a combat historian attached to the 7th Division after the operation, knew many of the participants and has been able to give details that do not appear in the official records. Much of the material in this chapter is based on his manuscript.

[10] 184th Inf Unit Jnl, 21 Oct 44.

[11] 32d Inf Regt Jnl, 21 Oct 44.

[12] 7th Div, Detailed Division Narrative, King II, p. 4, DRB AGO.

continue the advance of the regiment and straighten the line between the battalions, he ordered the battalions to bypass the strong point, while the 1st Battalion under Maj. Leigh H. Mathias was ordered to move from its assembly area and reduce it. The lines were straightened somewhat, but the swamps and the heavy foliage made contact very difficult.

The 2d and 3d Battalions came under fire from 75-mm. guns emplaced in bunkers; tanks reduced these bunkers and the advance continued. A report of the 32d Infantry boasts that "the reduction of pillboxes was right down our alley." [13] By 1520 the 3d Battalion, 32d Infantry, had reached the regimental beachhead line; shortly thereafter the 2d Battalion came abreast of the 3d.

The 1st Battalion of the 32d Infantry, however, experienced difficulty in reducing the bypassed strong point, which it reached in the middle of the afternoon. The Japanese defenses consisted of one 75-mm. and one antitank gun emplaced in bunkers and four machine guns in pillboxes; these were completely surrounded by an elaborate system of trenches and foxholes and were occupied by approximately two platoons of riflemen.[14] When the battalion reached the position, Companies A and B, with Company A on the right, were on a line behind five medium tanks and one M8 self-propelled 75-mm. howitzer from the Cannon Company. As the troops moved across an open field toward a hedgerow, the Japanese opened fire upon Company A. Company B also received fire as it moved beyond the hedgerow. After several men had been killed and others wounded, Company B halted until

the Japanese positions could be neutralized by the tanks and the howitzer.

As the tanks emerged from the hedgerow they came under heavy fire from the Japanese antitank gun. Although some of the tanks were hit, no serious damage was done; but the howitzer received a direct hit that set it ablaze and exploded its ammunition.[15] The crew abandoned the burning vehicle. Pfc. Fedele A. Grammatico crawled up under enemy fire, removed the machine guns, which were intact, and brought them safely back behind the lines. In the meantime, Company A tried to advance and knock out the enemy antitank gun but the Japanese stopped the company with direct fire.

Both companies were halted. The struggle resolved itself into a battle between the tanks and the Japanese in entrenched positions. The tanks finally silenced the enemy, and the infantrymen moved in with rifles and bazookas and cleared out the foxholes. After the reduction of this strong point, the 1st Battalion tried to overtake the 2d and 3d Battalions. This was not possible, and at 1800 the 1st Battalion formed its own perimeter.

The 184th Infantry found little opposition in its area, but excessive heat and the difficulty of maintaining communication in the high cogon grass rendered its progress difficult. At 0900 the regiment secured the Dulag airstrip and continued its forward movement against sporadic rifle and machine gun fire. Contact had been broken with the 32d Infantry, and at 1245 a gap of 3,000 yards existed between the regiments. At 1515 the 184th Infantry was ordered to hold up its advance and establish contact with the 32d.[16] It had advanced

---

[13] 32d Inf Opns Rpt Leyte, p. 5.
[14] *Ibid.*

[15] *Ibid.*
[16] 184th Inf Regt Jnl, 21 Oct 44.

approximately 1,000 yards beyond the division beachhead line.

On 21 October an unidentified Japanese soldier wrote in his diary:

Finally the enemy's gunfire and bombardment has reached our field and road area (except the runway). Gunfire seems to fade to Dulag area during the night. It seems that enemy tanks are approaching San Pablo vicinity. We are preparing for them. . . . Barracks and fuel dumps are to be burned. I am awaiting the opportune moment. . . .

I feel alive during the night and dead during the day. Though life and death are separated by a thin sheet of paper I will not die until I see a face of a Yankee.[17]

During the night of 21–22 October all field artillery battalions delivered harassing fires, and just before the assault they fired a fifteen-minute barrage.

At 0800 the 32d Infantry moved out to the attack. The 2d Battalion on the right faced difficult and swampy terrain lying along the winding, steep-banked Calbasag River, which the troops had to cross twelve times during the day's advance. In the afternoon a platoon of amphibian tractors and another of amphibian tanks were sent to the aid of the battalion, and engineers from the 13th Engineer Battalion constructed temporary bridges over the river when necessary.[18] The 3d Battalion of the regiment paced its speed of advance with that of the 2d.

In the meantime the 1st Battalion overtook the others and at 1000 moved to the right of the 3d Battalion, bringing the three units into line. Earlier, at 0925, the 3d Battalion was advancing just to the right of the Dulag–Burauen road when it received enemy artillery fire, which came from four 75-mm. field pieces to the rear

of a hedgerow 600 to 700 yards ahead. When the companies reached the hedgerow, Company L received heavy fire from four machine guns which had been emplaced to protect the field pieces.

Light machine guns and mortars were brought up, and the 31st Field Artillery Battalion placed a five-minute concentration on the enemy strong point. Three tanks from Company C, 767th Tank Battalion, were poised for an assault. As soon as the artillery lifted its fire, the tanks dashed forward and destroyed one machine gun and one 75-mm. field piece immediately. The tanks then covered the rest of the area with machine gun fire until Company L moved up and destroyed the remaining gun positions with rifles and grenades. The action ended at 1240.

As the 3d Battalion, 32d Infantry, was destroying the artillery position, Company G of the 2d Battalion received heavy enemy machine gun and rifle fire near the banks of the Calbasag River. The 3d Platoon of Company G walked into an ambush of machine guns, which fired from two pillboxes under native shacks. The platoon was pinned down, having suffered ten casualties from the first burst of fire. To keep the advance moving, Company G remained behind to knock out the bunkers while Company F went forward to continue the advance with Company E. Since the swamps prohibited the use of tanks, and the mutually supported pillboxes prevented envelopment, and since the nearness of friendly troops made the use of artillery dangerous, all of Company G was held up. The 3d Platoon hugged the ground until darkness enabled it to withdraw.

At 0900 on 22 October, planes from the Seventh Fleet bombed the Japanese fortifications in front of the 184th Infantry. As

---

[17] 7th Inf Div Opns Rpt Leyte, App. C to Annex 2.
[18] 13th Engr Bn Opns Rpt Leyte, p. 6.

on the previous day, the heat, tangled foliage, and deep swamps, rather than enemy action, slowed the advance of the regiment. Since the 184th Infantry's rate of advance was more rapid than that of the 32d Infantry, orders were issued to the 184th after it had moved forward an additional 2,800 yards to hold its position until the 32d Infantry could close the gap.[19] The 184th maintained contact with the 3d Battalion, 17th Infantry, by means of patrols.

The 184th Infantry waited most of the day for the 32d to come abreast. By 1800 the 1st and 3d Battalions of the 32d Infantry had advanced approximately half the distance to Burauen. The 3d Battalion, 17th Infantry, on the southern flank of the division, sent out reconnaissance patrols, which encountered small groups of the enemy 1,000 to 1,200 yards south. The rest of the 17th Infantry moved into an assembly area in the vicinity of the Dulag airfield.[20]

Changes in Plans

On the evening of 22 October both General Makino, commander of the *16th Division* on Leyte, and General Arnold, commander of the 7th Division, made changes in their plans.

The *16th Division* was divided into the *Northern* and *Southern Leyte Defense Forces*. The *Northern Leyte Defense Force*, consisting of the *9th Infantry Regiment* reinforced by elements of the *22d Field Artillery Regiment*, would defend the Catmon Hill area against the 96th Division. The *Southern Leyte Defense Force*, which opposed the 7th Division, was composed of the *20th Infantry Regiment*, less one battalion, the *2d Battalion* of the *33d Infantry Regi-*

ment, the *7th Independent Tank Company*, and two platoons of the *16th Engineer Regiment*. Some troops were to occupy the area in the vicinity of San Pablo and the Calbasag River. The main force was to be centralized in a prepared position near Hindang. Another group was to occupy Julita, from which it would make small night raids. At the same time part of this force was to operate along the right bank of the Daguitan River, protecting the *16th Division's* right flank. Another unit of approximately 600 troops was composed of the *98th Airfield Battalion*, the *54th Airfield Company*, and air-ground service units. It was to occupy the key positions—the high ground west of Burauen, the south end of Burauen, and the Buri airfield—and thus prevent the Americans from using the airfield and stop the advance of American tanks along the road. The main strength of the artillery (*22d Field Artillery Regiment*, less the *6th Battery*) would support the *Southern Leyte Defense Force*. The engineers were to be prepared to demolish the road between Dagami and Burauen and between Dagami and Tanauan. The main force of the engineers was to secure the road connecting Dagami, Hiabangan, Rizal, and Tingib. A naval unit was to protect a supply dump east of Dagami, and all remaining units, together with the *16th Division* command post, would occupy positions in the vicinity of Dagami.[21]

Three of the four airfields in the zone of the XXIV Corps were in the vicinity of Burauen. General Arnold wished to seize them as soon as possible, and at the same time he was anxious to advance so rapidly that the Japanese would not have time to

---

[19] 7th Div G–3 Periodic Rpt 3, 22 Oct 44.
[20] *Ibid.*

[21] 96th Inf Div Opns Rpt Leyte, Annex C, Part III, Trans, *KAKI* Operational Order A-837, 22 Oct 44.

DISABLED M4 TANK *on the Dulag–Burauen road.*

construct additional fortified positions near the airfields. He accordingly rearranged the assault troops. The 17th Infantry, less the 3d Battalion, with the 2d Battalion, 184th Infantry, attached, was ordered to pass through the 184th and 32d Infantry Regiments at 0830 on 23 October, attack west astride the Dulag–Burauen road, and capture the San Pablo airfield. The 767th Tank Battalion, in support of the regiment, was either to precede the 17th Infantry or to operate with it, as the terrain permitted. It was to jump off from the vicinity of the Dulag airfield thirty minutes earlier than the assault units of the 17th Infantry. The 32d and 184th Infantry Regiments were to follow 1,000 yards behind the 17th.[22] It was

[22] 7th Div FO 11, 22 Oct 44.

hoped that this "flying wedge" formation would catch the Japanese off balance and that the rear elements of the wedge would be able to take care of any disorganized enemy units that had been bypassed.

On to Burauen

The flying wedge was very successful. The tanks of the 767th Tank Battalion moved out at 0730 on the morning of 23 October. Though one of the tanks was knocked out about 3,000 yards west of Julita at 1000, the others reached the western edge of Burauen at 1712 and scattered the enemy forces in that area. At 0800 the assault units of the 17th Infantry jumped off, 400 yards to the rear of the tank battalion. Because of the narrow front the column of troops was elongated, and it was not until shortly after 0900 that the 1st Battalion, 32d Infantry, was able to move forward. Because of the difficult terrain and the blazing heat, the infantrymen experienced difficulty in keeping up with the tanks. The troops encountered sporadic opposition during the day, passed rapidly through the barrios of Julita and San Pablo, and secured San Pablo airfield. At 1115 General Arnold notified Colonel Logie that the 32d Infantry was to be responsible for the right flank of the 7th Division's zone of action, less the 200-yard front covered by the 17th Infantry.

At 1700 the units prepared their night perimeters, the 1st Battalion of the 32d, 400 yards south of the San Pablo airstrip; the 3d Battalion, 1,500 yards north of Julita; and the 2d Battalion in division reserve, 500 yards southeast of Julita.[23] At the same time the 17th Infantry was on the west end of the San Pablo airfield.[24] The 184th Infantry, minus the 2d Battalion, was south of the highway between San Pablo and Julita. During the day's action, the commanding officer of the Japanese *20th Infantry Regiment* was killed.[25] The action for the next few days resolved itself into two separate engagements—the seizure of the Buri airstrip and the battle for Dagami.

Securing the XXIV Corps Beachhead Line

Burauen

The 7th Division attacked at 0830 on 24 October, using the same formation employed on the previous day except that the

1st Battalion, 184th Infantry, reverted to regimental reserve. The 1st and 2d Battalions, 17th Infantry, continued along the road to Burauen; the 32d Infantry crossed San Pablo airfield and then went to the right in a north-northwest direction toward the Buri airstrip. The 2d Battalion, 17th Infantry, fought its way through the northeastern part of the town of Burauen and managed to reach the road to Dagami. As the main part of Burauen is south and west of the road, the barrio was in the zone of the 1st Battalion, 17th Infantry, which was advancing along the left side of the road.

The 17th Infantry reached the edge of Burauen at 1030. As the troops explored the situation, they found that though there was no organized resistance in the town, scattered throughout Burauen were elements of the *20th Infantry Regiment,* dug in under the buildings in spider holes and armed with satchel charges, Bangalor torpedoes made of bamboo, and antitank mines.[26]

As the American tanks moved through the barrio, some of the Japanese jumped out of their spider holes and held explosive charges against the tanks in an attempt to destroy them at the cost of their own lives. The assault forces of the 17th Infantry, despite the difficulty of flushing the enemy from the spider holes under the buildings, made steady progress and by 1400 had mopped up and secured the town. The battalions re-formed and were ready to go north to Dagami.

The Buri Airstrip

At 0800 on 24 October, Colonel Logie was transferred to the headquarters of the 7th Division and Lt. Col. John M. Finn

---

[23] 32d Inf Opns Rpt Leyte, p. 6.
[24] 7th Div G–3 Periodic Rpt 4, 23 Oct 44.
[25] *35th Army* Opns, p. 28.

[26] 17th Inf Opns Rpt Leyte, The Battle for Dagami, Annex A, p. 1.

BURAUEN *is searched for the enemy by troops of the 17th Infantry.*

assumed command of the 32d Infantry. Colonel Finn ordered the 1st Battalion, 32d Infantry, to advance to positions across the San Pablo airfield and then continue the attack northwest toward the Buri airstrip. The 2d Battalion remained in division reserve.

The Buri airfield was northeast of Burauen, with a heavily wooded area on its northern edge. On the northern and western edges the Japanese had constructed pillboxes in the high grass and heavy brush, together with mutually supporting machine gun pillboxes interlaced with extensive trench systems. On the southern side of the airstrip the enemy had twenty strong field fortifications. Approximately 1,000 enemy troops were defending the sector—elements of the *20th Infantry Regiment,* the *98th Airfield Battalion,* and the *54th Airfield*

Company. The airfield had been extensively mined with 100-pound aerial bombs buried nose up in the runway and scattered throughout the dispersal area. Some of these bombs had electric fuzes and could be detonated by enemy troops hidden in foxholes a short distance away.[27]

The 1st Battalion, 32d Infantry, met no resistance as it moved out from the vicinity of the San Pablo airstrip at 1123, but when the battalion was 1,000 yards northwest of the airfield it ran into well-camouflaged enemy positions. About 1400 the battalion attacked the emplacements with Company A on the right, Company C on the left, and Company B in reserve on the right rear of Company A. In the face of intense enemy resistance, Company A moved forward and

---

[27] 7th Inf Div Opns Rpt Leyte, p. 7.

placed heavy rifle and machine gun fire on the Japanese positions, which crumpled under the attack.[28]

Although Company C fought valiantly to keep abreast of Company A, the bulk of the enemy strength was in front of it. Heavy machine gun fire on its left flank and in front pinned the company down and kept it from moving forward. This delay created a gap between the two companies which a platoon from Company B was ordered to fill.

When he found that Company C could not move, Major Mathias, commander of the 1st Battalion, started out to locate Company A but was wounded before he could reach it. Maj. Robert C. Foulston, Jr., the battalion's executive officer, assumed command of the battalion as Major Mathias was evacuated.

Intense enemy rifle and machine gun fire hit both of the flanks and the front of Company C and forced the company to start a confused withdrawal. The 2d Platoon pulled back, but four of its men were cut off from the others and went the wrong way. These men, picking up another who was seriously wounded, proceeded three quarters of a mile behind the Japanese lines before they discovered their mistake. To cover the withdrawal of the rest of the company a holding force, consisting of one platoon from Company C and one platoon from Company B, together with a section of heavy machine guns, was set up about 500 yards to the rear of Company C.

As Company C started its withdrawal, the enemy moved forward. Keeping well concealed, the Japanese edged forward and laid down a heavy volume of rifle, machine gun, and mortar fire on the troops, but the holding force stopped the advance. An in-tense fire fight broke out in which both sides suffered many casualties. The Americans held on grimly.

At 1530 Colonel Finn ordered the 3d Battalion, 32d Infantry, to move to the left of the 1st Battalion, but the swamps and heavy foliage made progress slow. By 1630 the 3d Battalion was 600 yards to the left rear of the 1st Battalion.

During the fight Colonel Finn went forward. Grasping the seriousness of the situation, he ordered the 1st Battalion to withdraw to San Pablo airstrip and sent one platoon of the 3d Battalion to assist the 1st Battalion in its withdrawal. The rest of the 3d Battalion was to protect the withdrawal of the 1st. The troops rapidly carried out the orders and withdrew to the airstrip. The 2d Battalion, released from division reserve that evening, moved up on line with the 3d Battalion. The 32d Infantry formed a defensive perimeter for the night.[29]

During the day the 2d Battalion, 32d Infantry, captured a Japanese private, Isamu Nakamaru, who had been a mechanic with the *7th Independent Tank Company.* He informed his captors that his company originally had eleven tanks. Eight of these were lost in the action near Julita; the others were at Buri but were out of commission. All the tanks were obsolete and had been used mainly to clear and roll the airstrips.[30]

On the morning of 25 October the 49th Field Artillery Battalion fired concentrations from 0800 to 0830 in front of the 32d Infantry and covered an area of 400 yards on each side of the Buri airstrip.[31] At 0700 the 3d Battalion moved to the right and in front of the 1st. The 32d Infantry was to

[28] 32d Inf Opns Rpt Leyte, p. 7.

[29] *Ibid.,* pp. 7–8.
[30] Attachment to 7th Div G–2 Periodic Rpt 5, 24 Oct 44.
[31] 49th FA Bn Opns Rpt Leyte, p. 4.

move out at 0830 with the 2d and 3d Battalions abreast, each battalion to be preceded by a platoon of tanks.

At 0830 the battalions attacked, both advancing 1,500 yards before they encountered any serious obstacle. The 2d Battalion on the right ran into the system of bunkers that protected the Buri airstrip. The 3d Battalion halted and waited for the 2d to overcome the bunkers and move forward. Though an antitank gun was brought up to fire on the bunkers, two futile attacks were launched against them and it became apparent that the 2d Battalion would be considerably delayed. Colonel Finn therefore ordered the 3d Battalion to advance and secure the edge of the Buri airstrip, and, with its reserve company, to close the gap thus created.

Colonel Finn also ordered the 1st Battalion to move closer to the right flank of the 3d and prevent an enemy envelopment. Meanwhile, strong patrols which the 3d Battalion had sent to within 300 yards of the airstrip reported that they had encountered only one strong point in the 3d Battalion's zone of advance. In order that the 3d Battalion could be certain it was moving in the direction of the airstrip, Colonel Finn requested an artillery liasion plane to drop a flare over the southwest edge of the airfield. After this was done the battalion resumed its attack and at 1700 reached the edge of the airstrip. Fortunately the battalion immediately went into a defensive position, for at 1715 a sharp enemy assault had to be repulsed with machine gun and rifle fire.[32]

Meanwhile the 2d Battalion probed at the bunkers located at the edge of the heavy woods on the northern fringe of the Buri airfield. These defenses consisted of three bunkers connected by an elaborate system of trenches and spider holes. Both flanks of the 2d Battalion received machine gun fire, which became heavier upon any attempt to carry out an enveloping movement. Under cover of fire from American heavy machine guns, the 2d Battalion withdrew its wounded. It then formed a night perimeter and waited for heavier supporting weapons to be brought up.

On the following day the 2d Battalion was to move from its night perimeter on a 400-yard front and secure the western end of the airstrip. The 3d Battalion, 32d Infantry, was to follow the 1st Battalion and protect the regiment from an attack from the north. Each of the assault battalions was to have attached a platoon of medium tanks and a platoon from the Cannon Company.[33]

On the morning of 26 October, the 49th Field Artillery Battalion for ten minutes concentrated its fire for 500 yards on each side of the airstrip. At 0800 the 32d Infantry attacked. The artillery fire had been effective, and the 2d Battalion knocked out the pillboxes that had stopped its advance the previous day. Aided by tanks, the battalion was able to advance 700 yards along the south side of the airstrip by 1700.

The 1st battalion, on the right, passed through the 3d and attacked west on the north side of the airstrip on a 400-yard front toward the other end of the airstrip. The 1st Battalion immediately encountered a highly intricate system of pillboxes and bunkers, which slowed the attack until the tanks arrived. From that time on, a fiercely contested struggle continued throughout the afternoon. The battalion employed tanks,

---

[32] 32d Inf Opns Rpt Leyte, p. 8.

[33] 32d Inf FO 6, 25 Oct 44.

antitank guns, artillery, and mortars to cover its advance, and destroyed many bunkers with grenades, demolition charges, and automatic rifles.[34]

Company B bore the brunt of the assault and, fighting tenaciously, had battled through 900 yards of the fortified area by 1700. The 1st and 2d Battalions made contact on the edge of the airstrip and formed their night perimeters; the 3d Battalion protected the rear. During the night the 32d Infantry repulsed several light counterattacks.

On the following day, 27 October, the time for the attack was set an hour earlier in the hope that the Japanese would be caught off guard. At 0700 the 32d Infantry moved out, with the assault battalions in the same formation as on the previous day.[35] To their happy surprise the troops encountered little opposition as they readily secured bunker after bunker. The *20th Infantry Regiment* had spent its strength. The American troops found enemy dead "in every bunker, trench, foxhole and bush," and wreckage of enemy 75's, machine guns, grenade launchers, and rifles was scattered about. More than 400 Japanese dead were found in the sector of the 1st Battalion.[36] The infantrymen encountered only an occasional rifleman while mopping up. By 1130 the Buri airstrip was secured.

On 28 October the 2d Battalion was alerted to move to Abuyog at 0400 on the following day. The 3d Battalion was ordered to move to Guinarona for possible attachment to the 17th Infantry, which had committed all three of its battalions in the fight north along the Burauen–Dagami road.

On to Dagami

After securing the barrio of Burauen at 1300 on 24 October, the 17th Infantry had rested for an hour before attacking along the Burauen–Dagami road.[37] The 2d Battalion, 184th Infantry, remained attached to the 17th. As the 17th Infantry started north, a patrol of four jeeps was sent ahead to reconnoiter. It encountered a strong force of the enemy on a road that forked off to the Buri airfield, and after a short but determined fire fight the enemy withdrew north. On its return the patrol reported that the road to Dagami had been mined with aircraft bombs that were buried nose up in the road and covered with palm fronds and other vegetation. A platoon from Company A, 13th Engineer Battalion, removed the mines and the column continued forward.

About 1530 the right flank of the 17th Infantry came under mortar and machine gun fire which came from a ridge north of Burauen and east of the road to Dagami. The ridge was about 700 yards long, 50 feet high, heavily wooded, and covered with dense undergrowth. Most of the fire seemed to be coming from an eastern spur that overlooked the Bayug and Buri airfields. On the left (west) of the road the terrain was flat and marshy.

At 1630 the 17th Infantry began to form its night perimeter on the southern edge of the ridge. The 1st Battalion protected the left (west) flank and tied in at the road with the regiment's 2d Battalion. The lines of the 2d Battalion, 17th Infantry, covered the forward line of the ridge that extended

---

[34] 32d Inf Opns Rpt Leyte, p. 9.
[35] 32d Inf FO 7, 27 Oct 44.
[36] 32d Inf Opns Rpt Leyte, p. 9.

[37] Unless otherwise stated the material on the drive to Dagami is based on 17th Inf Opns Rpt Leyte, Annex A, The Battle for Dagami, pp. 1–9.

to the rear where the 2d Battalion, 184th Infantry, held the entrance to the eastern finger. The perimeter of the 2d Battalion, 184th Infantry, extended south to tie in with the 1st Battalion, 17th Infantry.

Only the 1st Battalion, 17th Infantry, was able to set up its night perimeter without incident. The 2d Battalion, 184th Infantry, ran into determined resistance but was able to establish a firm bivouac for itself, using the vacated enemy positions. The 2d Battalion, 17th Infantry, received scattered rifle fire but did not encounter any of the enemy. During the night the 2d Battalion, 184th Infantry, and the 2d Battalion, 17th Infantry, were harassed by patrols of ten to twenty Japanese each, probing for a break in the lines.

Shortly after nightfall there were two abortive charges against the American lines. As soon as the troops heard the enemy, they called for protective fire, which prevented any of the Japanese from entering the lines. The enemy, however, continually fired into the area throughout the night. Earlier in the day an American tank had bogged down in a swamp to the left of the road, and the crew was forced to abandon it under fire, leaving the guns intact. During the night the Japanese captured the tank and sprayed the areas of the 1st Battalion, 17th Infantry, and the regimental command post with the tank's 37-mm. and machine guns, and with four of their own machine guns. Fortunately the bullets passed harmlessly over the heads of the troops.

During the night Lt. Col. Francis T. Pachler discussed plans for the following day, 25 October, with his battalion commanders. He was faced with a choice between two courses of action. On the one hand, he could take advantage of the tactical surprise occasioned by his rapid advance,

attempt to bypass the Japanese forces on the ridge, and make a dash along the Burauen–Dagami road, disregarding losses that might be inflicted on his flank; or, on the other hand, he could destroy the enemy forces on the ridge before advancing to Dagami. The first alternative must allow for a strong possibility that fire from the 32d Infantry, which was pushing west, might fall upon the 17th Infantry if it continued its advance before the Buri airfield was secured. After prolonged discussion, Pachler decided to destroy the enemy forces on the ridge before proceeding to Dagami.

Colonel Pachler therefore ordered the 1st Battalion, 17th Infantry, to remain in its present position until the 2d Battalion, echeloned to its right rear, could swing up on line facing north. While waiting for the 2d Battalion to move up, the 1st Battalion would send a strong reconnaissance patrol along the road north to the barrio of Buri to determine Japanese strength, and the condition of the road and terrain. The 2d Battalion, 184th Infantry, would attack and destroy the enemy force on the finger of the ridge and then come up, also facing north.

The patrol moved out at 0730 on 25 October. A rifle platoon mounted the tops and sides of five tanks and headed north towards Buri. On its way, the platoon encountered and killed Japanese troops who were emplaced in spider holes and coconut log pillboxes under buildings, but a destroyed bridge at the edge of Buri prevented any further advance. The platoon returned at nightfall with the report that the road to Buri was clear and that it had killed forty-nine of the enemy.

The 2d Battalion, 17th Infantry, made its move without incident. The 2d Battalion, 184th Infantry, advancing from its position on the heavily wooded eastern finger of the ridge, was forced to meet and destroy the enemy force with bayonets and grenades. Its progress was slow until a platoon of the Cannon Company and a platoon of medium tanks made a wide encircling movement through the Bayug airstrip and were able to bring fire to bear on the Japanese. By 1300 the enemy threat was removed and the battalion commenced its swing to the north to join the other two battalions. At dusk the three units were in line; the combat teams had advanced 400 yards and formed their night perimeters.

At 1700 Colonel Pachler rearranged his troops and made plans for the following day. The 2d Battalion, 184th Infantry, was detached to guard the ridge. The 3d Battalion, 17th Infantry, which had been guarding the divisional left flank south of Dao since A Day, was brought forward by truck to rejoin the regiment. The 17th Infantry would move out along the highway in a column of battalions—the 1st, 2d, and 3d.[38]

The 1st Battalion, 17th Infantry, moved out at 0700, Company A on the left (west) and Company C on the right (east). Since the tanks were forced to remain on the road because of swamps on either side, tank support was reduced to a platoon. After having moved about 300 yards beyond the line of departure, Company C ran into a small pocket of enemy resistance which it soon destroyed with hand grenades and small arms fire; twenty-one of the enemy were killed and one was captured. Company A also met and overcame some resistance from enemy in foxholes in its zone, but was not held up. At 1000 the 1st Battalion received machine gun fire to its front and observed a movement in the marsh on its right flank.

When the heavy machine guns and 81-mm. mortars were brought to bear upon the marsh, approximately sixty Japanese began to run across the open fields. The 4.2-inch mortars of the 91st Chemical Company also fired on the fleeing enemy.

When the forward elements were about 1,100 yards south of Ginogusan, Company A encountered a rice paddy to its front. One platoon of the company went left to move around the rice field, and the support platoon was committed to close the gap thus created. As the leading elements got past the field, an enemy force, which was entrenched just beyond it, started firing. The rear elements of the 1st Battalion immediately closed in and killed fifteen of the enemy with grenades and small arms fire. In the meantime, Company C encountered about twenty-five Japanese who had dug in under native shacks. Two tanks were called up, and after they had knocked over the shacks the infantrymen closed in and destroyed the enemy.

During this action the 3d Platoon of Company F, 2d Battalion, 17th Infantry, reinforced by one squad of the antitank platoon of the battalion Headquarters Company, established a roadblock on one of the roads that led to the Buri airfield. The troops came under rifle and machine gun fire from their front. Within a few minutes the platoon leader and two other men were killed and another man was wounded. The platoon withdrew about one hundred yards and called for an 81-mm. mortar concentration on the area. The rest of Company F was committed against the Japanese south flank.

In the face of heavy fire Company F pushed through the difficult terrain and forced the enemy to withdraw. However, four Japanese machine guns remained in

---

[38] 17th Inf FO 3, 25 Oct 44.

ENGINEER TROOPS *of the 13th Engineer Battalion rebuild a bridge near Burauen.*

position and fired into the company. The leader of the antitank squad, though wounded in both legs, ran back to the battalion command post and asked for tanks in support. A cannon platoon which was sent up silenced the enemy guns. While continuing the fight during the enemy withdrawal, the company evacuated its wounded on improvised bamboo litters.

Company F was then relieved by the 2d Battalion, 184th Infantry, which established a roadblock nearer the main highway. Company F rejoined its battalion and the regiment formed its night perimeter about 600 yards south of Guinarona. The night was comparatively peaceful except for a minor bombing in the 2d Battalion area. The troops of the 17th Infantry were ordered to move out on 27 October in a column of battalions in the following order:

3d, 2d, and 1st, with a distance of 500 yards between battalions.[39] Since aerial photographs showed that all the bridges had been blown, a platoon of the 13th Engineer Battalion was attached to the 3d Battalion.

At 0700 the regiment moved out, with the 3d Battalion in the lead, on a 100-yard front on both sides of the highway. The tanks were forced to stay on the road. The 3d Battalion was able to cross a small stream south of Guinarona, although the bridge had been damaged. When it reached the northern bank of the stream the battalion ran into the enemy. Approximately twenty Japanese were dug in around a schoolhouse, with two machine guns mounted in the building. Company K, the lead company, under cover of machine gun and

---

[39] 17th Inf FO 4, 26 Oct 44.

mortar fire, successfully stormed the school-house and killed seventeen of its defenders. The engineer troops from the 13th Engineer Battalion advanced and quickly repaired the bridge, after which the rest of the 17th Infantry moved forward. Since the bridge north of Guinarona was also damaged, the same tactics were used. The infantrymen of the lead company crossed the stream and stood guard while the engineers repaired the bridge. For 2,500 yards the advance continued, unopposed except for small groups of Japanese. The heavy machine guns of the regiment fired from the flanks of the American forces and covered the swamps on both sides of the road. The 17th Infantry went into night perimeter about 2,200 yards south of Dagami and about 200 yards south of a demolished stone bridge. As the regiment started to dig in, enemy rifle and machine gun fire fell on the front of the 3d Battalion but mortars returned the fire and silenced the enemy. Although there was sporadic air and ground activity during the night, no attempt was made to penetrate the lines of the regiment.

Entrance Into Dagami

The 17th Infantry learned from Japanese prisoners that in addition to elements of the *20th Infantry Regiment* in the Dagami sector, the following units were present: the *2d Battalion, 33d Infantry Regiment* (about 200 men), together with scattered elements of the *16th Engineer Regiment* and the *9th Infantry Regiment.*[40]

The Japanese had firmly established themselves in positions in depth about 1,000 yards south of Dagami. These defenses consisted of mutually supporting pillboxes made of logs and sandbags, from which the Japanese could deliver interlocking bands of machine gun fire. They were situated on higher ground and could be approached only across open rice paddies.[41]

As the American forces came close to Dagami, the 17th Infantry was moving north along the Burauen–Dagami road, and the 382d Infantry, 96th Division, was approaching the road between Dagami and Tanauan.

Lt. Col. Kakuda, the commander of the Japanese *Central Area Unit* of the *20th Infantry Regiment,* issued a series of operational orders. At 1800 on 27 October he ordered the *20th Infantry Regiment* to take a position southwest of Dagami and annihilate the Americans.[42]

The 17th Infantry estimated that there were from 1,500 to 2,500 Japanese in the vicinity to oppose the regiment's advance and that about 500 of these withdrew from Dagami in orderly fashion.[43] The commander of the 17th Infantry prescribed a column of battalions for the attack of 28 October. The 2d Battalion would pass through the 3d Battalion, and the attack north would be in the order of 2d, 1st, and 3d. All of the supporting arms were attached to the 2d Battalion for its attack.[44]

At 0730 the 2d Battalion attacked and immediately met very strong opposition. The stone bridge and road were in the

---

[40] 7th Inf Div G–2 Periodic Rpt 9, 28 Oct 44. Unless otherwise stated the entrance into Dagami is based upon 17th Inf Opns Rpt Leyte, Annex A, The Battle for Dagami, pp. 1–9.

[41] 7th Div Opns Rpt Leyte, p. 9.

[42] *Central Area Unit* Opns Order 2, 27 Oct 44, trans in App. C to Annex 2, 7th Div Opns Rpt Leyte.

[43] 17th Inf FO 5, 27 Oct 44.

[44] These were the Cannon Company, a platoon of the Antitank Company, a platoon of the 13th Engineer Battalion, 767th Tank Battalion, and the 91st Chemical Company minus the 1st and 3d Platoons.

middle of a strip of waist-deep swamp 100 yards wide, which funneled out to form a larger swamp. A crescent-shaped coconut grove lay beyond the swamp, one end in front of the road and the other bent to the south about 800 yards west of the road. The road and the curve in the coconut grove divided the swamp into three segments— one on each side of the road, and the third west of and parallel to the road. In the face of intense rifle, machine gun, and mortar fire coming from an unknown number of Japanese, Company F and three tanks managed to cross the creek. The tanks continued north up the road. As Company F waded through the waist-deep swamp, it pushed through direct enemy fire and past a large tank trap and found a line of pillboxes to its front and left flank.

The company commander ordered his unit to hold its position and then returned south of the bridge to bring up more tanks. The 1st Platoon of Company F moved to the left rear to protect that flank, which was receiving considerable enemy fire. As the company commander rushed back to get the tanks, about twenty Japanese attacked the 1st Platoon in an attempt to envelop the left flank of the company. The platoon leader ordered his men to hold their fire until the enemy was only five yards away, and nearly all of the Japanese were killed in the initial volley. The platoon held its ground to prevent any further enveloping attempts by the Japanese. Meanwhile, Company F's commanding officer found that no tanks were available, since they could not cross the weakened bridge. He returned to Company F and ordered it to retire to the tank trap, reorganize, and evacuate the wounded.

In the meantime, in order to relieve the pressure on Company G (on the right),

which had run into somewhat the same situation, Lt. Col. William B. Moore, the battalion commander, committed Company E to the right (east) flank. Company E initially encountered determined opposition but managed to flank the enemy and assist Company G in its sector. At the same time the engineer troops of the 13th Engineer Battalion, working feverishly under heavy fire, tried to repair the damaged bridge. One of the armored bulldozers lost three drivers, successively, to enemy fire.

Under the close supervision of Colonel Moore, who was in the front lines, the 2d Battalion pressed the attack. Two M8 armored cars were brought wide around the right flank in order to avoid the swamp. With their aid, Companies E and G rolled up the cast flank of the *20th Infantry Regiment* and broke through the pillboxes in their own area.

Company C was committed to the left of Company F in order to aid it. Although this move was partially successful, Company C found itself pinned down by an enemy force entrenched in pillboxes and zigzag trenches. Since the Japanese defense line extended beyond the regiment's left (west) flank and around it to the south, Company B was committed further left to hit the southern flank of the enemy. Although Company B could not break through the line, it was able to locate the enemy right flank and neutralize the fire on that flank.

One of the three tanks that had gone north in the morning returned at 1400 and was guided into the sector of Company F. With all of its guns blazing, the tank broke through the enemy fortifications, and Companies C and F were then able to move in and mop up the enemy. The other two tanks had gone up the road some 250 yards when they met antitank fire which completely destroyed one and immobilized the other, trapping its crew. As soon as the bridge was made passable, two M8's, a medium tank, and a squad from Company F were sent to rescue the trapped crew. While the medium tank and the infantry covered the damaged tank, the M8's drew up to it and allowed its crew to escape into their open turrets. The detail withdrew, having suffered no casualties, and the immobilized tank was then destroyed.

At dusk the 2d Battalion, 17th Infantry, and the committed companies from the 1st Battalion pushed some 300 yards beyond the enemy strong point and formed a perimeter defense for the night.[45] Company B on the far left flank was withdrawn and closed into the perimeter. Although machine gun and mortar fire came from the left line of fortifications, there was no major action on the part of the Japanese. A few of the enemy, attempting to crawl through a trench into the position of Company F, became ensnarled in the concertina wire and were then destroyed by grenades.

Since the 2d Battalion had borne the brunt of the fighting on 28 October and had suffered numerous casualties, the regimental commander decided to have the battalion drop back into reserve. Although the drive to Dagami was to continue, the north-south line of enemy pillboxes on the left flank of the regiment could not be ignored. At 0800 on 29 October the regimental lines were to

be reorganized so that the 3d and 1st Battalions, less Company B, would pass through the 2d Battalion, which would become the regimental reserve. Company B with a platoon of M8's would attack the flank and rear of the enemy in the left line of pillboxes.

At 0800, under cover of a heavy artillery concentration from the 49th Field Artillery Battalion, the 1st and 3d Battalions, 17th Infantry, passed through the 2d Battalion without incident. Company B, reinforced by the platoon from the Cannon Company, moved out to destroy the enemy force on the regiment's left flank. The company fought the Japanese from pillbox to pillbox, catching the enemy on his flanks and rear by rifle and machine gun fire, together with time-burst fire from the self-propelled howitzers. This completely demoralized the Japanese, some of whom threw down their arms and tried unsuccessfully to escape. More than 120 enemy dead were counted in the area. The 1st Battalion entered the southern part of Dagami without encountering serious resistance. It then came under artillery fire from the hills west of the town.

The 3d Battalion proceeded east of the road in a column of companies in the order L, K, and I, and met no serious opposition until it reached a cemetery south of Dagami. Overgrown with weeds seven to ten feet high and containing stone crypts built off the ground, the cemetery was divided by a path running east to west. As Company L moved into the burial ground, Company I swung around the right (east) side to come into position for the night. The leading elements of Company L passed through the cemetery and Company I moved into position without incident, but as the 1st Platoon of Company L, the reserve platoon, crossed the path, a headstone tilted back and from the open grave four Japanese opened fire

---

[45] During the day's action, Pfc. Leonard C. Brostrom of Company F and Pfc. John F. Thorson of Company G so distinguished themselves that they were awarded the Medal of Honor. Private Brostrom singlehandedly destroyed a pillbox and killed six Japanese before collapsing from his wounds. Private Thorson sacrificed his life to save his comrades by throwing himself upon an enemy grenade that landed in his platoon's defensive position.

with an American Browning automatic rifle and other small arms. The small arms of the 1st Platoon had no effect and it became necessary to bring forward a flame thrower to burn the enemy out. At the same time the platoon received fire from other open graves, from which the Japanese had removed the bodies. By punching holes through the stone they used the crypts as individual foxholes. The platoon broke into small units and pushed through the cemetery, destroying the enemy forces wherever they could be located.

Company K, which followed Company I, placed two platoons abreast behind Company L. As it came through the weeds past the cemetery path a Japanese officer charged on the right flank with his saber and wounded one man before he could be brought down. Since the platoons were also receiving heavy fire from the tombs, the commander of Company K drew his men back to the path where they reorganized. Preceded by a battery of six flame throwers, the men then marched shoulder to shoulder through the cemetery and burnt out the enemy. About 1900 the regiment completed the action and formed its night perimeter.

During the fighting, the regimental operations officer, hearing the heavy fire and not being able to communicate with the 3d Battalion headquarters, called Company K direct to ascertain if the Japanese had broken through the American lines. "Hell no," was the reported reply, "we're breaking through theirs and fighting for our bivouac." [46] During the night small infiltration parties of Japanese tried unsuccessfully to penetrate the regiment's defenses, and sporadic artillery fire was received from the hills west of Dagami.

---

[46] 17th Inf Opns Rpt, Battle for Dagami, App., p. 9.

By 1040 on 30 October Dagami was securely in American hands, and the 17th Infantry continued to mop up for the rest of the day. The 19th Infantry Regiment of the 24th Division, X Corps, across the Binahaan River north of Dagami, was reached by an airdrop message from the artillery spotter plane, and patrols reached the 382d Infantry of the 96th Division on the east. The mission of the 17th Infantry Regiment—securing the town of Dagami and effecting junction with the X Corps and the 96th Division—was completed. The regiment spent the next two days in mopping up and patrolling the area around Dagami.

The 7th Division had secured the limits of its beachhead line, but the southern approaches to the line had not yet been secured. The road farther south, running across the island from Abuyog on the east coast to Baybay on the west coast, offered a potential route along which the Japanese might pour in reinforcements.

At 0530 on 29 October the 2d Battalion, 32d Infantry, left Burauen for Abuyog via Dao and the coastal road, Highway 1. Its progress was impeded by muddy roads and the previous destruction of the bridge over the Bito River. The battalion, less one company, crossed the river by DUKW's at 0940 and by 1000 was in Abuyog, having encountered no Japanese. The 7th Cavalry Reconnaissance Troop, acting as an advance guard for the battalion, pushed west from Abuyog inland four miles on the road toward Baybay.

On 30 and 31 October the 2d Battalion, 32d Infantry, remained at Abuyog, but on the latter day it sent Company G, reinforced, toward Baybay on the Abuyog–Baybay road, which corkscrewed through the mountains for about twenty-seven miles between the east and west coasts. The company encountered no Japanese. On 1 November no forward progress was made, but all elements of the 2d Battalion, 32d Infantry, patrolled. On 2 November Company G moved along the road and closed in on Baybay at 2200.

Far to the south the 21st Infantry Regiment, 24th Division, had been engaged since A Day in extensive patrolling of the Panaon Strait area. On 31 October the 1st Battalion, 32d Infantry, left the Bayug airfield for Dulag and at 2200 sailed from Dulag to relieve the 21st Infantry. The battalion arrived at Panaon Island at 0700 on 1 November and during the day effected the relief of the 21st Infantry, which then moved north to rejoin the 24th Division.[47]

The initial mission of the 7th Infantry Division—to land between the Calbasag and Daguitan Rivers, advance rapidly inland along the axis of the Dulag–Burauen road, seize hostile airstrips in its zone of action, secure the Burauen–Dagami road, and protect the XXIV Corps' left (south) flank—had been accomplished.

Since landing, the 7th Division had killed an estimated 4,211 Japanese and had taken 19 prisoners.[48] Up to 1000 on 1 November, 32 officers and 290 enlisted men of the division had been killed; 48 officers, 1 warrant officer, and 777 enlisted men wounded; 15 officers and 223 enlisted men injured; and 21 enlisted men were missing in action.[49]

By 2 November, General Hodge's XXIV Corps had finished its assigned role for the second phase of General Krueger's plan for the capture of the island of Leyte. It had seized the southern part of Leyte Valley with its important roads, airfields, and potential base sites. An element of the corps had pushed to the west coast of the island, and was preparing for the move toward the important port of Ormoc as part of the third phase of the plan. General Makino had been forced to give up his Dagami headquarters and other positions on the heights overlooking the town. Far to the north, the X Corps was engaged in securing the northern part of Leyte Valley.

[47] 7th Div G–3 Periodic Rpts 10–14, 29 Oct–2 Nov 44.

[48] 7th Div G–2 Periodic Rpt 13, 2 Nov 44.
[49] 7th Div G–1 Weekly Rpt 2, 31 Oct 44, Incl 2, Part 2, 1 Nov 44; 7th Div Opns Rpt Leyte, G–1 Rpt.

CHAPTER IX

Northern Leyte Valley: Part One

By the evening of 20 October the Tacloban airfield and Hill 522, overlooking the town of Palo at the northern entrance to Leyte Valley, were in the hands of the X Corps. The night of 20–21 October was free from enemy activity in the sector of the 1st Cavalry Division, and the exhausted troops were able to obtain an unquiet rest during their first night in the Philippines. Having secured the Tacloban airfield they were in position to march on Tacloban, the capital of Leyte, the following morning. Tacloban is situated on a peninsula at the head of San Pedro Bay. A string of low hills, stretching from Anibong Point along the base of the peninsula to the southeast, commands the approaches to the town.[1] Throughout the night the 61st Field Artillery Battalion delivered harassing fires on the hills south of the town.[2] (*Map 7*)

San Juanico Strait

Drive Toward Caibaan

General Krueger wished to push rapidly through Leyte Valley and secure its important roads and airfields before the Japanese could regroup and offer a firm line of resistance. In the north, securing San Juanico Strait would prevent any of the enemy from crossing over from Samar. Control of the road that led through the interior of northern Leyte Valley would give the possessor a firm hold on the northern part of the valley. With a successful two-pronged attack—elements of the 1st Cavalry Division driving north along San Juanico Strait and units of the 24th Infantry Division pushing along Highway 2—the X Corps would arrive at Carigara Bay. At that point the corps would be in position to contest any Japanese amphibious movement through Carigara Bay, and at the same time elements of the corps could drive south through Ormoc Valley and secure the important port of Ormoc.

Preceded by a naval and air bombardment and a preparation by the 61st Field Artillery Battalion,[3] the 1st Cavalry Division at 0800 on 21 October resumed the assault against the Japanese.[4] The division was to capture Tacloban and then secure control over San Juanico Strait.[5] The 7th Cavalry, 2d Brigade, had been assigned the mission of seizing Tacloban,[6] which was defended by elements of the Japanese *33d Infantry Regiment*.[7]

On the morning of 21 October the 1st Squadron, 7th Cavalry, joined the regi-

---

[1] 7th Cav Opns Rpt Leyte, Part II, Annex 2, Terrain Study of Operational Areas, pp. 1–3.
[2] 1st Cav Div Arty Opns Rpt Leyte, p. 2.

[3] *Ibid.*, p. 3.
[4] 1st Cav Div Msgs to X Corps, 21 Oct 44.
[5] 1st Cav Div FO 1, 2 Oct 44.
[6] 7th Cav Opns Rpt Leyte, p. 4.
[7] *35th Army* Opns, p. 28.

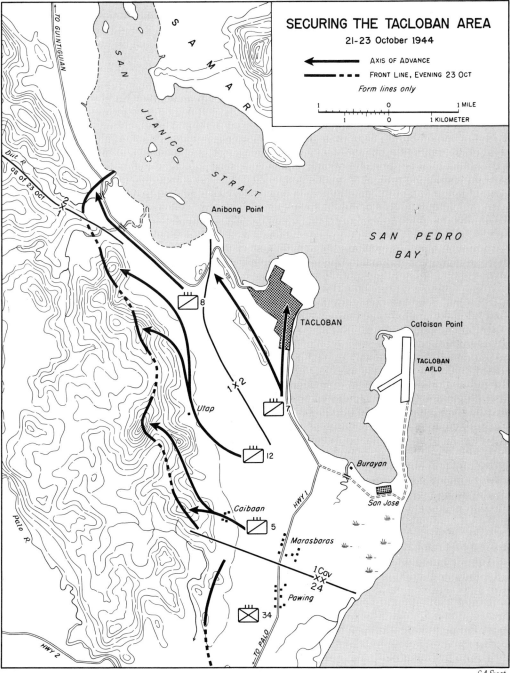

SECURING THE TACLOBAN AREA
21-23 October 1944

AXIS OF ADVANCE

FRONT LINE, EVENING 23 OCT

Form lines only

1 MILE

1 KILOMETER

S A M A R

SAN JUANICO STRAIT

TO GUINTIGUAN

Diit R. as of 23 Oct

Anibong Point

SAN   PEDRO
BAY

TACLOBAN

Cataisan Point

TACLOBAN
AFLD

Utap

Burayan

San Jose

Palo R.

Caibaan

Marasbaras

Pawing

HWY 1

TO PALO

C.A.Frost

MAP 7

ment's 2d Squadron in a drive on Tacloban. At 0800 the 7th Cavalry moved with squadrons abreast, the 1st Squadron on the right and the 2d Squadron on the left, astride the highway leading to Tacloban. Although the squadrons found the terrain extremely swampy and movement difficult, by 1400 the 1st Squadron was on the outskirts of the town and the 2d was halted at the foot of a hill overlooking Tacloban. The Japanese had dug into the hills overlooking the capital. The division artillery then shelled the hill and the high ground to the north.[8] At 1500 the fire was lifted and the forward movement proceeded.

The men of the 1st Squadron entered Tacloban to conduct a house-to-house search for concealed Japanese. They received a tumultuous welcome from the Filipinos who lined the sides of the narrow streets, waving American flags and urging gifts of eggs and fruit upon the troopers.[9] They were also welcomed by the governor of the province. The 2d Squadron, on the other hand, was held up by an estimated 200 Japanese who were entrenched in pillboxes and foxholes and behind the dense vegetation that covered the hilly area. As heavy fire from the enemy pinned down the troops, Col. Walter H. Finnegan, the regiment's commanding officer, sent the Antitank Platoon and elements of the Regimental Weapons Troop in support of the 2d Squadron, where that unit faced the southern end of the hill mass.[10]

The Weapons Troop was ordered to lay aside its automatic weapons and assault the hill with rifles, but it was pinned down by intense fire from an enemy bunker to the immediate front. Pfc. Kenneth W. Grove,

an ammunition carrier, volunteered to clear the Japanese from the position. He worked his way through the underbrush to the flank of the bunker, then charged in the open against its front and killed the gun crew.[11] The advance then continued.

The movements of the Weapons Troop and the Antitank Platoon were successful, and by 1800 the southern half of the hill and the town of Tacloban were in American hands. Shortly after the seizure of the capital, General Mudge, the division commander, inspected the town from a medium tank. At one point, where the Japanese had turned over a truck to form a roadblock, the general personally received the surrender of forty Formosan laborers.[12] The regimental command post was established in the building that had housed the Leyte Intermediate School for Girls.

The following day, after an intensive mortar, artillery, and air bombardment on a hill southwest of Tacloban, the 2d Squadron of the 7th Cavalry moved out against the hill at 0820. Although the terrain was rugged, the position was overrun by 1100. The 1st Squadron spent the day mopping up the town in search of the enemy. At 1108 General Mudge released the 8th Cavalry, commanded by Colonel Bradley, to 2d Brigade control.

By the end of 22 October the capital of Leyte and its hill defenses were securely in American hands. The 7th Cavalry was one day ahead of schedule, a fact partly explained by the unexpectedly light resistance of the Japanese and partly by the vigor of the 7th Cavalry's advance.[13]

On the morning of 22 October the 8th Cavalry made a "victory" march through

---

[8] 1st Cav Div Arty Opns Rpt Leyte, p. 3.
[9] 1st Cav Div Opns Rpt Leyte, pp. 19–20.
[10] 7th Cav Opns Rpt Leyte, p. 4.

[11] He was awarded the Silver Star.
[12] X Corps Opns Rpt Leyte, p. 18.
[13] 2d Cav Brig Opns Rpt Leyte, pp. 3–4.

A PATROL FROM THE 7TH CAVALRY *moves along Avenida Rizal in Tacloban (above). Flag-waving Filipinos greet the American troops (below).*

MAJ. GEN. VERNE D. MUDGE *(in tank) confers with Brig. Gen. William C. Chase in Tacloban.*

liberated Tacloban and went into perimeter to the west of the 7th Cavalry on the hills overlooking the town. Troop C went to Anibong Point in order to guard the brigade flank from a suspected Japanese barge landing through San Juanico Strait.

Shortly after the command post was opened at 1830, the 8th Cavalry received orders for the 1st Squadron to depart at 0700 on the following day. It was to pass through the 7th Cavalry and secure the bridge crossing the Diit River so as to protect the 2d Squadron, 8th Cavalry. The latter was directed to move northwest across the mountains, seize Santa Cruz, which was on Carigara Bay about sixteen miles northwest of Tacloban, and locate the remnants

of the Japanese who had opposed the 7th Cavalry in its advance through the city.

The 1st Squadron, 8th Cavalry, passed through the 7th Cavalry at 0900 on the morning of 23 October. By nightfall the squadron had crossed and secured the Diit River bridge and routed small groups of the enemy. The 2d Squadron experienced difficulty in securing Filipino carriers for the trip up the Diit River and across the unmapped and unknown mountains to Santa Cruz. It resolved the situation by driving a truck through the streets and seizing every able-bodied Filipino in sight. These "volunteers" were sufficient to get the squadron to its night bivouac on the Diit River. The "indignant carriers [then] dissolved into the

8-INCH HOWITZERS READIED FOR ACTION *against an enemy strong point southwest of Tacloban.*

jungle."[14] The 2d Squadron established its perimeter near the village of Diit.

Meanwhile, the 1st Brigade of the 1st Cavalry Division had been ordered to move west on 21 October. This maneuver was designed to protect the southern flank of the 2d Brigade and to prevent the Japanese from reinforcing their troops in Tacloban. The 1st Brigade moved out at 0800 toward Caibaan, the 12th Cavalry on the right and the 5th Cavalry on the left.[15] Troop B of the 12th Cavalry advanced toward the

barrio of Utap, and though it ran into enemy opposition it was able to secure the town after being reinforced by the regimental and brigade reconnaissance platoons. Swampy ground made the going very difficult. The troops captured a large Japanese supply dump which contained quantities of foodstuffs, vehicles, and equipment, and valuable documents.[16]

The 1st and 2d Squadrons of the 5th Cavalry advanced abreast toward Caibaan and the high ground beyond the town. They encountered only sporadic rifle fire in Caibaan but at the foot of one of the hills they met determined opposition from about half a company of Japanese. After an ex-

[14] 8th Cav Opns Rpt Leyte, pp. 6–7.

[15] At 0500 on 21 October Colonel Drake, the commanding officer of the 5th Cavalry, was killed while inspecting the regimental perimeter defenses in the vicinity of Caibaan. 5th Cavalry Opns Rpt Leyte, p. 2.

[16] 1st Cav Div G–3 Periodic Rpt 2, 21 Oct 44.

change of fire, the Japanese signified they wished to surrender by waving a white flag. The heavy machine guns were brought into position and the American soldiers signalled for the Japanese to disrobe in order to forestall their using concealed grenades or other weapons. The Japanese opened fire and wounded five men. The automatic weapons then returned the fire, killing thirteen of the enemy. The remaining Japanese withdrew over the hill, and contact was lost.

There was no enemy activity in the 5th Cavalry's sector during the night of 21–22 October, and at 0645 the advance elements of the 1st Squadron began to move up the steep east slope of a hill west of Caibaan. The squadron continued its advance, and at 1200 engaged in a short skirmish between the hill and Caibaan, killing ten Japanese. The difficult terrain, rather than the Japanese, slowed the advance. Hampered by tall cogon grass, which cut off every breeze, the troops struggled up steep slopes and sharp ridges. Exposed to the hot sun and burdened with equipment and ammunition, they were soon exhausted. At 1447 the 5th Cavalry received orders to halt all forward movement until further notice. The 1st Squadron was in bad condition physically, since it had been steadily on the move for a day and a half and had consumed all its rations and water. At the end of the day, 22 October, the squadron was still at the base of the hill, but the rest of the regiment had reached Caibaan.[17] On the following day elements of the 5th Cavalry were sent to Tacloban to act as a guard of honor for General MacArthur. The other units remained in position.[18]

---

[17] 5th Cav Opns Rpt Leyte, pp. 2–3.
[18] 1st Cav Div G–3 Periodic Rpt 4, 25 Oct 44.

Restoration of Civil Government

The guard of honor, consisting of 1st Lt. John Gregory and thirty enlisted men of the 5th Cavalry, arrived at Tacloban later on 23 October. President Osmeña of the Philippine Commonwealth was also present, having come ashore for the occasion.[19] A simple but impressive ceremony was held in front of the municipal building of Tacloban, though the interior of the edifice was a shambles of broken furniture and scattered papers. A guard of honor of "dirty and tired but efficient-looking soldiers"[20] was drawn up in front of the government building. General MacArthur broadcast an address announcing the establishment of the Philippine Civil Government with President Osmeña as its head. Lt. Gen. Richard K. Sutherland then read the official proclamation. President Osmeña spoke appreciatively of American support and of the determination of the Filipinos to expel the enemy. "To the Color" was sounded on the bugle, and the national flags of the United States and the Philippines were simultaneously hoisted on the sides of the building. Colonel Kangleon of the guerrilla forces was then decorated with the Distinguished Service Cross.

Few Filipinos except representatives of the local government were present for the ceremony. Apparently the inhabitants had not heard of it, or did not know that they were permitted to attend. Information quickly spread, however, that the civil government had assumed control, and as General MacArthur and his party left town the civil population cheered them.[21]

---

[19] 5th Cav Opns Rpt Leyte, p. 3.
[20] Rpt, Capt Ray Tarbuck, USN, Observers Rpt of King II Opn, 3 Nov 44, GHQ G–3 Jnl, 30 Oct 44.
[21] Ibid.

GENERAL MacARTHUR *announces the establishment of the Philippine Civil Govern-ment. Seen in the front row, left to right, are: Lt. Gen. George C. Kenney, Vice Adm. Thomas C. Kinkaid, Lt. Gen. Walter Krueger, Lt. Gen. Richard K. Sutherland, General MacArthur and President Sergio Osmeña.*

Drive up the Strait

Though the 1st Cavalry Division had secured Tacloban and the region surrounding it, there remained the important task of seizing San Juanico Strait to prevent the Japanese from bringing in reinforcements from Samar. San Juanico Strait, connecting the Leyte Gulf with Samar Sea, forms a narrow passage between Leyte and Samar Islands. Highway 1 ends on its western shore, some fourteen miles north of Tacloban at Guintiguian, a small barrio two miles north of San Isidro. A ferry between Guintiguian and La Paz, just across the strait on Samar, links the road networks of the

two islands. The 2d Brigade's mission was to seize Guintiguian on Leyte; La Paz on Samar (including the establishment of a bridgehead on the north bank of the Silaga River, three miles northeast of La Paz); and Babatngon on the north coast of Leyte. By shore-to-shore operations it was also to seize Basey on the island of Samar and the area north and west of it.[22]

General Hoffman had been warned that his 2d Brigade would be assigned the mission of securing San Juanico Strait and possibly landing on Samar; he therefore directed an overwater reconnaissance of the

---

[22] 2d Cav Brig FO, 22 Oct 44.

P R O C L A M A T I O N

TO THE PEOPLE OF THE PHILIPPINES:

I have returned. By the grace of Almighty God
our forces stand again on Philippine soil - soil
consecrated in the blood of our two peoples. We
have come, dedicated and committed, to the task of
destroying every vestige of enemy control over your
daily lives, and of restoring, upon a foundation of
indestructible strength, the liberties of your
people.

At my side is your President, Sergio Osmena,
worthy successor of that great patriot, Manuel Quezon,
with members of his cabinet. The seat of your government is now therefore firmly re-established on Philippine soil.

The hour of your redemption is here. Your
patriots have demonstrated an unswerving and resolute
devotion to the principles of freedom that challenges
the best that is written on the pages of human history.
I now call upon your supreme effort that the enemy may
know from the temper of an aroused and outraged people
within that he has a force there to contend with no
less violent than is the force committed from without.

Rally to me. Let the indomitable spirit of
Bataan and Corregidor lead on. As the lines of battle
roll forward to bring you within the zone of operations,
rise and strike. Strike at every favorable opportunity.
For your homes and hearths, strike! For future genera-
tions of your sons and daughters, strike! In the name
of your sacred dead, strike! Let no heart be faint.
Let every arm be steeled. The guidance of divine God
points the way. Follow in His Name to the Holy Grail
of righteous victory!

DOUGLAS MacARTHUR.

sector. Consequently, on 23 October the staff officers of the 8th Cavalry and of the 1st Squadron of the regiment boarded an LCI at the Tacloban dock. The landing craft made the trip through San Juanico Strait to the barrio of Babatngon on Janabatas Channel without incident. On the return trip, the officers observed some Japanese positions which overlooked the ferry crossing at the Guintiguian landing on Leyte. The party made a brief reconnaissance of the Guintiguian side of the ferry landing and of La Paz on the Samar side. There was no enemy contact.[23]

As a consequence General Hoffman, in issuing his orders for the next day, assigned the following missions: the 1st Squadron, 7th Cavalry, under Maj. Leonard E. Smith would embark at 0630 on 24 October, and move overwater to seize the town of Babatngon. This operation would seal off the western entrance into San Juanico Strait. Troop C, reinforced, of the 1st Squadron, 8th Cavalry, under Maj. F. Raymond King, was also to embark at 0630 from Tacloban and move north to seize the ferry crossing between Guintiguian and La Paz. At the same time the rest of the 1st Squadron, 8th Cavalry, under Lt. Col. Mayers Shore, would drive north along the highway and effect a juncture with C Troop at Guintiguian.[24]

The 1st Squadron, 7th Cavalry, sailed for Babatngon at 1030 on 24 October. The trip was uneventful, and at 1330 the squadron arrived at Babatngon, sent out security patrols, and established a perimeter defense. On 25 October the Japanese launched an air attack, hitting an LCI in the Babatngon harbor. Eight men were killed and seventeen wounded, all of them Navy personnel.[25] For the next few days the 1st Squadron, 7th Cavalry, made a series of overwater movements through Carigara Bay and exploited the lack of any strong Japanese resistance along the northeast coast of the Leyte Valley.[26]

Reinforced Troop C of the 1st Squadron, 8th Cavalry, was ready to sail by 0630 on 24 October but was delayed by a Japanese air attack on the shipping in Tacloban harbor and San Pedro Bay, made by about fifty medium bombers and Army fighters. Before they could reach the beachhead area, many of the Japanese planes were shot down by Navy combat air patrol fliers, who also beat off another wave of about thirty more planes. Two of the American planes crashlanded on the Tacloban airfield, while a third landed in the water.[27] There was minor damage to American shipping.

One of the Japanese planes crashed less than 200 yards from elements of Troop C but the force got under way. The troopers, after running down and killing five Japanese in a canoe, arrived at La Paz, Samar, their destination, without further excitement and established a roadblock on the road leading to Basey.

The 1st Squadron of the 8th Cavalry, which was to travel overland by Highway 1 to make junction with Troop C at the ferry crossing, broke camp at 0700 on the morning of the 24th. The squadron was accompanied by a platoon of light tanks and weapons carriers with rations and ammunition. Since the passage was through enemy-held territory and over unfamiliar terrain,

---

[23] 8th Cav Opns Rpt Leyte, p. 7.
[24] 2d Cav Brig FO 3, 23 Oct 44.

[25] 7th Cav Opns Rpt Leyte, pp. 6–7.
[26] 1st Cav Div Opns Rpt Leyte, pp. 24–25.
[27] Rad, CG Sixth Army to G–2 Sixth Army, Sixth Army G–2 Jnl, 24 Oct 44.

TACLOBAN *from the air (above). Close-up of the dock area (below), showing San Juanico Strait and the island of Samar in the background.*

and since the strength of the Japanese forces was unknown, it was estimated that it would take the squadron a minimum of two days to cover the sixteen and a quarter miles between the two forces. The commanding officer of the squadron, however, by utilizing stream-crossing expedients to the utmost in snaking tanks and vehicles across the many intersecting streams and by driving the troops, was able to complete the difficult march to Guintiguian and go into perimeter with all his men except a rear guard at 2130 on the same day. At the end of 24 October, the 8th Cavalry, less the 2d Squadron, was in a position from which it could defend its beachhead on Samar.[28]

At 2300 an estimated hundred Japanese from the *2d Battalion, 9th Infantry Regiment,* attacked the roadblock which had been established on the road leading to Basey. The Japanese opened up with machine gun fire and tossed several grenades against the position. The defenders repelled the attack with machine gun and mortar fire, but for the remainder of the night "confusion reigned supreme and the odds and ends were not rounded up until the next morning." [29] During the next three days the 8th Cavalry consolidated its position and extended its perimeter to include a bridgehead on the Silaga River.

By the end of 27 October the 1st Cavalry Division had seized Tacloban and gained control of San Juanico Strait. Because of supply difficulties the 2d Brigade on 25 October had ordered the 2d Squadron, 8th Cavalry, to discontinue its movement toward Santa Cruz, to remain in bivouac along the upper reaches of the Diit River and patrol that area. At this time the casualties of the 1st Cavalry Division amounted

to 4 officers and 36 enlisted men killed, 14 officers and 185 enlisted men wounded, and 8 enlisted men missing in action.[30] During the same period, the division reported it had killed 739 of the enemy and had taken prisoner 7 Japanese, 1 Formosan, and 1 Chinese.[31]

The opposition had been light—much lighter than had been expected. Elements of the division had therefore been sent south to reinforce the 24th Division, which had borne the brunt of the Japanese opposition in the X Corps sector in its drive through northern Leyte Valley toward Carigara Bay.

Leyte Valley Entrance

Defense at Pawing

At the end of 20 October the 24th Division had established a firm beachhead near Palo, averaging a mile in depth, and had secured Hill 522 which overlooked Palo.[32] (*Map 8*) The 24th Division was to seize Palo and drive astride the road that ran northwest through the Leyte Valley to Carigara. The 34th Infantry, in the vicinity of Pawing, had its 2d Battalion, commanded by Lt. Col. James F. Pearsall, Jr., 100 yards west of Highway 1, with the northern elements of the battalion in contact with the 5th Cavalry of the 1st Cavalry Division on the right. The 3d Battalion, 34th Infantry, was just short of the highway. The leading elements of the 19th Infantry were on Hill 522.[33]

---

[28] 8th Cav Opns Rpt Leyte, pp. 7–9.
[29] *Ibid.*

[30] 1st Cav Div G–1 Daily Strength Rpts, 20–27 Oct 44; 8th Army Opns Rpt, p. 14.
[31] 1st Cav Div G–3 Periodic Rpt 8, 27 Oct 44.
[32] Unless otherwise stated the subsection is based upon the 24th Div Opns Rpt Leyte, pp. 1–39.
[33] 34th Inf Unit Rpt 1, 21 Oct 44, 34th Inf Jnl, 21 Oct 44.

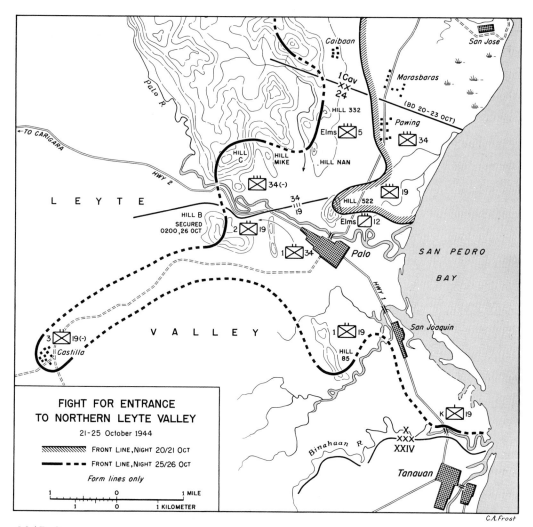

MAP 8

At 0100 on 21 October three companies of Japanese,[34] part of the *33d Infantry Regiment,*[35] under cover of darkness and aided by heavy machine gun and mortar fire, struck from the south along Highway 1. The leading elements made a double envelopment of the American flanks while the main force came down the road and attacked the

[34] 34th Inf Unit Rpt 2, 34th Inf Jnl, 21 Oct 44.
[35] *35th Army* Opns, p. 28.

perimeter of the 2d Platoon of Company G. By 0200 the enemy, still employing machine gun and mortar fire, had pushed to within a few yards of the American positions and had killed or wounded everyone but Pvt. Harold H. Moon, Jr., in the first two positions.

The Japanese then centered their fire upon Private Moon, who, although wounded by this fire, replied with his submachine gun. An enemy officer attempted to throw grenades at Moon's position and was killed. The Japanese then brought up a light machine gun to within twenty yards of his position. Moon called back the range correction to friendly mortars which knocked out the machine gun. For over four hours he held back the enemy. At dawn an entire platoon with fixed bayonets charged toward him. From a sitting position he fired into the Japanese, killed eighteen, and repulsed the attack. He then stood up and threw a grenade at a machine gun that had opened up on his right. He was hit and instantly killed.[36] The Japanese then resumed their attack, but the remnants of Moon's platoon fixed bayonets, charged, and succeeded in breaking through the enemy line.

In the meantime the enemy hit the perimeter of Company L. For several hours the Japanese felt out the company positions, and then, covered by three machine guns, they charged in platoon strength on the east side of the company's perimeter. The company, supported by mortar fire, retaliated and assaulted the Japanese in front of the perimeter. Attempted movements around both the enemy flanks failed. A frontal assault, protected by fire from both flanks, was then successfully made by the company, and the Japanese force was routed. There were 105 enemy dead in the immediate area of the company.

By this time it was dawn, and Pearsall's men began extensive countermeasures. Concentrated mortar fire was laid down, and, since Japanese artillery was shelling the American positions, artillery and air strikes were requested. At 0900 Battery A of the 63d Field Artillery Battalion fired 150 rounds on the Japanese.[37]

At a point 1,500 yards south of Pawing naval flyers from the Seventh Fleet strafed the enemy and, in co-operation with the artillery fire, successfully broke the back of the offensive. The enemy scattered into the rice paddies. Members of the 2d Battalion were then able to go down the road and mop up. More than 600 Japanese were killed during the engagement.[38] Company G, which had borne the brunt of the attack, lost fourteen men killed and had twelve wounded.

The battalion had scarcely finished breakfast when at 1000 it was given the mission of seizing a hill mass immediately west of its position at Pawing. After artillery and naval gunfire had been placed upon the hill for fifteen minutes,[39] E Company was to take the northern knoll of the hill mass and F Company to take the southern knoll. It was not until 1400, however, that the attack jumped off. Company E met no opposition, and within twenty-five minutes was able to occupy its objective.

Company F, commanded by Capt. Paul Austin, had more difficulty. Its objective was a steep hill, heavily covered with cogon grass ten to twelve feet high, which limited visibility to a few feet. A trail ran west from a small clump of trees to the top of the hill, and then south along the crest of the ridge where the grass was only six inches high. The company proceeded west in a column of platoons and at 1430 reached the foot of

---

[36] 24th Div Opns Rpt Leyte, p. 12. Private Moon was posthumously awarded the Medal of Honor.

[37] 63d FA Bn Unit Rpt 1, 21 Oct 44, 63d FA Bn Opns Rpt Leyte.

[38] 24th Div Opns Rpt Leyte, p. 13. This casualty figure from the 24th Division Operations Report seems excessive.

[39] 34th Inf FO 4, 21 Oct 44, 34th Inf Unit Jnl, 21 Oct 44.

TANK-SUPPORTED INFANTRYMEN OF THE 34TH REGIMENT *attack a hill near Pawing.*

the hill. At the western edge of the group of trees, the 1st and 3d Platoons turned left and advanced directly toward the highest point of the hill. The 2d Platoon, with machine guns, continued up the path.

As the 2d Squad of the 1st Platoon reached the crest and as the 1st Squad had nearly done so, an estimated 200 Japanese from the *33d Infantry Regiment* opened fire upon the troops with rifles and two machine guns that were emplaced upon a knoll overlooking the trail. Enemy riflemen also rolled grenades down upon the 1st Squad. These actions pinned down both of the squads.

Protected by the machine gun fire, other enemy riflemen worked north along the reverse slope of the ridge and began to throw grenades down upon the 2d Platoon. The Japanese possessed a seemingly inexhaustible supply of grenades, which they rolled down upon the Americans with telling effect. Company F was unable to advance. By 1500 the 1st and 2d Squads of the 1st Platoon were forced off the forward slope. The 2d Platoon also had been unable to go ahead, and the company had suffered fourteen casualties. Captain Austin ordered his company to disengage for reorganization. Since the American mortars could not fire directly upon the Japanese for fear of hitting friendly troops, they were forced to fire over the enemy and gradually shorten the range as the American troops disengaged. Consequently the fire at first was not too effective. By 1600 the reorganization was complete, but Colonel Pearsall decided to delay the attack until artillery support could be obtained. Company F formed its night perimeter 500 yards from Pawing.

The following morning arrangements were made for an air strike by Navy flyers on the positions of the *33d Infantry Regiment* on the hill. It was not until afternoon, however, that the strike could be effected. At 1345 the 63d Field Artillery Battalion marked with smoke the right and left limits for the air strike.[40] At 1410 naval dive bombers bombed and strafed the hill for ten minutes with very good results, and the Japanese power to resist was broken.[41] Captain Austin's Company F, accompanied by Colonel Newman, the regimental commander, then moved out. Supported by artillery fire, Company F captured the entire ridge by 1515 without a single casualty. The Pawing area was now securely in American hands. Farther south the 19th Infantry was engaged in fulfilling its mission of capturing the town of Palo.

Capture of Palo

At the end of the first day's fighting, C Company of the 19th Infantry had just secured the top of Hill 522 and Company B at dusk had been pinned down at the southern crest. The following morning artillery fire effectively knocked out some enemy pillboxes on the north crest. Both companies then simultaneously launched an attack down the far slope of the hill. In the sharp fight that followed fifty Japanese from the *33d Infantry Regiment* were killed and the hill was secured.[42] It was not until late in the day, however, that supplies could be brought to the troops and the wounded be evacuated. The 1st Battalion spent the next few days mopping up the area and sealing off the tunnels with grenades.

On the beach the 3d Battalion, 19th Infantry, on the morning of 21 October waited for naval gunfire to knock out positions that blocked the beach road to Palo. These defenses consisted of mutually supporting well-constructed pillboxes reinforced with logs and earth, with intercommunicating trenches and foxholes. They were designed to be used in resisting attacks from the beach and from the north. After an all-night mortar concentration, naval gunfire was directed against the positions, and at 1400 the 3d Battalion attacked. When within 200 yards of a road bend, Company I and elements of the Antitank Company, leading the main assault, met strong resistance, which forced the company to dig in. The other companies occupied the same positions they had held the previous day.[43] During the night Company C of the 85th Chemical Battalion, expending 500 rounds of ammunition, laid intermittent fire from the 4.2-inch mortars on the Japanese positions.[44]

At 0900 on 22 October the 3d Battalion, with Company I in the lead, attacked with the 1st Battalion, 34th Infantry, which had been released from division reserve, on its left flank. This co-ordinated advance pushed past the defensive positions of the *33d Infantry Regiment,* many of which had been abandoned. The positions of the 3d Battalion, 19th Infantry, were taken over by the 1st Battalion, 34th Infantry. The latter battalion patrolled the road and eliminated

---

[40] 63d FA Bn Unit Rpt 2, 22 Oct 44.
[41] 24th Div G–3 Periodic Rpt 3, 22 Oct 44.
[42] 19th Inf Unit Rpt 2, 21 Oct 44.

[43] *Ibid.*
[44] 85th Chemical Mortar Bn Hist 1943–44, p. 28.

PALO, *with the Palo River and the slopes of Hill 522 in the background (above), and the junction of Highways 1 and 2 (below).*

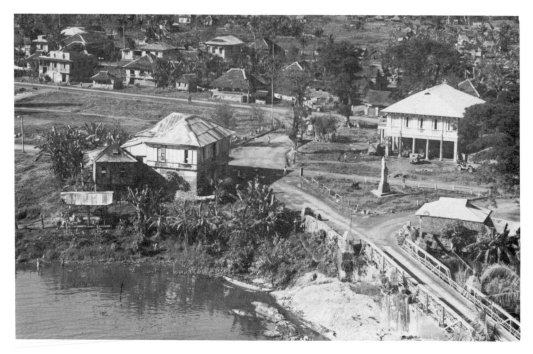

scattered Japanese pockets of resistance south to the Palo River.

The 2d Battalion, 19th Infantry, was to secure Palo, which is situated about one mile inland on the south side of the Palo River. The town is an important road junction, the meeting point of the Leyte Valley and east coast road systems. The coastal road, Highway 1, which goes through Palo, crosses a steel bridge over the Palo River on the edge of the town. Highway 2, a one-lane all-weather road for most of its length, extends west to Barugo and Carigara.[45] Just outside Palo are two hills, one on each side of the highway, which guard the entrance into the interior. The Americans termed them Hills B and C. Elements of the *33d Infantry Regiment* were guarding Palo.[46]

Early in the morning of 21 October, the 2d Battalion, 19th Infantry, moved west through enemy machine gun and rifle fire and bypassed the enemy defensive position that had held it up the previous day. At 1155 the battalion reached the junction of the beach road and Highway 1. During the movement two men were killed and two wounded. At the road junction, the battalion dispersed with machine gun fire a column of about thirty-five Japanese moving south on Highway 1. Artillery fire was then laid on a grove of trees, west of the road, to which the enemy had fled. As the battalion proceeded south along the highway between the road junction and the bridge, it came under artillery fire from an undetermined source. The tempo of the march into Palo was accelerated—"the troops wanted to move as rapidly as possible from that vicinity. They double timed across

the bridge." [47] At 1500 they entered Palo without further opposition.[48]

The residents of the town were crowded into the church. As the Americans entered, the church bell rang and the Filipinos came out and greeted the troops. After the first exuberant welcome had subsided, the soldiers ordered the civilians back into the church until they could secure the town. In the house-to-house search, the troops found some booby traps made from coconuts [49] and encountered Japanese entrenched under and between houses in the western sector of the town. Although the battalion had expected to outpost the entire town, the menace of the Japanese appeared so threatening that a night perimeter was established around the town square.

Defense of Palo

During the early part of the night there was continuous rifle fire from individual Japanese. The 13th Field Artillery Battalion had arrived and began to fire on the roads leading into the town, expending some 300 rounds of ammunition. At midnight some Japanese ammunition stored in a house exploded, and the ensuing fire lasted for three hours. At 0400 on 22 October elements of the *33d Infantry Regiment* counterattacked along Highway 2 [50] but were repulsed by fire from the outposts. The enemy then struck at the juncture of the left flank of Company F and the right flank of Company G. The 81-mm. mortars of the 2d Battalion fired on this point, expending all their ammunition. In the meantime Battery B of the 13th Field Artillery Battalion

[45] Allied Geographical Sec, Terrain Study 84, Leyte Province, 17 Aug 44.
[46] *35th Army* Opns, p. 28.

[47] 24th Div Opns Rpt Leyte, p. 16.
[48] *Ibid.*; 19th Inf Unit Rpt 2, 21 Oct 44.
[49] 24th Div G-2 Jnl, 21 Oct 44.
[50] 24th Div G-2 Jnl, 22 Oct 44.

and elements of the 63d Field Artillery Battalion moved up to within a hundred yards of the front outposts and fired. The enemy stubbornly continued to fight, throwing "everything he had into the attack." [51] At the same time nearly a platoon of the enemy came out at the curve of the beach road and started toward the bridge on Highway 1 at Palo, but these troops were dispersed by light machine gun fire. Artillery fire forced the Japanese to withdraw, and they were thrown back on all fronts.[52] Though the battalion had lost 16 men killed and 44 wounded, it had killed 91 Japanese. After the engagement, the battalion requested additional ammunition, supplies, and equipment, and transportation for the wounded.[53] The requests were complied with, though not without danger since the Japanese had mined the road.

At 1330 the regimental headquarters of the 19th Infantry moved into Palo. The regiment's 3d Battalion relieved the 2d Battalion at the same time, thus enabling the latter to attack Hill B at 1425.[54] The 3d Battalion spent the rest of the day and the following day mopping up in Palo and sending probing patrols southward in order to make contact with the XXIV Corps.[55] A patrol in Palo killed seven Japanese dressed in civilian clothing, one of whom, a lieutenant, had his insignia pinned inside his clothes.[56]

On the night of 23 October Col. Tatsunosuke Suzuki, the commanding officer of the *33d Infantry Regiment,* led a raiding detachment, armed with rifles, sabres, grenades, and mines, into Palo from the southwest.[57] Using Filipino civilians in front of them, the men of the detachment tricked the guards at the outpost into believing that they were guerrillas. The Japanese were thus able to capture two machine guns and a 37-mm. gun. They penetrated to the town square and charged, throwing explosives into houses, trucks, and a tank, and broke into an evacuation hospital where they killed some wounded. They then moved toward the bridge and mounted the captured machine guns on it,[58] firing until their ammunition was exhausted and then abandoning the guns. The American guards on the other side of the bridge, however, were able to fire upon the bridge and its approaches so effectively that they killed fifty Japanese, according to a count made the next morning. The raid was completely broken up, and sixty Japanese, including Colonel Suzuki, were killed. The American casualties were fourteen killed and twenty wounded.

The 3d Battalion, 19th Infantry, had sent Company K to reconnoiter to the south and if possible make contact with the XXIV Corps. On the morning of the 24th the company entered San Joaquin to the south of Palo. By 1600 the town had been secured and the company was prepared to defend it. Engineers began to repair the damaged bridge so that armored units could proceed southward along Highway 1. On the morning of 25 October Company K advanced south from San Joaquin and by 1200 had secured positions on the north bank of the Binahaan River, from which patrols were sent into Tanauan. At 1430 the patrols met a motorized unit of the 96th Division, establishing contact for the first time between the X and XXIV Corps. The rest of the

---

[51] 24th Div Opns Rpt Leyte, p. 18.
[52] 19th Inf Unit Jnl, 22 Oct 44.
[53] *Ibid.*
[54] *Ibid.*
[55] *Ibid.*
[56] 19th Inf Unit Rpt 3, 22 Oct 44.

[57] *35th Army* Opns, p. 28.
[58] GHQ Observer to G-2 Sixth Army, Sixth Army G-2 Jnl, 24 Oct 44.

battalion moved out of Palo the same morning and was able to advance rapidly with little opposition and set up a perimeter at Castilla, 8,000 yards southwest of Palo.

Thus the northern and southern approaches to Palo and the beachhead area east of the town had now been secured. But on the western edge of Palo were the two hills athwart Highway 2 and blocking passage into Leyte Valley. Hill B on the southern side of the highway and Hill C on the northern side would have to be secured before the Americans could advance. Preliminary reconnaissance had revealed that these hills were strongly held, and since the 24th Division, contrary to expectations, had encountered considerably stronger opposition than the 1st Cavalry Division, General Sibert decided to detach the 1st Brigade from the 1st Cavalry Division and place it under X Corps control. The 2d Squadron of the 5th Cavalry remained in position on the high ground west of Tacloban, while the regiment's 1st Squadron moved into position in Pawing, to relieve the 2d Battalion, 34th Infantry. The 12th Cavalry assembled in the vicinity of Marasbaras in X Corps reserve.[59]

Capture of Hill C

At 0800 on 23 October the 1st Battalion, 34th Infantry, commanded by Maj. Edwin N. Edris, and the 1st Platoon, 603d Tank Company, assembled 500 yards north of Hill 522 preparatory to launching an attack on Hill C.[60] It was reported that 300 Japanese were in a strong defensive position between Hills C and 331, the latter located west of Pawing. Consequently, an air strike

was called for and delivered on the area, after which the battalion started for Hill C. The first obstacle encountered was a small ridge known as Hill Nan, and just beyond this ridge was another hill mass known as Hill Mike. Company B advanced up Hill Nan in a skirmish line. When the company neared the crest of the ridge, a machine gun 200 yards to its front opened up, and at the same time the Japanese from dug-in positions on the reverse slope began to throw grenades over the crest. The company was halted. Three times during the afternoon it reached the crest, only to be driven back by enemy fire. Several counterattacks were repulsed, but the machine gun was not silenced.

At 1800 the company received orders to disengage so that artillery fire might be laid upon the enemy positions. The Japanese immediately counterattacked. An American lieutenant and a sergeant of the company rushed to the crest with grenades which they threw upon the advancing Japanese. This action enabled the company to disengage and return to the assembly area with only a few casualties.

During the night artillery and 4.2-inch mortar fires were placed on the ridge. As a result, on the following day, 24 October, the 1st Battalion secured it without meeting any resistance. With this ridge in American hands, the 3d Battalion was able to pass through the 1st Battalion and secure without opposition Hill Mike, the last remaining obstacle before Hill C. During the night artillery pounded Hill C.

On the morning of 25 October the 3d Battalion, 34th Infantry, moved out to attack Hill C, with Companies I and K abreast.[61] Although the troops found the hill difficult to climb, elements of Company

---

[59] 1st Cav Div G–3 Periodic Rpt 3, 24 Oct 44.
[60] 34th Inf FO 5, 22 Oct 44, 34th Inf Unit Jnl, 23 Oct 44.

[61] Fragmentary FO, 34th Inf Jnl, 25 Oct 44.

K reached its crest without opposition. The enemy started his usual tactics of throwing grenades over the crest of the hill at Company I as it neared the top. Since the company had suffered many casualties, a platoon from Company K was sent to reinforce Company I. Finally, at 1700, the company took the crest of the hill and dug in for the night.

The 2d Battalion, 34th Infantry, which had been relieved by the 1st Squadron, 5th Cavalry, moved out of Pawing at 0700 on 24 October. At 1030 it received orders to seize a small hill southeast of Hill C. With Company E in the lead, the battalion proceeded in single file up the hill, which was covered with cogon grass. As it had hitherto been the practice of the Japanese to withhold their main fire until the Americans neared the top of a hill, the troops expected little opposition before reaching the crest. But while the company was still a considerable distance from the top, elements of the *33d Infantry Regiment* opened up with rifles, machine guns, and grenades. This fire pinned the company down, and the men immediately sought concealment in the cogon grass. Light machine guns were brought up, but, because of the steepness of the slope, they were ineffective. Artillery and mortars fired for two hours against the entrenched Japanese positions. At 1610 Company E renewed the attack and this time secured the hill with little opposition. The 34th Infantry now occupied the hills on the north side of Highway 2.

Seizure of Hill B

On 22 October the 3d Battalion of the 19th Infantry had relieved the 2d Battalion of the regiment at Palo, and the regimental commander ordered the 2d Battalion to proceed against Hill B.[62] Earlier, the 2d Battalion had sent patrols out preparatory to attacking the hill. The 13th Field Artillery Battalion laid maximum supporting fires on Hill B as naval bombers strafed it.[63] The 2d Battalion moved out to the attack at 1425, and the concentrated artillery fire enabled it to secure without resistance a ridge east of Hill B and then push on down the road toward the hill. But as Company E, the lead company, reached the foot of Hill B, it was met by a large group from the *33d Infantry Regiment* coming east down the road and around the hill. The Japanese had left riflemen dug in on the steep banks of the road and had posted others in the trees along the road. Some of these riflemen allowed part of the American troops to pass and then opened fire. A sharp fire fight broke out in which Company E killed an estimated hundred of the enemy before being forced to withdraw to the ridge, where the 2d Battalion dug in for the night. During the night the 13th Field Artillery fired on Hill B. At 0730 the following day the 2d Battalion sent out two patrols to scout the enemy positions. The patrol on the right flank was stopped by machine gun fire at a point 200 yards west of the ridge and was forced to return. Mortar fire was placed on the enemy machine guns, after which the 2d Battalion advanced, reaching what was believed to be the crest of Hill B at 1530.[64]

As the forward progress was more difficult than had been expected, the 2d Squadron of the 12th Cavalry was sent to relieve the 1st Battalion, 19th Infantry, which had been engaged in mopping up Hill 522.[65] This

---

[62] 19th Inf Unit Jnl, 22 Oct 44.
[63] *Ibid.*
[64] 19th Inf Unit Rpt 4, 19th Inf Unit Jnl, 23 Oct 44.
[65] 1st Cav Div G–3 Periodic Rpt 3, 24 Oct 44.

relieved battalion was given the mission of attacking Hill 85, to the south of Palo, where the 24th Cavalry Reconnaissance Troop had located a strong enemy position. During the night the artillery placed concentrated fire upon Hill 85.

At 0800 on 24 October the men of the 2d Battalion moved out, attempting to complete the capture of Hill B.[66] They were held up by well-emplaced pillboxes and foxholes on the highest crest of the ridge, having discovered that the crest they had first occupied was not the true crest. Since the *33d Infantry Regiment* seemed to be well emplaced on the hill, Lt. Col. Robert B. Spragins had his battalion move to the right. It took up a position overlooking a narrow asphalt road that ran from Highway 2 to a Japanese supply dump to the south. Colonel Spragins decided to attack Hill B from this position on the following morning.

The 13th Field Artillery Battalion again pounded the enemy positions on the hill during the night. On the morning of 25 October the 2d Battalion attacked with Companies G and E abreast. The troops moved down the slope, across the road, and up the hill, with no opposition. On reaching the crest, they were met by heavy fire that came from well-constructed emplacements. Some of these positions were six feet deep and five feet wide. Very heavy fighting broke out in which the companies were barely able to hold their positions. The 11th and 52d Field Artillery Battalions fired in front of Hill B,[67] and the enemy fire was silenced. Company E was forced back, but Company G held on.

Although the hill was in American hands, the hold was very precarious. Colonel Spragins therefore moved the rest of the battalion up to Company G and ordered the latter to move out to a far ridge in order to secure the hill firmly. This move was accomplished at twilight. The rest of the battalion moved out to join Company G.

Starting in the dark, the battalion lost its way. At midnight the troops came to the true crest of the ridge where the enemy had an observation post surrounded by prepared positions. All were empty. The Japanese had formed the habit of going to the villages for the night and returning in the morning to man their posts. The night movement of the battalion "literally caught them napping away from their defenses." [68] The battalion had not reached Company G, but it set up a defensive perimeter for the night. The hills guarding Leyte Valley were now in American hands.

During the day the 1st Battalion, 19th Infantry, secured complete control of Hill 85 without opposition. The battalion found an abandoned position, mortar ammunition, and six dead Japanese.

By the end of 25 October the X Corps had made substantial progress toward securing northern Leyte Valley. After capturing Tacloban, the 1st Cavalry Division had pushed north and secured control over San Juanico Strait. The 24th Division had secured Palo and the hill fortresses that blocked the entrance into northern Leyte Valley. The corps was now in a position to launch a drive into the interior of the valley.

---

[66] 19th Inf Unit Jnl, 24 Oct 44.
[67] 24th Div Arty Unit Rpt 3, 26 Oct 44.

[68] 24th Div Opns Rpt Leyte, p. 27.

CHAPTER X

Northern Leyte Valley: Part Two

General Krueger had expected stronger Japanese resistance in the zone of action of the 1st Cavalry Division than in that of the 24th Division. He had therefore thought it safe to release the 21st Infantry for the landings at Panaon Strait. When events proved otherwise, a portion of the strength of the 1st Cavalry Division was shifted into the zone of the 24th Division to enable the latter to free itself of responsibility for rear areas and direct its effort to the advance into Leyte Valley.[1] (*Map 9*)

Drive up Leyte Valley

The Japanese planned to fall back into the mountains if the Americans were successful in seizing the Tacloban airfield. They expected to take with them "munition sufficient for one and one-half units of fire for one division . . . and food for 20,000 men for six month[s]."[2] The rapid advance of the Americans, however, prevented the execution of this plan. After 25 October the remaining elements of the *33d Infantry Regiment* withdrew to a position about three and three-fourths miles northeast of Jaro.[3] When the American forces had taken the hills dominating the entrance into Leyte Valley and overlooking Highway 2, Lt. Gen. Sosaku Suzuki, the commander of the

35th Army, concentrated his forces around Jaro on the southern edge of Leyte Valley. The *41st Regiment* of the *30th Division* and the *169th Independent Battalion* of the *102d Division,* both of which had but recently arrived on Leyte as reinforcements to the *16th Division,* on 26 October were ordered to proceed from Carigara to Jaro. On the same day the *17th Independent Battalion, 102d Division,* moved toward Jaro.[4]

The 34th Infantry Advances Into the Valley

After the successful capture of Hills B and C, the 24th Division resumed its attack west. With the 1st Cavalry Division protecting the 24th Division's northern flank, the 34th Infantry was to proceed westward into the interior along Highway 2. The 19th Infantry, as the 24th Division's southern prong, was to follow an almost parallel route to Pastrana.[5] The 1st Cavalry Brigade was to relieve the combat troops of the 24th Division in the rear areas in order to enable the division to continue its advance into the interior.

Highway 2 was a one-lane all-weather road, twelve feet wide with four-foot shoulders. It had a crushed rock and gravel

[1] Sixth Army Opns Rpt Leyte, p. 38.
[2] *14th Area Army Opns* Leyte, pp. 2–3.
[3] *35th Army Opns,* p. 35.

[4] 10th I&HS, Eighth Army, Staff Study Opns of Japanese *35th Army* on Leyte, Interrog of Maj Gen Yoshiharu Tomochika, CofS *35th Army,* Pt. I, p. 2.
[5] 24th Div FO 3, 0700, 25 Oct 44.

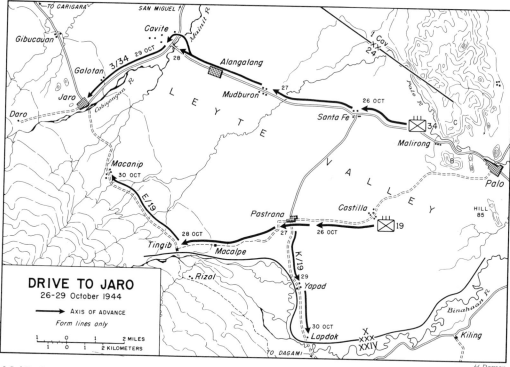

MAP 9

DRIVE TO JARO
26-29 October 1944

→ AXIS OF ADVANCE

Form lines only

H. Damon

surface. In general it ran through level ground, with occasional groves of light timber, bamboo, and abaca. Much of the area was under cultivation. At Santa Fe a one-lane all-weather branch road ran four miles south to Pastrana, at which point a seasonal one-lane road ran southward for about five miles to Dagami and another northwest for about eight and a half miles to Jaro.

At 1000 on 26 October the 2d Battalion of the 34th Infantry, commanded by Colonel Pearsall, moved out of its assembly area at Malirong in a column of companies and pushed westward on Highway 2. The battalion met slight resistance at the Malirong River bridge, but mortar fire knocked out the enemy opposition, and the advance continued. Since the battalion encountered few

Japanese, the flank protection, which had to traverse difficult terrain, was called in, and the advance then proceeded at a much more rapid pace. The 2d Battalion met, and killed or routed, small groups of the enemy. It crossed streams where the bridges had been destroyed. The 3d Engineer Battalion put temporary structures in for two of these bridges in order that the first elements might proceed, and it placed a Bailey bridge over a third stream. The 1st Battalion, which followed the 2d, used Japanese handcarts to transport supplies between the destroyed bridges and the forward troops.[6] By 1730 Colonel Pearsall had all of his battalion in Sante Fe. The following day, Lt. Col. Thomas E. Clifford, Jr., who had become

---

[6] 34th Inf Unit Jnl, 26 Oct 44.

the commanding officer of the 1st Battalion, pushed his unit through the 2d Battalion and advanced 7,000 yards without opposition to the Mudburon River, where the troops established their night perimeter at 1545.[7]

Mainit River Bridge

On the morning of 28 October Colonel Clifford ordered the 1st Battalion to move out in a column of companies along Highway 2 toward the town of Alangalang about a mile and a quarter northwest. At 0900 the battalion moved out. Company A, the lead company, entered Alangalang without incident, set up local security, and then fell to the rear of the battalion, which passed through Alangalang [8] without pausing and moved toward the Mainit River about one and a half miles farther on.

As Company C reached the Mainit River it made contact with the enemy, who had dug in on both steeply sloping banks of the river at the steel bridge crossing. The company suffered five casualties. It was opposed by the remaining elements of the *33d Infantry*, which had been considerably mauled by the Americans.[9] Company C withdrew 300 yards as Companies B and A pressed forward on the left side of the road under continuous rifle fire. Colonel Pearsall's 2d Battalion had followed the 1st Battalion, and both units were to make an assault against the *41st Infantry Regiment,* which

had arrived in the area. Three batteries of the 63d Field Artillery Battalion shelled the enemy positions for a depth of 300 yards on the eastern side of the river and 100 yards on the western side.

After the artillery concentration was over, the two battalions were to move out to the attack—the 1st on the left and the 2d on the right. The regimental commander ordered the 1st Battalion to attack, destroy the enemy resistance, and secure the eastern bank of the river. Five tanks were to follow in the rear of the assault companies and fire at targets of opportunity. Five hundred yards away, to the right of the 1st Battalion, Companies E and F of Pearsall's battalion were to cross the river, destroy enemy resistance on the western side, and then go south on Highway 2 to contact the enemy at the bridge.[10]

The 1st Battalion moved to the water's edge, where it was pinned down by enemy fire. Companies E and F of the 2d Battalion, however, were able to push north 500 yards through the heavy brush, and amid a driving rain they managed to ford the river unobserved. Once on the other side they charged the entrenchments of the *41st Infantry Regiment* on the river, with Company F in the lead. As Company F neared the bridge it overran three mortar positions without stopping but was finally halted by heavy machine gun fire. After the company's 60-mm. mortar had knocked out the machine gun, the unit continued to advance and passed the bridgehead before it ran out of ammunition. Company E then relieved Company F, while the latter set up heavy machine guns to silence enemy machine guns in the woods to the west. By 1500 the bridge was in American hands. The Japanese had placed a demolition

---

[7] 1st Bn, 34th Inf, Unit Jnl, 27 Oct 44.

[8] There is an interesting anecdote about the town: "Sergeant [Charles W.] Capps and Pvt. [Harold O.] Mottlet of G-3 got some help from a Jap sniper when they were hunting for Alangalang on a situation map. There was a 'ping' and they hit the dirt. When they resumed work they found a bullet puncture practically through Alangalang on the map." 24th Div Opns Rpt Leyte, p. 78.

[9] Tomochika, True Facts of Leyte Opn, p. 15.

[10] 1st Bn, 34th Inf, Unit Jnl, 28 Oct 44.

charge on the bridge, but the American advance had been so swift that the enemy never had an opportunity to set off the charge.

The 3d Battalion had meanwhile moved up to the rear of the other two battalions and established contact south of Santa Fe with the 19th Infantry, which was protecting the southern flank of the division.

Seizure of Pastrana

On 25 October the 3d Battalion, 19th Infantry, advancing toward Pastrana, had pushed against slight opposition into Castilla and established a perimeter there.[11] On the morning of the same day, Maj. Elmer C. Howard, the battalion commander, told Lt. Col. George H. Chapman, Jr., of the 19th Infantry that he had learned from the Filipinos that there was no organized resistance along the three miles from Castilla to Pastrana. He therefore asked permission to go to Pastrana and establish a roadblock. Colonel Chapman told Major Howard to stay out of Pastrana but to send patrols to locate defenses around the town.[12] Colonel Chapman later rescinded this order, and at 1300 on 26 October Major Howard moved his battalion out from Castilla to attack Pastrana, which was 5,000 yards southwest of Santa Fe. Company I, the lead company, proceeded over a trail that was too narrow to accommodate vehicles. At 1600 the point of Company I reached the outskirts of Pastrana but came under heavy enemy fire. The battalion pulled back and then attacked with Companies I and K abreast. The companies were stopped by fire that came from an unusual fortifica-

tion—a star-shaped fort, with a tin roof, which looked like three or four native shacks in a cluster. The sides were banked with earth, over which grass had been allowed to grow—a feature so exceptional that it aroused suspicion and gave away the nature of the installation. Pillboxes flanked the fortification, which was backed by a system of trenches. Colonel Chapman ordered another attack at 1630, but casualties were so heavy that the troops dug in after getting within 100 yards of the fortress.

At 1750 Battery C, 11th Field Artillery Battalion, placed fire on the fortification, but after forty-two rounds of ammunition had been expended, the battery reported that the muddy ground "caused [the] guns to go out of action."[13] From 1850 to 1905, Battery A of the 14th Field Artillery delivered harassing fire on Pastrana,[14] and from 2200 to 2400 the 13th Field Artillery Battalion took over the task of placing fire on the sector around the town.[15] With the coming of daylight, the 4.2-inch and 81-mm. mortars took up the shelling. The night-long pounding of the Japanese positions around Pastrana was so effective that on the morning of 27 October Company K of the 3d Battalion was able to move around the town and establish a roadblock at a demolished bridge a few hundred yards southwest. The rest of the day the 3d Battalion, assisted by Colonel Zierath's 1st Battalion, which had followed the 3d Battalion, mopped up in the town and sent out patrols to investigate the terrain and enemy dispositions west and south of the town.

The 19th Infantry was to continue to protect the southern flank of the 24th Division,

---

[11] 19th Inf Unit Rpt 6, 25 Oct 44, 19th Inf Unit Jnl, 25 Oct 44.
[12] 19th Inf Unit Jnl, 25 Oct 44.

[13] 11th FA Bn Unit Rpt 6, 28 Oct 44. There was no report for 27 October.
[14] Ibid.
[15] 13th FA Bn Unit Rpt 7, 27 Oct 44.

PASTRANA *was left a mass of smoldering ruins after the shelling of 26–27 October.*

which was driving toward Carigara, by moving toward Jaro—the proposed assembly point of the *35th Army.* On the morning of 28 October, Colonel Zierath had the 1st Battalion establish a roadblock north of the Binahaan River in the vicinity of Macalpe. The 2d Battalion pushed forward to Tingib and established a perimeter there. For the next two days the 19th Infantry sent out patrols in all directions; they met only scattered resistance from the Japanese. On 29 October Company K left Pastrana and established a roadblock at Ypad. On the following day it moved south from Ypad to Lapdok, where it established contact with elements of the XXIV Corps. On the 30th two platoons from Company C encountered about 100 Japanese at Rizal. The enemy fought aggressively, but resistance ceased after artillery fire had been placed on the

town. It was estimated that the majority of the enemy force was killed. As a result of the skirmishes and patrols, General Makino was unable to establish contact between elements of the *16th Division* at Dagami and those at Jaro.[16]

Fall of Jaro

At the crossing of the Mainit River, a one-lane all-weather branch road runs southwest for about three and a half miles to Jaro, and then northwest along the western edge of Leyte Valley for about ten and a half miles to Carigara on the north coast. At Jaro many dirt roads and trails branch out in all directions.

The drive of the 24th Division toward Carigara was continued as the 34th Infan-

[16] *35th Army* Opns, p. 43.

try, protected by the 19th Infantry on its flank, moved toward Jaro. After the seizure of the Mainit River bridge, two tanks of the 1st Platoon, 603d Tank Company, attached to the 34th Infantry, scouted north and made contact with forward elements of the 2d Squadron of the 8th Cavalry, which had arrived in the San Miguel area.

On the evening of 28 October Colonel Newman issued orders to the 34th Infantry for the following day. The 3d Battalion, under Lt. Col. Edward M. Postlethwait, was to pass through Colonel Clifford's 1st Battalion and Colonel Pearsall's 2d Battalion and resume the offensive with Company L in the lead. From Cavite the battalion would move southwest along the road to capture Jaro. Company L would be sufficiently in advance to make reconnaissance of the route before the rest of the battalion arrived.[17]

At 0900 on 29 October, Company L moved out from Cavite, meeting no resistance until an hour later when it ran into some of the enemy at a point about 100 yards from Galotan.[18] The leading scout spied a man, whom he thought to be a Filipino, dashing into a shack. When he shouted for the man to come out, the scout was shot in the head. The company came on and killed the man. It then came under machine gun fire. Platoons attacked from both flanks against Galotan. Since the enemy troops had dug in under the shacks, it was slow, bloody work digging them out with rifles and grenades. The 3d Platoon, which had been in reserve, closed in when the center of the town was reached and helped finish the job. In the meantime another unit of the company, which had been

sent to the right on a wide enveloping movement, came under fire from a wooded knoll. Artillery and mortar fire soon drove the Japanese off. Unable to retreat westward, the enemy moved northward down a stream bed and set up a defensive position 500 yards west of the road and opposite the center of the advancing column of the 3d Battalion. Fortunately, since the Antitank Platoon had displaced forward by sections, one section was in position at this point and was able to quickly eliminate the enemy threat. The 3d Battalion resumed its march and secured Jaro at 1700 without further difficulty.

By this time the 19th Infantry had gained control of the area south and east of Jaro. Junction between the 34th Infantry and 19th Infantry was accomplished on 31 October when the 1st Battalion, 19th Infantry, moved into Jaro. Other elements of the 19th Infantry were engaged in mopping up in the Pastrana sector. The 19th and 34th Infantry Regiments had been able to advance rapidly in their drives through Leyte Valley, had maintained contact with the 1st Cavalry Division, and had arrived within ten miles of Carigara Bay.

By 28 October the XXIV Corps had nearly secured the southern portion of Leyte Valley. General Sibert was anxious to have the X Corps advance rapidly to the shore of Carigara Bay and thus bring all of the valley under control of the Sixth Army. The 24th Division was relieved by the 1st Cavalry Division of responsibility for protecting the rear areas from Santa Fe to Cavite. The 24th Division, thus freed, was to continue pressing the attack to its front with the utmost vigor.[19]

The American advance had been so rapid that General Suzuki did not have sufficient time to put into effect his plan

---

[17] 34th Inf Unit Jnl, 28 Oct 44.
[18] The battalion journal laconically notes that Company L "meets slight resistance—kill appx. 50 Japs and continues." 3d Bn, 34th Inf, Unit Jnl, 29 Oct 44.

[19] X Corps FO 3, 28 Oct 44.

U.S. ANTITANK PLATOON *under enemy fire at Jaro. Soldier in foreground is taking cover behind a 37-mm. antitank gun M3.*

for making Jaro the assembly ground for the *35th Army*. He was forced to use the Carigara area as the new point of rendezvous for his troops. On the evening of 28 October Colonel Newman planned his attack for the remaining distance to Carigara. He hoped that the troops would make a swift passage, but later events proved that the Japanese intended to contest the advance bitterly.

Drive From the North

At the close of 27 October the 7th Cavalry, less the 1st Squadron, was in reserve, while the 1st Squadron was at Babatngon sending patrols along the north coast of Leyte and the southwest coast of Samar. The 1st Squadron of the 8th Cavalry was

patrolling Samar in the La Paz area and the 2d Squadron of the regiment was patrolling from its bivouac area in the upper reaches of the Diit River. In order to protect the rear of the 24th Division in its forward advance, the 1st Squadron of the 12th Cavalry, which had been in reserve, was ordered to Castilla. The squadron closed on Castilla at 1200 on 28 October.[20]

In accordance with orders from General Sibert, General Mudge reassigned the various elements of the 1st Cavalry Division. On 28 October General Hoffman issued orders for his 2d Cavalry Brigade to move toward Carigara. The 2d Squadron, 8th Cavalry, was to establish a base at San Miguel, secure Cavite with one troop, patrol and mop up the north and northwest

---

[20] 1st Cav Div G–3 Periodic Rpt 8, 28 Oct 44.

area up to and including the Barugo road, and maintain contact with patrols of the 1st Squadron, 7th Cavalry, that would be operating southeast from Barugo. The 1st Squadron, 7th Cavalry, while maintaining a platoon at Santa Cruz and a troop at Babatngon, was to move to the Barugo–Carigara area and mop up and patrol the area to the south and southeast.[21]

In accordance with this plan, Troop C of the 7th Cavalry was to proceed by water from Babatngon to Barugo and then overland to feel out the enemy position in Carigara. Troop C, under 1st Lt. Tower W. Greenbowe, on 28 October made the overwater and overland movements without incident. The troop entered the eastern end of Carigara without opposition, but as it neared the main intersection it received fire from several buildings. In anticipation of this contingency, the men of Troop C had been well deployed when they entered the town, and were able to return the fire immediately. As the fight progressed, the Japanese transported their dead and wounded to five trucks near the beach road. The fire fight continued until late in the afternoon when Lieutenant Greenbowe withdrew his force to Barugo, and evacuated his dead and wounded with him. The enemy had suffered an estimated 75 casualties; Greenbowe's force had 3 men killed, 9 wounded, and 1 missing. The mutilated body of the missing man was found later.[22]

Since intelligence reports stated that as many as 5,000 Japanese were in Carigara, General Sibert decided that the attack on the town should be a two-division operation. While the 24th Division was fighting its way up the road from Jaro to Carigara, additional 2d Cavalry Brigade units assem-

bled in the Barugo area. The 1st Squadron of the 7th Cavalry joined its C Troop at Barugo on 29 October; the 2d Squadron, 8th Cavalry, moved from San Miguel to Barugo on 31 October; and the advance headquarters of the 7th Cavalry Regiment and the 2d Cavalry Brigade arrived at Barugo on 31 October and 1 November, respectively. Attached to the 7th Cavalry Regiment was the 2d Squadron, 5th Cavalry, which closed into the Barugo area on 1 November via Cavite and San Miguel.[23]

Drive to Tunga

On 29 October the Japanese had prepared new plans for the defense of Leyte. In order to simplify planning, the *35th Army* headquarters was relieved of command responsibility for Samar by the *14th Area Army*. Almost simultaneously, the *35th Army* received the erroneous report that the Japanese naval forces had destroyed a large part of the U. S. Navy on 24 and 25 October in engagements off Leyte and that the losses would prevent the Americans from continuing the operation. On the contrary, the American naval forces had secured a decisive victory. The Japanese reverse seriously affected General Suzuki's attempt to put his new plans for the *35th Army* into effect.

The plans provided for the calling up of the *102d Division* from Panay and the *1st* and *26th Divisions* from Luzon. These divisions were to land at Ormoc and then pro-

---

[21] 2d Cav Brig FO 6, 28 Oct 44.
[22] 2d Cav Brig Opns Rpt Leyte, p. 6.

[23] The 5th Cavalry Regiment had moved behind the 34th Infantry on its advance along Highway 2 to the Mainit River bridge. When the 34th Infantry moved south to Jaro the 5th Cavalry took over the Cavite area and, during the Carigara attack, the regiment (less its 2d Squadron) was responsible for the protection of the line of communication from Cavite to Barugo. 5th Cav Opns Rpt, p. 5; 1st Cav Div FO 6, 1 Nov 44.

ceed in three columns northward along Highway 2 through Ormoc Valley to the shores of Carigara Bay. They were then to advance eastward and destroy the American forces in the area between Tacloban and Tanauan. Since it was assumed that Carigara would remain in Japanese hands, the *68th Brigade,* serving as *35th Army* reserve, was expected to land in the north in the vicinity of Carigara. At the same time the *30th Division* was to land at Albuera on the west coast and drive overland to Burauen, in order to support the operations of the main body of the *35th Army.*[24]

Although the American naval victory and rapid advance of land forces prevented the Japanese from bringing this plan to full fruition, sizable enemy forces opposed the drive of U.S. troops toward Carigara. About 28 October the *41st Infantry Regiment* moved from Carigara to the southeast section of Jaro. The *169th Independent Infantry Battalion* of the *102d Division,* together with a battalion (*Tempei Battalion*) of the *57th Independent Mixed Brigade,* was in the Carigara area. The advance elements first engaged the Americans about 30 October.[25] These units, however, continued out past Jaro and took up positions in the mountains.

On the night of 29 October the 34th Infantry had captured Jaro and was about ten miles from Carigara along the Jaro–Carigara highway. (*Map 10*) At 0800 on 30 October Colonel Newman ordered the 3d Battalion of the 34th Infantry to start for Carigara down the highway. As the battalion left the outskirts of Jaro, with Company L in the lead, it came under fire from

Japanese who were dug in under shacks along the road. Upon a call from the commanding officer of Company L, the tanks came up in a column, fired under the shacks, and then retired. The leading platoon was drawn back so that artillery fire might be placed on the Japanese, but the enemy could not be located precisely enough to use the artillery. Colonel Newman then ordered a cautious movement forward without artillery support, a squad placed on each side of the road and two tanks in the center. The squads had advanced only fifty yards when Japanese fire again pinned them down.

When Colonel Newman came forward and discovered why the advance was held up he declared, "I'll get the men going okay." [26] Upon hearing that the regimental commander was to lead them, the men started to move forward. The Japanese at once opened fire with artillery and mortars, and Colonel Newman was hit in the stomach. Although badly wounded he tried to devise some means of clearing the situation. After sending a runner back with orders to have Colonel Postlethwait fire on the Japanese position, he said, "Leave me here and get mortar fire on that enemy position." [27] As soon as possible Colonel Newman was put on a poncho and dragged back to safety.[28]

Meanwhile the troops, unable to move forward, broke contact with the Japanese in an orderly fashion. Lt. Col. Chester A. Dahlen, the regimental executive officer, assumed command and at 1209 ordered that the attack be resumed.[29] The 3d Battalion was to move northwest along the road to Carigara for 3,000 yards and then set up a night perimeter. The 2d Battalion, in sup-

---

[24] 10th I&HS Eighth Army, Stf Study of Opns of Japanese *35th Army* on Leyte, Part I, p. 5; Part IV, p. 3, OCMH.

[25] 10th I&HS, Eighth Army Stf Study of Japanese *102d Division* on Leyte and Cebu, *passim,* OCMH.

[26] 24th Div Opns Rpt Leyte, p. 33.

[27] *Ibid.,* p. 34.

[28] Colonel Newman was awarded the Distinguished Service Cross.

[29] 34th Inf Unit Jnl, 30 Oct 44.

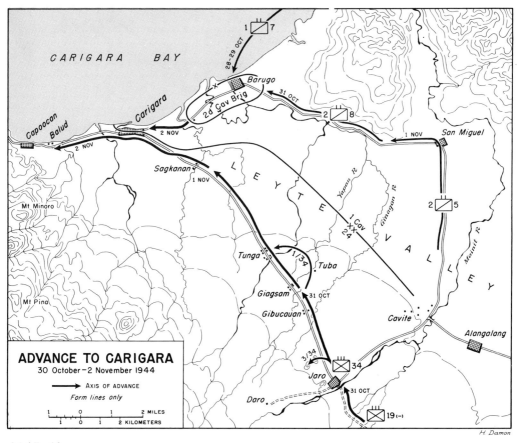

MAP 10

port astride the highway, was to secure the high ground 500 yards northwest of Jaro, while the 1st Battalion was to move to the town of Jaro from its position at the Mainit River bridge.

The artillery concentrated its fire on the area to the front, and at 1230 the 3d Battalion renewed the attack with Company K on the left of the road and Company I on the right. After the troops had proceeded about 200 yards, heavy artillery, machine gun, mortar, and rifle fire pinned them down. Company L in the rear thereupon attempted a flanking movement to the left across an open field but came under heavy

fire from a ridge that commanded the road. All the companies were forced to pull back. At the end of the day's action, the forward elements were still on the outskirts of Jaro.

During the night, the 11th, 52d, and 63d Field Artillery Battalions fired continuously in support of the 34th Infantry. The corps artillery placed harassing and interdiction fire along the Jaro–Carigara road.[30]

On the morning of 31 October Colonel Dahlen ordered the 3d Battalion to move toward Tunga along the Jaro–Carigara road. The 2d Battalion was to pass through

---

[30] 24th Div Arty Unit Rpt 8, 31 Oct 44.

the 3d along the highway, and the 1st Battalion was to be prepared to follow the 2d.[31] The 19th Infantry was to protect the rear of the 34th Infantry and forestall any attempt by the Japanese to send reinforcements from north of the Binahaan River. The 1st Battalion, 19th Infantry, was to move to Jaro via Tingib and Macanip to assist the 34th Infantry.[32]

At 0820 the 3d Battalion, 34th Infantry, supported by the 2d Battalion, attacked along the Jaro–Carigara highway. Company L went down the highway and then to the rear of the hill from which it had been repulsed the previous day; Company I moved forward astride the road; and Company K was in reserve. As advanced elements of Company I reached a stream, they came under intense fire but moved to a position from which they could attack the reverse slope of the hill. Other elements of the company moved off the road to the top of the hill. When they pushed westward along the crest they discovered another hill behind it.

In the meantime the troops that had attacked the reverse slope came under intense fire from the second hill. Concentrated fire was laid on the second hill and a heavy machine gun was sent to the top of the first. Company I, protected by the fire, was thus able to assault and take the first hill. Company K, the reserve company, thereupon occupied the hill. These assaults drove the enemy into Company L, which was at the foot of the hill. A determined three-hour fight followed, and, although at one time elements of the company were driven across the highway, the company retaliated and eventually cleared the area of Japanese.

---

[31] 34th Inf Unit Jnl, 31 Oct 44.
[32] 19th Inf Unit Jnl, 31 Oct 44.

While this fight was going on the 2d Battalion, with Company E as the point, moved along the highway toward Tunga. At 1130 the Japanese opened fire on Company E at the Ginagan River. Tanks, which had been brought up, fired with machine guns at the enemy positions on the left of the road. The Japanese retaliated with mortar and artillery fire, pinning down an antitank gun crew and Company E's mortar section. The artillery fired a concentration on the Japanese positions and the advance was able to continue.

At 1430 the enemy reopened fire on the 2d Battalion at the Yapan River. Company G was in the lead, with the 2d Platoon on the left of the road and the 3d Platoon on the right. Company E was on Company G's left flank. With all the troops in a skirmish line, the 2d Battalion, with tanks, moved down the road to attack. When Company G came under fire the tanks went to its assistance, and the Japanese then concentrated their fire on the armor.

Meanwhile Company E pushed down the left side of the road but was halted by fire from an enemy pillbox on a knoll. A self-propelled 105-mm. howitzer was brought up, and fire from this weapon completely disorganized the Japanese and forced them to desert their position. When the howitzer had exhausted its ammunition, another was brought up to replace it. By this time, however, the enemy's artillery was registering on the spot and the second was disabled before it could fire a shot.

Elements of the *41st Infantry Regiment*, protected by artillery, gathered in front of Company E and emplaced machine guns in a position from which they could enfilade the company. Thereupon Company E committed its reserve platoon to its left flank but shortly afterward received orders to protect the disabled howitzer and dig in for the night. A tank was sent up to cover the establishment of the night perimeter. Company G received orders to fall back and dig in for the night, and upon its withdrawal the Japanese concentrated their fire on Company E. Although badly shaken, Company E held on and protected the howitzer. A tank was sent forward to tow the weapon, but since it was untowable because of broken treads the crew sent a shell through it to prevent its use by the enemy. Company E then disengaged and fell back through Company F, as Company G had done.

Under the protective cover of night, the *41st Infantry Regiment* retreated.

During the day the 19th Infantry had followed closely, protecting the rear of the 34th Infantry and the southern flank of the 24th Division and blocking off the enemy escape routes. That night General Irving gave the plan of action for the following day—1 November—for the 24th Division. The 19th Infantry was to continue to block the enemy escape routes and protect the southern flank of the division along the Binahaan River east from Tingib to Yapad, move a battalion into Jaro, establish a roadblock in the vicinity of Jaro, and protect the line of communications behind the advance of the 34th Infantry as far as Gibucauan. The 34th Infantry was to continue advancing along the Jaro–Carigara highway, seizing every opportunity to make a wide envelopment, especially from the northeast.[33]

In accordance with this order, Companies A and B, 34th Infantry, were sent at 0820 to make a wide flanking movement eastward to Tuba and then strike at Tunga from the northeast. At 0900, after patrols had reported no enemy contact, the 2d Bat-

talion moved on down the Jaro–Carigara highway.

Both battalions proceeded rapidly. At 0900 the 1st Battalion was in Tuba, and at 1100 the 2d had passed through the scene of the previous day's fighting and was in Giagsam. The troops found much matériel, including two 37-mm. guns and numerous range finders, machine guns, rifles, packs, and helmets, which the enemy had left in his precipitous flight. Both battalions closed on Tunga. They paused for rest and then moved on down the highway toward Carigara. At 1600 when the 34th Infantry formed its perimeter for the night, its advance unit, the 1st Battalion, was 1,000 yards from Sagkanan, and its rearmost unit, the 3d Battalian, was at Tunga.[34]

On the previous day the regimental headquarters had moved into Jaro. It had been a bloody road to Carigara, but the 24th Division was knocking at the back door for admittance as the 1st Cavalry Division on the north was demanding entrance at the front door.

Capture of Carigara

By 31 October it became evident to the Americans that there was unusual activity on the part of the Japanese, who were apparently building strong defensive positions around Carigara and pouring reinforcements into the town. Statements by reconnaissance parties and reports from guerrillas led to the belief that 2,000 to 3,000 Japanese were in the town and its environs.[35] The enemy was capable of bringing up a considerable number of reinforcements along the Ormoc road, or of attacking the

---

[33] 34th Inf Unit Jnl, 31 Oct 44.

[34] 34th Inf Unit Rpt 13, 34th Inf Jnl, 1 Nov 44.
[35] One guerrilla unit estimated the number of Japanese as high as 5,000.

155-MM. GUNS FIRING ON CARIGARA

American left flank from the south.[36] The situation remained unchanged on 1 November.

Plans of X Corps

In view of the apparent strength of the Japanese defenders, General Sibert felt that no means should be left untried to insure the successful reduction of the strong point. Both the corps and division artillery were to fire on the town, with a heavy 15-minute preparation from 0745 to 0800 on the front of the 24th Infantry Division to a depth of 1,000 yards. Immediately thereafter a series of concentrations covering 1,000 yards in depth would be fired from 0800 to 0840, advancing at the rate of 100 yards every four minutes. All available artillery except one light battalion of the 24th Infantry Di-

vision would then fire in front of the 1st Cavalry Division to a depth of 1,000 yards from 0845 to 0900. Thereafter the artillery of each division would support its own division.[37]

The 2d Brigade, reinforced, was to seize Carigara from Barugo,[38] while the 34th Infantry would attack along the Jaro–Carigara highway. General Hoffman of the 2d Cavalry Brigade commanded the attack against Carigara. In preparation for the combined assault, the forces of the 1st Cavalry Division had been gathering in the Barugo area.

On 1 November General Hoffman arrived at Barugo, examined the troops, and made last-minute arrangements. The assault from the north was to be in a column of

[36] X Corps G–2 Periodic Rpt 10, 31 Oct 44.

[37] X Corps FO 5, 1 Nov 44.
[38] 1st Cav Div FO 6, 1 Nov 44.

squadrons: 1st Squadron, 7th Cavalry; 2d Squadron, 8th Cavalry; and the 2d Squadron, 5th Cavalry, in reserve. The squadron last mentioned was to establish and maintain communication with the 34th Infantry, which was to move out in a column of battalions, wait on the outskirts of Carigara until the town had been secured by the 2d Cavalry Brigade, and then flank the town and move on to Capoocan.[39]

During the day of 1 November and the night following, General Suzuki withdrew his troops from Carigara and established very strong positions in the mountains southwest of the town in the vicinity of Limon. By "clever deception as to his strength and intentions," the enemy completely deluded the Americans into believing that his major force was still in Carigara.[40]

Seizure of Carigara

Unaware of the Japanese withdrawal, the Americans proceeded with the execution of their plans. During the American artillery fire on the morning of 2 November some of the shells landed in the sector of the 7th Cavalry, an accident which delayed the attack until 0935. At that hour the 1st Squadron, 7th Cavalry, followed by the 2d Squadron, 8th Cavalry, jumped off. Since the bridge over the Canomontag River had been destroyed by the enemy and the river was not fordable, it was necessary to utilize native canoes, only two of which were available. This procedure consumed much time, but by 1130 the troops completed the crossing. Troop E, 5th Cavalry, made contact with the 34th Infantry at 1100. Since the troops encountered no resistance, the 1st Squadron,

7th Cavalry, followed by the 2d Squadron, 8th Cavalry, entered the town at 1200 and established a perimeter. General Mudge, the commander of the 1st Cavalry Division, entered the town with the assault cavalry troops.[41] The 2d Squadron, 8th Cavalry, outposted the western and southern sections of the town. Patrols from the 34th Infantry were already in Carigara.

At 0800 on 2 November the 34th Infantry moved out, the 1st Battalion leaving its bivouac area 1,000 yards southeast of Sagkanan and going down the highway, followed by the 2d Battalion, less Company G, and the 3d Battalion. Company G of the 2d Battalion was to reconnoiter the western side of Carigara in case an enveloping movement became necessary.[42]

By 0900 the 1st Battalion, 34th Infantry, reached a small bridge at the outskirts of Carigara and awaited word from the 1st Cavalry Division. After a wait of one and a half hours, patrols were sent into the western portion of Carigara, but they reported no enemy contact. All was quiet and the town deserted. The battalion then skirted Carigara and proceeded along the coast toward Capoocan. It encountered difficulty in crossing the Carigara River, since the bridge had been destroyed, but was able to get as far as Balud, where it set up a night perimeter after being halted by enemy fire. The 2d Battalion moved to the Carigara River, where it dug in for the night and was rejoined there by G Company. The 3d Battalion set up its perimeter just behind the 2d, and the regimental headquarters of the 34th Infantry was set up in Carigara.

In the advance through northern Leyte Valley the 24th Division had lost 210 killed,

---

[39] 34th Inf FO 7, 2 Nov 44.
[40] Sixth Army Opns Rpt Leyte, p. 38.

[41] 7th Cav Unit Jnl, 2 Nov 44.
[42] 34th Inf Unit Jnl, 2 Nov 44.

U.S. PATROL CROSSING THE CANOMONTAG RIVER *(above). Engineer troops replacing a Capoocan River bridge blown up by retreating Japanese.*

859 wounded, and 6 missing in action, but it had killed an estimated 2,970 Japanese and taken 13 prisoners.

With the capture of Carigara, the second phase of General Krueger's plan for the liberation of Leyte was completed. Panaon and San Juanico Straits, respectively south and north of the island, had been seized. Elements of the Sixth Army were on the west coast in the vicinity of Baybay on the shores of Ormoc Bay, and others were at Carigara near the northern entrance to Ormoc Valley. The two forces were poised for a co-ordinated drive toward Ormoc Valley—the last important Japanese stronghold on the island. Nearly all the tactically significant airfields and ports, together with Leyte Valley, were in the hands of the Sixth Army. Victory appeared to be in sight—but continued reinforcement of the island by the Japanese and delay in the construction program for building Leyte Valley into a major air and supply base were matters of grave concern.

CHAPTER XI

Logistics and Civil Affairs

The old saw that for want of a horseshoe nail the kingdom was lost is applicable in some degree to the story of logistics on the island of Leyte. Fortunately the outcome in Leyte was less serious than that recounted in the proverb. But the cumulative effect of many unfavorable conditions, each capable of being overcome in itself but each entangled with the others, resulted in a protraction of the campaign and a slowing of the schedule for future operations in the Pacific.

Despite the forebodings of Sixth Army engineers with regard to developing major logistical and air bases in Leyte Valley, General MacArthur had assigned logistical missions to the Sixth Army which, even under the best of circumstances, would have taxed its facilities to the utmost. General Krueger thought that in the planning stages greater emphasis should have been placed on an appreciation of terrain when selecting landing beaches and their exits, as well as sites for base development, airdrome construction, and headquarters installations. Terrain information should have been carefully analyzed by competent personnel in order that tactical and development plans could be based on the utilization of suitable terrain. The target dates and phase lines should have been flexible enough to allow for unsatisfactory terrain features. "Airdromes cannot be built speedily across rice paddies and swamps; bivouac areas, depots and dumps cannot properly be established in swamps and rice paddies." [1]

Logistics

Scarcely had the assault troops landed when the gloomy predictions of Colonel Ely that conditions of soil and weather on the island would make it unfit for the establishment of major bases began to be realized. Nevertheless, the necessity for early establishment of land-based air forces to support the operation made it imperative that the engineers start work immediately on rehabilitation of existing airfields. Before this task could be carried out, however, it would be necessary to strengthen and widen the roads in order to move heavy construction equipment to the airfields. A breakdown of the transportation system for even a few days could affect adversely all aspects of the Leyte operation. Because of the shortage of engineer troops, the lack of road metal, and the continuous traffic, the construction and maintenance of roads presented a critical and continuing problem.

Road Construction

The troops found their progress greatly hampered by the poor quality of roads leading to the interior of the island. The type of soil made it difficult to provide sufficient ap-

[1] Ltr, CG Sixth Army to CG X Corps *et al.*, 25 Nov 44, p. 24.

proach roads and to maintain all-weather roads. Drivers did not dare come too near the edge of the pavement in passing, even on the major two-lane roads, since their vehicles would probably become mired on the shoulder. The edges of hard-surfaced roads broke down under the constant wear until the roads were no longer wide enough for two-way traffic. Vehicles would often sink to their axles on the shoulders of the highway and on the many access roads, and frequently the roads into camp areas became unsuitable for traffic of any sort.[2]

In the 24th Division zone the engineers undertook to build an ancillary road, from the beachhead area to the existing coastal road, over the deep swamps and flooded rice paddies. After twenty-four hours' labor they abandoned the project as not feasible and in a few days rebuilt a trail that skirted the swamp along higher ground. This new thoroughfare was pronounced an "excellent" three-lane egress road.[3]

By utilizing a narrow road leading inland to Highway 1, egress from the 1st Cavalry Division beachhead area was accomplished. Since the road forked near the beach and ran north to Cataisan Point it became an access road to the Tacloban airfield. All supplies were routed along Highway 1 into the interior. When this road went to pieces under the heavy rains of 25 October, no means remained of getting overland from the area of the 24th Division to that of the 1st Cavalry Division. The open country back of the Dulag area made the road problems of the XXIV Corps zone a little more manageable than those in the X Corps area. Dulag itself offered graveled streets for traffic, but un-

fortunately only one very narrow road, with deep ditches on both sides, led west toward the mountains. With the coming of heavy rains, this road was chewed to bits by heavy traffic.

In order to preserve the roads as far as possible, the transportation officer of the Sixth Army decided to allow their use only to vehicles having the highest priority and to hold the transportation of civilians to a minimum. He forbade the use of trucks and other heavy vehicles for carrying personnel when lighter transportation was available.[4] Throughout the Leyte operation, though the engineering troops worked unceasingly, the condition of the roads remained a tremendous unsolved problem. A rainfall of 23.5 inches during the month of November forced a continuous contest with the mud, and men and equipment employed on the airstrips had to be diverted to the roads, some of which were closed for days at a time while under repair. Traffic censuses were made as a basis for many corrective measures that were introduced to control, reduce, and equalize the flow of traffic. Supplies were issued at night to avoid congestion at peak periods. ASCOM made strong efforts to keep the road construction equipment in use and in workable condition, and placed stress upon provision for proper drainage. Filipino pick-and-shovel crews were used as much as possible. In spite of these measures, at the end of November the condition of the roads was "a major hindrance to base development and operations." [5]

Airfields

The condition of the airstrips produced an even more perplexing problem than the

---

[2] Hist of Fifth Air Force, Ch. 5, pp. 34–35, AAF Archives.

[3] Sturgis, *Engineer Operations in the Leyte Campaign*, p. 6. Unless otherwise cited, the material on construction is taken from this study.

[4] Draft of Memo, 30 Oct 44, Sixth Army G–4 Jnl, 30 Oct 44.

[5] ASCOM Opns Rpt Leyte, pp. 8–9.

ACCESS ROAD FROM WHITE BEACH *under repair (above). Filipino road workers on Route 2 (below).*

roads. Immediately upon their arrival, engineer reconnaissance parties followed the assault infantry and examined the various sites which had been selected during the planning for airfields. By 22 October they reported that all the proposed airdrome sites except Tacloban were unfit for use during the rainy season.

Elements of the Sixth Army had captured both the Dulag and Tacloban airstrips within twenty-four hours after landing, but the Dulag airstrip was found to be out of use and unserviceable.[6] Since the Tacloban field was shorter than had been estimated and was in need of resurfacing, it was necessary to construct practically a new airfield. Although Japanese air resistance was moderate for the first few days and the weather temperate, progress was slow because of the condition of the roads and congestion of traffic. Trucks bearing gravel moved at a snail's pace.

On 25 October the 7th and 8th Fighter Squadrons of the 49th Fighter Group assisted in the work on the Tacloban strip. The 8th Squadron was dismayed. The entire Cataisan Peninsula, on which the airstrip was located, was an "unadulterated bog" and the "confusion was awe inspiring." Labor details were called to work and then dismissed. Upon returning to their bivouac area, they would be recalled, and the process repeated.[7] On 25 and 26 October the Japanese air force came over the airfield in great waves. Many times the men were forced to drop their tools and sprawl into gullies and slit trenches as the Japanese "returned for more blood." [8]

With the naval battle of Leyte Gulf under way, activities on the airfield were further hampered. Construction crews attempted to lay a base of coral on the airfield for the steel matting at the same time that Navy planes used the field for emergency landings. About a hundred aircraft used the field on 25 October, and twenty-five of these were destroyed in crash landings, one of which set the fuel dump afire at night.[9] In spite of enemy air raids, the landing of naval aircraft, and the wrecked planes littering the airstrip, construction continued. By 30 October some aircraft were arriving and making satisfactory landings on the runway, which at that time had nearly 4,000 feet of matting.[10]

On 27 October the Fifth Air Force took over the mission of supplying air support. Because of the poor condition of the airstrips and the scarcity of available aircraft, however, it was announced on 31 October that only "sporadic bomb support by the heavy bombers" and strafing could be accomplished. Work on the airstrips had barely got under way at the end of October.[11]

At the same time General Casey, commanding the Army Service Command, painted a dark picture of the future. He stated that the construction of airfields in the Dulag area would require more effort than had been anticipated during the planning phase, since the Japanese, contrary to expectations, had placed little or no surfacing material on the runways and since soil conditions were such that an eight-inch sand and gravel base covered with steel mat would be

[6] RAD, CTF 78 to CG Sixth Army, MC 1280, 22 Oct 44, Sixth Army G-3 *Wasatch* Jnl, 23 Oct 44.

[7] Hist 8th Fighter Squadron, October 1944, p. 7, AAF Archives.

[8] Hist 7th Fighter Squadron, October 1944, pp. 4-5, AAF Archives.

[9] Opns Rpt, Comdr Support Aircraft to Comdr Seventh Fleet, no serial, 2 Nov 44.

[10] Hist 8th Fighter Squadron, 49th Fighter Group, 86th Wing, V Fighter Command, Fifth Air Force, October 1944, p. 7, AAF Archives.

[11] Rad, Col Quinn to the 6, 8, and 9 Air Liaison Parties, Sixth Army G-3 Jnl, 31 Oct 44.

required to support bomber traffic.[12] Furthermore, the labor crews that were to have been used in airfield construction were being diverted to road building, still further reducing "the already insufficient amount of engineer effort available for drome construction."[13] Aside from labor shortages, the chief causes for the disappointing delay in airfield construction were poor soil conditions, enemy air raids, and rain.[14] Under such inauspicious circumstances, the Allied Air Forces undertook the mission of furnishing air support on Leyte. Because of the poor condition of the airfields, only a token force from the Fifth Air Force was able to come in.

Much ingenuity was exercised by the engineers in overcoming difficulties. In enlarging the Tacloban airstrip, one of the greatest impediments to progress was the limited supply of coral for surfacing the runways. The engineers conceived the idea of having the dredge *Raymond*, which had been brought forward to dredge the navigational channel, used to pump coral from the channel bottom onto the runways. The 2,800-horsepower pumps could transport solid matter one mile through pipes that extended across the bay and onto the land, and they could also raise the dredged matter as much as 300 feet above sea level. The engineers found that this pipeline was the quickest way to transport material to the Tacloban airstrip, though mechanical difficulties sometimes developed.[15]

Despite constant work on the morasses that constituted the San Pablo and Buri air-

fields, these strips continued to be in a generally unusable condition. Finally, on 25 November, ASCOM dropped all construction work on them. The Fifth Air Force, however, felt that it was necessary to continue using the Bayug airfield, and at least one aviation battalion remained at work on that strip.

When work on the airstrips at Buri and San Pablo was abandoned, the Sixth Army units thus released began the construction of a new airfield on the coast at Tanauan, midway between Tacloban and Dulag. This field became operational on 16 December 1944.[16] The fact that the main part of the Fifth Air Force was unable to displace forward to Leyte made it possible for the Japanese to reinforce their Leyte garrison and thus prolong the campaign.

Although his engineers, before the opening of the campaign, had protested vigorously to General Headquarters against the establishment of a major base upon Leyte, General Krueger felt constrained to take the responsibility. Said he:

There is no doubt that if I could have made adequate airdromes available on Leyte as scheduled we would have had ample air forces on hand to stop all Jap reinforcements from coming in. But this proved to be impossible, because of terrific rains that flooded all level areas on the island. In consequence, we lacked the air support necessary adequately to support the operation. This was not the fault of the Allied Air Force, however, but mine.[17]

Base Construction

After the assault troops had cleared the beach areas, a perplexing problem came to the fore. In the plans for the Leyte operation

---

[12] Ltr, Maj Gen Hugh J. Casey, CG ASCOM, to Gen Krueger, CG Sixth Army, 31 Oct 44, Sixth Army G-4 Jnl, 7 Nov 44.

[13] *Ibid.*

[14] Hist Fifth Air Force, Ch. 5, p. 33, AAF Archives.

[15] Hist of Engineer Corps in the Pacific, Ch. VI, Philippine Campaign, pp. 327–29. Copy in OCMH.

[16] Sixth Army Opns Rpt Leyte, p. 69.

[17] Ltr, Gen Krueger to Gen Ward, 13 Aug 51, OCMH.

TANAUAN AIRSTRIP *built to replace San Pablo and Buri airfields.*

General Krueger had assigned to the various commands areas for such facilities as their supply dumps and hospitals. Upon arrival on Leyte, the Army Service Command discovered that many of the sites were swamps; the tactical situation delayed reconnaissance for others.

Throughout November the allocation of areas to the units continued to present difficulties. On 12 November General Krueger formed the Area Allocation Group, which consisted of representatives from MacArthur's General Headquarters, the Sixth Army, the Air Forces, the Navy, and the Army Service Command. The various units submitted requests for particular areas to this group, which accepted or rejected the requests, or allocated different sites. Since many of the applicants wished to be in the Tacloban area, some of the requests could

not be granted because of insufficient space. Many of the sites best suited for hospitals or storage were occupied by MacArthur's advance headquarters and other headquarters. The search of ASCOM for suitable storage areas continued throughout the month.[18] On 28 November General Krueger moved the Sixth Army command post from Tanauan to Tolosa so that an airstrip could be constructed in the Tanauan area.[19]

By 20 November General Krueger's program for hospital construction was far behind schedule. Of the eight hospitals planned for the area only one was as much as 34 percent complete, and one was only 5 percent complete.[20] The lack of hospital facilities, which continued throughout De-

---

[18] Army Service Comd Opns Rpt Leyte, pp. 6, 9.
[19] Sixth Army Opns Rpt Leyte, p. 69.
[20] 5201st Engr Const Brig Opns Rpt Leyte, p. 5.

cember, was somewhat offset by the rate of evacuation and the use of hospital ships and LST's operating under naval medical procedure. Next to airfields and roads the construction of hospitals was given priority. But "an adequate number of engineer battalions . . . to do justice to the original requirements" was not available. At the same time General Krueger ordered that the hospitals be given first priority on structural materials and on portable buildings. No lumber, including ship dunnage, could be used in constructing quarters for either officers or enlisted men until the hospitals were completed.[21] All units that could be spared from airdrome and road construction were used to build either hospitals or port and POL (petrol, oil, and lubricants) installations.

As for port facilities, the Japanese failed to destroy two existing deepwater berths at Tacloban. Despite numerous enemy aerial attacks on these docks and on shipping, no material damage resulted. By 1 December ASCOM had constructed an additional dock and several lighterage wharves. During November the Army Service Command established, in addition to the main supply base at Tacloban, a subbase at Dulag for the southern areas and a supply point at Carigara for the troops of X Corps.[22]

Supplies

Since the assault troops had brought with them only limited supplies and ammunition and since they were deep inside Japanese territory and 1,500 miles from their nearest supply base, at Hollandia, the need for immediate establishment and stocking of supply bases was especially urgent.[23]

Because some of the LST's offshore in the vicinity of Hill 522 and Palo were heavily shelled by the Japanese on A Day, the remaining LST's were directed to the Cataisan Peninsula, where many of them discharged their loads on the Tacloban airfield, over which the supplies were scattered. The proposed runway and dispersal areas were strewn with hundreds of vehicles, together with thousands of tons of ammunition, rations, and petroleum products. Since there was only one egress road, the airstrip became tremendously congested.[24]

Another important cause of the congestion was the dictum of General Headquarters that certain airfields were to be operational by an early date. The Air Forces had therefore loaded the vessels with a considerable number of service troops and a quantity of equipment which could not be used until the airfields were in operation. When construction of the airfields was delayed, these troops and equipment were unemployed for many days, thus cluttering the beaches and adding to the congestion. Ironically, because of limited shipping space, they had displaced "engineers and other service troops which would have been of great value." [25]

On 8 November an estimated 120,000 American troops were on Leyte. The rations of some of these were on board the vessels that had brought them to the island, and cargo was not being discharged at a satis-

[21] Sturgis, *Engineer Opns in Leyte Campaign*, p. 15.
[22] Army Service Comd Opns Rpt Leyte, p. 9; Memo, G–4 Sixth Army for DG ASCOM, 11 Nov 44, Sixth Army G–4 Jnl, 11 Nov 44.

[23] Sturgis, *Engineer Opns in Leyte Campaign*, p. 5.
[24] *Ibid.*, p. 6.
[25] Ltr, Gen Decker, formerly CS Sixth Army, to Gen Ward, 9 Jul 51, copy in OCMH.

LST'S UNLOADING AT TACLOBAN AIRFIELD. *The causeways leading from the beach to the ships were built by bulldozers scraping sand and earth to each ship as it landed.*

factory rate. Col. William N. Leaf, the supply officer of the Sixth Army, did not believe that more than sufficient rations, clothing, and construction equipment to meet minimum requirements could be unloaded unless the discharge capacity of the ports was substantially increased. While this condition was not entirely satisfactory, it was not as bad as appeared, since incoming units brought and discharged thirty days' supply for themselves.[26] General Krueger set up a committee to determine the priority of discharge for the various classes of cargo. On 9 November the committee gave top priority to the following items, in order of preference: ammunition, 1,400 tons a day; ra-

tions, 1,000 tons a day; bridge timber, no specified amount; landing field mats, 500 tons a day; and aviation gasoline, 1,000 drums a day.[27]

On 27 November the priorities committee reviewed the status of shipping in the harbors and established new priorities for the unloading of cargo. In order of priority, the following commodities were given preference: rations, ammunition, landing mats, and aviation gasoline.[28] Not all the vessels followed the priorities that had been set up for the discharge of cargo. General Krueger ordered that "appropriate disciplinary ac-

---

[26] Memo, G–4 Sixth Army for Transportation Sec Sixth Army, 8 Nov 44, Sixth Army G–4 Jnl, 8 Nov 44.

[27] Rpt of Conference on Establishment of Priorities, 9 Nov 44, Sixth Army G–4 Jnl, 30 Nov 44.

[28] Rpt of Conference on 27 Nov for the Establishment of Unloading Priorities, 28 Nov 44, Sixth Army G–4 Jnl, 30 Nov 44.

tion" be taken against any Army personnel who were responsible.[29]

Since successive resupply convoys arrived at Leyte before vessels of the preceding echelon had been unloaded, thus congesting the harbor, and since the Japanese were bombing the vessels, the assistant G–4 of Sixth Army suggested on 2 December that the number of vessels to be called forward from the rear area to be kept to an absolute minimum.[30] The time allocated for the discharge of cargo was steadily increased: from 20 October to 3 November it was twelve hours a day, from 4 November to 8 November eighteen hours a day, and from 9 November until Christmas, twenty-four hours a day.[31]

During the first thirty days the supplies in tons, stockpiled on Leyte or available on board ship for discharge, over and above current needs, increased as follows: 20 October, 30,313; 21 October through 30 October, 128,051; 31 October through 9 November, 193,838; and from 10 November through 19 November, 319,418.[32]

After the supplies were ashore and stored, the problem of getting them to the divisions and thence to the front-line troops presented tremendous difficulties. Nearly all types of transportation were utilized. As the roads disintegrated, more and more dependence was placed upon water transportation. Naval vessels and amphibian vehicles were used to carry the supplies as close as possible to the front-line troops, and motor vehicles transported them for the remaining distance whenever feasible. At other times the troops

and Filipino civilians often had to hand-carry supplies to the assault forces. In addition there were many airdrops to troops who were otherwise completely cut off from the rest of the Sixth Army.

Medical Support

As the assault forces moved across the beaches, medical units accompanied them. The 110th Portable Surgical Hospital supported the operations of the 6th Ranger Infantry Battalion in the islands of Leyte Gulf. In the northern part of Leyte the 19th and 27th Portable Surgical Hospitals went ashore with the 1st Cavalry Division in the Tacloban area, while the 16th Portable Surgical Hospital supported the 24th Infantry Division in the Palo area. The 38th and 58th Evacuation Hospitals also landed on A Day in the X Corps zone but did not establish themselves in positions to receive patients. In the zone of action of XXIV Corps in the vicinity of Dulag, the 7th and 96th Infantry Divisions were accompanied by the 51st and 52d Portable Surgical Hospitals, the 394th Medical Clearing Company, and the 644th and 645th Medical Collecting Companies. Later in the day a platoon from the 69th Field Hospital landed and before nightfall was ready to receive patients. Earlier on the same day the 7th Portable Surgical Hospital had accompanied the 21st Infantry Regiment to Panaon Strait.[33]

Evacuation of Casualties

General Bradley attached to each assault battalion a platoon from one of the collecting companies of the 96th Division Medical

---

[29] Ltr, CG Sixth Army to CG ASCOM, 30 Nov 44, Sixth Army G–4 Jnl, 1 Dec 44.

[30] Memo, Asst G–4 Sixth Army to QM *et al.* Sixth Army, 2 Dec 44, Sixth Army G–4 Jnl, 2 Dec 44.

[31] Sixth Army Opns Rpt Leyte, p. 218.

[32] Memo, G–4 Sixth Army to Transportation Off, 27 Nov 44, Sixth Army G–4 Jnl, 27 Nov 44.

[33] Rpt of Surgeon, Sixth Army Opns Rpt Leyte, p. 262.

ROAD CONDITIONS. *Disintegration of the roads greatly increased the supply problem. Filipino carriers unload an amphibious LVT(4) (above); carriers for the 1st Cavalry Division near Carigara (below).*

Battalion. These platoons landed with the assault waves, collected the casualties on the beach, gave them the necessary treatment, and then evacuated them to designated ships by landing craft. After the Navy beach parties had established aid stations the medical units cleared casualties through them.[34]

As the battle moved on beyond the beaches, the remaining medical units came ashore and hospitals were put into operation. For the first few days, however, the medical units evacuated all casualties to naval vessels in the harbor, whereupon the vessels sailed for a rear area base. It frequently happened that a man with a minor wound or illness, or a nonbattle injury, would be well and fit for further duty by the time the vessel reached the rear area.[35]

After the campaign had progressed beyond the beaches, both the corps evacuated to rear areas only those casualties who required prolonged hospitalization. The Filipino civilian employees of the Army and members of the Filipino armed forces received treatment but were not evacuated from the island without approval from Sixth Army headquarters. Wounded or sick Japanese prisoners were segregated in the hospitals but, otherwise, they received the same treatment as other patients.[36] Within three days after landing, the XXIV Corps set up a field hospital which was ready to receive patients on the following day. Consequently, all casualties who had already been evacuated to the ships but who required hospitalization for less than fifteen days were brought ashore and held in the shore party medical section or admitted to the hospital.[37]

Co-operation between the medical services of the Sixth Army and those of the Seventh Fleet was excellent. Col. William A. Hagins, Sixth Army Surgeon, praised the medical service of the Seventh Fleet in unstinting terms: "The LST's equipped to provide surgical service conformed to the highest professional standards and they, together with the APH's (transports for wounded) and the small PCE(R)'s (patrol craft, escort (rescue)) formed a floating hospital reserve that varied between 3,000 and 5,000 beds. Without this service, which relieved the hard pressed hospitals of many cases, the level of medical and surgical care on Leyte would certainly have been sub-standard." [38]

After the action had progressed beyond the beaches, the evacuation of troops became more difficult. Each medical collecting company of the 96th Division was furnished nine ¼-ton trucks and three other cargo carriers. The swamps and steep hills precluded the use of trucks, however, and the number of cargo carriers was insufficient for the task. The latter were most useful in evacuating casualties across swamps and rice paddies. It was necessary to use litter bearers in the mountains, but the narrow trails permitted the use of only two men to carry each litter. For some unexplained reason, attempts to use Filipinos as litter bearers were not successful.[39] The 24th Division, unlike the 96th, found the Filipinos to be excellent litter bearers and recommended their use whenever possible, since they were willing workers who conserved the efficiency of a combat unit by replacing the combat soldiers.[40]

---

[34] 96th Div Opns Rpt Leyte, p. 95.
[35] Rpt of Surgeon, Sixth Army Opns Rpt Leyte, p. 262.
[36] X Corps Rpt of Medical Service Leyte Campaign, pp. 3–4.
[37] XXIV Corps Opns Rpt Leyte, p. 38.

[38] Rpt of Surgeon, Sixth Army Opns Rpt Leyte, p. 263.
[39] 96th Div Opns Rpt Leyte, pp. 95–96.
[40] 24th Div Opns Rpt Leyte, p. 197.

Medical Treatment

With very few exceptions, all casualties were treated within one hour after the wound had been inflicted. At the forward aid stations the wounded soldier received only initial treatment necessary before evacuation to the collecting station. When the casualty arrived at that point, he was bathed and prepared for further evacuation to a clearing station. There the necessary surgery was performed to make the patient safe for further evacuation, and he was then taken to a rear area. Because of the swamps and steep hills in the 96th Division sector, the time lag in evacuation from the forward aid station to the clearing station varied from one hour to thirty hours.[41] In the 24th Division zone, the clearing stations remained mobile. Only in rare instances, where it was impossible to remove patients because of heavy fighting, was a casualty more than four hours in reaching the clearing station.[42]

Initial measures at the aid stations consisted of treatment for shock, stopping hemorrhage, administering plasma, applying splints, and dressing wounds. At the clearing stations and portable surgical hospitals, the initial surgical care consisted mainly of *débridements*, emergency laparotomies, and amputations. The medical officer performed surgical operations in these forward medical facilities only when it was thought that the wounded soldier could not stand the arduous trip to the rear or when his condition would not permit the delay necessary for evacuation.[43]

A great many chest wounds and compound fractures were treated. The fractures were cleansed, injured tissue was removed, and a splint or cast applied. The biggest problem in fractures was the immobilization of the humerus. If the nerves could be readily found they were anchored. Plasma was extensively used, and whole blood, considered indispensable by the surgeons, was generally available.[44]

In the first days of the Leyte Campaign, because of the prelanding bombardment, more civilians than soldiers required treatment by medical units. In the 7th Division sector for the first two days, 75 percent of the medical facilities of the only clearing company in operation were used in caring for civilian casualties. On 24 October the Army established a separate hospital on Leyte for civilians.[45]

The Sixth Army made a survey of 519 patients who died from injuries suffered in battle. Of these 1 died of bayonet wounds, 2 of blast concussion, 249 of gunshot wounds, 170 of fragment wounds, and 97 of unclassified injuries, many of which were believed to have been inflicted by bomb or shell fragments. The location of the gunshot wounds was as follows: 66 in the abdomen, 21 in the back, 7 in the buttocks, 67 in the chest, 49 in the head, 18 in the lower extremities, 9 in the upper extremities, 3 of multiple character, and 9 of unclassified location. Of the fragment wounds 25 were in the abdomen, 7 in the back, 6 in the buttocks, 30 in the chest, 33 in the head, 37 in the lower extremities, 11 in the upper extremities, 12 multiple, and 9 unclassified.[46]

Medical Supply

The Sixth Army plan called for the assault troops to go in with five days' medical

---

[41] 96th Div Opns Rpt Leyte, p. 96.
[42] 24th Div Opns Rpt Leyte, p. 134.
[43] *Ibid.*

[44] *Ibid.*
[45] 7th Div Opns Rpt Leyte, Medical Rpt, App. C to G–4 Rpt, p. 5.
[46] Sixth Army Opns Rpt Leyte, p. 263.

A LITTER SQUAD EVACUATES A CASUALTY *in mountainous terrain.*

A CASUALTY RECEIVES TREATMENT *at a forward aid station.*

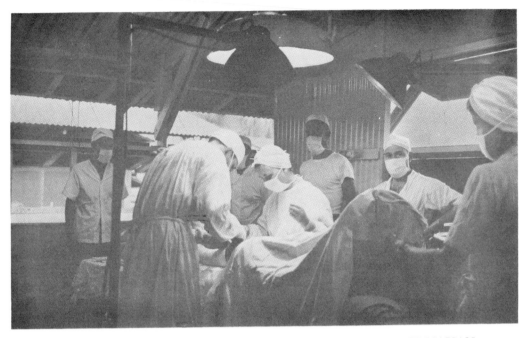

AN OPERATING ROOM AT THE STATION HOSPITAL, TANAUAN

A CASUALTY IS EVACUATED BY SHIP TO A REAR AREA

supplies. The other units would go in with thirty days' supply. The original plan provided for 300,000 troops over a sixty-day period only. Thereafter, it was expected that Sixth Army would depend upon resupply shipping and the diversion to Leyte of shipments intended to fill theater requirements of the Southwest Pacific area. The resupply shipping consisted of medical maintenance units. Since the average medical maintenance unit contained less than 700 items as compared to the 3,000 to 3,500 items eventually needed for a balanced supply, the medical plan of the X Corps called for loading three days' supply on their organic transports and on their personnel. The rest of the supplies were bulk loaded. The X Corps also had an emergency resupply of two medical maintenance units, one of which was never unloaded because of damage to the ship on which it was carried.[47]

When the XXIV Corps was ordered to prepare for the Yap operation, the 7th Division began to make its medical plans. After receiving permission to take a thirty-day supply for 22,000 men on its assault shipping, the division separated the stock into two sections, consisting of a ten-day supply and a twenty-day supply. The former was packed in ten identical units with one unit to a pallet, each weighing 1,840 pounds and having a volume of seventy-two cubic feet. One of these units was allotted to each battalion of the division and one to the division headquarters. The twenty days' supply was packed in three identical units, each weighing about 21,648 pounds and having a volume of about 864 cubic feet.[48]

The 24th Division drew approximately thirty tons of medical supplies from the base medical supply. The division then mobile-loaded twenty of these tons on five 2½-ton trucks and assigned a truck to each collecting company. The remaining medical supplies were bulk loaded. Each medical unit also carried a five-day supply for immediate use upon commitment.[49]

When put into practice, however, this system of the 24th Division was not entirely satisfactory. Because of the rapid advance of the assault troops and the lack of transportation, the system of supply became an acute problem. Resupply became co-ordinated with the chain of evacuation. Forward units would submit informal requisitions to the clearing companies at the second echelon of evacuation, whereupon the supplies would be issued and brought forward by ambulances on their return to the front. The clearing companies would submit requisitions to the main dump. The difficulty of resupply can be appreciated when considerations of time and distance are understood. For instance, the round trip from Carigara to Tacloban, where the main dump was located, amounted to about seventy miles.[50] As greater and greater dependence was placed upon human carriers to bring out the wounded and bring in supplies, it proved indeed fortunate that the Sixth Army had established amicable relations with the Filipino civilians.

Civil Affairs

Although the United States Government had interested itself in the civil affairs of the Philippines as early as 13 January 1944, it was not until 10 November, after the Leyte Campaign had been launched, that General

---

[47] Army Service Forces Monthly Rpt, Sec 7, Health, Jun 45, p. 10.

[48] 7th Div Medical Rpt, App. C to G–4 Opns Rpt Leyte, p. 3.

[49] 24th Div Opns Rpt Leyte, pp. 135–36.

[50] Ibid., p. 136.

MacArthur received his first directive on civil affairs. Between the two dates strong disagreements developed between the War and Interior Departments as to who should administer civil affairs in the Islands. The Interior Department insisted that a civil representative of the High Commissioner of the Philippines should accompany the assault troops, and General MacArthur was equally insistent that he should not. The President finally resolved the question in favor of MacArthur.[51] Lacking a directive from the Joint Chiefs of Staff, General MacArthur devised his own policy for civil affairs during the reoccupation of the Philippines.

The formulation of this policy may be said to have started on 22 July 1944 with a memorandum from Brig. Gen. Bonner F. Fellers, personnel officer of General Headquarters, to General MacArthur. He stated that although President Manuel Quezon had established a Division of Civil Affairs in the Philippine Army, the actual work would have to be done by the United States Army. General Fellers, therefore, recommended that General Headquarters immediately assume full responsibility for civil administration during the reoccupation. Administration in the occupied areas should be done, however, in the name of the Philippine Commonwealth and in complete co-operation with its official representatives.[52]

On 30 August General MacArthur issued a directive creating a civil affairs unit in his headquarters and outlining the broad policies that were to be followed in the Philippines.[53] This directive was subsequently expanded on 28 September[54] but it was not until 9 October, eleven days before the landing on Leyte, that MacArthur issued detailed instructions on the procedures to be followed.[55]

During the combat stage General Krueger, the senior tactical commander, was to be responsible for such civil administration and relief as would be possible under the existing tactical situation. General MacArthur would delegate the administration of civil affairs and relief in the liberated areas as promptly as possible to the authorized representatives of the Commonwealth Government. The only restrictions placed upon the Filipino people were to be those required by military necessity. By arrangement with General MacArthur the Philippine Commonwealth was, in general, to determine the guilt or innocence of suspected collaborationists, though the U. S. Army commanders were to retain complete authority to deal with the suspects if necessary.

General MacArthur also established the financial policies to be followed. A new series of Philippine Treasury certificates called "Victory Pesos" would be introduced in the liberated areas. The exchange rate would be two for an American dollar. All prewar currency and all emergency currency officially determined to be bona fide would be accepted at face value. All other Philippine or enemy currency would be worthless. Wage rates to be paid Filipino labor were established and ceiling prices consistent with the approved wage scale were set.

General Krueger delegated authority for civil administration and relief to Generals Hodge and Sibert for their respective corps areas. The commanding general of the

---

[51] History of Civil Affairs Div, WD Special Staff, Philippines, pp. 1–17, typescript in OCMH.

[52] Memo, Gen Fellers for CINCSWPA, 23 Jul 44, U. S. Army Forces, Pacific, Report on Civil Affairs (2 vols), II, 1.

[53] GHQ SWPA Staff Memo 35, 30 Aug 44; Rpt cited n. 52, pp. 6–9.

[54] GHQ SWPA Staff Memo 40; *Ibid.*, 28 Sep 44, pp. 12–15.

[55] GHQ SWPA, Standing Operating Procedure Instns 26, 9 Oct 44; *Ibid.*, pp. 22–42.

AN OFFICER OF A CIVIL AFFAIRS UNIT *pays off civilian workers with the new*
"Victory Pesos."

Army Service Command was responsible for the recruitment and maintenance of civilian labor. General MacArthur attached to the Sixth Army eight Philippine civil affairs units, which were to assist the field commanders in the administration of civil affairs and relief. Two of these were retained by Sixth Army, two were attached to each of the corps, and two to the Army Service Command.[56]

As soon as the conflict had passed by an area, a civil affairs unit of the Sixth Army stepped in and started to restore the normal community life. Temporary appointments of Filipino officials were made, such appointments going to men who had been screened by the Counter Intelligence Corps

or who were sponsored by Filipinos whose loyalty was unquestioned. In nearly every case the Philippine Commonwealth ratified these appointments. In every area reached by the Sixth Army, civil officials were appointed as soon as the tide of battle passed, and without exception cordial relations were established. The civil affairs officers of the Sixth Army did not attempt to interfere with civil operations unless requested to do so, or unless the military situation made it necessary.

Relations With Filipino Refugees

While the American assault forces were hitting the shores of Leyte, a delegation of Filipinos boarded the *Blue Ridge* and gave General Irving of the 24th Division infor-

---

[56] Sixth Army Admin O 14, Annex 8, Civil Affairs Plan. 30 Sep 44.

mation regarding conditions on the island. They received a cordial welcome, the Filipino steward's mates giving them much of their spare clothing.[57]

Many refugees who had been driven from their homes by the naval bombardment came into the American lines on the beaches seeking comfort and aid. These Filipinos had been without food or water for a considerable time, some of them for as long as twenty-four hours. Many of those who had remained in foxholes during the naval shelling were badly shaken up.

Palo Sector

In the area around Palo [58] fifty to seventy-five civilians had arrived by nightfall on A Day, 20 October. The Army gave them food and drink and then quartered them in two houses on the beach. By the following morning the influx of Filipinos had become very great and the arrival of many more was expected. The civil affairs officers therefore secured two more dwellings, had latrines dug, and maintained constant policing of the area, which was finally encircled by wire enclosures. The Army set up an evacuation hospital unit in the bivouac area to take care of the wounded and sick. A baby was delivered in an emergency obstetrical tent, "both mother and child faring well."

Wells were dug to provide water for washing. During 21 October between 1,500 and 2,000 refugees crowded into the area. By 22 October the congestion had become so great that a larger site was imperative. General Sibert decided to move the civilians to Palo, even though the town had not yet

been cleared of Japanese. After an Army chaplain had said Mass, the refugees proceeded on foot, in single file, to Palo. The Army adopted this mode of advance in order to minimize interference with troops, supplies, and equipment and also to protect the refugees from mines and booby traps which the Japanese had placed on the shoulders of the road. Many of the civilians carried all of their effects with them; children, as young as three or four years, were impressed into carrying their share of the family's meager possessions.

Because of the inpouring of refugees from surrounding districts, Palo suddenly grew from a normal population of about 6,000 to one estimated at 12,000 to 15,000. Nearly 5,000 people with their animals crowded into a church and its adjacent compound. Sanitary conditions were very bad.

The Army fed these refugees from captured stocks of rice and appointed a force of civilian police. After a survey of the area, the Army instituted sanitary measures for cleaning up the church and its compound, with removal and burial of the dead animals. Civilian laborers who had been checked for their loyalty undertook the burial of American and Japanese dead and the unloading of ships in the harbor. The Army disarmed all Filipinos except guerrillas and enforced security regulations, which prohibited civilians from appearing on the streets after dark. As more military units entered the town, 5,000 of the refugees were moved to its outskirts. The Army set up a hospital in the compound and surgeries in the schoolhouses, with separate wards for men and women. Teachers and other qualified women assisted as practical nurses. Within one week the Army had organized the town and begun work toward rehabilitation.

---

[57] Tarbuck Report.

[58] The material on refugees in the Palo area is taken from 24th Inf Div Opns Rpt Leyte, Annex 13, pp. 146–48.

REFUGEE AREA ON ORANGE BEACH NEAR DULAG

Dulag Sector

On the beaches of XXIV Corps a naval civil affairs unit controlled the Philippine civilians.[59] This unit arrived ashore at 0700 on 21 October. The area which had been previously allocated for a civilian compound was found to be a swamp. Approximately 1,500 refugees were scattered around the landing beaches. The Army assembled these and moved them to a new site in the town of Dulag, but the location had undergone a three-day naval bombardment which had reduced it to smoldering rubble. The Army recruited laborers to clean the area.

The military police assisted in control of

the civilian population and procured and distributed food and water. A medical officer and several enlisted men from the 7th Division gave medical aid to large numbers of civilians who were treated for minor wounds, injuries, tropical ulcers, and other ailments. By 22 October the medical officer had referred at least 100 of the more serious cases to an Army field hospital near by. Fifteen unclaimed and unidentified civilian dead were buried in the Filipino cemetery.

By the morning of 22 October, since the civilian population of Dulag had grown to approximately 10,000, General Hodge issued orders to move the refugees to a new location. By 23 October, when a suitable place had been found, the number of refugees had risen to approximately 30,000. The mass migration to the new location, which was two miles from Dulag, was most

---

[59] Material on refugees in the Dulag area is based on the Report of Naval Civil Affairs Unit, 7 Dec 44, 7th Inf Div Opns Rpt Leyte, Incl 1, App. G to Annex 1.

difficult, and not until the civil affairs officers had sent food and water to the new site could civilians be persuaded to move. The selected area measured about 1,000 by 600 yards and consisted of a coconut grove and a beach. Except for its inadequate size and its infringement upon military installations, it was completely satisfactory. After 24 October the civilians were removed from camp and sent back to their home villages as soon as the latter were declared secure.

Issuing of Supplies

By the morning of 24 October the Sixth Army was taking care of some 45,000 people, most of the population of about fifty-six communities. Although at first there was a shortage of food and water, by 24 October there was an adequate supply. Before that time the Army supplied the civilians with C and K rations, since it could not locate an appreciable quantity of the civilian food supplies. Seventy percent of these supplies, consisting of fish, rice, and meat, were later found and distributed by the civil affairs officers.

The Army originally distributed food to individuals but later made distribution through leaders in the barrios until it could establish a general store. The civil affairs officers distributed 28,700 full rations, fifty cases of condensed milk for infant use, and five tons of captured Japanese rice. About 5,000 full rations were stolen or not accounted for. An Army purification unit set up a 3,000-gallon canvas water tank and furnished water to the area.

A general store was in operation by 26 October for the sale of necessities. Clothing, rice, biscuits, salmon, and candles were the items most in demand. Some articles were ill adapted to the use or customs of the Filipinos. "The people would not buy or use the 4,000 rat traps or the rolls of toilet paper furnished nor would they buy or use canned or powdered milk." [60] Prices were fixed at prewar levels.

The civil affairs units of the Sixth Army opened about 500 schools in the principal barrios, those in Tacloban being the first to open. Many school buildings were either rebuilt or repaired under the direction of civil affairs officers and with funds furnished by them. Since there were no primary textbooks, in one instance the civil affairs units mimeographed a series of three schoolbooks which were illustrated by an Army artist. The teachers of Leyte not only provided excellent service in school work but also acted as relief workers, sanitarians, and assistants in the dispensaries and hospitals.

At first, a number of improvised hospitals were opened up. When the civilian hospital supplies arrived, however, modern hospitals were established at Tacloban, Baybay, and Carigara. These were staffed by local doctors and nurses, but the civil affairs unit continued to furnish food and supervision. Twenty-seven permanent dispensaries were also established. These were greatly needed, since the Japanese had not given the people any medical aid and had stopped all preventive medical measures. Dental treatment was given to more than 2,000 Filipinos, and smallpox inoculations were administered to more than 8,000. Also, when they seemed to be required, inoculations were given for typhoid, typhus, and cholera.

The prescribed amount of civilian medical supplies proved to be inadequate, a situation which placed an undue burden upon

---

[60] Civil Affairs, Sixth Army Opns Rpt Leyte, p. 279.

the medical units and facilities of all echelons of the Sixth Army. The food supplies, however, were more than adequate. The sizes of clothing and shoes were often too large and there was not a sufficient supply of women's and children's garments. On the island 10,000 tons of civilian supplies were landed, of which 6,830 tons were distributed. About 1,102 tons of rice were sold or given away, a figure which does not include captured Japanese stocks of rice. More than 400,000 refugees were fed and 287,000 relief clients were cared for.[61] By 25 December the relief rolls included only the aged, sick, and infirm, and members of families without a breadwinner.

Recruitment of Filipinos

"Hundreds of self appointed guerrillas whose only claim to participation in the guerrilla organization was a recently realized ambition to be of service to their country and to their allies" confronted the assault forces on the beachheads. These individuals caused endless confusion, since it was practically impossible for the Americans to distinguish between the genuine guerrilla and his opportunistic counterfeit. After the first few days, however, the Army made contact with guerrilla headquarters and established liaison with the bona fide guerrillas.[62]

General Krueger made the guerrillas a part of his armed forces, and they became a source of additional strength to the Sixth Army. These men frequently operated and patrolled in enemy-held territory and brought the Americans valuable information on Japanese movements and dispositions; the unit commanders of Sixth Army,

however, tended to discount reports from such sources with regard to the size of Japanese forces. The guerrillas also guarded supply dumps and depots, bridges, and other installations in the rear areas.

The generosity of the American soldier in giving away supplies made it difficult to recruit civilian labor. Since gifts of food to prospective laborers diminished their incentive to work, the Sixth Army issued an order prohibiting such gifts. As early as 21 October the Army got in touch with political and labor leaders to serve as advisers and assistants, telling them from day to day how many laborers would be needed. The Filipino leaders were very co-operative and made arrangements to secure the necessary labor. Good results were obtained by enlisting the support of local leaders, especially the parish priests. General Krueger declared: "In all reported instances, the priests lent willing assistance and their information on individuals and conditions was found reliable and outstandingly impartial." [63] As the fighting reached past Carigara and Dagami and into the central mountain range the Filipinos acted as supply carriers for the troops and worked on the roads and trails. At one time there were as many as 8,000 Filipinos engaged in this labor. Army furnished transportation to the site of the work and paid wages according to the Commonwealth Government wage scales.

Throughout November the logistical situation on Leyte remained bad. Work on roads, together with that on airfields and other installations, consisted largely of temporary expedients. The difficult problem of getting supplies ashore and to the troops had

---

[61] *Ibid.*, p. 279.
[62] 1st Cav Div Opns Rpt Leyte, pp. 22–23.

[63] Ltr, CG Sixth Army to CG X Corps and others, 25 Nov 44.

not been completely solved, a situation which hampered the progress of the tactical troops. The lag in construction of airdromes made it impossible for land-based air forces to give adequate close air support to the ground forces. This lack of support was another handicap to General Krueger's men as they fought their way into the mountains.

CHAPTER XII

The Mountain Barrier: Part One

The successful completion of the campaign for the entire Leyte Valley on 2 November enabled General Krueger to embark on the next phase of his plan for the liberation of Leyte.

This action was to consist of two drives converging on Ormoc: one south through Ormoc Valley by X Corps and the other north from Baybay by XXIV Corps. The remaining Japanese on the island would thus be forced into the mountains west of Ormoc Valley where they could not offer effective organized resistance. At first, while some elements of the XXIV Corps continued to push west to reinforce the troops on the shores of Ormoc Bay and mopped up in southern Leyte Valley, the X Corps was to secure control of the coast of Carigara Bay from Carigara to Pinamopoan. With the completion of this assignment, the northern elements of the Sixth Army would be in a position to drive south along Highway 2 which twisted and turned through the northern mountains and central plains of Ormoc Valley to the port of Ormoc.[1] (*Map 11*)

General Sibert ordered elements of the 1st Cavalry Division to occupy Carigara while the 24th Division secured the coastal corridor that ran from Carigara to Pinamopoan and then drove south along Highway 2 and occupied Ormoc. A battalion from the 24th Division was to move to the Jaro area and protect the 155-mm. howitzers of the 947th Field Artillery Battalion which was to assist the advance south by covering a trail that ran from Jaro to Ormoc.[2]

Since the 21st Infantry had encountered virtually no opposition in the vicinity of Panaon Strait and since it was desirable that the regiment rejoin the 24th Division, General Krueger on 30 October had directed General Hodge to relieve the 21st Infantry with one battalion of the 32d Infantry.[3] General Irving ordered the 34th Infantry to continue its attack and secure Capoocan. When the town was captured the 19th Infantry was to move into it on 4 November while the 34th Infantry continued the drive west and secured Pinamopoan.[4]

The Coastal Corridor

Capoocan and Pinamopoan

At 0700 on 3 November the 34th Infantry moved west from its perimeter at Balaud in a column of battalions, with the 1st Battalion, under Colonel Clifford, in the lead. The 1st Battalion entered Capoocan at 0755 and within ten minutes had secured the town.[5]

At 0830 the battalion moved out and continued west along the coastal road to Pina-

---

[1] Sixth Army FO 28, 3 Nov 44.

[2] X Corps FO 6, 3 Nov 44.
[3] Sixth Army FO 27, 30 Oct 44.
[4] 24th Div FO 5, 2 Nov 44.
[5] 1st Bn, 34th Inf, Unit Jnl, 3 Nov 44.

mopoan. After an advance of about 1,000 yards, Company B, the point, encountered an enemy force, estimated at about 100 men, entrenched on the west bank of a stream. The column halted and placed mortar fire on the Japanese but failed to dislodge them. The company then withdrew while the howitzers of the 63d Field Artillery Battalion pounded the enemy position.

In the meantime a platoon of Company B moved south to secure a ridge which paralleled the road. When the platoon located some Japanese dug in on the reverse slope Colonel Clifford sent Company A to its assistance. The guides took Company A over the wrong trail and the troops ran into the strong enemy entrenchments well concealed by underbrush on the western bank of the stream. Company A launched a frontal assault, but after the first platoon had passed the hidden positions the Japanese opened fire and forced the company to withdraw. Colonel Clifford rushed Company C to the assistance of Company A, ordering it to deploy around the left flank of Company A and onto the next ridge. The platoon from Company B returned to its morning position.

Companies A and C then started against the Japanese emplacements on the opposite bank of the stream.[6] The leader of the advance squad of Company A was killed and Sgt. Charles E. Mower assumed command. As he started to lead his men across the stream, Sergeant Mower was severely wounded. From his exposed position in the middle of the stream he directed his squad in the destruction of two enemy machine guns and numerous riflemen, but he was killed when the Japanese turned their fire against him. Sergeant Mower was posthumously awarded the Medal of Honor.

At 1530 Colonel Clifford withdrew Company A. After the 63d Field Artillery Battalion had blasted the ridge parallel to the road, Company B attacked, while Company C made its envelopment around the south flank and destroyed the Japanese pocket of resistance. At 1800 the 1st Battalion formed its night perimeter.[7]

Earlier, at 1430, Company K had made a reconnaissance in amphibian tractors from Capoocan to a point just west of Pinamopoan. Since it encountered heavy enemy fire, the company withdrew and returned to Capoocan.[8]

During the night the 11th and 63d Field Artillery Battalions massed their fires and laid interdiction fire up and down the highway. Under cover of darkness, the Japanese force opposing the 1st Battalion withdrew. On the following morning patrols sent out by the 1st Battalion scouted 1,000 yards to the front but encountered no enemy. The battalion therefore moved out at 0730 to Colasian where it set up a defensive position. The 2d and 3d Battalions then passed through the 1st. The 2d Battalion entered Pinamopoan and dug in, while the 3d passed through the town and continued west along the highway 1,700 yards. There it set up a defensive position just short of a ridge of hills that was later to be known as Breakneck Ridge.[9] Between Capoocan and Pinamopoan the Japanese had abandoned three 75-mm., one 40-mm., and five 37-mm. guns, together with ammunition dumps, signal equipment, and many documents. The 34th Infantry found some land mines on the road and destroyed them. Since the regiment had quickly secured the coastal

---

[6] 1st Bn, 34th Inf, Unit Jnl, 3 Nov 44.

[7] 1st Bn, 34th Inf, Unit Jnl, 3 Nov 44.
[8] 24th Div Opns Rpt Leyte, pp. 39–40.
[9] *Ibid.,* p. 40.

corridor and had started to move down Highway 2, the X Corps was now in a position from which it could drive south.

Defense of the Coastal Corridor

Some elements of the *26th Division* had arrived on Leyte during the naval battle, and on 1 November most of the *1st Division* and the *12th Independent Infantry Regiment* of the *26th Division* landed at Ormoc. The *1st Division*, which had been activated in Tokyo, had served in Manchuria during the "China Incident" and had been transferred to Shanghai in August 1944. Though it had no combat experience, this division was considered by General Tomochika to be the best equipped division of the Japanese Army. Under the command of Lt. Gen. Tadasu Kataoka, it had been held in reserve by *Imperial General Headquarters* for the decisive battle, and it was sent to Manila with great expectations.[10]

The arrival of these troops was in accord with a plan devised after the Battle of Leyte Gulf. The *102d Division*, coming from Panay, and the *1st* and *26th Divisions*, sailing from Luzon, were to land at Ormoc. General Suzuki planned to have these troops move north along the Ormoc–Limon road (Highway 2) through Ormoc Valley, from which they were to diverge in three columns and capture the Carigara–Jaro road. After seizing the road, the Japanese troops were to advance east and destroy the American forces in the area between Tacloban and Tanauan. After the *1st Division* had secured Carigara, the *68th Brigade* was to land in the north as *35th Army* reserve. At the same time the *30th Division* was to land at Albuera on Ormoc Bay and advance over

mountainous trails to Burauen and later neutralize all resistance in the Dulag area.[11]

When General Suzuki received information that the Americans had secured Carigara, he realized that it would be impossible to drive toward San Pedro Bay with the Americans on his left flank. He believed, however, that the reinforced *1st Division* could easily wipe out the American forces in the Carigara area. On 3 November he ordered the *1st Division* to speed up its passage through Ormoc Valley and the *102d Division* to consolidate its forces with those of the *1st Division* for an all-out attack to annihilate the American troops near Carigara. The *26th Division* was to advance on Jaro.[12] No alternative to this plan had been prepared in case the projected operations were not successful.[13] On 3 November, American aircraft struck at the *1st Division* as it moved up Ormoc Valley in a ten-mile-long convoy of trucks, tanks, and artillery. They destroyed about thirty trucks and left two tanks burning. The aircraft received heavy and accurate ground antiaircraft fire, and two of the planes were shot down by the Japanese.[14]

---

[10] Tomochika, True Facts of Leyte Opn, p. 18.

[11] 10th I&HS, Eighth Army, Stf Study of Opns of Japanese *35th Army* on Leyte, Part I, p. 5.

[12] *Ibid.*, Part I, pp. 5–6.

[13] *Ibid.*, Part IV, p. 2, interrog of Col Junkichi Okabayashi, CofS *1st Div.* Colonel Okabayashi makes the following statement about Japanese planning: "It is not the ordinary practice in the Japanese Army for higher headquarters to provide unit commanders with alternate plans. When conferences are held between unit commanders and the staff of higher headquarters, all possible alternatives are, of course, discussed. At any rate, unit commanders are invariably oriented with the general plan of higher headquarters. In the event an original order cannot be carried out because of the changing battle situation, the responsibility for making changes in plans devolves upon the commander of the unit concerned."

[14] Rpt of Sixth Army G–3 Liaison Sec, 3 Nov 44, Sixth Army G–3 Jnl, 3 Nov 44.

The lack of defense at Carigara had come as a surprise to General Krueger, since the Americans had observed the Japanese reinforcing the area. General Suzuki had cleverly concealed from the Americans his strength and intentions and thus had gained time for a withdrawal by a "very successful" delaying action.[15] At the same time, the *57th Infantry Regiment* of the *1st Division* had been able to move north through Ormoc Valley and establish itself in the northern mountains surrounding Highway 2.

The bringing in of reinforcements by the Japanese brought into sharp focus the lack of American aerial strength on Leyte. Although the Fifth Air Force had numerous aircraft in the rear areas, these could not be brought forward because of the very poor condition of the available airstrips. The few aircraft based on Leyte could not prevent the flow of additional enemy forces into the island or give direct support to the ground troops of Sixth Army.

Since the Japanese had been able to send without difficulty about 13,500 troops into the Ormoc area, General Krueger recognized that they were capable also of landing troops on the shores of Carigara Bay. This landing, if successful, would isolate the American forces in the Carigara area. To meet this threat, several courses of action were open to General Krueger: he could devote the full energy of the X Corps to preparing a defense against a sea force attack; he could disregard the threat and have the X Corps push vigorously south and secure a position on ground south of Limon, which was about two and a half miles southwest of Pinamopoan, before the Japanese could build defensive positions; or, finally, he could advance south with some elements, leaving others to guard the Carigara area.

If the Japanese Navy and amphibious assault forces entered Carigara Bay, the possibilities for effective countermeasures were not very promising. The escort carriers of the Seventh Fleet, greatly weakened by the Battle of Leyte Gulf, could not give support, and it was quite possible that any assistance that could be furnished by the Third Fleet might not arrive in time.

Ranking officers of the Seventh Fleet, however, did not believe it likely that the Japanese would launch an amphibious assault through Carigara Bay. The reasons given were as follows: The Japanese had never made an assault landing against defended beaches in the past; they were short of equipment to make a sustained amphibious assault; and they would be landing in the face of the combined fire of the X Corps artillery which would cover the beachhead area from positions well behind the beaches.[16]

Although General Krueger realized that the high ground in the Limon area was the key to operations farther south, he decided that the threat to the Carigara area could not be ignored. Since he had insufficient forces to drive south and at the same time to prepare the Carigara area for defense, on 4 November he directed General Sibert to protect the Carigara area from a seaborne attack before the advance to the south was continued. At the same time the X Corps was to send out units to explore for trails that led from Daro, about three miles southwest of Jaro, to Ormoc with the view of emplacing an artillery battalion of 155-mm. guns within effective firing range of Ormoc.[17]

---

[15] Sixth Army Opns Rpt Leyte, p. 38.

[16] Memo, Maj Reppert for Col Clyde D. Eddleman, Rpt of Conf with Rear Adm William M. Fechteler, 5 Nov 44, Sixth Army G–3 Jnl, 5 Nov 44.

[17] Ltr of Instns, CG Sixth Army to CG X Corps, 4 Nov 44, Sixth Army Opns Rpt Leyte, p. 199.

General Sibert immediately told General Irving to defer until further orders the advance south by the 24th Division. At the same time he directed Generals Irving and Mudge to have their divisions prepare defenses to ward off a seaborne attack against the Barugo–Carigara–Capoocan area. Patrols of the 24th Infantry Division and the 1st Cavalry Division were to maintain contact at the Carigara River.[18]

General Mudge thereupon ordered the 1st Cavalry Brigade to patrol the Carigara–Jaro road and to protect the movement of supplies and troops along the road. The 2d Cavalry Brigade was to establish two squadrons in the Carigara–Barugo area to protect the seaward approaches to the area, guard the bridge between Barugo and Carigara, and maintain the security of San Juanico Strait. The brigade was to be prepared to reinforce the 24th Division.[19]

General Irving, also, redisposed his forces. All the field artillery battalions had been at Carigara but, with the issuance of the order to protect the coast of Carigara Bay, the 13th and 52d Field Artillery Battalions moved to Colasion Point on 4 November, while the 63d and 11th took positions east and west of Capoocan.[20]

On 5 November General Sibert returned the 21st Infantry to the 24th Division and recommended that General Irving send the regiment to Pinamopoan to relieve the battle-weary 34th Infantry.[21] By the end of the day the 1st and 3d Battalions, 21st Infantry, had relieved the 34th Infantry and were on the edge of Breakneck Ridge west of Pinamopoan.[22]

The American aircraft made two strikes at the convoy of the *1st Division* as it moved north up Highway 2. The first one at about 1430 destroyed about thirty trucks, several tanks, and an ammunition dump and killed fifty to seventy-five men and thirty to forty horses. The second strike at about 1745 hit trucks loaded with Japanese soldiers who scattered when attacked. All the vehicles were camouflaged with palm leaves.[23]

By 6 November, since the X Corps had disposed its force to protect the seaward approaches and since the Navy had given assurance that an amphibious assault was unlikely, General Krueger felt that the attack south could be continued. He was anxious to have the Sixth Army drive rapidly down Highway 2 and secure the port of Ormoc, through which the Japanese had reinforced the Leyte garrison. He also wished to guard against the possibility that the Japanese, as more and more of their troops moved up Ormoc Valley, would attempt to debouch into northern Leyte Valley. He therefore directed General Sibert to expend his main effort in the drive south but also to send elements of his force into the mountains east of Ormoc Valley. These units were to seize the mountain passes and secure positions in the Daro area from which the artillery could deliver long-range fire upon Ormoc in support of the advance south. At the same time, elements of the XXIV Corps were to guard the mountain passages into southern Leyte Valley.[24]

---

[18] Ltr, CG X Corps to CG's 24th Div and 1st Cav Div, 4 Nov 44; X Corps G–3 Jnl, 5 Nov 44.

[19] 1st Cav Div FO 7, 4 Nov 44.

[20] 24th Div Opns Rpt Leyte, p. 103.

[21] X Corps Opn Plan, 5 Nov 44, Sixth Army G–3 Jnl, 5 Nov 44.

[22] 24th Div Opns Sum, 5 Nov 44, X Corps G–3 Jnl, 5 Nov 44.

[23] Msg, G–2 X Corps to G–3 Sixth Army, 5 Nov 44, Sixth Army G–3 Jnl, 6 Nov 44.

[24] Sixth Army FO 29, Nov 44.

Battle of Breakneck Ridge

The Battle Begins

On 5 November General Sibert instructed the 24th Division to complete the relief of the 34th Infantry and at the same time to push strong, aggressive patrols to the south. The 1st Battalion, 19th Infantry, was to protect a battalion of 155-mm. guns, which was to deliver long-range fire on Ormoc, about fourteen miles to the southwest. The attack south was to begin on 7 November.[25]

Accordingly, General Irving ordered the 21st Infantry, after the completion of its relief of the 34th Infantry, to reconnoiter Breakneck Ridge to its front on 6 November and on the following day to launch its drive south. A battalion of the 19th Infantry was to move to Pinamopoan and protect the line of communications of the 21st Infantry as the attack progressed. The rest of the 19th Infantry was to move to the mountains in the vicinity of Daro and Jaro to protect the 226th Field Artillery Battalion and secure the mountain passes that led into Leyte Valley.[26]

The 21st Infantry relieved the 34th Infantry in the vicinity of Pinamopoan without difficulty and sent out strong patrols to Breakneck Ridge. One of these patrols was led by Lt. Col. Frederick R. Weber, the regimental commander.

Breakneck Ridge, over which Highway 2 corkscrewed its way between Pinamopoan and Limon for about 7,200 yards, was actually a hill mass with many spurs branching off from an irregularly shaped crest line toward the shores of Carrigara Bay to the north and the Leyte River valley to the

south. Shoulder-high cogon grass was thick on the low ground, and the pockets between the hills were heavily forested. The valleys were deep, with precipitous sides. The *1st Division* had heavily fortified the area, taking advantage of the innumerable thickly wooded pockets that served as natural forts. The Japanese had also built an elaborate system of trenches and other defensive positions and had honeycombed the area with spider holes. Many of the latter were on reverse slopes some distance below the crests and were protected from direct fire. In front of each spider hole the enemy had cut fire lanes through the cogon grass, which was left so short that even a crawling soldier would be exposed to fire. The constant rainfall made the hills slippery and treacherous, and, more important, provided a protective curtain in the day and covered movements of the enemy at night.[27]

On 5 November, before the relief of the 34th Infantry, Maj. Kemuel K. Blacker, leading an artillery forward observer's party from the 52d Field Artillery Battalion and a patrol from the 34th Infantry, had reconnoitered far forward on Breakneck Ridge to the top of a knoll, later called OP Hill, which was some 2,500 yards west of Pinamopoan, and was directing fire from that point.[28] The party was attacked by a group of about platoon strength from the *57th Infantry Regiment* and took refuge in an abandoned position. At 1230 Colonel Weber ordered the 3d Battalion, 21st Infantry, to move out to the party's assistance. Company K, on the right side of the highway, was able to secure the northern approaches

---

[25] X Corps Amendment to FO 6, 5 Nov 44.
[26] 24th Div FO 7, 5 Nov 44.

[27] Col William J. Verbeck, *A Regiment in Action* (n. p., n. d., copy in OCMH), p. 16; 24th Div Opns Rpt Leyte, p. 42.
[28] 24th Div Opns Rpt Leyte, p. 42.

to the hill and rescue the observation party, though it ran into heavy machine gun and rifle fire. In the meantime Company I moved to the left and against stiff resistance secured a ridge later known as Corkscrew Ridge, which was about 1,200 yards southeast of OP Hill and which formed the southeastern spur of Breakneck Ridge. Since both companies needed more ammunition, vehicles with the required supply were sent up along the road. After hidden Japanese riflemen had punctured the tires, the vehicles withdrew and the ammunition was carried up by hand. A platoon of riflemen from Company I cleared out the enemy position but received mortar fire from an unknown source.[29]

Both companies were so far in advance of the rest of the 21st Infantry that only limited supplies of ammunition and rations could reach them. As the afternoon hours wore on, the pressure from the *57th Infantry* increased but the companies dug in and held their positions. During the night they repulsed three counterattacks of about fifty men each.[30] On the following morning the *57th Infantry* placed mortar fire upon the companies,[31] augmented at first by fire from one artillery piece and later by fire from a four-gun battery.[32] The intensity of this fire forced the companies to withdraw from their position and rejoin the rest of the 3d Battalion on the beach near Colasion.[33]

During the day the 1st Battalion tried unsuccessfully to secure positions to support the attack through Breakneck Ridge. At the close of 6 November the *57th Infantry*

of the *1st Division* securely occupied Breakneck Ridge and its northern approaches. For the assault the following day, General Irving attached the 3d Battalion, 19th Infantry, to the 21st Infantry. The 3d Battalion, 21st Infantry, had reorganized about 2,000 yards east of Pinamopoan. The 1st Battalion was on the regiment's right, the 2d Battalion was in the center astride the highway, and the 3d Battalion, 19th Infantry, was on the 21st Infantry's left.[34]

The 2d Battalion, 21st Infantry, was the object of a night attack that started at 2000 and lasted for two hours. The enemy used mortars and grenades against the battalion but was unable to penetrate its perimeter.[35] Colonel Weber ordered the 21st Infantry to be prepared to move out at 0800 on 7 November. The assault was to be made in column of battalions, the 2d Battalion in the lead, with a spur of Breakneck Ridge as the initial objective. This spur or branch ridge extended east and west across the road 400 yards south of the front line. General Irving ordered the 52d Field Artillery Battalion to mass its fire immediately in front of the troops for fifteen minutes just before they jumped off and then to shift its fire to the ridge. Attached to the 2d Battalion for support were a platoon from the 44th Tank Company, a company from the 85th Chemical Battalion, and a company from the 632d Tank Destroyer Battalion.[36]

At 0940 the 308th Bombardment Wing bombed the headquarters of General Suzuki at Ormoc and strafed the highway near by. Ormoc had also been under constant fire from the battalion of 155-mm. guns in Jaro, at a range of 25,000 yards. Only a

---

[29] 24th Div G-3 Jnl, 5 Nov 44.
[30] 24th Div G-2 Jnl, 6 Nov 44.
[31] Rad, Maj Clark, X Corps, to G-2 Sixth Army, BA 669, Sixth Army G-3 Jnl, 6 Nov 44.
[32] Msg, S-2 21st Inf to CG 24th Div, 6 Nov 44, 24th Div G-2 Jnl, 6 Nov 44.
[33] 24th Div Opns Rpt Leyte, p. 42.

[34] Sixth Army G-3 Jnl, 7 Nov 44.
[35] Msg, S-2 21st Inf to G-2 24th Div, 7 Nov 44, 24th Div G-2 Jnl, 7 Nov 44.
[36] 21st Inf FO 19, 7 Nov 44, 24th Div G-3 Jnl, 8 Nov 44.

few houses were left standing after the bombardment was completed.[37]

The troops moved out as scheduled. Company E, on the west of the road, reached the branch ridge at 0915 and came under fire from enemy automatic weapons on the right. Company G ran into about 200 men from the *3d Battalion, 57th Infantry Regiment.* They were well entrenched at a bend of the road on the forward slope of the high ground, and Colonel Weber had the self-propelled guns of the tank destroyer battalion brought forward. These fired into the pocket, and although they killed the commander of the *3d Battalion* the unit held fast.[38] Weber then called two tanks forward, but as they moved along the road a Japanese soldier jumped out of the high cogon grass and disabled one of the tanks by planting a magnetic mine against it. The other tank then withdrew.[39]

General Sibert was dissatisfied with the progress of the 21st Infantry and felt that Colonel Weber was not sufficiently aggressive. Accompanied by his G–2, Col. William J. Verbeck, he visited the command post of Colonel Weber at noon. Dispensing with the usual command channels and in the presence of General Irving, he relieved Colonel Weber and made Colonel Verbeck the commanding officer of the 21st Infantry. Colonel Weber was retained in the regiment as its executive officer.[40]

Colonel Verbeck ordered Company L, in support of the 2d Battalion, to make a wide flanking movement to the east and secure the ridge which had been denied to Company G. The company moved out at 1630 but was unsuccessful. As it withdrew it made contact with Company F which had successfully pushed forward but because of an unexplained misunderstanding of orders had withdrawn.[41] Night perimeters were established on the edge of Breakneck Ridge.

On the same day Colonel Chapman, commander of the 19th Infantry, ordered his 2d Battalion to send a reinforced rifle company to Hill 1525 about 2,600 yards southeast of Limon, seize this ground, and, in support of the advance south by the 21st Infantry, direct artillery fire on Highway 2 Company G, 19th Infantry, moved out on this mission with only two thirds of a ration per man, since its kitchens were still in the Jaro area. The guides with Company G lost their way, and the company set up a night perimeter after a patrol had located a strong enemy position on a ridge west of its course. The company position was thought to be in the vicinity of Hill 1525, but it was actually far east of the hill.[42]

As the 2d Battalion, 21st Infantry, had failed to secure the ridge 400 yards to its front, Colonel Verbeck that night ordered the battalion, with Company L attached, to continue the attack toward the ridge after an artillery barrage on the following morning. The 1st Battalion was to secure Hill 1525, establish contact with the 2d Battalion, 19th Infantry, and from the hill envelop the southern flank of the *1st Division.*[43]

On the morning of 8 November a typhoon, moving in from the west, swept

[37] Msg, 308th Bombardment Wing to Sixth Army, 7 Nov 44, Sixth Army G–3 Jnl, 7 Nov 44.

[38] Msg, CO 21st Inf to CG 24th Div, 7 Nov 44, 24th Div G–3 Jnl, 7 Nov 44; *35th Army* Opns, p. 57.

[39] Msg, S–3 21st Inf to CG 24th Div, 7 Nov 44, 24th Div G–2 Jnl, 7 Nov 44.

[40] Interv with Col Verbeck, 26 Sep 51. Colonel Verbeck stated that for the remainder of the campaign Colonel Weber was an excellent and loyal executive officer.

[41] Msg, S–3 21st Inf to G–3 24th Div, 7 Nov 44, 24th Div G–3 Jnl, 7 Nov 44: 24th Div Opns Rpt Leyte, p. 43.

[42] 24th Div Opns Rpt Leyte, p. 43.

[43] 24th Div G–3 Jnl, 7 Nov 44.

ENGINEERS REMOVE LAND MINES *from a bridge on Breakneck Ridge.*

over the entire island. Jan Valtin, a member of the 24th Division, graphically describes it: "From the angry immensity of the heavens floods raced in almost horizontal sheets. Palms bent low under the storm, their fronds flattened like streamers of wet silk. Trees crashed to earth. In the expanse of . . . [cogon] grass the howling of the wind was like a thousand-fold plaint of the unburied dead. The trickle of supplies was at a standstill. On Carigara Bay the obscured headlands moaned under the onslaught of the . . . seas. Planes were grounded and ships became haunted things looking for refuge. Massed artillery . . . barrages to the summit of Breakneck Ridge sounded dim and hollow in the tempest. Trails were obliterated by the rain. The sky

was black." [44] In the midst of the storm, the infantry attacked.

The 2d Battalion, 21st Infantry, effectively used flame throwers to drive the enemy troops out of spider holes and caves. [45] Although shelled by sporadic artillery fire, the battalion continued to advance. Strong elements of the *57th Infantry* hotly contested the American assault. Meanwhile Company E pushed farther along the road until it was halted at the site of a bridge which had been destroyed by the enemy. The Japanese had flanked the site with emplacements from which rifle, automatic weapons, and mortar fire resisted the frontal attack of

---

[44] Jan Valtin [Richard J. Krebs], *Children of Yesterday* (New York, The Readers Press, Inc., 1946), p. 187.
[45] 24th Div G–3 Jnl, 8 Nov 44.

the company.[46] At nightfall Company E fell back to its morning position. The *57th Infantry* continued to make a determined stand against the 2d Battalion. Concealed Japanese riflemen fired continuously on the front, flanks, and rear of all positions and small enemy detachments infiltrated through the lines. In concert with the attack of the 2d Battalion, the 1st Battalion had moved out that morning toward Hill 1525. Since the maps were grossly inaccurate, the precise location of the hill was unknown, but the battalion reported that it had reached the southern slope of the hill at 1600 and was digging in under automatic weapons fire. At 0700 the 2d Battalion, 19th Infantry, under Colonel Spragins, moved out through a driving rain and over precipitous trails to join the battalion's Company G. During the day Company G drove the enemy off the ridge where the company's advance had been halted the previous afternoon. In their flight the Japanese abandoned much equipment, most of which was new. Of more importance, a significant field order of the *1st Division* was found on the body of a Japanese officer.

When the consolidation of the battalion was made, Colonel Spragins determined that he was east of Hill 1525 as shown on the maps. Although the battalion was in a position to observe Leyte Valley, it would have to move westward in order to get a view of Ormoc Valley. At 1530 Colonel Spragins therefore sent Company E to occupy a ridge 1,000 yards to the west. The battalion then dug in for the night.[47] On the following morning General Irving placed the battalion under the operational control of the 21st Infantry.

Immediately in front of the 21st Infantry was a Japanese force estimated to be of battalion strength. To the east was an undetermined number of enemy machine guns. In front of Company E a bridge was out and tanks could not pass. On the steep sides of the gulch around this bridge site, elements of the *57th Infantry* with rifles, automatic weapons, and mortars stopped all attempts of Company E to move forward.[48]

Through the night torrential rains fell. At dawn of 9 November two begrimed, soaked, and weary battalions of the 21st Infantry jumped off to the attack, the 2d Battalion, less Company F, on the west side of the road and the 3d Battalion on the east. Heavy artillery preparations had already pounded the Japanese front lines. As the attack progressed, mortars and artillery placed fires on targets of opportunity. In destroying pockets of resistance in the gulch, grenades, rifles, and flame throwers were used, together with heavy machine guns.

At 0930 Company I, 21st Infantry, reached the crest of the intermediate ridge on the east side of the road which ran southward toward the center of Breakneck Ridge. An hour later Company E, 21st Infantry, moved out from the perimeter it had held for two days. Its mission was to cut west of the road and secure the commanding high ground in the rear of the emplaced Japanese at the bridge site where the advance of the company had been stopped on the previous day. At the same time Company L, 21st Infantry, passed through Company I and attacked the center of Breakneck Ridge as Company G started a wide envelopment to the west from Company E's position to assault OP Hill from the west. Artillery forward observer parties went with the com-

---

[46] 24th Div G–2 Periodic Rpt 20, 8 Nov 44.
[47] 24th Div Opns Rpt Leyte, p. 45.

[48] Msg, CO 21st Inf to CofS 24th Div, 8 Nov 44, 24th Div G–2 Jnl, 8 Nov 44.

panies and called artillery fires on targets of opportunity.

At 1150 Company L encountered determined opposition from enemy rifle and mortar fire but doggedly pushed ahead for several hours and secured the top of the ridge. Company G reached its objective, but upon receiving intense enemy fire was forced to retire to the eastern slopes of a ridge 300 yards to the north, where it reorganized. Company E also reached its objective and then formed its night perimeter. At 1815 the Japanese launched a counterattack against the perimeter of Company G but the attack was repulsed. For the night a platoon of heavy machine guns was attached to each rifle company to protect its perimeter.

Since the position of the 2d Battalion, 19th Infantry, had by this time become clear, Colonel Verbeck ordered the battalion to move from the east and to relieve the 1st Battalion, 21st Infantry, on Hill 1525. One company was to be established on a ridge overlooking Highway 2 while the remainder of the battalion was to block the trail that passed Hill 1525.[49] The 1st Battalion, 21st Infantry, was to push westward from its position on Hill 1525 and cut the Ormoc road some 1,800 yards south of Limon in order to forestall the escape of Japanese troops from Breakneck Ridge. Company A was to remain on the hill and hold it until the 2d Battalion, 19th Infantry, arrived.

The 1st Battalion, less Company A, jumped off at 0730. After it had advanced about one and a half miles and was within sight of Highway 2, the battalion was halted by heavy enemy fire from the front and both flanks. It renewed the attack and informed

Colonel Verbeck that it was moving slowly northwest and was less than a mile from Limon. In the meantime the enemy attacked Company A on Hill 1525, and the company was able to maintain its position with difficulty. Because of this fight and the fact that no contact had been established with the 2d Battalion, 19th Infantry, Colonel Verbeck ordered the battalion to rejoin Company A. The troops therefore returned and took part in the fight to repel the Japanese. The 1st Battalion withstood the enemy force until 1400, when an estimated battalion of fresh troops from the *57th Infantry* was thrown into the fight.[50] The Americans then broke off the engagement, and the battalion, covered by Company A, withdrew from Hill 1525 to the vicinity of Pinamopoan.[51]

Information that the 1st Battalion, 21st Infantry, was being attacked on Hill 1525 reached the 2d Battalion, 19th Infantry, shortly after noon as it was on its way to relieve the 1st Battalion. Colonel Spragins pushed forward immediately with two companies, hoping to reach the 1st Battalion by 1500, but progress was slowed by steep, slippery slopes that were often blocked by huge fallen trees. At 1630, without having heard any sounds of battle, which they had hoped would guide them to the 1st Battalion's position, the troops reached what they believed to be the western slopes of Hill 1525. Patrols reported no contact either with friendly or enemy units and the 2d Battalion set up its night perimeter.

"At this time," states the 24th Infantry Division operations report on Leyte, "it began to dawn on all concerned that Hill 1525, as shown on the map, was not a single hill mass, but a long ridge of many knolls and hilltops."[52]

---

[49] Msg, G–3 24th Div to G–2 24th Div, 9 Nov 44, 24th Div G–2 Jnl, 9 Nov 44.

[50] 24th Div G–3 Periodic Rpt 21, 9 Nov 44.
[51] 24th Div Opns Rpt Leyte, p. 47.
[52] *Ibid.*, p. 48.

VIEW FROM THE RIDGES LOOKING NORTH UP THE LIMON VALLEY

Breakneck Ridge: Second Phase

On 9 November the Japanese *26th Division* arrived at Ormoc in three large transports with a destroyer escort. The troops landed without their equipment and ammunition, since aircraft from the Fifth Air Force bombed the convoy and forced it to depart before the unloading was completed. During the convoy's return, some of the Japanese vessels were destroyed by the American aircraft.[53]

The arrival of these troops was in accord with a plan embodied in the order which had been taken from the dead Japanese officer on the previous day. This plan envisaged a grand offensive which was to start in the middle of November. The *41st Infantry Regiment* of the *30th Division* and the *169th* and *171st Independent Infantry Battalions* of the *102d Division* were to secure a line that ran from a hill 3,500 yards northwest of Jaro to a point just south of Pinamopoan and protect the movement of the *1st Division* to this line. With the arrival of the *1st Division* on this defensive line, a co-ordinated attack was to be launched—the *1st Division* seizing the Carigara area and the *41st Infantry Regiment* and the *26th Division* attacking the Mt. Mamban area about ten miles southeast of Limon. The way would then be open for a drive into Leyte Valley.[54]

General Krueger was quick to realize the significance of this order. Since General Suzuki apparently wished to make the mountains of northern Leyte the battleground for

[53] *35th Army* Opns, p. 59.

[54] *Ibid.;* Sixth Army Opns Rpt Leyte, p. 50; Sixth Army G–3 Jnl, 9 Nov 44.

the island, Krueger disposed his forces to meet the enemy threat. The X Corps was to continue its drive south down Highway 2 but at the same time was to dispose units in the central mountain range to protect the exits from Ormoc Valley into Leyte Valley. The XXIV Corps was to send a reinforced regiment into the hills northwest of Dagami to prevent any Japanese from infiltrating into Leyte Valley, and the corps was also to be prepared to assist elements of the X Corps that guarded the trail running from Daro to Dolores, a village about six miles northeast of Ormoc. A regiment of the XXIV Corps was to be placed in Sixth Army Reserve at Dagami, where the central mountain range began.[55]

General Sibert then ordered the 24th Division to continue its attack south. The 112th Cavalry Regimental Combat Team, under Brig. Gen. Julian W. Cunningham, which was expected to arrive on 14 November, was to relieve elements of the 1st Cavalry Division that guarded the beaches in the Carigara–Barugo area. The 1st Cavalry Division was then to drive southwest from the central mountains and relieve some of the pressure against the 24th Division.[56]

General Hodge at the same time ordered the 96th Division to seize the high ground between Jaro and Dagami, secure all routes of exit from the west coast through the central mountain range, and send patrols through the passes to the west coast of Leyte. The division was also ordered to maintain in the vicinity of Dagami one infantry regiment in Sixth Army Reserve. At the same time elements of the 7th Division had reached the shores of Ormoc Bay in the vicinity of Baybay and were ordered to send

patrols toward Ormoc and to prepare the route for a future advance in strength.[57]

If the attention of the Japanese could be fastened upon the X Corps in the north and northeast, it might be possible for General Krueger to put into effect his plan to send a strong force from the XXIV Corps over the mountains far to the south along the Abuyog–Baybay road to the eastern shores of Ormoc Bay in order to reinforce elements of the 7th Division already there. This force was to drive north toward Ormoc while elements of the X Corps pushed south toward the town along Highway 2. It might even be possible later to land an amphibious force, perhaps as large as a division, at a point just below Ormoc. But first it was all-important that the Japanese be contained in Ormoc Valley and that their attention continue to be directed to the north.[58]

On 9 November General Irving ordered the 24th Division to launch a co-ordinated assault on the following day to drive the *1st Division* from Breakneck Ridge and also deny it commanding ground from which the Japanese could conduct delaying actions just south of the barrio of Limon. (*See Map 11.*) The 21st Infantry was to drive south along Highway 2 and the 2d Battalion, 19th Infantry, was to proceed west from its position on the east flank of the enemy and establish a roadblock on Highway 2 about 2,000 yards south of Limon. The 1st Battalion, 34th Infantry, was to make a wide enveloping movement around the west flank of the *57th Infantry* and seize the high ground known as Kilay Ridge which was about 700 yards from Highway 2 and west of the proposed roadblock of the 2d Battalion, 19th Infantry. General Irving announced: "Success of the Leyte Campaign

[55] Sixth Army FO 30, 11 Nov 44.
[56] X Corps FO 12, 12 Nov 44.

[57] XXIV Corps FO 23, 10 Nov 44.
[58] Sixth Army Opns Rpt Leyte, p. 57.

depends upon quickly and completely destroying hostile forces on our front." [59]

By the morning of 10 November the 1st Battalion, 21st Infantry, had reorganized and re-equipped itself. The 2d and 3d Battalions of the regiment were disposed along a ridge southwest of Pinamopoan. The companies of the two battalions were intermingled.[60]

The rains continued to pour down upon the troops, and the thick mud was slippery and treacherous underfoot. After the artillery had fired a ten-minute concentration on Breakneck Ridge, the 21st Infantry attacked at 0945. Company A, the lead company, passed through Company E and pushed south. At 0955 Company G seized OP Hill. Simultaneously, Company I moved to the site of the destroyed bridge 300 yards east of OP Hill. Company L moved toward the high ground 300 yards southeast of its position and at 1120 secured this ground.

Colonel Verbeck then ordered the 1st Battalion to attack a ridge 200 yards to its front by maneuvering through the defiles on each side of the enemy-held spur. The maneuver was unsuccessful and the 1st Battalion resumed its former position.[61] The Japanese resisted all efforts of the 2d Battalion to move down the reverse slope of OP Hill.[62] During the day the 1st Battalion, 34th Infantry, and the 2d Battalion, 19th Infantry, moved out to secure the commanding positions south of Limon.[63]

The ten guns of the *2d Battalion, 1st Artillery Regiment* of the *1st Division,* were moved to a position east of Limon where they could be used to assist the *57th Infan-*try *Regiment.*[64] During the night of 10–11 November the *57th Infantry* severed the telephone lines from the headquarters of the 21st Infantry to all of the regiment's battalions.

That night the American artillery fired heavy interdiction fires, and before 0900 on 11 November it delivered preparations, including white phosphorus shells, on enemy pockets and strong points on Breakneck Ridge. Company C of the 85th Chemical Battalion maintained constant harassing fires on the reverse slopes of the east ridge and OP Hill, at the rate of approximately two 4.2-inch mortar rounds every five minutes.[65] Colonel Verbeck attached Company L to the 2d Battalion.

The 21st Infantry resumed the attack at 0900 with the 1st and 2d Battalions abreast, the 1st Battalion to the north of OP Hill and the 2d Battalion south and west of the parts of Breakneck Ridge previously captured.

Strong elements of the *57th Infantry* from the south and from positions in the wooded ridges east of Corkscrew Ridge immediately fired upon the 2d Battalion and pinned it down for the rest of the day. The 1st Battalion encountered little opposition until it reached a point about 300 yards south of the crest of Breakneck Ridge, where the Japanese strongly resisted. The troops then moved west of the enemy left flank about 200 yards to enable the tanks from Company A, 44th Tank Battalion, to make an attack against the main position of the *57th Infantry* on Breakneck Ridge.[66]

The tanks proceeded along Highway 2 up Breakneck Ridge and down its reverse slope. They destroyed an estimated twenty-five enemy positions which contained automatic

---

[59] 24th Div FO 8, 9 Nov 44.
[60] 24th Div G–3 Periodic Rpt 22, 10 Nov 44.
[61] 24th Div Opns Rpt Leyte, p. 49.
[62] 24th Div G–2 Jnl, 10 Nov 44.
[63] *Ibid.,* pp. 53, 61.

[64] *35th Army* Opns, p. 60.
[65] 24th Div Opns Rpt Leyte, p. 49.
[66] 24th Div G–3 Jnl, 11 Nov 44.

weapons. One tank got stuck when it went off the edge of the road. As darkness approached, its crew was rescued by another tank which then put a 75-mm. shell into the stalled vehicle to prevent its use by the Japanese.[67]

At 1600 the 308th Bombardment Wing dropped twenty-eight 500-pound bombs on the Valencia airfield in the middle of Ormoc Valley and twenty-four 500-pound bombs on a Highway 2 bridge in the vicinity of the airfield.[68]

At nightfall the 1st Battalion had secured its objective, a ridge 300 yards to the southwest of OP Hill, and all positions were consolidated. During the night the 226th and 465th Field Artillery Battalions placed harassing fire on the enemy positions. In order to shake the morale of the Japanese, the artillery fired its rounds at exact five-minute intervals but scattered the fire throughout the enemy-held area.[69]

On the morning of 12 November the 3d Battalion, supported by six tanks and a platoon from the 632d Tank Destroyer Battalion, moved out along the road skirting the crest of Breakneck Ridge. By 1115 it had passed over the crest and was moving down the reverse slope. After the 3d Battalion crossed the hill, the 1st Battalion attacked

on the right of the road with the mission of enveloping the Japanese left (north) flank.[70] There was little resistance, and soon after 1200 the crest of Breakneck Ridge was in the hands of the 21st Infantry. But shortly afterward the *2d Field Artillery Battalion* of the *1st Division* shelled the regiment and stopped all forward advance.[71]

On 13 November the 1st and 2d Battalions took up the fight, with machine guns from the vicinity of OP Hill firing in support. The 1st and 2d Battalions advanced 600 and 400 yards, respectively. By 14 November it appeared to General Irving that the 21st Infantry had eliminated nearly all resistance on Breakneck Ridge. The regiment controlled the ridge proper, but several adjacent spurs, notably Corkscrew Ridge, were still controlled by the *57th Infantry*. On 15 November the 1st Battalion, the most advanced unit, was about 1,500 yards north of Limon. On 16 November the 128th Infantry of the 32d Division relieved the 21st Infantry. The battle of Breakneck Ridge had not been an easy one for the 21st Infantry; it had lost 630 men killed, wounded, and missing, together with 135 men from other causes. By actual count it had killed 1,779 Japanese.[72]

---

[67] 24th Div Opns Rpt Leyte, p. 50; 44th Tank Bn Opns Rpt Leyte, p. 2.
[68] Msg, 308th Bombardment Wing to Sixth Army, 11 Nov 44, Sixth Army G–3 Jnl, 11 Nov 44.
[69] X Corps Arty S–3 Periodic Rpt 22, 12 Nov 44.

[70] 24th Div G–3 Jnl, 12 Nov 44; 24th Div Opns Rpt Leyte, p. 50.
[71] 24th Div G–3 Periodic Rpt 24, 12 Nov 44; *35th Army* Opns, p. 62.
[72] 24th Div Opns Rpt Leyte, p. 51.

CHAPTER XIII

The Mountain Barrier: Part Two

By the middle of November both the Americans and the Japanese realized that the struggle for the island of Leyte was going to be long and costly—far longer and costlier than either had anticipated.

On 9 and 10 November, Field Marshal Hisaichi Terauchi, the senior officer of the Japanese forces in the Philippines, held a series of conferences on the progress of the campaign. General Yamashita, commanding general of the *14th Area Army*, strongly urged that the Leyte operation be discontinued and offered reasons for this stand: There was little likelihood that additional reinforcements would reach the Philippines, and the vital manpower needed for the defense of Luzon would be drained off uselessly at Leyte. The naval battle of Leyte Gulf, he also thought, had been "unsatisfactory" and there was reason to believe that the air battle off Formosa had been equally disappointing. The shortage of shipping and escort strength greatly aggravated the already difficult problem of troop transportation. Finally, the land operations were not proceeding favorably.[1] But Yamashita's superior, Field Marshal Terauchi, commanding general of the *Southern Army*, insisted that the reinforcement program be

continued and that the battle for Leyte be brought to a successful conclusion. General Yamashita is said to have replied, "I fully understand your intention. I will carry it out to a successful end." [2]

Reinforcements

At the same time General Krueger was anxious to complete the third phase of the American campaign, the two-pronged drive toward the port of Ormoc. He felt, however, that there were insufficient troops to both protect the mountain passes into Leyte Valley and make the drives toward Ormoc.

In preparing for the Leyte Campaign, General Krueger had asked that the units which were to participate be embarked with a 10 percent overstrength. This request was disapproved. Just before the embarkation, however, he received 5,000 untrained replacements.[3] He had also requested that during the course of the operation 18,800 replacements be delivered to the combat zone, the first 10,000 to arrive by A plus 10. During the first thirty days of the operation he would need the following replacements: 14,300 Infantry, 1,300 Field Artillery, 1,130 Corps of Engineers, 750 Medical Corps, 375 Antiaircraft Artillery and Coast Artillery, 185 Quartermaster Corps, 185 Ordnance,

---

[1] GHQ FEC, MI Sec, Hist Div, Statements of Japanese Officials of World War II, Vol. II, p. 687, Statement of Maj Gen Toshio Nishimura [Asst CofS *14th Area Army*], copy in OCMH.

[2] *Ibid.*, I, 541.
[3] G–1 Rpt, Sixth Army Opns Rpt Leyte, p. 152.

Table 1—Sixth Army Daily Strength Reports, 12 November–25 December 1944

Date	Authorized strength		Difference Between Effective and Authorized Strength	
	Officers	Enlisted Men	Officers	Enlisted Men
12 Nov 1944	6,978	107,461	−1,050	−11,754
19 Nov 1944	9,290	147,497	−1,099	−15,058
26 Nov 1944	11,977	185,462	−1,603	−17,977
2 Dec 1944	11,637	191,060	−1,819	−19,012
9 Dec 1944	10,721	174,148	−1,194	−18,261
16 Dec 1944	10,905	176,466	−1,361	−21,059
25 Dec 1944	11,019	176,628	−1,228	−22,536

Source: Sixth Army Operations Report Leyte, 20 October–25 December 1944, p. 153.

185 Signal, and all others 375. Approximately 6 percent of these should be officers.[4]

As the fighting extended into the mountains, the lack of sufficient replacements began to be greatly felt. At no time did General Krueger know when replacements would arrive, or whether they would be combat or service troops, or what their individual specialties would be. During the course of the operation he received only 336 officers and 4,953 enlisted men as replacements.

To add to these difficulties, General MacArthur's headquarters used figures for "assigned strength" rather than "effective strength," that is, the number actually present with a unit, in computing the need for replacements. Such figures gave an entirely erroneous picture, since evacuations were to change rapidly the figures for medical installations, and dispositions reports were delayed for long periods. For example, on 12 November the assigned strength of the Sixth Army was only 289 officers and 1,874 enlisted men short of its Table of Organization strength, but its effective strength

was 1,050 officers and 11,754 enlisted men short of the Table of Organization strength. By 20 December this shortage had pyramided to about 21,000—considerably more than a division. (Table 1) General Krueger was seriously concerned about the situation, especially since nearly 79 percent of the casualties occurred in the infantry.[5]

Fortunately, the 32d and 77th Infantry Divisions—the Sixth Army reserve—were due to come in soon or had already done so, and there were on the island additional units that were to have used Leyte as a shipping area for subsequent operations. The availability of the 11th Airborne Division, under Maj. Gen. Joseph M. Swing, and the 112th Cavalry Regimental Combat Team,[6] under General Cunningham, was most timely. They could be used to help guard the mountain passes into Leyte Valley and also to give support to the drive of X Corps south down the Ormoc Valley.

At the same time General Krueger proposed that as soon as there were sufficient troops and supplies available, an amphibious landing be made near Ormoc to capture

---

[4] Ltr, CG Sixth Army to CINC SWPA, 29 Aug 44, sub: Replacements for Forthcoming Opn, Sixth Army G-3 Jnl, 29 Aug 44.

[5] Ltr, Gen Krueger to Gen Ward, 12 Sep 51, OCMH.

[6] This unit was a separate regimental combat team.

the town. This operation would speedily reduce the Japanese opposition south of Ormoc, cut the enemy's line of communication
at Ormoc, and place the hostile forces in
Ormoc Valley "in a vise which could shortly
squeeze them into extermination." [7]

The supporting naval forces, however,
could not make available sufficient assault
and resupply shipping to mount and support such an operation. The Navy also
thought that there was insufficient air support on the island to insure the safe arrival
of a convoy into Ormoc Bay. There was a
strong possibility that severe losses might
result from the suicide bombing techniques
of the Japanese pilots. General Krueger
therefore set aside his plan until it could be
introduced at a more opportune time.[8]
When the 11th Airborne Division arrived,
General Krueger could attach it to the
XXIV Corps in southern Leyte. General
Hodge could then relieve some of the troops
that had been guarding the mountain entrances into the valley and also send additional support to the troops on the shores of
Ormoc Bay, thus enabling the XXIV Corps
to launch a strong drive toward Ormoc
from the south.

General Krueger originally had planned
to have the 32d Division, under Maj. Gen.
William H. Gill, establish control over southern Samar, but in view of the limited number of Japanese on that island, he decided to
make use of the division to add momentum
to the attack of X Corps and to give rest to
the weary troops of the 24th Division.[9] On
14 November General Krueger therefore directed General Sibert to relieve the units of
the 24th Division with elements of the 32d
Division. At the same time, the 112th Cav-

alry was attached to the 1st Cavalry Division
in order to give impetus to the attack.[10]

32d Division Assumes the Offensive

General Sibert made arrangements for
the introduction of the 32d Division and the
112th Cavalry into the battle. The 2d Battalion, 19th Infantry, and the 1st Battalion,
34th Infantry, which had reached positions
overlooking Highway 2 south of Limon,
were to remain in those locations and temporarily under the operational control of
General Gill. The 112th Cavalry was to
operate in the mountains between Ormoc
and Leyte Valleys and assist the 1st Cavalry
Division in a drive to the southwest toward
Highway 2. A regimental combat team from
the 32d Division was to relieve the 21st Infantry on Breakneck Ridge. Another regiment from the division would mop up in
the vicinity of Hill 1525 and prepare to
assist in the drive south. Elements of the
division were to relieve the units of the 24th
Division in the Daro area, from which the
artillery had been shelling Ormoc. The 24th
Division artillery was to support the advance of the 32d Division until relieved.[11]
The flanks of the 32d Division were protected. The 2d Battalion, 19th Infantry, had
established a roadblock on Highway 2,
about 2,000 yards south of Limon, and the
1st Battalion, 34th Infantry, was on the high
ground known as Kilay Ridge, which was
700 yards from the road and west of the
roadblock of the 2d Battalion, 19th
Infantry.

General Gill directed the 128th Infantry
of the 32d Division, commanded by Col.
John A. Hettinger, to pass through the 21st
Infantry and attack south astride Highway

[7] Sixth Army Opns Rpt Leyte, p. 62.
[8] Ibid.
[9] Ibid.

[10] Sixth Army FO 32, 14 Nov 44.
[11] X Corps FO's 12–15, 12–16 Nov 44.

2, to push through Breakneck Ridge, and to capture Limon, 1,500 yards to the south. Colonel Hettinger ordered the regiment to move out on 16 November at 0800 with battalions abreast—the 3d Battalion, commanded by Lt. Col. William A. Duncan, on the right (west) of Highway 2, and the 1st Battalion, commanded by Lt. Col. James P. Burns, on the left.[12] (*Map 12*)

The forward elements of the 1st and 3d Battalions moved out of their assembly areas on time. They were followed by the remainder of the troops as fast as rations and ammunition could be distributed. The battalions assembled immediately in the rear of the 21st Infantry and at 1200 pushed through that regiment and entered upon their first battle on Leyte.[13]

Colonel Hettinger ordered Colonel Burns to overcome the enemy opposition on Corkscrew Ridge. The 1st Battalion made little progress. Company A was immediately pinned down by machine gun, mortar, and rifle fire, and Company B went forward only 150 yards. The 3d Battalion encountered no opposition and advanced to a point 350 yards south of its line of departure, from which Company M delivered machine gun fire and Company L rifle fire at long range on the enemy in the vicinity of Limon.[14]

On the morning of 17 November the 1st Battalion reached the slopes of Corkscrew Ridge, where it dug in. At 0737 the 3d Battalion moved out along Highway 2 with companies abreast—Company K on the right and Company L on the left. Company K met no resistance, advanced about 1,000 yards, and reached a ridge about 500 yards north of Limon. Elements of the *57th In-*

fantry stopped Company L almost immediately, but a platoon from the company moved fifty yards west around the pocket of resistance and destroyed it. The company then continued its advance to the ridge.[15] Companies K and L dug in on the ridge for the night.[16]

On the following morning Colonel Hettinger ordered the 3d Battalion to hold its position until the 1st Battalion could come abreast. The 3d Battalion therefore limited its activities to sending out patrols. The 1st Battalion again attacked Corkscrew Ridge but made very limited gains.

Elements of the *57th Infantry* had dug in on the reverse slope of the ridge, and heavy jungle prevented complete observation of these enemy positions. The Japanese regiment had placed automatic weapons to command the only routes of approach, thus forcing the American troops to move uphill in the face of hostile fire. The *2d Artillery Battalion* had placed its guns so that they covered Highway 2.[17]

The 1st Battalion continued to besiege Corkscrew Ridge until 20 November, while the 3d Battalion remained on the ridge overlooking Limon. Late in the afternoon of 21 November, Colonel Hettinger ordered the 128th Infantry to seize Limon, and then move south to secure a bridge-crossing over a tributary of the Leyte River. The 1st Battalion was to contain the enemy on Corkscrew Ridge. The two assault battalions of the regiment got into position on the ridge north of Limon, the 2d Battalion on the

---

[12] 128th Inf FO 4, 15 Nov 44.
[13] 3d Bn, 128th Inf, Opns Rpt Leyte, p. 1.
[14] 128th Inf Unit Rpt 1, 16 Nov 44.

[15] Capt Julius A. Sakas, The Operations of the 3d Battalion, 128th Infantry . . . at Limon . . ., p. 29, Advanced Infantry Officers Course, 1949–50, The Infantry School, Ft. Benning, Ga.
[16] 128th Inf Unit Rpt 2, 17 Nov 44.
[17] *35th Army* Opns, p. 66; 128th Inf Opns Rpt Leyte, p. 2.

east side of Highway 2 and the 3d on the west side.[18]

During the night the 120th Field Artillery Battalion delivered harassing fire along the road between Limon and the Limon bridge.[19] At 0800 the assault troops moved out. The 3d Battalion met little opposition, but the 2d met strong resistance from the *57th Infantry*.[20] Company I encountered no resistance as it moved along a bluff which was just west of the town and which overlooked Limon and the bridge. Company K and the 2d Battalion pushed through Limon and at 1400 the leading elements crossed a tributary of the Leyte River south of the town. A determined Japanese counterattack forced back the left flank of the 2d Battalion and exposed Company K. A sudden flood of the stream, caused by heavy rains, cut off the advance elements of Company K south of the river from the rest of the company. These troops moved to the right and joined Company I on the bluffs. The rest of the company and the 2d Battalion established a night perimeter along a ridge east of the village. The 3d Battalion, less Company K, established itself for the night around the positions of Company I that overlooked the bridge and the tributary of the river.[21]

On 23 November the 128th Infantry straightened out its lines and consolidated its positions. For the next three days activity was limited to extensive patrols and the placement of harassing fire on an east-west ridge that overlooked the highway about 1,000 yards south of Limon. Entrenched on this ridge, elements of the *1st Division* suc-

cessfully resisted until 10 December all efforts of the 32d Division to dislodge them.[22]

With the occupation of Limon, the battle of Breakneck Ridge was over, but a number of bypassed pockets of resistance were not eliminated until mid-December. The battle cost the 24th and 32d Divisions a total of 1,498 casualties, killed, wounded, and missing in action, as compared with an estimated 5,252 Japanese killed and 8 captured.[23]

The Japanese had failed in their attempt to block off Highway 2 at the northern entrance to Ormoc Valley. In no small measure, the establishment and maintenance of a roadblock south of Limon by the 2d Battalion, 19th Infantry, and the defense of Kilay Ridge in the rear of the Japanese front lines by the 1st Battalion, 34th Infantry, had made this achievement possible. (*See Map 11.*) Under constant fire and greatly outnumbered, these units had prevented General Suzuki from sending additional troops into Limon. From 12 to 23 November the 2d Battalion, 19th Infantry, had defended the roadblock under extremely difficult conditions. The operations report of the 24th Division graphically summarizes the deeds for which the battalion received a presidential citation:

These bearded, mud caked soldiers came out of the mountains exhausted and hungry. Their feet were heavy, cheeks hollow, bodies emaciated, and eyes glazed. They had seen thirty-one comrades mortally wounded, watched fifty-five others lie suffering in muddy foxholes without adequate medical attention. Yet their morale had not changed. It was high when they went in and high when they came out. They were proud that they had rendered invaluable aid to the main forces fighting in ORMOC CORRIDOR,

---

[18] 128th Inf Unit Rpt 6, 21 Nov 44; 128th Inf Opns Rpt Leyte, p. 3.

[19] 32d Div Arty Unit Rpt 2, 20 Nov 44.

[20] X Corps G–2 Jnl, 23 Nov 44.

[21] X Corps G–3 Periodic Rpt 34, 22 Nov 44; X Corps G–2 and G–3 Jnls, 22 Nov 44.

[22] 32d Div Opns Rpt Leyte, p. 7.

[23] X Corps Opns Rpt Leyte, p. 29.

AMERICAN TROOPS IN LIMON *(above), and taking cover there as enemy shells hit the area (below).*

by disrupting the Japanese supply lines and preventing strong reinforcements from passing up the ORMOC ROAD. They were proud that they had outfought the Emperor's toughest troops, troops that had been battle trained in Manchuria. They were certain they had killed at least 606 of the enemy and felt that their fire had accounted for many more. And they were proud that this had all been accomplished despite conditions of extreme hardship. Two hundred and forty-one of the battalion's officers and enlisted men were hospitalized for skin disorders, foot ulcers, battle fatigue, and sheer exhaustion.[24]

The 1st Battalion, 34th Infantry, under Colonel Clifford, operated west of Highway 2 on Kilay Ridge, behind the Japanese front lines. It "wrote a brilliant page in the history of the campaign"[25] but, since its influence on the situation was not appreciated until later and since it affords an excellent example of a battalion fighting independently, the operation of "Clifford's Battalion" will be discussed separately.

Battle of Kilay Ridge

When General Krueger told General Sibert to push the X Corps south with all possible speed down Highway 2 toward Ormoc, the latter had selected the 24th Division to make the drive. General Irving wished to protect the sides of the road and prevent the Japanese from sending reinforcements north up the highway. On 9 November he therefore ordered the 34th Infantry to send a battalion around the Japanese west flank to harass the enemy's rear and thus relieve the pressure that was holding up the frontal attack of the 21st Infantry on Breakneck Ridge.

Nipponese Caught Napping

At 0100 on 10 November Colonel Dahlen, commander of the 34th Infantry, alerted the 1st Battalion, 34th Infantry, for an amphibious landing to take place at 0700. The battalion had been in contact with the enemy for twenty-one days and was reduced to an effective strength of 560 men. The 1st Battalion, with an observer's party from the 63d Field Artillery Battalion, was ordered to move from Capoocan in eighteen LVT's and proceed seven miles northwest up the coast of Carigara Bay.[26] It was then to move inland and seize Kilay Ridge, which was west of the Ormoc road some 3,000 yards behind the Japanese front lines.[27]

At 0700 the battalion, under Colonel Clifford, moved out, taking every available man on the mission and leaving only a minimum of cooks and drivers behind. Since the troops had to hand-carry their equipment the Headquarters Company left the antitank guns behind, and Company D took only one section of heavy machine guns and one section of 81-mm. mortars. Colonel Clifford used the men thus released to carry other weapons and ammunition. Because of the scant time allowed by the orders, the battalion left without sufficient rations.

At 0750 Clifford's battalion went aboard the LVT's and at 0930 arrived at its destination. Debarking without opposition it pushed rapidly inland and at 1145 reached a hill approximately one mile from the landing area. At dusk the 1st Battalion reached a ridge in the vicinity of Belen and about 2,000 yards north of Agahang.

---

[24] 24th Div Opns Rpt Leyte, p. 59.
[25] X Corps Opns Rpt Leyte, p. 27.

[26] 1st Bn, 34th Inf, Unit Jnl, 10 Nov 44.
[27] 24th Div Opns Rpt Leyte, p. 61. Unless otherwise stated this subsection is based on the above report, pages 61–68.

There it set up a night perimeter. Since his maps were inaccurate, Colonel Clifford relied upon the services of Filipino guides from this time until the end of the mission. The rugged and muddy hillsides, made considerably worse by almost constant rain and fog, were similar to those encountered by other units fighting in the area.

At 0730 on 11 November Colonel Clifford sent out patrols to pick up a promised airdrop of rations. The battalion had been without food since the morning before. At 0910 Colonel Dahlen ordered Colonel Clifford not to move on to Agahang, which was about 3,800 yards northwest of Limon, until he received rations. The rations were not forthcoming but at 1400 Dahlen told Clifford to obtain the promised rations at Agahang, to which the battalion then proceeded. No supplies were received, but Filipinos furnished the unit with bananas, cooked rice, boiled potatoes, and a few chickens. A night perimeter was set up.[28]

At 0850 on the following day Colonel Clifford's men received their first airdrop of rations. Ten minutes later the commanding officer of the 1st Battalion of the guerrilla 96th Infantry made contact with Colonel Clifford and gave him a résumé of the enemy situation. (The guerrillas rendered invaluable aid to the 1st Battalion, 34th Infantry, throughout the Kilay Ridge episode by furnishing intelligence and protecting the rear of the unit.) The battalion moved out at 1200 for Consuegra near the Naga River and entered the town at 1240. At 1310 Colonel Clifford outlined to the officers the plan for the next two days. For the rest of the day, the battalion was to advance to Cabiranan and bivouac for the night. On the morning of 13 November it

was to split into two columns and make a fast advance by separate routes to Kilay Ridge, where it would reorganize. As Colonel Clifford was briefing his officers, LVT's entered Consuegra with rations for the troops. The LVT's had left Carigara Bay, passed through Biliran Strait, gone down Leyte Bay and into the Naga River, and then proceeded up the river to the vicinity of Consuegra.

At 0855 on 13 November a column of Filipino men, women, and children entered the perimeter and brought approximately thirty-five boxes of rations from Consuegra. The battalion left the area at 0930 and reached the ridge without opposition. Trenches and prepared gun positions without a man in them honeycombed the ridge from one end to the other. It was evident that elements of the *1st Division* had intended to occupy the area in the latter stages of the battle for Limon.[29]

Kilay Ridge ran from southeast to northwest, with its northern tip about 2,500 yards directly west of Limon and its southern end about 3,000 yards south and slightly west of the same point. The ridge was approximately 900 feet high and though narrow in some places in others it widened to 400 yards. The summit was broken into a series of high knolls from which the entire Limon area and some parts of the Ormoc road could be observed. A view of the latter feature was obstructed to some extent by a ridge, hereafter called Ridge Number 2, between Kilay and the road. Kilay Ridge was about 3,900 yards southwest of Breakneck Ridge. It would be necessary to maintain control of Kilay Ridge and deny its use to the enemy in order to give complete support to units advancing south from Breakneck Ridge.

---

[28] 1st Bn, 34th Inf, Unit Jnl, 11 Nov 44.

[29] 1st Bn, 34th Inf, Unit Jnl, 13 Nov 44.

LT. COL. THOMAS E. CLIFFORD, JR., *discusses plans with his staff as Filipino guerrillas look on.*

Preliminary Attack

On 14 November Colonel Clifford ordered his battalion to entrench itself along the ridge in positions that would afford the best tactical advantage. The battalion established strong points and observation posts on the knolls, placed blocks on the trails leading through the area, and sent out reconnaissance patrols to locate enemy positions. Colonel Clifford made arrangements to utilize the Filipinos as carriers. These men were to use a trail on the north end of the ridge and bring supplies to the battalion from a supply dump at Consuegra. The first human pack train arrived in the area at 1010 with twenty-eight cases of rations and a supply of batteries for the radios.[30]

At 1125 enemy artillery shelled the southern end of the ridge and twenty minutes later shifted its fire to the Limon area. The battalion did not succeed in establishing physical contact with the 2d Battalion, 19th Infantry, which was operating east of the road, but it was able to make radio contact. Throughout the day, patrols of the battalion were active in searching out enemy positions.

On 15 November Company A sent a patrol to Ridge Number 2, which was 600 yards east of the battalion's positions and which overlooked the Ormoc road. The pa-

---

[30] 1st Bn, 34th Inf, Unit Jnl, 14 Nov 44.

trol found numerous enemy emplacements and approximately fifty Japanese, who began firing with mortars. After killing five of the Japanese the patrol retired.[31] During the day the 24th Cavalry Reconnaissance Troop reported to Colonel Clifford and was assigned the mission of patrolling the west flank of the battalion. Although patrols from the 1st Battalion pushed east of the Ormoc highway south of Limon, they again were unable to make contact with the 2d Battalion, 19th Infantry. On 16 November Colonel Clifford again sent out patrols which tried, still unsuccessfully, to establish physical contact with this battalion.[32]

A platoon from Company B, on 17 November, carried on a running fire fight with the Japanese and forced its way past Ridge Number 2. It crossed the Ormoc road and made contact with the 2d Battalion, 19th Infantry, at its roadblock. A line of communication between the battalions could not be established because of the strong enemy forces between them. At the same time parts of Companies B and D engaged the enemy on Ridge Number 3, six hundred yards south of Ridge Number 2 and slightly lower. Approximately 200 of the enemy with rifles, machine guns, mortars, and artillery were entrenched on Ridge Number 3. The American fire killed at least fifty Japanese. A patrol from Company D probed the Japanese defensive position but was forced to retire with two men missing and one wounded. Then Company B entered the fray, and the fire fight grew in intensity. The Japanese directed fire from at least three automatic weapons as well as strong rifle fire against the Americans.

Colonel Clifford went to investigate and found Company B engaged in a bitter fight.

While he was there the company sustained six casualties. One of the men had been shot through the thigh and was unable to walk. Since the heavy underbrush and bad trails made it impossible for two men to carry him on a litter, Colonel Clifford carried the wounded soldier on his back for about a mile to the command post, over a difficult mountain trail which ran for several hundred yards in the bed of a swift stream.[33] Colonel Clifford was awarded a Distinguished Service Cross.[34]

At nightfall Company B was separated from the rest of the battalion. Colonel Clifford decided to pull the company off the ridge and replace it with Company C. He was determined to hold what he had "at all costs." [35] During the day General Sibert attached the battalion to the 32d Division.

Red Badge of Courage

At daylight on 18 November Colonel Clifford brought heavy machine guns into place on the perimeter of the battalion and began to fire on the enemy positions on Ridge Number 3, catching a group of about twenty-five Japanese who were cooking their breakfast. At 0700 a carrying party with rations and medical supplies moved out toward the besieged Company B, and at 1100 Company C started forward to relieve the company. Colonel Clifford decided to displace a platoon at a time during the day. Under intense rifle fire, Company C succeeded in relieving Company B. The fire fight continued throughout the day, and approximately fifty more Japanese were

---

[31] 1st Bn, 34th Inf, Unit Jnl, 15 Nov 44.
[32] 1st Bn, 34th Inf, Unit Jnl, 16 Nov 44.

[33] 1st Bn, 34th Inf, Unit Jnl, 17 Nov 44.
[34] Curiously enough, while on leave in the United States, he had been caught without his dog tags and arrested for "impersonating an officer." 24th Div Opns Dpt Leyte, p. 78.
[35] 1st Bn, 34th Inf, Unit Jnl, 17 Nov 44.

killed. At 1200 the battalion conducted burial services for Henry Kilay, a Filipino soldier and guide who had served the battalion well.[36] During the night and continuing into 19 November, Japanese heavy machine guns fired into the perimeter on Ridge Number 2.

In the meantime the enemy began to deliver heavy fire against Company B, which had moved to the south flank of the battalion on Kilay Ridge. Colonel Clifford estimated the Japanese assault force to be one reinforced company well equipped with mortars and light machine guns. By 0905 on 19 November the Japanese had destroyed one heavy machine gun and had begun a flanking movement to the east of the southernmost outpost of Company B.

The artillery liaison party moved south and directed artillery fire on the enemy. By 1150, however, Company B was being surrounded and its ammunition was very low. Colonel Clifford made a reconnaissance of the area and ordered the besieged company to fall back 100 yards to the north and set up a strong point with the assistance of Company A. The next morning Company A was to attack and retake the knoll from which Company B had been forced to retire. Because of strong Japanese resistance, the gradual attrition of the battalion's forces, and the "extreme scarcity" of ammunition, Colonel Clifford also decided to have Company C withdraw from Ridge Number 2 to Kilay Ridge on the following morning.[37]

Rain fell constantly upon the troops and churned the surface of the ridge into a "slick mass of mud and slime."[38] Men were tired. With insufficient rations, broken sleep in sodden foxholes, and constant harassing fire, many had sickened. Fever, dysentery, and foot ulcers were commonplace.

Early on the morning of 20 November Company C withdrew silently in the rain without the knowledge of the Japanese, who threw an attack of company strength against the position thirty minutes after it had been vacated. Company C established a strong position 200 yards south of the battalion command post. The artillery fired intermittently on the enemy to the south until 1200, when it concentrated its fire in front of Company B. So intense was the rain that although artillery shells were falling only 150 yards away, the artillery liaison party had to adjust the fire almost entirely by sound. At 1225 Company B moved out in an effort to retake the knoll from which the enemy had launched his attacks the previous day, but it came under intense rifle and mortar fire which forced it to retire. At this point the battalion's supply of ammunition became critically low.[39]

The downpour continued through the night and the next day. Patrols, sent to search for a means of flanking the Japanese, were unsuccessful, but they brought back information which made it possible to place artillery and mortar fire on enemy positions. At 1430 Colonel Clifford received the report that two strong Japanese columns were converging on the battalion from the southeast and northeast. One of the platoons from Company C moved to the north end of the ridge to assure that the supply line to Consuegra would be kept open. A carrying party from Consuegra brought in rations and at

---

[36] 1st Bn, 34th Inf, Unit Jnl, 18 Nov 44. Jan Valtin in *Children of Yesterday,* page 247, states that Henry Kilay was the owner of the ridge. Properly the ridge bears his name.

[37] 1st Bn, 34th Inf, Unit Jnl, 19 Nov 44.

[38] 24th Div Opns Rpt Leyte, p. 63.

[39] 1st Bn, 34th Inf, Unit Jnl, 20 Nov 44.

1705 the battalion received an airdrop of blankets, ammunition, and litters.[40] There was no major enemy contact.

The rains persisted during the night and the next day, 22 November. Throughout the morning, patrols probed the area. At 1130 the battalion received an airdrop of ammunition, medical supplies, and ponchos. The main perimeter lines were comparatively quiet until 1430 when the enemy pinned down Company B with heavy fire and assaulted Company A. These attacks rapidly grew in intensity. The Japanese with fixed bayonets charged against the perimeters and almost completely surrounded both companies.

At 2000, since the enemy completely surrounded Company B, Colonel Clifford ordered the company to break through and withdraw through Company A to the rear of the battalion command post. Under cover of machine gun and artillery fire, the company withdrew. When a litter train of the wounded was ambushed, one of the bearers was killed by enemy fire.

Within the new perimeter of Company B, 750 yards north of the battalion command post, Colonel Clifford established a rear command post and all communications moved to it. From this new location the mortars from Company D began to fire in front of Company A, the most advanced company. The battalion cached all supplies and ammunition in case the enemy should suddenly break through. The rains continued.

Colonel Clifford made tentative plans to withdraw during the night but abandoned them when General Gill ordered him to hold the ridge at all costs. Advance elements of the 32d Division had entered Limon, and the withdrawal of Clifford's battalion would

have left their western flank completely exposed.[41]

Fortunately the Japanese did not follow up the attacks on 23 November, but there was scattered automatic weapons and artillery fire. Next day American artillery and mortar fire repulsed a small enemy attack at 0830. A platoon from the battalion slipped through the enemy lines and brought information on the situation to General Gill. It returned with orders that the battalion was to hold fast. Two airdrops of supplies, although they drew enemy fire, were successfully recovered.

For the next two days there was comparative quiet in the sector except for patrol activity and intermittent fire. At 1000 on 25 November, General Gill sent Colonel Clifford the following message: "You and your men are doing a superb job. Hang on and keep killing the Japs. . . ."[42]

At nightfall on 25 November, however, the semiquiet was shattered when an enemy force armed with automatic weapons, mortars, and artillery began a heavy assault against the perimeter of Company A. The company beat off the attack with losses to both forces. On the following morning, Colonel Clifford had Company C relieve Company A. At 1630 Colonel Dahlen informed him that he, Clifford, was "in a tight spot," since the 32d Division could give "no immediate help," and advised him to "use artillery and hang on."[43] It became apparent that the Japanese were so disposed that they could launch attacks from different directions. Further evidence to this effect was supplied on 27 November, when a Japanese patrol of almost platoon strength

[40] 1st Bn, 34th Inf, Unit Jnl, 21 Nov 44.

[41] 1st Bn, 34th Inf, Unit Jnl, 22 Nov 44.
[42] 1st Bn, 34th Inf, Unit Jnl, 25 Nov 44.
[43] 1st Bn, 34th Inf, Unit Jnl, 26 Nov 44.

got astride the supply line to Consuegra on the northern front of Kilay Ridge. A patrol from Company B dispersed the unit and killed three of the enemy. Colonel Clifford estimated that elements of the *1st Regiment* were disposed as follows: a minimum of one reinforced company was south of him, at least two reinforced companies were on the ridge about 1,000 yards to the east, and a strong but unknown number of the enemy opposed him on the west. If this last force pushed northward Clifford's supply line to Consuegra would be severed. From 1725 to 2020 on 27 November, Company C came under a strong long-range attack from enemy positions on the ridge to the east. A patrol from the 128th Infantry, 32d Division, brought Colonel Clifford the welcome information that reinforcements were en route.

The Main Effort

At 1000 on 28 November the battalion repulsed a small party of the enemy that attacked from the south. There was a lull until 1930 when the Japanese unleashed a strong effort to drive the defenders from Kilay Ridge and recapture it. The opening was marked by 90-mm. mortar fire upon the outposts of the battalion. Heavy weapons from the ridge on the east then began firing as at least two machine guns and many small arms began to rain lead from the west. The enemy fire rose to a crescendo as the mortars joined in and directed their heaviest fire at a platoon of Company C on the southwestern end of the ridge. The Japanese began to deploy troops, apparently in an attempt to reach a gulch to the west of the battalion's positions. A heavy assault was launched from the south against Company C.

By 1955 the mortars of the battalion were brought to bear against the advancing Japanese as the crews worked in feverish haste to break up the assault. At 2015, although Company C now had mortar support, the enemy charged with bayonets and grenades. Fighting was at close quarters and the Japanese began to infiltrate the forward positions. An hour later the advance platoon of Company C pulled back to join the company, which had been cut off from the rest of the battalion. The fire fight continued throughout the night with constant rifle fire, numerous attempts at infiltration by the Japanese, and intermittent mortar fire.[44]

At dawn on 29 November the Japanese forces were still on the ridge in strength and their automatic weapons began to fire anew. All forward elements of the battalion were under attack and Company C was still separated from the rest of the battalion. A reinforced platoon from Company B, at 0730, was able to break through to Company C, kill six of the enemy, and seize two machine guns en route. As Company C's ammunition was practically exhausted, Colonel Clifford immediately sent a carrying party forward. Since the Japanese had blocked off the trail immediately after the passage of the platoon from Company B, the carrying party was pinned down.

In the meantime two carrying parties from Consuegra entered the perimeter of the battalion with food and ammunition. One carried the "Thanksgiving ration of roast turkey and . . . fresh eggs." The battalion therefore hoped for "a good meal" if the situation permitted.[45]

Colonel Clifford urgently requested General Gill to send reinforcements. At 1325

---

[44] 1st Bn, 34th Inf, Unit Jnl, 28 Nov 44.
[45] 1st Bn, 34th Inf, Unit Jnl, 29 Nov 44.

Gill told Clifford that he had ordered the 2d Battalion, 128th Infantry, 32d Division, to proceed to Kilay Ridge immediately and come under Clifford's control. Colonel Clifford forcibly reopened the trail to Company C and had food and ammunition brought into the forward position. A short time later, Company G, 128th Infantry, arrived and Clifford immediately committed it to reinforce Company C. The remainder of the 2d Battalion, 128th Infantry, arrived at 1835 and was held in reserve. (*See Map 12.*)

The action for 1 December began at 0800 when a patrol from Company B proceeded down a draw to the west of Kilay Ridge. The patrol was to swing wide and approach the right rear almost directly south of the enemy-held knolls on Kilay Ridge. These were thought to be the Japanese strong points and were the objectives for the day. A preparatory concentration from supporting artillery and from mortars of both battalions was first laid. The heavy machine gun section of the 128th Infantry moved into the draw to the west and set up its guns on the right flank of the ridge in order to be in a position to fire across the face of the ridge when the main assault began. Company E of the 128th Infantry then passed through Company C and launched an attack against the Japanese-held knolls on the southeastern end of the ridge. Heavy and light machine gun fire from Company C protected the flanks of Company E.

The company took the first knoll easily, but heavy fire from behind a huge log on the second knoll halted Company E. Company A sent a bazooka team forward to knock out the position and Company C sent all of its grenades forward, but by 1320 the Japanese soldiers were still resisting all attempts to dislodge them. The patrol from Company B returned at 1345 with the report that it had been to the rear of its objective and had seen no enemy activity. No unit made any further progress that day. At 1720 General Gill ordered Colonel Clifford to withdraw the 1st Battalion, 34th Infantry.[46]

At 0925 on 2 December, Company E, 128th Infantry, attacked the knolls at the south tip of Kilay Ridge, while Company F moved down the ridge and swung to the right to attack the ridge to the south—the objective of the two-battalion assault. The 1st Battalion, 34th Infantry, withdrew one unit, but at 1245 Colonel Clifford received orders to halt all further withdrawals pending orders from the commanding officer, 128th Infantry. By then Company E had taken its objective but Company F had encountered determined resistance fifty yards from the top of the ridge. It doggedly advanced and by 1625 reached the crest and dug in, though still receiving hostile mortar fire.

The next day examination of the battlefield where the two battalions had been fighting revealed numerous enemy dead and the following abandoned equipment: three 70-mm. mountain guns, four heavy machine guns, seventeen light machine guns, one 90-mm. mortar, and many rifles, pistols, sabers, and field glasses. Documents containing valuable intelligence were also found. On 4 December the 1st Battalion, 34th Infantry, started to withdraw. During the next two days elements of the battalion moved through Consuegra and Calubian to Pinamopoan. The battalion had lost 26 men killed, 2 missing, and 101 wounded, but it

---

[46] The message to Colonel Clifford, a former all-American football player from West Point, concluded: "You and your men have not been forgotten. You are the talk of the island, and perhaps the United States. Army beat Notre Dame 59 to 0, the worst defeat on record." 24th Div Opns Rpt Leyte, p. 67; 1st Bn, 34th Inf, Unit Jnl, 1 Dec 44.

estimated that it had killed 900 men of the *1st Infantry Regiment*. The 1st Battalion, 34th Infantry, had acquitted itself well. It had prevented the Japanese from reinforcing the Limon forces and imperiling the 32d Division. For its work the battalion received the presidential unit citation.

Central Mountain Range

1st Cavalry Division

As elements of the X Corps were pushing south on Highway 2 through Breakneck Ridge, other units from the corps were engaged in securing the central mountain range that divided Leyte and Ormoc Valleys in order to prevent any Japanese forces from debouching into Leyte Valley. General Suzuki had ordered the *1st Division* commander to place the *57th Infantry* in the Limon area while the *1st* and *49th Infantry Regiments* were to go to the central mountain range. The two regiments last mentioned were to prevent any American attempts to infiltrate into Ormoc Valley and to exploit any favorable opportunity to break through into Leyte Valley. About 8 November the *102d Division*, including its signal, artillery, and engineer units, arrived at Ormoc and General Suzuki immediately sent them into the mountains of central Leyte.[47]

General Krueger had already anticipated this movement and had stationed elements of the X and XXIV Corps at the principal entrances into Leyte Valley. On 10 November General Mudge sent elements of the 1st Cavalry Division to patrol the area extensively.[48]

The northern mountains between Ormoc and Leyte Valleys were high and rugged,

with precipitous sides. The area was heavily forested, and there were many ground pockets which constituted natural, heavily wooded fortresses for the Japanese. The very few trails in the sector were scarcely better than pig trails. The area had not been properly mapped and at all times the troops were seriously handicapped by insufficient knowledge of the terrain. The nearly constant rainfall bogged down supply and made the sides of the hills slippery and treacherous. From 5 November through 2 December, elements of the 1st Cavalry Division extensively patrolled the central mountain area and had many encounters with small forces of the enemy. At all times the supply situation was precarious.

The 1st Cavalry Division utilized motor transport, LVT's, tractors and trailers, native carriers, and airdrops to get supplies to forward troops. Motor transport hauled supplies from the warehouses in Tacloban to Carigara, a distance of thirty miles. At this point LVT's of the 826th Amphibian Tractor Battalion hauled the supplies, through rice paddies churned into waist-deep morasses, to Sugud, three miles south of Carigara. The supplies were manhandled from the LVT's into one-ton two-wheeled cargo and ammunition trailers, which were towed by the tractors of the artillery battalions that fired in support of the division. The tractors wound their way laboriously into the foothills through boulder-strewn streams and up steep inclines that made it necessary for the tractors to be arranged in tandem. There was always mud, which made traction difficult, and the LVT's were better able than the tractors to navigate through slick, soft mud which had little body texture.

The 12th Cavalry established high in the foothills, at the entrance to the passes through the mountains, a supply base that

---

[47] *35th Army* Opns, pp. 47–48.
[48] 1st Cav Div FO 9, 10 Nov 44.

FILIPINO CARRIERS HAUL SUPPLIES *over slippery mountain trails for the 12th Cavalry.*

was also a native camp, a hospital, and a rest camp. About 300 Filipino carriers were kept here under the protection of the guerrillas. The carriers had been hired for six days at a time and were not allowed to leave without a pass from their Filipino leader. This precaution was necessary, since the ration-carrying assignment was extremely arduous.

Under armed escort, the long train of carriers, two men to each fifty-pound load of rations, ammunition, and other types of supply, began immediately to struggle forward from the supply camp over narrow, slippery trails, across waist-deep rivers and streams, and through heavy undergrowth.

In the never-ending climb to gain altitude, it took five hours to traverse a track that measured less than three miles. At the base of a vertical descent of more than 500 feet, there was a second supply base, the relay station. From this station it was another day's forced march to the forward troops. An additional 300 Filipinos were stationed at the relay station in the mountain wilderness, surrounded by elements of the enemy. These carriers made the last half of the tortuous journey, while the others returned to the base camp for resupply. It took four days to get supplies from the warehouses to the front-line troops.[49]

---

[49] 1st Cav Div Opns Rpt Leyte, pp. 43–45.

The 112th Cavalry Regimental Combat Team, under General Cunningham, had arrived at Leyte on 14 November.[50] At this time the 21st Infantry was advancing very slowly along Breakneck Ridge, against strong resistance, and the units of the 1st Cavalry Division were spread thinly over the central mountain area.[51] In order to strengthen the defense line, the 112th Cavalry was committed upon its arrival and passed to the control of X Corps.[52] On 15 November General Sibert attached the 112th Cavalry to the 1st Cavalry Division and ordered it to operate in the Carigara area.[53] General Mudge directed the 112th Cavalry to assume, on 16 November, the responsibility for beach defenses in the Capoocan–Carigara–Barugo area and to mop up in the Mt. Minoro area about 3,000 yards south of Capoocan.[54]

The 112th Cavalry patrolled the Mt. Minoro area until 22 November. In accord with General Krueger's desire to relieve some of the pressure that was being exerted against the 32d Division in its drive south down Highway 2, General Mudge on 23 November ordered the 112th Cavalry to move southwest from Mt. Minoro toward the highway. The combat team encountered sporadic resistance and on the morning of 30 November reached a ridge about 2,500 yards east of Highway 2 and about 5,000 yards southeast of Limon.[55] A strongly entrenched enemy force on the ridge resisted all attempts of the 112th Cavalry to dislodge it.

The ridge was covered with a dense rain forest, and the lower slopes were thickly spotted with bamboo thickets and other extremely dense vegetation. Clouds covered the tops of the peak and rain fell almost continuously, churning the ground into ankle-deep mud. Visibility was limited to only a few yards. The enemy defensive field works consisted of foxholes, prone shelters, communication trenches, and palm-log bunkers. These positions presented no logical avenue of approach. They were complete perimeters and employed all-round mutually supporting automatic weapons fire. Although the fields of fire were limited, the weapons were so effectively placed that they covered all approaches.[56]

The strong resistance made further progress impossible and the 112th Cavalry established its perimeter. During the night the Japanese subjected the 1st and 2d Squadrons, 112th Cavalry, to heavy artillery fire and launched several patrol attacks against the perimeter of the 2d Squadron. The night assaults were beaten off.[57]

The next two days were spent by the 2d Squadron, 112th Cavalry, in trying unsuccessfully to dislodge the Japanese from the ridge. At 1310 on 2 December the 112th Cavalry received orders to move northnorthwest toward the Leyte River, from which point they were to send out patrols to make contact with units of the 32d Division.[58] At this time, however, the 112th Cavalry was still opposed by a strong enemy force. Troop A nevertheless moved out to make contact with the 32d Division and to reconnoiter to the west for further enemy concentrations and for routes by which the 112th Cavalry could advance to Highway 2.

[50] 112th Cav Opns Rpt Leyte, p. 1.
[51] Sixth Army G–3 Periodic Rpt 514, 14 Nov 44.
[52] Sixth Army FO 32, 14 Nov 44.
[53] X Corps FO 14, 15 Nov 44.
[54] 1st Cav Div FO 11, 14 Nov 44.
[55] X Corps G–3 Periodic Rpt 47, 5 Dec 44.

[56] 7th Cav Opns Rpt, Leyte, Part IV, S–2 Rpt, Tactical and Technical Characteristics of the Enemy, pp. 2, 5.
[57] 1st Cavalry Division G–3 Periodic Rpt. 42, 1 Dec 44.
[58] 112th Cav S–2 and S–3 Jnls, 2 Dec 44.

FOOTHILLS OF CENTRAL MOUNTAIN RANGE *are patrolled by elements of the 1st Cavalry Division.*

On 3 December, after an artillery concentration, Troop G, 2d Squadron, 112th Cavalry, started out toward the enemy-held ridge. The slope was so precipitous that the troops could not climb and shoot at the same time. The Japanese were able to throw grenades upon Troop G without exposing themselves, and the troop retired to the bottom of the hill. An artillery concentration was called for and delivered on the ridge, after which the troop again started up the hill. The Japanese, however, quickly regained their former positions after the artillery fire ceased and again repulsed Troop G with grenades and small arms fire. The troop withdrew to its former position at the bottom of the hill. For the remainder of the day, the artillery placed harassing fire on the enemy strong point while patrols probed

to the south and west around the flanks of the Japanese position, seeking better avenues of approach.[59]

Troop A journeyed without incident toward Highway 2, at 1415 on 3 December made contact with the left rear of the 126th Infantry west of Hill 1525, and at the end of the day was moving southwest to make contact with the leading elements of the 126th Infantry. No contact had been made with the enemy and there was little sign of enemy forces. The 1st Squadron received orders to proceed to the Leyte River and locate a dropping ground.[60]

---

[59] 1st Cav Div G–3 Periodic Rpt 45, 4 Dec 44; 112th Cav Opns Rpt Leyte, p. 6; 112th Cav S–2 and S–3 Jnl, 3, 4 Dec 44.

[60] 112th Cav S–2 and S–3 Jnl, 3, 4 Dec 44; 112th Cav Opns Rpt Leyte, p. 6.

Henceforward, until 10 December, the 2d Squadron, 112th Cavalry, was stalemated by the strongly entrenched Japanese force. Each day repeated attacks were made against the enemy position, but to no avail, and patrols that probed the flanks of the enemy to discover a means of enveloping the hostile force had no success. On 8 and 9 December the 1st Squadron, 112th Cavalry, attempted to locate and cut off the supply line of the Japanese force that was holding up the advance of the 2d Squadron.[61]

On 10 December the 2d Squadron, 7th Cavalry, which had been in the Barugo–Capoocan area, relieved the 2d Squadron, 112th Cavalry, which passed to the control of Sixth Army. In the meantime the 1st Squadron, 112th Cavalry, less Troop A had moved west toward the Leyte River. Troop A reached the left flank of the 126th Infantry. The progress of the 1st Squadron was slow because of the hilly terrain, but on the morning of 7 December it arrived at the Leyte River and established physical contact with Troop A and the 126th Infantry.[62] At the end of 10 December, the 1st Squadron, 112th Cavalry, was on the Leyte River.

The 2d Squadron, 7th Cavalry, after relieving the 2d Squadron, 112th Cavalry, sent out patrols to study the terrain and attempt to find avenues of approach to the flanks and rear of the enemy strong point which had long held up the 2d Squadron, 112th Cavalry. An aerial reconnaissance was made of the area. The aerial observer reported that the Japanese position was

"definitely as bad" as the 2d Squadron, 112th Cavalry, had reported it to be, and that the approach from the rear was even worse than the one from the front.[63]

The 2d Squadron, 7th Cavalry, spent 11 December in sending out patrols on both sides of the enemy-held ridge. The Japanese let the patrols through and then fired, wounding two of the men. The patrols then returned. An artillery concentration was placed upon the enemy position, and at 1245 the 2d Squadron, 7th Cavalry, moved out behind a barrage which lifted twenty-five yards at a time. One platoon attacked frontally while the other platoons attempted to flank the Japanese. The platoon on the right flank suffered three casualties and was immediately pinned down. After the other platoons got to within fifty yards of a Japanese machine gun position, they also were pinned down. At 1600 they dug in for the night at the base of the hill.

During the engagement fifteen to twenty enemy bunkers were observed on each side of the ridge and four machine guns were definitely spotted. A night infiltration party armed with hand grenades, rifles, and knives was sent to knock out these bunkers. It destroyed two machine guns and killed four Japanese.

At 0730 on the morning of 13 December, the 2d Squadron, 7th Cavalry, moved out and came under fire from two Japanese machine guns well emplaced on a cliff. The ridge narrowed to ten feet with sixty-degree slopes, making forward passage almost impossible. The troops were pinned down. In the meantime, Troop F of the squadron worked south in an attempt to envelop the rear of the enemy force but was unable to do so and returned. The 2d Squadron estab-

[61] 112th Cav Opns Rpt Leyte, pp. 6–8; 112th Cav S–2 and S–3 Jnl, 4–10 Dec 44; 1st Cav Div G–3 Periodic Rpts 46–51, 5–10 Dec 44; 1st Cav Div Opns Rpt Leyte, pp. 46–50.

[62] 112th Cav Opns Rpt Leyte, pp. 6–8; 1st Cav Div Opns Rpt Leyte, pp. 47–50; 112th Cav S–2 and S–3 Jnl, 4 Dec 44, 6–9 Dec 44; 1st Cav Div G–3 Periodic Rpts 46–51, 10 Dec 44.

[63] 112th Cav S–2 and S–3 Jnl, 10 Dec 44.

lished night perimeters near the same positions it had held the previous night.

On the following morning the 75-mm. and 105-mm. artillery and the 4.2-inch and 60-mm. mortars began to register heavy fire on the Japanese strong point. At 1200 Troop G of the 2d Squadron jumped off, attacking the enemy position frontally while Troop F moved in from the rear. Employing flame throwers, Troop G steadily pushed forward and by 1445 had knocked out four enemy bunkers and destroyed several machine guns. Of more importance, it was fifty yards beyond the enemy front lines. Troop F also continued to advance. By the end of the day the enemy force had been rooted off the high ground, and the 2d Squadron, 7th Cavalry, was in firm possession of the ridge. The unit captured a quantity of enemy ordnance, including 12 light and 3 heavy machine guns, 9 grenade launchers, and 73 rifles, together with considerable quantities of grenades and ammunition. Before the ridge was secured, "over 5000 rounds of artillery fire had been placed on [the] . . . position without appreciably affecting it." [64]

The 96th Division

By the end of October the XXIV Corps, having secured the southern part of Leyte Valley, the Dulag–Burauen–Dagami–Tanauan road net, and all airfields in the area, was ready for the next phase of its mission. General Hodge thereupon immediately initiated operations whereby the XXIV Corps was to liberate southern Leyte concurrently with the drive of the X Corps in the north.

General Hodge's plan called for the 96th Division to make a holding attack east of the mountains while the 7th Division drove north from Baybay up the coast of Ormoc Bay.[65] He therefore ordered the 96th Division to defend the Tanauan–Dagami–Burauen–Dulag area and to relieve as rapidly as possible all elements of the 7th Division in the area. Finally it was to mop up all enemy forces in its zone and to furnish security for all the principal roads and installations in the area.[66] General Bradley on 2 November ordered Colonel Dill's 382d Infantry to relieve the 17th Infantry of the 7th Division in the vicinity of Dagami, to send strong reconnaissance and combat patrols into the hills to the west and northwest, and to destroy all enemy forces encountered.[67]

General Suzuki was desirous of pushing through to Leyte Valley, one of the best entrances to which was through the Dagami sector. At the foot of the central mountain range, Dagami was the center of a network of roads that led to all parts of Leyte Valley and to the airfields. Since it was one of the key positions for control of the valley, its recapture would be of great advantage to the *35th Army*. Just west of Dagami, the central mountain range served as a natural fortification. The mountains consisted of a series of ridges separated by deep gorges which were usually covered with a dense tropical growth. At key points in the area, the *16th Division* had built coconut-log and concrete pillboxes.

There were substantial parts of the *9th, 20th,* and *33d Infantry Regiments* of the *16th Division* in the mountains west of

---

[64] 112th Cav S–2 and S–3 Jnl, 9–14 Dec 44; 7th Cav Div Opns Rpt Leyte, pp. 11–12; 112th Cav Opns Rpt Leyte, pp. 7–9; 1st Cav Div G–3 Periodic Rpts 53–56, 12–15 Dec 44.

[65] XXIV Corps Opns Rpt Leyte, p. 9.
[66] XXIV Corps FO 22, 8 Nov 44. This order confirmed previously issued oral orders.
[67] 96th Div FO 3, 2 Nov 44.

Dagami. In the latter part of October the *16th Division* became short of food and General Makino asked that it be supplied by air. The *4th Air Army* therefore attempted with six light bombers to supply the division, but for some unexplained reason it failed. The *16th Division* henceforward was forced to supply itself and forage off the land.[68]

On 2 November the 382d Infantry started to relieve the 17th Infantry. The 2d Battalion at 1500 relieved the 3d Battalion, 17th Infantry, just north of Dagami and at 1430, the 1st Battalion relieved the 1st Battalion, 17th Infantry, about 1,000 yards west of Dagami.[69]

Elements of the *16th Division* were entrenched on "Bloody Ridge," a small promontory on the left side of the road west of Dagami just short of Hitomnog in front of the 382d Infantry. A waist-deep swampy rice paddy was between the ridge and the road. The 1st Battalion, 382d Infantry, after moving into this area engaged the enemy, but at nightfall it broke off the fight and established its night perimeter.

At 0805, the 1st Battalion renewed the attack and met increased heavy resistance as it advanced through the rice paddy. The companies came under mortar and automatic weapons fire at 1445 as they came into the open.

The Japanese took full advantage of the exposed troops and from machine guns and mortars delivered heavy fire which immobilized the 1st Battalion. The unit was unable to move in any direction until nightfall, when, with the aid of some artillery smoke, the troops began to withdraw. "Men threw away their packs, machine guns, radios and even rifles. Their sole aim was to crawl back through the muck and get on solid ground

once more. Some of the wounded gave up the struggle to keep their heads above the water and drowned in the grasping swamp." [70] After every officer in Companies B and C had been killed or wounded, 1st Sgt. Francis H. Thompson took charge and organized the evacuation. He silenced an enemy machine gun and also assisted in removal of the wounded. As a result of his leadership both companies successfully withdrew and reorganized.[71]

At 1745 five enemy planes strafed the battalion. The advance units of the 1st Battalion withdrew some 300 yards in order to consolidate their defensive positions for the night. During the day Company E of the 2d Battalion reached Patok, and Company G moved out at 2100 to reinforce the 1st Battalion.[72]

During the night of 3–4 November the *16th Division* launched a strong counterattack of an estimated two-company strength against the perimeter of the 1st Battalion. Mortar and artillery fires repulsed the assault. There was no further enemy activity during the night. On the morning of 4 November the 1st Battalion moved out against light resistance, advancing about 800 yards and past the scene of the bitter fighting of the previous day. Colonel Dill ordered the 2d Battalion (minus Company E) and one platoon from Company G to move west from Dagami and join the 1st Battalion. The 2d Battalion joined close behind the 1st Battalion in a column. At 1430 the 1st Battalion encountered increased

---

[68] *14th Area Army* Opns Leyte, p. 8.

[69] 382d Inf Unit Rpt 14, 2 Nov 44.

[70] Orlando Davidson, J. Carl Willems, and Joseph A. Kahl, *The Deadeyes: The Story of the 96th Infantry Division* (Washington, Infantry Journal Press [now Combat Forces Press], 1947), p. 49.

[71] Sergeant Thompson was awarded the Distinguished Service Cross.

[72] 96th Div Opns Rpt Leyte, p. 54; 96th Div G–3 Periodic Rpt 14, 3 Nov 44; 382d Inf Unit Rpt 15, 3 Nov 44; Davidson *et al.*, *The Deadeyes*, p. 49.

enemy resistance and committed its reserve company on the left flank. The 2d Battalion received orders from Colonel Dill to move up to the left flank of the 1st, but the 2d arrived too late for the two battalions to launch a co-ordinated assault before nightfall. They therefore consolidated their positions for the night, having advanced about 1,000 yards.[73]

The night of 4–5 November was not quiet. The Japanese delivered harassing fire on the 1st Battalion, and at 2205 elements of the *16th Division* launched a heavy assault against the perimeter of the 2d Battalion. An artillery concentration immediately stopped the attack, and the Japanese fled, leaving 254 dead and wounded behind them.

The following morning, after the artillery had fired a preparation in front of the 1st and 2d Battalions, the two battalions renewed the attack at 0900 and two companies from the 3d Battalion protected the regimental left (south) flank. The battalions advanced about 1,000 yards before they encountered any strong resistance. The defenses of the *16th Division* consisted of a great many concrete emplacements, concealed spider holes, and connecting trenches. By nightfall, at 1700, the two battalions, assisted by the tanks from Company A, 763d Tank Battalion, successfully reduced the enemy to their front and captured the ridge. Each battalion formed its own perimeter and made plans to renew the attack on 6 November.[74]

At 0830 the 1st Battalion, with light tanks in support, moved out in the attack westward against a strong enemy force that was well entrenched in foxholes and pillboxes. Each of these defensive positions had to be reduced before the advance could continue. At 1300 the 2d Battalion moved to the high ground on the right flank of the 1st. The 1st Battalion encountered a strong concrete enemy pillbox which was believed to be a command post, since there were no firing apertures. As grenades had no effect it became necessary finally to neutralize the pillbox by pouring gasoline down the ventilation pipes and setting it afire. Two officers and nineteen enlisted men of the enemy were killed in the pillbox. The Japanese continued to fight tenaciously. There was no withdrawal, but by the end of the day only isolated pockets of enemy resistance remained.[75]

The Japanese *16th Division* was taking a bad beating. Its supply of provisions had run out. All the battalion commanders, most of the company commanders, and half the artillery battalion and battery commanders had been killed. On the night of 6 November the *16th Division* contracted its battle lines and on the following day took up a new position in the Dagami area. The new position ranged from a hill about four and a half miles northwest of Dagami to a point about three and three-fourths miles northwest of Burauen.[76]

On 7 November all three battalions of the 382d Infantry engaged the enemy and maintained constant pressure against his positions. The 1st and 3d Battalions advanced west, while the 2d Battalion drove north and west. The 3d Battalion encoun-

[73] Davidson *et al., The Deadeyes,* p. 51; 96th Div Opns Rpt Leyte, p. 54; 382d Inf Unit Rpt 16, 4 Nov 44; 96th Div G–3 Periodic Rpt 15, 4 Nov 44.
[74] Davidson *et al., The Deadeyes,* p. 51; 382d Inf Unit Rpt 17, 5 Nov 44; 96th Div Opns Rpt Leyte, p. 55; 96th Div G–3 Periodic Rpt 16, 5 Nov 44; 763d Tank Bn Opns Rpt Leyte, p. 5.
[75] 96th Div Opns Rpt Leyte, p. 55; 382d Inf Unit Rpt 18, 6 Nov 44.
[76] *35th Army* Opns, pp. 57–58.

tered the more determined resistance. Advancing, preceded by tanks, it met heavy enemy machine gun and rifle fire. A large enemy force assaulted the troops at close quarters and tried to destroy the tanks, but when the 382d Infantry introduced flame throwers and supporting machine guns, the attackers fell back in disorder. The regiment overran the Japanese defensive positions and killed an estimated 474 of the enemy.[77] Company E of the 2d Battalion had remained in the Patok area, engaged in patrolling and wiping out isolated pockets of enemy resistance.

On 8 November strong patrols from the 1st and 2d Battalions probed west into the hills. They encountered the left flank of the enemy supporting position at a point about 2,600 yards west of Patok. A very heavy rainfall on the night of 8–9 November made an assault against the position impossible on 9 November. After all-night artillery fire, the 1st and 3d Battalions moved out at 0900 on 10 November. They met no resistance, but progress was slow because of the swamps. By 1225 the two battalions, supported by a platoon of light tanks, occupied the ridge formerly held by elements of the *16th Division*. The 1st Battalion had advanced 2,500 yards.[78] The 382d Infantry had destroyed all organized enemy resistance

in its sector and removed the threat to Dagami.

By this time General Krueger was devoting the main effort of the Sixth Army toward preventing the *35th Army* from debouching into Leyte Valley. The 96th Division received orders from General Hodge to halt the relief of the 7th Division and to move north to the Jaro–Palo road and secure the mountain entrances in that sector. The 7th Division was to relieve the 96th Division on the Dagami–Burauen road. A regiment was also to be made available for immediate motor movement to the north and another for a proposed operation on northern Mindanao.[79]

The 96th Division moved to the mountains northwest of Dagami and sent extensive patrols into the central mountain range along a ten-mile line that extended from Dagami to Jaro. Constant small contacts with the enemy continued until the end of the campaign. The 7th Division patrolled the Burauen area.

The Sixth Army had prevented the Japanese from debouching into Leyte Valley. The X Corps had secured Limon, the entrance to Ormoc Valley, and was in a position to drive south down the valley to the port of Ormoc. Although General Krueger's troops had performed well, they had made mistakes which gave their commander serious concern.

---

[77] 382d Inf Unit Rpt 19, 7 Nov 44.
[78] 382d Inf Unit Rpt 22, 10 Nov 44.

---

[79] XXIV Corps Opns Rpt Leyte, p. 11.

CHAPTER XIV

Measure of the Fighting

By the latter part of November, the fighting on the island had entered a crucial stage. The additional troops received from General MacArthur had enabled General Krueger to put into effect his squeeze play against the Japanese. While the X Corps continued to apply unremitting pressure on the *1st* and *102d Divisions* in the northern mountains of Ormoc Valley near Limon, elements of the XXIV Corps would drive north against the *26th Division* along the shores of Ormoc Bay toward Ormoc.

General MacArthur had full confidence in the ability of General Krueger to carry out this plan and thus bring the Leyte Campaign to a successful conclusion. Once having given the Sixth Army commander the assignment for the operation, General MacArthur did not interfere with General Krueger's prosecution of the battle. But from his headquarters on Leyte, he closely followed the progress of the campaign, frequently visited the command posts of the Sixth Army units, and made available to General Krueger additional troops upon request.

Similarly, General Krueger allowed his corps commanders to exercise their independence of judgment and kept his orders to the minimum. He, too, made frequent visits to the front lines, observed the progress of the fighting, inspected the living conditions of the men, and noted the status of the construction program. General Krueger's concern is made evident by a critique issued on 25 November in which he analyzed the performance of the Sixth Army on Leyte.[1]

The Americans had had time to test their experience on Leyte against past operations, as well as to determine the good and bad features of their training and tactics and the performance of their weapons and to contrast them with those employed by the Japanese. An evaluation of American methods at this point serves to explain in concrete terms the nature of the fighting that had occurred and of that which would occur in the critical days ahead.

The American Ground Forces

Tactics

Following the customary procedure, the divisions went ashore with two regiments abreast. Within the regiments there were variations, some going ashore with the battalions abreast and others with the battalions in column. The size of the landing beach and the nature of the expected opposition determined the type of landing formation that was employed. Once ashore, the nature of the tactical situation resulted in numerous

---

[1] Ltr, CG Sixth Army to CG X Corps *et al.*, sub: Mistakes Made and Lessons Learned in K–2 Operation, 25 Nov 44, Sixth Army Opns Rpt Leyte, pp. 204–212. Unless otherwise stated this chapter is based upon General Krueger's critique.

GENERAL MacARTHUR AND MAJ. GEN. ARCHIBALD V. ARNOLD *at Headquarters, 7th Division.*

independent actions by subordinate units. The formation most frequently used was the normal one of two units in the assault and one in reserve.

Frontal assaults were usually employed against enemy positions, and not enough use was made of envelopments. When envelopments were tried they were nearly always successful. It was sometimes advantageous to bypass isolated enemy strong points, leaving them to be mopped up by the follow-up units.

Although the primary mission of the infantry is to close with the enemy and destroy or capture him, the natural reluctance of American infantrymen to engage the enemy in close quarters had to be overcome. There were several instances in which the

American attacking force felt out the Japanese position and then sat back to wait it out. In one area no progress was made for four days. On several occasions strong combat patrols of platoon or company strength were sent to feel out enemy positions, but as soon as they made contact with the Japanese the patrols withdrew. They accomplished nothing except to determine the presence of an unknown number of enemy soldiers.

If more than minor resistance was encountered, the troops frequently fell back and called for fire from supporting weapons. On one occasion a company called for artillery fire upon a roadblock and then withdrew 350 yards while the concentration was delivered. After the lifting of the artillery fire, it was very difficult to reorganize the company and get it back to the objective. Meanwhile the Japanese had again covered the roadblock and the whole process had to be repeated.

The American soldiers were too road-bound. Sometimes resistance along the road stopped the advance of an entire division. This opposition could have been eliminated quickly by the employment of simple envelopments and flanking attacks. Although the presence of swamps, jungle, and rice paddies tended to channelize the attack, the Japanese had displayed superior adeptness, and willingness to go into the swamps and stay there until rooted out.

The standard employment of artillery in close support of the infantry again proved to be very effective and was used extensively. However, since the artillery fire enabled the infantry to secure many heavily fortified positions with few casualties, the infantrymen tended to become too dependent upon the artillerymen and expected them to do the work of the infantry. General Krueger insisted that the infantry must be prepared to close in immediately after the cessation of the artillery fire.

The Americans had developed a strong tendency to telegraph their punches. In the morning, before an assault by the infantry, the artillery pounded the Japanese positions, after which the mortars opened up. The mortar fire nearly always lasted for a half hour, and then the infantry moved out. Upon occasion, the infantry did not attack immediately after the preparation by the supporting weapons. This delay gave the Japanese time and opportunity to regroup and consolidate their forces, and thus nullified the effects of the preparatory fires.

Parenthetically, it may be remarked that although the actual casualties per artillery shell were few, the cumulative effect of the heavy and prolonged fire of the artillery and mortars was very great. Col. Junkichi Okabayashi, chief of staff of the Japanese *1st Division*, estimated that the losses sustained by the division were distributed as follows: by artillery, 60 percent; by mortars, 25 percent; by infantry fire, 14 percent; and by aircraft, 1 percent.[2]

The employment of tanks singly, or in small groups, materially aided the infantrymen, since the tanks could be used effectively to reduce enemy pillboxes and to flush out bamboo thickets. Although light tanks were more mobile it was found that the mediums were more efficient in reducing pillboxes. For successful employment, it was necessary that the tanks have close infantry and engineer support. In some instances the tanks secured objectives when no infantrymen were present to consolidate and hold the positions. For example, a regiment supported by a tank battalion received orders to attack and secure an objective. The tanks quickly moved out and secured the objective with little resistance. Since the infantrymen did not arrive during the day, the tanks withdrew at nightfall. During the night the Japanese mined the area and four of the tanks were lost when they returned next morning.

Likewise, tanks were often disabled because the engineers had failed to remove mines and give support in the crossing of streams. In one case, the engineers failed to repair a bridge, which collapsed after three tanks had crossed over it. The Japanese completely destroyed one of the tanks and disabled the other two. It was necessary for the Americans to destroy the disabled tanks

---

[2] 10th I&HS Eighth Army, Stf Study of Japanese *35th Army* on Leyte, Interrog Col Okabayashi, pp. 5–6.

with their own gunfire in order to prevent their use as stationary pillboxes by the enemy.

It was found advantageous to establish a night perimeter before dusk. An early establishment of the perimeter enabled the troops to take effective countermeasures against Japanese infiltrations and night assaults.[3] The soldiers also had an opportunity to become familiar with their surroundings and were less likely to fire indiscriminately during the night. In spite of this precaution, there was considerable promiscuous firing during the night and at dawn. One corps commander effectively stopped this practice in his command post area by the adoption of two simple measures. First, he employed a reserve battalion to cover an area extending outward for one mile and when no Japanese were found the fact was announced over the loudspeaker. Second, any man caught firing before dawn was immediately court-martialed and fined fifty dollars. "There was very little promiscuous firing thereafter." [4]

Although there were three war-dog platoons available for the Leyte operation, their combat value was practically nil. The unit commanders to whom they were attached knew little of their capabilities or limitations. Some expected the dogs to spot a Japanese position exactly at a distance of 200 or more yards. One unit took the dogs on a four-day patrol without sufficient dog rations. Another unit attempted to use dogs in a populated area; the presence of so many civilians thoroughly confused the dogs.

In general, the troops found that their training had been sound and that the methods which in the past had been employed in overcoming the Japanese were also useful on Leyte. It was felt, however, that greater emphasis in training should be placed on night patrols and night movements near the enemy lines, as well as on closer co-ordination between the infantry and the supporting weapons. Finally, it was believed that the service troops should be given training in basic infantry tactics and prepared to maintain their own defenses.[5]

All units were in agreement that there could be "no substitute for aggressive leadership." [6] An infantry unit could be no better than its leaders. General Krueger said in this connection:

Infantry is the arm of *close combat*. It is the arm of *final* combat. The Jap is usually most tenacious particularly when in entrenched and concealed positions. Individual enemy soldiers will remain in their holes until eliminated. Although the supporting arms are of great assistance, it ultimately becomes the task of the small infantry units to dig them out. The American soldier has demonstrated on many battlefields that he can and will do it, but he must be aggressively led. There can be no hesitating on the part of his leaders.[7]

Welfare of the Men

At the same time, in order to obtain the best results from the troops, the unit commanders must concern themselves with the well-being and comfort of their men. Many commanders were indifferent to such matters. One corps, for example, had sufficient rations of all types available, but the meals served the men were poorly prepared and monotonous. Another corps, at the time it landed, was prepared to live indefinitely on

---

[3] 7th Div Opns Rpt Leyte, Annex, Tactics, n. p.
[4] Krueger's Critique, Sixth Army Opns Rpt Leyte, p. 205.

[5] 24th Div Opns Rpt Leyte, Incl 1 to Annex 3, n. p.
[6] *Ibid.*
[7] Krueger's Critique, Sixth Army Opns Rpt Leyte, p. 205. Italics are Krueger's.

field rations. As late as ten days after the landing, no unit—not even any of the fixed installations, including higher headquarters—operated a mess or served hot meals. Some units did serve hot coffee after the first few days.

Although there was considerable rain and mud, few units made a genuine effort to get their men under shelter even when the tactical situation permitted. Night after night, officers and men slept in wet foxholes even when no enemy troops were within shooting distance. "It must never be forgotten," said General Krueger, "that the individual soldier is the most important single factor in this war. . . . He is expected to do a lot including risking his life. But to get the most out of him he must have the feeling that everything possible under existing circumstances is being done for his well being and comfort. This is a prime responsibility of command. . . ." [8]

Weapons and Vehicles

The basic weapons—the U.S. .30-caliber rifle Model 1903, the U.S. .30-caliber rifle M1, the BAR, bayonets, and grenades— with which the rifle squads and the individual soldiers of the heavy weapons company were equipped were generally satisfactory and notably superior to comparable weapons of the Japanese.

The troops used a variety of hand grenades. The white smoke grenade was considered to be defective and was frequently discarded. The white phosphorus grenade was extensively used, mainly as an antipersonnel weapon. It was thrown with telling effect into foxholes, caves, and heavy under-

brush. An Australian grenade was introduced, but because the troops were unfamiliar with its use, it was not too successful. Incendiary hand grenades were effectively used against enemy weapons, ammunition dumps, and supplies. Colored grenades were employed to mark strips for the air dropping of supplies.[9] The fragmentation grenade was most favored by the troops, and after that the phosphorus grenade.[10]

The Browning automatic rifle was very popular, the best results being obtained when two were allotted to a squad. The increased fire power thus obtained was very effective in night defense.

The 81-mm. mortar continued to be highly esteemed as a close support infantry weapon. The 4.2-inch chemical mortars of the attached chemical mortar battalions were extensively employed, affording excellent results when emplaced on firm ground. On marshy or swampy ground, however, their base plates would sink and cause inaccurate firing or put the weapons out of commission. The most popular mortar was the 60-mm., which was very mobile and especially suitable for use in close terrain. This mortar fired an illuminating shell which was used constantly for night defense, but its base plate also tended to sink into the ground.

Flame throwers were employed with very good effect in reducing strongly fortified positions. The M2-2 flame thrower was an excellent incendiary weapon against bamboo thickets and shacks. The cartridge type was considered to be more satisfactory, since the spark-ignited flame thrower was not dependable in rainy weather. The flame

---

[8] *Ibid.*, p. 206.

[9] 24th Div Opns Rpt Leyte, pp. 113–14.
[10] 7th Div Opns Rpt Leyte, Annex, Effectiveness of Weapons, n. p.

thrower was considered "a very important factor in overcoming the enemy's inherent 'will to resist.' " [11]

The .50-caliber machine gun again proved its value in defense, being highly effective not only against ground targets but also against aircraft. The 96th Division found the Thompson submachine gun excellent for use by patrolling units but "some difficulty . . . has been encountered with the M3 machine gun in its failure to feed properly." [12]

The 7th Division found the 75-mm. self-propelled howitzer, because of its superior mobility, to be the most effective infantry weapon for reduction of Japanese pillboxes. The 105-mm. howitzers of the field artillery battalions again proved their worth by the speed, accuracy, and effectiveness of their fire. The greater striking range of the 155-mm. howitzer had special value for general support missions.

Demolition charges were used effectively by patrols for the destruction of enemy ammunition dumps in inaccessible locations and not salvageable because of the tactical situation. Except for this purpose, demolitions were not extensively used. [13]

The 37-mm. gun was an antitank weapon only occasionally employed by the 7th Division because there were few Japanese armored vehicles against which to use it. The excessive difficulty of manhandling it into a position from which fire could be delivered against Japanese pillboxes and machine guns rendered it ineffective for that purpose. The 90-mm. guns of the antiaircraft artillery had a considerable number of erratic bursts because of corroded fuzes and worn fuze setting lugs.

The tanks and tank destroyers could have been used more frequently and with greater versatility. Situations often arose in which an infantry platoon was held up by enemy machine gun and mortar fire, but "the use of indirect artillery fire was impracticable either because of overhead cover for the enemy weapons or because of undue risk to our enveloping infantry." General Krueger recommended that the infantry employ direct fire by the tanks or tank destroyers. He felt that "the tank destroyer commanders lacked aggressiveness and skilled direction." [14] The tank destroyer commanders admitted that they were idle but added that the infantry had not called for them. The tanks and tank destroyers were ideal weapons for the destruction of machine guns, mortars, and other heavy infantry weapons, but the infantry commanders seemed to be unaware of their capabilities. Many commanders employed their armored vehicles down the middle of the road when they could have used them more effectively on the flanks and for envelopments.

The 96th Division found the Cannon Company's self-propelled 105-mm. howitzer extremely mobile in swamps and mountainous terrain. It was able to go several miles farther up the mountains than any other vehicle and gave excellent support in covering the mountain passes. [15]

The cargo carrier M29 (weasel) proved to be a most useful supply vehicle. The commanders used it for reconnaissance and visits to units in isolated areas and over roads that were impassable to wheeled vehicles. It also was employed to carry sup-

---

[11] 96th Div Opns Rpt Leyte, p. 85.
[12] *Ibid.* p. 83. Presumably the .45-caliber submachine gun M3 is intended by the term "M3 machine gun."
[13] 7th Div Opns Rpt Leyte, Annex, Effectiveness of Weapons, n. p.

[14] Krueger's Critique, Sixth Army Opns Rpt Leyte, p. 208.
[15] 96th Div Opns Rpt Leyte, p. 82.

plies and to evacuate the wounded from inaccessible areas. The weasel was much less destructive of roads than any of the other tracked vehicles, but the tendency to use it on dry roads resulted in worn-out tracks and excessive maintenance requirements.

The 96th Division found the DUKW to be an excellent vehicle when waterborne but on land, regardless of the condition of the roads and terrain, it was not half as effective as the 2½-ton cargo truck. On roads the DUKW was a traffic hazard and an obstacle to other cargo traffic.[16]

The 7th Division landed with seventeen one-ton trailers. They were found to be of little value and the division recommended that they should not be used in any future operation unless a hard-surfaced, all-weather road net existed at the anticipated target.[17]

Intelligence

General Krueger pointed out that prompt, aggressive reconnaissance should have been instituted immediately upon the landing of the troops. The fact that knowledge of the terrain was very limited before the assault—inaccuracies in the distances on existing maps were as high as 50 percent—gave urgency to the need for immediate reconnaissance.

The sources of information on the Japanese were as follows: ground and aerial reconnaissance, Filipino civilians, guerrillas, captured documents, and prisoners. Air observation was of limited value because of the Japanese ability at camouflage and because the inclement weather prevented aerial observation of many areas. The tend-

ency of the Filipinos to say "yes" to everything was also a handicap. In general, the guerrilla reports were more accurate than those of civilians. Considerable information was obtained from patrols, which were especially valuable for on-the-spot intelligence.

In interrogating prisoners the best results were obtained by employing Nisei, who obtained more information from prisoners when the latter were not subjected to questioning by an officer through an interpreter. Since most of the prisoners had been separated from their units for a considerable time and were seriously wounded, their information was sparse and generally out of date.

Captured documents were the most fruitful source of intelligence. Although the Japanese made a few attempts to destroy dog tags and other means of identification before going into battle, they were not too successful. The fact that General Krueger obtained information on the proposed ground offensive of the Japanese for the middle of November from papers found on the body of a Japanese officer was not an isolated incident. Many officers carried on their persons sets of orders and maps.

The Japanese received much of their information on the American order of battle from broadcasts emanating from San Francisco. At first, the Japanese on the island were unable to find out the American order of battle for Leyte but within a few days the Americans gratuitously furnished them the information. Said General Tomochika:

> At the time of the landing, *35th Army Headquarters* did not know the number or name of the American units which had landed . . . but within a day headquarters learned. . . . We found out . . . by tuning in on the San Francisco broadcasts; Japanese troops in the combat area were unable to determine

---

[16] *Ibid.,* p. 95.

[17] 7th Div Opns Rpt Leyte, Annex, Deficiencies in Equipment, n. p.

their identity. From the same source, we later obtained information which was of considerable help in planning. In fact, that was the only way we could get information. . . . Information was always received through the San Francisco broadcast before reports from our front line units reached headquarters. . . . Since the information came much sooner from the American broadcast than from the Japanese communications, the Army Headquarters depended on the American broadcasts for much intelligence.[18]

Japanese Warfare

The 24th Division found the Japanese troops on Leyte to be better trained in combat and more skillful than those the division had encountered during the Hollandia–Tanahmerah Bay operation.[19] In general the Japanese fought a delaying action, and when forced to yield ground they would fall back to previously prepared positions. During a bombardment by American heavy weapons, the enemy troops would withdraw but when the fire lifted they would quickly reoccupy the vacated positions.[20]

The 21st Infantry was impressed with the Japanese "excellence in battle" on Breakneck Ridge. There were few instances of "reckless charges, needless sacrifices or failure to observe known tactical principles." The most notable characteristics exhibited were the excellent fire discipline and the effective control of all arms. Without exception individual soldiers withheld their fire until it would have the greatest possible effect. The heaviest firing would generally start about 1530 and increase in intensity until about dark, the fire being accompanied by counterattacks from the front and on the flanks. These assaults usually came when the Americans' energy and ammunition were at their lowest point during the day and when they would prevent proper consolidation of the front lines before dark.[21]

The Japanese employed reverse slope defense tactics with much skill and were successful in utilizing terrain for their defensive positions. Caves and other natural formations were exploited to the limit and positions were dug in deeply and expertly camouflaged. The Japanese frequently sacrificed fields of fire for cover and concealment, a fact which made it very difficult for the Americans to locate hostile positions.

Captured documents indicated that the Japanese attacks were generally well conceived but that there were not enough troops at the time of the assault. The documents also gave repeated indications that units either did not receive their orders or did not reach the appointed place on time. The Japanese employed two main types of attack. The first, which was similar to that employed by the Americans, utilized a base of fire from supporting weapons, followed by infantry fire and movement. This type of attack was not usually accompanied by artillery or mortar support. The other method consisted of a localized charge in which the Japanese by sheer force of numbers tried to crack the American lines. The heavy weapons fire of the Americans was nearly always able to break up both types of attack. Enemy forces, generally in small numbers, tried repeatedly to infiltrate through the American lines. The objectives

---

[18] 10th I&HS Eighth Army, Stf Study of Japanese *35th Army* on Leyte, Interrog Gen Tomochika, pp. 2–3.

[19] 24th Div Opns Rpt Leyte, p. 86.

[20] 96th Div Opns Rpt Leyte, p. 88.

[21] 24th Div Opns Rpt Leyte, Annex, Enemy Tactics on Breakneck Ridge, n. p.

were artillery pieces, supply dumps, and key installations. Rarely did they accomplish even minor damage.

Artillery weapons were seldom used by the Japanese to maximum effect. The gunnery techniques were "remarkably undeveloped" and inefficient, the pieces being used singly or in pairs and only rarely as batteries. Their fire was never massed. The gun positions generally were well constructed but they were frequently selected with such high regard for concealment that the fields of fire were limited. The use of mines and demolition charges was poor, the mine fields being hastily and obviously laid.

The troops were well trained and led by officers imbued with a sense of duty. Conse-quently, "as long as any officers remain alive, the remnants of a . . . force are capable of determined action." [22]

The Japanese view of American methods was summed up by General Tomochika as follows: "The strong points of the American strategy in the Leyte Operation were numerous but the two outstanding points were (1) the overwhelming striking power of the American Army, and (2) the American operations were planned in minute detail and on the whole were carried out scrupulously." [23]

---

[22] 7th Div Opns Rpt Leyte, Annex, Japanese Opns, n. p.

[23] 10th I&HS, Eighth Army, Stf Study of Opns of Japanese *35th Army* on Leyte, Interrog Gen Tomochika, p. 26.

CHAPTER XV

Battle of the Ridges

American Plans and Preparations

With the securing of the beachhead areas in the last week of October and the first days of November, General Krueger was ready to launch that part of his plan that concerned a drive north along the west coast of Leyte. Since a preliminary reconnaissance indicated that there were not a great many Japanese troops in the southern half of the island, elements of the 32d Infantry had already started to push west through the mountains to the west coast along the road from Abuyog to Baybay. After the attention of the Japanese had been diverted to the struggle in the northern mountains, the X Corps could launch a drive against Ormoc, proceeding north from Baybay on Highway 2 along the shores of the Camotes Sea and of Ormoc Bay. At the same time elements of the X Corps—the 24th Division and later the 32d Division—could drive down the Ormoc corridor to Ormoc. The enemy forces would then be caught between the jaws of a trap, with their freedom of maneuver limited and most of their strength employed in defensive action. But the need for blocking the exits from the central mountain range and the scarcity of combat troops made it necessary for General Krueger to postpone sending a strong force to the shores of the Camotes Sea until additional reinforcements arrived on Leyte in the middle of November. General Hodge was to be prepared, however, to send strong elements of the XXIV Corps over the mountains.

American Plans

On 30 October General Hodge directed the 7th Division to move elements, not to exceed one battalion, over the mountain road from Abuyog to Baybay, the western terminus of the road. He also ordered the 7th Division to be prepared to move to the west coast when relieved in the Burauen area.[1] In anticipation of this plan, the 2d Battalion, 32d Infantry, had moved to Abuyog on 29 October to occupy and defend that area. Company G had spearheaded the advance to Baybay. On 2 November General Arnold alerted the main body of the 32d Infantry, under Colonel Finn, for a move to Abuyog.

[1] XXIV Corps FO 12, 30 Oct 44. The operations of the 7th Division on the western coast of Leyte were more adequately covered than any other action in the Leyte campaign. Capt. Tucker Dean and 1st Lt. Russell A. Gugeler, two combat historians, prepared very complete manuscripts on the battle of Shoestring Ridge. Gugeler's Battle of the Ridgelines and Dean's King II: the Liberation of Leyte, on file in the Office of the Chief of Military History, have much information that is not given in the official reports. In addition Col. John M. Finn, who commanded the 32d Infantry which bore the brunt of the Shoestring Ridge battle, wrote an account of the engagement that appeared in the September and October 1945 issues of the *Infantry Journal*. (Unless otherwise stated, this chapter is based upon these accounts and the 32d Infantry Operations Report Leyte, pp. 10–26.)

As soon as word was received that the Americans were on the west coast, General Suzuki, believing these forces to be a small unit of American and Philippine troops, sent a company from the *364th Battalion* south from Ormoc to hold Albuera until the *26th Division* could arrive.[2] Albuera was important tactically, since from it ran a mountain trail that the Japanese had tried unsuccessfully to develop into a road to the Burauen airfield in Leyte Valley.

On 9 November the *26th Division* landed at Ormoc after a rough voyage from Manila. The transport vessels had been repeatedly attacked by Allied aircraft, which damaged many of the landing barges and ship hatches. These damaging attacks hindered the unloading of equipment, which did not proceed as planned. Many of the landing barges were run aground and destroyed by Allied aircraft, and the transports were forced to sail away before being completely emptied. They carried most of the ordnance, provisions, and munitions of the division with them. On their return trip, all the vessels were sunk by aircraft. The division consequently came ashore underequipped. The strength of the *26th Division* consisted of *Division Headquarters,* one battalion of the *11th Independent Infantry Regiment,* three battalions of the *13th Independent Infantry Regiment,* and the *2d Battalion* of the *12th Infantry Regiment.* These units had only light, portable weapons, and none was equipped with machine guns except a bat-

talion of the *13th Independent Infantry Regiment.*

General Suzuki had intended to use the *26th Division* in the Carigara area but the arrival of American forces in the Baybay area forced him to change his plans. On 13 November he received word from Manila that the *26th Division* was to be used in the Burauen area and consequently the main force of the *26th Division* was directed to Albuera. General Suzuki first sent the *13th Independent Infantry Regiment,* under Col. Jiro Saito,[3] but eventually the entire *26th Division,* including the division headquarters, was committed to the Albuera area.

As the troops of the 2d Battalion, 32d Infantry, moved over the mountains to Baybay, guerrillas informed them that about three hundred Japanese soldiers were pushing south toward the Abuyog–Baybay road. These enemy troops were "six marauding units" of the company which had been sent south to make contact with the American forces and contain them until the *26th Division* could arrive.[4] Company E set up an ambush, killed many of the Japanese, and forced the others to disperse.

By this time the appearance of Japanese reinforcements going north from Ormoc caused General Krueger to shift the weight of the Sixth Army to the north to meet the new threat, and to order General Hodge to hold up on the relief of the 7th Division in the Burauen area. It was not until after the arrival of the 11th Airborne Division that the 7th Division, on 22 November, was able to move in force to the west coast.[5]

At 1025 on 14 November General Arnold ordered Colonel Finn to start moving the 32d Infantry north to the Damulaan–Cari-

---

[2] The Japanese historians make the following ambiguous statement: "The Army had doubts as to the authenticity of this broadcast, but from past experience with U. S. broadcasts, the Army estimated it to be a small unit of U. S. and Philippine troops which had landed there." *35th Army Opns,* p. 51. Unless otherwise stated the part of this section dealing with Japanese plans is based upon this study, pp. 51–84.

[3] Tomochika, *True Facts of Leyte Opn,* p. 24.
[4] *Ibid.,* pp. 51–52.
[5] XXIV Corps Opns Rpt Leyte, pp. 11–12.

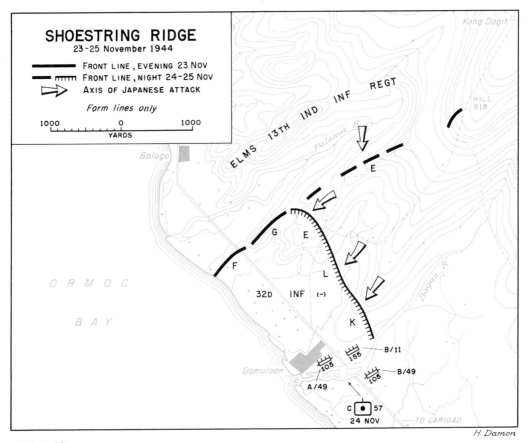

SHOESTRING RIDGE
23-25 November 1944

━━━━━ FRONT LINE, EVENING 23 NOV
━ ▥▥▥ FRONT LINE, NIGHT 24-25 NOV
⇨   AXIS OF JAPANESE ATTACK

Form lines only

1000   0   1000
        YARDS

MAP 13

H. Damon

dad area and to be prepared to advance
upon Ormoc on further orders.[6] The units
of the 32d Infantry moved to their assigned
areas near the Palanas River, and both the
Japanese and Americans made ready their
positions for the clash. (*Map 13*) The battle
that was about to be fought over the ridge
lines along the Palanas River was later
called the "Battle of Shoestring Ridge" by
troops of the 32d Infantry. This name applied to the supply technique rather than
to any terrain features of the ridge, since
the supply of the 32d Infantry throughout

the battle was precarious. Said Colonel
Finn: "The old slogan 'Too little and too
late' became 'Just enough and just in time'
for us." [7]

The Palanas River runs in a southwesterly
direction between two ridges that end
abruptly on reaching the road. The ridges
slope sharply toward the river and are separated by a narrow valley. Colonel Finn chose
to stand on Shoestring Ridge, the southernmost of the two, which rises steeply from
the fields. Its northerly face drops precipi-
tately for more than 125 feet to the valley,

---

[6] Fragmentary Order, CG 7th Div to CO 32d Inf,
14 Nov 44, 7th Div G-3 Jnl, 14 Nov 44.

[7] Col. John M. Finn, "Shoestring Ridge," *Infantry Journal*, LVII, 3 (September, 1945), 47.

where dense bamboo thickets cover the river banks. The main body of the ridge is covered with cogon grass, interspersed with palms and bamboo, growth being especially heavy in the gullies. Between the western tip of the ridge and the sea are rice paddies and clusters of palm trees, while at a point 3,000 yards northeast of the road the ridge falls into a saddle and then rises to join Hill 918.

Offensive Preparations

While the *26th Division* was building up positions on the opposite bank of the Palanas River, Colonel Finn had to solve problems that existed to the rear. Since enemy barges still operated freely a few thousand yards offshore and two Japanese destroyers had cruised by, General Arnold thought that the enemy might try to land forces and seize Baybay in order to separate the American units and sever their line of communications. There were only three infantry battalions on the west coast. The mud and floods on the narrow route that connected this force with the source of supplies at Dulag, on the east coast, made the road so undependable that the 7th Division could not rely on a quick transfer of reinforcements to the west.

Lt. Col. Charles A. Whitcomb's 3d Battalion, 32d Infantry, had moved from Baybay to a position just south of the 2d Battalion on 21 November [8] and established defensive positions in depth. To have increased the defensive strength on Shoestring Ridge would have placed the bulk of the forces in a position where they would be surrounded if the Japanese breached their line. General Arnold, to prevent such an envelopment,

directed that the 2d Battalion, 184th Infantry, should not be used to reinforce the front lines without his permission.[9] This order left only Lt. Col. Glenn A. Nelson's 2d Battalion, 32d Infantry, to hold the front. The 1st Battalion had been sent to the vicinity of Panaon Strait to relieve the 21st Infantry. In addition to the infantry there was a concentration of artillery at Damulaan for support. Batteries A and B of the 49th Field Artillery Battalion (105-mm. howitzer) had moved up and registered fire by 21 November,[10] and on the morning of 23 November Battery B of the 11th 155-mm. Marine Gun Battalion arrived at Damulaan.[11] The regimental Cannon Company brought two more pieces, which boosted the total to fourteen. All the artillery pieces were only about 1,500 yards behind the front lines, concentrated in a small area in the vicinity of Damulaan. The light weapons were situated so that their fire could be placed as far forward as possible, and the 155-mm. guns were in positions from which they could shell Ormoc.[12] The defenses of the infantry and the artillery were consolidated on ground that afforded the best protection.

A platoon from the 7th Reconnaissance Troop patrolled the road between Baybay and Damulaan, and a platoon of light tanks from the 767th Tank Battalion at Damulaan was the only armor on the west coast.[13]

---

[9] 7th Inf Div G–3 Jnl, 20 Nov 44.

[10] 7th Inf Div G–3 Periodic Rpt, 21 Nov 44.

[11] 7th Inf Div G–3 Jnl, 23 Nov 44. The 11th 155-mm. Gun Battalion and the 5th 155-mm. Howitzer Battalion were Marine artillery units and part of the V Amphibious Corps artillery which had been designated for Yap. With the cancellation of that operation, these two battalions had been assigned to the XXIV Corps as part of the corps artillery for Leyte.

[12] Msg, XXIV Corps to 7th Inf Div, 21 Nov 44.

[13] 32d Inf Regt S–3 Periodic Rpt, 23–24 Nov 44.

---

[8] 7th Inf Div G–3 Periodic Rpt, 21 Nov 44.

For several days preceding the 23d of November, Filipinos moving to the south through the lines reported that large enemy forces were massing on the opposite side of the Palanas River and emplacing field guns. Artillery observers on Shoestring Ridge could see the Japanese constructing trenches, machine gun pits, and other installations on the opposite ridge. The Japanese forces consisted of the *1st* and *2d Battalions, 13th Independent Infantry Regiment,* and two battalions from the *11th* and *12th Independent Infantry Regiments.*[14] Colonel Saito was ordered to hold back the American advance, which threatened to cut off a trail the Japanese had been building at Albuera over the mountains to Burauen.

On 23 November the defenses of the 32d Infantry were stretched very thin. Because of the great distance involved it was not possible to have a continuous front line extending from the sea to the mountains, and therefore some passages of approach had to be left open to the enemy. Only the longest and most difficult were undefended.[15] The main defensive sector of the 32d Infantry, just south of the Palanas River, was astride the highway and on that part of the ridge which overlooked the regiment's artillery and command post installations. The defensive sector of Companies F and G was 1,500 yards in width. Company F occupied the flat, marshy land between the sea and the hills to the east. The men built barricades of dirt and sandbags at intervals of seventy-five yards and mined the area in front of them. Company E and guerrillas of Companies F and G, 94th Philippine Infantry, which were attached to the 2d Battalion, were on a ridge that extended to Hill 918. Some guerrillas were also out-

posted between Companies G and E. Regimental headquarters was at Baybay.[16] "The main strength of the line was American guts and fighting spirit." [17] During the night, Battery B of the 11th 155-mm. Gun Battalion had moved in and was in position at 0800 to start firing. The battery was so well camouflaged that during the ensuing engagement it was never discovered by the enemy. The regiment now had in support two batteries of 105-mm. howitzers and one of 155-mm. guns.

Battle of Shoestring Ridge

The Battle Begins

At about 1830 on 23 November, the *26th Division* opened up the long-expected attack.[18] The signal for the commencement of hostilities was an artillery concentration, the first rounds of which fell in the area of Battery A, 49th Field Artillery Battalion. The next rounds were scattered. Enemy mortars joined the artillery and concentrated their fire on the front lines of the 32d Infantry. Counterbattery fire of the 105-mm. howitzers from Battery B of the 49th Field Artillery temporarily silenced the Japanese fire. At 2000 the enemy artillery and mortars again opened up against the front lines of the 32d Infantry and cut all communications between the 2d Battalion and the regimental headquarters at Baybay. Communications were later re-established by relay from the 3d Battalion at Caridad.

---

[14] 32d Inf Opns Rpt Leyte, p. 22.
[15] *Ibid.,* p. 17.

[16] That evening General Arnold, acting on instructions from the Sixth Army that "guerrillas not be given missions beyond their capabilities," ordered Colonel Finn to use guerrillas only as outposts and not as part of the main line of resistance. 7th Inf Div G–3 Jnl, 23 Nov 44.
[17] 32d Inf Opns Rpt Leyte, p. 17.
[18] *35th Army* Opns, p. 74.

At 2100 the Japanese infantry launched a well-planned attack, supported by artillery, mortars, and machine guns, against the lines of Company E. Although the company retaliated with all weapons at its command, the Japanese continued to come on, despite heavy casualties, through the covered draws, high cogon grass, and bamboo thickets. The guerrilla outpost between Companies G and E withdrew when the Japanese attacked Company E. The enemy force, which consisted of two reinforced rifle companies from the *13th Independent Infantry Regiment,* seized portions of the ridge and dug in.

Colonel Nelson, the commander of the 2d Battalion, ordered Capt. John J. Young, commanding officer of Company E, to withdraw his troops. Since the Japanese had penetrated the lines and were digging in, the withdrawal was difficult. At about 2200, when Capt. Roy F. Dixon, commanding officer of Company G, received word that Company E was to withdraw to a position behind Company L and thus leave the right flank of Company G exposed, he ordered the right platoon leader to move his right from a position in front of the ridge to one on the ridge facing east, refusing this flank.[19] The two right squads moved back and secured the right of Company G.

At dawn on 24 November Colonel Nelson re-formed the 2d Battalion. A patrol from Company F went to the Palanas River and found no enemy troops. At 0800 three companies moved to the east toward Hill 918. The troops succeeded in pushing back a Japanese force that had penetrated south of the Palanas River and east of Hill 918. Colonel Finn ordered Company K to move up from Caridad, and he attached it to the 2d Battalion.

Battery C of the 57th 105-mm. Howitzer Battalion, which had just arrived, was placed on the left, south of the Bucan River.[20] By 1800 the troops had regained some of the ground lost the previous night and occupied a perimeter approximately 2,000 yards long and less than 1,500 yards deep.

During the day, as far as their limited ammunition would allow, the artillery units fired at enemy troop concentrations and possible observation posts. The service troops worked feverishly to move badly needed ammunition to the front lines. The two most critical items were 105-mm. and 81-mm. ammunition, and by nightfall the front lines had received 1,400 rounds of the first item and 1,600 rounds of the second. General Arnold attached the 1st Battalion, 184th Infantry, to the 32d Infantry but Colonel Finn was forbidden to commit it to action without permission from the 7th Division.

Japanese Counterattack

The enemy forces did not wait. That night, under a full moon, they attacked American positions with great ferocity, opening the engagement with the heaviest artillery barrage the 32d Infantry had yet experienced.[21] The first rounds fell on the front-line troops, but the fire then shifted and centered on Battery A, 49th Field Artillery Battalion, and the infantry and artillery command posts in the rear at Damulaan. At the same time the enemy pounded the front lines of Companies G, L, E, and K with heavy mortar fire. Additional mortars joined the battle and shifted the greater

---

[19] 32d Inf Opns Rpt Leyte, p. 18.

[20] 49th FA Bn Opns Rpt Leyte, p. 10.

[21] Msg, CO 32d Inf to CG 7th Div, 25 Nov 44, 32d Inf Unit Jnl, 25 Nov 44.

part of their fire against Battery B. The cannoneers held fast and returned the fire.

After this thirty-minute artillery and mortar preparation, the Japanese *13th Independent Infantry Regiment* attacked the front lines of the Americans, concentrating the assault against three main positions: the right flank of Company G, the draw between Companies L and K, and the center of Company K. At the same time, combat patrols moved from the north against Companies F and G. The companies easily threw back these patrols.

Colonel Nelson ordered all supporting weapons of the 2d Battalion to fire. All three artillery batteries fired at the maximum rate for seven minutes, while the mortars placed their fire directly on the assault force in order to chop it up or drive it back into the artillery fire. Colonel Nelson then put the Ammunition and Pioneer Platoon of the 2d Battalion and a squad from Company B, 13th Engineer Battalion, in previously prepared positions between Companies G and E. Company G was thus able to strengthen its lines at the heaviest point of pressure and repel the frequently repeated assaults.

At about 1900 a strong force of the enemy gathered on the ridge in front of the right flank of Company L. The American mortars fired on the ridge but the American machine guns kept silent in order to conceal their locations. A group of about fifty Japanese came to within thirty yards of the right platoon of Company L and showered it with grenades. Mortar fire also fell on this platoon, and at the same time the platoon of Company K in the draw came under heavy fire. At least twelve emplaced machine guns, in addition to those carried up by the assaulting troops, raked the positions of Companies K and L with intense fire. Company L employed all weapons and

threw back the assault with heavy casualties to the Japanese.

Company K did not fare so well, since it was operating at little more than half strength and there were only nineteen men in the platoon that guarded the draw on the company's left flank. Under the protection of machine gun and mortar fire, the Japanese moved against the platoon, which was ringed by machine gun fire that cut off any avenue of withdrawal. The platoon seemed to be faced with imminent extermination. A Marine machine gunner from the 11th 155-mm. Gun Battalion, who was stationed on the high ground just south of the draw of the besieged platoon, opened fire and knocked out the enemy machine guns which had cut off the line of withdrawal. He then directed his fire against the Japanese weapons on the ridge across the draw and raked the ridge from one end to the other. After the enemy guns had been silenced the platoon made an orderly withdrawal to the foot of the ridge to positions on its right rear, from which it could cover the draw.[22] Many enemy dead were left in the vacated positions.

The Japanese then attempted to break through the center of Company K's line, but were driven off by the use of artillery, together with the mortars, machine guns, grenades, and rifles of the company. For the rest of the night the Japanese kept probing the left flank of the company and placing machine gun and mortar fire along the entire line. At one time about twenty-five of

---

[22] "The platoon leader, a technical sergeant, insisted that the Marine gunner either transfer to the Army or he would have to transfer to the Marines, as he couldn't get along without him." (Finn, *op. cit.*, p. 52.) A check of Marine Corps records, and interviews with Marine Corps historians and Colonel Finn failed to disclose the name and rank of the Marine gunner.

the enemy pushed past the outer perimeter to within fifty yards of the perimeter of the command post and set up two machine guns. Headquarters personnel, medical men, and engineers who were manning the perimeter drove the group off.

Meanwhile, the Japanese forces in front of Company L withdrew and were regrouping, preparatory to launching a new attack. Since there was no artillery observer with the company, 1st Lt. William C. Bentley, of the Cannon Company, with two men went to a vantage point from which they could observe the draw and the ridge where the enemy force was assembling. Lieutenant Bentley directed an artillery concentration on the draw. Three times the Japanese tried to pierce the right flank of Company L and three times the artillery drove them back with heavy casualties. The enemy then tried unsuccessfully to get through the left flank of the company. The front line of Company L had comparative quiet for the rest of the night, except for a few infiltrators.

Having failed to pierce the front lines, the 26th Division troops tried desperately to knock out the artillery supporting the 32d Infantry—Batteries A and B of the 49th Field Artillery Battalion receiving the heaviest blows. Battery B had all four of its guns knocked out, but by "cannibalizing" the damaged guns the battery had one of them back in operation by dawn. The enemy shelling gradually slackened in intensity, and by 0400, except for occasional outbursts of fire, all was quiet.

At dawn of 25 November each company sent scouting patrols 2,000 yards to its front in order to forestall any Japanese attempts to move in. The patrols remained out all day. The front lines were reinforced by Company I, which moved into the draw between Companies K and L. The troops prepared

positions but occupied them only at night, since they were located in a swampy rice paddy. Headquarters and B Battery of the 57th Field Artillery Battalion moved into the Damulaan area to provide additional artillery support. Four 105-mm. howitzer batteries and one 155-mm. gun battery were then available. The troops of the 3d Battalion reverted to the control of the 3d Battalion commander, Colonel Whitcomb. Because of the intense firing during the night, the ammunition in the front lines had been nearly exhausted, but a sufficient supply was brought forward to the guns by the next evening.

At 2200 the enemy, using the same tactics as on the previous night, again assaulted the eastern positions of the 32d Infantry with approximately one battalion, after an artillery preparation. Although apparently well led and well organized, they were in less strength than before and were driven back, but not without a grenade battle and some hand-to-hand fighting.

While the infantry troops were thus engaged, eight Japanese led by an officer moved unnoticed along the Bucan River about one and a half miles south of the Palanas River. Coming up on the right of B Battery, 49th Field Artillery Battalion, these enemy troops threw a shower of grenades at the gun crews and tried to clamber over the river bank and get at the guns. One man made it, and by placing a satchel charge behind the breechblock of a howitzer he put it permanently out of commission. All of the Japanese were killed.

The troops of the 32d Infantry spent the 26th of November improving their positions, moving automatic weapons, restocking ammunition, and securing much-needed rest. The only important change in the lines was the moving of B Company, 184th Infantry,

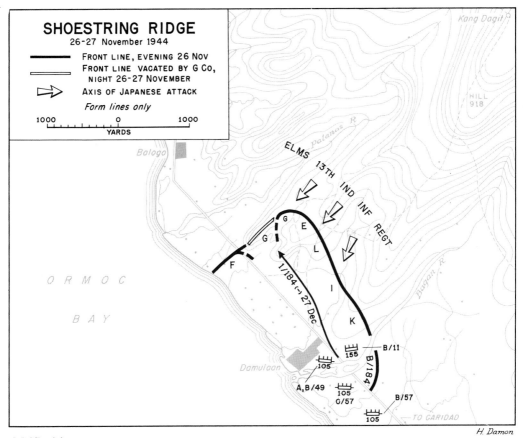

SHOESTRING RIDGE
26-27 November 1944

FRONT LINE, EVENING 26 NOV
FRONT LINE VACATED BY G CO,
NIGHT 26-27 NOVEMBER
AXIS OF JAPANESE ATTACK

Form lines only

1000   0   1000
YARDS

H. Damon

MAP 14

less one platoon, into the position of B Battery, which was made part of A Battery.[23]
(*MAP 14*)

Bloody Bamboo Thicket

At 2100 Colonel Saito renewed the assault against the American position, following the pattern set by the previous night
actions. The Japanese first laid down mortar and machine gun fire,[24] and then heavy-

[23] Msg, 32d Inf to 7th Div, 1520, 26 Nov 44, 32d
Inf Unit Jnl, 26 Nov 44.
[24] Msg, 32d Inf to 7th Div, 2213, 26 Nov 44, 32d
Inf Unit Jnl, 26 Nov 44.

weapons fire of the *13th Infantry Regiment*
hit the right platoons of Company G, shift-
ing to the east in about fifteen minutes. Immediately afterward, about a battalion of
Japanese infantry attacked Company G,
while twelve machine guns started to fire
from a ridge 1,200 yards to the east. The
Japanese moved into the fire of their own
heavy weapons. The 32d Infantry, using all
of its artillery batteries, mortars, machine
guns, and rifles, started throwing lead
against the enemy force as fast as its men
could load and fire. The Japanese, employing an estimated fifty machine guns, con-

tinued to come on. "All hell broke loose" [25] as the enemy shot off flares to guide their own artillery fire. The sharp declivity in front of the American lines did not allow for a close concentration of friendly artillery fire. Just as it appeared that the lines were to be overrun, some more enemy flares went up, and the Japanese withdrew, covered by heavy machine gun and mortar fire. Colonel Finn, taking advantage of this fortunate circumstance, hastily rearranged riflemen to fill gaps caused by casualties and replenished his ammunition supplies. The mortars of the regiment continued to fire into the draw.

After a short lull Colonel Saito renewed the attack. There was no preparatory artillery fire, but the mortars and machine guns introduced the assault. The attack did not seem as determined as the previous one, though the number of troops was apparently about the same. The 32d Infantry again called down all types of fire upon the enemy. Elements of the *13th Infantry Regiment* continued to advance, although "the carnage was terriffic," [26] and attempted to pass through the American lines. A strong enemy group moved into a bamboo grove on a nose in front of the center platoon of G Company. From this position the enemy launched an attack which the company resisted with grenades and bayonets. As Colonel Finn later reported: "The battle continued to flare up and die down as the valiant soldiers fought like devils to hold our lines." [27] The 81-mm. mortars from the mortar platoon of H Company fired 650 rounds in five minutes, and fire from the

60-mm. mortars was "practically automatic." [28] After an hour's intense fighting, the enemy force withdrew.

The Japanese had not attacked the left flank of G Company. These troops heard the battle raging to the right and the sounds of the Japanese forming below them. A noncommissioned officer in charge of a listening post sent a man to get permission for his three-man group to withdraw. After receiving permission he shouted the order from a distance of fifty yards. As the men from the listening post started back, they were joined by the left platoon and two squads from the center platoon. Within forty-five minutes the two platoons, less one squad, plus the section of heavy machine guns, were moving south on the highway. "There was no thought in their minds that the withdrawal was not authorized." [29] After proceeding down the road 250 yards they met the executive officer of Company H who ordered them back. It was too late, the damage was done. Though the left platoon was able to regain its position without trouble, the two squads from the center platoon found the enemy well dug-in in the bamboo thicket where the squads had been. It was later learned that there were about two hundred hostile troops with twenty machine guns in the thicket.

The Japanese were within the American lines and in a position from which they could fire on A Battery and the flanks of Companies E, L, I, and K.[30] Colonel Finn immediately took steps to contain the penetrators. The reserve platoon from I Company moved behind E Company to face north in order to stop any enemy troops moving south

---

[25] The Japanese give the number of enemy troops as two and a half battalions while the 32d Infantry estimated it as three battalions. *35th Army* Opns, p. 78; 32d Inf Opns Rpt Leyte, p. 22.

[26] 32d Inf Opns Rpt Leyte, p. 22.

[27] *Ibid.*, p. 23.

[28] *Ibid.*

[29] *Ibid.*

[30] Msg, CO 32d Inf to CG 7th Div, 0220, 27 Nov 44, 32d Inf Unit Jnl, 27 Nov 44.

along the high ground. The squad of the center platoon of Company G that had remained in position was faced to the west in order to forestall any attempt to roll up the line of G Company. That part of G Company which had withdrawn was moved along the high ground behind E Company where it established contact with the rest of G Company that faced the bamboo thicket. The right of F Company was turned south along the highway. Although the enemy could not be denied access to the flat, open ground leading to Damulaan, the rear of E and G Companies was protected and the flat ground could be covered by fire. The Japanese apparently did not realize the predicament of the Americans, since they made no attempt to exploit it.

At the same time that G Company was fighting, the other companies, E, L, and I, were also hit, though the assault was not so heavy as the one against G Company. The commanding officer of E Company, next to G Company, felt that the situation left him "in a hell of a spot," [31] but he held his position. The Japanese steadily persisted in their pressure against the lines of the companies and the fighting continued throughout the night. The defenders yielded no ground and effectively used many supporting fires to disrupt the attack of the *26th Division*. The Americans counted 400 Japanese dead the next morning, but casualties of the 32d Infantry, despite the heavy fighting, had been surprisingly light. For the twenty-four hour period ending at 1430 on 27 November, four officers and fifteen enlisted men had been wounded and one enlisted man killed.[32]

Colonel Finn made plans for the recapture of the ground lost by G Company, and General Arnold made available to him part of the 1st Battalion, 184th Infantry, which was at Caridad. The 1st Battalion, less B Company and two platoons from C Company, left Caridad at 0415 on 27 November, and by 0515 it was in Damulaan in readiness for the assault. Company G, 2d Battalion, 32d Infantry, was also available.

At the same time, the enemy was in the midst of preparing new plans. The Japanese felt that if they could recapture the Burauen airfields, all the American forces on Leyte would be in jeopardy. General Suzuki therefore ordered his troops to prepare for an operation at Burauen. In order to concentrate the *26th Division* for his daring move across the mountains to strike at the Americans in the vicinity of the Burauen airfields, General Suzuki risked his right flank, leaving only a detachment consisting of the *12th Independent Infantry Regiment,* one and one-half battalions of the *13th Independent Infantry Regiment,* and one battery of the *26th Artillery Battalion* with two mobile guns to prevent the Americans from reaching Albuera and cutting off the base of his attack. At the same time, staff members of the *26th Division* moved south to direct operations against the 7th Division.[33]

These Japanese measures were taken just as General Krueger was able to reinforce the attack toward Ormoc. The commanding officer of the 1st Battalion, 184th Infantry, at dawn on 27 November got his troops ready for the drive toward Albuera. He moved his battalion behind L and E Companies, 32d Infantry. Because of the limited

[31] Msg, CO 32d Inf to S–3 2d Bn, 0305, 27 Nov 44, 32d Inf Unit Jnl, 27 Nov 44.
[32] Msg, 32d Inf to 7th Div, 1443, 27 Nov 44, 32d Inf Unit Jnl, 27 Nov 44.
[33] *35th Army Opns,* p. 84.

area involved, the battalion commander decided that only A Company would make the attack. The artillery, mortars, and machine guns placed heavy fire on the bamboo thicket. At 0855 the troops moved out but were stopped by heavy machine gun fire after they had advanced about 200 yards. They then withdrew about fifty yards while the artillery and mortars again covered the area.[34] A second attack was also halted, and A Company again pulled back. At 1430 a very heavy artillery concentration was placed on the thicket.[35] Immediately thereafter C Company moved in swiftly and cleared out and secured the area by 1600. A total of 109 enemy dead was counted and twenty-nine machine guns were removed.

The defensive perimeters of the 32d Infantry were set up. With the addition of the 1st Battalion, 184th Infantry, the lines were much stronger. During the night of 27 November elements of the *13th Independent Infantry Regiment* made minor attempts to infiltrate through the lines but were easily repulsed.

By now the Sixth Army had received substantial reinforcements. General Hodge therefore ordered the 7th Division to assemble all forces in the Baybay area as rapidly as the logistical situation would permit.[36] By 27 November sufficient troops had assembled to enable him to order General Arnold to make "an early and vigorous attack" to destroy the Japanese in the area and then capture Ormoc.[37] On 28 November all the assault elements of the 7th Division, with the exception of the 1st Battalion, 32d Infantry,

which was patrolling in the vicinity of Panaon Strait, were either on the eastern shore of the Camotes Sea or on the way there. The 1st Battalion, 184th Infantry, and the 2d and 3d Battalions, 32d Infantry, were still engaging the enemy at a bamboo thicket on Shoestring Ridge south of the Palanas River and east of Damulaan.[38]

The troops of Colonel Finn's 32d Infantry were weary. They had prevented the Japanese *26th Division* from going south along the eastern shore of the Camotes Sea and had held back the best the enemy had to offer. General Arnold desired that the 7th Division push through the enemy lines with two regiments abreast toward Ormoc. The tired 32d Infantry was to be drawn back and replaced by the 184th and 17th Infantry Regiments.

On 28 November, after receiving orders from General Arnold, the commanding officer of the 184th Infantry, Col. Curtis D. O'Sullivan, outlined to his battalion commanders the new roles they were to play. The 184th Infantry was to relieve the 32d Infantry and then attack to the front and cover the division's left sector. The 1st Battalion of the regiment was to relieve Company F, 32d Infantry, from the beach inland to a clump of trees held by the enemy 600 yards inland. Parts of Companies A and C were already at the edge of the grove. The 2d Battalion, 184th Infantry, with the 57th Field Artillery Battalion in direct support, was to relieve Companies G and E of the 32d Infantry, tie in with Company L of the 32d Infantry, and attack in the direction of Hill 918. The 3d Battalion, in regimental reserve, was to take a position in San Agustin. The 32d Infantry was to fall back to Tinagan.[39] At 1700 the 2d Battalion, 184th

---

[34] 32d Inf Opns Rpt Leyte, p. 24; Msg, 2d Bn to 32d Inf, 27 Nov 44, and Msgs, Exec Off 32d Inf to CO 32d Inf, 1005, 1120, and 1210, 27 Nov 44, 32d Inf Unit Jnl, 27 Nov 44.

[35] 32d Inf Opns Rpt Leyte, p. 24.

[36] XXIV Corps FO 28, 22 Nov 44.

[37] XXIV Corps FO 30, 27 Nov 44.

[38] 7th Div G–3 Periodic Rpt 40, 28 Nov 44.

[39] 184th Inf Unit Jnl, 1200, 28 Nov 44.

Infantry, relieved the 2d Battalion, 32d Infantry, at Damulaan.[40]

At 1945 on 28 November elements of the *26th Division* attacked from the southeast and northeast the right flank of Company A, 184th Infantry, at the bamboo thicket and pushed it back fifty yards. Battery B, 57th Field Artillery Battalion, fired at the southern point of the enemy infiltration and also 100 yards to the west.[41] The Japanese attack was stopped, and the 1st Battalion held fast and dug in.[42]

Company E, 2d Battalion, hurriedly moved into a position from which, if requested, it could support the 1st Battalion. The 81-mm. mortar section of the 2d Battalion was prepared to place fire in front of the zone of Company A, and two platoons from Company C were in position to fill a gap existing between the 1st and 2d Battalions.[43] By 2045 the 3d Battalion, 32d Infantry, and the 2d and 1st Battalions, 184th Infantry, were on a line from right to left.[44] The night was quiet except for sounds of enemy activity in front of the 2d Battalion.[45]

At 0900 on 29 November Company A of the 1st Battalion and Company F of the 2d Battalion, after a mortar barrage, attacked to retake the lost ground and to overrun the Japanese position in the bamboo thicket. They regained the ground without opposition, but as the troops approached the thicket they met strong resistance. For the rest of the day the battle seesawed back and forth as elements of the 184th Infantry

and the *26th Division* contested for control of "Bloody Bamboo Thicket," as it came to be called. Between 1820 and 1920, Company A repulsed three heavy enemy attacks and killed an estimated fifty to eighty Japanese.[46] At 1800 Companies A and F made a co-ordinated but unsuccessful attack against the Japanese. They dug in for the night in positions from which they successfully withstood enemy attacks.[47]

The following morning both battalions sent patrols to scout out the strength and installations of the enemy. At 1045 Company A, which had been in action for several days, was relieved by Company C and moved to the old position of the latter.[48] At 1400, after a ten-minute artillery preparation, Company C and two platoons from Company F on its right were to move out toward a ridge 150 yards north in order to strengthen the lines and secure positions on the commanding terrain—part of which was the bamboo thicket over which Company A and the enemy had fought.

The companies moved out on time and met little resistance until they had penetrated twenty to thirty yards into the thicket, when the enemy strongly opposed any further advance. The troops of the 184th Infantry, however, steadily pushed on, and by 1603 Company C, with the platoons from Company F just behind it, had cleared the bamboo thicket. Since the line of Company C extended over a wide front, it was tightened and shortened and tied into Company B. By 1730 the troops of Companies C and F had consolidated their positions and formed a night perimeter on the forward slope of the ridge.[49] Shoestring Ridge was firmly in American hands.

---

[40] 184th Inf Opns Rpt Leyte, p. 6. Unless otherwise stated the material on the 184th Infantry is based on this operations report of the regiment.

[41] 184th Inf Unit Jnl, 2005, 28 Nov 44.

[42] 184th Inf Unit Jnl, 2045, 28 Nov 44.

[43] Msg, S–3 2d Bn to 184th Inf, 2010, 28 Nov 44, 184th Inf Unit Jnl, 28 Nov 44.

[44] Msg, CO 184th Inf to CG 7th Div, 2045, 28 Nov 44, 184th Inf Unit Jnl, 28 Nov 44.

[45] 184th Inf Unit Jnl, 0125, 29 Nov 44.

[46] 184th Inf Unit Jnl, 2020, 29 Nov 44.

[47] 184th Inf S–3 Periodic Rpt 42, 30 Nov 44.

[48] 184th Inf Unit Jnl, 30 Nov 44.

[49] *Ibid.*

Battles of the Hills

The attempts of the *26th Division* to drive the Americans back had been checked, but the front lines remained practically the same as they had been at the outset of the battle for Shoestring Ridge. It had become apparent that the most one regiment could do was to conduct a holding action and that if the 7th Division was to continue the advance it would be necessary to commit a stronger force against the Japanese. Elements of the *26th Division* were by now firmly ensconced in the hills that overlooked Highway 2 and were in a position to contest bitterly any forward movement of the 7th Division.

A series of sharply edged ridges with many spurs, heavily overgrown with bamboo thickets and high cogon grass, rose from the coastal plain to the central mountain range. (*Map 15*) One of these, Hill 918, was especially important tactically, since from it one could observe the entire coast to the south, and as far as Ormoc to the north. About four fifths of a mile northeast of Hill 918 was the barrio of Kang Dagit, and about one and a half miles north of the hill was Kang Cainto.[50] Other important high points were Hill 380, between the Palanas and Tabgas Rivers and about one and a third miles east of Balogo on Highway 2, and Hill 606, between the Tabgas River and Calingatngan Creek and approximately one and a third miles east of Calingatngan on Highway 2.

General Arnold wished to attack north with two regiments abreast. He therefore ordered Colonel O'Sullivan to send out a strong patrol to the front of the 184th Infantry but not to attempt any advance until the 17th Infantry could arrive from the east

coast. On 3 December, when most of the 17th Infantry had reached the west coast, General Arnold called a meeting of his regimental commanders. He told them that the 7th Division was to renew the attack north at 0800 on 5 December with regiments abreast, the 17th Infantry on the right and the 184th Infantry on the left, and secure the Talisayan River about three and a half miles north, together with the intervening enemy positions on Hills 918, 380, and 606. The boundary between the regiments was to be roughly 2,000 yards from the beach.[51] At this time the front-line units of the *26th Division*, which had been occupying a hill about two miles northwest of Damulaan, withdrew to the Palanas River and a hill northeast of the river. A battalion of the *26th Division* was on the western slope of a hill north of the river.[52]

On 4 December the 184th Infantry prepared for the attack and sent patrols from the 1st and 2d Battalions to the front. These patrols penetrated as far north as Balogo. The 17th Infantry spent the day in moving forward the various elements of the regiment.[53] By nightfall the units of the 7th Division were in readiness for the offensive which was to start the following morning.

Hill 918

On 4 December General Arnold ordered Lt. Col. O'Neill K. Kane to move the tanks of the 776th Amphibian Tank Battalion by water under cover of darkness to a position 1,000 yards at sea to the west of Balogo, the next coastal town, about a mile to the north

---

[50] Cainto is also known as *Caintic*. The Army spelling, Cainto, will be followed here.

[51] 184th Inf Unit Jnl, 3 Dec 44.
[52] *35th Army Opns*, p. 91.
[53] 17th Inf Opns Rpt Leyte, Annex B, The Battle of the Ridgelines, p. 1. Unless otherwise stated, the part played by the 17th Infantry during this engagement is based upon the above report, pp. 1–9.

of the front lines. The tanks at dawn on the 5th were to assault the beaches in that vicinity and fire on the town and on the north slopes of hills and ravines in the area. These movements of the tank battalion were to be closely co-ordinated with the 184th and 17th Infantry Regiments, into whose areas the attack was to be made.

At 0635 on the 5th, the tank battalion in a column formation started to move north over water. The tanks advanced toward Balogo until they were at a point offshore about 200 yards from the town. They then continued north in a column formation and fired into the town of Tabgas. At the mouth of the Tabgas River, just short of Tabgas, the tanks attacked in line formation. Moving ashore at 0700, they sent approximately 2,550 rounds of 75-mm. ammunition in direct fire against the northern slopes of the hills that confronted the 7th Division.

The tanks completed their mission, took to the water again, and headed north for a mile to reconnoiter the area around Calingatngan. They then turned south and started for the bivouac area. On the return, Colonel Kane, elated over the success of their previous landing and wishing to use up the remaining ammunition, ordered the tanks to land 500 yards south of the Tabgas River. From here the tanks fired and then withdrew unhindered by enemy fire. At 1045 they were back in their bivouac area.[54]

At 0800 on 5 December the 184th and 17th Infantry Regiments moved out with the 184th Infantry on the left. The 1st Battalion, 184th Infantry, on the extreme left, reached the Palanas River without incident and without having to fire a single shot.[55]

The Japanese historians, however, claimed that one of the amphibian tanks was set on fire and that the *2d Battalion, 12th Independent Infantry Regiment,* repulsed the advance of the 184th Infantry.[56]

There were numerous finger ridges inland which were cut by deep ravines and gorges that came to within a few hundred yards of the coast line. The entrenched Japanese, using reverse slope tactics, were able to deliver deadly fire on the advancing infantry. In many cases the reverse slopes were so steep that effective artillery fire could not be placed upon them.[57] The 2d Battalion, 184th Infantry, moved forward slowly toward a small hill which faced the Palanas River, and at 0858 it encountered enemy small arms fire from the western slope of the hill. Using grenades, the battalion pushed forward, but at 0938 the Japanese opened up with three light machine guns. The supporting weapons of the 2d Battalion fired on the enemy positions to the front. At 1037, as the battalion reached the military crest of the hill, the Japanese launched a small counterattack on the left flank of Company E. This attack was repulsed, but the companies continued to receive small arms and machine gun fire.

At 1325 the 1st Battalion renewed its advance and proceeded without incident, finding the situation "very quiet" to its front. At 1435 the battalion dug in for the night approximately 300 yards south of Balogo.[58] The 3d Battalion moved through the gap between the 1st and 2d Battalions and across the front of the 2d Battalion on the right toward Hill 380, which consisted of a series of ridges. As the 3d Battalion advanced toward the hill, it came under machine gun

[54] Armor on Leyte, a research rpt prepared by Committee 16, Officers Advanced Course, The Armored School, 1948–49, Ft. Knox, Ky., May 1949, pp. 89–91, copy in OCMH.
[55] 184th Inf. Opns Rpt Leyte, p. 7.
[56] *35th Army* Opns, p. 93.
[57] Armor on Leyte, p. 89.
[58] 184th Inf Unit Jnl, 5 Dec 44.

fire on each flank. With artillery support, the troops reached the top of the second ridge of Hill 380 and dug in, nine of the men having been wounded.[59] At 1635 the battalions of the 184th Infantry received orders to set up night defense positions in depth and to hold the "positions at all costs."[60] Colonel O'Sullivan decided that the 3d Battalion was to bear the brunt of the advance of the 184th Infantry on 6 December and push on to Hill 380.[61]

On the right of the 184th the 17th Infantry had had a busy day in working toward its objective, Hill 918. At 0800 on 5 December the 1st and 2d Battalions of the 17th Infantry, with the 1st Battalion on the left, had moved through the 32d Infantry. At 0906 the advance elements of the 1st Battalion secured a ridge south of the main ridge leading from Hill 918, and at 1000 the entire battalion closed on this ridge. In the face of sporadic rifle and machine gun fire, the leading platoons pushed forward to secure a ridge that led west from Hill 918. As the advance platoons neared the crest of this ridge, they received intense rifle, machine gun, and mortar fire to the front and on both flanks from the *2d Battalion, 12th Independent Infantry Regiment.* At the same time the rest of the battalion, in attempting to reach a forward ridge and support the leading platoons, also encountered cross fire that came down the intervening draw. As enemy gunfire pinned down the troops, the 1st Battalion lost contact with Company G, 2d Battalion, and a gap developed between the 1st and 2d Battalions. The *12th Independent Infantry Regiment,* quickly alert to exploit this opportunity to drive a wedge between the two

forces, threw approximately a company armed with machine guns and mortars into the gap. Although they did not penetrate completely, the enemy troops were able to secure a position which would make any forward movement of the 1st Battalion very costly. The 1st Platoon of Company B and the 3d Platoon of Company A were still out on the forward ridge and cut off from the rest of the battalion. The reserve platoon of Company A tried an envelopment around the right flank of the 1st Battalion but was stopped by the enemy in the gap. Company C moved up to protect the rear of Company A. Eventually the forward platoons withdrew to the battalion lines and preparations were made for the night. Under cover of darkness the 1st Battalion reorganized and moved into positions on top of the first ridge.[62]

Earlier that day the 2d Battalion had driven forward with Company E on the right and Company G on the left. Company E went east along the Bucan River for approximately 1,000 yards and then turned northeast to ascend Hill 918. At first, however, the company had to secure a small ridge southwest of Hill 918 on which was a small but dense banana grove. Company E encountered and destroyed a small enemy force on this ridge, after which the company reorganized and at approximately 1300 began to ascend Hill 918 itself. When Company E reached the military crest of the hill, the Japanese began heavy firing with grenade launchers and at least three machine guns. The enemy fire swept the crest of the hill and prevented any movement over the lip of the ridge.

Meanwhile, Company G went to the left of Company E and secured a small ridge about 1,200 yards from the line of departure

---

[59] *Ibid.*
[60] *Ibid.*
[61] *Ibid.*

[62] 17th Inf Unit Jnl, 5 Dec 44.

and west of Hill 918. The advance platoon of Company G then received fire from automatic weapons that were emplaced in a draw to the left front of the platoon. The rest of the company attempted to move around to the right of the ridge but also encountered automatic weapons fire coming from another draw. Since high cogon grass covered the area, observation was limited to a matter of inches. At about 1300, elements of the *13th Independent Infantry Regiment* counterattacked through a gap between Company G and Company A of the 1st Battalion. A machine gun platoon, which was thrown in to plug the gap, succeeded in stopping the attempted Japanese advance.

Company G, however, continued to be pinned down by the enemy fire directed at its front. Company F, the reserve company, was then committed to take a position between G and E Companies. Its mission was to come abreast of Company E, take Hill 918, and then turn west and wipe out the resistance in front of Company G. At 1415 Company F moved up Hill 918 and reached Company E without opposition.

Three spurs led down from Hill 918. The one occupied by Company E ran southwest, that occupied by Company F ran west, and the third ran northwest. As the two commanders started to launch a co-ordinated assault from their respective spurs, their companies received a concentration of about fifty rounds of mortar fire but pushed through this fire and secured the crests of both spurs. They immediately came under automatic weapons and rifle fire from the northwest ridge.

Since the left flank of Company F was in the tall cogon grass, it was practically impossible for the company to observe the enemy. On the other hand, Company E

was on bare and open ground which exposed it to machine gun and mortar fire from Hill 918. Both companies also came under long-range machine gun fire from the vicinity of Kang Dagit, northeast of Hill 918. It was impractical to attempt an envelopment to the right, since the flank of Company E rested on a deep ravine which ran to the bed of the Bagan River. An envelopment to the left would have necessitated going down the hill, circling behind Company G, and attacking east from the positions of the 1st Battalion. Because of these unfavorable conditions, Companies E and F with their wounded withdrew to make a line with Company G.[63]

In support of the advance of the 17th Infantry, the 49th Field Artillery Battalion fired 577 rounds of ammunition during the day. The fires "varied from knocking out machine guns to fire on mortars and on troops in the open." [64] The 17th Infantry had forced the *1st Battalion, 12th Independent Infantry Regiment,* to start withdrawal to a hill farther north. At the same time, Japanese engineer and artillery units at Albuera "were erecting anti-landing obstacles along the beach and putting up antitank defenses." [65]

At the end of 5 December the 17th Infantry had secured the ridge west of Hill 918 and the 184th Infantry had secured a line extending from the beach 300 yards south of Balogo east to the high ground southeast of the Palanas River. Company K, 32d Infantry, had filled a gap that had existed between the 17th and 184th Infantry Regiments, while the 3d Battalion, 184th Infantry, had crossed the Palanas River and, advancing up the southwest slope of Hill

---

[63] *Ibid.*
[64] 49th FA Bn Opns Rpt Leyte, p. 13.
[65] *35th Army* Opns, p. 93.

380, reached the top of the first ridge. There were no enemy attacks during the night.

Hill 380

General Arnold ordered the regiments to capture all of Hill 918, the northern slope of Hill 380, and the Palanas River valley. The 1st and 2d Battalions, 17th Infantry, aided by the 2d Battalion, 184th Infantry, were to move northeast until their front lines were on an east-west line south of the Palanas River. They were then to launch an attack to the north and capture the slope of Hill 380 in their zone of action. The 3d Battalion, 17th Infantry, was to attack to the north on the eastern slope of Hill 918 and capture the slope of Hill 380 in its zone of action. The 184th Infantry was to capture the northern slope of Hill 380 and assist the 17th Infantry in its movement north.[66]

The 184th Infantry started out at 0800 on 6 December with the 1st Battalion on the left and the 3d Battalion on the right. Supported by eight tanks, the 1st Battalion pushed through rifle fire, moved into Balogo, and cleared the town. The battalion commander then ordered Company B to seize a ridge just east of Balogo. Though the company temporarily secured the ridge, at 1155 the Japanese drove the men off. At 1210 artillery and mortar fire was placed against the Japanese positions on the ridge. As soon as the supporting fire lifted, at 1305, Company B sent a platoon through Company K to hit the ridge from the right flank.[67] Company B secured the ridge at 1510 but fifty yards farther north on the southern slope of the next ridge strong elements of the 26th Division had dug in, making it impossible for the troops to move forward. Before

the jump-off of the 3d Battalion, 184th Infantry, a platoon from Company K secured the first ridge north of the battalion position. At 1000 the rest of the battalion reached the top of Hill 380 and secured an enemy field artillery observation post from which it could see enemy activity in a deep valley north of Hill 380. Elements of the 26th Division set up machine guns and delivered mortar and artillery fire on Hill 380 throughout the afternoon.[68] The 1st and 3d Battalions, 184th Infantry, covered by mortar and artillery fire, set up night perimeters, the latter on Hill 380 and the former on the ridge east of Balogo. The 2d Battalion, 184th Infantry, remained in the Palanas River valley throughout the day.

The 1st and 2d Battalions of the 17th Infantry jumped off abreast. The 1st Battalion reached the ridge which led west from Hill 918 and overlooked the Palanas River, where it found strong enemy positions that had been abandoned. While the 1st Battalion reorganized, advance platoons, one each from Companies B and C, went across the Palanas River to the next ridge, which overlooked the Tabgas River. The 1st Battalion, in conjunction with the 2d Battalion, 184th Infantry, followed the platoons at a distance of about 500 yards. Company B moved behind a "protective nose" which led south from the main ridge and Company C pushed "a knife edge east of Company B."[69] As Company C reached a point just short of the main ridge, the men moved in single file and were pinned down by heavy machine gun cross fire from both flanks and to their front. Company B, attempting to envelop the entrenched enemy from the west,

---

[66] 184th Inf FO B, 5 Dec 44.
[67] 184th Inf Unit Jnl, 6 Dec 44.

[68] 184th Inf S–3 Periodic Rpt 48, 6 Dec 44; 7th Div G–3 Jnl, 6 Dec 44.
[69] 17th Inf Opns Rpt Leyte, Annex B, The Battle of the Ridgelines, p. 4.

encountered heavy fire on its left front, which made any envelopment in that direction impossible. At 1500 a strong column of the enemy counterattacked the left flank of Company C, but six machine guns from Company D broke up the enemy attack. The 1st Battalion dug in for the night halfway up Hill 380.[70]

Meanwhile, at 0800, the 2d Battalion, 17th Infantry, had started for Hill 918. The 49th Field Artillery Battalion established a smoke screen on the hill to cover the advance of the infantry,[71] and at 1100 Company E reached the crest of the hill. A patrol located a trail that led down to the Palanas River. As Company E moved down this trail, Company G, though under machine gun fire, pushed straight ahead through the saddle to its front.[72] By 1715 all elements of the 2d Battalion had reached the Palanas River and were moving left to establish contact with the 1st Battalion. From dug-in positions in the dense bamboo thickets on the northern bank of the river, the Japanese opened fire upon the 2d Battalion. Nothing serious developed, however, and the troops formed their night perimeters. The elements of the 1st and 2d Battalions, 17th Infantry, were now in contact on a line along the Palanas River.[73]

The 3d Battalion, 17th Infantry, swung to the extreme right towards Kang Dagit and Kang Cainto in order to hit Hill 380 from the east, but it was hampered by ravines two to three hundred feet deep. Though the advance was very slow, the 3d Battalion in a column of companies with

Company L in the lead was able to reach Kang Dagit where it closed for the night.[74]

At the end of the day the 7th Division had secured the barrio of Balogo, had overrun Hill 918 and occupied Kang Dagit, and had established elements of the division on the banks of the Palanas River and on part of Hill 380.

The night of 6–7 December was quiet. General Arnold ordered the 7th Division to attack north at 0800 on 7 December and secure Hills 380 and 606. The 184th Infantry was to capture the high ground south of the Tabgas River.[75] Colonel Pachler ordered the 17th Infantry, with its 1st Battalion on the left and its 2d Battalion on the right, to attack north to secure the portion of Hills 380 and 606 in its sector. The 3d Battalion, 17th Infantry, was to secure Kang Cainto and to be prepared to attack Hill 380 from the east or to continue north. At 0630 patrols went out to make reconnaissance and determine the enemy strength and dispositions to their front.[76]

At 0913 the 184th Infantry moved out. It met little opposition, and at 1643 the regiment reached the high ground overlooking the Tabgas River and dug in for the night.[77]

At dawn the 17th Infantry sent out patrols. The one from the 1st Battalion located an enemy heavy machine gun, two light machine guns, and a mortar, emplaced 150 yards from the battalion's lines. When the patrol returned, mortar fire was placed on the position and it was wiped out. The 1st Battalion moved out at approximately 0900. Though long-range fire fell on the troops and small arms fire hit the left flank of Com-

[70] 17th Inf Unit Jnl, 6 Dec 44.
[71] 49th FA Bn Opns Rpt Leyte, p. 13.
[72] 32d Inf S–3 Periodic Rpt, no number, 6 Dec 44; 7th Div G–3 Jnl, 6 Dec 44.
[73] 17th Inf Unit Jnl, 6 Dec 44.

[74] *Ibid.*
[75] 184th Inf FO C, 6 Dec 44.
[76] 184th Inf Unit Jnl, 7 Dec 44.
[77] *Ibid.*

pany C, the men continued to push forward. The battalion found several ridges leading up Hill 380—a knifelike ridge in front of Company C and a double ridge in the form of a horseshoe, with its closed end toward the hill, in front of Company B.

Company B moved across the double ridge while Company C forced its passage through machine gun and rifle fire across the closed part of the horseshoe. At 1600 the two companies re-established contact on the northernmost ridge leading to Hill 380. At 1630 the Japanese with machine guns launched a counterattack against the right flank of the 3d Battalion, 184th Infantry, and the left flank of the 1st Battalion, 17th Infantry. The 3d Battalion, 184th, was pinned down but did not yield any ground. The troops on the front lines of the 1st Battalion, 17th Infantry, at first were forced back slightly but in a few minutes regained the lost ground. They dug in for the night on the crest of the ridge.[78]

After its dawn patrols had reported on 7 December, the 2d Battalion, 17th Infantry, jumped off to the attack. Company E secured the first of the three spurs leading from Hill 380, and continued forward to the middle spur in the face of light fire that came from in front of the company in the area the 17th Infantry wished to secure. Presently the fire grew to considerable intensity and the company's section of light machine guns and two platoons of heavy machine guns moved onto the middle spur, where they neutralized the enemy position.

While this action was going on, Companies G and F moved to the first spur. Company G received orders from the battalion commander to make a wide envelop-

ment of Hill 380 and then assault the hill from the east. At 0930 the company dropped below the military crest of the southern slope of Hill 380 unobserved and made its way very slowly over the steep terrain and through the thick cogon grass. At 1200 the 49th Field Artillery Battalion laid a five-minute preparatory fire in front of the battalion.[79] The American troops then routed the surprised Japanese defenders and killed the majority of them as the others fled into the mountains northeast of the hill.

Apparently realizing that Hill 380 was the key to defense of the Tabgas River valley and Hill 606, troops of the *26th Division* poured long-range machine gun fire from Hill 606 into Company G and at the same time halted the company with small arms fire from the immediate left along the ridge. At 1355, after a heavy mortar barrage, about fifty men from the *26th Division* counterattacked the positions of Company G, but the company held firm and mowed down the attackers with fire from its rifles and automatic weapons. The position on the hill was maintained.

Although Company G occupied the top of Hill 380, it was not in a position to aid the advance of Company E. The Japanese troops were dug in on the reverse slopes and could only be rooted out by close-in fighting. The commanding officer of the 2d Battalion committed Company F down the main spur from the east, supported by Companies E and G and the machine guns from Company H. As soon as Company F started down the ridge, the enemy concentrated fire upon it both from the north and the west. In a matter of minutes Company F was reduced to a point where the number

---

[78] 17th Inf Unit Jnl, 7 Dec 44.

[79] 49th FA Bn Opns Rpt Leyte, p. 13.

of its riflemen hardly equaled one platoon. The company commander secured an additional platoon from Company G and renewed the assault behind a concentration of 100 rounds of 60-mm. mortar fire and 80 rounds of 81-mm. mortar fire. The attack succeeded, and the enemy force was overrun and annihilated. Company E thereupon moved to the main ridge and helped mop up the area.[80]

At 0700 the 3d Battalion, 17th Infantry, moved out, reaching the source of the Palanas River at 1400. An enemy force of about fifty men was observed in a natural bowl to its immediate front. The battalion placed long-range rifle and machine gun fire on the group as two platoons from Company K attacked from the flank. They destroyed the entire Japanese force without any casualties to the American troops. The 3d Battalion then crossed the Palanas River and went into night perimeter at Kang Cainto. At 1907 eight rounds of artillery fire fell into the area, killing seven men and wounding eighteen others.[81]

At the end of the day the 184th Infantry was on the banks of the Tabgas River and

the 17th Infantry had secured Hill 380, which commanded the Tabgas River valley.

Although several days of hard going still lay ahead before the 7th Division was to reach its objective, the Talisayan River, the backbone of the Japanese resistance had been broken and the Battle of the Ridges was virtually won. The division had achieved what the Japanese had considered impossible. It had pushed through Leyte over the tortuous mountain road between Abuyog and Baybay, it had held the enemy back at Shoestring Ridge, and it had then pushed north along the shores of Ormoc Bay toward Ormoc, decimating the right flank detachment of the *26th Division* in the process. General Suzuki had been forced to send south much of his tactical strength, which was to have been used for the defense of Ormoc. The 7th Division had assisted in no small way in tightening the ever-shortening noose about the Japanese who remained on the island.

On this day, 7 December, the 77th Division landed at Deposito just below Ormoc. The *26th Division* was caught between two strong American divisions. It was doomed. At this point the action of the 7th Division merged with that of the 77th Division in the drive of the XXIV Corps against Ormoc.

---

[80] 17th Inf Unit Jnl, 7 Dec 44.
[81] *Ibid.*

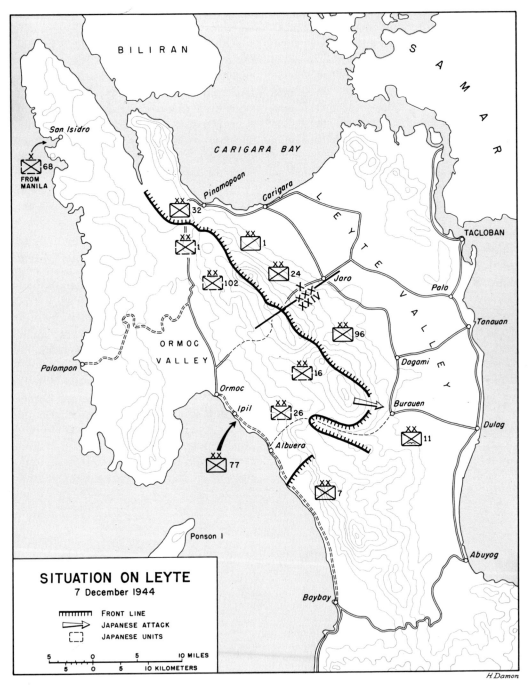

SITUATION ON LEYTE
7 December 1944

 FRONT LINE
→ JAPANESE ATTACK
⌐⌐ JAPANESE UNITS

5   0   5   10 MILES
5   0   5   10 KILOMETERS

MAP 16

CHAPTER XVI

The Fall of Ormoc

It was a time for decision. By the first of December the two adversaries had taken the measure of each other, but neither felt satisfied with the progress of the campaign.

The tide of battle was slowly turning against the Japanese. They had wagered major stakes that the battle of Leyte should be the decisive one of the Philippines. Someway, somehow, the Japanese felt, they must regain the initiative or Leyte, for which so much had been sacrificed, would be lost to them. The days had dwindled to a precious few.

Imperial General Headquarters was loath to write off the Leyte Campaign. A daring plan was conceived whereby the ground and air forces, working in close co-ordination, would attempt to wrest the initiative from General Krueger's forces. Before the main effort, suicide aircraft carrying demolition teams were to crash-land on the Dulag and Tacloban airstrips and render them unfit for use. Thereafter, the *2d Raiding Group* of the *4th Air Army* would transport two paratroop companies to the Burauen airfields. The paratroops in conjunction with elements of the *35th Army*, including the *26th Division*, would then seize the Burauen airfields. The time was to be the evening of 5 December. With the loss of the airfields, the U. S. Sixth Army, it was hoped, would be in a perilous situation.[1]

_____

[1] Japanese Studies in World War II, 7, *14th Area Army* Opns Leyte, pp. 10–13, OCMH.

General Krueger was also making plans. By the middle of November strong elements of the Sixth Army were trying to force their way into the Ormoc Valley and others were on the eastern shore of Ormoc Bay. The plan of General Krueger was simple. He wanted to secure control of the valley and the port of Ormoc and thus force the Japanese into the mountains near the western coast, from which they could escape only by sea.

At this time the XXIV Corps was with difficulty driving west and north from the center of the island. The 96th Division was engaged in mopping up in the mountains overlooking Leyte Valley. Units of the 7th Division, far to the south, were moving westward toward Baybay on the shore of the Camotes Sea. The 1st Cavalry Division and the 24th and 32d Infantry Divisions of the X Corps were making slow progress in driving down the Ormoc corridor from the Limon–Pinamopoan–Carigara area.

Several courses of action were now open to General Krueger. He could concentrate on the drive of the 32d Infantry Division and the 1st Cavalry Division south down the Ormoc corridor, or on the advance of the 7th Division north along the coast of Ormoc Bay from Baybay to Ormoc. A third course also presented itself. An amphibious overwater movement might be attempted by landing troops just below Ormoc in the midst of the enemy force, thus dividing the

Japanese strength. After landing, the troops could push north, seize Ormoc, and then drive up the Ormoc corridor and effect a juncture with elements of the X Corps. This move, though highly hazardous, would considerably shorten the Leyte Campaign if successfully carried out.

In mid-November, therefore, General Krueger proposed that an amphibious movement and a landing at a point just below Ormoc be made. At that time, however, the naval forces did not have the necessary assault and resupply shipping on hand to mount and maintain such an operation and to execute as well the Mindoro operation scheduled for 5 December. Since there was insufficient air support, the local naval commander felt that a convoy entering Ormoc Bay might be in jeopardy and that Japanese suicide bombing tactics could cause heavy losses. Unable to secure the necessary assault shipping, General Krueger temporarily set aside his plan.[2]

Plan for Amphibious Movement

On 30 November General MacArthur postponed for ten days the Mindoro operation.[3] The postponement would make available the amphibious shipping and naval support that were necessary for a landing in the Ormoc area. From a naval point of view, however, the operation was very precarious, since the Japanese were still making aerial attacks that could seriously damage the shipping needed for the forthcoming Mindoro and Luzon operations. After careful consideration of the risks involved, Admiral Kinkaid decided to make available to General Krueger the shipping required for an am-

phibious movement to a point below Ormoc.[4]

After issuing a warning order on 1 December, General Krueger on 4 December ordered the two corps to make their "main effort," starting 5 December, toward the defeat of the enemy forces in the Ormoc area. The X Corps was to advance "vigorously south astride Highway 2 so as to support the effort made by the . . . XXIV Corps." The commanding general of the XXIV Corps was to arrange with the commander of the naval task group for the shipping and naval gunfire support necessary to transport and land a division just below Ormoc. General Hodge, also, was to arrange with the commanding general of the Fifth Air Force for close air support for the landing and subsequent operations ashore.[5] The 77th Division was selected to make the amphibious movement to the Ormoc area.

In planning for the Leyte operation the Sixth Army had designated Maj. Gen. Andrew D. Bruce's 77th Infantry Division, then on Guam, as the second of its two reserve divisions. As a result of the successes in the first days of the campaign, however, General MacArthur thought it would not be necessary to use the division on Leyte. On 29 October, without General Krueger's concurrence, General MacArthur transferred control of the division from General Krueger to Admiral Nimitz, Commander in Chief, Pacific Ocean Area.[6] Shortly afterward the Japanese began their reinforcements of Leyte and a captured Japa-

---

[2] Sixth Army Opns Rpt Leyte, p. 62.
[3] Rad, CINCSWPA to AGWAR, CM-IN 2966, 30 Nov 44.

[4] Sixth Army Opns Rpt, pp. 69–70.
[5] Sixth Army FO 36, 4 Dec 44.
[6] Rad, MacArthur to Halsey, Nimitz, and Krueger, CM-IN 29353, 29 Oct 44. General Krueger later wrote: "The 77th Division was actually taken away from me without my knowledge and I complained about it." Ltr, Gen Krueger to Gen Ward, 13 Aug 51, OCMH.

nese field order revealed that an all-out offensive would be launched against the Americans in the middle of November. These developments led General MacArthur to request Admiral Nimitz to divert the 77th Division, which was on its way to New Caledonia, to the Tacoloban area on Leyte.[7] Admiral Nimitz acquiesced and told General MacArthur that the division was being sent to Manus. After its arrival there, operational control over it would pass to General MacArthur.[8]

Upon arrival of the 77th Division at Seeadler Harbor on Manus at 1330, 15 November, General MacArthur ordered it to go to Leyte and come under the control of General Krueger.[9] After the ships' stores had been replenished, the convoy sailed out of the anchorage at 1700, 17 November, and made the voyage to Leyte without incident.[10] The units commenced landing on the eastern shores of Leyte in the vicinity of Tarragona and Dulag about 1800, 23 November, and came under the control of General Krueger who assigned the division to General Hodge. From 23 to 25 November it was engaged in unloading the transports and establishing bivouac areas.

On 19 November, while it was still at sea, General Krueger had ordered the 77th Division to furnish immediately after landing a ship-unloading detail of about 1,200 men for the projected operation at Mindoro.[11] At 1600 on 27 November the detail, a bat-

talion of the 306th Infantry, boarded LCI's at Tarragona Beach and departed for the staging area for the Mindoro operation.

In conformity with General Krueger's plans, General Hodge ordered the 77th Division to make preparations for the amphibious operation below Ormoc. (*Map 17*) It was to be assisted by the 7th Division, which was to attack and capture the high ground south of the Panilahan River. General Bruce, once ashore, was to direct and co-ordinate the attack of the 7th Division with that of the 77th Division.[12] General Krueger informed General Hodge that he did not approve of this arrangement and added that such co-ordination as was necessary should be exercised by Hodge as corps commander.[13]

At a point about three and a half miles southeast of Ormoc was the barrio of Deposito where the 77th Division was to land. Along the eastern shore of Ormoc Bay, south from Ormoc, there were many areas which offered suitable landing beaches. These were crossed by numerous rivers and streams which discharged into Ormoc Bay. None of these would be a handicap, since all could be forded except during the monsoon season. The beach area selected, though narrow, was suitable for landing, having a surface of hard sand and gravel that could be used as a road by vehicles.

---

[7] Rad, MacArthur to Nimitz, CM-IN 10478, 10 Nov 44.

[8] Rad, Nimitz to MacArthur, CM-IN 10683, 10 Nov 44.

[9] Rad, GHQ to Comdr Allied Naval Forces, CX 52239, 16 Nov 44, Sixth Army G–3 Jnl, 17 Nov 44.

[10] 77th Div Opns Rpt Leyte, p. 2.

[11] Memo, CofS XXIV Corps for G–3 XXIV Corps, 19 Nov 44, XXIV Corps G–3 Jnl, 23 Nov 44.

[12] XXIV Corps FO 33, 4 Dec 44. In a lecture delivered before the Command and General Staff College on 19 January 1951, General Bruce indicated that his previous study of the Civil War was helpful in planning for the 77th Division's part in the operation: "May I suggest that you do not sell short the study of history. One does not parallel history, but the previous study of Jackson's Valley Campaign in friendly territory influenced the mind OCMH.

[13] Ltr, Gen Krueger to Gen Ward, 13 Aug 51, of the Division Commander in this campaign."

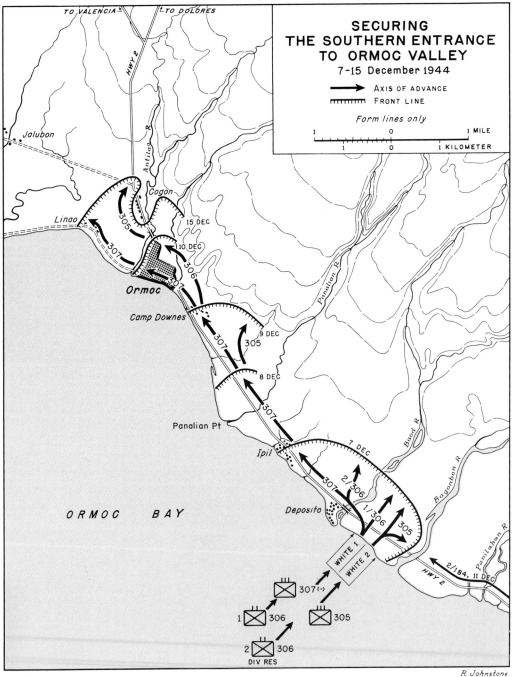

**SECURING
THE SOUTHERN ENTRANCE
TO ORMOC VALLEY**
7-15 December 1944

⟶ AXIS OF ADVANCE

〓〓〓〓〓 FRONT LINE

Form lines only

1 ————— 0 ————— 1 MILE

1 ————— 0 ————— 1 KILOMETER

TO VALENCIA

TO DOLORES

HWY 2

Antiloa R.

Jalubon

Cogon

Linao

15 DEC

10 DEC

Ormoc

Camp Downes

9 DEC

8 DEC

Panalian R.

305

307

306

307

305

307

Panalian Pt

307

Ipil

7 DEC

Baod R.

ORMOC BAY

Deposito

2/306

1/306

305

307

Bagonbon R.

WHITE 1

WHITE 2

HWY 2

Panilahon R.

2/184, 11 DEC

307(-)

1 306

305

2 306
DIV RES

MAP 17

The terrain was level for about a mile and a half inland from the beach, and then rose gradually to a height of twenty to thirty feet. Half a mile farther inland, the mountain slopes began. Highway 2, which was ten feet wide and composed of sand and gravel, ran along the entire length of the east coast of Ormoc Bay. Several roads ran from Highway 2 to the beach: one was about a hundred yards south of the Baod River and skirted the rice paddies in the middle of the landing beach area; another, just south of the rice paddies, extended inland about two miles from the beach.[14]

Naval Plans

When the naval forces were informed that the overwater movement to Ormoc would take place and that the Mindoro operation was postponed, the shipping reserved for the Mindoro operation was turned over to the Ormoc force. Rear Adm. Arthur D. Struble was given command of Task Group 78.3, which was to transport and land the 77th Division, together with its supplies and equipment, in the Ormoc Bay area and support the landing by naval gunfire.[15]

Admiral Struble divided his task group into six units, in addition to the destroyer which was his flagship. These consisted of: a Fast Transport Unit of eight transports; a Light Transport Unit of twenty-seven landing craft and twelve LSM's (medium landing ships); a Heavy Transport Unit of four LST's (tank landing ships); an Escort Unit of twelve destroyers; a Mine-Sweeping Unit of nine mine sweepers and a transport; and a Control and Inshore Support Unit made up of four LCI(R)'s (infantry rocket landing craft), two submarine chasers, and one tug. The landing was to be made between the Baod and Bagonbon Rivers but clear of the Bagonbon River delta. The northern half of the beach was called White I and the southern half White II. Six destroyers would bombard the landing beaches.

The line of departure was fixed at 2,000 yards from the beach, but if the shore fire became heavy the line of departure would be moved back 1,000 yards. There would be five assault waves with two LCI(R)'s flanking the first wave to the beach. Each craft would fire so as to cover the sector of the beach in its area to a depth of 600 yards. After completion of the bombardment the LCI(R)'s would reload and remain on the flanks to engage targets of opportunity.

Air Support Plans [16]

The Fifth Air Force would provide both day and night air cover for the journey of the assault convoy to the target, for the landings, and for the return convoy. It was estimated that on 5 December, for the journey to the target, seventeen night fighter sorties and seventy-two day fighter sorties would be required. Protection would also be furnished by the bombers, and forty-six aircraft would be available on call for strikes against enemy installations and targets of opportunity, as well as for special missions.

On the day of the landings, the tempo would be accelerated. There would be nine-

---

[14] 77th Div FO 13, App. 4 to Annex Baker; Allied Geographical Sec, GHQ SWPA, Terrain Study 84, Leyte Province, 17 Aug 44; Allied Geographical Sec, GHQ SWPA, Special Rpt 55, Airfields, Landing Beaches and Roads—Samar, Leyte, and Dinagat Group, 10 Jul 44.

[15] Opn Plan Comdr Task Group 78.3, Attack Order Comphib Grp NINE, 5-44, 1 Dec 44.

[16] Fifth Air Force Fighter Cover Plan for Ormoc Bay Opn, 731.326, AAF Hist Archives.

teen night fighter sorties and ninety-six day fighter sorties; ten flights of forty bombers to cover the beachhead; six flights of twenty-four bombers to cover the return of the assault convoy; and eleven night fighters to cover the LST and main assault convoys, the beachhead, and the return convoy. There would also be available sixteen bombers for interception or additional cover for the beachhead and convoy; twenty-four P–47's for interception, ground support, and attacks against enemy shipping or targets of opportunity; sixteen P–40's for ground strikes; and thirty-four F4U's for cover or interception.

The 77th Division continued to assemble its troops on Tarragona Beach, on the east coast of Leyte, and during the night of 5 December the loading of supplies and equipment on the landing ships began. The loading was slowed by frequent air alerts. The division had previously been told that the convoy would be unable to stay in the landing area more than two hours and consequently there was no attempt to bulk load supplies, since they would take too long to unload. All supplies and equipment to support the initial assault had to be mobile-loaded, that is, loaded on the vehicles taken with the division so that the supplies could be brought ashore in the vehicles upon debarkation. There were only 289 vehicles in the initial convoy, including tanks, M8's, and M10's that could not carry supplies. The LVT's (tracked landing vehicles) were filled with supplies rather than troops in order that they could be discharged from the landing ships into the water and go ashore fully loaded. Furthermore, since the supplies were mobile they could be moved either by water or inland by motor.[17] The

77th Division gave the highest priority to ammunition, water, and rations.

About 0700 on 6 December the assault shipping rendezvoused off Tarragona and Rizal Beaches, and one hour later the assault troops began to board the vessels. The loading was completed at 1200 and the convoy assembled offshore from Dulag to await the arrival of the twelve escorting destroyers.

The Movement Overwater

The Convoy Sails

Two mine sweepers swept the Canigao Channel between Leyte and Bohol on 27 November and again on 4 and 6 December, but they encountered no mines of any sort.[18] At 1200 on 6 December the convoy's escorting destroyers departed from San Pedro Bay and moved to the point of rendezvous offshore, near the Tarragona–Rizal area. The principal convoy was formed and got under way at 1330, having been preceded by four slower-moving LST's escorted by two destroyers. The commander of the destroyer unit gave additional protection to the transports with four destroyers until 2300, when the destroyers departed for a prelanding raid on Ormoc Bay. They were also to intercept any Japanese surface vessels that might be attempting to bring reinforcements into Ormoc harbor.

The journey through Leyte Gulf, Surigao Strait, and the Camotes Sea was uneventful. Several unidentified planes flew over the convoy but did not launch an attack. The only alert during the voyage was about twilight on the 6th of December, when an unidentified group of eighteen bombers flew over the formation in the direction of

---

[17] Ltr, Gen Bruce to Gen Ward, 16 Aug 51, OCMH.

[18] Opns Rpt, CTU 78.3.6 to COMINCH, Ser 0017, 22 Dec 44, Off Nav Rcds and Library.

TROOPS OF THE 77TH DIVISION BOARD LCI'S AT TARRAGONA

Tacloban. The convoy encountered numerous small native craft en route and checked several of these but found no Japanese.[19]

Throughout the night the vessels steamed toward the target. Silently they took their stations in Ormoc Bay, off the coast of Deposito, before dawn. At 0634 on 7 December an enemy shore battery opened fire, which was answered at 0640 as the destroyers commenced firing upon their assigned targets. Behind Ipil, in the vicinity of the northern fire support group, a number of enemy 3-inch gun positions were observed. The destroyers took the positions under fire and quickly silenced them. At 0655 a large number of Japanese were observed in the town

of Albuera and these also were taken under fire. The destroyers covered the landing beaches until ordered to lift fire just as the first wave of the landing party was approaching the beach.[20]

As the American convoy steamed into position, it received word that an enemy convoy was on the way to Ormoc with reinforcements. Aircraft of the V Fighter Command flew to intercept the Japanese vessels, which comprised six transports and seven escort vessels. During the morning occurred one of the most intense aerial battles of the Leyte Campaign. Fifty-six P–47's of the 341st and 347th Fighter Squadrons dropped ninety-four 1,000-pound and six 500-pound bombs on the enemy shipping and strafed the vessels. The Army and Marine land-based air-

[19] Opns Rpt, CTU 78.3.5 to COMINCH, 056–60/A163, Ser 0016, 22 Dec 44, Off Nav Rcds and Library.

[20] Ibid.

CONVOY CARRYING 77TH DIVISION APPROACHES DEPOSITO *(above)*.
Bombardment of enemy positions at Ipil (below), with stack of sugar mill visible. Village is near center of picture.

craft destroyed two cargo vessels and two passenger transports.[21] Nearly all the available American aircraft were engaged in the attack. General MacArthur in his daily communique estimated that the entire convoy was wiped out and that 4,000 enemy troops lost their lives.[22]

"Land the Landing Party"

The landing of the first wave, scheduled for 0630, was delayed until 0707 to take advantage of better light for the naval bombardment. There were to be five waves for each regiment.[23] At 0701 the first wave of small landing craft left the line of departure and raced for the shore. The first wave was landed at 0707, co-ordinating its spacing and timing with that of the LCI(R)'s supporting the landing. There was no opposition, and the troops moved inland.

The dispatch and landing of the fourth wave of LCI(R)'s was delayed because the third wave had been unable to disembark the troops and retract according to schedule. The fifth wave of LSM's was delayed for the same reason. Since the tide was rapidly falling and the sand bar was exposed, a tug was used in several instances to pull the craft off. At 1100 the commander of the task group pulled out, leaving behind one LCI

and four LSM's stranded on the beach. The tug left at the same time, and Admiral Struble ordered the grounded craft to retract at high tide and proceed back to San Pedro Bay under cover of darkness.[24]

With the departure of the landing waves for the shore, the destroyers turned their fire upon targets adjacent to the landing beaches. The *Laffey* at 0830 opened fire against some enemy troops approaching the barrio of Ipil from the north and turned them back. At 0930 the *Conyngham* fired upon a possible concentration south of Ipil and at 1000 this destroyer's shore fire control party requested additional support against enemy troops that were moving into Ipil.[25]

At 0820 the Japanese launched a strong aerial offensive against the American vessels in Ormoc Bay. The enemy air attacks continued for nearly nine and a half hours. The Fifth Air Force, beginning at 0700, gave air cover throughout the day and "did an excellent job."[26] Upon a number of occasions, however, the enemy airplanes slipped through the antiaircraft fire and the air protection and hit the shipping. Japanese suicide aircraft struck and badly damaged five vessels. At 0945 the destroyer *Mahan* and the high-speed transport *Ward* received such damaging blows that they later had to be sunk by gunfire.[27] The Japanese made

---

[21] The Joint Army-Navy Assessment Committee, *Japanese Naval and Merchants Shipping Losses During World War II by all Causes* (Washington, 1947), p. 77.
[22] Hist of V Fighter Command, Ch. 4, pp. 62–63, AAF Hist Archives.
[23] 77th Div FO 13, 4 Dec 44, Annexes 5 and 6. In each small landing craft there were thirty-six men—a platoon leader or sergeant, messenger, aid man, flame thrower and bazooka operators, a rifle squad, and a machine gun or mortar crew. The composition of the second wave was about the same. The third wave, consisting of LCI's, included engineer and heavy weapons personnel, artillery units, and other troops and vehicles. The fourth wave consisted of LCI's and the fifth wave of LSM's.

[24] Opns Rpt, CTU 78.3.7 to COMINCH, no serial, 17 Dec 44, Off Nav Rcds and Library.
[25] Opns Rpt, CTU 78.3.5 to COMINCH, Ser 0016, Off Nav Rcds and Library.
[26] Sixth Army G–3 Jnl, 7 Dec 44.
[27] "By a coincidence, Commander W. W. Outerbridge, USN, the commanding officer of the *O'Brien*, which sank the *Ward* by gunfire, had been the commanding officer of the *Ward* at Pearl Harbor on 7 December 1941, when that vessel fired the first shot of the war in sinking a Japanese submarine attempting to enter Pearl Harbor, just three years previously to the day." CINCPAC–CINCPOA Opns in the Pacific Ocean Areas During the Month of December 1944, Ser 002910, 25 Jun 45, p. 41, Off Nav Rcds and Library.

sixteen different raids on the shipping, during which an estimated forty-five to fifty enemy aircraft attacked the formation. Thirty-six of these were believed to have been shot down.[28]

The landing waves arrived ashore without incident and without casualties. Within thirty-five minutes the advance echelon of division headquarters, including the assistant division commander and the general staff sections, were ashore.[29] Approximately 2,000 men were placed on a 1,000-yard beach every five minutes. Mobile-loading of supplies had made this speed possible. "Logistically it was a difficult operation to push that mass of troops and equipment on a beach in so short a time and had there been any considerable unexpected enemy mortar or artillery fire at any time during the period, great casualties might have resulted." [30] At 0930 General Bruce assumed command ashore.

Japanese Plans

Until the middle of November, the commander of the Japanese *35th Army* had failed to put any beach obstacles along the shores of Ormoc Bay,[31] since he believed that there was little likelihood of an American thrust up the bay. General Suzuki thought that the Americans would be deterred by the presence of a Japanese naval base on Cebu in front of Bohol Strait. As American naval activity increased along the

coast in the last part of November, however, the Japanese finally conceded that there was "a great possibility" of an American landing at Ormoc Bay. By the middle of the month the *Ormoc Defense Headquarters* was organized under the command of Colonel Mitsui, the commanding officer of the *Shipping Unit*. The main force of the *Defense Headquarters* was the *Shipping Unit*, but the *Antitank* and *Antiaircraft Gun Units*, the *Automatic Gun Company*, and other units were added. In addition, all units then in Ormoc were temporarily placed under Colonel Mitsui. The enemy plan of defense was simple. At the town of Ormoc the Japanese, from their main defensive positions, were to stop the advance and then, gathering as much strength as possible, they were to counterattack.

The Japanese defenses, however, were not completed at the time of the American landings. Only individual trenches had been dug along the coast, and the field positions in the northern part of Ipil were elementary. Upon being alerted that the Americans had landed, the *Shipping Unit* of Colonel Mitsui took up its main defensive positions in the Ipil area. At the same time, troops of the *Nonaka Battalion* of the *30th Division*, consisting of an infantry company and a machine gun company, were placed under the command of Colonel Mitsui. The major part of the *30th Division* remained on Mindanao. The American strength was estimated to be one regiment.

Drive Toward Ormoc

Ipil

The assault elements of the 77th Division advanced inland immediately after landing. The 1st Battalion of Col. Vincent J. Tanzola's 305th Infantry, with two companies

---

[28] Opns Rpts, CTU 78.3.5, Ser 0016, 22 Dec 44; CTU 78.3.3, Ser 082, 22 Dec 44. Both in Off Nav Rcds and Library.

[29] 77th Div Opns Rpt Leyte, p. 11.

[30] Study, Hq Army Ground Forces, 319.1/3 (POA), 16 May 45, in OPD 319.1 Sec. XII.

[31] The material in this subsection on Japanese planning is based on Japanese Studies in World War II, No. 11, *35th Army* Opns, 1944–45, pp. 94–98, OCMH.

abreast, was to seize the crossings over the Bagonbon River in the vicinity of Highway 2.[32] The 307th Infantry was to move rapidly inland and establish an initial beachhead line about 1,300 yards east near a bridge over the Baod River. The 305th Infantry landed in a column of battalions with the 1st, 3d, and 2d Battalions going ashore in that order. The 1st and 3d Battalions moved rapidly inland to the objective while the 2d Battalion remained in regimental reserve. The 307th Infantry also reached the bridge without difficulty. In the town of Deposito, enemy foxholes had been dug in the tall grass and apparently were to be used only as a protection against Allied air attacks, since they had no field of fire. Immediately upon landing, a reconnaissance patrol went to locate a trail leading from the beach to Highway 2. About 300 yards north of the Bagonbon River, the patrol found a small access road which was put to immediate use.[33] The initial beachhead line was achieved within forty-five minutes after landing. Most of the Japanese *26th Division* which had been in the area were either moving over the mountains to participate in a battle for the Burauen airfields or were engaging the 7th Division south of Deposito. Little besides service troops remained to oppose the 77th Division.

General Bruce originally had planned to hold the beachhead line, establish a defensive position, and await the arrival of additional supplies and reinforcements on the following day. But because of the lack of organized resistance, the speed with which the troops moved inland, and his desire to fully exploit the situation before the Japanese could counterattack, he very early decided to continue the attack northward astride the highway and extend the division's beachhead to Ipil.[34]

The 307th Infantry (less the 2d Battalion which was on Samar), under Col. Stephen S. Hamilton, together with the 2d Battalion of Col. Aubrey D. Smith's 306th Infantry, which was attached to the regiment after the landing, was ordered by General Bruce to move northward and take Ipil.[35] At about 1045, with the 1st Battalion in the lead, the regiment moved out northward astride Highway 2 toward Ipil. At the same time the division artillery was in position to support the advance. The 306th Field Artillery Battalion had been previously placed in the 7th Division area at a position from which it could fire as far north as Ipil and 6,000 yards inland.[36] At first there was little enemy opposition, but the troops observed many well-camouflaged foxholes under the houses, and many stores of Japanese food and ammunition.

Within ten minutes after starting, the 1st Battalion, 307th Infantry, was 300 yards north of Deposito and by 1215 had advanced 500 yards farther north. Japanese resistance became heavier as the troops neared Ipil. The remaining troops of the *Nonaka Battalion* of the *30th Division,* consisting of an infantry company and a machine gun company, had landed at Ormoc from junks and "fought bravely" under the command of the *Shipping Unit.*[37] The enemy had emplaced machine guns, and in one instance a cannon, in dugouts under the

---

[32] 305th Inf FO 1, 5 Dec 44, 77th Div G–3 Jnl, 8 Dec 44.
[33] 77th Div S–2 Recon Rpt for Leyte, p. 1.

[34] 77th Div Opns Rpt Leyte, p. 12; 305th Inf Opns Rpt Leyte, p. 1; 307th Inf Opns Rpt Leyte, p. 3.
[35] Msg, 307th Inf to CG 77th Div, 7 Dec 44, 77th Div G–3 Jnl, 7 Dec 44.
[36] Msg, Lt Col Douglas C. Davis, Div Arty, to CG 77th Div, 7 Dec 44, 77th Div G–3 Jnl, 7 Dec 44.
[37] *35th Army* Opns, p. 97.

houses.[38] By 1455 the 307th Infantry was on the outskirts of Ipil, but its advance was temporarily held up when the Japanese exploded one of their ammunition dumps.[39] By 1740 the 1st Battalion had cleared the barrio and set up a night perimeter on its northern outskirts. The regiment had killed an estimated sixty-six Japanese and had captured one prisoner of war, a medical supply dump, a bivouac area, and numerous documents.[40]

The 305th Infantry during the day moved south to the Bagonbon River without serious opposition. Patrols of platoon strength were sent to scout out enemy positions and, if possible, establish contact with the 7th Division which was fighting north along the coast from Baybay. These patrols went as far south as the Panalihan River, destroying three food dumps and knocking out an enemy pillbox.[41]

During the afternoon enemy aircraft that were molesting the shipping dropped some bombs ashore but no appreciable damage resulted. The division artillery established a command post approximately 200 yards inland on the southern banks of the Baod River. As the beachhead line extended, the artillery moved to the northern banks of the river. This position afforded better cover and concealment. The artillery fired on enemy machine guns, mortars, and troops.[42]

At 1640 General Bruce issued orders for the regiments to consolidate their positions and form night perimeters. The 77th Division had established a two-mile beachhead extending from Ipil in the north to the Bagonbon River on the south and had penetrated inland nearly a mile.

General Bruce's plan at this time was to push forward vigorously and capture Ormoc, after which he would drive north, take Valencia, and make contact with elements of the X Corps. Each day he would "roll up his rear" to form a defensive perimeter at night. Patrols would be sent east to locate enemy concentrations and destroy them by artillery fire, and at the same time other patrols would move to the east to search out routes and Japanese dispositions with a view to taking Valencia from the east.[43]

In planning for the amphibious landing, the Fifth Air Force had ordered the 308th Bombardment Wing to conduct bombing and strafing missions, in addition to providing cover for the movement.[44] The plans for 8 December called for the 308th Bombardment Wing to be prepared on request to bomb Camp Downes—a prewar military post south of Ormoc—maintain a close vigilance over Ormoc, and continue the overhead air patrols.[45] The 307th Infantry was to move north at 0800 astride Highway 2 and seize Camp Downes. The 305th Infantry was to withdraw from the south and move north in support of the attack of the 307th Infantry and at the same time protect the southern and southeastern flanks of the division. The 902d Field Artillery Battalion and Company A of the 776th Amphibian Tank Battalion would support the attack. At

---

[38] 307th Inf Opns Rpt Leyte, p. 3; Msg, S-2 307th Inf to 77th Div, 7 Dec 44, 77th Div G-3 Jnl, 7 Dec 44.

[39] Msgs, 307th Inf to G-3 77th Div, 1055, 1215, 1445, 7 Dec 44, 77th Div G-3 Jnl, 7 Dec 44.

[40] 307th Inf Opns Rpt Leyte, p. 3; Msg, 307th Inf to G-2 77th Div, 7 Dec 44, 77th Div G-2 Jnl, 7 Dec 44.

[41] 305th Inf Opns Rpt Leyte, p. 1.

[42] 77th Div Arty Opns Rpt, pp. 2-3.

[43] Observers Rpt, 20 Dec 44, Col Paul L. Freeman, Operation in the Ormoc area, OPD 319.1 SWPA (20 Dec 44) Sec X.

[44] 308th Bombardment Wing Fragmentary FO 341-C, 6 Dec 44, Sixth Army G-3 Jnl, 9 Dec 44.

[45] Msg, XXIV Corps to Sixth Army, 8 Dec 44, Sixth Army G-3 Jnl, 8 Dec 44.

least two patrols of the 305th Infantry would be sent south to disrupt enemy communications. All other units of the division were to be prepared to move north on division order.[46]

Camp Downes

Immediately north of Ipil, Colonel Mitsui had constructed a few small strong points, each of which consisted of two coconut log pillboxes, several trenches, and foxhole emplacements for machine guns. Between these positions and Camp Downes were groups of enemy riflemen and machine gunners on the banks of the streams and at the ends of wooded ridges that extended from the northeast toward the highway. They had dug in at the bases of the trees and on the edges of the bamboo clumps. In the sector between Ipil and Camp Downes the highway was nine feet wide, with three-foot shoulders, and surfaced with coral or gravel. Fields of sugar cane or grassy hills lay east of the road, which was fringed with clumps of acacia or coconut trees. At least one reinforced enemy company had taken up its last defensive stand at Camp Downes. Less than a mile from Ormoc, Camp Downes had been an important Philippine Army and Constabulary camp before the war. The plateau on which it was situated lay east of the highway and commanded all approaches, most of which were open and without cover. A ravine ran along the southern side of the barrio. At Camp Downes the Japanese had placed thirteen machine guns, two 40-mm. antiaircraft guns, and three 75-mm. field pieces under the porches and in the foundations of buildings. These were well camou-

flaged and mutually supporting and were protected by concealed riflemen.[47]

As the 77th Division consolidated its positions in Ipil, the Japanese started to use reinforcements to check any further advance toward Ormoc. The *12th Independent Infantry Regiment* had been assembling at Dolores, northeast of Ormoc. On the night of 7 December its commander, Colonel Imahori, ordered the newly arrived *Kamijo Battalion,* which consisted of two companies, to co-operate with the *Shipping Unit* under Colonel Mitsui in delaying the advance of the American forces until the arrival of the main body of the *12th Independent Infantry.*[48] By the morning of 8 December it became evident to the 77th Division that it had surprised the enemy.

At 0615 enemy planes flew over the command post area, and ten minutes later one of these was shot down by antiaircraft fire.[49] At 0800 Colonel Hamilton's 307th Infantry moved out.[50] By 1000 the regiment was 200 yards north of Ipil, but it encountered more determined resistance when it reached the Panalian River at 1200. General Bruce ordered the attacking force to continue north with the objective of reaching the ravine just south of the Camp Downes plateau. The 307th Infantry was to make the assault and employ if necessary all reserves, while the 2d Battalion of the 306th Infantry continued to be attached to the regiment in support. The 902d Field Artillery Battalion,

---

[46] 77th Div FO 14, 8 Dec 44.

[47] 77th Div Opns Rpt Leyte, G–2 Sum 3, App. 2; Allied Geographical Sec, GHQ SWPA, Terrain Study 84, Leyte Province, 17 Aug 44, pp. 57, 60, 65.
[48] *35th Army* Opns, p. 98.
[49] Msg, G–2 Observer to G–2 77th Div, 8 Dec 44, 77th Div G–2 Jnl, 8 Dec 44.
[50] Msg, 307th Inf to 77th Div, 8 Dec 44, 77th Div G–2 Jnl, 8 Dec 44.

A PATROL OF THE 307TH INFANTRY *warily approaches a river crossing near Camp Downes.*

Company A of the 776th Amphibian Tank Battalion, and Company A of the 88th Chemical Weapons Battalion were also to continue their support. Farther south, the 305th Infantry would move north to defend the bridgehead at the Baod River and the 77th Reconnaissance Troop would move at 1330 to an area 500 yards north of the Pani-lahan River to clear out a position for the division command post.[51]

Upon receiving its mission, a platoon from Company A of the 776th Amphibian Tank Battalion moved over water toward Camp Downes to secure information on the dispositions of the Japanese. The platoon proceeded north 500 yards offshore to the vicinity of Panalian Point where it received heavy enemy artillery fire from Camp

Downes. The platoon returned and reported the location of the enemy artillery.[52] The 902d Field Artillery Battalion thereupon shelled the Japanese artillery positions.[53]

The assault units of the 307th Infantry steadily pushed out against determined opposition in which the enemy used rifles, mortars, and small artillery from dug-in positions along finger ridges and streams. The Japanese had a prepared position 1,000 yards in depth from which they swept the rice fields which the troops had to traverse, but fire from the American automatic weapons and mortars forced the Japanese to fall back.[54] An enemy company counterattacked

---

[51] 77th Div FO 15, 8 Dec 44.

[52] 776th Amphib Tank Bn Opns Rpt Leyte, p. 18.
[53] 77th Div Arty Opns Rpt Leyte, p. 3.
[54] 307th Inf Opns Rpt Leyte, pp. 3–4.

and hit Company A of the 88th Chemical Battalion. The Japanese were repulsed on two separate occasions—the first time at 1320 and the second at 1520, when in company strength they charged the Americans. The chemical company stopped both charges with high explosive and white phosphorus shells.[55] The 307th Infantry pressed forward, capturing considerable quantities of small arms and artillery ammunition, and by nightfall had advanced some 2,000 yards. The 1st Battalion, 306th Infantry, was to relieve the regiment's 2d Battalion, which had been attached to the 307th Infantry as an assault battalion.[56]

Colonel Tanzola's 305th Infantry during the day protected the southern and southeastern flanks of the 77th Division in its advance northward. At night the regiment's defensive perimeter centered around Ipil but extended as far south as the Baod River.[57]

The Japanese forces suffered greatly in the course of the day. The commander of the *Kamijo Battalion* was severely wounded and the battalion itself had many casualties. Consequently, the *Tateishi* and *Maeda Battalions* of the *12th Independent Infantry Regiment*, which had been alerted to join the *Kamijo Battalion*, were ordered to take positions north of Ormoc, on the night of 9 December.[58] The Japanese troops in the sector opposing the 77th Division were two companies totaling 100 men of the *1st Battalion, 12th Independent Infantry*, with three machine guns and two battalion guns; three companies totaling 250 men of the *3d Battalion* of the same regiment with nine machine guns, two battalion guns, and four antitank guns; sixty men with three machine guns from the *30th Division;* a paratroop unit of eighty men; a ship engineer unit of 500 men; and 750 personnel from the Navy. The total effective military strength was 1,740 men.[59]

At 0400 on 9 December the first resupply convoy arrived carrying with it the rest of the 306th Infantry. The 3d Battalion, 306th Infantry, was placed on the eastern flank which connected the 305th Infantry on the south with the 307th Infantry on the north. Its mission was to protect the east and center of the beachhead. At 0530 the batteries of the 902d Field Artillery Battalion fired 110 rounds on a harassing mission and at 0820 they fired 192 rounds in preparation for the attack by the infantry against Camp Downes.[60] The 1st Battalion, 306th Infantry, was to pass through the 2d Battalion, 306th Infantry, and continue the attack with the 3d Battalion, 307th Infantry, on the left. The 1st Battalion, 307th Infantry, would protect the regimental right flank.[61] After the artillery concentration the 307th Infantry at 0830 moved out toward Camp Downes.

The 307th Infantry inched slowly forward. It became evident that the Japanese had regrouped and emplaced the forces on ridges and high ground which overlooked all possible approaches to Camp Downes and Ormoc. In selecting his defensive positions the enemy used "excellent judgment" [62] and defended the area with at least two companies heavily reinforced with automatic weapons. The assaulting forces received intense small arms and artillery fire.[63]

[55] Company A, 88th Chemical Bn, Jnl, 8 Dec 44.
[56] 307th Inf Opns Rpt Leyte, pp. 3–4.
[57] 305th Inf Opns Rpt Leyte, pp. 1–2.
[58] *35th Army* Opns, p. 98.

[59] *Ibid.*, p. 106.
[60] 902d FA Bn Opns Rpt Leyte, p. 3.
[61] 307th Inf Unit Jnl, 8 Dec 44.
[62] 307th Inf Opns Rpt Leyte, p. 4.
[63] Msg, CG 77th Div to CG XXIV Corps, 9 Dec 44, 77th Div G–3 Jnl, 9 Dec 44.

The 902d Field Artillery Battalion supported the attack from positions north of the Baod River. The 305th Field Artillery Battalion, which had just arrived, was sent forward to support the attack.[64] At one of the Japanese strong points that had been overrun were found eleven heavy machine guns, two 40-mm. antiaircraft guns, and three 75-mm. guns. At 1700, Japanese aircraft strafed the regiment and inflicted several casualties. At 1750, however, the 307th Infantry entered Camp Downes, secured the area, and established a night perimeter. Its total advance for the day was about one thousand yards.[65]

At 1245 the 305th Infantry, which had been protecting the southern flank of the division, received a new assignment from General Bruce. The 2d Battalion of the 305th Infantry was to protect the division's rear by taking a position just south of Ipil. The 1st and 3d Battalions were to move north of the Panilahan River and 1,000 yards to the east in order to complete an all-around defense of Camp Downes.[66] At 1345 the battalions moved north. As soon as the 307th Infantry entered Camp Downes, General Bruce ordered his forward command post into that area, and the advance echelon of his headquarters moved out. Upon its arrival at the selected camp site, a coconut grove on a hill just south of Camp Downes, the advance echelon became involved in a fire fight between the 307th Infantry and the enemy forces on the hill. It dug in under fire in the new area. The Japanese defenders were driven out of the coconut grove as the rest of the command post moved in.[67]

During the day the 307th Infantry had advanced about 1,000 yards and captured Camp Downes. The 305th Infantry had secured the area northeast of Camp Downes and protected the northeastern flank of the 77th Division. The 306th Infantry had moved into an assembly area 600 yards north of Ipil.[68]

Two Sevens are Rolled in Ormoc

At 1830 General Bruce issued verbal orders for the attack on 10 December. Ormoc was the target. The 307th and 306th Infantry Regiments were to move out abreast. The 307th Infantry would attack along the highway to its front while the 306th Infantry would move to the northeast and attempt to envelop the opposing enemy force. The 305th Infantry initially was to remain in position and defend its part of the line.[69]

Ormoc, the largest and most important commercial center in western Leyte, possessed a concrete and pile pier at which a vessel with a sixteen-foot draft, and two smaller vessels, could anchor at the same time.[70] On the route to Ormoc and in the town itself, the Japanese dug strong defensive positions. The favored sites were in bamboo thickets, on reverse slopes, along creek beds, and under buildings. Individual spider holes about six feet deep were covered with logs and earth and "beautifully camouflaged." Against such positions, artillery and mortar fire did little more than daze the de-

[64] 77th Div Arty Opns Rpt Leyte, p. 3.
[65] 307th Inf Opns Rpt Leyte, p. 4.
[66] Msg, G-3 77th Div to S-3 305th Inf, 9 Dec 44, 77th Div G-3 Jnl, 9 Dec 44.
[67] 77th Div Opns Rpt Leyte, pp. 14-15.
[68] 306th Inf Opns Rpt Leyte, p. 6.
[69] 77th Div Plan of Action for 10 Dec 44, 77th Div G-3 Jnl, 9 Dec 44; 77th Div Opns Rpt Leyte, pp. 15-16.
[70] Allied Geographical Sec, GHQ SWPA, Terrain Study 84, Leyte Province, 17 Aug 44, pp. 10, 22, 60, 69.

fenders. Each position had to be searched out and destroyed.[71]

On 9 December the commander of the Japanese *35th Army* ordered the four companies of the *12th Independent Infantry Regiment* to return to their regiment from positions north of Ipil and to be prepared to help defend the Ormoc area.[72]

In preparation for the assault against Ormoc, the 902d Field Artillery Battalion at 0830 established an observation post at Camp Downes. At 0920 the battalion fired 100 rounds of ammunition during a ten-minute period in front of the area which the attacking forces were to traverse. At 0930 the artillery fire was directed at enemy positions observed in Ormoc.[73] General Krueger made arrangements with Admiral Kinkaid for LCM's, LCV's, and LVT's to operate along the coast at dawn and nightfall for an indefinite period.[74]

At 0900, Company A of the 776th Amphibian Tank Battalion with its 75-mm. howitzers moved into Ormoc—the first American troops to enter the city. The 2d and 3d Platoons of the company moved through the streets and sent high explosives and smoke shells into the buildings occupied by the Japanese.[75] The enemy defenders were also hit from the bay. LCM(R)'s from the Navy came overwater, moved near the Ormoc pier, and fired their rockets into the center of the town. As the rockets were being fired, the crews of the LCM's engaged the enemy defenders on the pier in a small arms fight, the antiaircraft machine guns on the

LCM's exchanging fire with the Japanese rifles and machine guns. After the last of the rockets were launched the LCM's withdrew, still under small arms fire.[76]

Colonel Smith's 306th Infantry was to move to the northeast with the 1st and 3d Battalions abreast and forestall any attempt to reinforce the Ormoc garrison. At 0945 the commanding officer of the 306th Infantry announced that both battalions had moved out on time.[77] The 1st Battalion on the left encountered only light opposition during the day. The 3d Battalion met light resistance in two deep ravines but was able to push through without difficulty. Throughout the day, however, the regiment received harassing fire from well-concealed riflemen, each of whom generally worked alone. By 1600 the 1st Battalion was at a bridge on Highway 2 north of Ormoc and the 3d Battalion was within 500 yards of the 1st but was slowed by the necessity for maintaining contact with the regiment's 2d Battalion. This unit had been committed on the right in order to secure contact with the 305th Infantry.[78]

At 0930 the troops of the 307th Infantry moved out.[79] They encountered little resistance until they neared the outskirts of Ormoc, where a deep ravine lay between the southern edge of the town and the front lines of the advancing troops. An enemy force, which had dug in on both sides and along the top of this ravine, had to be rooted out with bayonets, grenades, and mortars. In spite of the determined enemy resistance, American casualties were very light. Entering the western part of the city, the 307th

---

[71] Observers Rpt, 20 Dec 44, Col Freeman, Operation in the Ormoc Area, OPD 319.1, SWPA (20 Dec 44) Sec X.

[72] *35th Army* Opns, p. 97.

[73] 902d FA Bn Opns Rpt Leyte, p. 4.

[74] Rad, CG Sixth Army to CTF 77, 9 Dec 44, Sixth Army G–3 Jnl, 9 Dec 44.

[75] 776th Amphib Tank Bn Opns Rpt Leyte, p. 19.

[76] 77th Div Opns Rpt Leyte, p. 16; Msgs, 307th Inf to 77th Div, 1110, 1130, 10 Dec 44, 77th Div G–2 Jnl, 10 Dec 44.

[77] 306th Inf Unit Jnl, 10 Dec 44.

[78] 306th Inf Opns Rpt Leyte, p. 6.

[79] 307th Inf Opns Rpt, p. 4.

AERIAL VIEW OF ORMOC *after the bombardment. In the middle background is the Antilao River, with the mountains of western Ormoc Valley in the distance.*

Infantry hit the front line of the *Mitsui Unit* on the left flank of the *12th Independent Infantry Regiment.*[80]

Ormoc "was a blazing inferno of bursting white phosphorus shells, burning houses, and exploding ammunition dumps, and over it all hung a pall of heavy smoke from burning dumps mixed with the gray dust of destroyed concrete buildings, blasted by . . . artillery, mortar, and rocket fire." [81]

The 306th and 307th Infantry Regiments squeezed the enemy like a tube of toothpaste. The 306th Infantry enveloped

the northeast flank, while the drive of the 77th Division up the shore of Ormoc Bay banished any hopes that the Japanese might have entertained of escaping southeast by Highway 2. The Japanese were squeezed through Ormoc to the north.

Left behind, however, were some defenders who heroically but hopelessly fought to delay the American advance. Situated in spider holes beneath the buildings, they stubbornly fought back until overcome. Street by street, house by house, the 307th Infantry cleared Ormoc, which was a scene of gutted buildings and rubble. Many ammunition and signal supply dumps were captured, including a church that had been

---

[80] *35th Army* Opns, p. 107.
[81] 77th Div Opns Rpt Leyte, p. 16.

filled with artillery and small arms ammunition.[82]

As his troops were reducing Ormoc, General Bruce made a report to the commanding general of the XXIV Corps on the status of the attack and referred to a promise that had been made by the commanding general of the Fifth Air Force: "Where is the case of Scotch that was promised by General Whitehead for the capture of Ormoc. I don't drink but I have an assistant division commander and regimental commanders who do. . . ."[83]

At the same time that the 77th Division was entering Ormoc, the 32d Division was pushing southward toward Ormoc Valley, the 11th Airborne Division was working westward over the mountains toward the town, and the 7th Division was pushing northward along the eastern coast of Ormoc Bay in an attempt to make a juncture with the 77th Division. General Bruce advised General Hodge: "Have rolled two sevens in Ormoc. Come seven come eleven."[84]

The 307th Infantry pushed through the town and at 1730 established a night perimeter on the banks of the Antilao River on the western edge of Ormoc where it tied in with the front line of the 306th Infantry. At long last, Ormoc was in American hands.

In its drive north the 77th Division killed an estimated 1,506 Japanese and took 7 prisoners.[85] Its own casualties were 123 men killed, 329 wounded, and 13 missing in action.[86]

On 7 December, the 7th Division moved north from its position about seven miles south of Deposito to join the 77th Division, which had landed that day at Deposito. It advanced with two regiments abreast—the 184th Infantry on the left and the 17th Infantry on the right. The regiments made slow progress as they pushed over a series of hills and river valleys. On the night of 9–10 December the Japanese who were caught between the 7th and 77th Divisions withdrew into the mountains. At 1000 on 11 December an advance element, the 2d Battalion, 184th Infantry, reached Ipil and established contact with the 77th Division.

The XXIV Corps was now in undisputed control of the eastern shore of Ormoc Bay and the town of Ormoc. The capture of Ormoc had very important effects. It divided the Japanese forces and isolated the remaining elements of the enemy *26th Division*. It drew off and destroyed heretofore uncommitted enemy reserves, thus relieving the situation on all other fronts, and it hastened the juncture of the X Corps with the forces of the XXIV Corps. It denied to the Japanese the use of Ormoc as a port, through which so many reinforcements and supplies had been poured into the campaign. Finally, the Japanese were unable to use Highway 2 south of Ormoc and were driven north up Ormoc Valley.[87] General Krueger had realized an important part of his plan for the seizure of Ormoc Valley, since sealing off the port of Ormoc would enable the Sixth Army to devote its major effort toward completion of that plan.

---

[82] 307th Inf Opns Rpt Leyte, p. 4.

[83] Msg, CG 77th Div to CG XXIV Corps, 1400, 10 Dec 44, 77th Div G–3 Jnl, 10 Dec 44.

[84] Msg, CG 77th Div to CG XXIV Corps, 1645, 10 Dec 44, 77th Div G–3 Jnl, 10 Dec 44.

[85] 77th Div G–2 Summary Leyte Opns.

[86] 77th Div G–1 Daily Strength Rpts, 7–10 Dec 44.

---

[87] 77th Div G–2 Summary Leyte, No. 3.

CHAPTER XVII

Battle of the Airstrips

Immediately after Pearl Harbor, American submarines began to attack Japanese shipping to the Netherlands Indies. From the beginning they were successful. In September 1943 the submarines accelerated the tempo of their attack. The Japanese lost to the submarines "tremendous tonnages of shipping . . . all over the ocean. No route was secure from their attack; no ship was safe south of Honshu." [1] By the early fall of 1944 the Japanese line of communications to the Netherlands Indies was virtually cut.

With American land-based air strength on Leyte increasing steadily, a strong possibility existed that the line of communications between the Japanese homeland and the South Pacific area would be completely severed, especially if the main American air force should move up from New Guinea to Leyte. *Imperial General Headquarters* felt, therefore, that the Dulag and Tacloban airfields must be neutralized, and the Burauen airfields in southern Leyte Valley seized before the American air force could establish itself in strength on the island. Japanese control of the airfields would also facilitate the movement of Japanese supplies to the island and greatly assist the ground operations of the *35th Army*.[2]

In the latter part of November, Gen. Tomoyuki Yamashita, commanding general of the *14th Area Army,* sent a liaison officer from his headquarters in Manila with orders to Lt. Gen. Sosaku Suzuki, the *35th Army* commander, at Ormoc. General Yamashita is quoted as saying: "If the construction of air bases on Leyte is permitted to continue, the communications between the Southern areas and the homeland will be cut and this would be a serious situation. Therefore, we must occupy Burauen airfield as soon as possible and at the same time neutralize Tacloban and Dulag airfields. Moreover, we must annihilate the enemy's air power." [3]

Therefore, in a desperate attempt to gain the initiative, the Japanese embarked on a rash scheme to seize the airfields of Leyte. Their plan entailed a co-ordinated effort by both the ground and air forces. Beginning on 23 November and continuing through 27 November, the army air force was to launch a campaign to eliminate American air resistance. On the night of 26 November, aircraft carrying specially trained demolitionists were to crash-land on the Dulag and Tacloban airstrips and put them out of commission.[4]

---

[1] USSBS, *The War Against Japanese Transportation, 1941–1942* (Washington, 1947), p. 48.

[2] Japanese Studies, 11, *35th Army* Operations 1944–45, p. 74, OCMH.

[3] Tomochika, True Facts of Leyte Opn, p. 23.

[4] Japanese Studies in World War II, 7, *14th Area Army* Operations on Leyte, p. 11; 10th I&HS, Eighth Army, Stf Study of Japanese *35th Army* on Leyte, Part III, The Part Played by the Japanese Air Force . . . p. 5.

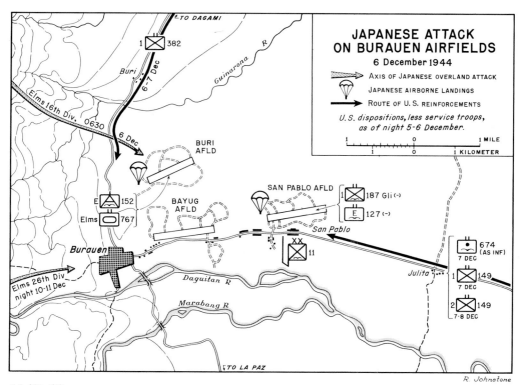

MAP 18

R. Johnstone

Plans were made for the *3d* and *4th Airborne Raiding Regiments* to descend from Luzon on the Burauen airfields. The *26th Division,* together with the *16th Division,* which had fought the Americans in Leyte Valley, and the *68th Independent Mixed Brigade* of the *35th Army* were to infiltrate through the mountains and attack and capture the Burauen airfields. The *16th Division* was to move from its position in the mountains west of Dagami toward Buri, the northernmost of the Burauen airfields. Elements of the *26th Division* which were engaging the 7th Division on the shores of Ormoc Bay were to break off the fight, move over the mountains, and attack Bayug and San Pablo, the southernmost of the Burauren fields. (*Map 18*) If all went well

they were to proceed east and capture the Dulag airfield, on the shores of Leyte Gulf. The airborne assault was to be made on the night of 5 December. The ground troops were to arrive early on the morning of 6 December and assist in the attack.

Because he felt that he had not made sufficient preparation, General Suzuki requested that the attack be postponed until 7 December. General Yamashita disapproved this request, but since bad weather was forecast for 5 December, he sent a message to General Suzuki changing the date of attack to the night of 6 December. This information was immediately transmitted to the *26th Division.* At the same time, efforts were made by General Suzuki's headquarters to relay the information to the *16th*

Division, but because of radio difficulties General Makino never received the message.

General Makino, after receiving the order for the airborne attack on the night of 5 December to be followed with an attack by his forces on the following morning, concentrated the remaining strength of the *16th Division* into one battalion. General Suzuki personally took command of the Burauen operation, and on 1 December he and a part of his staff moved east into the mountains near Burauen. General Tomochika was left in command of the Ormoc forces.[5]

Unwittingly, the Japanese were flogging a dead horse. General Krueger had stopped all work on these airfields on 25 November.

The American Dispositions

The Sixth Army planners for the Leyte operation had not envisaged the employment of the 11th Airborne Division during the campaign. This division, commanded by Maj. Gen. Joseph M. Swing, was to have staged on Leyte for subsequent operations.[6]

On 22 November, however, General Hodge ordered the relief of the 7th Division, minus the 17th Infantry, by the 11th Airborne Division in order to free the 7th Division for the drive up the eastern shore of Ormoc Bay. On the same day the 11th Airborne Division, along with the 17th Infantry, less the 2d Battalion, was ordered to seize and secure all exits from the mountains into Leyte Valley in its area. The division was then to advance through the central mountain range, and secure the western exits from the mountains in order to assist the attack of the 7th Infantry Division in its

drive north toward Ormoc.[7] Upon receipt of this order, General Swing assigned to the units of the 11th Airborne Division the mission of securing the mountain exits.

General Swing immediately started to relieve elements of the 7th Division and by 28 November the relief was completed. For several days the 11th Airborne Division sent patrols to the west and maintained small security guards at the Buri and Bayug airfields.

There were three airstrips—San Pablo, Bayug, and Buri—north of the Dulag–Burauen road in the area between San Pablo and Burauen. Both the Bayug and San Pablo airfields were on the Dulag–Burauen road. The Buri airstrip was almost directly north of the Bayug airstrip. The land between the Bayug and Buri airstrips was flat for a distance of about 800 yards. The northern half of this flat land was a swamp, sometimes five feet in depth. At the northern end of the swamp was a narrow stream, about fifteen feet wide, which ran along the base of a plateau. This plateau, which was directly north of the Buri airfield, was forested with palm trees and jungle growth. Buri airfield lay between the swamp and the plateau.[8]

By 27 November information from captured documents and prisoners interrogated by units of the Sixth Army indicated that the enemy was planning a co-ordinated ground and airborne attack to seize the airfields in the Burauen area. The intelligence officers of the XXIV Corps, however, thought that the Japanese were not capable of putting this assault plan into effect. The American patrols operating west of Burauen had found no new trails being constructed

---

[5] *35th Army* Opns, pp. 80–84.
[6] Sixth Army Opns Rpt Leyte, p. 62.

[7] XXIV Corps FO 28, 22 Nov 44.
[8] 149th Para-Glider Inf Opns Rpt Leyte, p. 1.

nor any old ones being extensively used. Furthermore, the American forces had blocked all known trails leading east over the mountains into the area. Although the enemy might be able to make an airborne attack, "he is not at this time capable of launching a co-ordinated ground airborne attack of major proportions in the Burauen area." [9]

Despite the trail blocks, however, elements of the *16th Division* were able to descend upon the Buri airstrip from the mountains southwest of Dagami. Only one battalion of the *26th Division,* which was to have attacked the airfields in the Burauen area on 7 December, ever reached the area. The movement over the mountains was difficult, and it was not until the night of 10–11 December that the unit arrived west of Burauen. It made a half-hearted attack, which was repulsed by elements of the 11th Airborne Division.[10]

Although the intelligence officers of the XXIV Corps believed there was no possibility of a co-ordinated ground and aerial assault, General Hodge alerted the XXIV Corps to a possible enemy paratroop landing. All units were directed to strengthen local defenses and establish in each sector a twenty-four-hour watching post. All men were to be armed and wear helmets, or to have arms and helmets within reach at all times. In the event of any unusual enemy activity, the headquarters of the XXIV Corps was to be notified immediately.[11]

In order to protect the airfields more adequately, a company of the 77th Division was furnished to the 11th Airborne Division to defend the Dulag airfield, while the latter division held one battalion alerted at Burauen in readiness to move against hostile forces at any of the three airfields in the area.[12] One battalion of the 306th Infantry Regiment and a platoon each from Companies A and B of the 767th Tank Battalion were stationed north of Burauen; the regiment was to be prepared to assemble two companies near the headquarters of the Fifth Air Force for motor movement in defense against airborne attack, and to maintain security detachments at the Bayug and Buri airstrips.[13]

First Japanese Effort

In the meantime the first phase of the Japanese plan to regain the initiative had begun. At 0245 on 27 November, three enemy air transports with lights on flew over Leyte Gulf at an altitude of about fifty feet. Ten minutes later one of these aircraft crash-landed in the water about twenty-five yards offshore in the area of the 728th Amphibian Tractor Battalion, which was about two miles south of Rizal and about three miles north of Tarragona.

A guard from the battalion, assuming the plane to be friendly, approached it and climbed on the wing to offer assistance. The Japanese emerged from the plane and threw grenades at the guard. The men of the tractor battalion, hearing the noise, came on and killed two Japanese with small arms fire. Three others, however, escaped and reached a swamp west of the landing point.

[9] XXIV Corps G–2 Periodic Rpt 39, 27 Nov 44.
[10] 11th Airborne Div After Action Rpt, 18 Nov–11 Dec 44.
[11] Msg, CG XXIV Corps to CG 7th Div *et al.,* 27 Nov 44, XXIV Corps G–3 Jnl, 27 Nov 44.

[12] Msg, G–3 XXIV Corps to CG 11th AB Div, 28 Nov 44, XXIV Corps G–3 Jnl, 28 Nov 44, and Sixth Army G–3 Periodic Rpt 528, 28 Nov 44.
[13] 11th Airborne Div FO 3, 29 Nov 44.

Ten or twelve more of the enemy moved south along the beach in the surf and also disappeared into the swamp.[14]

One of the other two planes crash-landed on the Buri airstrip and all its occupants were killed. The remaining plane crashed on the beach near the Bito River, north of Abuyog. Opposite, across the river, elements of the 11th Airborne Division were encamped.[15] With the exception of one soldier, who was killed at dawn, all of the Japanese in this plane escaped. The 728th Amphibian Tractor Battalion found many demolition charges abandoned in the plane. In view of this discovery, and the fact that the enemy made no attempt to follow up the landing by an airborne attack in force, the Americans concluded that the Japanese were on a suicide mission of demolition and destruction in the Dulag and Burauen airfield areas. Although the operation caused no damage, Radio Tokyo informed the Japanese people that it was "most successful." If the enemy believed that his attempt had been sucessful, however, the possibility existed that other airborne troops would be landed, either as raiding parties or in force.[16]

---

[14] 728th Amph Tractor Bn Unit Rpt 30, 27 Nov 44, and 20th Armored Gp Unit Rpt 5, in 20th Armored Gp Opns Rpt Leyte.

[15] The history of the 11th Airborne Division tells the following story about the landing of the third plane. "An antiaircraft machine gun crew, which outfit is forgotten now, was in position on the alert for enemy aircraft. When the plane landed and came to a halt, they called across the small river: 'Need any help?' 'No, everything OK,' someone yelled back, and the machine gun crew went back to watching the skies for enemy aircraft." Maj. Edward M. Flanagan, Jr., *The Angels, a History of the 11th Airborne Division, 1943–1946* (Washington, 1948), p. 34.

[16] XXIV Corps G–2 Periodic Rpt 43, 1 Dec 44, XXIV Corps G–3 Jnl, 2 Dec 44; XXIV Corps G–2 Periodic Rpt 45, 3 Dec 44, XXIV Corps G–3 Jnl, 4 Dec 44.

By 5 December the XXIV Corps was lulled into a sense of false security. The 2d Battalion, 511th Parachute Infantry, which had been in the Burauen area, had rejoined its regiment, which was fighting for the mountain passes on the trail to Albuera. The 3d Battalion, 306th Infantry, on the northwestern approaches to the airfields, reverted on 5 December to the control of the 77th Infantry Division, which was embarking for the Ormoc operation. The only infantry unit in the Burauen area at the time of the Japanese attack was the 1st Battalion, 187th Glider Infantry (less one company), which was on San Pablo airfield. The G–2 periodic report on 5 December at 2000 stated with regard to the general situation in the Burauen–Dagami–Mount Alto area: "An examination of reports of action in this area since 1 Nov may well warrant the assumption that organized resistance has about ceased." [17] But before morning, the remnants of the Japanese *16th Division* hit the Buri airfield.

Battle of Buri Airstrip

On or about 2 December General Makino, commanding general of the *16th Division*, had assembled from the hills southwest of Dagami the remaining elements of the division. The total strength thus massed was only about 500 men. The men rested, and then marched on toward the Buri airstrip. On the way, American artillery and tank fire killed approximately 200 of them. The remaining force moved to a new location—a deep gorge about 6,500 yards southwest of Dagami. On 5 December, this force was to move out of the gorge, join the paratroopers, and launch a combined assault against the Buri airstrip.

---

[17] XXIV Corps G–2 Periodic Rpt 47, 5 Dec 44.

BURI AIRSTRIP *as it appeared in 1946.*

The Americans later learned from interrogated prisoners that the morale of the men of the *16th Division* was very low at that time. They were living on coconuts and bananas, since the officers had taken the few remaining rations. Wounded men in the force had been abandoned.[18]

The *16th Division* was still unaware that the target date for the Burauen operation had been postponed to the night of 6 December, and consequently proceeded with its plans to attack the Buri airstrip on 6 December at 0630—over fourteen hours before the paratroopers were scheduled to land. On the night of 5–6 December, approximately 150 Japanese made their way quietly toward the Buri airstrip.

At 0600, the 287th Field Artillery Observation Battalion, northwest of Burauen, saw elements of the Japanese *16th Division* crossing the main road south of the battalion's position and heading east toward the Buri field. The battalion immediately relayed this information to the XXIV Corps headquarters.[19] After crossing the road, the enemy moved into the swamp near the airfield. One Japanese unit of about 15 men, armed with a machine gun, stationed itself at a Filipino shack 300 yards west of the highway in order to cover the road.[20]

At the Buri strip were about 47 men from the 287th Field Artillery Observation Bat-

---

[18] XXIV Corps G–2 Periodic Rpt 50, 8 Dec 44, XXIV Corps G–3 Jnl, 9 Dec 44.

[19] Msg, Corps Arty to G–2 XXIV Corps, 0710, 6 Dec 44, XXIV Corps G–3 Jnl, 6 Dec 44.

[20] Msg, 96th Div to CG XXIV Corps, 1350, 6 Dec 44, XXIV Corps G–3 Jnl, 6 Dec 44.

talion and 157 miscellaneous troops.[21] Small units of engineering troops and a signal company were at the foot of the bluff, on the northern edge of the strip.

At 0630, the *16th Division* launched its surprise attack. Led by a Filipino,[22] the Japanese broke into the American bivouac area while the men were still asleep. Some were bayoneted while in their blankets, or before they could seize their weapons. Others held the Japanese off until they could retreat, shoeless and in their shorts and undershirts, either up the bluff to the headquarters of the V Bomber Command, or to the road, where an infantry company had come up in support.[23] The service troops were "firing at everything that moves and . . . probably inflicting casualties among our troops." [24] The Japanese from the *16th Division* entrenched themselves in the woods north of the airstrip.

Meanwhile, General Hodge ordered that the 1st Battalion, 382d Infantry, be released from the 96th Division and placed under the operational control of General Swing of the 11th Airborne Division. The battalion was to proceed immediately to the aid of the two companies of the 11th Airborne Division in the Buri airfield area. General Hodge emphasized that the area was "critical" and "must be kept closed." It would be "dangerous" to let the enemy "get into the service troops along the road and around airfields." [25] One reinforced company of the

1st Battalion was already in the area and the rest of the battalion made ready to follow.[26]

Small patrols of combat troops held the enemy forces in check. At 1030 one patrol killed seventeen Japanese north of the Buri airfield, and another killed three of the enemy west of the airstrip. The 1st Battalion of the 187th Glider Infantry was moved from the San Pablo airfield to the Buri area and went into position near the airfield.[27] By 1800 on 6 December, the enemy had been driven off the Buri airfield, though pockets of resistance still remained on the edges of the airstrip. The battalion encountered a portion of the *16th Division* east of the strip and destroyed it.[28] Forty of the enemy were known to be dead, and it was believed that as many more had also been killed.

Attack From the Sky

San Pablo Airstrip

The Japanese air transports were scheduled to be over the airfields at 1840 on 6 December, with an escort of fighter aircraft. Fighters were to neutralize the airstrips and, just before the paratroopers jumped, medium bombers were to strafe the Buri, San Pablo, and Bayug airstrips. At the same time light bombers were to hit antiaircraft positions between San Pablo and Dulag and points west. Fifty-one aircraft in all (transports, bombers, and fighters) were assigned to the operation. The transports were allotted as follows: twenty to the Buri airstrip, nine to San Pablo airstrip, six to Bayug airstrip, and two each to the Tacloban and

---

[21] Msg, 287th FA Obsn Bn to XXIV Corps, 1350, 6 Dec 44, XXIV Corps G–3 Jnl, 6 Dec 44.

[22] This man was later caught and turned over to the Filipino guerrillas.

[23] Combat History, 5th Bomber Command, 8 June 44–May 45, pp. 5–6, AAF Archives.

[24] Msg, 11th Airborne Div to XXIV Corps, 1220, 6 Dec 44, XXIV Corps G–3 Jnl, 6 Dec 44.

[25] Msg, CG XXIV Corps to CG 96th Div, 1400, 6 Dec\44, XXIV Corps G–3 Jnl, 6 Dec 44.

[26] 96th Div G–3 Periodic Rpt 47, 6 Dec 44.

[27] XXIV Corps G–2 Periodic Rpt 48, 6 Dec 44, XXIV Corps G–3 Jnl, 7 Dec 44.

[28] Flanagan, *The Angels*, p. 49.

SAN PABLO AIRSTRIP *as it appeared in 1946.*

Dulag airstrips. Each transport carried fifteen to twenty men.[29]

The Japanese parachutists were well drilled as to their mission. The operation was to be divided into five phases. The first phase was to begin with the jump-off. The men, immediately after landing, were to attack and destroy aircraft on the ground, and one element was to attack the barracks and communications. This phase was to end when the moon rose. In the second phase, ending about 2230, the troops would destroy matériel, ammunition dumps, bridges, and remaining barracks. During the third phase, from 2330 to 0300, the paratroopers were to destroy the remaining aircraft and installations. In the fourth phase, lasting from 0300 to 0600, they were to build defensive positions. In the fifth phase, from 0600 on, preparations were to be made for future operations.

There were to be three assault waves. The first wave would consist of the headquarters unit with approximately 25 men; the signal unit with 7; the *1st Company* with 100; the *2d Company* with 86; the construction company with 97; and a platoon with 50 men. The second would be composed of 9 men from the headquarters unit; the *3d Company;* the *Heavy Weapons Company;* and the signal unit. The final wave would consist of the remaining troops—about 80 men.[30]

---

[29] Air Evaluation Board, SWPA, Leyte Campaign, p. 174, AAF Archives.

[30] Msg, CG XXIV Corps to CG Sixth Army, 1440, 9 Dec 44, XXIV G–3 Jnl, 9 Dec 44; XXIV Corps G–2 Periodic Rpt 50, Incl 1, 8 Dec 44, XXIV Corps G–3 Jnl, 9 Dec 44. Both are translations of Japanese documents giving plans for the airborne attack.

Just before dark, thirty-nine Japanese transports with supporting bombers and fighters roared over the Burauen airfields. Several incendiary bombs fell on the San Pablo strip, setting a gasoline dump afire and burning a liaison plane. Approximately eighteen enemy aircraft were shot down. Parachutists began to descend from the transports. The commander of the *3d Regiment* with about 60 of his men dropped on the Buri strip, while between 250 and 300 parachutists landed near the San Pablo strip.[31]

The parachutists, immediately after landing, ran up the north and south sides of the San Pablo strip. They talked in loud tones and allegedly called out in English, "Hello—where are your machine guns?" Most of the enemy forces assembled on the north side of the airstrip. They burned three or four more liaison planes, a jeep, several tents, and another gasoline dump, throwing ammunition on the latter.

The only American troops in the area, a small detachment of the 11th Airborne Division, consisted of elements of the 127th Airborne Engineer Battalion, the signal company, Headquarters Battery of the division artillery, special troops as well as Air Corps service troops. During the night of 6–7 December, confusion reigned on the airstrip. There was uncontrolled and disorganized firing and much difficulty arose in establishing a co-ordinated command.[32]

At dawn, after most of the paratroopers had assembled on the San Pablo airfield, they moved north and west to the northern

edge of the Buri airstrip and joined elements of the *16th Division.*

At the San Pablo airstrip, Lt. Col. Douglas C. Davis, the commanding officer of the 127th Airborne Engineer Battalion, organized the miscellaneous service troops into an infantry unit to protect the San Pablo airstrip. The 674th Parachute Field Artillery Battalion, which was at the mouth of the Bito River, north of Abuyog, was to leave its guns at that place and come to the assistance of Colonel Davis' force. At daylight, the troops of the 127th Airborne Engineer Battalion moved out toward the airstrip and met the 674th Field Artillery Battalion, under Col. Lukas E. Hoska. The artillery battalion swung into line and the two units moved out as a provisional infantry regiment under Colonel Davis—the airborne engineers on the left and the artillery battalion on the right.

They encountered strong resistance to the west of the San Pablo airstrip. After advancing north of the strip, the engineers ran out of ammunition. The field artillery battalion went forward to a coconut grove, also to the north of the airstrip. The gap between the two units was closed by a strong patrol. Since the food and ammunition situation remained uncertain, the composite force went into a perimeter in defense of San Pablo strip, where it remained for the next few days.[33]

Buri Airstrip

On the night of 6–7 December, the Air Corps service personnel had abruptly quitted the Buri airfield, leaving behind carbines, rifles, grenades, small arms ammunition, and machine guns. 2d Lt. Rudolph Mamula of the 767th Tank Battalion had been or-

[31] Davidson *et al., The Deadeyes,* pp. 67–68; Flanagan, *The Angels,* pp. 40–50; 408th Airborne QM Co, Opns Rpt Leyte, pp. 10–11; CG 11th AB Div to CG XXIV Corps, 2205, 6 Dec 44, XXIV Corps G–3 Jnl, 7 Dec 44.

[32] Rpt, Capt Charles Bellows to G–3 XXIV Corps, 8 Dec 44, Investigation of Enemy Paratroopers, XXIV Corps G–3 Jnl, 8 Dec 44.

[33] 127th AB Engr Bn Opns Rpt Leyte, pp. 1–2; Flanagan, *The Angels,* p. 51.

dered to take charge of the situation, co-ordinate the action of forces on the airstrip, and recover abandoned armament and ammunition. Apparently he was unsuccessful, because later in the day the Japanese made "the best use" of the same arms and ammunition. By the middle of the morning, on 7 December, the enemy had completely occupied the Buri airstrip.

In anticipation of the landing of Japanese paratroopers, General Krueger had requested General MacArthur to release elements of the 38th Division for employment against the enemy airborne troops. The 38th Division had arrived on Leyte to stage for future operations. General Headquarters assigned the 149th Infantry to the control of the commanding general of the Sixth Army; two battalions of the 149th Infantry were in turn released on 6 December to the control of General Hodge, the commanding general of XXIV Corps, who put them under the operational control of the 11th Airborne Division for employment against parachutists in the Burauen area. The remaining battalion of the 149th Infantry was alerted for the movement in the Burauen area on twenty-four hours' notice.[34]

The 1st and 2d Battalions of the 149th Infantry, 38th Division, were alerted at 0200 on 7 December for movement to the San Pablo airstrip. The advance elements of the 1st Battalion were greeted at the San Pablo airstrip by General Swing, who is reported to have said: "Glad to see you. I am General Swing of the 11th Airborne Division. We've been having a hell of a time here. Last night approximately seventy-five Jap paratroopers dropped on us of which we have accounted for about fifty. Fifteen hundred yards from here on an azimuth of

273° is another airstrip just like this one. Between here and there are about twenty-five Jap troopers. It is now 1400. I want that strip secure by nightfall." [35]

The commanding officer of the 1st Battalion decided to attack with Companies A and C abreast, Company A on the right, with approximately a 200-yard frontage for each company. A section of heavy machine guns was attached to each unit, and a platoon of 81-mm. mortars from Company D was to support the attack from positions on the San Pablo airstrip.

Moving out at 1430, the troops covered the first 400 yards without incident but were stopped by a rain-swollen swamp. Since attempts to bypass the swamp were fruitless, the men were forced to go through it. The water was shoulder-high in places, and the companies lost contact during the crossing. Company A proceeded to the Buri airstrip, arriving there about 1630. Company C, which had been delayed by a slight skirmish with the enemy, did not arrive until about 1800. Because of the lateness of the hour and the fact that observation had shown there were "many more Japanese" on the north of the airstrip than had been estimated by General Swing, it was decided to establish perimeters for the night.[36]

By the end of 7 December the 1st Battalion, 149th Infantry, had established a toe hold on the southwestern fringe of the Buri strip. During the day the 1st Battalion, 187th Infantry, northwest of the Bayug airstrip, had received machine gun fire from an estimated enemy platoon just west of the Burauen–Dagami road. This enemy force was contained throughout the day as ad-

[34] Sixth Army Opns Rpt Leyte, p. 72.

[35] Maj Martin C. Grigg, The Operations of the 1st Battalion, 149th Infantry . . . in the Battle for the Buri Airstrip . . ., pp. 6–7, OCMH.
[36] Ibid.

vances were made southeast toward the Buri airstrip. At 1630 the 1st Battalion, 187th Infantry, and the 1st Battalion, 149th Infantry, established contact at the western end of the Buri airstrip. The 1st Battalion, 382d Infantry, 96th Division, had been placed under the control of the 11th Airborne Division. At dusk of 7 December, it took a position near the 1st Battalion, 149th Infantry.[37] At 2000 the sector was reported quiet. It was impossible to estimate the total number of American and Japanese casualties for the day, but it was believed to be large.[38]

During the night of 7–8 December, the Japanese brought forward two machine guns and emplaced them directly in front of Company A of the 1st Battalion, 382d Infantry. At dawn the machine guns opened up. Their low, grazing fire pinned down the company, but Pfc. Warren G. Perkins, in the face of enemy bullets, located the guns and called mortar fire upon the site. The mortar concentration, falling within fifty yards of Perkins, silenced the machine guns and startled the Japanese. Pvt. Ova A. Kelley took advantage of the confusion and charged with his M1 rifle and a carbine. Kelley killed eight of the enemy before he himself was slain.[39] The rest of Company A followed Kelley and secured the edge of the airstrip where it set up a perimeter. During 8 December the Americans consolidated their positions.

At 1045 on 9 December the 1st Battalion, 149th Infantry, attacked north with Companies A, B, and C on a line. The companies got across the airstrip but then came under fire from Japanese weapons emplaced on high ground to the north. The 1st Battalion therefore withdrew to the southern edge of the strip. During the day it had killed fifty of an enemy force estimated to consist of two hundred men. The 2d Battalion remained in position throughout the day.[40]

At twilight the assault companies of the 1st Battalion, 382d Infantry, were sent out in various directions to locate enemy patrols said to be converging upon the airfield. Only a few mortar men and headquarters personnel were left behind to guard the perimeters. At midnight approximately 150 Japanese attacked. The headquarters and service troops with rifle fire, together with the mortar men, stopped the charge. They killed fifty of the enemy and suffered seven casualties.[41]

On 10 December, after a half-hour artillery concentration, the 1st Battalion, 149th Infantry, attacked with Companies A and C abreast, and Company B in the rear. After the 1st Battalion had pushed north 300 yards across the airstrip, Companies A and C moved northwest while Company B went to the northeast. The companies cleared the airfield area of individual riflemen and destroyed small pockets of enemy resistance. The 1st Battalion went into perimeter at 1700 on the Buri airstrip. The 2d Battalion remained in position throughout the day.[42]

At 1930 the Japanese launched their final concentrated attack against the airfields. They began to fire at the administration buildings of the Fifth Air Force, and some of the bullets went through the plywood walls of the house of Maj. Gen. Ennis C. Whitehead. "The General ducked a bullet, ordered

---

[37] Davidson et al., The Deadeyes, p. 67.

[38] Rpt, Capt Charles Bellows to G–2 XXIV Corps, 8 Dec 44, Investigation of Enemy Paratroopers, XXIV Corps G–3 Jnl, 8 Dec 44.

[39] Private Kelley was posthumously awarded the Medal of Honor.

[40] 149th Inf S–3 Periodic Rpt, 9 Dec 44, 149th Inf Opns Rpt Leyte.

[41] Davidson et al., The Deadeyes, p. 69.

[42] 149th Infantry S–3 Periodic Rpt, 1800, 10 Dec 44, 149th Inf Opns Rpt Leyte.

someone to find out who the blankety-blank was responsible and that he'd blankety-blank better stop or think up a blankety-blank good reason." [43]

A staff officer immediately started to investigate the situation. He got Lt. Col. Paul V. Kaessner of the 8th Aviation Signal Battalion on the telephone. The following conversation is reported to have ensued:

"Colonel," he said sternly, "you've got to stop that promiscuous firing down there immediately!"

"Like to, sir," answered the colonel, "but the Japs . . ."

"Japs," shouted the staff officer, "that can't be Japs. That fire is coming from our fifties."

"That's right . . . and the Japs are doing the shooting!"

"Where in the hell did the Japs get our machine guns?"

"How in hell should I know, sir?"

"The bullets are coming right through the general's quarters."

"Tell the general to get down on the floor. Incidentally, that yelling you hear is a Banzai raid on our mess hall." [44]

The air force personnel were pushed back until they reached the hospital, where they halted and held. They then counterattacked and drove the enemy away from the area. The Japanese left thirty of their dead behind them.

This action was the last major effort of the Japanese against the Burauen airfields. Only a little more than a battalion of the *26th Division,* which was to have assisted the *16th Division,* managed to reach the airstrips, and it had arrived in a very disorganized condition. Immediately afterward, General Suzuki, the commanding general of the *35th Army,* learned that the 77th Division had landed just below Ormoc on the eastern coast of Ormoc Bay. Since Ormoc was the southern entrance to Ormoc Valley, it was highly important that the town be defended at all costs. General Suzuki therefore ordered that the operations against the Burauen airfields be discontinued and that all troops repair to Ormoc Valley. The return through the mountains was difficult. Nearly all organization was lost, and the Japanese made their way back through the mountains as scattered individuals. [45]

The air transports allotted to Tacloban were destroyed by antiaircraft fire, while those destined for Dulag crash-landed, killing all their occupants. [46]

The Japanese had failed to achieve any major objective. Though they had destroyed minor fuel and supply dumps and a few American aircraft, delayed airfield construction, and isolated Fifth Air Force headquarters for five days, they had not appreciably delayed the Leyte operation. [47]

The Japanese attempt to take the initiative away from the Americans had failed. The Sixth Army was at the northern and southern entrances to Ormoc Valley. Elements of the X Corps had been battering for a long time at the northern portal. With the capture of Ormoc, the XXIV Corps had sprung the lock on the southern doorway and was in a position to drive north and thus relieve some of the pressure being exerted against the X Corps.

The arrival of the XXIV Corps at the entrance to Ormoc Valley brought the critical logistical situation on the island of Leyte to the fore. The tenuous supply line already had been stretched very thin, and, with the 77th Division extending its lines, a strong possibility existed that it might snap altogether.

[43] Maj Herbert O. Johansen, "Banzai at Burauen," *Air Force,* Vol. 28, No. 3, March 1945, p. 7.

[44] *Ibid.*

[45] Japanese Studies, 11, p. 86, OCMH.

[46] Air Evaluation Board, SWPA, Leyte Campaign, p. 174, AAF Archives.

[47] *Ibid.*

CHAPTER XVIII

Logistics

The conquest of Leyte was taking longer than had been anticipated. The decision of the Japanese to make Leyte the decisive battleground of the Philippines had forced the Americans to commit not only the reserve 32d and 77th Infantry Divisions but also the 112th Cavalry Regimental Combat Team, the 11th Airborne Division, and elements of the 38th Infantry Division. The inability of the Americans to establish considerable land-based air forces on Leyte, as well as the unexpected Japanese reinforcement program, had retarded the campaign. Not only was the timetable of future operations in the Pacific upset, but a strong possibility existed that it would not be feasible to establish a major logistical and air base on the island—the primary purpose of the operation.

The construction program on Leyte was hampered by conflicting priorities and, as had been foreseen, very poor terrain, bad weather conditions, and a shortage of service personnel.

Construction

Retelling the disagreements and describing the conflicts that arose over the ever-changing needs of the Army, Navy, and Air Forces would be involved, tedious, and unprofitable. But the progress of the construction program must be recounted, since it had direct bearing not only on the Leyte Campaign but also on the Mindoro and Luzon operations.

Airfields

The importance of the development of the airfields cannot be overemphasized. The inability of the Sixth Army to meet its construction dates on the airstrips, because of poor soil conditions and heavy rains, prevented the U. S. forces from stopping the flow of Japanese reinforcements and made it impossible for the Allied Air Forces to give sufficient land-based air support to the ground troops. It also forced a postponement of the Mindoro operation. It is well, therefore, to summarize just what had been accomplished in airfield construction.

Work on the Tacloban airstrip had been handicapped at first by the heavy concentration of troops, supplies, and equipment in the area during the early stages of the operation. Thereafter, work was further hampered by the insufficient supply of coral for surfacing the runway and by the very heavy traffic concentrated on the haul road because of the necessity for unloading cargo over White Beach. By 25 December, 1 runway, 50 dispersal areas, 536,000 square feet of alert apron, 1 diagonal taxiway, 1 parallel dispersal taxiway, and 8,943 feet of additional dispersal taxiways had been constructed.

OPERATIONAL LOSSES AT THE BURAUEN AIRFIELDS *forced their abandonment and the construction of the field at Tanauan.*

The Dulag airfield was located on the flat flood plain of the Marabang River. The difficulties encountered were numerous: time lost because of excessive rains that amounted to thirty-five inches in forty days; air alerts; very poor drainage, which required the construction of a system of dragline trenches to the river; and very poor access roads. The access roads required an excessive expenditure of time, labor, and material in order to maintain traffic to the airfield. One runway, 2 alert areas with gravel surface and 2 with mat surface, 1 matted transport parking area, 133 dispersal areas, and 24,200 feet of dispersal taxiways were constructed by 25 December.

In the latter part of November all construction work was stopped on the three air-

fields in the Burauen area, but not before considerable time and effort had been expended in futile attempts to make the airfields usable.[1] Since these airfields could not be made serviceable, General Krueger received permission from General MacArthur to construct an airfield in the Tanauan area, and moved his headquarters from Tanauan to Tologosa on 28 November in order that construction might be started. The new site had a good sandy surface, its drainage was satisfactory, and it proved to be an excellent location for an airfield. By 16 December the field became operational, and by the 25th there had been completed 1 runway with mat surfacing, 1 overrun, 90,000 square feet of warm-up area, 120,000 square feet of

[1] Sixth Army Opns Rpt Leyte, p. 233.

alert apron, 1 parallel taxiway, and 26 large dispersal areas.[2]

Roads

The rehabilitation of roads presented problems as vexatious as those in airfield construction. In southern Leyte Valley, the road that ran from Dulag through Burauen to Dagami soon became impassable for about two miles on each side of Burauen. This section of the road was completely rebuilt by dumping approximately three feet of gravel over it. The remainder of the road was kept open most of the time by permitting only one-way traffic. The other roads were just as bad. After heavy rains the road in the Army Service Command area was frequently under at least two feet of water. The streets in Tacloban disintegrated so rapidly that much engineer effort was required to keep them open. Such maintenance was necessary to assure continued operation of the many supply and administrative facilities located in the city.[3] The roads on the west coast were, if possible, even worse. Upkeep of the roads in general required a "profligate expenditure of engineer troops." It was found that a battalion could accomplish no more in a month than a platoon could have carried out in a week under good weather conditions. The roads required a rock or gravel foundation one to three feet thick, whereas a road-metal surface of three to four inches on an earth base was normally adequate. Since priority was given to work on the principal roads and airfields, the construction of access roads, as well as hardstands for hospitals, depots, and other needed installations was greatly delayed. In

this connection General Krueger stated: "This, in turn, greatly affected the supply situation, including construction materials, by lack of access to the depots, lack of storage space into which to discharge ships, and lack of facilities and spare parts to permit repair and servicing of engineer heavy equipment as well as other critical transportation and combat vehicles."[4]

On 21 December General Krueger estimated that after the elimination of certain projects on which informal agreements had been reached, the extent of completion by 5 January of the other projects would be as follows: main supply roads, 50 percent; access roads, 20 percent; Air Forces installations (exclusive of air depot and assembly plants), 44 percent; hospitals, 40 percent; base supply and services, 25 percent; oil and aviation gasoline storage (exclusive of naval oil storage which had not been started), 50 percent; Navy installations, 20 percent; and headquarters construction, 40 percent.[5] The gloomy prognostications of Sixth Army engineers had proven all too true.

Supplies

Inland Movement of Supplies

As the roads on Leyte became more and more unserviceable, greater reliance was placed on the use of naval vessels to transport supplies and personnel to various parts of the island. The Transportation Section, Sixth Army, maintained a small-boat pool that was used extensively to transport light cargo and personnel between Tacloban, San Ricardo, Palo, Tanauan, Tolosa, Dulag, and

---

[2] *Ibid.,* pp. 69, 233.
[3] *Ibid.,* p. 233.

[4] Ltr, CG Sixth Army to CINCSWPA, sub: Construction Program, 21 Dec 44, Sixth Army G-4 Jnl, 24 Dec 41.
[5] *Ibid.*

APPROACH ROAD TO QUARTERMASTER SERVICE CENTER *at Tacloban after a heavy rain (above). The 7th Cavalry motor pool on 17 December 1944 (below).*

TABLE 2—SHIPPING TONNAGE DISCHARGED IN LEYTE–SAMAR AREA, 28 OCTOBER–25 DECEMBER 1944

Period	Tonnage Discharge	Average Daily Rate of Discharge	Lighterage on Hand			
			LCT's	LCM's	DUKW's	Barges
Total	571,350					
28 Oct–3 Nov	33,901	4,843	11	54	107	18
4 Nov–10 Nov	32,421	4,632	35	63	315	33
11 Nov–17 Nov	141,238	20,177	26	69	219	33
18 Nov–24 Nov	110,494	15,785	18	59	253	39
25 Nov–1 Dec	47,744	6,821	28	71	289	38
2 Dec–8 Dec	56,786	8,112	24	53	297	43
9 Dec–15 Dec	53,387	7,627	21	53	294	42
16 Dec–22 Dec	68,677	9,811	39	68	300	49
23 Dec–25 Dec	26,702	8,900	39	69	287	49

Source: G–4 Report, Sixth Army Operations Report Leyte, p. 218.

Catmon Hill.[6] LCM's were widely employed on the northern and eastern coasts of the island and LSM's operated on the west coast.[7] (Table 2)

The troops that were fighting in the mountains were frequently supplied by air-drops by the 11th Air Cargo Resupply Squadron from supplies that were available in the Leyte area. From about the middle of November until the latter part of December, 1,167,818 pounds of supplies were either dropped or delivered by air. (Table 3) Two hundred and eighty-two plane loads of supplies were dropped, a total of 2,776 parachutes being used. Because of the nature of the terrain and the proximity of the Japanese, the proportion of airdropped supplies that could be recovered varied from 65 to 90 percent. Approximately 60 percent of the parachutes were recovered and returned to the 11th Air Cargo Resupply Squadron.[8]

Supplying the West Coast

The landing of the 77th Division on the west coast of Leyte brought into sharper focus the difficult job of giving adequate logistical support to the tactical units. The Sixth Army supply lines were tenuous. There was a shortage of shipping, and furnishing supplies to the troops fighting in the mountains was especially difficult.

In planning for the amphibious movement of the 77th Division, the resupply shipping set up for the division was as follows: on 9 December, two days after the division's landing at Deposito, 12 LSM's and 4 LCI's would bring in supplies; on 11 December, 12 LSM's and 5 LCI's would bring in additional supplies; and on 13 December 12 LSM's and 4 LCI's would carry further supplies to the division. Thereafter, 3 LSM's would be assigned the task of supplying the 77th Division.[9]

---

[6] Rpt of Transportation Off, Sixth Army Opns Rpt Leyte, p. 270.

[7] *Ibid.*

[8] G–4 Rpt, Sixth Army Opns Rpt Leyte, p. 218.

[9] Msg, G–3 XXIV Corps to G–4 XXIV Corps, n. d. (probably 4 Dec 44), XXIV Corps G–4 Jnl, Annex, Vol. III.

TABLE 3—AIRDROPS BY 11TH AIR CARGO RESUPPLY SQUADRON, 11 NOVEMBER–25 DECEMBER 1944

Branch	Supplies	Weight in Pounds	Percent of Total
Total		1, 167, 818	100. 0
Quartermaster	Rations	445, 916	38. 3
	Miscellaneous	357, 061	30. 4
Ordnance	Ammunition	337, 761	28. 9
Medical	Supply and Equipment	21, 308	1. 8
Signal	Supply and Equipment	4, 546	0. 4
Chemical	Chemical Warfare Supplies	1, 226	0. 2

Units Supplied	Weight	Percent of Total
Total	1, 167, 818	100. 0
11th Airborne Division	388, 570	33. 3
1st Cavalry Division	301, 058	25. 8
32d Infantry Division	167, 859	14. 3
24th Infantry Division	126, 004	10. 7
Guerrillas	91, 054	8. 7
96th Infantry Division	52, 973	4. 2
77th Infantry Division	14, 800	1. 1
112th Cavalry Regiment	10, 300	0. 8
7th Infantry Division	4, 200	0. 3
Others	11, 000	0. 8

Source: Report of Transportation Officer, Sixth Army Operations Report Leyte, p. 271.

The Japanese had sunk two LSM's near Baybay on 4 December and damaged several other vessels during the Deposito landing.[10] Because of the extreme shortage of shipping that resulted, General Hodge suggested to General Bruce on 8 December that thirty trucks, which had been scheduled for delivery on the first two convoys of resupply shipping, be sent overland along the Abuyog–Baybay mountain road and used to shuttle supplies of the division between the two towns. These supplies could be sent forward to the 77th Division when its beach-head merged with that of the 7th Division.[11] On the following day the first resupply for the 77th division left Abuyog in a convoy of trucks which went over the mountains to Baybay, where LCM's took the cargo and moved it to the area of the 77th Division.[12]

At 2100 on 10 December, General Hodge notified General Bruce that the second echelon of resupply was to arrive at 2359 on the following day at any beach that General Bruce desired. The supplies consisted of

[10] Sixth Army Opns Rpt Leyte, p. 79.

[11] Msg, CG XXIV Corps to CG 77th Div, 8 Dec 44, XXIV Corps G–4 Jnl, Annex, Vol. III.

[12] Msg, CG XXIV Corps to Col Gillette, 9 Dec 44, XXIV Corps G–4 Jnl, Annex, Vol. III.

40,000 rations, 1,000 gallons of 80-octane gasoline, 500 gallons of diesel oil, 100 tons of ammunition, and 10 tons of medical supplies. Certain tactical and service units were also to be sent forward. The third echelon, which was scheduled to arrive on the west coast on the night of 14–15 December, was to consist of the remaining units of the 77th Division and "considerable resupply." [13]

As the tide of battle swept the 77th Division farther northward, its line of supply and that of the 7th Division became very thin. About 15 December the supply officer of the XXIV Corps summarized the situation to the corps chief of staff. Between 19 and 25 December three resupply echelons, consisting of twenty-four LSM's and five LCI's carrying 3,250 tons of supplies, were to arrive on the west coast. He believed this amount was insufficient. According to his calculations, the daily requirements for two divisions in heavy fighting were 500 tons of supplies. He estimated that the supplies of the 77th Division could not last beyond 18 December. By 19 December the division would be in short supply unless 100 truck loads of supplies could be sent over the mountains before that time. The convoy that was to go forward on the 19th would carry only two days' supplies and there would be a three-day interval before the arrival of the next convoy. The XXIV Corps, therefore, was faced with the problem of moving 200 truck loads of supplies during those three days merely to keep even. After 25 December, one and a half days' supply would be sent overwater every three days. Since the supply officer of the XXIV Corps had strong

doubts that the road would stand "a movement involving 300 trucks every three days" it was believed that the supply situation would steadily worsen. [14]

On 15 December General Krueger sent a radio message to Admiral Kinkaid reviewing the critical supply situation and requesting that sufficient amphibious shipping be made available immediately to carry supplies to the forces on the west coast. Admiral Kinkaid acquiesced, and on 22 December a resupply convoy arrived at Ormoc with "sufficient supplies and equipment to alleviate the critical situation." [15]

By 26 December a general level of five to ten days' supply of all classes had been built up, a level that was maintained throughout the rest of the operation. The XXIV Corps utilized to the maximum the available space on the LSM convoys, and units on the west coast employed all available motor transportation to supplement the tonnage on the convoys. Finally, the supplies were pooled in dumps at Ipil and Ormoc and then allotted to the units.

On 25 December General Hodge received a Christmas message from his supply officer: "Best wishes for Merry Xmas and a New Year filled with supplies, resupplies, more supplies and no supply worries." [16]

The serious logistical situation was to affect definitely the progress of the Sixth Army as it fought its way into Ormoc Valley—the last important enemy stronghold on the island.

_____

[14] Memo, G–4 XXIV Corps to CofS XXIV Corps, n.d. (probably 15 Dec 44), XXIV Corps G–4 Jnl, Annex, Vol. IV.
[15] Sixth Army Opns Rpt Leyte, p. 80.
[16] XXIV Corps G–4 Jnl, 25 Dec 44.

_____

[13] Msg, CG XXIV Corps to CG 77th Div, 10 Dec 44, XXIV Corps G–4 Jnl, Annex, Vol. III.

CHAPTER XIX

The Entrances to Ormoc Valley

General Bruce's quick exploitation of the surprise landing of the 77th Division just below Ormoc had resulted in the capture of Ormoc on 10 December. With each successive advance, he had displaced his entire division forward. General Bruce, as he phrased it, preferred to "drag his tail up the beach." [1]

With the seizure of Ormoc, General Krueger's Sixth Army had driven the main elements of the Japanese *35th Army* into Ormoc Valley. The Japanese were caught in the jaws of a trap—the 1st Cavalry Division and the 32d Infantry Division were closing in from the north and the 77th Infantry Division from the south. General Krueger ordered the X and XXIV Corps to close this trap upon the Japanese.

Southern Entrance to Ormoc Valley

Japanese Plans

When General Suzuki, the commander of the Japanese *35th Army,* ordered the action against the Burauen airfields, his anticipations had been high. Accompanied by his chief of staff and six other staff officers, he had gone to the headquarters of the *26th Division,* in the mountains near Lubi, in

order to supervise the operation personally. General Tomochika, the deputy chief of staff, remained at Ormoc because of the advance of the Americans up the west coast, and took command of operations in the area.

A mixed battalion, consisting of four companies, reinforced the *12th Independent Infantry Regiment.* This regiment, under Colonel Imahori, was to be prepared at a moment's notice for action in the Ormoc sector.[2] The *16th* and *26th Divisions* received orders to retreat westward and establish defensive positions in the Ormoc Valley. The *16th Division,* which had less than 200 men, had ceased to exist as a fighting unit. The Japanese decided that henceforward their operations would be strictly defensive. The *26th Division* started to withdraw through the mountains, but its orders to retreat were very hard to carry out. The Americans had blocked the road, and the 11th Airborne Division units, which had advanced west from Burauen, were attacking in the vicinity of Lubi. As a result, the staff officers of General Suzuki's *35th Army* "disbanded and scattered." General Suzuki passed through the American lines and reached the command post at Huaton, four miles north of Ormoc, on 13 December; his chief of staff arrived there the following day. As for the *26th Division,* "all contact with

---

[1] Maj Charles V. McLaughlin, Operations of the XXIV Corps in the Invasion of Leyte Island, pp. 29–30. Advanced Infantry Officers' Course, 1947–48, Infantry School, Ft. Benning, Ga.

[2] *35th Army* Opns, p. 86.

the Division was lost by Army Headquarters until the early part of March." [3]

In the meantime General Tomochika had prepared new plans. On 6 December he was told by a staff officer of the *1st Division,* which was fighting the 32d Division in the north, that the *1st Division* had "reached the stage of collapse." [4] The mission of the *1st Division* was then changed to one of defense. Colonel Imahori by the night of 7 December had sent two companies south. [5] These companies, known as the *Kamijo Battalion,* were destroyed at Ipil by the 77th Division in its march to Ormoc. Colonel Imahori, fearful that the rest of his detachment would suffer the same fate, ordered his main force, the *Tateishi* and *Maeda Battalions,* to construct positions north of Ormoc. The remnants of the *Kamijo Battalion* established a position northeast of Ormoc. In his plan for the parachute attack on the Burauen airfields, General Suzuki had decided to use as a part of his attacking force the *4th Air Raiding Landing Unit.* In view of the unfavorable situation that had developed, the *14th Area Army* commander, General Yamashita, decided that after the *4th Air Raiding Landing Unit* landed at the Valencia airfield it was to be kept in the Ormoc area. From 8 to 13 December approximately 500 men from the unit arrived in the Ormoc area, '

and were attached to the *Imahori Detachment.* They had traveled only at dawn or dusk to avoid detection.

At the same time, "in order to ease the difficult Leyte Island Operation," General Yamashita dispatched from Luzon to assist the troops in the Ormoc sector the *Takahashi Detachment,* composed of the *5th Infantry Regiment* of the *8th Division,* an artillery battalion, a company of engineers, a transportation company, and a *Special Naval Landing Force* of 400 men with four light tanks and sixteen trench mortars. In order to suppress the guerrillas, who were active in the Camotes Islands off the west coast of Leyte and who were guarding the entrance to Ormoc Bay, the area army commander ordered a detachment, known as the *Camotes Detachment,* to those islands. This detachment was composed of one battalion (less two companies) of the *58th Independent Mixed Brigade,* an artillery battery, and an engineering platoon.

The transports carrying the troops to the Ormoc area underwent a severe aerial bombardment from American aircraft. As a consequence, only the *Special Naval Landing Force* arrived at its target. On the same day the transports carrying the *Takahashi* and *Camotes Detachments* were forced to put in at Palompon on the west coast. The subsequent advance of these detachments toward Ormoc was greatly delayed.

On 9 December the *77th Infantry Regiment,* the last of the Japanese reinforcements for Leyte, landed at Palompon and moved to Matagob. General Suzuki intended to assemble and integrate these units and to launch a counteroffensive against Ormoc starting on 17 December. [6]

---

[3] Tomochika, True Facts of Leyte Opn, p. 25; *14th Area Army* Opns Leyte, p. 13.

[4] Tomochika, True Facts of Leyte Opn, p. 25.

[5] General Tomochika was unqualified in his praise of the commander of the *Imahori Detachment.* He said, "Colonel Imahori had good personality and was a good leader. His subordinates were willing to join the suicide squads when the American forces increased in number. We did not have any worries about the attacking Americans on this detachment's front because the suicide squads brought good results . . . *Ibid.,* pp. 19–20.

[6] *35th Army* Opns, pp. 87–89.

HEAVY MACHINE GUNS COVER CROSSING *of the Antilao River by men of the 77th Division at Ormoc.*

Cogon Defenses

On 10 December General Bruce devised a new scheme of maneuver: the 77th Division was to break loose from its base and use Indian warfare or blockhouse tactics. At night each "fort" was to establish an all-round defense from any Japanese night attacks. In the daytime, an armed convoy was to go "from fort to fort." The Filipino guerrillas were to guard the bridges and furnish intelligence.[7]

By nightfall of 10 December the 77th Division had cleared Ormoc. (*See Map 17.*) The front lines of the 307th Infantry were on the western outskirts of the town along the bank of the Antilao River, a stream which flows past the entire western side of Ormoc. At the city's northern edge the river is crossed by Highway 2, which then proceeds directly north about 300 yards west of the river and parallel to it for a distance of about 1,000 yards. The 306th Infantry on the right of the 307th Infantry had come abreast of that regiment at twilight.

General Bruce's plan for 11 December provided for a limited attack north to enable the division to straighten out its lines. The 305th Infantry in the afternoon would come between the 306th Infantry on the right and the 307th Infantry on the left. The 305th Infantry was to be prepared to attack on the morning of 12 December with battalions abreast, one on each side of the highway.[8]

---

[7] Ltr, Gen Bruce to Gen Ward, 16 Aug 51, OCMH.

[8] 77th Div G–3 Jnl, 11 Dec 44.

At 0930 on 11 December the 306th and 307th Infantry Regiments jumped off with the 307th Infantry on the left. The assault battalions of the 307th Infantry and the 1st Battalion, 306th Infantry, attempted to cross the Antilao River but came under heavy fire and were pinned down.

The fire came from a well-fortified position of the *12th Independent Infantry Regiment* on the north bank of the river at Cogon, a small barrio on Highway 2 just north of Ormoc. The enemy position was on a small elevated plateau, adjacent to Highway 2, overlooking the river to the south and rice paddies to the east and west. Innumerable spider holes had been constructed throughout the area. The principal defensive position, slightly east of Cogon, was in the vicinity of a three-story reinforced concrete building that had been converted into a blockhouse. The well-camouflaged positions, with the exception of the fortress, were so situated in the underbrush and the waist-high cogon grass that it was impossible to detect them at a distance of more than ten feet. From these positions the Japanese could command the bridge over the Antilao River and deny the U. S. troops the use of Highway 2 to the north. An estimated reinforced battalion with machine guns, antitank guns, and field pieces, together with small arms, defended the area.

The artillery fired on the enemy front lines, which were only twenty-five yards in front of the American assault troops, but failed to dislodge the Japanese. The assault battalions of the 307th Infantry and the 1st Battalion, 306th Infantry, thereupon delivered point-blank fire from their tank destroyer guns, amphibian tank guns, light and medium machine guns, and infantry weapons on the Japanese position but still could not overcome it. The lack of shipping

had prevented the division from taking its medium tanks with it. Unable to move forward, the battalions established their front lines and perimeters for the night along a line just north of Ormoc.

On the division's right, the 3d Battalion, 306th Infantry, moved forward against increasingly strong resistance from the *12th Independent Infantry Regiment*. After advancing about 1,000 yards the 3d Battalion encountered a well-entrenched position. Elements of the *12th Independent Infantry Regiment* had dug in on a steep ridge in front of which was a deep ravine. Eight hundred yards of rice paddies lay between this position and the one opposing the other battalions, though both positions were part of the same defensive system. The artillery placed fire upon the ridge. Although able to utilize only a company and a half against the enemy position, the 3d Battalion, under cover of the artillery fire, attacked and succeeded in gaining a foothold on the ridge. The *12th Independent Infantry Regiment* at the same time directed two unsuccessful counterattacks against the right flank and rear of the 3d Battalion. Since the forward elements on the ridge were vulnerable and any further advance would have exposed both flanks of the 3d Battalion, the commanding officer of the 306th Infantry at 1600 ordered the 3d Battalion to withdraw the forward units on the enemy-held ridge and consolidate its position.[9]

At 1600 the 2d and 3d Battalions, 305th Infantry, moved north of Ormoc and took up the position held by the 1st Battalion, 306th Infantry, between the 307th Infantry

---

[9] 77th Div G–2 Periodic Rpt 15, 11 Dec 44; Company A, 88th Chemical Bn, Jnl, 10 Dec 44; 306th Inf Opns Rpt Leyte, p. 8; 77th Div Opns Rpt Leyte, p. 18; 307th Inf Opns Rpt Leyte, p. 5; 77th Div G–3 Jnl, 11 Dec 44; 77th Div G–3 Periodic Rpt 17, 12 Dec 44.

on the left and the 3d Battalion, 306th Infantry, on the right. The relieved battalion was ordered to take a position to reinforce the 2d and 3d Battalions, 306th Infantry. The 1st Battalion, 305th Infantry, remained just south of Camp Downes as the extreme right flank of the 77th Division.[10]

In his plan for the drive of the XXIV Corps up Ormoc Valley, General Hodge ordered the 7th Division to "continue the attack as directed and coordinated" by General Bruce.[11] To strengthen the Ormoc defenses, elements of the 7th Division were scheduled to be brought forward. General Bruce planned to attack daily towards Valencia, which was about six and a half miles north of Ormoc. The 77th Division would eventually cut loose from the Ormoc defenses and take up each night an all-round defense. The supply convoy, protected by strong guards, would move along Highway 2 and measure its advance by that of the assault units. The 305th Infantry was to proceed along Highway 2 and the 306th Infantry, while protecting the division right flank, was to be prepared to proceed 2,000 to 3,000 yards east of Highway 2, move north through the hills to a point due east of Valencia, and then turn west across Highway 2 and capture that town. The 307th Infantry, while protecting the division left flank, was to be prepared to relieve the 305th Infantry. The artillery of the division at the outset was to support the advance from Ormoc and eventually move with the forward element of the 77th Division when the latter cut loose from the Ormoc sector.[12]

---

[10] 305th Inf Opns Rpt Leyte, p. 2; 306th Inf Opns Rpt Leyte, p. 8; 77th Div Opns Rpt Leyte, p. 18; 77th Div G–3 Periodic Rpt 17, 12 Dec 44.
[11] XXIV Corps FO 33, 4 Dec 44.
[12] Ltr, CG 77th Div to CG XXIV Corps, sub: Future Plans, 11 Dec 44, 77th Div G–3 Jnl, 12 Dec 44.

Enemy Night Landings

At 2330 on 11 December the 77th Division beach defense units observed a Japanese convoy, which was transporting the *Special Naval Landing Force*, steaming into Ormoc Bay with the apparent intention of landing at Ormoc. The Japanese evidently thought that Ormoc was still in their hands. The first craft noticed by the U.S. forces was a landing barge with about fifty men, heading directly for the Ormoc pier. By the time the barge came within range of the shore weapons, all shore units were alert and waited with guns trained upon it. They withheld their fire until the barge was within fifty yards of the pier and then all weapons converged their fires upon the craft. The first rounds squarely hit the barge, which immediately burst into flames. The Japanese clambered atop the gunwales and are reported to have screamed, "Don't shoot," under the mistaken notion that their forces still occupied Ormoc.

The harbor was lit up by the burning barge and 60-mm. illuminating shells. During the night the Americans discovered that another enemy vessel, about the size of an LST, had pulled into shore northwest of the town under cover of darkness and was busily engaged in discharging troops and equipment. The tank destroyer guns of the 307th Infantry, emplaced along the beach within 1,000 yards of the vessel, opened fire on it while forward observers from the 902d Field Artillery Battalion directed artillery fire upon the landing area and inland. The enemy vessel attempted to pull out to sea, but after proceeding less than fifty yards it burst into flames and sank. About 150 men, two tanks, a number of rifles, mortars, and machine guns, and a quantity of ammunition had been unloaded before the vessel sank, but most of the supplies, including four ammunition trucks, had been destroyed by American fire while the vessel was unloading.

The early dawn of 12 December revealed another ship of the same type farther west near Linao. The artillery, mortars, and tank destroyer guns opened up against this vessel as it fled along the shores of Ormoc Bay, and their fire followed until it was out of range. Before the fire ceased, heavy clouds of smoke billowed from the vessel as it moved at a snail's pace. During the night the American fire had to be closely co-ordinated, since American vessels, including a resupply convoy, were in the bay. Not a single U. S. craft was damaged.

Troops of the *Special Naval Landing Force* who had disembarked got in touch with Colonel Imahori, who immediately ordered them to go to Highway 2 as the reserve unit of the *12th Independent Infantry Regiment*. It was impossible for them to carry out the order, since the 77th Division had advanced north from Ormoc. They thereupon decided to join a naval airfield construction unit at Valencia, but again they failed. In the latter part of December, the men of the *Special Naval Landing Force* were in the eastern part of the Palompon area without having taken part in the battle for the Ormoc corridor.[13]

Battle of the Blockhouse

Because the fighting on the previous day had been extremely intense, General Bruce on 12 December consolidated his positions and brought forward supplies and supporting artillery. The front-line units sent out strong combat and reconnaissance patrols to

the front and flanks to secure information on the dispositions of the Japanese.[14] Throughout the day and night the artillery battalions of the division placed harassing and interdiction fires on the enemy positions across the Antilao River.[15]

The 902d and 305th Field Artillery Battalions, two batteries of the 304th Field Artillery Battalion, and one battery of 155-mm. howitzers from the 306th Field Artillery Battalion fired continuously for five minutes on the morning of 13 December at the enemy position in front of the 305th Infantry. So intense was the fire that the enemy soldiers were bewildered and streamed toward the front lines of the division where they were cut down in great numbers by machine gun and small arms fire. The Japanese in and around the concrete building, however, lay low and weathered the barrage.

General Bruce attached Col. Paul L. Freeman, an observer from the War Department General Staff, to the 305th Infantry. Colonel Freeman was made the commander of a special attack force, consisting of Companies E and L, which was to storm the blockhouse. The 305th Infantry, which was to make the main effort, had the 3d Battalion on the right of Highway 2 and the 2d and 1st Battalions on the left of the road. The 3d Battalion in a column of companies moved out at 0830. In support of the 305th Infantry, the 2d Platoon, Company A, 88th Chemical Battalion, fired on and silenced two enemy machine guns. The Japanese held their fire until the infantrymen were upon them, making it necessary for the artillery to fire at very close range. The fire from the 305th Field Artillery Battalion came to

---

[13] 77th Div Opns Rpt Leyte, pp. 18–19; 305th Inf Opns Rpt Leyte, p. 5; *35th Army Opns,* p 8.

[14] 77th Div G–2 Jnl, 13 Dec 44.
[15] 77th Div Opns Rpt Leyte, p. 20.

within fifty yards of the American front lines.

After Company I, the lead company, reached the ridge at 0925, K Company moved up and attempted to consolidate the 3d Battalion's position by making an oblique turn to the right flank of Company I. It was hit at 1155 by the first of five counterattacks by the *12th Independent Infantry Regiment*. The enemy preceded the infantry assault by artillery, mortar, and automatic weapons fire. The 3d Battalion estimated the enemy force to be a reinforced battalion. All of the counterattacks were driven off with heavy casualties on both sides.

The 2d Battalion, 305th Infantry, on the left of the highway, jumped off at 0830 in a column of companies, Company F leading. At 0845 the troops ran into concentrated automatic weapons fire, which pinned them down. Company G moved around the left flank of Company F and also came under heavy fire. A Japanese force estimated as two reinforced companies opposed Companies F and G. With the right flank of Company F on the blockhouse, the 2d Battalion pivoted on this point until the line ran in a generally northern direction from the blockhouse and faced toward the east. The 1st Battalion faced north and tied in with the 307th Infantry on its left. Colonel Freeman's special attack force was unable to move forward. The 3d Battalion held the commanding ground east of Highway 2. The battalions of the 305th Infantry arranged co-ordinating fires that covered all open spaces.[16]

The 307th Infantry moved westward along the Ormoc–Linao road to forestall any enemy reinforcements and counterat-

tacks from that direction. The troops encountered few Japanese. The 307th Infantry in its advance of 1,000 yards took the barrio of Linao and captured three artillery pieces and two antiaircraft guns, as well as ammunition for those weapons.[17]

The 306th Infantry, protecting the right flank of the 305th, received no opposition during the day but assisted the attack of the 305th Infantry by fire. Patrols of the 306th Infantry explored the area in the vicinity of Donghol, about two miles northeast of Ormoc, but made no contact with the enemy.[18]

Although the 77th Division had extended its western boundary during the day by about 1,000 yards, the front lines in the center remained generally where they had been in the morning. The 1st and 2d Platoons of Company A, 88th Chemical Battalion, laid a continuous smoke screen in front of the troops from 0930 to 1630, enabling the aid men to remove the wounded from the front lines and carry them to the rear.[19]

During the night of 13–14 December the artillery of the 77th Division delivered harassing and interdiction fires to the front, the principal target being the concrete house that had withstood the onslaught of the previous two days. The 1st Battalion, 305th Infantry, received enemy mortar fire during the night, and both it and the 2d Battalion received light machine gun fire in the early morning hours. The 2d Battalion destroyed one machine gun with mortar fire.

At 0930 on 14 December Colonel Freeman prepared his special assault force to

[16] 307th Inf Opns Rpt Leyte, pp. 3–4; Company A, 88th Chem Bn, Jnl, 0900, 13 Dec 44; 77th Div Opns Rpt Leyte, pp. 20–21; 77th Div Arty Opns Rpt Leyte, p. 5; 77th Div G–2 Jnl, 13 Dec 44.

[17] 307th Inf Opns Rpt Leyte, p. 5; 77th Div Opns Rpt Leyte, p. 21; 77th Div G–2 Jnl, 0850, 13 Dec 44.

[18] 306th Inf Opns Rpt Leyte, p. 8; 77th Div Opns Rpt Leyte, p. 21.

[19] Company A, 88th Chem Bn, Jnl, 0930, 1000, 13 Dec 44; 77th Div Opns Rpt Leyte, p. 21.

renew the attack. Before the jump-off, artillery and mortars laid their fire on the blockhouse and beyond. Under cover of artillery fire the troops cautiously moved out at 1030 with Company L on the right and by 1105 they had advanced 100 yards. Company L knocked out two pillboxes with flame throwers and a tank destroyer gun. Company E found every step of the way contested. The troops used hand grenades and bayonets and literally forced the enemy out of the foxholes in tough hand-to-hand fighting.[20] Capt. Robert B. Nett, the commanding officer of Company E, although seriously wounded, refused to relinquish his command. He led his company forward and killed seven Japanese with his rifle and bayonet. Captain Nett was awarded the Medal of Honor.

While Company E was so engaged, Company L on its right advanced through dense foliage and burnt the Japanese out of their foxholes and the bamboo thicket with flame throwers. The company was assisted by armored bulldozers from the 302d Engineers. For a hundred yards on all sides of the blockhouse, the enemy had dug many deep foxholes only a few yards apart. All the foxholes were covered, some with coconut logs and earth, and others with improvised lids of metal and earth. One was protected by an upturned bathtub. The armored bulldozer drove over the positions, its blades cutting off the tops of the foxholes, after which small arms fire into the holes killed the occupants. The crews of the tank destroyers not only fired point-blank at targets but opened the escape hatches and dropped grenades into the foxholes.[21] At 1240 the blockhouse, or what remained of it, was secured.

[20] 305th Inf Opns Rpt Leyte, p. 5.
[21] Ltr, Gen Bruce to Gen Ward, 16 Aug 51, OCMH.

In the meantime the 1st Battalion, 305th Infantry, flanked the blockhouse at 1225 and wheeled 1,000 yards to the east, cutting off the enemy line of communications on Highway 2. The 3d Battalion, 305th Infantry, remained on the high ground. By 1510 the crossroad north of Ormoc was taken. At the end of the day, the front lines of the 305th Infantry ran south to north along Highway 2 with Company L in the blockhouse sector. A large pocket of the enemy, which had been bypassed by the 1st Battalion, was centered generally in front of the 2d Battalion. The 307th Infantry was on the left flank of the 305th, while the 1st Battalion, 184th Infantry, which had relieved the 306th Infantry, was on the right flank in Ormoc.[22]

During the day the 307th Infantry continued its mission of protecting the left flank of the 77th Division in its northward advance and sent patrols and a strong reconnaissance force, consisting of two reinforced rifle companies, one dismounted cannon platoon, and four tanks, west to the banks of an unnamed river near Jalubon. The reconnaissance force killed twenty-one of the enemy, also capturing and destroying great quantities of Japanese matériel and supplies. By the time the perimeter of the 307th Infantry was established in the late afternoon of 14 December, as reported by General Bruce, "the coast line from Ormoc to Jalubon was dotted with fires and the explosions of burning Japanese ammunition dumps."[23]

[22] 305th Inf Opns Rpt Leyte, p. 5; 77th Div G–3 Periodic Rpt 20, 15 Dec 44; 77th Div Opns Rpt Leyte, p. 22; 77th Div G–2 Summary Leyte Opn, p. 2; 77th Div Arty Opns Rpt Leyte, p. 5.
[23] "This force succeeded in destroying 6 amphibious tanks, 7 landing barges, 1 eighty-foot two-masted schooner, 50 tons of ammunition, approximately twenty-five tons of miscellaneous supplies, 4 40-mm. AA guns, 4 20-mm. AA guns, 1 77-mm.

Two other patrols, composed of volunteers from the 306th and 307th Infantry Regiments, reconnoitered approximately 3,000 yards to the west of the 307th Infantry for possible trails for a wide envelopment.[24] These patrols met only scattered groups of the enemy and advanced within 2,000 yards of Valencia, returning with the information that an envelopment was feasible.[25] During the day the 184th Infantry relieved the 306th Infantry of its mission of holding the coastal defenses, freeing the latter unit for an enveloping movement to the north.

On 15 December the 77th Division consolidated its lines and sent out small patrols. The enemy continued to be very active in the sector of the 305th Infantry. During the night the artillery operating in the 1st Battalion sector knocked out four 2½-ton trucks and killed seventeen of the enemy, while the 2d Battalion beat off two Japanese counterattacks. In the 3d Battalion sector all was quiet.

By 15 December the port of Ormoc had been sealed off. It was through this port that the Japanese had sent in a profusion of men, supplies, and equipment, thus prolonging the battle for the island beyond the time anticipated in the original American plans for the operation. The 77th Division estimated

that for the period from 11 through 15 December it had taken 9 prisoners and killed 3,046 of the enemy.[26] Its own casualties were 2 officers and 101 enlisted men killed, 22 officers and 296 enlisted men wounded, and 26 enlisted men missing in action.[27]

The Mountain Passage

As a result of General Suzuki's abortive attempt to seize the Burauen airfields, a number of Japanese soldiers remained in the mountains west of Burauen. Most of these were from the *26th Division* and they were trying to rejoin the main part of the *35th Army* in Ormoc Valley. Earlier, the 11th Airborne Division had started out over the mountains from Burauen in order to relieve enemy pressure on the eastern flank of the XXIV Corps in its drive toward Ormoc. (*Map 19*)

Mahonag

Just west of Burauen the central mountain range rises abruptly from Leyte Valley to peaks that are 4,000 feet or more in height. Many of the deep, precipitous gorges were impassable even for foot soldiers. No roads went through the mountains but there were short footpaths from one locality to another. Some of these trails led over boulder-strewn, swiftly running streams and frequently bridged deep gorges with a single log where a slip meant a drop of thirty to forty feet. The paths were often so steep that footholds had to be cut into the hillsides, and soldiers were forced to use their hands to avoid falling as much as forty to a hundred feet.[28]

---

dual purpose gun [probably a 75-mm. gun], several machine guns, a radio transmitter and generator, 1 seacoast range finder and had burnt about half the town of Linao in order to destroy Japanese positions dug in that vicinity. . . .
Although the force was unable to carry back much of the equipment it captured owing to its small size and the necessity of mobility, it managed to return 1 seacoast range finder, 1 large radio transmitter and 2 20-mm. AA guns." 77th Div Opns Rpt Leyte, p. 23.
[24] 77th Div Opns Rpt Leyte, p. 22.
[25] *Ibid.*, pp. 22–23; 77th Div G–3 Periodic Rpt 20, 15 Dec 44; 306th Inf Opns Rpt Leyte, p. 9; 307th Inf Opns Rpt Leyte, p. 9.

[26] 77th Div G–3 Periodic Rpts Nos. 17–21, 13–16 Dec 44.
[27] 77th Div G–1 Daily Strength Rpts, 11–15 Dec 44.
[28] 188th Prcht Regt Opns Rpt Leyte, p. 1.

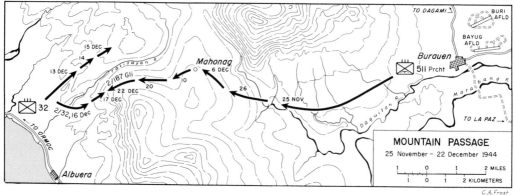

MAP 19

On 25 November the 511th Parachute Infantry Regiment moved west from Burauen for Mahonag, ten miles away. The almost impassable terrain, heavy rainfall, and pockets of lurking Japanese made passage very difficult. It was impossible for the regiment to move as a unit. In small parties, sometimes even less than a squad, the 511th moved forward. "The journey to Mahonag defies description. Sucking mud, jungle vines, and vertical inclines exhausted men before they had marched an hour. Though it rained often during any one trip, still there was no drinking water available throughout the journey." [29] The 3d Battalion, 511th Parachute Infantry Regiment, after considerable hardship entered Mahonag on 6 December.[30]

On 9 December the 2d Battalion, though encountering heavy fire from enemy machine guns, mortars, and rifles, pushed steadily forward and established contact with the other units of the 511th Parachute Infantry Regiment at Mahonag. For several days thereafter, this regiment was busily engaged in sending out patrols. Company G, patrolling in force for two miles to the front, was cut off from the rest of the regiment,

which was held down because of strong enemy action. On 13 December the 32d Infantry pushed northeast from Ormoc Bay in an effort to make juncture with the 11th Airborne Division and assist it in moving out of the mountains.

Drive of 32d Infantry

The 32d Infantry also encountered very precipitous hills and its advance was bitterly contested by the Japanese. By the evening of 14 December the regiment had considerably reduced the distance between itself and the 511th Parachute Infantry.

At 0700 on 15 December, as the 3d Battalion was moving out, a patrol of six men from Company G, 511th Parachute Infantry, entered the battalion's lines. The rest of Company G was only 700 yards east of the ridge. The patrol reported that Company G had been cut off from the rest of the regiment for four days and was without food.

---

[29] 511th Prcht Inf Regt Opns Rpt Leyte, p. 6; 11th Airborne Div Special Study Leyte, p. 5.

[30] During the movement Pvt. Elmer E. Fryar of Company E was killed on 7 December when he voluntarily got in the way of enemy fire in order to shield his platoon leader. Private Fryar posthumously received the Medal of Honor.

The 3d Battalion encountered only slight resistance and at 0950 was on top of the ridge. A platoon moved out to make contact with Company G of the 511th Parachute Infantry. The platoon reached the company, and at 1855 Company G entered the lines of the 3d Battalion, which fed and sheltered its men for the night.

In the meantime the 1st Battalion had moved out at 0800 and encountered scattered resistance. To the east and south of the 32d Infantry was an impassable canyon, several hundred feet deep. In order to reach the 511th Parachute Infantry, it would be necessary for the regiment to go either north for an undetermined distance or down the ridge toward the coast and then up again. A third possibility involved crossing the Talisayan River in the foothills several miles to the west. With these facts in mind Colonel Finn asked his executive officer, "Are we to actually contact the 511th personally[?] What is the purpose of the contact and are we to lead them out by hand[?]" [31]

At the same time, General Arnold advised the 511th Parachute Infantry of the situation and that "present orders" from General Hodge required the displacement of the 32d Infantry from its positions in order to wipe out pockets of resistance that remained near Ormoc. The 511th Parachute Infantry was to make every effort to drive toward the position of the 32d Infantry, since the latter would soon be withdrawn. The 511th would then have to fight it out alone. General Arnold finally decided that the 1st and 3d Battalions, 32d Infantry, would be withdrawn and that the 2d Battalion, which was fresher, would move up and attempt to establish contact with the 511th Parachute Infantry.[32]

At 0700 on 16 December the 2d Battalion started eastward along the south bank of the Talisayan River. For the next few days the battalion made slow progress, meeting and destroying small groups of the enemy pushing west. As the troops advanced they were confronted with steep and heavily wooded ridges which were separated by gorges several hundred feet deep. The Japanese, well concealed by the heavy foliage and entrenched in caves, were most difficult to dislodge, but the distance between the 2d Battalion and the 511th Parachute Infantry daily diminished. On 20 December the 2d Battalion was held up by the terrain and strong enemy opposition on two ridges to its front. For the next two days the battalion pounded at the Japanese force in attempts to dislodge it. At this time the distance between the 2d Battalion and the 511th Parachute Infantry had narrowed down. Enemy resistance was overcome on the morning of 22 December. In the meantime the 187th Glider Infantry Regiment passed through the 511th Parachute Infantry Regiment and continued the attack. At 1330 on 22 December the 2d Battalion of the 187th Glider Infantry Regiment passed through the 2d Battalion, 32d Infantry, and pushed on to the coast. The difficult mountain passes had been overcome.[33]

The Drive South

Regrouping of Japanese Forces

When the Americans took Limon, the key point of entrance on Highway 2 into Ormoc Valley from the north, the Japanese

---

[31] 32d Inf Unit Jnl, 15 Dec 44.
[32] 32d Inf Opns Rpt Leyte, pp. 29–30; 32d Inf S–3 Periodic Rpt, no number, 15 Dec 44; 32d Inf S–2 Periodic Rpt, no number, 15 Dec 44; 32d Inf Unit Jnl, 15 Dec 44.
[33] 32d Inf Opns Rpt Leyte, pp. 30–31; 32d Inf Unit Jnl, 16 to 22 Dec 44; 11th Airborne Div Opns Rpt Leyte, p. 10.

forces were thrown into confusion. The Americans, unknown to themselves, had successfully divided the Japanese *1st* and *102d Divisions* that had been charged with the defense of northern Leyte. The Japanese were forced to regroup their various units in an attempt to correct the rapidly deteriorating situation along their front lines. The strong American infantry assaults, which had been co-ordinated with heavy mortar and artillery fire, induced General Kataoka, the commanding general of the *1st Division,* to redistribute his forces along Highway 2.[34]

The onslaught of the X Corps had forced General Suzuki to abandon the earlier plan of advancing the *35th Army* north along three widely separated routes. Instead he had to concentrate the main strength of the *1st Division* along the highway to check the American advance. The plan to use the *1st Division* as a strong offensive force had to be discarded in favor of using it in a strictly defensive role.

The *1st Division* had suffered much: as of 2 December, 3,000 of its men had been killed or wounded. Furthermore, one third of the infantry weapons of the *1st Infantry Regiment* and two thirds of those belonging to the *57th Infantry Regiment* had been rendered inoperable. The infantry was short of grenades and ammunition for the 50-mm. grenade dischargers. "The men were suffering from the effect of continuous fighting, from lack of provisions, overwork, and especially from the lack of vitamins." [35]

By this time communications between the *1st Division* and other units had broken down. Telephonic and telegraphic communications between the division and *35th Army* headquarters were out for long periods of time, and liaison between the division headquarters and front-line units was carried out by messengers moving on foot. The supply lines had also broken down. The *1st Division Transport Regiment* found it virtually impossible to supply food and ammunition to the *1st* and *57th Infantry Regiments* and the *1st Artillery Regiment.*

General Kataoka grouped his forces along Highway 2 in the Limon–Pinamopoan area in order to concentrate the maximum strength along Highway 2. The *1st Reconnaissance Regiment* was to attack the left flank of the *32d Division,*[36] which was already opposed by the *57th Infantry* in the Limon sector; the *1st Battalion,* less *Company 3,* and the *2d Battalion,* plus *Company 11,* of the *49th Infantry* were to occupy the 1,900-yard sector two miles southeast of Limon in order to hold back American forces in that area; and the *1st Artillery Regiment* was to defend its prepared positions south of Limon. The troops of the *1st Engineer Regiment* and other noncombat units were issued small arms and ordered to take part in the defense of Highway 2.[37]

---

[34] The part of this section dealing with Japanese plans and maneuvers is based upon the following documents: Tomochika, True Facts of Leyte Opn; *35th Army* Opns; 10th I&HS, Eighth Army Stf Study, Opns of Japanese *35th Army* on Leyte.

[35] *35th Army* Opns, p. 91.

[36] The *1st Reconnaissance Regiment* could not carry out this assignment, since it had been attacked by a larger American force.

[37] General Tomochika made the following comments on the *1st Division:*

The personnel were brave but the officers lacked sufficient training in modern warfare and it finally did not live up to the expectations of its leaders. The division commander, Lt. Gen. Kataoka worried about the loss of his troops, lacked brave command ability and did not establish any set battle policy. [He refused to commit one of his important units to the defense of Highway 2.] . . . therefore the Chief of Staff, Deputy Chief of Staff and senior staff officers were dispatched from Army to Division on three different occasions to urge General Kataoka to submit to these orders. . . . Regardless of how much we urged General Kataoka to change his views he would not budge. Colonel Ikeda, the Chief of Staff

Drive of the 32d Division

In order to support the amphibious landing of the 77th Division at Deposito and its subsequent movement northward, General Krueger had ordered the X Corps to make its main effort, beginning on 5 December, by advancing vigorously south astride Highway 2 from the vicinity of Limon.[38] Acting on Corps orders, General Gill prepared to move out with two regiments abreast. The 32d Division consolidated its positions on 5 December, and readied itself for a strong assault south down Highway 2.[39] (*See Map 12.*)

The 127th Infantry had pushed past the 3d Battalion, 128th Infantry, which was south of the Leyte River and west of Limon. The 127th encountered very determined resistance from the Japanese entrenched on the high ground 1,000 yards south of the Leyte River bridge. The well-camouflaged enemy defenses consisted of numerous foxholes and ten-foot-deep spider holes, many of which were connected by interlacing communication trenches.

The terrain that the troops traversed was adapted to defensive fighting, and the *1st Division* took full advantage of this fact. There were deep ravines and steep hills where the enemy had dug in on both the forward and reverse slopes. The entire area was covered by heavy rain forest with dense underbrush. The nearly constant rainfall made observation difficult and the maps for the area were very inaccurate.

By 12 December the 32d Division had "detoured" around the *1st* and *57th Infantry Regiments* of the *1st Division* and was assaulting the Japanese artillery positions south of Limon. On this date the division straightened out its lines, established physical contact between the assault battalions, resupplied the assault units, and sent out patrols. The sector in which the greatest Japanese resistance was encountered continued to be that of the 2d Battalion, 126th Infantry. Employing mortars and four tanks, this battalion was able to make only limited gains.[40]

During the night of 12–13 December the artillery battalions of the 32d Division fired harassing missions near the perimeters of the 126th and 127th Infantry Regiments and southward on Highway 2 as far as the vicinity of Lonoy.

The *14th Area Army* had planned to land the *39th Infantry Regiment* and an artillery company from the *10th Division* near Carigara on 16 December, but in view of the American 77th Division's advance to Ormoc the plan was canceled on 11 December. On 13 December General Suzuki attached an

---

of the 1st Division [until 13 December] was partially deaf and further because of a former lung ailment, he was unsuited to hold his important position. (Tomochika, True Facts of Leyte Opn p. 18.)

General Tomochika was less than fair to the *1st Division*. From its positions in the mountains of nothern Leyte, the division contested every foot of advance of the X Corps. General Krueger said of the *1st Division*: "This unit more than any other hostile unit on Leyte was responsible for the extension of the Leyte Operation." (Sixth Army Opns Rpt Leyte, p. 41.)

[38] Sixth Army FO 36, 4 Dec 44.

[39] During the action of 5 December, Pfc. William A. McWhorter sacrificed his life that a companion might live. He deliberately held next to his body and away from his comrade a Japanese grenade which had been thrown into his position. The charge exploded and killed him instantly but did not harm his companion. He was awarded posthumously the Medal of Honor.

[40] "However for a patrol from Company I [127th Infantry] it was a red letter day in that the patrol found a bottle of U.S. Golden Wedding Wiskey [sic] at an evacuated Jap hospital. It was consumed." 127th Inf Unit Jnl, 12 Dec 44. See also 127th Inf Opns Rpt Leyte, p. 9; 126th Inf Unit Jnl, 12 Dec 44; 32d Div G–3 Jnl, 12 Dec 44; 32d Div Leyte Opn Diary, pp. 21–22.

infantry company of about 100 men from the *102d Division* to the *1st Division* in order to strengthen the latter's lines.

On the morning of 13 December the 2d Battalion, 126th Infantry, with the assistance of its tanks and heavy mortars, pushed past the Japanese who had held up its advance. In the face of most determined opposition the battalion moved south, destroying the pockets of resistance which had been bypassed. At the end of the day the 2d Battalion had advanced 400 yards to a position 200 yards north of a roadblock set up by the 3d Battalion, 126th Infantry. The 3d Battalion, less Company L, which was to remain on the high ground overlooking the road, was to attack south on the east side of Highway 2 and come abreast of the 1st Battalion, 126th Infantry.

At 1521 the 3d Battalion reported that six enemy tanks were coming up the highway. After heavy fighting, the Japanese tanks withdrew at nightfall and returned to the south. The 1st Battalion, 126th Infantry, the southernmost unit of the division, made plans to dislodge the enemy force between it and the 3d Battalion. The contested ground consisted of an open space 600 to 700 yards long and 200 to 300 yards wide, at the southern end of which were two knolls. The 1st Battalion had men on both knolls but did not control the northern end of the sector where the Japanese had dug in and were using machine guns, mortars, and rifles. The 1st Battalion charged against the Japanese and rooted them out with grenades and mortar fire. Except for this action, only slight gains were registered during the day. The men of the battalion were hungry, having been without food since the previous afternoon. The commanding officer of the battalion renewed a request for additional rations and ammunition, since the one-third

ration that had been received the day before was insufficient.

The 1st and 2d Battalions of the 127th Infantry received orders from the regimental commander to advance south with the 1st Battalion on the left, pinch out the 3d Battalion, 126th Infantry, and link up with the 1st Battalion, 126th Infantry. The 1st Battalion, 127th Infantry, moved out in a column of companies and had advanced 400 yards when it encountered forty to fifty Japanese on a ridge to its front, about 150 yards west of the road. The enemy threw blocks of TNT and grenades against the battalion, effectively pinning down the troops. A night perimeter was established.

The 2d Battalion, 126th Infantry, moved abreast of the regiment's 1st Battalion throughout the day. Its advance was bitterly contested by the Japanese, who employed machine guns, mortars, and rifles against the battalion, which dug in for the night under fire.[41] At 1630 the 11th Field Artillery Battalion fired upon fifteen Japanese who were walking along the road south of Lonoy and killed twelve of them.[42]

The night of 13–14 December was not quiet. At 2300 an enemy force from the *1st Infantry Regiment* broke into the command post of the 126th Infantry. The Japanese set up a machine gun in the area and attacked with grenades and rifles. Bitter hand-to-hand fighting ensued but by 0325 the enemy force was evicted and the area had quieted down. At 0630, with the coming of dawn, the Headquarters Company got things in order and everyone was "happy to hear sound of comrade's voices." Six Japanese

---

[41] 32d Div G–3 Periodic Rpt 27, 13 Dec 44; 32d Div Opns Diary Leyte, pp. 23–24; 126th Inf Unit Jnl, 13 Dec 44.
[42] 32d Div Arty Daily Rpt, 14 Dec 44.

CHAPTER XX

Seizure of Ormoc Valley

General Krueger wished the two corps to attack aggressively through Ormoc Valley toward Valencia, about six and a half miles north of Ormoc. The X Corps, pushing south along Highway 2, was to seize the high ground north of Valencia and the XXIV Corps was to continue its drive north, capture Valencia, and establish contact with the X Corps. (*Map 20*) Driving north along Highway 2, the 77th Division was to seize Valencia and its airfield and effect a juncture with the X Corps to separate the enemy forces in the mountains east of its zone of action from those on the west coast in the Palompon area. General Bruce was to co-ordinate all artillery fires and air support missions in the Ormoc–Valencia area.[1]

After the seizure of Ormoc, although the *35th Army* still controlled Ormoc Valley, the Sixth Army had closed the northern and southern entrances. There remained available to the Japanese as a principal port only Palompon. A road from this town through the mountains joined Highway 2 in the vicinity of Libongao and constituted the only main route from the west coast of Leyte to Ormoc Valley. The Americans noticed that the Japanese were moving supplies, men, ammunition, and artillery to the Valencia area and concluded that the Japanese would make a defensive stand in Valencia.[2]

By the end of 15 December the forces of General Bruce had cleared the Japanese defenders from the Ormoc area and were ready for the next phase of the drive north up the Ormoc corridor. Reports made the previous day by the reconnaissance patrols from the 306th and 307th Infantry Regiments indicated that there was little enemy resistance to the west of Highway 2. These led General Bruce to decide in favor of a plan for enveloping the enemy from the west. The 306th and 307th Infantry were to strike the flanks and rear of the Japanese defending the highway and thus permit a more rapid advance along this road by the 305th Infantry.[3]

General Hodge had informed General Bruce that the commanding general of the Sixth Army desired to have the attack pushed "with all possible vigor." The operations of the 77th Division were to depend upon the situation and conditions then existing.[4] On 14 December General Hodge visited General Bruce, who explained his plans. General Hodge thought they were "sound"[5] and later told General Bruce to keep his plans flexible in order to take advantage of every break to speed the advance north. It was imperative that the XXIV

---

[1] XXIV Corps FO 37, 18 Dec 44.
[2] Sixth Army G–2 Wkly Rpt 68, 13 Dec 44, p. 14.

[3] Ltr, Gen Bruce to Gen Ward, 16 Aug 51, OCMH.
[4] Msg, CG XXIV Corps to CG 77th Div, 13 Dec 44, XXIV Corps G–3 Jnl, 13 Dec 44.
[5] Msg, CG XXIV Corps to G–3 Sixth Army, 14 Dec 44, Sixth Army G–3 Jnl, 14 Dec 44.

Corps secure control of the roads north before the Japanese could establish positions.

Drive From the South to the Libongao Area

Seizure of the Road Junction

According to its plan of attack for 16 December the 305th Infantry, from the vicinity of Cogon, was to continue its assault north on Highway 2, liquidate the remaining enemy forces in Cogon, and finally secure a large defensive position centered around the road junction north of Cogon. All three battalions of the regiment were to consolidate around the point while the 306th and 307th Infantry Regiments were to drive toward Valencia.

The Cannon and Antitank Companies and the heavy weapons units of the other two regiments were attached to the 305th Infantry for movement only and were to be used solely in case of emergency. These units were to be sent to the 306th and 307th Infantry Regiments upon call by those regiments.

At 0930 on 16 December the assault units of the 305th Infantry moved out. The 1st Battalion, on the left of Highway 2, was to attack north, and the 3d Battalion, on the right of Highway 2, was to attack north and then northeast to effect a juncture with the 1st and 2d Battalions at the road junction north of Cogon. The 2d Battalion was to attack east to flank the enemy positions along the highway. The operation was to be assisted by artillery.

During the morning the artillery in support of the 1st Battalion knocked out two antitank guns, a heavy machine gun, and an enemy dugout position. At 1035 the 1st Battalion had advanced several hundred yards. As the 3d Battalion came forward,

Company L moved in on the right flank of the 1st Battalion. At 1100 the 2d Battalion had reached the enemy positions along the highway and by 1215 had cleared out the enemy pocket and the road in its sector. A light tank platoon from the 706th Tank Battalion was attached to the 1st Battalion at 1255 in order to assist the battalion in clearing the Japanese from their foxholes. Although progress was slow, it was thorough. The localized envelopments of the enemy's right (west) flank resulted in the capture of Cogon at the end of the day. The 305th Infantry advanced 400 yards north of the road junction and established night positions around it.[6]

Envelopment of Valencia

In the meantime, the 306th and 307th Infantry Regiments had been ordered to make a series of sweeping envelopments on the Japanese right (west) flank toward Valencia. The 307th Infantry was to move northwest about six and a quarter miles through the barrios of Jalubon, Liloan, and Bao to Catayom on the Bao River, then swing northeast to the barrio of San Jose and continue northeast to the Valencia airstrip. The 306th Infantry was to follow the 307th Infantry northwest and then drive east and cut Highway 2.[7]

The 306th Field Artillery Battalion, though in general support, was to give priority to the 307th Infantry. The 902d and 305th Field Artillery Battalions were to support elements of the reconnaissance

---

[6] 77th Div Opns Rpt Leyte, pp. 24–25; 305th Inf Opns Rpt Leyte, p. 5; 305th Inf Unit Rpt 11, 16 Dec 44; 77th Div G–3 Periodic Rpt 22, 16 Dec 44; 77th Div G–3 Jnl, 16 Dec 44.

[7] XXIV Corps FO 37 (Confirmatory of Oral and Fragmentary Orders), 18 Dec 44; 77th Div FO 17, 15 Dec 44.

troops operating on each flank of the division. The artillery battalions would fire in the regimental zones of action only on call from or with the approval of the regiments.[8]

On 16 December the 307th Infantry crossed the line of departure on time. Since there were no roads and the route was across rice paddies, through waist-deep rivers, and over terrain impassable for vehicles, the troops hand-carried their supplies. Arrangements were also made for Filipinos to carry supplies, and, as the advance progressed, more and more Filipinos joined the column of the 307th Infantry for this purpose.[9] The regiment met only scattered resistance. Some Japanese troops encountered in the vicinity of Liloan were dispersed. At 1525 leading elements of the 307th Infantry passed through Bao and moved on toward San Jose. On the outskirts of that barrio, the troops met and destroyed two platoons of the enemy. At 1645 the 307th Infantry dug in for the night in San Jose. The regiment had covered eight miles, a rapid rate of advance considering the nature of the terrain and the load carried. At 2340 General Bruce told the 307th Infantry that an incendiary air strike would be made on Valencia before 0900 the following day and that the regiment was to hold its present position until further orders.[10]

At 0900 on 16 December the 306th Infantry moved past the initial point of departure on the northwestern edge of Ormoc. At 1035 the regiment was 1,000 yards west of the starting point and close "on the tail" of the 307th Infantry. The 306th waited until the 307th cleared and then moved north. Although it did not encounter any Japanese its progress was very slow because the route of advance ran through deep rice paddies. At 1730 the regiment established its night perimeter about 700 yards south-southwest of Tipic.[11] During the day the 305th Infantry had cleared Cogon and occupied defensive positions around the road junction north of the town.

The Japanese had constructed defensive positions along Highway 2 in the southern part of Ormoc Valley. At the road junction of Highway 2 with the road to Liloan were many trenches three to four feet deep and parallel to the highway. Trenches had also been dug along the sides of a machine gun emplacement that occupied a slight elevation commanding Highway 2 both to the north and to the south. On both sides of the road from Cogon to Catayom foxholes lined Highway 2, in the ditches and under the shacks. Some of these positions were dug on a slant and were six to seven feet deep. At Tambuco the foxholes extended along the highway for 400 yards, with machine gun emplacements on the sides of the foxholes. Other positions along Highway 2 consisted of poorly integrated foxholes and machine guns that covered the road. The field artillery pieces between Tambuco and Catayom were placed along the highway, with the exception of a 75-mm. gun that guarded a bridge and was well concealed inside a roadside shack.[12]

The *14th Area Army* had planned to reinforce the *35th Army* by dispatching the *Takahashi Detachment*, which consisted of the *5th Infantry Regiment*, one artillery

[8] 77th Div FO 17, 15 Dec 44.
[9] Ltr, Gen Bruce to Gen Ward, 16 Aug 51, OCMH.
[10] 77th Div G–3 Jnl, 16 Dec 44; 77th Div G–3 Periodic Rpt 22, 16 Dec 44; 77th Div Opns Rpt Leyte, p. 25; 307th Inf Opns Rpt Leyte, p. 6.

[11] 306th Inf Unit Jnl, 16 Dec 44; 77th Div G–3 Periodic Rpt 22, 16 Dec 44; 77th Div Opns Rpt Leyte, pp. 24–25; 306th Inf Opns Rpt Leyte, p. 9.
[12] MI Div, War Dept, "Leyte Field Fortifications," *Tactical and Technical Trends*, No. 57 (April, 1945), pp. 108–10.

JAPANESE DUG-IN POSITIONS ALONG HIGHWAY BANKS *delayed the advance of the 77th Division north of Ormoc.*

battalion, and one engineer company and one transport company each from the *8th Division,* together with the *Ito Naval Landing Force* of 400 troops from Luzon.

The *77th Infantry Regiment* had landed at Palompon on or about 9 December from Cebu and moved to Matagob where, after assembling its troops, it began to move southeast toward Huaton, the new headquarters of the *35th Army.* Huaton was a small barrio on Highway 2 about three and a half miles north of Cogon. On 13 December General Suzuki, the commander of the *35th Army,* arrived at Huaton from the Burauen area. After the *12th Independent Infantry Regiment,* the *4th Airborne Raiding Regiment,* the *Mitsui Shipping Unit,* the *Ito Naval Landing Force,* and the *77th Infantry Regiment* were assembled, General

Suzuki on 15 December ordered an attack, which was to start 17 December, against the American forces in the Ormoc area.[13]

The fall of Cogon and the envelopment to the west forced General Suzuki to change his plans again. The 305th Infantry had captured the positions of the *Tateishi Battalion* of the *12th Independent Infantry Regiment,* and the position of the *77th Infantry Regiment* was greatly weakened. As the attack against Ormoc could not be successfully completed, the *12th* and *77th Infantry Regiments* were to carry out a delaying action.[14]

Since the fall of Valencia might break the organized resistance of the Japanese in Ormoc Valley, General Bruce decided to push

---

[13] *35th Army* Opns, pp. 99–101.
[14] *Ibid.,* p. 101.

forward rapidly and take the barrio before the enemy could regroup.[15] General Krueger asked General Whitehead for air strikes against Valencia. If the weather permitted, a strike would be made at 0900 and another would be delivered on call. In addition, nearly all available artillery of the division that could arrive within firing distance, as well as the 226th Field Artillery Battalion from positions east of the mountains near Daro, would shell the town until ordered to lift the fire.

The 305th Infantry was to drive rapidly north on Highway 2 and clear out the Japanese for a distance of 200 to 300 yards on each side of the road, even though it might mean bypassing groups of the enemy on the flanks. A patrol from the regiment was to operate east of its sector to locate enemy forces. The 306th Infantry was to drive rapidly east toward Highway 2 and then advance north up the highway, clearing a lane 200 to 300 yards wide. At a point 500 to 600 yards north of Cabulihan, it was to await further orders. The regiment was to be prepared to send a battalion south to assist the 305th Infantry in its advance.

General Bruce organized an armored column to carry rations and ammunition to the 306th and 307th Infantry Regiments. This column, which was to move north on Highway 2, consisted of five light tanks from the 7th Division, the Cannon and Tank Destroyer Companies of the 306th and 307th Infantry Regiments, part of Company C, 302d Engineer Battalion, a platoon from the 305th Infantry, and sufficient LVT's to carry men and supplies. An artillery observer accompanied the column.

Elements of the 302d Engineer Battalion were to repair immediately the highway between Ormoc and Valencia and at night re-

tire within the nearest infantry defensive perimeter. The order was summed up as follows: "The action will be pressed with the utmost vigor by careful planning but every effort will be made to save casualties." [16]

At 0830 on 17 December the 305th Infantry moved out along Highway 2. At 1000 the 1st Battalion reported that it was advancing at the rate of 100 yards every ten minutes against light opposition. By 1145 the 305th Infantry was fighting through Tambuco. At a road junction just north of Tambuco, it eliminated some enemy resistance and the advance slowed down. The regiment moved forward to a point about 300 yards north of the road junction and established its night perimeter, which extended 300 yards to the northeast along the Tambuco–Dolores road in order to forestall any Japanese counterattacks from that direction.[17]

On the same day the 306th Infantry pushed its attack northeast at 0800. The advancing troops almost immediately encountered Japanese who, apparently taken by surprise, were unable to offer organized resistance. At 1040, when the forward elements were 1,000 yards southwest of Cabulihan, the opposition stiffened and the regimental commander therefore committed the 3d Battalion on the left of the 2d Battalion. The advance continued. As the regiment neared Highway 2, resistance became more intense. The 306th Infantry encountered the Japanese who were fleeing northwest from the assault of the 305th Infantry

---

[15] 77th Div Opns Rpt Leyte, pp. 26, 27.

[16] 77th Div FO 18, 17 Dec 44; 77th Div Opns Rpt Leyte, pp. 25–26.
[17] 77th Div G–3 Jnl, 17 Dec 44; 77th Div G–2 Jnl, 17 Dec 44; 77th Div Opns Rpt Leyte, p. 27; 305th Inf Opns Rpt Leyte, p. 6; 77th Div G–3 Periodic Rpt 23, 17 Dec 44.

and the heavy artillery that accompanied it. (Unknown to the Americans, General Suzuki and his staff were among the retreating Japanese. Suzuki succeeded in escaping to Libongao, where he established a new headquarters for the *35th Army*.) At 1440 the 306th Infantry reached Highway 2 between Catayom and Cabulihan and proceeded north toward Cabulihan, its objective. Advance elements of the 3d Battalion reached the outskirts of the town but withdrew three or four hundred yards to take advantage of more commanding terrain. After combat patrols had cleared the area, the 306th Infantry established its night perimeter five hundred yards south of Cabulihan at 1600.[18]

General Bruce had ordered the 307th Infantry to remain in San Jose until further notice. Since the guerrilla forces had reported a large number of Japanese in the area, General Bruce had made arrangements to soften the sector with an aerial bombardment and artillery fire before the infantry attack. In response to Bruce's request, fifteen P–40's from the V Fighter Command had been made available by General Whitehead for an air strike against the Valencia area.

The 155-mm. guns of the 226th Field Artillery Battalion at Daro began firing on Valencia and the airstrip on the morning of 17 December and hit a Japanese ammunition dump. At 1245 the artillery fire was halted for the air strike, and for fifty minutes the area was bombed and strafed. With the conclusion of the air attack, at 1335, the artillery began anew to pound the area. "The medium artillery . . . reached out from Ormoc and the 'Long Toms' . . .

from Daro joined in the fighting." [19] In the meantime the 902d Field Artillery Battalion moved forward to a point from which it could support the advance of the 307th Infantry. At 1415 the artillery fire stopped and the 307th Infantry moved out astride the San Jose–Valencia road toward Valencia. Though the artillery fire and aerial bombardment had driven some of the Japanese from the area, a strong well-equipped force, including a number of paratroopers, remained to oppose the 307th Infantry. The regiment pushed forward, however, and at 1640 its leading elements were on the southwestern edge of the airstrip and within 1,000 yards of Valencia. The 307th Infantry formed its night perimeter on the edge of the airfield and made preparations to continue the attack on 18 December.[20]

During 17 December, despite the disorganization of the Japanese forces, Colonel Imahori of the *12th Independent Infantry Regiment* tried to reach Ormoc, but he was unsuccessful.[21] A few enemy artillery shells landed in the Ormoc area but that was all. General Bruce wrote later: "The men got a laugh because the General's latrine, unoccupied, was struck. He wished about that time that he had remained up front which he had reached by landing in a cub plane on an unimproved jungle road." [22]

On the morning of 18 December, since supplies and ammunition for the 306th and 307th Infantry Regiments were becoming dangerously low, General Bruce pushed the armored column vigorously forward through

---

[18] 77th Div G–3 Jnl, 17 Dec 44; 306th Inf Unit Jnl, 17 Dec 44; 77th Div G–3 Periodic Rpt 23, 17 Dec 44; 306th Inf Opns Rpt Leyte, p. 9; *35th Army* Opns, pp. 101–103.

[19] Ltr, Gen Bruce to Gen Ward, 16 Aug 51, OCMH.
[20] 307th Inf Opns Rpt Leyte, p. 7; 77th Div Arty Opns Rpt Leyte, pp. 5–6; 77th Div G–3 Jnl, 17 Dec 44; 77th Div Opns Rpt Leyte, p. 27; 77th Div G–3 Periodic Rpt 23, 17 Dec 44.
[21] *35th Army* Opns, p. 101.
[22] Ltr, Gen Bruce to Gen Ward, 16 Aug 51, OCMH.

JAPANESE LIGHT TANK *destroyed during the fighting along Highway 2. Note dugouts in the sides of banks behind the tank.*

the 305th Infantry. The column swept past enemy strong points and succeeded in bringing supplies to both regiments.

The attack of the 305th Infantry was consequently delayed. The 3d Battalion of the regiment, however, jumped off in a northeast direction on the Dolores road in order to cut off any Japanese reinforcements from that area. At 0945 the rest of the 305th Infantry started out along Highway 2 and encountered little resistance. By 1400 the battalions had passed through the barrios of Dayhagan and Huaton (the former and short-lived headquarters of General Suzuki), and knocked out fifteen enemy trucks and three tanks. The 3d Battalion proceeded northeast from the road junction along the road to Dolores, and crushed all resistance. The battalion then moved west

toward Highway 2, leaving a platoon behind to seal off the Dolores road from Highway 2.[23]

At 0830 on 18 December the 306th Infantry renewed its attack. At first the 2d Battalion moved south astride Highway 2 in order to make contact with the 305th Infantry, which was pushing north along the highway, but since there was little resistance the battalion withdrew and rejoined the regiment. As the rest of the regiment continued north it met moderate opposition but pushed ahead steadily. The troops encountered many strong points along the road but no organized main line of resistance.

---

[23] 305th Inf Unit Rpt 15, 18 Dec 44; 77th Div G–2 Jnl, 18 Dec 44; 77th Div G–3 Jnl, 18 Dec 44; 77th Div G–3 Periodic Rpt 24, 18 Dec 44; 305th Inf Opns Rpt Leyte, p. 6; 77th Div Opns Rpt Leyte, p. 28.

The 306th Infantry proceeded astride the highway against moderate to strong opposition. An enemy force estimated as two battalions had dug in under the houses and in foxholes along the sides of the road. The Japanese tried to halt the advance with heavy machine guns and a few mortars, but without avail. Patrols from the 306th Infantry made contact with the 305th Infantry at 1500. The 306th Infantry reached the southern edge of Valencia at 1630 and tied in with the 307th Infantry. Night perimeters were established.[24]

At 0830 on 18 December the 307th Infantry from the southwestern edge of the Valencia airstrip renewed the attack. There was no opposition and at 0905 the airfield and the town of Valencia were in the hands of the regiment. General Bruce considered the heavy artillery and aerial assaults of the previous day "most effective." The airfield was in "fair" condition; it was safe for light aircraft and with minor repairs could be made suitable for other aircraft. The 307th Infantry spent the rest of 18 December consolidating its positions and conducting extensive patrols to the north and east. At 1630 it established physical contact with the 306th Infantry.[25]

In three days of relatively fast fighting and maneuvering the 77th Division had shaken the Japanese forces badly and disrupted the plans of General Suzuki. The 307th Infantry, by making a wide envelopment of the west flank, had captured Valencia and its airfield, and the 306th Infan-

try, making a smaller envelopment, had bisected Highway 2 at Cabulihan while the 305th Infantry moved up the highway from Cogon. All of southern Ormoc Valley from Ormoc to Valencia, a distance of about six and a half miles as the crow flies, was securely in American hands. All units were in contact and ready for the next phase of their mission.

Drive to Palompon Road Junction

Since elements of the XXIV Corps had been able to make more rapid progress through Ormoc Valley than the X Corps units, General Krueger on 19 December enlarged the zone of action of the XXIV Corps to include Libongao, the barrio just below the juncture of Highway 2 with the Palompon road.[26] General Hodge thereupon ordered the 77th Division to continue north and seize Libongao and then to secure the Palompon road and establish contact with the X Corps.[27]

General Bruce ordered the 305th Infantry to assume responsibility for the defense of Valencia and its airfield, and thus free the 306th and 307th Infantry Regiments for new assignments. The 307th was to move north astride Highway 2 to Libongao and then continue to the junction with the Palompon road. The 306th was to move across country and strike northwest toward the Palompon road. Although its advance would parallel that of the 307th, the 306th was to be about 2,300 yards west of the other regiment. After reaching the Palompon road in the vicinity of the Togbong River the 306th Infantry would strike west for the crossing and then move east to the road

---

[24] 306th Inf Unit Jnl, 18 Dec 44; 77th Div G–2 Jnl, 18 Dec 44; 77th Div G–3 Jnl, 18 Dec 44; 306th Inf Opns Rpt Leyte, pp. 9–10; 77th Div Opns Rpt Leyte, p. 28; 77th Div G–3 Periodic Rpt 24, 18 Dec 44.

[25] 77th Div G–3 Jnl, 18 Dec 44; 77th Div G–3 Periodic Rpt 24, 18 Dec 44; 307th Inf Opns Rpt Leyte, p. 7; 77th Div Opns Rpt Leyte, p. 28.

[26] Sixth Army FO 39, 19 Dec 44.

[27] XXIV Corps FO 38 (Confirmatory of Oral and Fragmentary orders), 21 Dec 44.

junction. The 304th, 305th, and 902d Field Artillery Battalions were to remain in the Valencia area while the 306th Field Artillery Battalion was to be prepared to move forward on call.[28]

At Libongao, General Suzuki prepared his defense. In the area he had his headquarters guard and a part of the *4th Airborne Raiding Regiment,* in addition to a field artillery battalion, an engineering company, and a transportation company. An advance battalion of the *Takahashi Detachment* arrived in the sector from Palompon on the night of 17 December. General Suzuki ordered it to proceed south from Libongao and destroy the American forces in the Valencia area.[29]

As the 307th Infantry advanced north at 0900 on 19 December, it became apparent that General Suzuki had organized a defense of the highway. Many machine gun and light artillery emplacements were dug in along the road, and the enemy resistance became more determined as the troops moved north. A force estimated to be of battalion strength was dug in in depth along streams and ridges. With the use of grenades the 307th routed the defenders, the battalion from the *Takahashi Detachment.* The 307th Infantry pushed steadily north and at 1800 established a night perimeter; it had advanced nearly three miles and captured much enemy equipment during the day.[30]

The 306th Infantry moved out at 1100 and proceeded rapidly, without meeting resistance, to a point about 500 yards south of the Palompon road where it encountered elements of the *5th Infantry Regiment.* At 1530 a battery of artillery and infantry

mortars and machine guns fired upon the Japanese. In co-ordination with fire from these weapons, the 306th Infantry was then able to push forward. At 1800, though patrols from the regiment had reached the Palompon road, the regiment itself dug in for the night at a point 300 yards south of the Palompon road.[31]

On 20 December, after a five-minute artillery preparation to its front, the 307th Infantry moved out at 0830 and encountered the "strongest fortified positions" since it had left Camp Downes. The Japanese *5th Infantry Regiment* and other elements of the *1st Division* resisted any forward advance. By 1000 the 307th Infantry had "mowed down" and annihilated two suicide counterattacks of fifty men each on its right flank. An additional force, estimated at 2,000 men, well equipped with machine guns, mortars, and a limited amount of artillery, opposed the 307th Infantry from hastily constructed defensive positions. The attack of the enemy forces was not well co-ordinated; consequently the regiment, though slowed down, was able to continue forward. At 1549 the leading elements of the 307th Infantry were at Libongao. The enemy defensive fire increased in intensity on the northern outskirts of the village. At 1710, about 200 yards north of Libongao, the regiment repulsed a force estimated to consist of 200 Japanese armed with machine guns and mortars. The 307th Infantry established its night perimeter about 1,000 yards south of the road junction. During the day the regiment had captured many tons of ammunition and matériel in supply dumps, to-

---

[28] 77th Div FO 19, 19 Dec 44.

[29] *35th Army* Opns, p. 103.

[30] 77th Div G–3 Jnl, 19 Dec 44; 77th Div G–3 Periodic Rpt 25, 19 Dec 44; 307th Inf Unit Jnl, 19 Dec 44; 307th Inf Opns Rpt Leyte, p. 7.

[31] 306th Inf Opns Rpt Leyte, p. 10; 306th Inf Unit Jnl, 19 Dec 44; 77th Div G–3 Jnl, 19 Dec 44; 77th Div Opns Rpt Leyte, p. 29; 77th Div G–3 Periodic Rpt 25, 19 Dec 44.

gether with more than thirty enemy trucks. The 307th Infantry put many of the latter into serviceable condition and made immediate use of them.[32]

For the same day, 20 December, the 306th Infantry, on the left of the 307th, was assigned the mission of advancing to the Palompon road. Upon reaching the road, the 1st Battalion on the left would turn west along it to seize a bridge crossing the Togbong River and the 3d Battalion would turn east to seize the junction of the road and Highway 2.[33] During the night the enemy artillery heavily shelled the sector of the regiment. After a ten-minute artillery preparation the assault battalions moved out at 0830, and by 0925 they had reached the Palompon road. Each of the battalions thereupon started to execute its part of the mission.

The 1st Battalion pushed steadily forward and reached the eastern banks of the Togbong River at the bridge crossing, the bridge itself having been destroyed by the enemy. From a commanding ridge upon the western banks of the river, just north of the bridge site, a Japanese force estimated to be a battalion in strength opposed any further advance. The company on the left forced a passage across the river south of the bridge site, but the company on the right, despite repeated attempts, was unable to cross the river. At 1630 the 1st Battalion received orders to take up a night defensive position on the eastern banks of the river. During the night the enemy unsuccessfully launched three counterattacks against the 1st Battalion. In the morning the battalion counted

more than 400 Japanese dead around its position.

The 3d Battalion, 306th Infantry, upon reaching the Palompon road turned east and encountered steadily increasing enemy opposition. By 1500, however, Company K reached the road junction. At the same time the 3d Battalion received orders to withdraw west 300 yards so that the 307th Infantry could register unrestricted fire to its front. This withdrawal was carried out and the 3d and 2d Battalions of the 306th Infantry established night positions 300 yards west of the road junction.

At 1900 General Bruce ordered the 306th Infantry to deliver harassing fire on the enemy forces to the west during the night of 20–21 December and the 307th Infantry to fire 500 yards to its front up Highway 2 and east of the highway.[34]

The Japanese *5th Infantry Regiment* had assembled in the Libongao sector with orders to proceed to the Valencia sector, but the 77th Division had advanced so rapidly that it was attacking the *35th Army Headquarters*. The *Takahashi Detachment* suffered heavy casualties and withdrew to Matagob, on the Palompon road between Palompon and Libongao. The field artillery battalion and the engineering and transportation companies that had been left at Matagob were absorbed by the *Takahashi Detachment*. On 21 December General Suzuki ordered the regiment to make a defensive stand, so that the main force of the *35th Army* could withdraw to the Palompon sector on the shore of the Camotes Sea.[35]

---

[32] 77th Div G–3 Periodic Rpt 26, 20 Dec 44; 77th Div Opns Rpt Leyte, p. 31; 77th Div G–2 Jnl, 20 Dec 44; 77th Div G–3 Jnl, 20 Dec 44; 307th Inf Opns Rpt Leyte, pp. 7–8; 307th Inf Unit Jnl, 20 Dec 44.

[33] 306th Inf FO 11, 19 Dec 44.

[34] 77th Div Opns Rpt Leyte, pp. 30–31; 77th Div G–3 Jnl, 20 Dec 44; 77th Div G–2 Jnl, 20 Dec 44; 306th Inf Unit Jnl, 20 Dec 44; 306th Inf Opns Rpt Leyte, pp. 10–11; 77th Div G–3 Periodic Rpt 26, 20 Dec 44.

[35] *35th Army* Opns, pp. 103–104.

During the night of 20–21 December the 77th Division artillery expended half a unit of fire, intermittently bombarding enemy positions west of the 77th Division and to the east of Highway 2. The bombardment was the most intensive made by the 77th Division during the campaign. Just before renewal of the attack on 21 December, the artillery delivered a concentrated thirty-minute preparation. General Bruce ordered the 306th Infantry to move out at 0630. Since the 1st Battalion was short of ammunition, it was to await the arrival of Company E, which had been attached to the battalion, with additional ammunition. At 1250, having received the ammunition, the battalion moved out and at 1330 secured the ridge (overlooking the bridge site), which had blocked its advance the previous day.

Immediately afterward General Bruce ordered the battalion to proceed west along the Palompon road and secure the bridge over the Pagsangahan River. The ridge was thereupon outposted as the 1st Battalion withdrew to prepare for continuation of the assault, but elements of the *5th Infantry Regiment* drove the outposts off the ridge and immediately occupied it. At 1500 the 1st Battalion attacked unsuccessfully in an effort to retake the position. It formed a night perimeter at the river crossing at 1600, and at 0750 concentrated a ten-minute artillery preparation on the enemy positions on the ridge. The 1st Battalion then moved out toward the high ground and secured the ridge within twenty minutes, the Japanese offering only slight resistance.[36]

---

[36] 306th Inf Opns Rpt Leyte, pp. 11–12; 306th Inf Unit Jnl, 21 Dec 44. During this action Pfc. George Benjamin, Jr., a radio operator from Company A, killed the crew of a machine gun nest at the cost of his life. He was posthumously awarded the Medal of Honor.

The 77th Division had reached the Palompon road. In its drive north the division had destroyed the major elements of the *5th* and *77th Infantry Regiments* and the *4th Airborne Regiment*.

The 32d Division Resumes the Offensive

Elements of the X Corps were slowly moving south in an attempt to effect a juncture with the XXIV Corps. On 14 December the 126th and 127th Infantry Regiments of the 32d Division had pushed south down Highway 2 against very determined resistance and through mountainous terrain to the main defense line of the *1st Division*. The Japanese were well entrenched on a series of ridges overlooking Highway 2. A heavy rain forest covered the ridges and the deep ravines in between. The enemy had carefully selected his defensive positions and camouflaged his machine guns, which were flanked by hidden riflemen. Targets could not be spotted beyond a range of about seventy-five feet. The employment of mortars was very limited because of the lack of visibility, and the hazards of tree burst were equally dangerous to both the Japanese and the Americans. The troops had to "approach within spitting distance of the [Japanese machine] guns" before they could locate the weapons.[37]

For the next few days the regiments of the 32d Division fought valiantly against a foe that limited the division's advance to a few score yards a day. Of the many acts of individual bravery, those of Pfc. Dick J. Vlug and Sgt. Leroy Johnson were outstanding. Private Vlug single-handedly destroyed five enemy tanks that were moving north along the highway. Sergeant Johnson threw himself upon an enemy grenade that killed him

---

[37] 32d Div G–3 Periodic Rpt 30, 16 Dec 44.

but did not hurt those comrades near him. Both men were awarded the Medal of Honor.

On the morning of 17 December advance elements of the 126th Infantry were about 4,000 yards south of Limon. After a preparation of heavy mortar fire the 1st Battalion moved out at 0730, encountering about a platoon of the enemy on a knoll 300 yards east of the road. A bitter fire fight broke out and continued throughout the day. The battalion was unable to advance farther and set up a night perimeter. During the fight the 1st Battalion captured four enemy machine guns.

In the zone of the 2d Battalion, east of the highway, all the battalion's mortars, machine guns, and 37-mm. guns, together with four medium tanks, massed their combined fires on the enemy positions to the front. These positions consisted of numerous foxholes, pillboxes of coconut logs, and L-shaped fortifications dug into the mountain sides. A rain of steel descended upon the Japanese on the high ground directly east of the battalion. This preparatory fire had excellent results and the 2d Battalion, after moving out at 1100, quickly secured the ridge and consolidated its position. It captured three 47-mm. antitank guns, three 75-mm. mountain guns, and two 70-mm. battalion guns. About 150 of the enemy were killed by the preparatory fire and the battalion attack.

Company I, 3d Battalion, quickly secured and destroyed a roadblock that the enemy had constructed the previous day. Accompanied by the four tanks, the company then advanced down the highway just behind the 2d Battalion without encountering opposition. For the rest of the day the 3d Battalion protected the road and patrolled five or six hundred yards to the rear. The

127th Infantry to the south remained in position awaiting the 126th Infantry.[38]

By the following morning, 18 December, the 126th Infantry was on a line that extended east of Highway 2. To the front of the regiment, elements of the *1st Division* occupied three positions on an east-west line approximately 800 yards in length and extending across Highway 2. There were actually three ridges along this line. The first ran north and south beside the road, and on it was located the western position of the enemy. From this site the Japanese were able to roll hand grenades down on the road. About 200 yards to the east was another strongly fortified north-south ridge, east of which was a small valley with a banana grove. Still farther east was a small knoll upon which was located a strong enemy defensive position. An estimated two reinforced enemy companies, well supported by automatic weapons and well dug in, occupied this position. The whole area was covered with a dense rain forest, and it was impossible to spot any Japanese fortified position more than thirty yards away.

Before the troops moved out, the mortars and tanks placed heavy fire on the Japanese positions for twenty minutes. At 1010 on 18 December the 126th Infantry attacked with the 1st Battalion on the right and the 2d Battalion on the left. In advancing to the ridge nearest the road, the American troops received considerable small arms fire just east of the road. The 1st Battalion moved ahead up the ridge east of the road and by 1230 it had advanced 200 yards to the top of the ridge. The Japanese resisted strongly and heavy fighting occurred in which both sides used machine guns, grenades, and

---

[38] 32d Div G–3 Periodic Rpt 31, 17 Dec 44; 32d Div G–3 Jnl, 17 Dec 44; 126th Inf Unit Jnl, 17 Dec 44; 32d Div G–3 Periodic Rpt 31, 17 Dec 44.

bayonets. By 1800 the 1st Battalion was in firm possession of the ridge. The 2d Battalion, supported by machine guns and mortars, was able to creep up through the forested ravine to within thirty yards of the enemy position on the knoll before it was fired upon. A bitter engagement then ensued. After five hours of intense fighting the battalion drove the Japanese defenders off the knoll. The 1st and 2d Battalions formed their night perimeters within fifty yards of the enemy front lines. The 3d Battalion of the 126th Infantry moved south along the road and closed the gap between the 126th and 127th Infantry Regiments.[39] The artillery fired upon several buildings about 800 to 1,500 yards southwest of the forward elements of the 32d Division. Lucrative artillery targets were practically nonexistent.[40]

On the morning of 19 December the 126th Infantry followed the same procedure that had been used the previous day. A heavy machine gun and mortar concentration was placed upon the Japanese positions on the crest of a ridge fifty yards to the front. At 1100 the 126th Infantry moved out with battalions abreast, the 1st Battalion on the right and the 2d on the left. Six heavy machine guns immediately fired on the left flank of the 1st Battalion. The battalion withdrew and placed a concentration of more than 200 rounds of mortar fire on the position while its machine guns raked the Japanese force "fore and aft." The troops then renewed the assault but the Japanese continued to resist. Elements of the *1st Division* had dug in on the top and both sides of a ridge and had utilized caves to construct a defensive position in which there were more than 100 foxholes with com-

municating trenches. Heavy fighting continued throughout the day. The 1st Battalion used mortars, flame throwers, white phosphorus grenades, hand grenades, rifles, and supporting flanking fire from its heavy and light machine guns, but was able to advance only seventy-five yards. Although the battalion overran many emplacements, a determined Japanese force remained to be overcome when the battalion established its night perimeter on the eastern slope of the ridge.

The 2d Battalion, 126th Infantry, encountered only scattered rifle fire that came principally from the enemy position on its right flank. During its advance the battalion delivered flanking machine gun and rifle fire in support of the 1st Battalion on its right. By 1200 the 2d Battalion had advanced 200 yards and secured the area in its zone of action. At 1530 the 1st Squadron, 112th Cavalry, which had been protecting the eastern flank of the 32d Division, relieved the 2d Battalion, which withdrew to an assembly area in the rear.

During the night of 19–20 December, the commanding officer of Company B, 126th Infantry, which had borne the brunt of the enemy resistance, placed one platoon of the company along the eastern side of the ridge and another platoon on the western side. At the same time he continued the pressure from the south. Throughout the night the company kept firing at known enemy positions and the sector in general. The company commander also required each of his men to throw hand grenades periodically. At first light and without any breakfast the troops rushed the enemy position. The Japanese had lost the power to resist and by 1000 the company had taken the last of the three enemy positions. Two hundred Japanese dead were counted in the area.

---

[39] 32d Div G–3 Periodic Rpt 32, 18 Dec 44; 32d Div G–3 Jnl, 18 Dec 44; 126th Inf Unit Jnl, 18 Dec 44.

[40] 32d Div Arty Daily Rpt, 18 Dec 44.

At 1245 on 20 December the 127th Infantry took over the conquered sector and the 1st Battalion, 126th Infantry, withdrew to an assembly area in the rear.[41]

Debouchment From the Mountains

Since the 32d Division had borne the brunt of the assault, General Sibert ordered the 1st Cavalry Division to make the main attack south. It was to assist the advance of the 32d Division to a bridge 1,000 yards north of Lonoy and then move south and make contact with the 77th Division.[42] The 1st Cavalry Division had been operating in the central mountain chain on the eastern flank of the 32d Division and had been opposed by the *102d Division*. The latter, after its arrival at Ormoc, had gone directly into the mountains in the vicinity of Mt. Pina.[43] The *102d Division* did not play a significant role in the Leyte campaign.

The 112th Cavalry Regimental Combat Team had moved south on the eastern flank of the 32d Division. The 1st Squadron of the 112th Cavalry had been able to keep pace with the 32d Division, but the 2d Squadron had encountered a very strong enemy force on a ridge overlooking the Leyte River south of Limon. The Japanese resisted all the squadron's efforts to dislodge them. The 2d Squadron, 7th Cavalry, relieved the 2d Squadron, 112th Cavalry, and on 14 December it had succeeded in overcoming the Japanese and had seized the ridge.

Spearhead of the Assault

While the 112th and 7th Cavalry Regiments were busily engaged in defending the east flank of the 32d Division in its push south along Highway 2, the 12th Cavalry was mopping up enemy groups entrenched in the mountains farther to the east. Particularly strong enemy resistance had been encountered in the Mt. Badian and Hill 2348 sector, which was about five miles northeast of Kananga, a barrio on Highway 2.[44] In the process of reducing the Japanese-held area, it was estimated that an enemy force of 500 to 600 men had been wiped out. From 28 November to 9 December, the 12th Cavalry remained in the Mt. Badian and Hill 2348 sector, sent out westward patrols, and slowly moved westward.

On 10 December, General Sibert decided to have elements of the 1st Cavalry Division debouch from the mountains onto Highway 2 south of the 32d Division and in the Lonoy area. This move was to be concurrent with the expected advance of the 32d Division down the highway.[45] The 1st Squadron, 12th Cavalry, was in the vicinity of Mt. Cabungaan, and the 2d Squadron, on Hill 2348, was 2,000 yards northeast of the 1st Squadron. An enemy strong point existed to the north of the perimeter of the 1st Squadron. The 12th Cavalry spent 10 December in making preparations for a two-squadron assault against this enemy force. The plan was for the 1st Squadron to attack at 0830 while the 2d Squadron from Hill 2348 supported the attack by enveloping the left flank of the enemy. In further-

---

[41] 32d Div G–3 Periodic Rpt 33, 19 Dec 44; 32d Div G–3 Jnl, 19 Dec 44; 126th Inf Unit Jnl, 20 Dec 44; 32d Div G–3 Jnl, 20 Dec 44.
[42] X Corps FO 22, 20 Dec 44.
[43] 10th I&HS, Eighth Army Stf Study of Opns of Japanese *102d Division* on Leyte and Cebu, Interrog of Maj Chuji Kaneko, p. 3.

[44] Unless otherwise stated the part of this subsection dealing with the 12th Cavalry is based on: 12th Cav Opns Rpt Leyte, pp. 20–30, 76–85; 1st Cav Div G–3 Periodic Rpts 51–63, 10–22 Dec 44; and 12th Cav Unit Rpts 54–65, 11–22 Dec 44.
[45] 1st Cav Div Opns Rpt Leyte, p. 52; 1st Cav Div FO 17, 10 Dec 44.

ance of this plan Troop E of the 2d Squadron moved off Hill 2348 at 0800 toward the southwest and dug in for the night just north of Mt. Cabungaan.[46]

On the morning of 11 December, an intense mortar and artillery concentration was placed upon the enemy position in front of the 1st Squadron. The fire was so close that fragments frequently fell on the waiting assault troops. After this fire, the 1st Squadron with Troop A in the lead moved out at 0715. At the same time Troop E attacked from the northeast. The enemy defenses consisted of seven or eight pillboxes and many caves dug into the very rugged terrain. The men of Troop A, closely followed by Troop B, charged up the hill "throwing grenades and firing from the hip."[47] The hill fell to the 1st Squadron at 1003 after very heavy hand-to-hand fighting. Troop E had been held up by the terrain and was unable to assist the 1st Squadron. After the capture of the Japanese position, patrols established contact with Troop E at 1200. The regimental reconnaissance platoon returned from the vicinity of Lonoy with the information that the Japanese had prepared strong defensive positions in that area. The platoon had gained a good observation point 900 yards east of Lonoy.[48] The next several days were spent in sending out patrols and moving the 2d Squadron to the position of the 1st Squadron.

On 14 December, the 12th Cavalry was ordered to continue west to Highway 2 and assist the advance of the 32d Division, to establish a roadblock on the highway, and to attack the hostile forces to the north between it and the 32d Division.[49] In furtherance of this order, the 1st Squadron, less A and C Troops, moved west on 15 December toward a previously reconnoitered area that was about 1,800 yards east of the barrio of Lonoy. This site, a banana plantation, was chosen for its observation facilities to the west and as an excellent dropping ground for supplies. The 1st Squadron, having encountered little opposition, closed on the area before dusk. Thereupon the rest of the regiment was ordered to close in on the area before nightfall on 17 December.

Lonoy

The 12th Cavalry on 18 December sent out patrols to Lonoy, Kananga, and to the northwest to make contact with the nearest friendly troops. The patrols to Lonoy and Kananga, although they ran into scattered groups of the enemy, were able to locate suitable approaches to Lonoy for their squadrons.[50]

At 2235, on 18 December, the 12th Cavalry received orders to move out the following morning, seize Lonoy, and be prepared to seize Kananga. The commanding officer of the regiment decided to have the 1st and 2d Squadrons move out abreast with the 2d Squadron on the left. During the entire night the artillery was to deliver harassing fire on the highway north of Lonoy and on the area between the routes of approach of the two squadrons.

After a preparation on 19 December, the 1st and 2d Squadrons moved out at 0800. The 1st Squadron met only light, sporadic resistance. The troops observed many Jap-

---

[46] 12th Cav Unit Rpt 53, 10 Dec 44; 1st Cav Div G–3 Periodic Rpt 52, 11 Dec 44. The spelling of *Mt. Cabungaan* used here follows that of the maps employed by the combat troops. The Board of Geographic Names gives the spelling as *Mt. Cabungangan.*

[47] 12th Cav Opns Rpt Leyte, p. 24.

[48] 12th Cav Unit Rpt 54, 11 Dec 44; 1st Cav Div G–3 Periodic Rpt 53, 12 Dec 44.

[49] 1st Cav FO 18, 14 Dec 44.

[50] 1st Cav Div G–3 Periodic Rpt 60, 19 Dec 44.

anese proceeding north along the highway and had mortar and artillery fires placed upon them. At 1200, the 1st Squadron seized Lonoy, captured much enemy equipment, and destroyed many supply dumps. The 1st Squadron moved to assist the 2d Squadron in the capture of a knoll southeast of the barrio. The 1st Squadron closed on the knoll about 1400, and aided the assault of the 2d Squadron by fire and by sending a troop east to assist it.

The 2d Squadron jumped off on schedule but at 0930, when it was 800 yards short of its objective, the squadron came under heavy rifle and machine gun fire from the thick woods. The 271st Field Artillery Battalion placed fire on the area and a great many of the enemy were killed, the remainder fleeing south. The squadron received additional machine gun fire from the north but a patrol quickly silenced it. In the meantime the mortar platoon from Troop D, in support of the 1st Squadron, fired upon Lonoy. The Japanese immediately responded with fire from a 105-mm. gun, which they had cleverly concealed in the gap between the two squadrons and about 600 yards from the regimental observation post at which the gun directed its fire. The enemy gun killed one man and wounded fifteen others of the command-post group. The heavy machine guns from the Weapons troop and the artillery from the 271st Field Artillery Battalion began concentrating their fires upon the enemy gun. The Antitank Platoon was sent out to destroy the gun and its crew. Following the machine gun and artillery fire, the enemy gun was silent for about half an hour. It then suddenly opened up against the 2d Squadron at a range of about 300 yards. The enemy fire resulted in tree bursts which killed five men and wounded fifteen others. Troop G, which suf-

fered the most casualties, and the Antitank Platoon immediately turned and attacked to the north to destroy the gun. The 2d Squadron, less Troop G, renewed the attack towards Lonoy, receiving scattered rifle fire. At 1730 it reached Lonoy and was in contact with the 1st Squadron.

Meanwhile, Troop G sideslipped to the west and with the Antitank Platoon attacked and destroyed the enemy gun and four of its crew. A patrol located another enemy 105-mm. gun but, because of darkness and point-blank fire from the weapon at a range of about twenty-five feet, it was unable to knock out the gun. At 2200 Troops G and H, the medical group, and the Antitank Platoon formed a joint night perimeter.[51]

Late that night the regimental commander ordered the 2d and 1st Squadrons of the 12th Cavalry to move south on the morning of 20 December along Highway 2 in a column of squadrons, with the 2d Squadron in the lead. During the night, in preparation for this advance, the 271st Field Artillery Battalion fired 1,096 rounds on Kananga, on the road north of Lonoy, and on sectors occupied by the enemy artillery. This fire destroyed the enemy 105-mm. gun.

At 0715 on the morning of 20 December the 2d Squadron, less Troop G, moved out and immediately came under heavy fire from enemy forces that had dug in underneath houses and behind small pieces of cover along the road. The squadron eliminated these pockets of resistance by direct fire and by flanking movements on both sides of the highway. At 1200 the 2d Squadron forced the Japanese off a ridge which was just east of the highway and about 500 yards north of Kananga. The squadron then

---

[51] 1st Cav Div G–3 Periodic Rpt 61, 20 Dec 44; X Corps G–2 Periodic Rpt 59, 19 Dec 44; 1st Cav Div G–3, Jnl, 19 Dec 44.

encountered heavy rifle and machine gun fire that came from a coconut grove and some houses about 200 yards south of the ridge.

In the meantime, the 1st Squadron, at 0830, moved south to support the attack of the 2d Squadron. At about 1230, the 1st Squadron arrived behind the ridge occupied by the 2d Squadron and then continued south, at 1500, seizing and completely dominating a ridge about fifty yards east of Kananga. The 2d Squadron and a platoon from the 1st Squadron attacked north, parallel to the highway, and by nightfall cleaned out the coconut grove and set up a night perimeter.

General Mudge, commanding general of the 1st Cavalry Division, said of the 12th Cavalry:

As a result of the stout-hearted efforts of the 12th Cavalry Regiment, elements of the Division are within 2,500 yards of making contact with forward elements of the 77th Division. Considering the fact that the regiment has been reduced to 50% strength by the rigors and deprivations of 40 days in the mountains, the display of courage, stamina, and drive on the part of the 12th Cavalry is a credit to the best traditions of the United States Cavalry.[52]

During the night General Mudge ordered the 12th Cavalry to move out at 0800 21 December, seize Kananga, and then make physical contact with the 77th Division, which was pushing north from Libongao. He attached the 1st Squadron, 5th Cavalry, to the 12th Cavalry.

Juncture of Forces

On the morning of 21 December the 1st and 2d Squadrons of the 12th Cavalry, supported by the 271st Field Artillery Battalion,

moved out in a co-ordinated assault against Kananga. The 1st Squadron attacked from the north while the 2d Squadron drove in from the ridge on the east. The first elements of the regiment reached Kananga at 1157 and by 1425 the 12th Cavalry was in the town. The regiment methodically cleared out every hut, ferreted out each Japanese, and destroyed every installation. While the mopping up was going on, patrols from the 12th Cavalry pushed to the south to make contact with the 77th Division.

The regimental commander ordered the commander of the 3d Battalion, 306th Infantry, to push east at 0730 on 21 December along the Palompon road to the juncture of the road with Highway 2 and then turn north for 1,000 yards and attempt to establish contact with the 1st Cavalry Division. The 3d Battalion moved out on time, and within fifteen minutes reached the road junction and turned north. The battalion had gone only 200 yards north when its left-flank company came under intense fire from a ridge overlooking the road. The 2d Battalion complied with orders from the regimental commander to "put out something" on the 3d Battalion's left flank and sent out one rifle company to envelop the enemy position. This move relieved the pressure to some extent but the advance was still slow and costly.

In the meantime, the 307th Infantry reached the road junction at 0800, having advanced without incident. With the slowing up of the 306th Infantry, General Bruce ordered the commander of the 307th Infantry Regiment to send forward additional troops. The 2d Battalion, 307th Infantry, and the Cannon and Antitank Companies of the regiment were sent to the front to reinforce the 306th Infantry. This maneuver

[52] 1st Cav Div G–3 Periodic Rpt 62, 21 Dec 44.

was successful and the attacking forces pushed forward.

At 1645, the 306th Infantry and Troop A of the 12th Cavalry made physical contact. At 1115 on 22 December, Col. John H. Stadler, the commanding officer of the 12th Cavalry, representing General Mudge, met General Bruce at a bridge south of Kananga. The X and XXIV Corps had joined hands. Highway 2 was at long last open for its entire distance from Ormoc to Pinamopoan.[53]

The Ormoc Valley, in which the Japanese had so tenaciously resisted the American advance, was now securely in the hands of the Sixth Army. The northern and southern prongs of the trap had closed. There remained only Palompon as an exit for the Japanese forces. To the securing of that port, the X and XXIV Corps, acting in concert, could concentrate their main efforts. Plans had been readied. The Sixth Army was poised in a position from which it could drive westward to the sea and bring the Leyte campaign to a successful conclusion.

[53] 77th Div G–3 Jnl, 21 Dec 44; 77th Div G–3 Periodic Rpt 27, 21 Dec 44; 77th Div Opns Rpt Leyte, pp. 31–32; 307th Inf Unit Jnl, 21 Dec 44; 307th Inf Opns Rpt Leyte, p. 8; 306th Inf Unit Jnl, 21 Dec 44; 306th Inf Opns Rpt Leyte, pp. 11–12.

CHAPTER XXI

Westward to the Sea

The co-ordinated pressure exerted from the north and south on the Japanese forces in the Ormoc area had compelled the commander of the *35th Army* to make successive changes in his plans. General Suzuki had abandoned the aerial and ground assault against the Burauen airfields, transferred the field base of the *35th Army* from Ormoc to Palompon and, finally, had found it necessary to order the remaining Japanese units on Leyte to retreat to the hills behind Ormoc Valley. General Tomochika said afterward, "The best that the *35th Army* could do from then on was to hold out as long as possible." [1]

The northwestern mountains of Leyte west of Ormoc Bay provided a difficult barrier to any movement toward the northwest coast. The area was the last one available to the Japanese either for escaping from Leyte or for staging defensive actions. In general, the terrain was rough, increasing in altitude from broken ground and low hills in the north to steep rocky ridges and high hills in the south. The northern part was either under cultivation or covered with cogon grass. Toward the south, the cultivated fields and grasslands were gradually supplanted by dense forests.

Palompon had been extensively used by the Japanese as an auxiliary port of entry to Leyte. The town was the western terminus of the road that ran north and eastward across the northwestern hills to join Highway 2 near Libongao. (*Map 21*) It was this road junction that the X and XXIV Corps had seized. The Palompon road, as it was called, followed the lower slopes of the hills until the flat interior valley floor was reached. The confining hills were steep-sided with many knife-edged crests. [2] Such was the area into which the forces of the Sixth Army had driven remnants of the Japanese *35th Army*.

When the 77th Infantry Division and the 1st Cavalry Division joined forces on 21 December just south of Kananga, Highway 2 between Ormoc and Pinamopoan was opened to the Americans. The Sixth Army, anxious to deliver the *coup de grâce*, arranged its troops for a four-division thrust to the west coast on a long front. In the south the 77th Division was to drive west along the Palompon road. To its right (north) there would be, from left to right, the 1st Cavalry Division and the 32d and 24th Infantry Divisions. The Sixth Army had started the Leyte Campaign with two corps on a four-division front and was ending its part in the campaign with two corps on a four-division front.

---

[1] 10th I&HS, Eighth Army Stf Study of *35th Army* on Leyte, Part 1, p. 24, Interrog of Maj Gen Yoshiharu Tomochika.

[2] Sixth Army G–2 Wkly Rpt 69, 20 Dec 44, pp. 14–18.

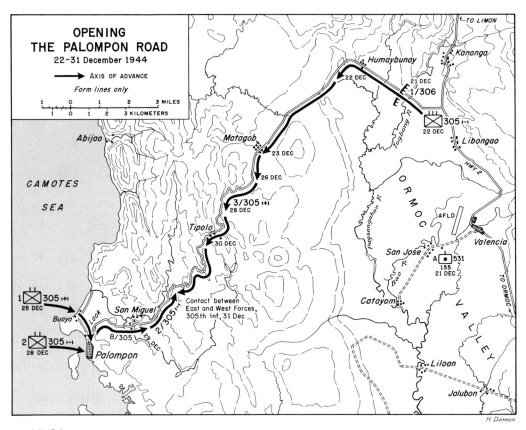

MAP 21

The 77th Division Goes West

Overwater to Palompon [3]

Guerrillas had informed General Bruce
that the bridges on the road that wound

through the mountains from the vicinity of
Libongao to Palompon either were intact
or could be quickly repaired. General Bruce
decided to verify this by having an engineer
patrol work with the guerrillas and by having a reconnaissance made over the area in a
cub plane. On 19 December General Bruce
directed that a fast-moving force be organized to operate along the road to Palompon.
The engineers later informed him that because of the condition of many of the bridges
it would be impossible to send an advance
column along the road. [4]

[3] Unless otherwise indicated, this subsection dealing with the 77th Division is based upon the following: 77th Div Opns Rpt Leyte, pp. 32–35;
77th Div Supp Opns Rpt Leyte, pp. 1–8, 28–29;
77th Div G–3 Periodic Rpts 33–37, 27–31 Dec 44;
77th Div G–2 Summary Leyte Campaign; 305th
Inf Opns Rpt Leyte, pp. 7–8; 305th Inf Hist Rpt
1944, pp. 5–7; 77th Div G–3 Jnl, 23–30 Dec 44;
77th Div Admin O 7, 24 Dec 44; 77th Div FO 20,
19 Dec 44; 77th Div FO 22, 24 Dec 44; 1st Bn,
305th Inf, FO 3, 23 Dec 44; 305th Inf Unit Jnl,
25 Dec 44–2 Jan 45.

[4] Ltr, Gen Bruce to Gen Ward, 16 Aug 51,
OCMH.

On 21 December General Hodge, anticipating the juncture of the X and XXIV Corps, ordered the 77th Division to be prepared after that event to move rapidly west and seize the Palompon area.[5] On 22 December General Krueger, acting on a recommendation that had been made by General Bruce through General Hodge,[6] informed Admiral Kinkaid that it might be possible to expedite the capture of Palompon by having an infantry battalion, utilizing amphibian vehicles and LCM's, make an amphibious movement from Ormoc to the vicinity of Palompon. He therefore asked Admiral Kinkaid if naval support to escort and guide this movement could be furnished for either the night of 23–24 or that of 24–25 December. If possible, the amphibious force should have a destroyer escort.[7] Admiral Kinkaid stated, in reply, that because of preparations for other operations it would be "most difficult" to provide a destroyer escort but that he could furnish a PT escort which he believed would be sufficient protection.[8] This was satisfactory to General Krueger and he ordered the XXIV Corps to make plans for the amphibious movement.[9] In turn General Hodge told General Bruce to prepare for the operation.

On 22 December, General Bruce put his plan into operation. The 1st Battalion, 305th Infantry, was to make the amphibious landing in the vicinity of Palompon while the 2d and 3d Battalions were to proceed west along the Palompon road, after moving in

trucks from Valencia to the Palompon road near the Togbong River. Previously, on 21 December, Battery A of the 531st Field Artillery Battalion (155-mm. gun) was brought with a great deal of effort to a position near San Jose from which it could fire on Palompon, which the guerrillas and civilians had received instructions to evacuate.[10]

The 1st Battalion was to commence loading at 1400 on 23 December at Ormoc. The convoy was to be protected en route by patrol torpedo boats and close air support. Upon arriving at Palompon at 0500 on 25 December, the mortar-firing LCM's were to bombard the shore before the assault forces moved in. Beginning 23 December, the artillery of the 77th Division was to bombard Palompon and to continue as long as Lt. Col. James E. Landrum, the task force commander, desired it.[11]

The 1st Battalion was to move ashore on the beach about 1,500 yards north of Palompon with Companies C and B in assault, Company C on the left. Its mission was to destroy the enemy force in Palompon and then turn north.[12]

In support of the proposed landing, aircraft from the Fifth Air Force bombed Palompon on 23 December. The results were "hot stuff," an overenthusiastic observer reported, claiming that "only half of two houses were left standing in the whole town." [13]

On 23 December, the reinforced 1st Battalion moved to Ormoc to prepare for the amphibious landing and at 1930 on 24

[5] XXIV Corps FO 38, 21 Dec 44.
[6] Ltr, Gen Bruce to Gen Ward, 16 Aug 51, OCMH.
[7] Rad, CG Sixth Army to CTF 77, 22 Dec 44, Sixth Army G–3 Jnl, 22 Dec 44.
[8] Msg, CTF 77 to CG Sixth Army, 23 Dec 44, Sixth Army G–3 Jnl, 23 Dec 44.
[9] Memo for Col Guerard, unsigned, 23 Dec 44, XXIV Corps G–3 Jnl, 23 Dec 44.

[10] Ltr, Gen Bruce to Gen Ward, 16 Aug 51, OCMH.
[11] 77th Div G–3 Jnl, 25 Dec 44.
[12] 77th Div FO's 20 and 21, 19 Dec 44; 1st Bn, 305th Inf, FO 3, 23 Dec 44.
[13] Rad, 9th Air Liaison Party to Fifth Air Force, X Corp G–3 Jnl, 24 Dec 44.

PALOMPON AFTER ALLIED BOMBINGS. *Note bomb craters in foreground.*

December the troops embarked.[14] The convoy departed at 2000. The vessels included, in addition to the mechanized landing craft, the LVT's of the 718th and 536th Amphibian Tractor Battalions. They made the tedious ten-hour trip without incident as far as enemy action was concerned, al-

though three of the LVT's "sank owing to mechanical failure."

The vessels took position off the landing beaches on the morning of 25 December. After the 155-mm. guns of the 531st Field Artillery Battalion had fired from positions near San Jose, twelve and a half miles east of Palompon, the mortar boats of the 2d Engineer Special Brigade softened up the beaches. The landing waves then started for the shore, the first wave landing at 0720 and the last one at 0755. They received no hostile fire.

"Meanwhile," wrote General Bruce, "the Division Commander could stand it no longer and called for a plane, flew soon after daylight across the mountains and seaward, located the amphibious forces still at

[14] In addition to the 1st Battalion, 305th Infantry, the Special Task Force included: the Amphibian Tractor Company; Company A, 776th Amphibian Tank Battalion; one platoon of Company D, 706th Tank Battalion; three guns from the regimental Cannon Company; the 2d Platoon of Company A, 302d Engineer Battalion; a detachment from Company A, 302d Medical Battalion; the 292d JASCO detachment; the 305th Field Artillery Battalion; a detachment of the 306th Field Artillery Battalion; a detachment from Battery A, 531st Field Artillery Battalion. 77th Div Opns Rpt Leyte, p. 33.

sea, . . . witnessed the preparatory fires by the 155-mm. guns and that from the mortar boats . . . saw them going in . . . and advance to the beach. (He obeyed a rather boyish impulse and flew from 25 to 50 feet above the heads of the troops in the assault boats and leaned out, giving a boxer's victory sign with both hands.)" [15]

The troops quickly organized on the beach. A light fast armored column moved north to clear the road and to forestall any Japanese counterattack from that direction as the rest of the task force went rapidly south through the barrio of Look to Palompon, which fell at 1206. This closed the last main port of entrance on the island to the Japanese. Within four hours after hitting the beaches the battalion had secured the barrios of Buaya and Look as well as Palompon, and had strong patrols operating to the northeast and south. The troops met no opposition at any point. It was doubtless with great satisfaction that General Bruce sent the following message to the Commanding General, XXIV Corps: "The 77th Infantry Division's Christmas contribution to the Leyte Campaign is the capture of Palompon, the last main port of the enemy. We are all grateful to the Almighty on this birthday of the Son and on the Season of the Feast of Lights." [16] The 1st Battalion received "warm congratulations and thanks" from General Krueger. [17]

The 1st Battalion occupied a defensive position in the vicinity of Look on 25 December, and rested on 26 December, which was Christmas Day back home. It spent the next five days sending out patrols and awaiting the arrival through the mountains of the rest of the 305th Infantry. On 30 December, Company C made a reconnaissance in force and an amphibious landing at Abijao, about seven miles north of Palompon. The company overcame some Japanese resistance and burned down the town to prevent its reoccupation. It then pushed 1,300 yards north and established radio contact with elements of the 1st Cavalry Division, which had pushed through the mountains to the vicinity of Villaba. [18]

The Palompon Road

The Palompon road wound through the mountains and crossed many rivers, over which some forty bridges would have to be built or repaired. It ran northwest two and a half miles from the Togbong River to the barrio of Humaybunay and then cut sharply to the southwest for about four miles to Matagob, at which point it went into the hills almost directly south for about 2,000 yards, and then turned south-southwest for 1,000 yards. At this point it turned and twisted to the southwest for approximately five and a half miles to the vicinity of San

---

[15] Maj Gen A. D. Bruce, The Operations of the 77th Division in Leyte, 19 January 1951, pp. 27, 28, MS in OCMH.

[16] 77th Div G–3 Jnl, 25 Dec 44.

[17] 77th Div G–3 Jnl, 26 Dec 44. It is possible that the weary soldiers were more interested in the following administrative order of General Bruce:

  1. Supply
    a. Rations
      (1) Turkey ration—distribution from Valencia ration dump at 0900, 25 Dec 1944. Ration and mess personnel will exercise great care and

speed in handling turkey and keep covered at all times.

      (2) Organization commanders will serve turkey to every man in this command on 26 Dec 1944. The Division commander has made arrangements for air drop to troops located in areas not accessible by road.

General Bruce wished the troops to have turkey on the same day that Christmas is observed in the States. 77th Div Admin Order 7, 24 Dec 44.

[18] 77th Div Opns Rpt Leyte, pp. 32–35 and Supplemental Opns Rpt, pp. 1–8, 305th Inf Opns Rpt Leyte; 77th Div G–3 Jnl, 26–30 Dec 44.

Miguel, from where it arched 3,500 yards to Look, on the Camotes Sea.

The Japanese had pockmarked Matagob and the area surrounding it with foxholes and emplacements and had dug spider holes under the houses. South of Matagob, where the road climbed into the hills, the enemy had utilized natural caves, gullies, and ridges on both sides of the road and dug many deep defensive positions. Some of these were eight feet deep, two feet in diameter at the top, and widened to six feet at the bottom. The Japanese had emplaced machine guns in culverts and had constructed several well-camouflaged coconut log pillboxes on the forward slopes of the ridges. An excellent, almost invisible installation, which served as an observation post, was dug in on the forward slope of a ridge about three miles north of San Miguel. It had a concealed entrance on the reverse slope. From this post eight miles of the road to the north and east could be observed.

The Japanese *5th Infantry Regiment* was the principal enemy unit in the sector, although remnants of other units retreating west from Highway 2 were in the area. The following Japanese units were identified: *1st, 3d,* and *6th Batteries* of the *8th Field Artillery Regiment;* elements of the *8th Division Signal Unit;* the *8th Transport Regiment;* and the *8th Engineer Regiment.* Although intelligence officers estimated that there were between 2,000 and 3,000 enemy troops in the sector, only a force of about battalion strength opposed the 305th Infantry. The rest had scattered into the hills to the northwest.

At 0700, on 22 December, the 2d Battalion, 305th Infantry, left Valencia followed at 1035 by the 3d Battalion. The 2d Battalion crossed the Togbong River, moved through the 1st Battalion, 306th Infantry,

and at 1030 attacked along the Palompon road. The battalion had advanced 1,600 yards northwest by 1230 and secured the Pagsangahan River crossing. The assault continued with the 3d Battalion coming up on the right flank of the 2d. The battalions moved through rice paddies and through Humaybunay and established a night perimeter about one mile southwest of the barrio.

The 302d Engineer Battalion, which followed behind the assault battalions, fought the "battle of bridges." [19] The engineers worked around the clock, frequently without any infantry protection, to restore the bridges as soon as possible. The bridges were to be sufficiently strengthened initially to support 2½-ton truck traffic for infantry supply, then they were to be reinforced to carry 20 tons in order to bring M8's forward, and eventually to 36-ton capacity to carry the M10's. General Bruce had hoped that sufficient Bailey bridges could be made available for important crossings to carry traffic while engineers built wooden bridges under the Bailey bridges. Only a limited number of Bailey bridges were furnished, however, and engineer progress to the west was slowed down.[20]

The assault battalions of the 305th Infantry that were astride the Palompon road spent a quiet night. They had before them the enemy's strongly fortified positions at Matagob. At 0830 on 23 December, the 2d Battalion moved out, followed at 1130 by the 3d Battalion. The 2d Battalion moved forward west of the road while the 3d advanced east of the road. Intermittent enemy rifle fire fell upon the 2d Battalion but it pushed ahead steadily. At 1500, the 2d Bat-

---

[19] 77th Div Opns Rpt Leyte, p. 35.
[20] 77th Div and 305th Inf Opns Rpts Leyte; 77th Div G–3 Jnl, 22 Dec 44.

talion was 500 yards beyond Matagob and the 3d was 300 yards behind the 2d. The troops came under heavy fire from two enemy 75-mm. guns on the hills west of Matagob and suffered several casualties. The mortars and artillery with the 305th Infantry silenced the Japanese guns. The regimental commander issued orders for the battalions to move out for the assault at 1000 on the following day against the regimental objective, a road bend that was 2,000 yards to its front. The 2d Battalion set up its night perimeter in place while the 3d Battalion withdrew to a point 1,000 yards east of Matagob. The regimental command post moved from Humaybunay to the 3d Battalion perimeter.[21]

During the night the Japanese made several attempts to penetrate the American lines. The 3d Battalion destroyed a demolition squad that entered its position, while the 2d Battalion beat back one attack at 0245 and another one, which was accompanied by mortar fire, at 0630. The 305th Infantry killed an estimated 100 Japanese with no casualties to the regiment.[22]

At 1000 on 24 December the assault troops jumped off. The Japanese resistance was light and intermittent, but American progress was slow because of the rough, irregular hills in which the enemy had established positions in foxholes, spider holes, and caves. Since it was not possible to bypass these positions, the regiment had to clear each one before the advance could continue. The force received some artillery fire but a mortar platoon from Company A, 88th Chemical Weapons Battalion, silenced the enemy guns. At 1500 the battalions set up their night perimeter 500 yards short of

the road bend. During the night a Japanese force of twenty men, which tried to penetrate the defenses of the 3d Battalion, was killed.[23]

At 0800 on 25 December the attack was renewed, but made very slow progress. The enemy, dug in in small pockets along the road, resisted stubbornly. The 3d Battalion advanced 200 yards and was pinned down by machine gun, mountain gun, and rifle fire. The 2d Battalion attempted to envelop the enemy strong point on the Japanese right (south) flank but was repulsed.[24]

On 26 December the regiment limited its activity to patrolling. Since it was Christmas Day in the States, "All guns of the Division Artillery fired . . . at . . . 1200 as a salute to the nation on Christmas Day. This was followed by one minute of silent prayer for the dead and wounded of the 77th Division."[25] That night General Bruce ordered the troops to build bonfires and sing, and employ other ruses in the hope that the Japanese might believe that the troops were celebrating Christmas and might therefore try to enter the defensive perimeters. These ruses were unsuccessful in the sectors of the assault battalions, but a similar one employed in the area of the regimental command post attracted some Japanese patrols, which were either destroyed or driven off.

At dawn on 27 December the 3d Battalion moved around the Japanese left flank toward the high ground six hundred yards from the line of departure. Despite enemy artillery and machine gun fire and the difficult terrain, the battalion reached the objective, killing 160 Japanese. The remainder fled to the hills.

---

[21] 77th Div Opns Rpt Leyte, p. 35; 77th Div G–3 Jnl, 23 Dec 44; 305th Inf Opns Rpt, p. 7.
[22] 77th Div G–3 Jnl, 24 Dec 44.

[23] 77th Div Opns Rpt Leyte, p. 36.
[24] 77th Div Opns Rpt Leyte, p. 37; 77th G–3 Jnl, 25 Dec 44; 305th Inf Unit Rpt No. 19, 25 Dec 44.
[25] 77th Div Supplemental Opns Rpt Leyte, p. 2.

When it became apparent that the Japanese resistance was strong and determined and might unduly delay the progress of the 305th Infantry, General Bruce decided to move the 2d Battalion of the regiment overwater to the vicinity of Palompon at the western terminus of the road. The 2d Battalion could then attack east along the road while the 3d Battalion continued the attack west. The Japanese defenders would thus be under fire on their front and rear. This eastern attack force, which was called the Provisional Mountain Force, moved to Ormoc and thence, after arrangements had been made with the naval representatives of Krueger's staff, overwater by LCM's to Palompon. It arrived at the latter without incident at 1500 on 28 December. On the same day the 3d Battalion, reinforced, continued the attack westward. The Japanese resisted strongly with small arms fire from pillboxes and with artillery. The 3d Battalion advanced approximately 1,000 yards during the day.[26]

At 0800 on 29 December, the 3d Battalion moved out. The battalion had advanced 650 yards at 1000 when it encountered very determined resistance from an enemy force in very well camouflaged, dug-in positions. The troops were pinned down for the rest of the day. The Provisional Mountain Force moved out of Look at 1200 to a position from which it could launch its assault eastward along the road.

At 0930 on 30 December the 305th Infantry struck along the Palompon road, the 3d Battalion driving west, and the Provisional Mountain Force attacking east. The Mountain Force encountered only scattered resistance until 0930, when the Japanese, from well-entrenched positions in the precipitous sides of the road at a point about four miles east of Palompon, directed strong machine gun fire along the road. The Mountain Force dug in for the night on high ground overlooking the point at which its advance had been halted. The 3d Battalion succeeded in overcoming the opposition which had halted it the previous day, and pushed forward to a point about 1,000 yards southwest of Tipolo. The Japanese had emplaced artillery on curves in the road and could fire directly on the advancing American troops. Although the 305th Infantry lost one tank to enemy artillery fire, it was able to destroy three 75-mm. guns and capture two others intact.[27]

During the night, the Japanese force withdrew; only scattered troops were left to delay the advance. At 0800 on 31 December, the assault forces of the 305th Infantry resumed the attack, and encountered only sporadic rifle fire. At 1225 at a point two miles northeast of San Miguel the 3d Battalion and the Provisional Mountain Force met. This ended all organized resistance along the Palompon road and secured an overland route from Highway 2 in the Ormoc Valley to Palompon on the west coast.[28] The 77th Division made the astounding estimate that for the period from 21 through 31 December 1944, it had killed 5,779 Japanese, taken 29 prisoners, and had lost 17 men killed, 116 wounded, and 6 missing in action.[29]

X Corps Goes West

Meanwhile, to the north of the 77th Division, elements of the 1st Cavalry Division and the 32d Infantry Division had turned

---

[26] *Ibid.*, p. 4; 305th Inf Supplemental Opns Rpt, p. 2.

[27] *Ibid.*, p. 5.

[28] *Ibid.*, p. 6.

[29] 77th Div G–1 Casualty Rpts; 77th Div Supplemental Opns Rpt Leyte, pp. 2–7.

off Highway 2 and were pushing over the mountains to the west coast.[30]

The 1st Cavalry Division

With the clearing of Highway 2 and the junction of the X and XXIV Corps at a point just south of Kananga, the 1st Cavalry Division was in readiness to push toward the west coast in conjunction with assaults by the 77th Division on its left and the 32d Division on its right. The troops were on a 2,500-yard front along Highway 2 between Kananga and Lonoy.

On the morning of 23 December the assault units of the 1st Cavalry Division moved out from the highway and started west. None encountered any resistance. The 1st Squadron, 12th Cavalry, established a night perimeter on a ridge about 1,400 yards slightly northwest of Kananga. The 1st Squadron, 5th Cavalry, set up a night perimeter 1,000 yards north of that of the 1st Squadron, 12th Cavalry, while the 1st Squadron, 7th Cavalry, dug in for the night on a line with the other two squadrons.

This first day's march set the pattern for the next several days. The regiments pushed steadily forward, meeting only scattered resistance. The chief obstacles were waist-deep swamps in the zone of the 12th Cavalry. These were waded on 24 December. The tangled vegetation and sharp, precipitous

ridges that were henceforward encountered also made the passage slow and difficult.

On 28 December, the foremost elements of the 5th and 12th Cavalry Regiments broke out of the mountains and reached the barrio of Tibur on the west coast, about 2,800 yards north of Abijao. By nightfall on the following day, the 7th Cavalry was also on the west coast but farther north. In its advance it had encountered and destroyed many small, scattered groups of the enemy, most of whom showed little desire to fight. The regiment arrived at Villaba, two and one-half miles north of Tibur, at dusk, and in securing the town killed thirty-five Japanese.

During the early morning hours of 31 December, the Japanese launched four counterattacks against the forces at Villaba. Each started with a bugle call, the first attack beginning at 0230 and the final one at dawn. An estimated 500 of the enemy, armed with mortars, machine guns, and rifles, participated in the assaults, but the American artillery stopped the Japanese and their forces scattered. On 31 December, the 77th Division began to relieve the elements of the 1st Cavalry Division, which moved back to Kananga.

On the morning of the 30th of December, the 7th Cavalry had made physical contact northeast of Villaba with the 127th Infantry, 32d Division, which had been driving to the west coast north of the 1st Cavalry Division.

The 32d Division

On 22 December the 127th Infantry had reached Lonoy and made contact with the 7th Cavalry. On the following day the troops rested.[31] The 128th Infantry had been

---

[30] The subsection dealing with the elements of the 1st Cavalry Division is based upon the following: 1st Cav Div Opns Rpt Leyte, pp. 59–69; 1st Cav Div Supplementary Opns Rpt Leyte, pp. 1–7; 1 Cav Div FO No. 21, 24 Dec 44; 1st Cav Div G–3 Periodic Rpts Nos. 65–84, 23 Dec 44–11 Jan 45; 1st Cav Div G–2 Periodic Rpts Nos. 64–75, 23 Dec 44–3 Jan 45; 5th Cav Opns Rpt Leyte, pp. 28–29; 1st Cav Div Arty Opns Rpt Leyte, pp. 21–22; 1st Cav Div Brig Opns Rpt Leyte, pp. 6–7; 12th Cav Unit Rpts Nos. 66–68, 23–25 Dec 44; 5th Cav S–3 Periodic Rpt 72, 2 Jan 45; 1st Cav Div G–3 Jnl, 26–31 Dec 44. Sixth Army Opns Rpt Leyte and 8th Army Opns Rpt Leyte.

[31] 127th Inf Opns Rpt Leyte, p. 13.

engaged in sending out patrols throughout the Limon area from 11 to 18 December. These patrols were successful in wiping out pockets of resistance that had been bypassed by the advance forces of the 32d Division in the division's drive along Highway 2 to the south. On 20 December, the 128th received orders from General Gill to prepare for a move to the west coast.[32]

Both the 127th and 128th Infantry Regiments sent out patrols on 23 December to reconnoiter the terrain. At 0800 on 24 December the two regiments started for the west coast. Throughout the march to the sea, they encountered only small parties of the enemy, who put up no effective resistance, but heavy rains, dense, almost impassable forests, and steep craggy hills slowed the advance.

The commanding officer of the 127th Infantry said of the hills encountered on 24 December:

The morning was spent in climbing to the top of a mountain ridge. The climbing was difficult but as we later found out, the descent was much worse. The trail led almost perpendicular down the side. After reaching the bottom, another ridge was encountered, this almost straight up, everyone had to use hand holds to pull themselves up. All in all there were seven ridges from the bottom of the first descent to the first possible bivouac area.[33]

The hills were less rugged from then on. On the morning of 25 December, the 1st Battalion, 127th Infantry, encountered and dispersed 300 to 400 Japanese. Throughout the march both regiments received supplies by airdrop, which was not completely satisfactory since none of the drops was made at the requested time and frequently there was a wide scattering of supplies.

On the afternoon of 29 December the two regiments were on their objectives: the 128th Infantry on the high ground overlooking Tabango and Campopo Bays and the 127th Infantry on the high ground overlooking Antipolo Point, approximately three miles to the south. Patrols were sent out to scout the terrain and establish contact with the 1st Cavalry Division on the south and with the 24th Infantry Division on the north.[34]

The 24th Infantry Division [35]

The 24th Division, after having been relieved by the 32d Division on Breakneck Ridge, had protected the rear areas on a trail leading from Jaro to Ormoc. Two weeks before the march to the west coast a large Japanese convoy had been attacked by U. S. aircraft and forced into San Isidro Bay on the northern part of the west coast. Although the vessels were destroyed, some of the troops were able to get ashore. On 9 December they headed toward Calubian, on Leyte Bay about six miles northeast of San Isidro. General Woodruff, who had replaced General Irving on 18 November, ordered Colonel Clifford's 1st Battalion, 34th Infantry, which had been defending Kilay Ridge, to wipe out the part of the enemy force that had landed at San Isidro and fled northeastward to the vicinity of Calubian.

---

[32] 128th Inf Opns Rpt Leyte, p. 11.
[33] 127th Inf Opns Rpt Leyte, p. 13.
[34] 32d Div Supplementary Opns Rpt Leyte, pp. 1–5; 127th Inf Opns Rpt Leyte, pp. 12–14; 32d Div Leyte Opn Diary, pp. 31–43; 128th Inf Opns Rpt Leyte, pp. 10–12.
[35] The material in this subsection is based upon 24th Div Opns Rpt Leyte, pp. 73–76; 34th Inf Unit Jnl, 9–30 Dec 44; 34th Inf Unit Rpts Nos. 51–71, 9–29 Dec 44; 2d Bn, 34th Inf, FO No. 8, 26 Dec 44; 34th Inf FO No. 17, 18 Dec 44; 34th Inf FO No. 18, 26 Dec 44; 24th Div G–3 Periodic Rpts Nos. 45–67, 2–25 Dec 44; 24th Div FO No. 12, 8 Dec 44 and FO No. 13, 17 Dec 44.

At 2300 on 21 December, Colonel Clifford notified Colonel Dahlen, the commanding officer of the 34th Infantry, that a Japanese force of about 160 men was at Tuktuk, about four miles south of Calubian. He added that at 0800 on the following morning the 1st Battalion would move out and destroy the force.

At 0300 a force consisting of a platoon from Company C and a platoon from Company A moved toward the high ground northwest of Tuktuk in preparation for the assault, but because of very poor trails the force was delayed. In the meantime four LVT's with a platoon of mortars moved overwater to Tuktuk. At 0830 the attack started, with machine guns mounted on the LVT's and mortars furnishing supporting fire. The Japanese resistance was sporadic, although some mortar fire was received. As the troops of the 34th Infantry neared the barrio, the enemy defenders broke and fled, and the town was deserted as the soldiers entered. Approximately thirty enemy dead were counted in the barrio and vicinity. The fleeing enemy force was later destroyed by patrols that worked over the sector. The Japanese had obviously been looting because linens, silverware, and women's clothing were found in their packs. One soldier had a baby's high chair tied on the top of his pack.

On 23 December, Col. William W. Jenna, former commanding officer of the 34th Infantry, returned from sick leave in the States and assumed command of the 34th Infantry. With his arrival plans were expedited to clean up the northwestern end of the Leyte peninsula in conjunction with the assaults of other units of the Sixth Army.

From 23 to 26 December, extensive patrolling was conducted along the west coast of the Leyte peninsula. On 26 December the 34th Infantry issued orders for clearing the part of the Leyte peninsula in its zone. The 1st Battalion was to secure all trails and high ground in the interior, prevent any enemy movement to the north and to the east, and, finally, be prepared to assist the 2d Battalion in the capture of the San Isidro Bay area.

At 2245 on 26 December the LCM's at Villalon (a barrio on Biliran Strait and about six miles northwest of Calubian) began to load Companies F and G. By 2300 the embarkation was completed and the craft moved to Gigantangan Island, arriving there fifteen minutes after midnight. The troops disembarked and slept. At 0530 they again embarked and proceeded to Taglawigan, arriving there at 0730. After strafing the shore the companies landed, meeting no resistance. At the same time Company F completed its assignment without opposition, pushing east and south and encircling Taglawigan. Before noon, some elements of the 2d Battalion were moving overland to Daha, about two miles to the south, while others had re-embarked and were making an overwater movement toward it. By noon Taglawigan and Daha had fallen to the 2d Battalion.

Company G, reinforced, left Company F at Daha, re-embarked on the landing craft, and headed toward the San Isidro Bay area, 6,000 yards to the south. As the convoy neared San Isidro, it came under machine gun fire from the barrio and the hills to the southwest. A frontal attack on the town was abandoned and the landing craft moved to the southwest of the jetty to make their landing. The LVT's mired in the mud about 100 to 150 yards offshore. The rest of the force, which was in the LCM's, waded ashore. Some of the troops from the LVT's met with great difficulty in trying to get ashore but the LVT's finally succeeded in retracting and picked them up. Approximately 150 soldiers with supplies for the task force returned to Gigantangan Island. The convoy had only one casualty.

In the meantime, the 1st Battalion had received orders at 1300 to take San Isidro. The battalion moved overland from Calubian and at nightfall it dug in on the high ground overlooking San Isidro.

At 0800 on 28 December, the co-ordinated assault was made against San Isidro, with elements of the 2d Battalion attacking from the north while the 1st Battalion attacked from the east. The troops encountered light resistance, the Japanese defenders being only partially armed. Fifty-five of the enemy were killed and one prisoner was taken. By 1230, the 1st Battalion was outposting San Isidro.

With the capture of San Isidro, the last main point on the Leyte peninsula was safely in the hands of the 34th Infantry. The troops moved south along the coast and destroyed small, poorly equipped groups of the enemy. One group of Japanese, whose only weapons were bayonets attached to bamboo poles, tried hopelessly to break through the lines.

On 1 January 1945, the 77th Division was ordered to relieve the 32d and 24th Infantry Divisions and the 1st Cavalry Division. The relieved divisions were to move to staging areas and prepare for future operations.

The Japanese Retreat

Condition of Japanese Forces

The morale and physical condition of the Japanese Army were very low. With the juncture of the American X and XXIV Corps, the 35th Army had begun to disintegrate. Desertion became common. The wounded would not assemble with their units. The problem of the wounded became serious since there were no proper facilities for medical treatment. General Tomochika later said: "Commanders employing persuasive language frequently requested seriously wounded soldiers at the front to commit suicide; this was particularly common among personnel of the 1st Division and it was pitiful. However the majority died willingly. Only Japanese could have done a thing like this and yet I could not bear to see the sight." [36]

Those of the slightly wounded that could not march with the able-bodied soldiers walked by themselves. They became separated from their units and some, although able to do so, refused to rejoin their outfits, giving their wounds as an excuse. In addition there were deserters who fled to the hills. The 35th Army began the policy of sending the slightly wounded back to the front lines. Many of the service units, such as the Mitsui Shipping Unit and the air corps ground crews, refused to fight since they were not trained as combat troops. "Even the artillery and antiaircraft units retreated without facing the enemy. Their excuse was that they were not trained to fight as infantry and were useless without their guns." [37]

Doubtless, some of the unwillingness of the Japanese service troops to serve on the front lines was due to their physical condition. When the 1st Division arrived on Leyte on 1 November it brought with it enough food and ammunition for one month, and by 1 December this supply was exhausted. On 3 December an additional one-half month's supply was brought in at Ormoc;

[36] Tomochika, True Facts of Leyte Opn, p. 28.
[37] Ibid., p. 29.

but this was destroyed or captured by the 77th Division in its advance. Consequently after the 1st of December all Japanese troops on Leyte "were on a starvation diet and had to live off the land." [38] The *1st* and *57th Infantry Regiments* were the principal sufferers. The men were forced to eat coconuts, various grasses, bamboo shoots, the heart fibers of coconut tree trunks, and whatever native fruits or vegetables they could forage. When the troops received orders to withdraw to the west coast of Leyte, "they were literally in a starved condition, . . . many instances occurred in which men vomited seven to ten times a day because they could not digest some of the food due to their weakened stomachs." [39]

The *1st Division* abandoned much equipment, ammunition, and rations along the highway through the Ormoc Valley. Many of the stragglers and deserters clothed and fed themselves with the abandoned matériel. The chief of staff of the *35th Army* stated that when the Americans captured army headquarters, he left the headquarters without any clothing. However, he picked up "a new uniform and sufficient food while on the road." [40]

Withdrawal Plans

On 19 December, General Suzuki, the commander of the *35th Army* on Leyte, had received word from the *14th Area Army* in Manila that henceforth the *35th Army* was to subsist on its own resources and what it could obtain within its operational area. [41]

On the same day, probably because of the information received from Manila, General Suzuki ordered a conference of the staff officers of the *1st* and *102d Divisions*. At this meeting, General Suzuki ordered the *1st Division* to retreat to the northern sector of the Matagob area and the *102d Division* to the southern part of the same sector. At Matagob the divisions were to reorganize for a counterattack. The order did not give any specific time for the withdrawal; each division was to take action according to the situation in its sector. On 20 December, General Suzuki moved his headquarters farther west to a point approximately three and a half miles north of Palompon. [42]

On 21 December, the *102d Division*, which had about 2,000 men, began to withdraw to the vicinity of Matagob. The division, having failed to get in touch with the *35th Army*, moved to the west coast near Villaba, approximately ten miles north of Palompon. [43] It made contact with the *1st Division* at the end of December, and also with the *68th Infantry Brigade* and the *5th Infantry Regiment*, which were already in that sector. [44] The *1st Division* also began to withdraw on 21 December, making the withdrawal in two columns. The southern column consisted of about six hundred men of the *49th Infantry Regiment, 1st Division Transport Regiment*, and other units. On its way west, it was met on 23 December by the *68th Brigade* which, unaware of the loss of the Ormoc road, was proceeding toward the highway. The brigade joined the southern column, which reached the Bagacay

---

[38] 10th I&HS, Eighth Army Stf Study of the Japanese *35th Army* on Leyte, Interrog of Col Junkichi Okabayashi [CofS *1st Div*] pp. 10–11.
[39] *Ibid.*
[40] Tomochika, True Facts of Leyte Opn, p. 28.
[41] *35th Army* Opns, p. 114.

[42] Tomochika, True Facts of Leyte Opn, p. 27.
[43] *35th Army* Opns, p. 115.
[44] 10th I&HS, Eighth Army Stf Study of Japanese *102d Division* on Leyte and Cebu, Interrog of Maj Chuji Kaneki [G–2 *102d Division*], p. 5.

sector the following day. (The barrio of Bagacay is six miles northeast of Villaba.) The northern column also had about six hundred men and consisted of elements of the *Division Headquarters,* the *1st Infantry Regiment,* the *57th Infantry Regiment,* and other units. The detachment was forced to cut its way through dense jungle. On 25 December it was attacked by the Americans and further decimated. That night the northern and southern columns met at Bagacay and on the following day started towards Matagob. On the 28th, following orders from General Suzuki, they turned north and established defensive positions on the eastern slope of Mt. Canguipot, two and a half miles southeast of Villaba.[45]

As the Japanese, pursued by the forces of the X and XXIV Corps, spiritlessly retreated toward the mountains of western Leyte, *Imperial General Headquarters* notified the Japanese people: "Our forces are still holding the Burauen and San Pablo airfields and continue to attack the enemy positions. Our forces are fighting fiercely on the eastern mountain slopes near Ormoc and Albuera.[46]

---

[45] 10th I&HS, Eighth Army Stf Study of Japanese *35th Army* on Leyte, Part IV, Col Junkichi Okabayashi, Opns of the *1st Division* on Leyte, p. 18.

[46] Tomochika, True Facts of Leyte Opn, p. 25.

CHAPTER XXII

Leyte Is Liberated

On 15 December, General MacArthur had directed General Eichelberger's Eighth Army to be prepared to assume control of nearly all Sixth Army units in the Leyte area at 0001 on 26 December 1944 in order to relieve the Sixth Army for future operations. The Eighth Army was to relieve the Sixth of all duties and missions in the area except certain ones dealing with logistics and construction. These were assigned to the USASOS (SWPA). The Allied Naval and Air Forces were directed to continue, in support of the Eighth Army, the missions which hitherto had been specified for the Sixth.[1]

In furtherance of General MacArthur's instructions, General Krueger issued orders covering the transfer to Eighth Army control of certain Sixth Army units. On 21 December he named the units over which he was relinquishing control as of 0001, 26 December, and stated that the responsibility for continuing assigned duties and missions in the area would then pass from him to the Commanding General, Eighth U. S. Army, the Commanding General, USASOS (SWPA), and the Commander, Allied Naval Forces.[2]

General Eichelberger, also, prepared orders for the forthcoming transfer of authority. The supply and evacuation procedures of the Sixth Army would remain in effect. The X and XXIV Corps would "continue on their present assigned missions of destroying Japanese wherever found, and . . . be prepared to conduct overland or amphibious shore to shore operations to seize enemy supply points and bases, and ports of entry." [3]

On 25 December, when elements of the 77th Division had seized Palompon, the last important port on Leyte, General Mac-Arthur declared that all organized resistance had ended. He said in a message to General Krueger: "Heartiest congratulations on capture of Palompon. This closes a campaign that has had few counterparts in the utter destruction of the enemy's forces with a maximum conservation of our own. It has been a magnificent performance on the part of all concerned." [4]

The Eighth Army Assumes Control

On 26 December, General Eichelberger assumed control of all combat units in the Leyte–Samar area. It was not until the first part of January 1945 that the American troops secured the west coast of Leyte. Thereafter only isolated pockets of enemy resistance remained.

Assembly of Japanese Forces

On 25 December 1944, General Yamashita, commanding the *14th Area Army,*

---

[1] GHQ SWPA Opns Instns 81, 15 Dec 44.
[2] Sixth Army FO 40, 21 Dec 44.
[3] Eighth Army FO 8, 20 Dec 44.
[4] Quoted in Sixth Army Opns Rpt Leyte, p. 84.

notified General Suzuki, the *35th Army* commander, that he had written off the Leyte Campaign as a loss; henceforward the *35th Army* on Leyte would be self-sustaining and self-supporting, the units on Leyte would be transferred to other areas, and, finally, the units on the island would be assembled at a point from which raiding operations could be conducted. Since these orders were ambiguous and apparently contradictory, General Suzuki asked that the message be repeated but he never received an answer. Accordingly, in the latter part of December, he sent his chief of staff to Manila for further clarification of the orders. The chief of staff arrived at Manila, by way of Cebu, in late January, but he was unable to obtain any further information for General Suzuki.

The decision of General Yamashita to abandon the Leyte operation followed a series of rapidly moving events. On the 14th of December, he canceled an optimistic plan for an amphibious assault through the shallow waters of Carigara Bay against Carigara, an assault that had been scheduled for 16 December. This cancellation followed the sighting of an Allied convoy en route to Mindoro.[5] The convoy reached Mindoro and the troops landed successfully on 15 December. On 19 December, two days prior to the junction of the X and XXIV Corps on Highway 2, General Yamashita told General Suzuki that he could no longer send any reinforcements and supplies to Leyte and that the *35th Army* would have to become self-supporting. On the same day, General Yamashita assigned to the defense of Luzon three divisions that *Imperial General Headquarters*

had earmarked for Leyte. Shortly afterward, at a conference with representatives from the *Southern Army* and *Imperial General Headquarters,* the representative from the latter told General Yamashita to forget the Leyte operation.

In the meantime, General Suzuki interpreted his orders to mean that units of the *35th Army* would assemble at a common point at which they could be self-supporting. He had selected the western area of Matagob–Palompon in the vicinity of the road leading from Highway 2 at Libongao over the mountains to Palompon on the west coast. Palompon was to have been used as the rear center of the line of communications and the army headquarters was to have been established at Kompisao, but the seizure of Palompon on 25 December by the 77th Division forced Suzuki to change the location of his army headquarters.[6] He then selected as a base of operations an area in the vicinity of Ginabuyan that overlooked Silad Bay and was about three kilometers north of Villaba.

The new area was a plateau with an elevation of about 1,200 feet, heavily forested and having rocky eastern and western slopes that made it "a natural fortress." From it one could command a view of Ormoc Valley to the east and the Camotes Sea and Cebu to the west. There were a few Filipino huts, and cultivated fields and coconut groves, interspersed with salt beds, lay along the beach. The area "was admirably suited for an extended period of defensive action."[7] General Suzuki ordered the units of the *35th Army* that were retreating westward to repair to the vicinity of the new base of operations.

---

[5] See M. Hamlin Cannon and Robert Ross Smith, Luzon and the Southern Philippines, a forthcoming volume in this series.

[6] *35th Army* Opns, p. 119.

[7] Tomochika, True Facts of Leyte Opn, p. 32.

The units continued to straggle westward towards the selected area. By 1 January, most of them had taken up positions in the Balanac sector, which was about three and a half miles southeast of Villaba and over-looked the Palompon road. They had been hard pressed. The *68th Brigade* and the *1st Division* made contact and successfully con-centrated south of Villaba in early January. The *12th Independent Regiment* (the *Imahori Detachment*), the *Mitsui Shipping Unit,* the *4th Airborne Raiding Regiment* and the remaining troops of the *77th In-fantry Regiment,* which had been operating northeast of Ormoc, reached the southern Matagob area about the middle of January. It was not until the beginning of February that these units made contact with the *35th Army.* The few remaining elements of the *16th Division* stayed in the vicinity of Valencia until the end of February. The *26th Division* also remained in this area until the middle of January, when it moved west and established contact with the *35th Army.*[8]

The *102d Division* presented certain diffi-culties. There had been instances of forty to fifty deserters fleeing to Cebu or Negros on boats they had built for themselves. Deserters that were apprehended were court-martialed. General Suzuki for some time had been out of touch with Lt. Gen. Shimpei Fukue, the commanding general of the *102d Division,* which was in the Mt. Pina area. By chance, one of Suzuki's offi-cers learned that Fukue was planning to evacuate to Cebu. General Suzuki was in-censed since he and his staff felt that Fukue "was violating the military code in taking these steps without consent." He thereupon sent the following message to Fukue: "Lt. General Fukue and his headquarters will

remain in Leyte and at the same time I am attaching other units and groups in the Visayan and Mindanao sectors to your Di-vision. General Fukue and his Chief of Staff will report to me in person at Army Head-quarters." The commander of the *102d Di-vision* did not answer but his chief of staff sent the following reply: "We appreciate the efforts of Army but at the present time we are very busy preparing for retreat. The division commander and chief of staff are unable to report to Army Headquarters."[9]

General Suzuki was "entirely displeased" with the reaction of Fukue and sent his chief of staff, General Tomochika, to investigate the situation. When Tomochika arrived he found that Fukue, with his chief of staff and some headquarters personnel, had already left for Cebu. This fact was communicated to General Suzuki by Tomochika, who states that "for several days I had a difficult time in consoling the general."[10] The sequel to these events was that General Suzuki re-lieved General Fukue of his command and ordered him to remain on Cebu until he received further orders. Upon the arrival of Suzuki in Cebu in the spring of 1945, Fukue was sentenced to confinement for thirty days. General Suzuki asked *Imperial Gen-eral Headquarters* in Tokyo for authority to court-martial General Fukue; no reply was forthcoming. General Fukue was released and later returned to command of the *102d Division.*[11]

In the meantime, the leaderless *102d Di-vision,* with a strength of approximately 2,000 men, crossed Highway 2 north of Li-bongao and reached the southern area of

---

[8] *35th Army* Opns, pp. 115–16.

[9] Tomochika, True Facts of Leyte Opn, p. 29.

[10] *Ibid.,* p. 30.

[11] 10th I&HS, Eighth Army Stf Study of Opns of Japanese *102d Division* on Leyte and Cebu, App., p. 3; Tomochika, True Facts of Leyte Opn, pp. 29–31.

Matagob about 24 December. The troops failed to contact the *35th Army* and after remaining for a short time at Matagob moved to the vicinity of Villaba.

The units that arrived on the west coast were much understrength and very poorly equipped. All artillery had been lost. There were only five to ten machine guns per regiment in addition to individual weapons. Each man had an average of sixty rounds of ammunition and several hand grenades.

On the 30th of December, General Yamashita sent the following message to General Suzuki:

Sixty days have already elapsed since the American forces invaded Leyte Island, during which period the *Thirty-fifth Army,* under the forceful leadership of its commander, has waged many a heroic battle against superior enemy forces and in the face of numerous difficulties. The Army gave a great blow to the enemy. Moreover, the *Thirty-fifth Army* by containing the opposing enemy for this long period of time deprived him of freedom of action for the coming operation, thereby facilitating the general conduct of our operations in this battle and rendering great services to our cause. I am deeply impressed, particularly with the fact that the *Takachiho Unit* captured the hostile airfield at BURAUEN after the *Thirty-fifth Army,* despite its inferiority in equipment and number of men, and the stoppage of supply, made a timely and resolute attack against the enemy with the commander himself leading them. However, the enemy, who has increased his material power and war potential, now threatens, solely on the strength of his material superiority, to bear down on Luzon Island despite the heroic and desperate efforts of our sea and air forces as well as of the *Thirty-fifth Army.* In view of the sudden change in the situation, we shall seek and destroy our enemy on Luzon Island, thereby doing our part in the heroic struggle of the Army and avenging many a valiant warrior who fell before the enemy. As munitions have not been supplied adequately, I cannot keep back tears of remorse for tens of thousands of our officers and men

fighting in Leyte Island. Nevertheless, I must impose a still harder task upon you. Please try to understand my intentions. They say it is harder to live th....... .You, officers and men, be patient en...... endure the hardships of life, and help guar..... maintain the prosperity of the Imperial Throne through eternal resistance to the enemy, and be ready to meet your death calmly for our beloved country. I sincerely instruct you as above.[12]

General Suzuki took steps to make the force on Leyte self-supporting. In January 1945, he established two principles for his troops. First, the troops were to utilize as much of the local food and material as possible and plant sweet potatoes and Indian corn. Second, all provisions in the area outside of the operation base were to be purchased. The execution of the first part of his first precept worked reasonably well but the constant American air raids and mopping-up operations prevented the Japanese from being too successful in planting and harvesting the corn and potatoes. They were also not very fortunate in purchasing supplies from outside the area, although some supplies were obtained each time the men could pass through the American protective screen.

The Japanese arrived on the western shores of Leyte at the end of the harvest season. They secured large quantities of provisions which the Filipinos had stored and also a great number of coconuts and sweet potatoes. The soldiers used the carabaos of the island as meat and obtained salt from sea water. For vegetables, the army's chief reliance was upon wild ferns, tokay grass, and wild spinach.

---

[12] Msg, Gen Yamashita to Gen Suzuki, 1535, 30 Dec 44. Translation of HS–23A, file of *35th Army* Headquarters documents held by former Maj. Takahash Kohet, P8, GHQ FEC, MI Sec, ATIS. Copy in OCMH.

In conclusion, "although there was not enough food to increase the fighting power of the Army, no on̲e ̲died of starvation and some units stor̲e̲d ̲enough supplies for two to three ̲m̲on̲t̲hs̲."[13]

The Mop-up

By the end of December, most of the enemy troops were in northwest Leyte, west of Highway 2 and north of Palompon. Another large enemy concentration was located in the hills south of Palompon.[14]

The mop-up of any operation is dangerous, difficult, and unglamorous, but it is highly essential. The activities of the 7th Division on Leyte during January and February 1945 are typical of the large-scale mop-up in which many small units are sent out daily in all directions. This division was assigned all of the west coast area south of a line from Palompon to Valencia. Its records state that the division "sent out as many as forty combat patrols daily to hunt down and destroy thousands of Japanese stragglers wandering throughout the area."[15]

Eight divisions were engaged in mopping up for varying lengths of time on Leyte, but only an outline of their activities will be attempted here. The operation may be divided into three phases: XXIV Corps activities from 1 January to 15 February 1945; X Corps activities from 1 January to 24 February 1945; and Eighth Army Area Command operations from 24 February to 8 May 1945.[16]

During the XXIV Corps phase, the 11th Airborne Division encountered an enemy force well dug in on the southern slopes of Mt. Majunag, five miles northwest of Burauen. After much bitter hand-to-hand fighting the Japanese were destroyed. The 96th Division engaged in extensive patrolling, relieved the 11th Airborne Division, and relieved the X Corps of all tactical responsibility east of the mountains. The 7th Division sent out numerous patrols in the southern part of the island, and sent out a reinforced battalion that destroyed all enemy forces in the Camotes Islands. The 77th Division, which operated in the northwestern part of the island, cleared up many pockets of enemy resistance.

In the X Corps phase, the island of Samar was cleared of Japanese troops. The Americal Division, advance elements of which arrived on 24 January, extensively patrolled both the islands of Leyte and Samar.

During the Eighth Army Area Command phase, the constant searching out of isolated groups of enemy soldiers continued. In addition to the Americal Division, the 1st Filipino Infantry Regiment patrolled Leyte. On 8 May, the control of the Eighth Army over the area came to an end.[17]

The Japanese Withdrawal

At the time that General Suzuki made his plans for the units of the *35th Army* on Leyte to become self-sufficient, he felt that there were too many soldiers on the island to make the plan fully effective. General Suzuki decided therefore to transfer to other islands those who, because of their good physical condition and morale, would be able to withstand the rigors of a long fight.

---

[13] *35th Army* Opns, pp. 120–24.

[14] Eighth Army Opns Rpt Leyte, p. 3.

[15] *Ibid.*, p. 9.

[16] Eighth Army Opns Rpt Leyte, p. 3. Unless otherwise cited, this subsection is based upon this operations report, pp. 1–18.

[17] Eighth Army Opns Rpt Leyte, pp. 7–17.

Consequently the sick, weak, and wounded were dropped from the units that were to be withdrawn.[18] General Suzuki also considered the selection of the location of the new headquarters for the *35th Army*. Since there were 15,000 Japanese residents in and around Davao on Mindanao, it was finally decided to remove the army headquarters to Davao. As a preliminary step, the *1st Division* was to be sent to Cebu.[19]

General Suzuki had plans drawn up showing the order of precedence by which the units on Leyte were to be withdrawn and their destinations. All available landing barges on Leyte and additional vessels from Cebu and other areas would be used. The order of the proposed withdrawal and the destinations of the units were as follows:

*1st Division*_____	northern Cebu and later to Negros
41st and *77th Infantry Regiments* _____	Mindanao
*102d Division*_____	Visayan area
*26th Division*_____	Bacolod sector of Negros
*Takahashi Detachment*_____	northern Cebu
Units of the *68th Independent Mixed Brigade*_____	northern Cebu

General Suzuki and *35th Army Headquarters* would leave Leyte about the same time as the *26th Division*. The *16th Division*, the *68th Independent Mixed Brigade*, and other small units were to remain on Leyte and would be under the command of Lt. Gen. Shiro Makino, the *16th Division* commander.[20]

When these plans were announced Lt. Gen. Tadasu Kataoka, the commanding general of the *1st Division*, suggested that as the *1st Division* had lost so many men and officers in the Leyte operation it might

be better to use the *68th Independent Mixed Brigade*, which had fresh troops and would be better suited for the assignment to Cebu. He was overruled.[21] There were, however, other officers who were more anxious to leave Leyte. General Tomochika later wrote: "Many of the troops rushed to join this movement and Staff Officer Nakamura experienced difficulty in controlling them. However, quite a number of men succeeded in transferring without the commander's orders. The commander was displeased because only a small number of staff officers were willing to stay on Leyte." [22]

On the morning of 12 January, four launches arrived at Abijao to begin evacuation of the *1st Division*. The Americans attacked and damaged the vessels, but three were repaired. By 2300, with the embarkation of the first party, composed of elements of the *49th Infantry* and *Division Headquarters*, the evacuation got under way. This group left Abijao at 0130 on 13 January and reached Tabogon, in northern Cebu, about 0730. At about the same time, the remnants of the *57th Infantry* reached Cebu. The rest of *1st Division Headquarters*, the *1st Infantry Regiment*, and part of the *1st Transport Regiment* left Leyte on the 18th, and on the 20th the rest of the *49th Infantry Regiment* and the *1st Division Transport* quitted the island.

Between the 13th and 20th of January the three launches, each carrying about seventy men, made four round trips. After the second trip, the Americans spotted the operation. The hiding place of the craft at Tabogon was frequently strafed by aircraft and shelled by submarines and motor torpedo boats, which kept the channel waters

---

[18] Tomochika, True Facts of Leyte Opn, p. 34.
[19] *35th Army* Opns, pp. 118, 127.
[20] *Ibid.,* pp. 127–28.

[21] 10th I&HS, *35th Army* Opns on Leyte, Part IV, Opns of Japanese *1st Division* on Leyte, pp. 19–20.
[22] Tomochika, True Facts of Leyte Opn, p. 34.

under sharp surveillance. On the night of the 20th, American aircraft sank three launches. Although additional craft were sent up from Liloan on Cebu, these were also sunk. It was impossible to evacuate any more personnel until the middle of March.[23]

The number of men from the *1st Division* evacuated to Cebu was estimated to be as follows: *1st Division Headquarters*, 73; *1st Infantry Regiment*, 72; *49th Infantry Regiment*, 208; *57th Infantry Regiment*, 178; and *1st Transport Regiment*, 212; a total of 743 men. The equipment evacuated included 332 rifles, 4 heavy machine guns, 11 light machine guns, 5 grenade launchers, and a small amount of small arms ammunition.[24] In addition several hundred men obtained their own transportation and left for other islands in the Philippines.

The Road Ends

From 20 January on, the remaining Japanese forces stayed in the Villaba sector, hoping that succor would come. On 20 January General Tomochika "waited on the beach" for a boat that never came. The men were "plunged into the depths of despair." Time passed. On the evening of 17 March, two Japanese vessels appeared. General Suzuki and part of his staff boarded the craft and at 0030, 18 March, left the island of Leyte. For days the vessels sailed from island to island in the Visayas only to find that they were too late. The Americans were already in possession. On the evening of 16 April, the vessel bearing General Suzuki was bombed by American aircraft off the coast

of Negros Island and Suzuki was killed.[25] The Leyte Campaign had ended.

The liberation of Leyte had been accomplished at no slight cost. During the peak month, January 1945, there were 257,766 American Army, including Air Forces, troops on Leyte.[26] The total Army casualties for the Leyte Campaign were over 15,500, including more than 3,500 killed and nearly 12,000 wounded. (*Tables 4 and 5*)

It is impossible, with data now available to determine with any degree of exactitude the number of Japanese who participated in the campaign or their casualties. The estimates of the Sixth and Eighth Armies vary greatly, as do those of the various Japanese sources. The Sixth Army estimated that it had killed 56,263 and captured 389 men.[27] and that as of 26 December 1944 when it relinquished control to Eighth Army about 5,000 of the Japanese remained on the islands of Leyte and Samar.[28] The Eighth Army estimated that, for the mop-up period from 26 December 1944 to 8 May 1945, it

---

[23] 10th I&HS, *35th Army* Opns on Leyte, Part IV, Opns of Japanese *1st Division* on Leyte, pp. 21–22.
[24] *Ibid.*, p. 21.

[25] During his travels, General Suzuki composed two poems which he presented to his "dear brother Tomochika." One of these, entitled "A Farewell Poem," ran as follows:

Every soldier must expect to sacrifice his life in War,
Only then has his duty been done;
Be thankful that you can die at the front,
Rather than an inglorious death at home.

Tomochika, True Facts of Leyte Opn, pp. 34–39.
[26] Strength Accounting Br, AGO, STM–30, 1 Feb 45. These figures must be treated with caution as they include, in addition to those who had actually participated, troops who were merely staging on the island and had played no part in the operation. It is important to remember that at all stages of the Leyte Campaign troops and units were constantly coming and going.
[27] Sixth Army Opns Rpt Leyte, p. 84.
[28] Eighth Army Opns Rpt Leyte, p. 3.

TABLE 4—U. S. ARMY BATTLE CASUALTIES AT LEYTE, 20 OCTOBER 1944–8 MAY 1945

Organization	Total	Killed	Wounded	Missing
Total	15, 584	3, 504	11, 991	89
Sixth Army Troops	961	141	813	ᵃ 7
Eighth Army Troops	404	61	340	3
X Corps	7, 126	1, 670	5, 384	72
Americal Div and 164th RCT	731	162	566	3
24th Infantry Division	2, 342	544	1, 784	14
32d Infantry Division	1, 949	450	1, 491	8
38th Infantry Division	272	68	171	33
1st Cavalry Division	931	203	726	2
11th Airborne Division	532	168	352	12
1st Filipino Division	52	14	38	0
108th RCT	53	14	39	0
112th RCT	160	32	128	0
Corps Troops	104	15	89	0
XXIV Corps	7, 093	1, 632	5, 454	7
7th Infantry Division	2, 764	584	2, 179	1
77th Infantry Division	2, 226	499	1, 723	4
96th Infantry Division	1, 660	469	1, 189	2
Corps Troops	443	80	363	0

ᵃ Estimated.

Source: Reports of the Commanding Generals, Eighth U. S. Army, Inclosure 1, and Sixth U. S. Army, on the Leyte–Samar Operation, p. 155.

killed and found dead 24,294 and captured 439 Japanese.[29] General Eichelberger stated that his forces killed "more than twenty-seven thousand Japanese." [30]

The Japanese historians of the Leyte operation estimate that the total strength of their army ground troops was 70,000 men.[31] General Tomochika, the chief of staff of the *35th Army*, was interrogated several times after the war. On one occasion he estimated that the total number of Japanese involved in the Leyte operation, including naval and air personnel and those who lost their lives in transports sunk en route to Leyte, was 59,400 men, approximately one fifth of all Japanese forces in the Philippine Islands.[32] On another occasion General Tomochika estimated that 61,800 Japanese had been on Leyte, and that 13,010 were alive and 48,790 had been killed by 17 March 1945.[33]

In the plan for the defeat of Japan the objective sought in reconquering the Philippines was not only to liberate the Filipinos

[29] *Ibid.*, p. 16.
[30] Robert L. Eichelberger, *Our Jungle Road to Tokyo* (New York, 1950), p. 181.
[31] *35th Army Opns*, p. 126.

[32] 10th I&HS, Eighth Army Stf Study of Opns of Japanese *35th Army* on Leyte, Interrog of Gen Tomochika, pp. 9–10.
[33] Tomochika, True Facts of Leyte Opn, Interrog of Gen Tomochika, p. 7.

TABLE 5—SIXTH ARMY BATTLE CASUALTIES BY ARM OR SERVICE, 20 OCTOBER–25 DECEMBER 1944

Arm or Service	Killed		Wounded and Injured		Missing in Action		Total	
	Number	Per Cent	Number	Per Cent	Number	Per Cent	Number	Per Cent
Infantry	2,380	82.42	7,749	78.61	85	52.80	10,214	79.14
Engineer	132	4.58	762	7.73	46	28.57	940	7.28
Medical	100	3.47	375	3.80	8	4.97	483	3.74
Field Artillery	96	3.33	328	3.33	5	3.11	429	3.32
Coast Artillery	47	1.59	248	2.52	1	.62	296	2.30
Ordnance	45	1.56	100	1.01	1	.62	146	1.13
Quartermaster	41	1.42	67	.68	9	5.59	117	.91
Signal	12	.42	76	.77	0	.00	88	.68
Transportation	7	.24	73	.74	1	.62	81	.63
Chemical Warfare	13	.45	44	.45	0	.00	57	.44
Military Police	13	.45	27	.27	4	2.48	44	.34
Chaplain	0	.00	0	.00	0	.00	0	.00
Miscellaneous	2	.07	9	.09	1	.62	12	.09
Total	2,888	100.00	9,858	100.00	161	100.00	12,907	100.00

Source: Sixth Army Operations Report Leyte, 20 October–25 December 1944, p. 155.

but also to cut off the Japanese from the rich empire that they had acquired in the Netherlands Indies, and at the same time to establish a base for the final assault on the enemy's homeland. As early as 1942 Allied submarines had begun to gnaw at the lifeline between Japan and its new empire, rich in rubber, tin, rice, and, above all, in oil, without which Japan could not remain in the war. By the fall of 1944 the submarines had virtually cut this lifeline, which ran past the Philippines. The loss of the Philippines to the Allies would finally sever it.

The object of the Leyte Campaign had been to force an entry into the Philippines and establish a solid base for their reconquest. It had accomplished this object, though the base had not been secured and developed as promptly or as effectively as the planners had anticipated. The construc-tion program on the island had been a disappointment. Leyte never became a major air base. But the campaign had other and more important effects that had not been foreseen when it was launched. In their determination to make Leyte the decisive battle of the Philippines, the Japanese had committed the major portions of their fleet and air force in a vain attempt to stay the American advance. In the Battle of Leyte Gulf the Japanese Navy suffered irreparable damage—all of the carriers were lost and most of the capital ships were sunk or damaged. The air force was now almost completely dependent upon the suicidal kamikaze pilot. Finally, the dispatch of reinforcements and supplies to Leyte had seriously crippled the defenses of Luzon— the strategic heart of the Philippine Archipelago.

The Americans had established an air base in the midst of the Japanese-held Philippine Islands—a base within medium bomber range of Luzon, the principal American target in the archipelago.[34] As General Yamashita, commanding officer of all Japanese Army troops in the Philippines later said: "After the loss of Leyte . . . I realized that decisive battle was impossible. . . ."[35]

Three years of hard fighting over jungle trails had finally brought the U. S. forces back to the Philippines. Ahead lay months of weary struggle but ultimate victory was no longer in doubt.

---

[34] See Cannon and Smith, Luzon and the Southern Philippines.

[35] U. S. Military Commission, U. S. Army Forces Western Pacific, United States of America vs Tomoyuki Yamashita, Testimony of General Yamashita, XXVIII, 3527.

Appendix A

GHQ Operations Instructions Number 70, 21 September 1944
GENERAL HEADQUARTERS
SOUTHWEST PACIFIC AREA

A. P. O. 500
21 September 1944.

OPERATIONS INSTRUCTIONS⎤
NUMBER . . . . 70⎦

1. a. See current Intelligence Summaries and Annex No. 3—Intelligence.

b. Allied Forces occupy the line: MARIANAS–ULITHI–PALAU–MOROTAI and control the approaches to the southern and eastern PHILIPPINES.

c. The THIRD FLEET, Admiral W. F. Halsey commanding, covers and supports the LEYTE GULF–SURIGAO STRAIT Operations by:

(1) Containing or destroying the Japanese Fleet.

(2) Destruction of hostile air and shipping in the FORMOSA, LUZON, VISAYAS and MINDANAO areas during the period A—9 through A—3 and from A Day through A+30 as necessary to maintain their continued neutralization.

(3) Destruction of ground defenses and installations and shipping in the objective and adjacent enemy supporting areas from A—2 until the escort carriers assume the mission of direct support.

(4) Providing direct support of the landing and subsequent operations by fast carrier aircraft as required.

d. Coordination of operations of THIRD FLEET and SOUTHWEST PACIFIC Naval and Air Forces will be published later.

e. I Time (Zone-9) of Z Time will be used during the operation.

2. a. Forces of the SOUTHWEST PACIFIC, covered and supported by the THIRD FLEET, will continue the offensive to reoccupy the PHILIPPINES by seizing and occupying objectives in the LEYTE and western SAMAR areas, and will establish therein naval, air and logistic facilities for the support of subsequent operations.

b. Target Date for A Day: 20 October 1944.

c. Forces

(1) SIXTH US ARMY—Lt General Walter Krueger, US Army. As constituted, less elements assigned by subsequent orders to EIGHTH US ARMY.

SIXTH US ARMY reserve:

77th US Infantry Division—GUAM

6th US Infantry Division—CAPE SANSAPOR, DUTCH NEW GUINEA. Forces allocated for the operation as designated in Annex No. 1. Tentative Troop List for the Operation. The exact composition of the landing force as designated by Commanding General SIXTH US ARMY.

(2) FIRST AUSTRALIAN ARMY—Lt General V. A. H. Sturdee, CBE

As constituted.

(3) EIGHTH US ARMY—Lt General Robert L. Eichelberger, US Army.

As later specified.

(4) ALLIED NAVAL Forces—Vice Admiral T. C. Kinkaid, US NAVY.

As reinforced.

(5) ALLIED AIR Forces—Lt General George C. Kenney, US Army.

As constituted.

(6) USASOS—Maj General J. L. Frink, US Army.

As constituted.

3. a. The SIXTH US ARMY, supported by the ALLIED NAVAL and AIR Forces, will:

(1) By overwater operations seize and occupy:

(a) Objectives in the TACLOBAN and DULAG areas in LEYTE and such adjacent areas as are required to initiate and insure uninterrupted naval and air operations therefrom.

(b) Objectives in the HOMONHON and DINAGAT ISLANDS and such adjacent areas prior to the main assault in LEYTE as will insure the uninterrupted access for amphibious shipping into LEYTE GULF.

(c) Objectives in the PANAON STRAIT area that will permit passage of naval forces through the PANAON STRAIT for operations in the CAMOTES SEA. This objective will be secured simultaneously with (1) (a) above.

(2) Establish control of SAN JUANICO STRAITS in order to permit passage of naval forces through the SAN JUANICO STRAITS for operations in the SAMAR SEA.

(3) In subsequent operations, establish control over the remainder of LEYTE ISLAND; occupy and consolidate the western portion of southern SAMAR to include the TAFT-WRIGHT Highway and seize objectives that will permit opening of SURIGAO STRAITS for naval operations.

(4) Prepare to conduct such operations as may be later directed by this headquarters to:

    (a) Complete the consolidation of SAMAR.

    (b) Destroy or contain hostile garrisons in the VISAYAS.

(5) Occupy and defend sites for radar and air warning installations as arranged with the Commanders ALLIED NAVAL and AIR Forces.

(6) Assume control of and direct the operations of FILIPINO Forces of the 9th Military District (LEYTE–SAMAR).

(7) Establish facilities for minor naval operations at the earliest practicable date in the LEYTE–SAMAR area as arranged with the Commander ALLIED NAVAL Forces and initiate the establishment of naval, air and logistic facilities for the support of subsequent operations to reoccupy the PHILIPPINES as directed in Annex No 4, Logistics, and Annex No 6, Engineer, and as later directed by this headquarters.

(8) Establish air facilities in the LEYTE area with objectives as follows:

(a) First Objective: Immediately following the assault and by a+5 for:	1 fighter gp (P–38) 1 fighter gp (P–40) 1 night fighter sq
(b) Second Objective: Additional by A+15.	1 tactical reconnaissance sq 1 photo sq 1 medium bomb gp plus 1 sq P. O. A. 3 PBY sqs (tender-based) 1 VMR sq (Marine)
(c) Third Objective: Additional by A+30.	2 light bomb gps (A–20) 1 air-sea rescue sq 1 tactical reconnaissance sq 1 fighter gp (P–38)
(d) Fourth Objective: Additional by A+45.	1 fighter gp (P–47) 1 PB4Y sq (Air Ech) 2 heavy bomb gps 1 LAB sq
(e) Fifth Objective: Additional by A+60.	1 photo sq (F–5) 1 PB4Y sq (Air-Ech) 2 troop carrier gps 1 combat mapping sq (Air Ech)
(f) As later designated.	

b. The Commanding General EIGHTH US ARMY, supported by the ALLIED NAVAL and AIR Forces will:

    (1) Relieve the SIXTH US ARMY of missions in NEW GUINEA, the ADMIRALTIES, NEW BRITAIN, and the MOROTAI area as later directed by this headquarters.

    (2) Prepare to relieve the SIXTH US ARMY in the VISAYAN area as later directed by this headquarters.

    (3) Assist the Commanding General SIXTH US ARMY by training, staging and mounting units of the SIXTH US ARMY in the EIGHTH US ARMY area of responsibility as arranged with the Commanding General SIXTH US ARMY.

c. The FIRST AUSTRALIAN ARMY, supported by the ALLIED NAVAL and AIR Forces, will continue:

    (1) The defense of naval and air installations within assigned areas of combat responsibility.

    (2) The neutralization of Japanese forces within assigned areas, seizing every opportunity for the destruction of hostile forces.

d. The Commander ALLIED NAVAL Forces, while continuing present missions, will:

    (1) Transport and establish landing forces ashore in the LEYTE GULF–SURIGAO STRAIT area as arranged with the Commanding General SIXTH US ARMY

    (2) Support the operations by:

        (a) Providing air protection for convoys and naval task forces and direct air support for the landing and subsequent operations, supplemented as arranged with the Commander THIRD FLEET and the Commander ALLIED AIR Forces.

        (b) Arranging direct air support and cover with carrier aircraft for minesweeping and preliminary landings in the LEYTE GULF area during the period A–2 to the time escort carriers assume the mission of direct support on A Day.

        (c) Transporting supporting troops and their supplies as required to the LEYTE GULF–SURIGAO STRAIT area in naval assault shipping.

        (d) Denying Japanese reinforcement of the LEYTE area from the SAMAR, western VISAYAS and northeastern MINDANAO areas.

        (e) Clearing the SURIGAO STRAIT area of hostile naval forces and shipping and sweeping the SURIGAO STRAIT to open it for naval operations and shipping in the CAMOTES SEA and adjacent waters, in conjunction with operations of the SIXTH US ARMY.

(3) Provide submarine offensive reconnaissance along probable routes of hostile naval forces and of water-borne reinforcements and supplies.

(4) Provide lifeguard services as required.

(5) Transfer to the Commander ALLIED AIR Forces the mission of direct air support when land-based fighters and light bombers are established in the LEYTE area, at a time as arranged with the Commander ALLIED AIR Forces.

(6) Escort and protect shipping on the lines of communication into the LEYTE and SAMAR areas.

(7) Establish in VISAYAN waters, naval forces required to support current and future operations.

   e. The Commander ALLIED AIR Forces, while continuing present missions, will:

(1) Support the operation by:

(a) Providing aerial reconnaissance and photography as required.

(b) Neutralizing, in coordination with carrier and land-based aircraft of the THIRD FLEET, hostile naval and air forces in areas within range in the PHILIPPINE ARCHIPELAGO, intensifying the neutralization in the western VISAYAS and MINDANAO areas from D–9 to cover the movement of naval forces, the landing and subsequent operations. (Cooperation of air operations of the THIRD FLEET and SOUTHWEST PACIFIC Air Forces will be published later.)

(c) Providing protection of convoys and naval forces and direct support of the landing and subsequent operations within capabilities and as requested by Commander ALLIED NAVAL Forces.

(d) Assuming the mission of direct support of the operations in the LEYTE–SAMAR area at the earliest practicable date after the establishment of fighters and light bombers in the LEYTE area, as arranged with the Commander ALLIED NAVAL Forces.

(2) Continuing the destruction of hostile naval and air forces and shipping in the ARAFURA and CELEBES SEA areas and by initiating strikes on northeastern BORNEO and the SULU ARCHIPELAGO at the earliest practicable date; denying use of naval facilities in the SULU ARCHIPELAGO to the Japanese and protecting the western flank of the operation.

(3) Destroying hostile installations and sources of war materials in Eastern NETHERLANDS EAST INDIES.

(4) Establishing and operating radar and air warning facilities as required in the LEYTE–SAMAR area, as arranged with the Commanding General SIXTH US ARMY.

(5) Establishing air forces in the LEYTE area in the priority as listed in paragraph 3a (8).

x. (1) For the coordination of planning the Commander ALLIED NAVAL and AIR Forces will cause their respective close support commanders to report to the Commanding General SIXTH US ARMY, who is charged with the coordination of plans.

(2) A brief of the coordinated plan of operations will be furnished this headquarters by the Commanding General SIXTH US ARMY by 5 October 1944.

(3) Commanders ALLIED NAVAL and AIR Forces, SOUTHWEST PACIFIC AREA, will submit to this headquarters by 1 October 1944 their respective plans for general support to be afforded by their forces during the period of operations.

(4) During the amphibious movement and landing, the Commander Naval Attack Forces is in command of the amphibious operations; his command continues until the landing forces are established ashore. Command of the forces ashore is then passed to the Landing Force Commanders. The exact time of transfer of command from the Commanders Landing Forces will be announced by radio. The controlling considerations for fixing the time when the landing forces are established ashore will be as agreed by the Commander ALLIED NAVAL Forces and the Commanding General SIXTH US ARMY, and will be announced by them to this headquarters and appropriate subordinates.

(5) For coordination of land-based and naval aircraft in support of the operation, see Standing Operating Procedure Instructions Number 16/1, this headquarters, dated 10 August 1944.

(6) To coordinate the attack of THIRD FLEET carrier aircraft, the Commander ALLIED NAVAL Forces, in concert with the Commander ALLIED AIR Forces and Commanding General SIXTH US ARMY, will furnish the Commander THIRD FLEET at the earliest practicable date the following:
(a) Schedule and tracks of echelons.
(b) Target maps of air and surface bombardment.
(c) Communication plans.
(d) Naval gunfire plans.
(e) Other plans and data necessary for the support of the operation by the fast carrier forces.

(7) Areas of responsibility for naval and air operations of the THIRD FLEET and SOUTHWEST PACIFIC Forces will be designated later.

(8) Instructions for long range reconnaissance, and bombing and attack restrictions will be issued in subsequent Operations Instructions.

(9) Annex No. 1 indicates the tentative troop list for the Operation, and Annex 2 indicates the troop movements for the concentration.

4. See Annex No. 4—Logistics. (to be issued later)

5. a. See Annex No. 5—Communications.

   b. Command Posts.

   PACIFIC OCEAN AREAS—HAWAII

   THIRD FLEET—AFLOAT

   GENERAL HEADQUARTERS, SOUTHWEST PACIFIC AREA—HOLLANDIA

       Rear Echelon—BRISBANE

       Advanced Echelon—LEYTE (date and hour of opening to be announced later)

   SIXTH US ARMY—LEYTE (as announced by Commanding General SIXTH US ARMY)

       Rear Echelon—HOLLANDIA

   FIRST AUSTRALIAN ARMY—LAE

   EIGHTH US ARMY—HOLLANDIA

   ALLIED NAVAL FORCES—HOLLANDIA

       Rear Echelon—BRISBANE

   ALLIED AIR FORCES—HOLLANDIA

       Rear Echelon—BRISBANE

   UNITED STATES ARMY SERVICES OF SUPPLY—HOLLANDIA

       Rear Echelon—BRISBANE

       By command of General MacARTHUR:

                       R. K. SUTHERLAND,

                       Lieutenant General, U. S. Army,

                       Chief of Staff.

OFFICIAL:

  /s/ S. J. Chamberlin,

    S. J. CHAMBERLIN,

  Major General, G.S.C.,

  Asst. Chief of Staff, G–3.

ANNEXES: (Omitted)

Appendix B

Basic Military Map Symbols*

Symbols within a rectangle indicate a military unit, within a triangle an observation post, and within a circle a supply point.

Military Units—Identification

Antiaircraft Artillery . . . .

Armored Command . . . .

Army Air Forces . . . .

Artillery, except Antiaircraft and Coast Artillery . . . .

Cavalry, Horse . . . .

Cavalry, Mechanized . . . .

Chemical Warfare Service . . . .

Coast Artillery . . . .

Engineers . . . .

Infantry . . . .

Medical Corps . . . .

Ordnance Department . . . .

Quartermaster Corps . . . .

Signal Corps . . . .

Tank Destroyer . . . .

Transportation Corps . . . .

Veterinary Corps . . . .

      Airborne units are designated by combining a gull wing symbol with the arm or service symbol:

Airborne Artillery . . . .

Airborne Infantry . . . .

*For complete listing of symbols see FM 21-30, from which these are taken.

Size Symbols

The following symbols placed either in boundary lines or above the rectangle, triangle, or circle inclosing the identifying arm or service symbol indicate the size of military organization:

Squad . . . . ●

Section . . . . ●●

Platoon . . . . ●●●

Company, troop, battery, Air Force flight I

Battalion, cavalry squadron, or Air Force squadron II

Regiment or group; combat team (with abbreviation CT following identifying numeral) III

Brigade, Combat Command of Armored Division, or Air Force Wing . X

Division or Command of an Air Force XX

Corps or Air Force XXX

Army XXXX

Group of Armies XXXXX

EXAMPLES

The letter or number to the left of the symbol indicates the unit designation; that to the right, the designation of the parent unit to which it belongs. Letters or numbers above or below boundary lines designate the units separated by the lines:

Company A, 137th Infantry . . . . A ⊠ 137

8th Field Artillery Battalion . . . . ● 8

Combat Command A, 1st Armored Division . . . . A ⬯ I

Observation Post, 23d Infantry . . . . ◬ 23

Command Post, 5th Infantry Division . . . . ⊠ 5

Boundary between 137th and 138th Infantry . . . . . . —III— 137 / 138

Weapons

Machine gun . . . . ●→

Gun . . . . ●

Gun battery . . . . ⊔⊔⊔

Howitzer or Mortar . . . . ●

Tank . . . . ◇

Self-propelled gun . . . . ⬭●

List of Abbreviations

AA	Antiaircraft
AAF	Army Air Forces
Admin O	Administrative Order
AFPAC	U.S. Army Forces, Pacific
AGO	Adjutant General's Office
AGS SWPA	Allied Geographic Section, Southwest Pacific Area
AGWAR	Adjutant General, War Department
AIB GHQ SWPA	Allied Intelligence Bureau, General Headquarters Southwest Pacific Area
AKA	Cargo Ship, attack
Amph	Amphibious, amphibian
APA	Transport, attack
APH	Transport for wounded
Arty	Artillery
ASCOM	Army Service Command
ATIS	Allied Translator and Interpreter Section
BAR	Browning automatic rifle
Bn	Battalion
Br	Branch
Bull	Bulletin
Cav	Cavalry
CCS	Combined Chiefs of Staff
CG	Commanding General
CINC	Commander in Chief
CINCPAC	Commander in Chief, U.S. Pacific Fleet
CINCPOA	Commander in Chief, Pacific Ocean Area
CINCSWPA	Commander in Chief, Southwest Pacific Area
CM–IN	Classified Message, incoming
CM–OUT	Classified Message, outgoing
CO	Commanding Officer
CofS	Chief of Staff
Com3dFlt	Commander, Third Fleet
COMINCH	Commander in Chief, U.S. Fleet
CTF	Commander, task force
CTG	Commander, task group
CTU	Commander, task unit
CVE	Aircraft carrier, escort

Div	Division
DNI	Division of Naval Intelligence
DUKW	Amphibian, 2½-ton, 6 x 6 truck, used for short runs from ship to shore
Engr	Engineer
ESB	Engineer Special Brigade
FA	Field Artillery
FE	Far East
FEAF	Far East Air Forces
FEC	Far East Command
Flt	Fleet
FM	Field Manual
FO	Field Order
G–2	Intelligence section of divisional or higher staff
G–3	Operations section of divisional or higher staff
G–4	Supply section of divisional or higher staff
GHQ SWPA	General Headquarters, Southwest Pacific Area
Gp	Group
GS	General Staff
Hist	History, historical
Hq	Headquarters
HRS DRB AGO	Historical Records Section, Departmental Records Branch, Adjutant General's Office
Inf	Infantry
I&HS	Information and Historical Service
Instns	Instructions
Intel	Intelligence
JCS	Joint Chiefs of Staff
Jnl	Journal
LCI	Landing craft, infantry
LCI (R)	Landing craft, infantry (rocket)
LCM	Landing craft, mechanized
LCM (R)	Landing craft, mechanized (rocket)
Log	Logistics
LSD	Landing ship, dock
LSM	Landing ship, medium
LST	Landing ship, tank
Ltr	Letter
LVT	Landing vehicle, tracked
M29	Weasel
MC	Medical Corps
MI	Military Intelligence
Mil	Military

Msg	Message
Mtg	Meeting
OCMH	Office of the Chief of Military History
OCNO	Office of the Chief of Naval Operations
Off	Officer
ONI	Office of Naval Intelligence
OP	Observation post
OPD	Operations Division, War Department General Staff
Opns	Operations
PCE (R)	Patrol craft, escort (rescue)
POL	Petrol oil and lubricants
Prcht	Parachute
QM	Quartermaster
Rad	Radiogram
Rcds	Records
Regt	Regiment
Rpt	Report
S–2	Intelligence section of regimental or lower staff
S–3	Operations section of regimental or lower staff
Sec	Section
Ser	Series
Sq	Squadron
SSUSA	Special Staff, U.S. Army
Stf	Staff
SWPA	Southwest Pacific Area
Tel Conf	Teletype Conference
USA	U.S. Army
USASOS	U.S. Army Services of Supply
USMC	U.S. Marine Corps
USN	U.S. Navy
USNR	U.S. Naval Reserve
USSBS	U.S. Strategic Bombing Survey
WD	War Department
WDGS	War Department General Staff
Wkly	Weekly

Bibliographical Note

Records and studies on the Leyte operation fall into eleven general classes: Joint Chiefs of Staff records, U.S. Army Air Forces records, U.S. Army records, U.S. Marine Corps records, U.S. Navy records, guerrilla records, Japanese studies, interviews, manuscript histories, special studies, and published works.

Joint Chiefs of Staff Records

The official records of the Joint Chiefs of Staff, as well as those of the Combined Chiefs of Staff, are now in the custody of the Research Analysis Section, Joint Chiefs of Staff. They consist primarily of the formal papers and minutes of the Joint Chiefs of Staff. An almost complete file of these JCS and CCS papers and minutes was kept for the Army during the wartime period by the Operations Division of the War Department General Staff and is now in the possession of the G–3 Division, the successor to the Operations Division. This Army file contains plans for projected operations, the working papers of the Army planning personnel, and correspondence with officers in the Pacific theaters, as well as the copies of the JCS and CCS minutes and papers.

Army Air Forces Records

The archives of the United States Army Air Forces contain manuscript histories of the various units and commands, written during or shortly after the war. The quality of these varies considerably. The following

histories are of especial value for a study of the Leyte Campaign: those of the 7th, 8th, and 9th Fighter Squadrons of the 49th Fighter Group, 86th Fighter Wing, V Fighter Command, Fifth Air Force; V Fighter Command; V Bomber Command; XIII Bomber Command; Fifth Air Force; Thirteenth Air Force; and Far East Air Forces. Two studies are also useful: Far East Air Forces Staff Study Operation KING II, 12 July 44; and Fifth Air Force Fighter Cover Plan for Ormoc Bay Operation, file 731.326.

Army Records

The voluminous Army records on the Leyte Campaign vary considerably in quality and content. The documents range from messages between the Chief of Staff and theater commanders to company journals.

The Chief of Staff's Log, 1944, which is in the Staff Communications Office, Office of the Chief of Staff, contains the daily high level radiograms and telephonic communications between Washington and the theaters. These give a concise daily summary of the strategic situation throughout the world, shed considerable light on joint and combined command, and summarize important plans and decisions.

Most of the records of General MacArthur's headquarters are in Japan. Available in the Historical Records Section of the Adjutant General's Office is a nearly complete file of the G–3 journals for the entire war period. The "Top Secret" messages are not included. In addition there is a nearly complete file of Allied Translator Interpreter Section, GHQ SWPA, "Current Translations" and "Enemy Publications." The Allied Geographical Section, GHQ SWPA, made terrain studies of the geographical regions in the Southwest Pacific Area. Although they contain errors three of these were of value—Special Report 55, Airfields, Landing Beaches and Roads, Samar, Leyte and Dinagat Group, 10 July 1944; Terrain Study 84, Leyte Province, 17 August 1944; and Terrain Handbook 34, Tacloban, 25 September 1944. The Military Intelligence Section prepared information bulletins on the guerrillas that were of some use. These are: The Resistance Movement on Leyte Island, 7 October 1944, and The Resistance Movement on Samar Island, 10 October 1944.

The records of the Sixth Army for the campaign are very complete and in excellent condition. In addition to a fine operations report, there are complete G–2, G–3, and G–4 journals. These journals contain the daily messages, reports, and memoranda exchanged between Sixth Army, General Headquarters, responsible naval commanders, and subordinate units of the Sixth Army, as well as planning papers, periodic reports of Sixth Army and subordinate units, field and administrative orders, interrogations, and estimates of the enemy situation. For the period after 26 December 1944 the operations report of the Eighth Army is useful.

The operations report of the X Corps is helpful but too brief. The journals (G–2, G–3, and G–4) of the corps, however, are good. The XXIV Corps prepared an inadequate and incomplete operations report and its journals as a whole are inferior to those of the X Corps. The sections and subsections of the headquarters of the XXIV Corps completed "histories." These consist mainly of photographs of individuals and notations of changes in personnel. The "history" of the Sixth Army Service Command is poor and there are few records of ASCOM in the Historical Records Section, Adjutant General's Office.

The records of the 1st Cavalry Division and subordinate units are generally adequate, although those of the two brigades are inferior to those of the division and of the regiments. The narrative of the operations report of the 7th Division is inferior but the appendixes are excellent and very complete; the journals of the division are good. In general the operations reports and journals of the infantry regiments are very helpful. The operations report of the 32d Infantry is excellent and a model for a perfect regimental operations report. In contrast, the operations reports and journals of the 11th Airborne Division and subordinate units are very poor and incomplete. The 24th Infantry Division prepared a superb operations report and kept good journals. The records of the regiments of the division are sparse and incomplete and their operations reports are either inadequate or nonexistent. The records and operations reports of the 32d Division and its regiments are extremely sketchy and inexact. The 38th Division used Leyte as a staging area; when the Japanese parachuted into the Burauen airfields, its 149th Infantry was committed. The operations report of that regiment for the resultant action is far too brief. The 77th Infantry Division and its regiments have very good operations reports but their journals are inadequate. The operations reports and journals of the 96th Division are good.

The journals and operations reports of the Americal Division are only fairly good. There are "histories" and operations reports of small independent or attached units, but these are frequently one to three pages in length and very incomplete. Finally, it should be noted that the operations reports of the various artillery units are in the main poor and incomplete and the journals are highly technical.

Marine Records

Special Action Report of Corps Artillery, V Amphibious Corps, 28 December 1944.

Navy Records

The naval records that were consulted include the operation plans and reports by naval commanders. Copies of most of these are among the records of the Historical Records Section, Adjutant General's Office, Department of the Army. All of the documents are in the files of the Office of the Naval Records and Library, Department of the Navy.

Guerrilla Records

There is in the Office of the Chief of Military History a large, completely disorganized collection of heterogeneous materials by and about the guerrillas in the Philippine Islands. These are incomplete, inadequate, and controversial. Some of the guerrilla bands had no records and all that is known of others is from violently prejudiced sources. Some of the American guerrillas published books on their experiences. These are impressionistic, generally replete with derring-do, and consequently possess scant value as sources. The Combat History Division, G–1 Section, AFWESPAC, prepared a four-volume work—"Triumph in the Philippines," the third volume of which, entitled "Guerrillas: Enemy Occupation," is colorful, but poor history.

Japanese Studies

At the cessation of hostilities, General MacArthur ordered the former Japanese War and Navy Ministries to prepare studies on Japanese plans and operations in World War II. The resulting studies, translations and originals, of which those mentioned below deal with the Leyte Campaign, are on file with the Office of the Chief of Military History. Although there are errors in dates, designations of units, and frequently in facts, these are the best sources for information on Japanese plans and operations. An exception is the independent study by General Tomochika, which despite its garish title is very good and contains much human interest. Tomochika, evidently a man of strong prejudices, at times was unduly critical of some of his fellow officers. Japanese Studies used in this volume are:

Tomochika, Maj. Gen. Yoshiharu, The True Facts of the Leyte Operation, typescript of translation, 10th I&HS, Eighth Army, 3 December 1946

Japanese Studies in World War II, 5, *4th Air Army Operations*, 1944–45

―――, 7, *14th Army* Operations on Leyte

―――, 11, *35th Army* Operations, 1944–45

―――, 14, Naval Operations in the Philippine Area, 1942–45

―――, 21, History of the *Southern Army*, 1941–45

————, 72, History of the *Army Section, Imperial General Headquarters,* 1941–45

————, 102, Philippine Area Naval Operations, October 1944–December 1944, Part II, The Battle of Leyte Gulf

Interviews

The following U.S. Army officers furnished the author valuable information on the Leyte Campaign: Lt. Gen. Robert L. Eichelberger, Maj. Gen. George H. Decker, Col. W. J. Verbeck, Col. Fred Weber, Col. Sidney F. Mashbir, Col. John M. Finn, Capt. Francis Cronin, Capt. Robert Ross Smith, and 1st Lt. James J. Frangie. Fleet Admiral William D. Leahy, Lt. Comdr. Henry M. Dater, Lt. Comdr. Russell L. Harris, Lt. Comdr. Philip A. Crowl and Lt. Roger Pineau of the U.S. Navy were very co-operative, helping to clear up moot points that arose. Capt. Samuel E. Morison furnished information on the Pearl Harbor Conference of July 1944.

Manuscript Histories

There are in the files of the Office, Chief of Military History, the following manuscript histories of certain phases of the campaign:

Dean, Captain Tucker—The Liberation of Leyte. A preliminary work based principally upon the earlier study by Capt. Russell A. Gugeler.

Gugeler, Captain Russell A.—The 7th Division on Leyte. A good study although poorly documented.

History of the Engineer Corps in the Southwest Pacific, Chapter VI, Philippine Campaign.

Special Studies

There are available in the Office, Chief of Military History, copies of special studies that bear upon the Leyte Campaign. As a group they are capably done, although, of course, some are better than others.

Air Evaluation Board, POA, Leyte Campaign, 1944. Highly critical of Army close air support.

Committee 16, Officers Advanced Course, The Armored School, Fort Knox, Kentucky, Armor on Leyte, May 1949.

Division of Naval Intelligence, Office of the Chief of Naval Operations, O. N. I. No. 93, Field Monograph of the Philippines, 3 parts, III, Visayan Islands, January 1944.

Grigg, Maj. Martin C., The Operations of the 1st Battalion, 149th Infantry . . . in the Battle for the Buri Airstrip . . . Advanced Infantry Officers Class, 1948–1949, The Infantry School, Fort Benning, Georgia.

MacLaughlin, Maj. Charles V., Operation of the XXIV Corps in the Invasion of Leyte Island, Advanced Infantry Officers Class, 1947–1948, The Infantry School, Fort Benning, Georgia.

Military Intelligence Division, War Department, "Leyte Field Fortifications," *Tactical and Technical Trends,* April 1945.

Military Intelligence Service, General Staff, War Department, Survey of the Philippines, 3 volumes, 15 February 1943.

National War College, Analytical Study, Japanese Opposition at Leyte and Okinawa, 1948.

Fellers, Col. Bonner F., Psychological Warfare in the Southwest Pacific Area, 1944–45, 15 March 1946.

Staff Study of Operations of the Japanese *35th Army* on Leyte, typescript of translation, 10th I&HS, Eighth Army (not dated), 4 parts.

Staff Study of Operations of the Japanese *102d Division* on Leyte and Cebu, typescript of translation, 10th I&HS, Eighth Army (not dated).

United States Strategic Bombing Survey, Employment of Forces Under the Southwest Pacific Command, February 1947.

Williams, Maj. E., Intelligence Activities During the Japanese Occupation (not dated).

Publications

Arnold, General Henry H., *Global Mission* (New York, Harper and Brothers, 1949).

Cronin, Capt. Francis D., *Under the Southern Cross, The Saga of the Americal Division* (Washington, Combat Forces Press, 1951).

Davidson, Orlando R., Williams, J. Carl, and Kahl, Joseph A., *The Deadeyes: The Story of the 96th Infantry Division* (Washington, Infantry Journal Press (now Combat Forces Press), 1947). A divisional history definitely above the average.

Wesley Frank Craven and James Lea Cate, eds., *The Army Air Forces in World War II: V, The Pacific: Matterhorn to Nagasaki* (Chicago, University of Chicago Press, 1953).

Eichelberger, Robert L., *Our Jungle Road to Tokyo* (New York, The Viking Press, 1950).

Field, James A., Jr., *The Japanese at Leyte Gulf, The Shō Operation* (Princeton, Princeton University Press, 1947). An excellent study based upon Japanese documents and interrogations. There are many superb photographs, maps, and charts.

Flanagan, Maj. Edward M., Jr., *The Angels: A History of the 11th Airborne Division, 1943–1946* (Washington, Infantry Journal Press, 1948). A popular history written for the men of the division.

Halsey, Fleet Admiral William F., and Bryan, Lt. Comdr. J., *Admiral Halsey's Story* (New York, Whittlesey House, 1947). An interesting and popular account, of value in showing Halsey's strong interest in an early return to the Philippines.

Johansen, Maj. Herbert O., "Banzai at Burauen," *Air Force*, XXVIII, 3 (March, 1945). A popular account based entirely on American sources.

Kenney, George C., *General Kenney Reports* (New York, Duell, Sloan and Pearce, 1949).

Karig, Capt. Walter, USNR, Harris, Lt. Comdr. Russell L., and Manson, Lt. Comdr. Frank A., *Battle Report, Victory in the Pacific* (New York and Toronto, Rhinehart and Co., Inc., 1949) (5 vols.), V. A highly readable journalistic salty account based upon documentary sources and interviews. There are many excellent photographs.

Leahy, Fleet Admiral William D., *I Was There* (New York, Whittlesey House, 1950). Excellent. Based entirely on his diary and notes written at the time.

Biennial Report of the Chief of Staff of the United States Army, July 1, 1943, to June 30, 1945, to the Secretary of War (Washington, 1945).

The Medal of Honor (Washington, 1948). A history of the Congressional Medal of Honor and the official citations of the men who had been awarded the medal.

Morton, Louis, "American and Allied Strategy in the Far East," *Military Review*, XXIX, 12 (December, 1949). An excellent analysis of prewar strategy up to the summer of 1941.

Reel, A. Frank, *The Case of General Yamashita* (Chicago, The University of Chicago Press, 1949). An able pleading for General Yamashita by one of his defense counsel at his trial as a war criminal.

Sturgis, Brig. Gen. S. D., Jr., "Engineer Operations in the Leyte Campaign," reprint from *The Military Engineer,* November, December 1947, and January 1948.

United States Strategic Bombing Survey, Pacific, Naval Analysis Division, prepared two studies on the Pacific campaigns which are valuable for the student of the Leyte operation. *The Campaigns of the Pacific War* (Washington, 1946) is excellent for a study of the Battle of Leyte Gulf. The *Interrogations of Japanese Officials* (2 vols., n. d.) contains much highly important material but it should be remembered that the interrogated Japanese officers were naturally desirous of making a good case for themselves and at the same time were anxious to give an answer which would please the interrogator.

Valtin, Jan [Richard J. Krebs], *Children of Yesterday* (New York, The Reader's Press, 1946). An excellent popular account of the activities of the 24th Division.

Verbeck, Col. W. J., *A Regiment in Action,* (n. p., n. d., privately printed, copy in OCMH). The story of the 21st Infantry Regiment which consists mainly of excerpts from the operations reports and journals of higher echelons.

Woodward, C. Vann, *The Battle for Leyte Gulf* (New York, The Macmillan Co., 1947). An extremely readable popular account based upon American and Japanese sources and interviews with which Dr. Woodward became acquainted while an officer on duty with the Office of Naval Intelligence during the war. The book is valuable in spite of a few minor errors of fact.

UNITED STATES ARMY IN WORLD WAR II

The following volumes have been published:

The War Department
Chief of Staff: Prewar Plans and Preparations
Washington Command Post: The Operations Division
Strategic Planning for Coalition Warfare: 1941–1942
Strategic Planning for Coalition Warfare: 1943–1944
Global Logistics and Strategy: 1940–1943
Global Logistics and Strategy: 1943–1945
The Army and Economic Mobilization
The Army and Industrial Manpower

The Army Ground Forces
The Organization of Ground Combat Troops
The Procurement and Training of Ground Combat Troops

The Army Service Forces
The Organization and Role of the Army Service Forces

The Western Hemisphere
The Framework of Hemisphere Defense
Guarding the United States and Its Outposts

The War in the Pacific
The Fall of the Philippines
Guadalcanal: The First Offensive
Victory in Papua
CARTWHEEL: The Reduction of Rabaul
Seizure of the Gilberts and Marshalls
Campaign in the Marianas
The Approach to the Philippines
Leyte: The Return to the Philippines
Triumph in the Philippines
Okinawa: The Last Battle
Strategy and Command: The First Two Years

The Mediterranean Theater of Operations
Northwest Africa: Seizing the Initiative in the West
Sicily and the Surrender of Italy
Salerno to Cassino
Cassino to the Alps

The European Theater of Operations
Cross-Channel Attack
Breakout and Pursuit
The Lorraine Campaign
The Siegfried Line Campaign
The Ardennes: Battle of the Bulge
The Last Offensive
Riviera to the Rhine
The Supreme Command

Index